# Reading Scripture in the Fellowship of the Spirit

The Koinonia Role of the Holy Spirit in Biblical Hermeneutics

Trevor Reynolds

WIPF & STOCK · Eugene, Oregon

Wipf and Stock Publishers
199 W 8th Ave, Suite 3
Eugene, OR 97401

Reading Scripture in the Fellowship of the Spirit
The Koinonia Role of the Holy Spirit in Biblical Hermeneutics
By Reynolds, Trevor
Copyright©2017 Apostolos
ISBN 13: 978-1-5326-6980-4
Publication date 9/23/2018
Previously published by Apostolos, 2017

*To my beloved wife Margaret*

# ACKNOWLEDGEMENTS

The interpretive dynamic between Word and Spirit is a topic of vital interest to all preachers and Bible students, so my appetite was whetted when Robin Parry of Paternoster Press kindly suggested this as a possible PhD topic some years ago. The final title of the PhD thesis upon which this book is based was 'An Investigation into the Spirit's Guidance of the Community as Custodian and Interpreter of Scripture.' The 'community' element was suggested to me by Dr Tom Holland, of the Wales Evangelical School of Theology (now Union School of Theology), and I am very grateful to him for encouraging me to investigate the idea of a 'corporate' reading of Scripture, which ties in with the work of the Holy Spirit as the Spirit of fellowship, or rather, *koinonia*.

I would like to sincerely thank Dr Holland and Professor D. Davies, of the University of Wales, my PhD supervisors, for all the support, guidance and theological input they gave me during my research, and also to Rev Dr David Spriggs of the Bible Society for his helpful critique of my work. The final stages of my research also benefited from the stimulus of a visit to the International Baptist Theological Seminary (then in Prague) and participation in a 'Bible as Pastor' Symposium organized by the Bible Society and the School of Religious and Theological Studies of Cardiff University.

I owe a particular debt of gratitude to my PhD examiners, the late Professor I. Howard Marshall and Dr William Campbell, for all the helpful comments they made on my chapters whilst examining my thesis before its approval in 2007. I am also grateful to the librarians at the Union School of Theology for their continuous assistance. I would like to thank Mathew Bartlett, commissioning editor at Apostolos Publishing, for all his encouragement, careful reading and practical help in preparing this book for publication. Finally, I wish to give special thanks to my wife Margaret, without whose unfailing and loving support I would never have been able to complete my PhD and this subsequent book, which I gratefully dedicate to her.

As I have pursued my studies, I have been continually challenged by the wide-ranging implications that arise from following through a 'Spirit through community' hermeneutic. The topic has involved my straddling several different specialities—pneumatology, hermeneutics, New Testament studies, historical and Trinitarian theology, cultural studies, and so on. In so doing, I have stumbled across numerous complex debates, to which I have attempted to make some reference in the footnotes. I have also sought to engage with some of the more recent literature relating to my subject since my PhD was completed. I am, however, aware of the limitations of my research, as well as those limitations (and of course benefits) afforded by the interpretive understandings that I have because of my background and convictions.

In my case, these understandings have been shaped by the influences of a close-knit family; Sunday schools and day schools (with Christian assemblies) in England; American student evangelism in my conversion at University; my early work as a lawyer in London and my ongoing involvement with the Lawyers' Christian Fellowship; evangelical Anglicanism in early theological training; the expository preaching and spirituality associated with reformed thought; the warmth and fervour of charismatic friends; the pastoral experience from nearly 30 years as a Baptist Minister in 3 churches in England and Wales; the blessings of studying and teaching at the Union School of Theology, Bridgend, Wales; and finally the stimulus of international connections, particularly with Europe, Africa and China. All these influences have enriched my understanding of 'the fellowship of the Holy Spirit.' I trust that as this book is read, it will encourage others to reflect on their own experiences of reading Scripture in the *koinonia* of the Spirit.

# CONTENTS

ACKNOWLEDGEMENTS ................................................................. 4
PART 1 ............................................................................................ 12
PNEUMATOLOGY, HERMENEUTICS AND KOINONIA ................ 12
INTRODUCTION TO PART I ......................................................... 13
CHAPTER ONE: THE HOLY SPIRIT IN BIBLICAL INTERPRETATION ...... 14
The Case for a 'Community' Approach ........................................ 14
The Spirit's Role in Biblical Interpretation: History of Scholarship ............... 15
   An Overview ............................................................................. 15
   Some Recent Developments ................................................... 17
   Conclusion ................................................................................ 19
Definitions of Terms ...................................................................... 19
   Hermeneutics ........................................................................... 19
   Community ............................................................................... 20
   Corporate/Individualistic Readings .......................................... 20
Individualism in Biblical Interpretation ........................................ 21
The Case for a 'Community' Approach ........................................ 29
Dangers of a 'Community' Approach ........................................... 35
   Community Absolutism ........................................................... 35
   Pneumatic Vagueness .............................................................. 37
   Erosion of Textual Autonomy ................................................. 38
   Over-emphasis upon the Community/ Individual Dichotomy ........... 39
Conclusion to the Chapter ............................................................ 41
CHAPTER TWO: THE KOINONIA OF THE SPIRIT ....................... 42
Introduction ................................................................................... 42

Contemporary Pneumatology ........................................................................ 43

The Concept of Κοινωνία ............................................................................. 43

    Trinitarian ................................................................................................ 46

    Dialogical ................................................................................................. 53

    Historical .................................................................................................. 58

    Eschatological .......................................................................................... 69

Conclusion to and Summary of the Whole Section ................................. 73

    The Dimensions of Κοινωνία ................................................................ 74

    Implications for Biblical Hermeneutics ................................................ 74

Conclusion to the Chapter .......................................................................... 85

CHAPTER THREE: THE SPIRIT AT THE INTERFACE OF THE OLD AND NEW TESTAMENTS ................................................................................... 86

Introduction ................................................................................................. 86

The Spirit in Contemporary Judaism ........................................................ 89

    The 'Spirit of Prophecy' ......................................................................... 89

    Corporate Solidarity .............................................................................. 90

The Use of Testimonia ................................................................................. 93

The Spirit-anointed Messianic Exegete ..................................................... 96

    Jesus as a Model of Spirit-inspired Exegesis ....................................... 98

    Jesus as a Promiser of Spirit-inspired Exegesis ................................. 100

Presuppositions of NT Writers ................................................................ 105

    Charismatic Exegesis ........................................................................... 105

    Corporate Solidarity ............................................................................ 107

    Typology, Correspondences in History and Intertextuality ............ 108

    Eschatological Fulfilment ................................................................... 113

    Messianic Presence, or Christocentricity .......................................... 114

Conclusion to the Chapter ................................................................................. 115

PART 2 ..................................................................................................................... 119

INTRODUCTION TO PART 2 ............................................................................ 120

CHAPTER FOUR: THE PROMISE OF THE PARACLETE (JOHN 14–16) ... 122

Introduction ............................................................................................................. 122

    Methodological Approach to 'Community' ............................................... 122

    Relevance of John 14–16 to the Subject of this Book .............................. 123

    Spirit, Individual and Community in John ................................................ 124

    The Paraclete Sayings ..................................................................................... 125

The Nature of the Paraclete ................................................................................. 126

    (a) The Legal Aspect as 'Advocate' ............................................................. 126

    (b) The Paraclete as the Alter Ego ('Other I') of Jesus ............................ 127

    (c)   The 'Personal' Paraclete .................................................................. 128

    (d)   The Spirit of Truth ............................................................................ 129

    (e)   The Didactic Spirit ............................................................................ 130

The Hermeneutical Functions of the Paraclete ................................................ 131

    Historical and Didactic (14:25–26) ............................................................. 131

    Dialectical and Convictional (15:26–27; 16:7–11) ................................... 134

    Eschatological and Interpretive (16:12–15) .............................................. 136

    Trinitarian and Exegetical (14:16; 16:13–15 and previous verses) ......... 139

Conclusion to the Chapter ................................................................................... 141

CHAPTER FIVE: SPIRIT AND HERMENEUTICS IN THE FIRST CHRISTIAN COMMUNITY ....................................................................................................... 143

Introduction ............................................................................................................. 143

Spirit, Scripture and Community ......................................................................... 144

    Lukan Pneumatology ..................................................................................... 144

The Use of Scripture in Speeches ............................................................. 147

Spirit, Word and Community ..................................................................... 149

The Spirit-enabled Hermeneutics of the Early Christian Community ........... 150

    Acts 1: 15–26 The Election of Matthias: Reconstitution of the Apostolic Group ................................................................................................................ 151

    Acts 2 Pentecost: Spirit, Scripture and the Birth of the Church ................ 154

    Acts 4:23–31 Scripture in the Prayer Meeting ........................................... 164

    Acts 6–7 The Spirit's Witness through Stephen and the Old Testament Before the Sanhedrin ............................................................................................ 167

    Acts 15: Spirit and Scripture at the Council of Jerusalem ........................ 173

Conclusion to the Chapter ......................................................................... 180

# CHAPTER SIX: SPIRIT, COMMUNITY AND HERMENEUTICS IN PAUL. 182

Introduction ............................................................................................... 182

    The Flow of the Spirit .............................................................................. 182

    Corporate Terminology in Paul ................................................................ 184

    Recapitulation ......................................................................................... 185

    Foreword ................................................................................................. 186

Sources of Paul's Pneumatology ................................................................ 186

    Paul as a Jew ........................................................................................... 186

    The Old Testament ................................................................................. 189

    The Jesus Encounter and Tradition ........................................................ 191

Paul's Use of the Old Testament ............................................................... 193

    Source of Authority ................................................................................ 193

    Influence of Allusions ............................................................................. 193

    Jewish and Contemporary Interpretation ............................................... 194

    Christian Convictions and Ecclesial Concerns ........................................ 195

## 1 Corinthians 2:6–16: The Spirit of Understanding .................................. 196
### The Communal Dimensions ................................................................. 197
### Spirit-led Hermeneutics ...................................................................... 200
### Conclusion to 1 Corinthians 2 .............................................................. 206

## 2 Corinthians 3: The Spirit of Glory ....................................................... 207
### Incarnation ........................................................................................... 208
### Disjunction .......................................................................................... 210
### Liberation ............................................................................................ 211
### Contemplation ..................................................................................... 215
### Transformation ................................................................................... 216
### Glorification ........................................................................................ 217
### Conclusion to 2 Corinthians 3 ............................................................. 217

## Romans 8: The Spirit of Sonship ............................................................ 218
### The Life-giving Spirit (τοῦ πνεύματος τῆς ζωῆς in v. 2 and ζωή in vv. 6, 10, 11) ...................................................................................... 219
### The Spiritual Mindset (vv. 4–13) ......................................................... 220
### The Family Setting (vv. 14–17) ............................................................ 222
### Eschatological Tension/'Groaning' (vv. 17–25) .................................. 224
### Support in Weakness (vv. 26–27) ........................................................ 224
### Conclusion to Romans 8 ..................................................................... 225

## The Pastoral Epistles: The Spirit and Tradition ..................................... 226
### The Epistolary Form ............................................................................ 228
### Use of Theological Concepts, Sources and Traditions ....................... 229
### The Pneumatological Undergirding .................................................... 232
### Guidance for Interpreters ................................................................... 235
### Conclusion to the Pastoral Epistles .................................................... 239

Conclusion to the Chapter ........................................................................ 239

CHAPTER SEVEN: SPIRIT AND HERMENEUTICS IN THE JOHANNINE COMMUNITY ........................................................................ 241

Introduction........................................................................ 241

Corporateness and Pneumatology in 1 John ................................................ 243

χρῖσμα and Community in 1 John 2:20 and 27 ............................................ 246

    (a) Antichrists (2:18–19) ........................................................................ 246

    (b) Anointing (2:20, 27) ........................................................................ 247

    (c) All (2:20c) ........................................................................ 249

    (d) Abiding (2:19, 24, 27) ........................................................................ 252

Testing the Spirits in 1 John 4:1–6............................................................ 253

Conclusion to the Chapter ........................................................................ 264

CHAPTER EIGHT: READING SCRIPTURE IN THE FELLOWSHIP OF THE SPIRIT ........................................................................ 266

Summary of Chapters ........................................................................ 266

Some Implications of a 'Spirit Through Community' Hermeneutic .............. 269

    For the Hermeneutical Task........................................................................ 270

    For the Doctrine of Scripture ........................................................................ 276

    For the Use of Scripture........................................................................ 279

    For the Custodianship of Scripture ........................................................ 292

Final Word ........................................................................ 292

BIBLIOGRAPHY ........................................................................ 294

# PART 1

## PNEUMATOLOGY, HERMENEUTICS AND *KOINONIA*

*EXPLORING THE CORPORATE DIMENSIONS OF BIBLICAL INTERPRETATION OPENED BY THE SPIRIT IN THE FACE OF HISTORICAL AND CONTEMPORARY INDIVIDUALISM.*

# INTRODUCTION TO PART I

How does the Holy Spirit guide the Christian community in its custodianship and interpretation of Scripture? How can we understand the New Testament's 'community' reading of Scripture as opposed to an 'individual' reading of Scripture? And what are the implications of such a corporate/Spirit-led hermeneutic for the church's understanding of and use of Scripture today? These are some of the basic questions that this book addresses, seeking to find answers primarily from within Scripture itself.

My argument is not that individuals cannot read and understand the Bible for themselves. Rather it is seeking to underscore the essentially communal nature of biblical interpretation if it is being truly undertaken with the help of the Spirit whose nature is *koinonia*, whether the interpretation is being done by individuals or in a group.

In Part I, 'Pneumatology, Hermeneutics and *Koinonia*', I will set out the theological basis for my study. In chapter 1, I will investigate the role assigned to the Holy Spirit in biblical interpretation and the common exclusion of a corporate perspective. I will look at some examples of 'individualistic' approaches to interpretation, followed by the arguments for more of a 'community' approach, alongside some of the dangers of such an approach.

In chapter 2, I will explore the notion of the '*koinonia* of the Spirit' as a basis for a corporate approach to biblical interpretation in four different dimensions: Trinitarian, dialogical, historical, and eschatological.

In chapter 3 I will survey the general but complex question of the New Testaments's interpretation of the Old Testament, and the extent to which this can be understood to be driven by a corporate/Spirit-led hermeneutic.

Finally, in Part 2, I will examine specific chapters from Acts, John, and the letters of Paul to explore how the New Testament writers understood the Spirit's role in the interpretation and custodianship of Scripture, and in particular noting their essential communal components.

# CHAPTER ONE: THE HOLY SPIRIT IN BIBLICAL INTERPRETATION

The Case for a 'Community' Approach

Before his departure, Jesus told his disciples 'When the Spirit of truth comes, he will guide you into all the truth' (John 16:13). Despite this comforting promise, the role of the Holy Spirit in the interpretation of Scripture has been characterised by Kevin Vanhoozer as 'a justly famous problem.'[1] It has, nevertheless, been remarked that 'most works on hermeneutics [still] do not linger long over the Spirit's role.'[2] Pentecostal scholars in particular have lamented that 'despite the self-attestation of Scripture and the presuppositions of its writers, little attention is given ... to the role of the Holy Spirit in [modern] biblical hermeneutics.'[3] References to the Spirit's help are certainly not lacking; but more thorough attempts are needed to integrate pneumatological and interpretive insights within a biblical framework. This book represents one such attempt.

At the same time, I seek to combine the notion of the Holy Spirit's interpretation of Scripture with a 'community' reading emphasis which is increasingly being acknowledged as in need of being restored to a proper theological interpretation of the New Testament. The community/corporate emphasis will be shown to be a fundamental theological presupposition of the writers of the New Testament, as illustrated by their use of the Old Testament. I will argue that this corporate emphasis needs to be recognized and incorporated more fully into our own understanding of the interpretive process, especially when viewed from the perspective of the guidance of the Spirit whose distinctive characteristic is κοινωνία (*koinonia*).[4] This will have implications not just for biblical hermeneutics, but also for the doctrine of Scripture and its use in the church.

This introductory chapter will set the scene for the study by giving a brief historical survey of how the role of the Spirit in the church's interpretation of Scripture has been understood over the centuries. We will also define some terms and outline some trends toward individualism in biblical interpretation, along with the case for a more corporate approach.

---

[1] Kevin J. Vanhoozer, *Is there a Meaning in this Text? The Bible, the Reader and the Morality of Literary Knowledge* (Leicester: Apollos, 1998), 407.
[2] Richard Briggs, *Anvil* Vol. 20 No. 4, 2003, 323, reviewing E. Brown, *The Holy Spirit and the Bible* (Fearn: Mentor, 2002).
[3] Kevin L. Spawn and Archie Wright, 'The Emergence of a Pneumatic Hermeneutic in the Renewal Tradition' in *Spirit and Scripture: Exploring a Pneumatic Hermeneutic,* ed. Kevin L. Spawn and Archie Wright (London: Bloomsbury; T&T Clark, 2013), 10.
[4] 2 Cor 13:14. The κοινωνία theme is explored in chapter 2.

# The Spirit's Role in Biblical Interpretation: History of Scholarship

## An Overview

In the early Christian centuries, primary concern was given to affirming the deity of the Spirit,[5] his place and role within the Trinity, as well as in the life of the Christian. It was the polemics of the Reformation, however, that evinced more precise formulations of the Spirit's role vis-à-vis our understanding of Scripture.[6] Luther spoke of how we must first 'hear the Word, and then afterwards the Holy Ghost works *in our hearts*; he works in the hearts of whom he will and how he will, but never without the Word.'[7] Against the darkness of understanding resulting from the fall, Calvin asserts the necessity of illumination by the Spirit. 'There is no benefit from the word, except when God shines in us by the light of his Spirit; and thus the *inward* calling, which alone is efficacious and peculiar to the elect, is distinguished from the *outward voice of men*.'[8] The latter, in Calvin's writings, was often associated with the 'corrupt' churchmen of Rome.

For this reason, the resulting Reformation doctrine of *sola Scriptura* has been accused of separating biblical interpretation from the life of the church.[9] This, however, could not be said of one 'left wing' group that was an offshoot of the Reformation, the Anabaptists. Their strong congregationalist/pneumatic emphasis led them to believe that 'the Spirit is an interpreter of what a text is about only when Christians are gathered in readiness to hear it speak to their current needs and concerns.'[10] Here, then, was an anti-individualistic, community approach that 'made the common people supreme Bible interpreters in an even more concrete way than in the mainline Reformation.'[11] From the Puritan movement following the Reformation, John Owen stands out as a

---

[5] Hence his designation as 'the Lord and giver of life' in the Nicene-Constantinople Creed of 381.

[6] See J. I. Packer, '"Sola Scriptura" in History and Today' in *God's Inerrant Word: An International Symposium on the Trustworthiness of Scripture*, ed. John Warwick Montgomery (Minneapolis, MN: Bethany House, 1974), 46–48. Note the Westminster Confession of Faith (1646): 'We acknowledge the inward illumination of the Spirit of God to be necessary for the saving understanding of such things as are revealed in the Word (1:6) ... The supreme judge by which all controversies of religion are to be determined, and all decrees of councils, opinions of ancient writers, doctrines of men, and private spirits, are to be examined, and in whose sentence we are to rest, can be no other but the Holy Spirit speaking in the Scripture (1:10).'

[7] T. S. Kepler, ed., *The Table Talk of Martin Luther* (New York, NY: World, 1952), 143, cited in D. G. Bloesch, *The Holy Spirit: Works & Gifts* (Downers Grove, IL: IVP, 2000), 275. Italics mine.

[8] John Owen, ed. and trans., *Commentaries on the Epistle of Paul to the Romans* (Edinburgh: Calvin Translation Society, 1849), 400–401, as quoted in Bloesch, *The Holy Spirit*, 275. Italics mine. For more on the Word/Spirit relationship in Calvin, see John Calvin, *Institutes of the Christian Religion*, ed. John T. McNeill (Philadelphia, PA: Westminster, 1960), 78–81; 94–96.

[9] See further, pages 23–24 and 38–39.

[10] John Yoder, "The Hermeneutics of Anabaptists", in *Essays on Biblical Interpretation: Anabaptist-Mennonite Perspectives*, ed. Willard M. Swartley (Elkhart, IN: Institute of Mennonite Studies, 1984), 21. The Anabaptists also emphasized obedience to the Bible along with the concepts of 'a gathering church' and 'an inclusive community.' See Keith G. Jones *A Believing Church – Learning from some contemporary Anabaptist and Baptist Perspectives* (Didcot: Baptist Union of Great Britain, 1998).

[11] Veli-Matti Kärkkäinen, *Pneumatology: The Holy Spirit in Ecumenical International and Contextual Perspective* (Grand Rapids, MI: Baker Academic, 2002), 56.

primary advocate for the view that 'the principal efficient cause of the due knowledge and understanding of the will of God in the Scripture ... is the *Holy Spirit of God himself alone.*'[12]

In response to the subsequent rise of critical studies, B. B. Warfield formulated an influential doctrine of biblical inspiration[13] as an integral part of his defence of biblical inerrancy. Warfield held the view that the Word could not 'savingly' be understood without the Spirit, although it could be 'rationally' grasped by the unregenerate.[14] From the neo-orthodox angle, Karl Barth, with his dialectical approach, emphasized 'the Holy Spirit as the subjective side in the event of revelation.'[15] Barth's description of the Spirit as 'Lord of the hearing'[16] is matched by J. I. Packer's description of God as the 'Lord of Communication' who 'overcomes all muddles of the mind through the power of the Holy Spirit.'[17] For Packer, then, the Spirit is 'the great hermeneut who by leading and enlightening us in the work of exegesis, synthesis and application, actually interprets the Word in our minds and to our hearts.'[18]

Gordon Fee's description of the Spirit as 'God's Empowering Presence'[19] is a reflection not just of his Pauline theology, but of a wider appreciation of the role of the Holy Spirit, particularly as a result of the charismatic movement that began in the second half of the twentieth century. Pentecostal scholars in particular are now seeking to address some of the concerns of modern hermeneutics by appealing to the Spirit's help. Hence Arrington's statement that 'no one but the Holy Spirit provides the bridge that enables the ancient author and modern interpreter to meet and to span the historical and cultural gulf between them.'[20]

---

[12] To complete the quotation: 'for there is an especial work of the Spirit of God on the minds of men, communicating spiritual wisdom, light, and understanding unto them, necessary unto their discerning and apprehending aright the mind of God in his word.' John Owen, *The Causes, Ways, and Means of Understanding the Mind of God as Revealed in His Word, With Assurance Therein* (1678), as cited in *The Works of John Owen* Vol. IV (Edinburgh: Banner of Truth, 1967), 124–125. Italics original. See also C. Bennett, 'The Spirit in the Word - and Beyond?', *Foundations* No. 39 Autumn 1997, 10–20.
[13] For which his major texts were John 10:35, 2 Tim 3:16, and 2 Pet 1:20–21.
[14] See J. H. Gerstner, 'Warfield's Case for Biblical Inerrancy' in *God's Inerrant Word: An International Symposium on the Trustworthiness of Scripture*, ed. John Warwick Montgomery (Minneapolis: Bethany House, 1974), 138–139, where he highlights how Warfield follows Calvin's insistence upon the inseparability of Word and Spirit.
[15] Karl Barth, *Church Dogmatics* (Vol. 1.1): *The Doctrine of the Word of God* (Edinburgh: T&T Clark, 1975), 449. The 'objective' side of the revelation of the Father and Son is God coming to the world in Christ, as in John 1:18.
[16] Cited by Vanhoozer, *Is there a Meaning in this Text?*, 413.
[17] J. I. Packer, 'Understanding the Bible: Evangelical Hermeneutics' in *Collected Shorter Writings of J. I. Packer*, Vol. 3: *Honouring the Written Word of God* (Carlisle: Paternoster, 1999), 159.
[18] J. I. Packer, 'Infallible Scripture and the Role of Hermeneutics' in *Scripture and Truth,* ed. D. A. Carson and J. D. Woodbridge (Leicester: IVP, 1983), 347. See also J. I. Packer, *Keep in Step with the Spirit* (Leicester: IVP, 1984), 239 for a description of the processes that went into producing the Bible.
[19] G. D. Fee, *God's Empowering Presence: The Holy Spirit in the Letters of Paul* (Peabody, MA.: Hendrickson, 1994).
[20] French L. Arrington, 'The Use of the Bible by Pentecostals,' *Pneuma: Journal of the Society for Pentecostal Studies* Vol 16 (1994), 104.

This brief historical overview has hopefully highlighted the key role of the Holy Spirit in at least evangelical hermeneutics, but it has also pointed to two limitations. Firstly, the traditional explication of his interpretive role in terms of 'illumination' and 'revelation'[21] has at times been at the expense of a more nuanced approach that interacts with other kinds of interpretive insights from Scripture itself, not least from the complex ways in which the New Testament writers interpret the Old Testament, under the guidance of the Spirit. Secondly, the role of the Holy Spirit in interpretation has frequently been rather narrowly conceived in terms of the guidance of the individual interpreter, without reference to the corporate/community factors that are necessarily involved.

As an example, we cite Arrington's suggestion of four ways in which 'the interpreter' (an individual) relies on the Holy Spirit:

> (1) submission of the mind to God so that the critical and analytical abilities are exercised under the guidance of the Holy Spirit; (2) a genuine openness to the witness of the Spirit as the text is examined; (3) the personal experience of faith as part of the entire interpretive process; and, (4) response to the transforming call of God's word.[22]

Such summary formulations are certainly helpful, but nevertheless overlook the wider corporate dimensions of interpretation involved in being guided by the Spirit of *koinonia*.[23]

## *Some Recent Developments*

The relevance of the corporate factor has, in recent years, been increasingly recognised in theological disciplines generally, as we shall note later in this chapter, including the area of biblical hermeneutics, although the 'communal' dimension is not always linked with the work of the Spirit. Thiselton's monumental *New Horizons in Hermeneutics*, for instance, details how understanding is shaped by 'the communities to which the individual reader belongs';[24] but the reasoning for this owes more to literary reader-response theories, rather than the *koinonia* character of the Spirit.[25] Vanhoozer writes

---

[21] Eph 1:17–18.
[22] French L. Arrington, 'The Use of the Bible by Pentecostals', 105. Another example would be French L. Arrington, 'The Role of the Spirit' in *Grasping God's Word: A Hands-On Approach to Reading, Interpreting and Applying the Bible*, ed. J. Scott Duvall and J. Daniel Hays (Grand Rapids, MI: Zondervan, 2001). The otherwise helpful section 'The Spirit and the Christian Interpreter' is couched almost exclusively in individualistic terms.
[23] To be fair to Arrington, he does deal with the criticism of 'subjectivism' and acknowledges the importance of the 'community' aspect. Arrington, 'The Use of the Bible by Pentecostals', 105–107.
[24] A. C. Thiselton, *New Horizons in Hermeneutics* (Grand Rapids, MI: Zondervan, 1992), 65.
[25] But note Thiselton's more recent substantive work: A. C. Thiselton, *The Holy Spirit: In Biblical Teaching, Through the Centuries, and Today* (London: SPCK, 2013). On 454, commenting on A. Yong's *Spirit-Word-Community* (see below, fn 29), he refers to the need for '*a triadic balance between the author* [the Spirit of God and his agent], *the word* [Christ and the text], and the *response of the wider community* [Reader-Response theory] ... [for] *some or many situations*'. See also Thiselton, *New Horizons*, 558–619.

more fully about 'the *Spirit-Led* Interpretive Community',[26] often in the context of speech act theory. Grenz also highlights 'community' as 'theology's integrative motif,'[27] although he has been criticised by Vanhoozer for placing tradition and culture in equal weighting alongside Scripture in the 'triangulation' that 'constitutes the Spirit's community-forming speaking.'[28]

The most proliferous writing concerning Spirit-led hermeneutics comes, not surprisingly, from the Pentecostal stable. For instance, A. Yong's *Spirit-Word-Community: Theological Hermeneutics in Trinitarian Perspective*,[29] is an impressive work that aims 'to develop a Trinitarian hermeneutic and method from a pneumatological starting point.'[30] Its philosophical and psychological arguments spiral around the Spirit-Word-Community 'trialectic' in a methodology that engages with cultural and biblical insights. Archer similarly advocates a 'hermeneutical model … [that] encourages a tridactic dialectical and dialogical interdependent relationship between Scripture, Spirit and Community for the negotiation of meaning … [that] finds biblical support in Acts 15'.[31]

Mark Cartledge spells out the essentials of such a position:

> The most recent Pentecostal scholarship has articulated its theological method in terms of an interrelation between 'text-community-Spirit.' That is, the inspired text of Scripture functions normatively within the community of faith, the church, as the Holy Spirit mediates between the horizon of the text and the horizon of the community. Therefore, the Holy Spirit inspires the contemporary reading of the text, just as he inspired the original authors … Scripture is not viewed in a static sense, as a series of received true propositions simply to be believed and applied, but as the locus of God's continuing act of revelation.'[32]

---

[26] Vanhoozer, *Is There a Meaning in this Text?*, 410. Italics mine.
[27] S. Grenz and J. R. Franke, *Beyond Foundationalism: Shaping Theology in a Postmodern Context* (Louisville, KY: Westminster John Knox, 2001), 203–238, although the Holy Spirit is only mentioned at the end of the relevant chapter on 'community' that is based more upon social and political theory.
[28] K. J. Vanhoozer, 'On the Very Idea of a Theological System: An Essay in Aid of Triangulating Scripture, Church and World' in *Explorations in Systematic Theology: Always Reforming*, ed. A. T. B. McGowan (Leicester: Apollos, 2006), 144–147.
[29] A. Yong, *Spirit-Word-Community: Theological Hermeneutics in Trinitarian Perspective* (Aldershot: Ashgate, 2002).
[30] Yong, *Spirit-Word-Community*, 1.
[31] K. J. Archer, *A Pentecostal Hermeneutic for the Twenty-First Century: Spirit, Scripture and Community* (London; Edinburgh; New York: T&T Clark, 2004), 185.
[32] Mark J. Cartledge 'Text-Community-Spirit: The Challenges posed by Pentecostal Theological Method to Evangelical Theology' in Kevin L. Spawn and Archie Wright (eds.), *Spirit and Scripture: Exploring a Pneumatic Hermeneutic,* (London: T&T Clark, 2013), 134.

Pentecostal hermeneutics often cite the deliberations of the Jerusalem Council in Acts 15 as a prime example of this 'text-community-Spirit' hermeneutic at work.[33] But there is a need for further exploration of the wider New Testament basis for such a hermeneutic, alongside some critical reflection thereon.

## *Conclusion*

This introductory overview of current scholarship has arguably shown how there is more scope for investigating the Spirit's role in biblical hermeneutics, and in this book I will attempt this in three ways:

(a)     I shall examine the corporate nature of biblical interpretation that arises from the *koinonia* character of the Spirit

(b)     I will use a methodology that is more thoroughly rooted in Scripture, rather than in the literary and philosophical theories of modern hermeneutics

(c)     In addition, I will study a selection of New Testament passages that not only speak of the interpreting work of the Holy Spirit, but which particularly demonstrate how New Testament writers interpret the Old Testament, with the Spirit's help.

## Definitions of Terms

### *Hermeneutics*

'Hermeneutics'[34] is a term that is commonplace in theological circles because of the somewhat stretchable way in which it can be deployed in the 'science' of interpretation. Strictly speaking, hermeneutics has been defined as 'the branch of knowledge that deals with interpretation, especially of Scripture or literary texts.'[35] As such, it should not be confused with biblical exegesis. The distinction has been explained by Donald Carson:

> Exegesis is concerned with actually interpreting the text, whereas hermeneutics is concerned with the nature of the interpretive process. Exegesis concludes by saying "This passage means such and such"; hermeneutics ends by saying, "This interpretive process is constituted by the following techniques and preunderstandings."[36]

---

[33] Cartledge 'Text-Community-Spirit', in Spawn and Wright, *Spirit and Scripture,* 13, 41, 116, 133. See also pages 173-179 of this book.
[34] And the related words 'hermeneut' and 'hermeneutical'.
[35] Della Thompson, ed., *The Concise Oxford Dictionary $9^{th}$ Ed.* (Oxford: Clarendon, 1995), 635. For other definitions of 'hermeneutics', see Graeme Goldsworthy, *Gospel-Centred Hermeneutics* (Nottingham: Apollos, 2006), 25 underlining common 'presuppositional baggage.'
[36] D. A. Carson, *Exegetical Fallacies* (Grand Rapids, MI: Baker, 1984), 23.

If hermeneutics refers 'the science of how we do interpretation', 'hermeneutic' is commonly used for what Vanhoozer calls 'a theory of interpretation'.[37] This book, then, is focussed upon a 'Spirit through community' hermeneutic, seeking to explore the ways in which the Spirit of God helps the Christian church to understand Scripture.

## Community

In contemporary culture, 'community' is certainly a popular 'buzzword'[38] with a wide range of meanings.[39] Grenz and Franke define it as being a group which 'is characterized by a shared frame of reference that includes shared meanings and values, a group focus that evokes a shared sense of group identity and group solidarity, and a person focus that leads the members to draw their identity from the community.'[40]

In this book, unless otherwise stated, such references to 'community' will be to the Christian community, ranging from two or three persons gathered in Jesus's name to the wider community of the church, both local and universal. I will not, however, limit my use of the word 'community' purely to persons meeting or associating in a group context, but following Yong, will also use it to 'symbolise the communal contexts of hermeneutical inquiry, interpretation, and discernment.'[41] This will allow us to investigate the notion of the Spirit's guidance of the 'community' in the New Testament—even though the relevant passages may be associated with the name of an individual such as John, Luke or Paul—on the basis of their operating as members and representatives of the community of 'the believing faithful',[42] the historic people of God.

## Corporate/Individualistic Readings

'Corporate' is a more focussed term than 'communal/community' and has been defined as 'forming one body of many individuals.'[43] In our context, this is 'the body of Christ' (1 Cor 12:27). By a 'corporate reading' of texts, we therefore mean a tradition of reading which issues from within this body (the church), and is directed primarily to that body as a whole, although also to the individual, albeit as a secondary application. Such a reading will be referred to as against its negative counterpart of an 'individualistic' reading.

---

[37] Vanhoozer, *Is there a Meaning in this Text?*, 9.
[38] Grenz and Franke, *Beyond Foundationalism*, 215.
[39] The *Concise Oxford Dictionary*, 268, lists no less than eight! The lack of a communal consensus on the meaning of 'community' is, perhaps, a good example of contemporary individualism!
[40] Grenz and Franke, *Beyond Foundationalism*, 225.
[41] Yong, *Spirit-Word-Community*, 16–17.
[42] Yong, *Spirit-Word-Community*, 17.
[43] *Concise Oxford Dictionary*, 299.

Individualism has been defined as 'the assumption that the self is autonomous, self-determining, and 'unencumbered'—that it exists independently of and outside any tradition or community.'[44] On this basis, interpretations of Scripture can be considered 'individualistic' in two different senses:

(i) When resulting from 'self-reliant'[45] readings which are out of tune with 'Spirit-reliant' readings that provide a link with the original Spirit-inspired writers of the Scripture and the tradition of their interpretation in church (cf. 2 Pet 2:20: 'no prophecy of Scripture comes from someone's own interpretation'[46]). Examples of this will be given in our next section.

(ii) When application is made exclusively with reference to the individual when the biblical context and wording, make it clear that the text demands a wider corporate application. As examples of this, Michael Griffiths cites the soldier of Ephesians 6, the guidance of the Spirit in Romans 8:14 and 16 and the use of spiritual gifts as in 1 Corinthians 12 and concludes: 'an individualistic interpretation of Scripture is... responsible, to a certain extent, for some of the distressing controversies which have divided Christians from time to time.'[47]

Which of these two meanings, (i) or (ii), we are adopting should be clear from the context of our discussion. Sometimes, of course, both meanings are applicable.

## Individualism in Biblical Interpretation

Although the term 'individualism' may be 'of relatively recent origin,'[48] the concept is, from a biblical perspective, endemic to fallen human nature. Bockmuehl says that the first result of the serpent's entrance in Genesis 3 was 'to place interpretation in the hands of the autonomous reasoning subject, isolated from the worshipping community: the serpent speaks to Eve, not to Eve and Adam, let alone to their fellowship with the Lord God himself who walks in the garden.'[49]

The continued breakdown of fellowship with God leads to Babel, with its confusion of tongues and a separation of peoples taking humanity further down the road of individualism.[50] That people lived independent, individualistic lives

---

[44] Grenz and Franke, *Beyond Foundationalism*, 207.
[45] From the *Concise Oxford Dictionary*'s definition of 'individualism': 'the habit or principle of being independent and self-reliant', 692.
[46] There is, however, a debate to whether the reference in this verse is to the original inspiration of Scripture or its subsequent interpretation.
[47] Michael Griffiths, *Cinderella with Amnesia: A Practical Discussion of the Relevance of the Church* (London: IVP, 1975), 26.
[48] Grenz and Franke, *Beyond Foundationalism*, 206, tracing it back to the nineteenth century.
[49] Markus Bockmuehl, *Seeing the Word: Refocusing New Testament Study* (Grand Rapids, MI: Baker Academic, 2006), 93.
[50] Gen 11:9.

is indicted in Judges 21:25: 'In those days there was no king in Israel. Everyone did what was right in his own eyes.' The ongoing perversion of the interpretive process—which was itself the result of sin—earned the regular tirades of the prophets against those 'prophesying lies... the deceit of their own minds' (Jer 14:14). In contrast to the true prophets who spoke by 'the Spirit of the LORD' (Ezek 11:5), Ezekiel had to rebuke 'the foolish prophets who follow their own spirit' (Ezek 13:3).

The coming of the Spirit upon the first Christians at Pentecost is often thought of as a reversal of the effects of Babel and was accompanied by a renewed life of community,[51] a *koinonia* of both people[52] and property.[53] What is more, the early church subsequently expressed its understanding of its reading of Old Testament texts in the words 'it seemed good to the Holy Spirit and to us,'[54] a phrase that reveals the church's understanding of itself as being a Spirit-inspired community. Paul's frequent references to *koinonia*[55] provide further evidence of this, for not only did Paul understand the true church to be a Spirit-inspired community, his own Scriptural readings were pneumatologically driven, and often expressed in corporate terms.[56]

By the end of the New Testament era, however, Dunn has argued that the corporate aspect of the Spirit's working was being stifled by increasing 'formalization of faith and institutionalization of church'[57] and a more 'individualised' conception of the working of the Spirit, purportedly shown in 1 John.[58] Burge, however, challenges this viewpoint relating to Johannine pneumatology in his work appropriately entitled *The Anointed Community*.[59] Whatever the exact state of 'community' within the church at the end of the New Testament era, it is clear that the further away the church moves from the first-hand effects of Spirit-inspired readings of the Word within the believing community, the greater the lapse into individualised readings that are the products of the peculiar understanding, bias, and historical and social circumstances of the interpreters involved.

---

[51] As in Acts 2:42–47; 4:32–37.
[52] Acts 2:42.
[53] Acts 2:44.
[54] Acts 15:28. See pages 173–179 for more detail on Acts 15.
[55] See chapter 2.
[56] See chapter 6.
[57] J. D. G. Dunn, *Jesus and the Spirit: A Study of the Religious and Charismatic Experience of Jesus and the First Christians as Reflected in the New Testament* (London: SCM, 1975), 349.
[58] 'For John, the 'vertical' relationship with God the Spirit is essentially an *individual* affair' ... 'everything is seen in terms of the individual's immediate relationship to God through the Spirit and the word,' Dunn, *Jesus and the Spirit*, 354–355.
[59] G. M. Burge, *The Anointed Community: The Holy Spirit in the Johannine Tradition* (Grand Rapids, MI: Eerdmans, 1987). See also chapter 7 of this book on 1 John.

As we briefly survey the complex history of biblical interpretation, the extent to which 'individualistic' tendencies are evident is a debatable matter upon which we can but point to six examples over the centuries which still have relevance today.

(a) In the patristic period, appeal to the *regula fidei*, certainly represented a commonly accepted 'hermeneutical consensus.'[60] Origen, however, was influential in promoting the *allegorical* approach to the Bible, stemming from Greek thought, in which the interpreter was invited to start with plain or grammatical meaning of the text but then 'rise from the letter to the spirit.'[61] This may have helped to provide applications of the text that encouraged the church to 'go on living with and under scripture,'[62] but also had the effect of creating a wedge between Word and Spirit[63] and of removing the meaning of Scripture from its narrative context.[64] As allegorical exegesis developed in the medieval period, Wright claims that 'almost anything could be "proved" from Scripture.'[65] The idiosyncratic interpretations that have followed, both historically[66] and today,[67] can be labelled 'individualistic' to the extent that the resultant readings are often peculiar to the interpreter who devised them.

(b) The eccentricities of the allegorical method were but one of the factors that led to the protests of the Reformers[68] in their overall concern to defend Christian truth against the doctrinal and moral corruption in the church in the sixteenth century. Their key doctrine of *sola Scriptura*—that Scripture is the only rule in matters of faith—has consistently encouraged Christians to 'get back to the Bible.' It has, however, as already noted, been accused of divorcing biblical

---

[60] Keith A. Matheson, *The Shape of Sola Scriptura* (Moscow, ID: Canon, 2001), 280. For *regula fidei*, see fn. 74.

[61] A. C. Thiselton, 'Hermeneutics' in *New Dictionary of Theology*, ed. S. Ferguson et al (Leicester: IVP, 1988), 294. As an example of the pervasive influence of the allegorical method, we could cite Arthur M. Climenhaga's tracing of universalist thinking back to Origen's methodology: 'on the basis of an allegorical interpretation of Scripture he developed the theory that all men (and even fallen angels) ultimately would be redeemed; thus the term 'cosmological universalism.' Arthur M. Climenhaga, 'Mission and Neo-Universalism,' *Evangelical Review of Theology* (2004) 28:1, 4.

[62] N.T. Wright, *Scripture and the Authority of God* (London: SPCK, 2005), 50.

[63] G. L. Bray, *Biblical Interpretation- Past and Present* (Leicester: Apollos, 1996), 83.

[64] Wright, *Scripture and the Authority of God*, 50.

[65] Wright, *Scripture and the Authority of God*, 52. Despite this, it has been claimed that 'at its best, precritical exegesis was not individualistic. Not all lay people could access the Scriptures, but those who could do so were seeking to orient their spiritual lives around participating in the divine liturgy and teaching others.' Daniel J. Treier, *Introducing Theological Interpretation of Scripture: Recovering a Christian Practice* (Nottingham: Apollos, 2008), 79.

[66] Thiselton cites, as an early example, Clement of Rome (c. AD 96) who, when commenting on Jos. 2:18 observes that the Israelite spies gave Rahab a sign 'that she should hang out a scarlet thread from her house, foreshowing that all who achieve and hope in God shall have deliverance through the blood of the Lord' (*1 Clem. 12:7*). A. C. Thiselton, 'Hermeneutics', in Ferguson et al, *New Dictionary of Theology*, 294. Wright cites the medieval Hugh of St Victor suggesting that 'Noah's Ark, being 300 cubits long, points to the cross – since the Greek letter T, in the shape of a cross, represents the number 300': Wright, *Scripture and the Authority of God*, 52.

[67] Such as 'this = that' approaches, as in dispensationalism, that can draw too straight lines between 'Bible prophecy' and contemporary happenings.

[68] They re-emphasized the grammatical and literal sense of biblical texts and elaborated a 'covenant' or 'federal' theology, which 'gave the church a way of reading the Old Testament as a Christian book without lapsing into allegory', Bray, *Biblical Interpretation - Past and Present*, 167.

interpretation from the control of the church, and thus making way for all kinds of private, indeed individualistic readings of Scripture,[69] sometimes leading to a form of bibliolatry that has little place for ecclesiology.

Bray points out, however, that it was not Calvin's intention to facilitate individualist readings of the text by *sola Scriptura* and the allied doctrine of the 'inner witness of the Spirit'.[70] 'This was not a subjective experience, as we might imagine it today, but an objective conviction that what was plain in the text was also true in experience. The idea that the inner witness might somehow lead to a private (and offbeat) interpretation of the Bible was the farthest thing from his mind.'[71]

Matheson recognizes that *sola Scriptura* has at times degenerated into an autonomous form of 'solo'[72] *Scriptura* in modern Western evangelicalism (due to the absorption of 'enlightenment rationalism and rugged democratic individualism'[73]), but argues that the Reformers never intended to jettison the place of the 'communion of saints' and tradition in the interpretation of Scripture. Rather, *sola Scriptura* means that 'Scripture must be confessed as the sole source of revelation; it must be confessed as the only infallible, final and authoritative norm of doctrine and practice; it is to be interpreted in and by the church; and it is to be interpreted according to the *regula fidei*.'[74]

---

[69] To cite a typical recent (1993) Catholic critique of 'fundamentalist' interpretation: 'In its attachment to the principle of "Scripture alone", fundamentalism separates the interpretation of the Bible from the tradition, which, guided by the Spirit, has authentically developed in union with Scripture in the heart of the community of faith ... It presents itself as a form of private interpretation which does not acknowledge that the church is founded on the Bible and draws its life and inspiration from Scripture.' J. L. Houlden, ed., *The Interpretation of the Bible in the Church: Report of Pontifical Commission* (London: SCM, 1995), 45.

[70] 'Scripture must be confirmed by the witness of the Spirit. Thus may its authority be established as certain; and it is a wicked falsehood that its credibility depends on the judgment of the church ... [a]s if the eternal and inviolable truth of God depended on the decision of men! For they mock the Holy Spirit when they ask: Who can convince us that these writings came from God?' John Calvin, *Institutes of the Christian Religion* Book 1 Ch. VII, 74–5 in *The Library of Christian Classics Vol. XX*, trans. F. L. Battles, ed. John T. McNeill (Philadelphia, PA: Westminster, 1960).

[71] McNeill, *The Library of Christian Classics Vol. XX*, 193. According to Carl Trueman, 'the Protestants overcame this [i.e. individualism in interpretation] by arguing that the subjective work of the Holy Spirit guaranteed, at least in the long run, that Christian individuals would arrive at positions marked by both orthodoxy and orthopraxy. In practice, they used pastoral authority, bolstered and applied by church courts and reinforced by catechetical and casuistical work, in order to make sure that the Holy Spirit's work was indeed effectively accomplished.' See Carl Trueman, 'The Impact of the Reformation and Emerging Modernism' in *The Bible in Pastoral Practice: Readings in the Place and Function of Scripture in the Church*, ed. Ballard and S. Holmes (London: Darton, Longman and Todd, 2005), 91.

[72] 'Solo' expresses an 'aberrant Evangelical version of *sola scriptura*' that elevates the autonomy of the individual in the interpretation of Scripture, discards the creeds and overlooks human fallibility and prejudice. Keith A. Matheson, *The Shape of Sola Scriptura* (Moscow, ID: Canon, 2001), 238.

[73] Matheson, *The Shape of Sola Scriptura*, 239.

[74] Matheson, *The Shape of Sola Scriptura*, 281. Matheson refers Irenaeus's use of *regula fidei* ('the rule of faith'), the historic faith of the church as defined in 'the ecumenical creeds [which] represent the hermeneutical consensus already reached by the church' (p. 280) and as confessed down the centuries. For a recent discussion of the role of tradition, the rule of faith and *sola Scriptura* in biblical interpretation; see C. Stephen Evans 'Tradition, Biblical Interpretation and Historical Truth' in *'Behind' the Text: History and Biblical Interpretation* Vol. 4 of Scripture and Hermeneutics Series ed. Craig Bartholomew et al (Carlisle: Paternoster, 2003), 320–336. Also C. D. Allert,

(c) This *regula fidei* received a fundamental attack by the eighteenth-century *Enlightenment*[75] in its challenge to '*sapere aude*' ('have courage to use your own understanding'). Hence Descartes's admission: 'as soon as age permitted me to emerge from the control of my tutors, I entirely quitted the study of letters.'[76] He went on to develop an influential philosophy in which the human mind was supreme, lording it over all tradition, and summed up in his famous dictum *ego cogito, ergo sum* ('I think, therefore I am'). According to Brueggemann:

> The perspective of Descartes represented an immense break with traditional, church-dominated reading of the Bible and initiated a practice of reading the Bible in academic contexts that was undisciplined, unfunded and unfettered by church practice, faith or doctrine.[77]

Cunningham says that one of the lasting legacies of the Enlightenment to Western thought has been its concept of 'the apotheosis of the ostensibly solitary human being.[78]... [T]he individualism of the Enlightenment, like its rationalism, has extended itself quite forcefully into the twentieth century.'[79] Thiselton similarly highlights 'the rationalism of Descartes [which] typically signals the transition into the [profoundly individualistic] modern era. He evolves a system of rationalism by placing the individual thinking self as the centre of thought, and submitting everything else to methodological doubt. This has coloured two centuries of method in biblical interpretation.'[80]

(d) One notable 'method' that evolved from Enlightenment rationalism— *historical criticism*—is particularly associated with nineteenth century German scholars and their successors. They sought to read the Bible in terms of their 'objective' investigations of its literary history. Their critical methodologies opened new insights into the origins and meaning of Scripture and underlined some of the communal aspects in the formative/interpretive process, such as form criticism's concern with the *Sitz im Leben* (life setting or situation in

---

'What Are We Trying to Conserve? Evangelicalism and *Sola Scriptura*' in *Evangelical Quarterly* 76.4 (2004), 327–348.

[75] Alister McGrath defines the Enlightenment as 'a loose term, defying precise definition, embracing a cluster of ideas and attitudes characteristic of the period 1720–80, such as the free and constructive use of reason in an attempt to abolish old myths which were seen to have bound individuals and societies to the past'; Alister McGrath, *An Introduction to the History of Christian Thought* (Oxford: Blackwell, 1998), 220.

[76] David Weissman, ed., *Discourse on the Method and Meditations on First Philosophy* (New Haven, CT: Yale University Press, 1996), 8: quoted by Roger Lundin, 'Interpreting Orphans: Hermeneutics in the Cartesian Tradition' in *The Promise of Hermeneutics*, ed. Roger Lundin, Clarence Walhout and Anthony Thiselton (Carlisle: Paternoster, 1999), 9.

[77] Walter Brueggemann 'The Re-emergence of Scripture: Post-liberalism' in *The Bible in Pastoral Practice: Readings in the Place and Function of Scripture in the Church*ed, ed.Ballard and S. Holmes (London: Darton, Longman and Todd, 2005), 153.

[78] David Cunningham, *These Three are One: The Practice of Trinitarian Theology* (Oxford; Malden, MA: Blackwell, 1988), 170.

[79] Cunningham, *These Three are One*, 170.

[80] A. C. Thiselton, *New Horizons in Hermeneutics* (London: HarperCollins, 1992), 143.

community) or redaction criticism's interest in editing/shaping of texts by the Christian community.

The critical approach has also been attacked for creating a form of individualism with its reliance upon the powers of reason of the scholar who could end up by 'dissecting and dismantling'[81] texts that have traditionally been 'read and reread as authoritatively within a particular community.'[82] Hence 'canonical' critics like Childs have argued that 'to take the concept of canon seriously is to assign to scripture a normative role and to refuse to submit the truth of its testimony to the criteria of human reason.'[83] Francis Watson refers to the great reasoning exploits of scholars such as Schweitzer in his renowned *Quest of the Historical Jesus* (1910), to which we could add Bultmann's 'demythologization' of texts. These could be cited as examples of what Watson has labelled a 'scholarly obsession with salvaging precious "authentic" material from the mass of inferior tradition in which it has been buried.'[84]

(e) There has in recent times been a shift in emphasis from the *diachronic* approach of historical-criticism (focussed upon the historical development of texts or traditions across the passage of time) to *synchronic* methods of understanding the text that concentrate upon the meaning created through the 'dialogical process'[85] between the final form of the text and its readers. 'Biblical interpretation' has now developed into 'hermeneutics' (the science of interpretation) into which many non-theological insights have been imported. The plurality of contemporary approaches now on offer[86] affords interpreters with a rich array of interpretive tools with which to work, although the lack of a commonly accepted approach could be cited as an example of modern individualism. This could certainly be said of the more extreme *reader response* theories[87] that claim that 'meaning resides not in the text but in the readers, the

---

[81] Houlden, *The Interpretation of the Bible in the Church*, 13.
[82] F. Watson, *Text Church and World - Biblical Interpretation in Theological Perspective* (Edinburgh: T&T Clark, 1994), 103.
[83] B. S. Childs, *The Book of Exodus* (Philadelphia and London: OTL, 1974), as cited in Watson, *Text Church and World*, 32.
[84] Watson, *Text Church and World*, 42.
[85] Watson, *Text Church and World*, 137.
[86] Including rhetorical and narrative analysis, semiotics, linguistic approaches (ranging from negative forms of 'deconstructionism' to the more positive aspects of 'speech/acts' theory), sociological, socio-political, anthropological, and psychological insights. Particular readings of scripture have also come out of various contemporary concerns, represented by such diverse movements as liberation theology, inter-faith dialogue, feminism, black theology, gay 'rights', and ecology.
[87] 'The most widely known uses of reader-response theory have been in particular fields where the complaint of relativism or perhaps *individual self-legitimation* [my italics] of some sort may be valid: one thinks primarily of liberation theology and feminist theology.' Richard Briggs, Let the Reader Understand: The Role of the Reader in Biblical Interpretation' in *Evangel* Autumn 1995, 72.

interpreters of the text.'[88] For literary theorists such as Stanley Fish, 'interpretation is the only game in town.'[89]

(f) The view that 'one person's interpretation is as good as another's',[90] since 'there are no such things as texts, only interpretations'[91] has been described by Wright as 'the classic postmodern position.'[92] *Postmodernism* has contributed to the fragmentation and individualisation of the hermeneutical task in various ways, with its absolutizing of personal choice. In consequence, Ward claims that 'religious faith has to a large extent been privatized and pluralized.'[93] Along with the influence of its accompanying materialism, the experience of many pastors would confirm the view that not infrequently, at least in the West, 'disciples have become consumers, with a take-away attitude to church,'[94] including a 'pick and mix' attitude to its teachings. One example would be the appeal of 'prosperity' teaching in which promises of spiritual blessing for God's people[95] are both over-materialised and individualised.

This is an example of a 'promise box' approach to Scripture which can, indeed, bring great comfort, but which can also be misleading when applied too selfishly, not least since much of Scripture was intended to be read out congregationally and applied corporately before ever being applied individually. Private reading is a practice that has only been possible in more recent times with the advent of mass education and the ready availability of individually owned copies of the Bible, at least in the Western world.[96] Personal devotions, of course, are vital for spirituality, but Fee refers to a common type of 'devotional reading of the Bible, where the "Word for the day" is received by one's direct encounter with the text

---

[88] D. A. Carson 'How to Interpret the Bible' in *The New Bible Commentary* 4th edition, ed. D. A. Carson et al (Leicester: IVP, 1994), 11. Ian Paul's summary: 'The heart of the matter is the question of where meaning is found in the process of reading. For the rationalist concerned with objectivity, meaning lies within (or behind) the text. For the postmodern relativist, meaning is found within the reader. But in fact, meaning lies in the interaction of reader and text; there is an objective element (a text cannot simply mean anything) and a subjective element (a text cannot mean something without a reader making sense of it).' Ian Paul, 'The theological interpretation of the Bible as Scripture,' *TransMission* Spring 2001, 13.
[89] Stanley Fish, *Is There a Text in This Class? The Authority of Interpretive Communities* (Cambridge, MA: Harvard University Press, 1980), 356.
[90] Wright, *Scripture and the Authority of God*, 81.
[91] Wright, *Scripture and the Authority of God*, 82.
[92] Wright, *Scripture and the Authority of God*, 81.
[93] Keith Ward, 'The Decline and Fall of Reason. From Modernity to Postmodernity' in *Faith and Praxis in a Postmodern Age*, ed. Ursula King (London: Cassell, 1998), 1–2. For a discussion of modern day individualism (from an American angle), see David Wells *No Place for Truth – Or Whatever happened to Evangelical Theology* (Leicester: IVP, 1992), chapter IV on 'Self Piety', and D. A. Carson, *The Gagging of God-Christianity Confronts Pluralism* (Grand Rapids, MI: Zondervan, 1996), 47.
[94] Chris Andre-Watson, in Spurgeon College's *The Record*, May 2003: reviewing Derek Tidball, *Discerning the Spirit of the Age* (London: Kingsway, 2002).
[95] For instance, from 2 Cor 9:10–11. Carson points the collective nature of the promise '*you* will be made rich in every way' (v 11a, NIV). 'It does not *necessarily* follow that each individual in the church is thereby promised to become "rich in every way" and not, say, die early of cancer' D. A. Carson, *For the Love of God* Vol. 1 (Leicester: IVP, 1998).
[96] T. S. Holland, *Romans and the New Exodus: A Study in the Paschal New Exodus Theology of the Apostle Paul*, Ph.D. thesis, University of Wales, Lampeter 1996, 39.

in a more free-floating, associative way of reading texts'[97] that can be divorced from the commonly accepted, exegetically-based meaning. In a more general sense, this is a symptom, in some branches of evangelicalism, of an overemphasis upon the 'personal' at the expense of the corporate.[98] Further examples of this include: an over concentration upon the individual testimony at the expense of the story of the church and the truths of the gospel;[99] upon 'me and God' expressions in worship and devotion at the expense of 'God and us';[100] undue vauntings of '*charismata* [so that they become] ... a threat to community;'[101] and a common distrust, in the modern day, of anything which may be thought of as 'tradition'.[102]

There are, of course, exceptions to these generalisations. I am not claiming that the Bible has not been, or is not being, interpreted correctly by people indwelt and guided by the Spirit. And, as we shall see shortly, there has been a recovery of interest in the corporate/communal element in both theology and hermeneutics in recent times. However, influences such as the eccentricities of the allegorical method, the misuse of *sola Scriptura*, the rationalism of critical methodology, the subjectivisms of over personalised spirituality and postmodernism still produce readings of the Bible which are too exclusively individualistic. As Vanhoozer says, 'self-love can pervert the course of interpretation as it does every other human activity. It is [only] the Spirit who enables us to transfer attention away from ourselves and our interests to the text and its subject matter.'[103] Similarly, Watson observes that 'theological reflection can be a purely individual and individualistic activity, or it can be addressed to communities other than the ecclesial one. If theology is to be Christian, however, the ecclesial community must be its primary point of reference.'[104] I shall now cite some arguments for this.

---

[97] G. D. Fee, *Listening to the Spirit in the Text* (Grand Rapids, MI; Cambridge: Eerdmans, 2000), 8.
[98] See J. B. Thomson 'Time for Church? Evangelicals, Scripture and Conversational Hermeneutics' in *Anvil*, Vol. 21 No. 4 2004, 247–248.
[99] For a positive Pentecostal evaluation of 'testimonies' in the life of the church, see John C. Thomas 'What the Spirit is Saying to the Church – the Testimony of a Pentecostal' in New Testament Studies, in *Spirit and Scripture: Exploring a Pneumatic Hermeneutic*, ed. Kevin L. Spawn and Archie Wright (London: T & T Clark, 2013), 118–119.
[100] In *The Complete Mission Praise* (London: Marshall Pickering, 1999), a songbook that has found acceptance in many churches as containing a balance of the old and the new, 100 of the songs begin with 'I', 40 with 'we' and 25 with 'God'.
[101] Dunn, *Jesus and the Spirit*, 266, referring to 'the Corinthians' over-evaluation of charismatic phenomena ...'
[102] According to Bray, 'the concept of *sola Scriptura* and the belief in the indwelling presence of the Holy Spirit today are often too strong for the claims of tradition to be highly regarded'; Bray, *Biblical Interpretation - Past and Present*, 562.
[103] K. J. Vanhoozer, 'The Spirit of Understanding: Special Revelation and General Hermeneutics' in *Disciplining Hermeneutics: Interpretation in Christian Perspective*, ed. Roger Lundin (Grand Rapids, MI: Eerdmans; Leicester: Apollos, 1997), 161.
[104] Watson, *Text Church and World*, 7.

## The Case for a 'Community' Approach

Whilst there is no doubt that the Holy Spirit does give highly *personal* guidance and inspiration to individuals,[105] not least in the realm of Bible study, and sermon preparation and delivery, the fact remains that most of the early Christian texts were written to churches in a community context, and consequently, much may be lost of the original meaning if this corporate setting is overlooked. Hence there is a strong case to be made for emphasizing the Spirit's guidance of the *community*, as opposed to the individual, as custodian and interpreter of Scripture. Just a brief look at some of the evidence, from both biblical and non-biblical disciplines, will make this plain.

(a) Most importantly, from the angle of the hermeneutical/pneumatological thrust of this book, the very *character of the Holy Spirit* as the Spirit of fellowship/communion, or more precisely κοινωνία,[106] should propel us towards a community reading of the Scripture, i.e. within the churchly context. It has, for instance, been pointed out by Dunn that 'the early church's sense of community stemmed basically not from the first resurrection appearances but from Pentecost... *from the common experience of the eschatological Spirit and the communal enthusiasm engendered thereby.*'[107] (The dimensions of κοινωνία will be discussed in more detail in the next chapter).

(b) It is to be noted that the insights of *cultural anthropology* have revealed a background to the New Testament very different to that of the individualist culture of the Western world of today. Malina says:

> Instead of individualism, we find in the first-century Mediterranean world... a strong group orientation. Persons always considered themselves in terms of the group(s) in which they experienced themselves as inextricably embedded. We might describe such a psychological orientation as "dyadism" (a pair, a twosome), as opposed to "individualism". The dyadic person is 'a group-embedded person ... who simply needs another continually in order to know who he or she really is.'[108]

Such a 'group orientation', of course, was not limited to the first century, but can be seen as a distinctive feature of the Jewish culture from which Christianity sprang and derived its essentially corporate identity, a feature that persists in Judaism to this day, as a former Chief Rabbi has written:

---

[105] Cf. Acts 8:29: 'And the Spirit said to Philip...' Note also Acts 10:19, 11:28, Luke 4:18.
[106] As in 2 Cor 13:14.
[107] Dunn, *Jesus and the Spirit*, 188. Italics his.
[108] Bruce Malina, *The New Testament World: Insights from Cultural Anthropology* (Louisville, KY: Westminster John Knox, 1993), 67. Many group orientated societies of course still exist, such as in African tribal culture.

> Judaism is an insistently communal faith. [Some] belief systems [have] emphasized the individual. Dean Inge once defined religion as 'what an individual does with his own solitude'. Walter Savage Landor called solitude 'the audience chamber of God.' Plotinus spoke of the 'flight of the alone to the Alone'. For them the primary religious experience is the private communion of the soul with God. That has never been the Jewish way. To be sure, we have had our share of mystics and contemplatives, but the greatest challenge as Judaism has seen it is not to ascend from earth to heaven through the journey of the soul, but to bring the Divine presence from heaven to earth and share it with others. That is an essentially collective task, which is why the covenant at Mount Sinai was made not with individuals but with an entire people. In biblical times it was the task of the nation. In the Diaspora it became the function of communities.[109]

Cultural anthropologists have also applied the concept of 'liminality' ('that stage of existence which is on the *threshold* of a new world, in transition from the order of a previous world'[110]) to the early Christian congregations and postulated that 'a necessary correlate of liminality is *communitas*,'[111] as the foundation for their new order.

(c) In addition to all this, Stephen Barton has pointed out how *sociological* studies have drawn attention to the essentially communal dimension of the life of the first Christians:

> [C]ommunity formation and maintenance were all-pervasive concerns in early Christianity.... [F]rom the beginning, following Jesus was a thoroughly social commitment, which involved the shaping of a corporate life engaged in an all-pervasive ... way with questions of morality, politics, economics, law and culture. From the perspective of Christian origins, therefore, it is impossible to justify a separation of personal salvation and spirituality, on the one hand, and corporate identity and responsibility on the other. [112]

Other studies have looked at the character of ancient Greco-Roman/Jewish associations as the social context for the community formation of the early church, alongside the distinctively spiritual dimension brought to it by the New Testament. [113]

---

[109] Jonathan Sacks, *Celebrating Life* (London: Continuum, 2003), 136.
[110] Richard L. Jeske, 'Spirit and Community in the Johannine Apocalypse,' *New Testament Studies* Vol. 31 1985, 458, referring to the work of A. van Gennup, V. Turner, and J. Gager.
[111] Jeske, 'Spirit and Community in the Johannine Apocalypse', 459.
[112] S. Barton, 'The Communal Dimension of Earliest Christianity: A Critical Survey of the Field,' *Journal of Theological Studies* Oct. 1992 Vol. 43 Part 2, 407, 426–427, tracing the recovery of the communal dimension in recent theological study.
[113] See, for example, R. N. Longenecker, ed., *Community Formation in the Early Church and in the Church Today* (Peabody, MA: Hendrikson, 2002).

(d) Other areas of scholarship have also argued for a more corporate interpretive approach. For instance, some *philosophers* have reacted against various forms of individualism in religious thought to produce diverse theories of communal ontology. Josiah Royce, for example, a century ago, insisted upon the essentially societal nature of religious experience, the necessity of 'a Community of Interpretation,' and of its being united and guided by a 'Spirit' of interpretation.[114] His definitions of 'Community' and 'Spirit' are admittedly somewhat unorthodox,[115] being part of his visionary goal of reaching an absolute ideal of 'complete mutual understanding,'[116] but his 'Beloved community'/Spirit directing notions at least show affinities with the kind of hermeneutical process that we are discussing here.

(e) Back within the Christian church, two worldwide *ecclesiastical movements* have, over the last century, also highlighted the importance of the community dimension, albeit from different angles. The *ecumenical* movement in its resistance to individualism[117] has described itself as 'On the way to Fuller Koinonia'[118] and 'The church as a hermeneutical community.'[119] As a follow-up to this, a recent report on discussions between Catholics and Evangelicals, 'Church, Evangelization, and the Bonds of *Koinonia*',[120] refers to the perceived need for 'Growing in *Koinonia*'[121] in the evangelistic witness of the church. On the other hand, the rise of *Pentecostalism*[122] has arguably brought 'a contribution to hermeneutics [which] is in the area of community participation and experiential understanding.'[123] Hence, for instance, a Pentecostal 'hermeneutic built on Acts 15 [which] has three primary components: the community, the activity of the Spirit and the Scripture.'[124]

---

[114] Josiah Royce, *The Problem of Christianity* (New York, NY: MacMillan, 1913). Royce is reacting against William James's *Varieties of Religious Experience* that confined it to the experience of individuals, and writes, 'All experience must be *at least* individual experience; but unless it is *also* social experience, and unless the whole religious community which is in question unites to share it, this experience is but as sounding brass...'xvi, Vol. I;211, Vol II.

[115] Josiah Royce, *The Problem of Christianity, Vol. II,* 220, 428-429.

[116] Josiah Royce, *The Problem of Christianity, Vol. II,* 220.

[117] Michael Kinnamon highlights ecumenism's consistent rejection of 'individualism' in favour of its insistence 'that diverse individuals committed to truth need each other, that *community* is the context within which various claims are continually tested and enriched'; Michael Kinnamon, *Truth and Community: Diversity and its limits in the Ecumenical Movement* (Grand Rapids, MI: Eerdmans, 1988), 10–11.

[118] T. F. Best and G. Gassman, eds., 'On the Way to Fuller Koinonia,' *Faith and Order* No.166, (Geneva: WCC, 1993).

[119] Anton Houten, 'Hermeneutics and Ecumenism: The Art of Understanding a Communicative God', in *Interpreting Together: Essays in Hermeneutics*, ed. Bouteneff and D. Heller (Geneva: WCC, 2001), 5.

[120] G. Vandervelde, 'A Report of the International Consultation between the Catholic Church and the World Evangelical Alliance (1993-2002)', *Evangelical Review of Theology* Vol. 29 No. 2 April 2005, 100-130.

[121] Vandervelde, 'A Report of the International Consultation,' 122.

[122] 'With a third of a billion adherents around the world, and the fastest growing part of the worldwide church, Pentecostals cannot be ignored' Paul Goodliff in *Baptist Times*, July 7th 2005.

[123] Kenneth J. Archer, 'Pentecostal Hermeneutics: Retrospect and Prospect' *JPT* 8 (1996), 81.

[124] John Christopher Thomas, 'Women, Pentecostals and the Bible: An Experiment in Pentecostal Hermeneutics', *JPT* 5 (1994), 50. The 'Scripture-Community-Spirit ... triad' is also highlighted by Paul Hanson as 'the basis for a biblically informed spiritual understanding of reality': Paul Hanson, 'Scripture, Community and Spirit: Biblical Theology's Contribution to a Contextualized Christian Theology'; *JPT* 6 (1995), 8. See also Kenneth J. Archer, *A*

(f) Such a focus shows how developments in *theological studies* have, in very different ways, sought to recapture the early Christian emphasis upon community. Critical studies have long emphasized the role of the early Christian community in the production of Scripture, not infrequently to the point of denying individual apostolic authorship of certain New Testament books.[125] From a more recent conservative perspective, canonical criticism has drawn attention to 'the function of the Bible as canon in the believing communities which formed and shaped it and passed it on to their heirs of today.'[126] In the realm of general theologizing, scholars such as Grenz and Franke have written about a 'New Communitarianism'[127] in its reaction to 'individualistic atomism linked to political liberalism'[128] and which, for them, is expressed in 'the concept of community as the integrative motif of Christian theology.'[129] Hence this motif in recent efforts to develop a more 'theological interpretation of the Bible'[130] with its concern for what Vanhoozer calls 'reading Scripture in and for the community of the faithful.'[131]

Biblical theologians generally have underlined the essentially corporate nature of primitive Christianity, a fact often missed in the world of 'liberal Protestantism', with its emphasis upon the individual's submission to God.[132] Thus Tom Holland has argued that a Paschal-new exodus motif undergirds the whole of Pauline soteriology, and that his theology is an outflow of the corporate solidarity of his Hebrew background rather than Hellenism, with its bias towards individualism.[133] The Pauline letters, moreover, were generally addressed to churches rather than individuals. Indeed, as Bockmuehl says, 'almost invariably, the implied readers [of the New Testament] are ecclesially situated.'[134] Hence Johnson's comment that the NT writings 'were not composed for private readership ... or for individual interpretation ... but written for *communities* ...

---

*Pentecostal Hermeneutic for the Twenty-First Century: Spirit, Scripture and Community* (Edinburgh; London; New York: T&T Clark, 2004).

[125] For example, in the authorship of the Pastoral Epistles, see pages 226–228.

[126] James A. Sanders, *Canon and Community: A Guide to Canonical Criticism* (Philadelphia, PA: Fortress, 1984), xv.

[127] Grenz and Franke, *Beyond Foundationalism*, 210. In connection with 'the retrieval of the communal tradition' (p. 208), they mention contemporary names such as Alasdair MacIntyre, Michael Sandel, Stanley Hauerwas, and James McClendon, but also refer to an earlier 'renaissance of communitarian thinking' (p. 210) in German Romantic thinkers such as Johann Herder (d. 1803) and G. W. F. Hegel (d. 1831).

[128] Grenz and Franke, *Beyond Foundationalism*, 208.

[129] Grenz and Franke, *Beyond Foundationalism*, 232.

[130] K. J. Vanhoozer et al, eds., *Dictionary for Theological Interpretation of the Bible* (Grand Rapids: Baker, 2005), 19.

[131] Vanhoozer et al, eds., *Dictionary for Theological Interpretation of the Bible*, 19. See also Treier, *Introducing Theological Introduction of Scripture*, 79–100.

[132] E. Stauffer, 'The Individualism of the Fourth Gospel' in *Essays in New Testament Interpretation*, ed. C. F. D. Moule (Cambridge: Cambridge University Press, 1982), 91.

[133] Holland, *Contours of Pauline Theology*.

[134] M. Bockmuehl, *Seeing the World*, 71–72: adding that they also 'evidently assumed to be "inspired" in the sense of Spirit filled.'

to be read aloud, and to be interpreted in preaching, and to be open to the discernment of all.'[135]

English has, furthermore, underlined the implications of New Testament plural terminology:

> The intense individualism of our culture often cloaks the corporate implications of New Testament teaching. The failure of the English language adequately to distinguish between second person singular and second person plural is also a great hindrance. Not least it masks the fact that most of the great commands and promises of the New Testament are stated in the plural. We need some equivalent of the southern United States expression 'y'all'![136]

In view of all this, says Holland, the New Testament needs to be interpreted through 'the lens of a corporate reading of the texts.'[137]

(g) As already mentioned, as tenets of *literary theory* have increasingly been employed to biblical interpretation, attention has been focussed upon the role of the reader(s) in supplementing, or even supplying textual meaning. Fish has influentially written about 'the *authority* of interpretative communities,'[138] whilst Fowler asserts that meaning is 'not buried... in the text... Rather, it is something produced in the act of reading through the unique interaction on the text and the particular reader doing the reading, at a particular moment, from a particular slant.'[139] Hauerwas has claimed that the Bible 'should only be made available to those who have undergone the hard discipline of existing as part of God's people.'[140] Understandable though such comments may be, reader-response theories can nevertheless seriously confuse the text with its interpretation and are open to a number of other objections from a Christian viewpoint.[141] They do, however, highlight the fact that 'readers do bring much

---

[135] Luke Timothy Johnson, *Scripture and Discernment* (Nashville, TN: Abingdon, 1996), 58.
[136] D. English, *The Message of Mark* B.S.T. series (Leicester: IVP, 1992), 38. Michael Griffiths regards the confusion between the second person singular and second person plural in the English language as 'one possible cultural reason for our Western individualism'; Griffiths, *Cinderella with Amnesia*, 24.
[137] Holland, *Contours of Pauline Theology*, 291, claiming that this has 'been missing from virtually all NT exegesis.'
[138] Stanley Fish, *Is There a Text in This Class? The Authority of Interpretive Communities* (Cambridge, MA: Harvard University Press, 1980).
[139] R. M. Fowler, *Let the Reader Understand: Reader-Response Criticism and the Gospel of Mark* (Minneapolis: Fortress, 1991), 50: as cited by Sean Winter, *More Light and Truth? Biblical Interpretation in Covenantal Perspective, Whitley Lecture 2007* (Oxford: Whitely, 2007), 12.
[140] Stanley Hauerwas, *Unleashing the Scriptures: Freeing the Bible from Captivity to America* (Nashville, TN: Abingdon, 1980), 9, as quoted in Timothy Ward, *Word and Supplement: Speech Acts, Biblical Texts, and the Sufficiency of Scripture* (Oxford: Oxford University Press, 2002), 187.
[141] For example, by all but obliterating any notion of textual objectivity or respect for authorial intention: 'the community of the interpreter influences the interpretation and the community must also appropriate the fruit of that interpretation. However, the context is not the text. The community is the context for interpreting the text, it is not the sacred text. Otherwise, the process becomes circular: we interpret the biblical text as a community and then interpret the community as a text.' H. K. Harrington and R. Patten, 'Pentecostal Hermeneutics and Postmodern Literary Theory' in *Pneuma: The Journal of the Society for Pentecostal Studies*, Vol. 16 No. 1 Spring 1994, 111. See further pages 35–41 of this chapter, and the critique of Fish and Hauerwas in Ward, *Word and Supplement*, 182–190.

of themselves to biblical interpretation'[142]—not least from their 'diverse identity, social location, gender, ethnicity, class, theological assumptions and denominational allegiance'[143]—a fact that has been explored philosophically by Hans-Georg Gadamer in his insistence upon the reader's location in a tradition of understanding. [144]

(h) We should, finally, note the widespread recognition that *contemporary Western culture* has been blighted and fragmented by a relentless tide of individualism that has affected every area of Western society, including the church. Fee claims that 'one of the sure members of the modern world's Trinity, along with relativism and materialism, is individualism.'[145] In the UK, a recent report commissioned by the Salvation Army bore the title '*The Responsibility Gap: Individualism, Community and Responsibility in Britain*'. It claims that growing individualism and 'time famine' has meant that adults are 'too busy to help the vulnerable.'[146] This is but one instance of the scourge of contemporary individualism which has led to many voices crying out for a recovery of 'community'.

It is the purpose of this book to challenge this kind of individualism and to argue that, as part of the church's response to the need for 'community', there should be a strengthening of the '*koinonia* of the Spirit' in biblical interpretation that will, in turn, be translated into the praxis of the church and its witness in society. The eight factors outlined in this section (pneumatological, anthropological, sociological, philosophical, ecclesiastical, theological, literary, and cultural) all underline the case for the key role of 'community' in church life and hermeneutics. Bible reading and understanding needs to be pursued in conscious and Spirit-given awareness of being part of the 'communion of the saints'.

Of course, the idea of 'community' is open to very different conceptions,[147] and in the secularised culture of the West, is often thought of in exclusively social terms. But from a Christian angle, however, the deepest form of sociality has a

---

[142] Ward, *Word and Supplement*, 191.
[143] Winter, *More Light and Truth?*, 13.
[144] See Ward, *Word and Supplement*, 193–197 and pages 68–69 of this book.
[145] G. D. Fee, 'The Spirit and the Church', lecture given at Trinity College, Bristol, 26th February, 2004.
[146] As reported in *The Daily Telegraph* January 13th 2004, 8.
[147] Discussions about 'community', of course, cross different disciplines, including theology, sociology, philosophy and political philosophy. See Grenz and Franke, *Beyond Foundationalism*, 203–239 for a sociological/theological discussion of 'The Concept of Community.' Archie Spencer notes that '[T]here is no consensus as to what constitutes [the] contemporary desire for community. In the long run, Christians and postmoderns are likely to disagree not only on what constitutes a community but also on why community is desirable ... Jacques Derrida, once referred to the word "community" as "a word I never much liked, because of its connotation of participation, indeed fusion, identification: I see in it as many threats as promises"... I rather suspect that no secular desire for community will ever overcome the secular fear of the loss of individual identity...'; Archie Spencer 'Culture, community and commitments: Stanley J. Grenz on Theological Method', *Scottish Journal of Theology* Vol. 57 No. 3 2004, 353.

## Dangers of a 'Community' Approach

Before we continue to explore the dimensions of 'community' in biblical interpretation, we need to point out some possible pitfalls. The very positive aspects of a community orientation need always to be balanced by an awareness of the corresponding dangers, both in hermeneutics and in the life and health of the church. Here, then, are four possible dangers when moving in a 'community' direction.

### *Community Absolutism*

The motto of 'let the people decide!' may be appropriate in the politics of *demo*cracy, but not always so in the realm of the Christian church, which in the final analysis is meant to be a *theo*cracy, under the rule of God. 'Community' focussed understanding can easily be dominated by human opinion rather that divine revelation, whilst corporate pride can precede a corporate fall.

The 'community' is, indeed, not always right. In the world, the clamour of the crowd can 'crowd out' the voice of God,[148] and the confusion of the crowd can stifle the voice of reason.[149] It is even more lamentable when this happens in the church, yet the Bible, especially the Old Testament, abounds with examples of God's people rebelling against God's voice. As Vanhoozer says, '[t]he believing community is all too often portrayed in Scripture as unbelieving or confused, and subsequent church history has not been reassuring either.'[150] He accordingly presses home the necessary hermeneutical warning. 'If the literal sense is a function of community conventions, if there is no text in itself, how can we guard against the possible *misuse* of Scripture?'[151]

A relevant contemporary, albeit controversial, example could be cited from the ongoing ecclesiastical debate on homosexuality. We cite a critical observation from Ashley Null, from a 'traditional' viewpoint, following the consecration of a gay bishop in the USA:

> The legislative leadership of the Episcopal Church ... believes that they have been called and, therefore, inspired by the Holy Spirit to establish the guidelines by which the Bible is to be interpreted. In keeping with

---

[148] As in Matt 27:22–23.
[149] As in Acts 19:32.
[150] Vanhoozer makes this point *contra* Hans Frei's argument that the 'community consensus on Scripture' is 'the stabilizing force for the notion of the literal sense'; Kevin J. Vanhoozer, 'The Spirit of Understanding: Special Revelation and General Hermeneutics' in *Disciplining Hermeneutics: Interpretation in Christian Perspective*, ed. Roger Lundin (Leicester: Apollos, 1997), 145–146.
[151] Lundin, *Disciplining Hermeneutics*, 146.

their commitment to religious truth as an experience of the inherent oneness of all things, they have selected those biblical texts which talk about the inclusion of 'outcasts' [viz. homosexuals[152]] as the true definition of the gospel of Christ.... Because of this selective biblical hermeneutic, homosexual practice is not automatically ruled out as wrong as in many other parts of the Anglican Communion.[153]

The whole homosexual debate highlights the variability of community interpretations when made under an ecclesial authority that is neither absolute nor committed to a particular biblical hermeneutic. It also illustrates the difficulties of achieving consensus in a 'Communion' (in this case, the Anglican) that includes such wide ranging opinions.[154]

On a more general level, the existence of so many denominations, sects, splinter movements, and house fellowships today is further testimony to the hermeneutical fickleness of groups, both large and small. Jones has also challenged free church models of decision making that can resemble 'a mock-Parliament debate and a vote'[155] rather than a listening, prayerful, and reflective consultation. Cartledge further has warned how 'the critical capacity of Scripture' can be 'domesticated by the community', which in turn can 'become the *norming norm*, rather than Scripture.'[156] All this underlines the perpetual danger of idealising 'community.'[157]

In view of this danger, we need to heed McClendon's reminder that ultimately authority belongs to God and that the authority of the community that is the church is therefore only permissible if 'it functions as a fellowship in the Spirit.'[158] Later in our book, we shall look at some of the tests for discerning a work of the Spirit,[159] but now point out another danger associated with the terminology of 'Spirit.'

---

[152] Author's insertion.

[153] Ashley Null 'Understanding the Episcopal Church and Why They Consecrated a Gay Bishop', *The Briefing* Jan. 2004, 14. For further comment on Anglican hermeneutics and the need for a wider ecclesial hermeneutic, see John B. Thomson, 'Time for Church? Evangelicals, Scripture and Conversational Hermeneutics,' *Anvil* Vol. 21 No. 4 2004, 245-257.

[154] In January 2016, the Primates of the Anglican Communion met and concluded that 'recent developments in the Episcopal Church with respect to their canon on marriage represent a fundamental departure from the faith and teaching held by the majority of our Provinces on the doctrine of marriage.... The traditional doctrine of the church in view of the teaching of Scripture upholds marriage as between a man and a woman in faithful, lifelong union. The majority of those gathered reaffirm this teaching ...' The Episcopal church was banned from taking part in certain decision making bodies for three years. <www.primates2016.org/articles/2016/01/14/statement-primates-2016>

[155] Keith G. Jones, *A Believing Church – Learning from Some Contemporary Anabaptist and Baptist Perspectives* (Didcot: Baptist Union of Great Britain, 1998), 39.

[156] Cartledge, *Spirit & Scripture*, 141-142.

[157] Note F. Watson's critique of Childs' canonical criticism: 'he is operating with a concept of an *ideal* community of faith to which real communities only occasionally and imperfectly correspond': Watson, *Text Church and World*, 44.

[158] James Wm. McClendon, *Systematic Theology: Doctrine* Vol. II (Nashville, TN: Abingdon, 1994), 477.

[159] See chapter 7.

## Pneumatic Vagueness

In 1919, Leisegang noted that *pneuma* is 'a word into whose mythical depths everyone has deposited all that fit into his range of ideas, and out of which everyone heard what he could or would, according to the level of his own understanding.'[160] Such an observation seems even more relevant today when there seems to be more interest in open-ended 'spirituality' than doctrinal 'Christianity'. Vanhoozer remarks upon postmodern 'death of the author'/ reader response literary theories that use the concept of 'spirit' to internalize the interpretive process.

> With the birth of the reader, the divine has been relocated: the postmodern era is more comfortable thinking of God not as the transcendent Author but as the immanent Spirit. The Shekinah cloud has settled on the interpreting community.[161]

Other conceptions of the Spirit highlight rather nebulous 'therapeutic' aspects. A recent edition of *Retreats*,[162] for instance, refers to the Holy Spirit as 'that amorphous, creative energy of our God, illuminating and paradoxical, and totally beyond our human control'; and further, 'the Spirit in our time is calling forth a new communion between humans and the whole of creation.'[163] Such a mystical/ecologically orientated pneumatology is understandable to a degree, but it can all too easily miss out on the necessary ethical demands inherent in the concept of *Holy* Spirit, as well as the necessary Christological origins implicit in the doctrine of *filioque*.

If it is believed that the 'Father and the Son' send the Spirit, it is also a risky business to build up a foundational theological system that 'begins with the Spirit', as for instance, does the Pentecostally-rooted theologian Amos Yong.[164] His view that a 'Trinitarian theological hermeneutic' necessarily needs a 'pneumatological starting point'[165] would doubtless be criticised by Bloesch who claims:

> Today there is a movement away from propositional theology to narrational theology, from logos to mythos. *A Christocentric theology is being overshadowed by a pneumatocentric theology in which the living voice of the Spirit is viewed as a higher authority than the written Word of God.* The appeal is no longer to what Scripture says but to the

---

[160] H. Leisegang, as cited by F. W. Horn, 'Holy Spirit' in *Anchor Bible Dictionary*, ed. D. N. Freedman et al (New York: Doubleday, 1992) Vol. 3, 264.
[161] Kevin J. Vanhoozer, 'The Spirit of Understanding: Special Revelation and General Hermeneutics' in *Disciplining Hermeneutics: Interpretation in Christian Perspective*, 136-137.
[162] *Retreats*, 2004.
[163] *Retreats*, 2004, in an article entitled 'Spirituality and the Holy Spirit' by Diarmuid O'Murcho, member of Sacred Heart Missionary Congregation.
[164] Yong, *Spirit-Word-Community*, 27.
[165] Yong, *Spirit-Word-Community*, 1.

sanctified imagination of the reader. The new light that breaks forth from God's holy word supersedes the old light contained in the sacred Scripture of the past.[166]

Such a statement rides rather roughshod over the complexities of the Word/Spirit relationship. Nevertheless, it does highlight the dangers of going too far in an exclusively pneumatological direction, a direction which can lead almost anywhere if set free from the constraints of classical Trinitarian and biblical theology. As Vanhoozer rightly asserts, 'the Spirit may blow where, but not *what*, he wills,'[167] for 'the Spirit's role [in relation to Scripture] ... is not to change the meaning but to *charge* it with significance.'[168]

## *Erosion of Textual Autonomy*

Complete capitulation to modern literary theory in shifting the focus of meaning from author to readers involves a repudiation of basic evangelical doctrines, two of which are 'inspiration' and *sola Scriptura*.

The claim that the human authors of Scripture wrote under the inspiration of the Spirit[169] invests the Bible with an authority of its own that no reader or readers have the right to usurp. As John Frame states, the Spirit as 'the author of Scripture,'[170] working through human authors,[171] necessarily entails that 'Scripture has objective authority over us', whereas 'the subjective authority of Scripture ... comes through the Spirit's witness.'[172]

This twofold Spirit-given authority to the text of Scripture means that Word and Spirit are for ever mutually-authenticating and mutually-interpreting. Hence Packer has argued that 'the "spiritual sense" of Scripture is nothing other than the literal sense—that is, the sense the writer's words express—'integrated with the rest of biblical teaching and applied to our individual lives.'[173] Therefore any so-called 'spiritual' reading, whether by community or individual, that detracts from this essential literal sense, goes beyond authorised limits.

---

[166] Donald G. Bloesch, *The Holy Spirit Works and Gifts* (Downers Grove, IL: IVP, 2000), 58. Italics mine.
[167] Vanhoozer, *Is There a Meaning in the Text?*, 429.
[168] Vanhoozer, *Is There a Meaning in the Text?*, 421.
[169] 1 Cor 2:9–10, 2 Tim 3:16 and 2 Pet 1:21 are often quoted in support.
[170] John M. Frame 'The Spirit and the Scriptures,' in *Hermeneutics, Authority and Canon,* ed. D. A. Carson and J. D. Woodbridge (Leicester: IVP, 1986), 217. This chapter discusses the Spirit's work in revelation, inspiration and internal testimony along Calvinist lines, but does not include the community perspective.
[171] For a discussion of the divine/human elements in inspiration, see K. J. Stewart, 'A Bombshell of a Book: Gaussen's *Theopneustia* and its Influence on Subsequent Evangelical Theology,' *Evangelical Quarterly* Vol. LXXV No. 3 July 2003, 215–237. This article traces the pervading influence of L. Gaussen's *Theopneustie ou Pleine Inspiration des Saintes Ecritures* (1840) with its alleged overstressing of the divine element at the expense of the human, along with a rather mechanical view of inspiration.
[172] Stewart, 'A Bombshell of a Book, 225. See Rom 8:14–17, 1 Cor 2:10–16 (both discussed in chapter 6), 1 Thess 1:5; 2:13 and 1 John 2:27 and 5:9 (see chapter 7), for Scriptures that speak about the internal witness and authenticating testimony of the Spirit to the Word.
[173] J. I. Packer, *Keep in Step with the Spirit* (Leicester: IVP, 1984), 240.

Closely linked to this line of thinking is a concern regarding *sola Scriptura* that is expressed by Vanhoozer:

> Because of both hermeneutic and theological influences, there is increasing pressure on Reformed churches to abandon the Reformers' position on *sola scriptura* in favour of a view that makes Scripture an inseparable aspect of the church's Spirit-led, living tradition.[174]
>
> [As a result], there is a danger of losing, or at least subordinating, the literal sense of Scripture ("what it meant") to its use by the Spirit in the community ("what it means").[175]

The reading of Scripture within the believing community must, then, always resist any 'pull' towards a community reading which leads in any sense to the 'objective' textual meaning collapsing into corporate relativism.

## Over-emphasis upon the Community/Individual Dichotomy

The notion of the Spirit guiding the community in the interpretation of Scripture should not exclude the importance of individual interpretation. For most of us, the question 'what does this mean to me?' is the first that comes to mind when hearing/reading Scripture. An overstressing of the corporate at the expense of the individual can indeed diminish the reality of the Christian's personal relationship with and responsibility towards God. This latter fact flows from the Christian conviction that God not only created *us*, but also created *me*, saved me, loves me, and will one day judge me.[176] The one who cares for every fallen sparrow[177] also cares for each unique individual made in his image.

Much Scripture is couched in highly personal terms, from the Psalmist's 'I am fearfully and wonderfully made'[178] to the 'woe is me'[179] protest of the prophet and the apostle's reference to 'the Son of God, who loved me, and gave himself for me.'[180] These words from the writers of Scripture would be endorsed by virtually every Christian, who would say with conviction: 'God speaks to me through Scripture.' Indeed, for Christians who have a daily 'quiet time' with their Bibles, their encounter with Scripture may well probably be taking place more frequently in a solitary rather than a group context, thus seemingly producing an interpretation that is more personal than communal. Hopefully this will also

---

[174] Vanhoozer, *Is There a Meaning in this Text?*, 410.
[175] Vanhoozer, *Is There a Meaning in this Text?*, 412.
[176] 2 Cor 5:10.
[177] Matt 10:29–31.
[178] Ps 139:14 AV. Note also Ps 138:8.
[179] Isa 6:5.
[180] Gal 2:20.

include the hymn writer's invocation, 'Spirit of God my teacher be, showing the things of Christ to me.'[181]

The Spirit's help in interpretation, however, should not be understood solely in terms of an immediate 'illuminist' functioning. It will also have been supplied in the form of community influences, both past and present, whether from family upbringing, church teaching and tradition, mass produced Bible study notes or whatever.[182] The same could be said of the preparation of the preacher. He may well conceive of his sermon alone in his study, but his interpretation will have been influenced by interaction with a whole host of community influences: the 'fellowship' of the commentators, the needs of his congregation, the contemporary situation, his past and present experiences, the influences of his theological training, viewpoints of fellow ministers, or even his spouse!

One's reading and interpretation of Scripture is, then, invariably the result of a highly complex web of individual yet also community-interacting influences,[183] as indeed was the original writing of Scripture. Paul Noble, for instance, gives the example of Paul and the Old Testament prophets:

> [Although] the Pauline epistles are very individual writings ... Paul did not write as an *isolated* individual, but from within a generally accepted framework of ideas and practices; and likewise more recent Old Testament studies have undermined the 'romantic' image of the prophet as a poet who spoke out of his or her own individual experience of God, by showing their dependence upon the inherited traditions. Yet nevertheless, we are indebted to Paul's 'personal genius' for the penetrating insights he has given into these generally accepted ideas; and similarly, many of the insights embodied in the Old Testament could perhaps be more plausibly explained as the work of gifted individuals or schools who refined the common traditions, rather than as community products *per se*.[184]

Concepts of individuality and community are not therefore mutually exclusive categories, but rather correlative ones.[185] The one should inform and enrich the other. And it is through the Spirit that this is to be effected. Thus Welker criticises pneumatologies that interpret 'the unity of the Spirit' by 'imposing an illusory homogeneity.'[186] The Pentecostal manifestation to peoples of different

---

[181] E. E. Hewitt, 'More about Jesus would I know,' No. 597 in *The Baptist Hymn Book,* ed. M. E. Aubrey et al (London: Psalms and Hymns Trust, 1962 ed.). Cf. John 14:26 and Ps 119:18.
[182] For more on the aspect of 'historical community' influence, see pages 79–82.
[183] See chapter 2.
[184] Paul R. Noble, *The Canonical Approach: A Critical Reconstruction of the Hermeneutics of Brevard S. Childs* (Leiden: Brill, 1995), 185–186. For a consideration of 'community' influences in Paul, see chapter 6.
[185] See also Grenz and Franke, *Beyond Foundationalism,* 214 for the interdependence of individualism and community.
[186] Michael Welker, *God the Spirit* (Minneapolis: Fortress Press, 1994), 25.

cultures and ages gives an example of the Spirit's respecting and indeed cultivating *difference*, in a special kind of pluralism.

> No one is totally the same as other, and no one is unique in every respect. The Spirit of God gives rise to a multiplace force field that is sensitive to differences. In this force field, enjoyment of creaturely, invigorating differences can be cultivated while unjust, debilitating differences can be removed in love, mercy, and gentleness.[187]

As Paul highlights in 1 Corinthians 12, the church is one body in which 'Jews or Greeks, slaves or free'[188] have been given of the one Spirit to drink. Welker comments on 'the unity of the body that consists in the interplay of a differentiated diversity that cannot be reduced to a simple unity (1 Cor 12:14ff).'[189] The Spirit, then, is not only the author of the best kind of individuality, but also uses it to enrich and edify the body in the knowledge of Christ and experience of what the New Testament has described as the 'variegated grace of God.'[190]

To summarise this section, then, we have seen that in focussing upon the Spirit's guidance of the *community* in the interpretation of Scripture, we must beware of: forms of community absolutism that overlook the possibility of ecclesial aberration; vague notions of 'spirit' that import extraneous material into interpretation; reader response notions that rob the text of its autonomy and relativizes meaning; and an overemphasis upon the dichotomy between the community and the individual.

## Conclusion to the Chapter

In this introductory chapter, we have briefly surveyed how the Spirit has been viewed in relation to the interpretation of Scripture, showing how the focus has frequently been upon his guidance of the individual as opposed to the community. We referred to some recent studies and concluded there was scope for a fresh investigation of the corporate reading of the text that arises from the κοινωνία character of the Spirit, using a methodology that is more thoroughly rooted in Scripture rather than literary theory. Having given some definitions of terms, we then outlined some trends to individualism in biblical interpretation, before finally listing some of the dangers we must avoid whilst seeking to explore the corporate nature of the reading and understanding of Scripture within the Spirit-inspired community—which is the church of Jesus Christ.

---

[187] Welker, *God the Spirit*, 21–22.
[188] 1 Cor 12:13.
[189] Welker, *God the Spirit*, 23.
[190] 1 Pet 4:10.

# CHAPTER TWO: THE KOINONIA OF THE SPIRIT
## An Exploration of Pneumatological Community

Introduction

What special understanding and focus should the Spirit's help bring to the interpretation of Scripture? What sort of communal dimensions to the process are opened by the essentially κοινωνία (*koinonia*) character of the Holy Spirit? In this chapter I shall take a general overview of this κοινωνία and argue that it is an essential component in biblical interpretation, as opposed to the frequently individualistic workings of the human spirit. As Thiselton says, 'the Holy Spirit is not "mine", but graciously "ours",'[191] a fact that must always be borne in mind when we set about the task of understanding Scripture with the help of the Spirit.

I shall approach the subject by way of an interaction with insights from contemporary pneumatology, Trinitarian theology, hermeneutical theory, and New Testament (especially Pauline) theology. These will be combined with both a historical perspective and a contemporary application. At various points, I will also seek to highlight differing emphases within different ecclesiastical traditions. As we follow the path of 'the Spirit [who] searches everything,'[192] our discussion will be wide-ranging and perhaps seemingly discursive in places. This simply illustrates the far-reaching scope and multi-dimensional nature of the Spirit's guidance of the Christian community in its custodianship and interpretation of Scripture. Later chapters will involve a more focussed and precise investigation of selected pneumatological passages in the New Testament, and in particular of the way in which the New Testament writers and early church—as members of a Spirit-led community—understood the Old Testament.

In this chapter, following a brief reference to contemporary pneumatology, I will engage in a detailed discussion of the κοινωνία operations of the Spirit regarding what I shall call its Trinitarian, dialogical, historical, and eschatological dimensions. From my findings, I shall suggest implications for praxis in terms of the church's need to maintain Spirit-led interpretation within the Christian community.

---

[191] Anthony C. Thiselton, *The Holy Spirit - In Biblical Teaching, Through the Centuries, and Today* (London: SPCK, 2013), 475.
[192] 1 Cor 2:10.

## Contemporary Pneumatology

The great explosion of interest in the Holy Spirit that occurred in the second half of the last century has produced what Kärkkäinen has described[193] as a veritable 'pneumatological smorgasbord'[194] whose flavours reflect a great diversity of theological views. But is this mixture of pneumatologies on offer today really an example of the wind of the divine *ruach/pneuma* 'blow[ing] where it wishes'?[195]

There has certainly been a healthy concern to develop a more comprehensive theology of the Spirit after centuries of relative neglect[196] and understatement. Too often his function in conventional Western theology has been too narrowly construed in terms of his role in the economy of salvation and of his enabling and enlightenment of the individual. The impetus of the charismatic and ecumenical movements has certainly greatly extended the perceived focus of operations for the Spirit.

It is arguable, however, that in several more recent pneumatologies, the broadening out process has gone too far. The Spirit is certainly the 'Lord and giver of life', to cite the words of the ancient creed,[197] but immanentist concepts of the Spirit,[198] not only in redemption, but also in creation[199] and the cosmos, that veer towards panentheism, pantheism, and universalism would probably horrify classic expositors of this part of the creed.[200]

## The Concept of Κοινωνία

A more theologically orthodox way to explore the wider role of the Spirit can be undertaken by looking at the New Testament, particularly Pauline, notion of κοινωνία,[201] especially as it is to be harnessed in support of the hermeneutical

---

[193] Veli-Matti Kärkkäinen, *Pneumatology: The Holy Spirit in Ecumenical, International, and Contextual Perspective* (Grand Rapids, MI: Baker, 2002), 105.
[194] Ibid., 105: the subheading of his chapter, 'Leading Contemporary Theologians of the Spirit.'
[195] John 3:8a.
[196] This neglect has been attributed to the Spirit's deference to Christ (John 16:13-14). Barth, however, interprets it as a symptom of human pride. 'By the doctrine of the deity and autonomy of the Spirit's divine mode of being man is, as it were, challenged in his own house' *Church Dogmatics*, Vol. 1.1: *The Doctrine of the Word of God* (Edinburgh: T&T Clark, 1975), 468. George Smeaton, *The Doctrine of the Holy Spirit* (London: Banner of Truth, 1958), 1, links later neglect of the Spirit with the advent of critical and rationalist theology.
[197] The First Council of Constantinople (AD 381)
[198] For example, G. W. H. Lampe in *God as Spirit* (London: SCM, 1977) speaks of 'an incarnation of God as Spirit within every man as human spirit' (p. 45).
[199] For example, Jürgen Moltmann, *The Spirit of Life* (London: SCM, 1992).
[200] Such as Barth who in *Church Dogmatics*, 469, speaks of the transcendent Lordship of the Spirit: 'With the Father and the Son He is the one sovereign divine Subject, the Subject who is not placed under the control or inspection of any other, who derives His being and existence from Himself.' See further ibid., 466-489.
[201] For a survey of the biblical concept of *koinonia* in an ecumenical perspective, see John Reumann, 'The Biblical Witness to Koinonia' in *On the Way to Fuller Koinonia*, ed. T. F. Best and G. Gassman, Faith and Order Paper No.166 (Geneva: WCC, 1993), 36-69. For a discussion of *koinonia* in terms of ecumenically-based evangelism, see G. Vandervelde, 'Church, Evangelization, and the Bonds of *Koinonia*' in A Report of the International Consultation

thrust of this book. Although the word is not employed in the gospels, 'the concept of κοινωνία ("fellowship") is a broad one in Paul,'[202] who uses it in its noun form no less than thirteen times.[203] In 2 Cor 13:14 and Phil 2:1, the expression 'the fellowship of the Holy Spirit' (ἡ κοινωνία τοῦ ἁγίου πνεύματος) links κοινωνία with the Spirit in a fundamental way. To quote Fee, '...what most characterizes the Holy Spirit is *koinonia*.'[204]

Κοινωνία can be translated 'association, communion, fellowship, participation.'[205] In its original root meaning in ancient Greek it had reference to having things in common, 'often in contrast to what is "private,"'[206] and hence the sharing of a common life, 'virtually the sense of brotherhood.'[207] Paul, however, invests it with a new meaning, transforming it from a social to a spiritual concept. 'Paul never used *koinonia* in a secular sense but always in a religious one.... [Hence] the "right hand of fellowship" (Gal 2:9) given to Paul and Barnabas by James, Peter, and John was not just a handshake over a deal but mutual recognition of being in Christ.'[208]

Ralph Martin highlights this aspect of participation in that which is beyond ourselves:

> The root idea of *koinōnia* is "taking part in something with someone." [But] which is more important to the biblical authors, the realities in which Christians share or the sense of sharing that binds them to one another? We ... give the chief place to the second part of the definition .... But the New Testament puts the emphasis on the "in something" aspect, and invariably the stress falls on the privilege which comes to us as we join with other Christians in participation in "objective realities" outside and independent of our experience because they are there before we lay hold of them and they exist irrespective of our feelings. This becomes crystal clear as we look at some texts in Paul.[209]

Martin proceeds to discuss 1 Cor 1:9, 1 Cor 10:16, Phil 2:1 and 2 Cor 13:14, showing how in each case their primary focus is upon 'having a share'[210] in the divine persons/realities of which they speak. He does, however, also show that 'in a natural transference of meaning ... *koinōnia* shades off from "participation

---

between the Catholic Church and the World Evangelical Alliance (1993-2002) *Evangelical Review of Theology* Vol. 29 No. 2, April 2005, 100-130.

[202] G. D. Fee, *God's Empowering Presence* (Peabody, MA: Hendricksen, 1994), 872.

[203] Rom 15:26; 1 Cor1:9, 10:16[twice]; 2 Cor 6:14; 8:4; 9:13; 13:14; Gal 2:9; Phil 1:5; 2:1; 3:10; Phlm 6. It is also used in the New Testament in Acts 2:42; Heb 13:16; 1 John 1:3, 6, 7.

[204] G. D. Fee, *Listening to the Spirit in the Text* (Grand Rapids, MI: Eerdmans, 2000), 27.

[205] J. Schattenmann, 'Fellowship,' *NIDNTT*, 639.

[206] J. Reumann, 'The Biblical Witness to Koinonia', 40.

[207] Schattenmann, op. cit., 640.

[208] Ibid., 643.

[209] Ralph Martin, *The Family and the Fellowship: New Testament Images of the Church* (Exeter: Paternoster, 1979), 36-37.

[210] Ibid., 36.

in" to include "sharing with" another person or a group'[211] in acts of generosity or community, as, for instance in 2 Cor 9:13, Rom 15:26 and Acts 2:42. Cranfield makes a similar comment when discussing Christian fellowship in Paul and the New Testament: 'the vertical is the origin of the horizontal, while the outward expression of the horizontal is at the same time the sign and pledge of the vertical.'[212]

Here I wish to underline the priority of the 'vertical' element in the Pauline use of κοινωνία in 2 Cor 13:14, which Fee has described as 'in many ways ... the most profound moment in the Pauline corpus.'[213]

> The grace of the Lord Jesus Christ and the love of God and the fellowship of the Holy Spirit be with you all.

In line with Martin's point above, the majority of modern commentators[214] now think that the genitive τοῦ ἁγίου πνεύματος ('of the Holy Spirit') is objective (i.e. the Spirit is the object in which one partakes), rather than subjective (referring to the fellowship produced by the Spirit). Accordingly, Paul's appeal for unity amongst the Corinthians is based upon their common participation in the Spirit (vertical), rather than the fellowship created by the Spirit (horizontal). Nevertheless, as Fee says, 'although [κοινωνία] refers chiefly to "a participation in the Spirit himself," such participation is common to them all [note μετὰ πάντων ὑμῶν ('be with you all') at the end] and thus also includes "the fellowship" created and sustained by the Spirit.'[215]

Fee further links the passage with the similar expression εἴ τις κοινωνία πνεύματος ('if any participation in the Spirit'—Phil 2:1) in which 'part of the basis of his appeal to unity and harmony in v. 1 is their common participation (both Paul's and theirs together) in the Spirit.'[216] Bockmuehl similarly comments on this passage, stressing that κοινωνία here 'denotes not togetherness so much as *partnership* of common interest, forged and empowered by the Holy Spirit.'[217]

---

[211] Ibid., 42.
[212] See C. E. B. Cranfield, 'Fellowship, Communion' in *A Theological Word Book of the Bible*, ed. Alan Richardson (London: SCM, 1950), 82. Cranfield speaks of the 'vertical' as 'the sharing together of Christians *in* and *with* Christ' and the 'horizontal' as 'the sharing *together* of Christians in and with Christ.'
[213] Fee, *God's Empowering Presence*, 363.
[214] For example, C. K. Barrett, *A Commentary on the Second Epistle to the Corinthians* (London: A & C Black, 1973), 344; M. E. Thrall, *2 Corinthians* (Edinburgh: T&T Clark, 2000), 919; R. Martin, *2 Corinthians* (Milton Keynes: Word (UK), 1991), 505; M. J. Harris, *The Second Epistle to the Corinthians: A Commentary on the Greek Text* (Milton Keynes: Paternoster, 2005), 941. Dunn writes, 'What is in view is not a physical entity (like a congregation), but the subjective experience of the Spirit as something shared ... [W]hat draws and keeps believers together for Paul was not simply a common membership of a congregation, but the common experience of the Spirit,' J. D. G. Dunn, *The Theology of Paul the Apostle* (Edinburgh: T & T Clark, 1998), 561. A subjective genitive (the fellowship brought about by the Spirit) is favoured by J. M. Scott, *2 Corinthians*, New International Commentary (Carlisle: Paternoster, 1998), 265 and Linda Belleville, *2 Corinthians* (Leicester: IVP, 1996), 338.
[215] Fee, *God's Empowering Presence*, 872.
[216] Ibid., 872.
[217] M. Bockmuehl, *The Epistle to the Philippians* (London: A & C Black, 1997), 106. Other commentators following the rendering 'participation in the Spirit' include R.Martin, *The Epistle of Paul to the Philippians* (London: Tyndale, 1959), 49 and *Philippians* (New Century) (London: Marshall, Morgan & Scott, 1980), 87;T. O'Brien, *The*

When, therefore, we come to think of the wider role of the Holy Spirit in relation to the great enterprise of biblical interpretation, we need to think of it in terms of his distinctive κοινωνία operations, primarily in creating a partnership with God himself, but then, secondarily, in partnership with others who 'live and breathe by the same Spirit.'[218]

In view of this special bonding/linking role of the Holy Spirit, I will now proceed to make a case for a form of 'relational pneumatology',[219] centred around the idea of κοινωνία, and providing a basis for a Spirit/community-based hermeneutic.[220] As we think of the Spirit as πνεῦμα or wind, we shall find that the theme of κοινωνία will certainly blow us into a number of different directions that reveal the various dimensions in which this κοινωνία operates. In this section, we will now take an extensive look at four of these, categorising them under the following major headings: Trinitarian, dialogical, historical and eschatological.

These categories are not intended to be exhaustive and, as we shall see, are capable of a number of further subdivisions. They do, however, provide a convenient, biblically-based way of classifying the multi-faceted κοινωνία operations of the Spirit. In the last section of this chapter, we will seek to spell out some of the implications for the interpretive process. We will also refer to this fourfold categorisation in our later exegetical chapters.

## Trinitarian

The fact that 'the κοινωνία of the Spirit' comes in a verse (2 Cor 13:14) that refers to Son, Father, and Spirit lifts the initial starting point for our investigation into the elevated realm of inter-Trinitarian relationships.[221] Not that Paul himself in this verse was thinking specifically in such conceptual terms, for his chief concern in this passage was 'to function as a pastor [viz. to promote reconciliation in the Corinthian church], not as a systematic theologian.'[222] Nevertheless, 2 Cor 13:14 reveals what Fee calls the 'presuppositional, experiential'[223] character of the Pauline Trinitarianism. Vanhoozer has indeed argued that all our hermeneutics are necessarily governed by theological

---

*Epistle to the Philippians: A Commentary on the Greek Text* (Grand Rapids, MI: Eerdmans, 1991), 174; I. Howard Marshall, *The Epistle to the Philippians* (London: Epworth, 1992), 42; G. D. Fee, *Paul's Letter to the Philippians* (Grand Rapids, MI: Eerdmans, 1995), 181.

[218] G. D. Fee, *Paul's Letter to the Philippians*, 181.

[219] Phrase borrowed from J. McIntyre, *The Shape of Pneumatology* (Edinburgh: T & T Clark, 1997), 172.

[220] J. Reumann seeks to encapsulate the blending together of the individual and corporate aspects of *koinonia* of the Spirit in 2 Cor 13:14: 'may participation in the Spirit continue to characterize the life of each of you and the life of all of you together'; Reumann, 'The Biblical Witness to Koinonia', 47.

[221] C. K. Barrett points out that 'the kind of threefold formula that we have here (cf. 1Peter 1:1f) provided a starting-point for such [viz. Trinitarian] speculative thinking and for its credal formulation.' Barrett, *A Commentary on The Second Epistle to the Corinthians*, 345.

[222] R. Martin, *2 Corinthians*, 497.

[223] Fee, *God's Empowering Presence*, 826.

presuppositions and that 'the best general hermeneutic is a Trinitarian hermeneutic.'[224] For him, the Trinity alone can explain 'the experience of meaningful communication,'[225] with 'God as author, as message, and as power of reception.'[226]

Many Trinitarian formulations such as this have had as their 'starting-point'[227] verses such as 2 Cor 13:14 and have noted that within the Trinity, the Spirit is particularly identified by κοινωνία. To quote Barth, 'This togetherness or communion of the Father and the Son is the Holy Spirit.'[228] It was 'togetherness' that Paul prayed might be experienced in the church of his day, and modern ecumenical dialogue strives for today, as recognised in Kärkkäinen's statement that '*koinonia* between Christians is rooted in the Trinitarian Communion.'[229]

These words reflect the recent resurgence[230] of interest in Trinitarian theology which has resulted in a reworking and refinement of several Trinitarian notions. Out of these, we will now briefly comment upon relevant insights from three areas: economic/immanent Trinity, 'being as communion,' and *perichoresis*.

*(i) Economic/Immanent Trinity*

Originating with Athanasius,[231] a distinction has commonly been drawn between the '*economic*' Trinity ('God *for* us'[232]—conceptions of God that flow from the pattern of his work of salvation in history) and the '*immanent*' (or '*ontological*') Trinity ('God *in himself*'[233]—the inherent nature and distinctiveness of the divine persons). Modern theologians, however, have questioned the reality of this distinction[234] when considering the dynamic of God's revelation within the spirit of κοινωνία, for something of the essence of the divine immanence is imparted to us in the economic process of his self-communication. To quote Torrance:

---

[224] Vanhoozer, *Is There a Meaning in this Text?*,456.
[225] Ibid., 456.
[226] Ibid., 161.
[227] Barrett, *Second Epistle to the Corinthians*, 345.
[228] *Church Dogmatics 1:1*, 469. Barth goes on to say 'He is the common element, or, better, the fellowship, the act of communion, of the Father and the Son. He is the act in which the Father is the Father of the Son or the Speaker of the Word and the Son is the Son of the Father or the Word of the Speaker', ibid., 470.
[229] Veli-Matti Kärkkäinen, 'Trinity, Spirit and Church' in *The Spirit and Church* 4:1 (May 2002),13.
[230] See John Thompson, in *Modern Trinitarian Perspectives* (Oxford: Oxford University Press, 1994),1–2 for some explanations of this resurgence. Renewed emphases on the relational/social aspect of the Trinity could also be seen as part of a response to the postmodern search for community, as explored in this book. On the other hand, 'social' conceptions of the Trinity that too readily identify the economic and immanent Trinity risk the charge of 'reducing God to a predicate of our language and experience', Archie Spencer, reviewing S. Grenz, *Theology for the Community of God* (Carlisle: Paternoster Press,1994) in 'Culture, community and commitments: Stanley Grenz on theological method' in *Scottish Journal of Theology* Vol. 57 No. 3, 350.
[231] T. Chester, *Delighting in the Trinity* (Oxford: Monarch, 2005), 89.
[232] T. F. Torrance, *The Christian Doctrine of God, One Being, Three Persons* (Edinburgh: T&T Clark, 1996, paperback ed. 2001), 7.
[233] Ibid.
[234] Karl Rahner has indeed argued that 'the economic Trinity is the immanent Trinity and vice versa [*umgekehrt*]' cited in Yves Congar, *I believe in the Holy Spirit* (New York, NY: Crossroad, 1997), Vol.111, 13. For a discussion of this, see Congar, ibid., 11–18.

> The economic Trinity and the ontological Trinity are not to be separated from one another for they are locked together in God's threefold *self*-revelation and *self*-communication to us as Father, Son and Holy Spirit.[235]

Similarly, Amos Yong:

> The economic 'fellowship of the Spirit' (2 Cor 13:14) reflects the immanent triune community wrought about by the Spirit who is the mutual love of the Father and the Son.[236]

Yong's talk of the Spirit as 'mutual love' here goes back to Augustine. He described the Spirit's special role within the Godhead as 'the bond of love' (*vinculum caritatis*) between Father and Son. Such terminology has been criticised for depersonalising the Spirit, but it did at least lay emphasis upon the vital bonding/relational aspect of his ministry. Word and Spirit have further been described by Irenaeus as the 'two hands' of the Father.[237]

From these two notions, which originated in the patristic period, Yong has concluded:

> Relationality is at the heart of the divine life, expressed coinherently and subsistently (two hands) as well as mutually and lovingly (mutual love). Further, Spirit ... is a constitutive of the dynamic mutuality between Father and Son. Spirit can therefore be conceptualized also as the dispositional vector of the divine life.[238]

Reference to the Spirit as the 'dispositional vector' may seem a far cry from the more personal *Paraclete* (παράκλητος) promised by Jesus,[239] but Paul Fiddes has nevertheless pointed out the common element of 'movement' inherent in many of the biblical metaphors for the Spirit that highlight his role as '"the opener" or "the disturber".'[240]

> [B]lowing wind,[241] pulsing breath,[242] trickling oil,[243] raging fire,[244] pouring water,[245] beating wings[246] and the outstreaming of light[247] ... [These] images of the Spirit constantly open up our sense of God. They

---

[235] Torrance, *The Christian Doctrine of God*, 7.
[236] Amos Yong, *Spirit-Word-Community: Theological Hermeneutics in Trinitarian Perspective* (Aldershot: Ashgate, 2003), 67.
[237] See Yong, ibid., 50.
[238] Yong, ibid., 78.
[239] John 14:16.
[240] Paul Fiddes, *Participating in God: A Pastoral Doctrine of the Trinity* (London: Darton, Longman and Todd, 2000), 264.
[241] Acts 2:2–3.
[242] John 20:22.
[243] Isa 61:1.
[244] Isa 4:4.
[245] Isa 44:3.
[246] Gen 1:2.
[247] 2 Cor 3:7–8, 17–18.

enable not only talk about God, but *participation* in God ... They [also] allow us to notice the way that the Spirit moves in human community, moving between people and building bridges of awareness and empathy.[248]

Just as the Spirit dynamically relates to and between Father and Son within the immanent Trinity, then, so too he relates believers to and with Father and Son within the economic Trinity.[249] He works, to quote Nigel Wright, as 'God on the Inside,'[250] recreating with and between believers the internal fellowship he sustains within the Godhead.[251]

In this connection, Tom Smail reminds us of two relational fundamentals:

> [T]he primary work of the Holy Spirit in the New Testament does not have to do with charismatic manifestations but with our initiation into the two central relationships that are summed up in the two confessions, "*Abba*, Father" [Gal 4:6] and "Jesus is *Kurios*, Lord" [1 Cor 12:3].'[252]

These two confessions encapsulate the heart of the Spirit's relational activity in the church, highlighting the ultimate direction towards which Yong's 'dispositional vector' should be pointing. As 1 John 1:3c puts it, 'our fellowship (κοινωνία) is with the Father and with his Son Jesus Christ.' This vertical aspect of κοινωνία is also closely linked with the horizontal: '... fellowship with us' 1:3b. Furthermore, calling God 'Father' implies being a member of a family, and Jesus 'Lord' implies a realm over which he has dominion. From the Christian perspective, this family and realm is experienced in the community of the church as the focus of the Spirit's relational operations.

*(ii) 'Being as Communion'*

In this ecclesiastical context, the recent engagement between Western and Eastern theological perspectives has highlighted what some have seen as an undue subordination of pneumatology to Christology in Western Trinitarian thinking.[253] In this, the Spirit is, according to Gunton, 'conceived as the motive

---

[248] Fiddes, ibid., 263–264, italics added.
[249] Jim Purvis refers to this as enabled by 'the ontic actuality' of the Spirit which embraces Christians so that 'they are "brought together ... [and] towards a participation with the Trinity ...."' Jim Purvis, *The Triune God and the Charismatic Movement: A Critical Appraisal from a Scottish Perspective* (Carlisle: Paternoster, 2004), 231.
[250] N. G. Wright, *God on the Inside: The Holy Spirit in Holy Scripture* (Oxford: Bible Reading Fellowship, 2006).
[251] Ibid., 22.
[252] Tom Smail, *The Giving Gift - The Holy Spirit in Person* (London: Darton, Longman & Todd, 1988 & 1994), 13.
[253] 'There has been a tendency historically to either neglect the Spirit in theological reflection or to theologize about the Spirit in such a way as to result in ... a ... subordination of the Spirit either to the Word or to both Word and Father', Yong, op. cit., 74. 'Much modern theology of the Trinity ... is highly critical of the neglect of ... the Holy Spirit...[T]here is a subordination of pneumatology to Christology or an inadequate view of the relationship of these to each other. In the West the relation of the Spirit to the Father and Son is seen as a mutual communion of both, a view which ... tends to depersonalize the Spirit and make him less than Father and Son.' J. Thompson, *Modern Trinitarian Perspectives*, 149.

power of an institution which is, so to speak, given, like an automobile already built and requiring only fuel (motor spirit!) to cause it to move.'[254]

In response to this, a number of Western theologians have embraced what they see as a pneumatologically corrective insight from Eastern Orthodoxy.[255] They refer to the significantly entitled work *'Being as Communion'* [256] by the Orthodox theologian John Zizioulas who asserts:

> The Spirit is not something that "animates" a church which already somehow exists. The Spirit makes the church *be*. Pneumatology does not refer to the well-being but to the very being of the church. It is not about a dynamism which is added to the essence of the church. It is the very essence of the church ... Pneumatology is an ontological category for ecclesiology.[257] [T]he Holy Spirit is not one who *aids* us in bridging the distance between Christ and ourselves, but he is the person of the Trinity who actually realizes in history that which we call Christ, this absolutely relational entity, our Savior. In this case, our Christology is *essentially* conditioned by Pneumatology, not just secondarily as in the first case; in fact it is *constituted* pneumatologically.[258]

Zizioulas goes on to argue that whereas Christ *institutes* the church—through his incarnation and saving work—it is the Spirit who *constitutes* the church, through his ongoing work of creating communion and fellowship. If this balance is maintained, then a proper balance between institution and community is more likely to be achieved.[259]

There is undoubtedly substance in Zizioulas's case for a heavier pneumatological weighting, although a number of things could be said in response,[260] not least that pneumatology should not be confused with ecclesiology, even though it

---

[254] Colin Gunton, 'The Spirit in the Trinity' in *The Forgotten Trinity: A Selection of Papers presented to the B.C.C. Study Commission on Trinitarian Debate Today* (London: B.C.C., 1991), 127.
[255] For example, Smail, *The Giving Gift*, 191ff; Gunton, *The Spirit in the Trinity*, 127-128; Yong, *Spirit-Word-Community*, 110–112.
[256] John D. Zizioulas, *Being As Communion: Studies in Personhood and the Church* (Crestwood, NY: St Vladimir's Seminary Press; London: Darton Longman & Todd, 1985).
[257] Ibid., 132.
[258] Ibid., 110–11.
[259] See J. Thompson, *Modern Trinitarian Perspectives*, 151. Tom Smail spells out the relevance of Zizioulas's distinction here: 'If we over-emphasize the given, "institutional" element in the church, as we often have in the West, we are in danger of imposing the gospel on people in a heteronomous and authoritarian way ... [But] church is not only instituted by the incarnate Son, but is constituted by the Holy Spirit. *Con* means together and ... the Holy Spirit is the Spirit of *koinonia*, togetherness. The Spirit creates atogetherness between Christ and his people.' Smail, *The Giving Gift*, 192–193.
[260] For one thing, the Western emphasis on Christology has principally stemmed from a rightful concern to exalt Christ as the head of the church (Eph 2:21–22) mirroring the Holy Spirit's concern to glorify Christ (John 16:14). The New Testament defines the church as the body of Christ (1 Cor 12:27) as well as the temple of the Holy Spirit (Eph 2:21–22). The Spirit-quenching dangers of hierarchialised institutionalism that stem from monarchical tendencies within Trinitarian thought are not limited to churches inculcated with Western theology.

remains vitally related to it. Few, however, would disagree that the prayer 'Come, Holy Spirit!'[261] should preface all ecclesiastical and interpretive endeavour.

*(iii) Perichoresis*

Historically, the Nicene's fourth-century notion of *homoousion* ('of one substance with the Father'[262]), a fundamental term but with rather static connotations, had been followed up in the sixth-century[263] by the more sophisticated and dynamic idea of *perichoresis*[264]—the mutual interpenetration and coinherence of Father, Son, and Holy Spirit. This notion has been developed over the centuries and particularly by some contemporary theologians. The result is that the ontology of the Trinity is for many no longer seen in terms of a fellowship of three distinct *personae*, but as a dynamic 'event of relationships.'[265] To quote three different theologians:

> God is *wholly constituted* by relationality. In other words, God is not (first) three independent entities who (then) decide to come into relation with one another'. God is, rather, "relation without remainder".[266]

> With God, Being, and Communion are one and the same.[267]

> God is the supremely communal being, eternally living and subsisting as a triune relationality.[268]

And in so far as people are 'made in the image of the triune God' ('let *us* make man in *our* image' Gen 1:26),[269] this perichoretic conception of the Trinity has been used as a means of underlining the need to define human personhood in terms of 'person-in-relationship', as opposed to notions of persons as solitary,

---

[261] Historically known as the *epiklesis* in Orthodox and Catholic sacramentalism. See Congar, op. cit., Vol. 111, 228, 267.

[262] The second article in the Nicene Creed of AD 381 refers to the Lord Jesus Christ as 'being of one substance (*homoousia*) with the Father', thus defending the deity of the Son and his oneness with the Father. In later Trinitarian formulations, *homoousia* was subsequently extended to include the Holy Spirit.

[263] L. Boff, *Trinity and Society* (Tunbridge Wells: Burns & Oates, 1988), 135–136.

[264] Torrance's elucidation: '*Perichoresis* derives from *chora*, the Greek word 'space' or 'room', or from *chorein*, meaning 'to contain', 'to make room', or 'to go forward'. It indicates a sort of mutual containing or enveloping of realities, which we also speak of as *coinherence* or *indwelling*.... It was then applied to speak of the way in which the three divine Persons mutually dwell in one another and coinhere or inexist in one another while nevertheless remaining other than one another and distinct from one another' op. cit.,102. The biblical basis for the concept is found in verses such as John 10:38, 14:10-11 and 17:21.

[265] Paul S. Fiddes, op. cit., 36, taking a clue from Karl Barth's insistence that 'with regard to the being of God, the word "event" or "act" is final' *Church Dogmatics* 11/1, 263.

[266] David S. Cunningham, *These Three are One: The Practice of Trinitarian Theology*, (Oxford: Blackwell, 1988), 165. Cunningham uses the musical analogy of 'polyphony' as an example of the harmony that can come through a combination of different sounding instruments thus picturing diversity, unity and participation within the Godhead.

[267] Torrance, *The Christian Doctrine of God*, 194.

[268] Yong, *Spirit-Word-Community*, 79.

[269] T. Chester, *Delighting in the Trinity*, 159, 161.

reasoning individuals.[270] The Trinity is therefore seen as 'the perfect community,' providing a model for 'mutual self-giving' and thus 'the deepest foundation possible within the Christian tradition for the rejection of the bias towards individualism.'[271]

There is, of course, still a distinct place for the individual, stemming from the distinct personhood of Father, Son, and Holy Spirit, but only within the overall context of a greater united whole. As Chester says, 'Trinitarian Christianity offers a way of being human together that integrates unity and diversity ... of perfectly integrat[ing] ... the one and the many.'[272] He goes on to speak of how, as Christians, we are '*re*made in the image of the triune community'[273] and uses John 17:20–26 as the basis for arguing how we 'participate in the Trinitarian life through our union with Christ,'[274] by the agency of the Holy Spirit. 'God is not only relational; he has opened up the Trinitarian relations to include us.'[275] As Grenz and Franke put it, 'the community we share is our shared participation ... in the perichoretic community of Trinitarian persons.'[276]

In such a context, the work of the connecting but self-effacing[277] Spirit within the Trinity provides a basis for understanding hermeneutics as an exercise that is not just as a reflection of *perichoresis*, but as an expression of the more biblical concept of κοινωνία. To return to our starting point in 2 Corinthians 13:14, we shall conclude with Torrance's remarks thereon relating to the 'Communion of the Holy Spirit':

> God's self revelation to us is actualised in the Communion of the Holy Spirit through whom God brings his divine Reality to bear personally and indeed experientially upon us, both in the address of his Word to us and in our hearing and understanding of that Word. It is through his own presence to us in his Spirit that God establishes the relation between us and himself which we need in order to know him.[278]

---

[270] Ibid., 164ff, drawing on insights from C. E. Gunton, *The One, The Three and the Many: God, Creation and the Culture of Modernity* (Cambridge: Cambridge University Press, 1993).

[271] Thomas J. Scirghi, 'The Trinity: A Model for Belonging in a Contemporary Society' in *Ecumenical Review* W.C.C. Vol. 54 No. 3 July 2002, 337, 341. In this article Scirghi is drawing on the insights of the Brazilian Catholic Liberation theologian Leonard Boff and in particular his work *Holy Trinity, Perfect Trinity* (Maryknoll, NY: Orbis, 2000). In this and *Trinity and Society* (Tunbridge Wells: Burns & Oates, 1988), Boff is arguing the case for a more equal and just society modelled on the community of the Trinity. This is a laudable aim but is open to the criticism that can be levelled against all liberation theologians, namely of an over-politicisation of theological concepts.

[272] Chester, *Delighting in the Trinity*, 162. He goes on to discuss how this 'unity-in-diversity' is worked out in Paul's model of the church as the body of Christ in 1 Cor 12, a dynamic community that is created by the Spirit (vv. 7, 11, 13).

[273] Ibid. 167, italics added.

[274] Ibid. 175.

[275] Ibid. 176.

[276] S. Grenz and J. R. Franke, *Beyond Foundationalism: Shaping Theology in a Postmodern Context* (Louisville, KY: Westminster John Knox, 2001), 228.

[277] Congar, *I Believe in the Holy Spirit*, Vol. 111, 5.

[278] T. F. Torrance, op. cit., 60. This statement comes as part of an exposition of the classic Nicene doctrine of the Trinity using the threefold framework of 2 Cor 13:14.

It is thus in the context of the (secondary) κοινωνία of the Spirit experienced within the church on earth that we can truly receive and interpret the word of God, a word that springs from that (primary) κοινωνία that characterises the triune Godhead in heaven.

To summarise this section, we began by remarking on the Trinitarian presuppositions of Paul. Recent Trinitarian discussions have highlighted the fact that God economically reveals himself in his triune immanent self. He is therefore known and understood through relational channels that are created by and received through the Holy Spirit, as explicated from his role within the Trinity. The perichoretic dynamic of Trinitarian relationship is not confined to the Godhead, but is shared with those who constantly call on the life and illumination of the Spirit. Thus God opens himself up to Christians so that, together, they actually participate in the life of the Trinity, with its rich blend of both diversity (the threeness of the divine persons) and unity (the oneness of God).

For biblical interpreters, this provides a model for distinctively individual insights but always within the parameters of the great united whole, the body of Christ which is his church. The Trinitarian focus involves an 'upward' look to the triune God but also, in consequence, a 'horizontal/outward' dimension in partnership with other Christians, a partnership modelled upon and sourced from the 'fellowship' of the Trinity, as enabled and energised by the κοινωνία of the Spirit. In the next section, we will seek to make more specific applications of the Trinitarian aspect of κοινωνία to the task of biblical interpretation.

## Dialogical

The Spirit does not just provide an 'upward' movement to God, with a consequent outward orientation to others who are also looking upwards. There is also a 'downward' movement of the Spirit as he proceeds from God to bring challenge and judgment. For despite human pleas for the Spirit to come and 'help' us, when the wind of the divine *pneuma* makes his initial presence felt, it is more often than not as a contrary rather than a comforting force. Barth has written of the Spirit:

> He has spoken and acted in direct contradiction of everything that I can say or thou canst hear—he contradicts even our questioning. He is completely the Other. Confronting Him, we are confronted with perfected speech and with perfected action.[279]

Jesus spoke of this kind of action of the Spirit on a global scale: 'And when he comes, he will convict the world concerning sin and righteousness and

---

[279] Karl Barth, *The Epistle to the Romans,* translated from 6th ed. by Edwyn C. Hoskins (Oxford: Oxford University Press, 1968), 275.

judgement.'²⁸⁰ Yet as the Spirit comes up against people in this way, it is in order to bring them to the point of repentance, that they might experience a restoration of fellowship and communion. As the Spirit confronts and deals with us in our problems and disputes, the ultimate result can often be a greater understanding of Scriptural truth and its application to us. We will now seek to show this by way of examples from the New Testament pattern, and in particular Pauline teaching, as well as from the life of the church, both past and present.

*(i) The New Testament Pattern*

Reading through the New Testament references to the Holy Spirit, one is constantly reminded of the dialogical aspect of the Spirit's workings. They do not occur in a vacuum, but are frequently described in terms of contrasts, opposites, tensions, and polarities that challenge and change people and situations.

A particularly pointed example occurs soon after the day of Pentecost in the ongoing life of the early church. The deceit of Ananias and Sapphira was a direct affront not just to believers who 'had everything in common' (αὐτοῖς ἅπαντα κοινά)²⁸¹ but was also a lying (ψεύσασθαί)²⁸² to and testing (πειράσαι)²⁸³ of the Spirit that brought God's immediate judgment. As Turner points out, 'the contrast between the united community becoming 'filled with the Spirit' in 4:31 and the heart of Ananias being 'filled by Satan to lie to the Spirit' (5:3) is evidently intentional, and indicates quite clearly that the Spirit's role in community is seen as part of a cosmic and soteriological dualism: the Spirit verses Satan; salvation versus judgment.'²⁸⁴ The result was a further stimulus to community, even if it was in the fact of 'the whole church' being united in 'great fear.'²⁸⁵

*(ii) The Pauline Antitheses*

The dialogical aspect of the Spirit's workings is particularly noticeable in Pauline pneumatology, undergirded as it is by that substratum of the Trinitarian 'trialectic',²⁸⁶ the dynamic of the Word/Spirit relationship.²⁸⁷ As F. W. Horn writes, 'Beginning with the Corinthian correspondence, the view that life in its entirety is determined by Christ and the Spirit is expressed in *antitheses*.'²⁸⁸ An appreciation of these antitheses helps us to understand something of the Spirit's

---

[280] John 16:8a.
[281] Acts 4:32c.
[282] Acts 5:3.
[283] Acts 5:9.
[284] Max Turner, *Power from on High – the Spirit in Israel's Restoration and Witness in Luke-Acts* (Sheffield: Sheffield Academic Press, 1996), 406.
[285] Acts 5:11.
[286] I have adopted this word from Yong's *Spirit-Word-Community*, for example at 7 and 109.
[287] 1 Cor 2:4; 1 Thess1:5.
[288] My italics. See F. W. Horn, 'The Holy Spirit' in *ABD*, 276. See also Max Turner, *The Holy Spirit and Spiritual Gifts* (Carlisle: Paternoster, 1996), 118.

purposes. As James Barr has remarked, albeit in a different context, 'an essential part of lexicography is the observation of oppositions between words, the points where they become contrasted.'[289]

In compiling our own dictionary of pneumatological contrasts, we could start with Gal 5:17 as a typical example, 'For the desires of the flesh are against the Spirit, and the desires of the Spirit against the flesh, for these are opposed to each other.' This πνεῦμα/σάρξ tension is the one most frequently highlighted in Paul,[290] followed by the 'Spirit'/'letter'[291] (πνεῦμα/γράμμα) and 'Spirit'/'law' (πνεῦμα/νόμος)[292] contrasts. The Holy Spirit is further set over against the human spirit,[293] mind,[294] and wisdom,[295] as well as the spirit of the world,[296] of wine[297] and of fear.[298] This is by no means a comprehensive list,[299] but it highlights various points of discordance and disjunction which the Spirit brings to light. One of the primary purposes of this is to show how the Spirit helps to resolve them into harmony and peace for believers as they obey his leading—in short, to create κοινωνία out of conflict.

This insight could be explored at many different levels, but for the purposes of this book, we should note how the Spirit superintends dissension and difference to bring about a greater κοινωνία of understanding. 'Truth emerges not only in the conflicts and struggles of the individual, but also in the conflicts and struggles of the believing community.'[300] These words from a Church of England report on the Holy Spirit see this as part of the fact that 'the Holy Spirit is given corporately to the community of God's people as "shareholders" in the common gift (*koinonia* of the Spirit ... in the sense of 2 Cor 13:14) ... [Hence] they are a *corroborative* community ... in which the Spirit guides "into all the truth" (John 16:13) and in which "iron sharpens iron" (Prov 27:17).'[301] The report goes on to

---

[289] James Barr, *The Semantics of Biblical Language* (Oxford: Oxford University Press, 1961), 220.
[290] Gal 3:3; 4:29; 5:17; 6:8; Rom 1:3-4; 8:4-5, 9, 13; Phil 3:3. See also Ferguson, *The Holy Spirit* (Leicester: IVP, 1996), 153-162, Fee, *God's Empowering Presence*, 816-822, and Dunn's positive comment thereon: 'The presence of conflict between flesh and Spirit is a sign that the Spirit is having effect in shaping the character.' Dunn, *The Theology of Paul the Apostle*, 496.
[291] 2 Cor 3:6; Rom 2:29; 7:6.
[292] Rom 7:6; 8:3-4. See Ferguson, op. cit., 162-166.
[293] Such as in Rom 8:16 and 1 Cor 2:11, though in a number of cases the reference to *pneuma* could be construed as either the Spirit of God or the spirit of man, for instance in Gal 6:1 and Eph 1:17. For more on Holy Spirit/human spirit see Dunn, *The Theology of Paul the Apostle*, 76-78; Moule, *The Holy Spirit* (London & Oxford: Mowbray, 1978), 7-21; and Fee, *God's Empowering Presence*, 23-25, where he speaks of 'Paul's apparent conviction that the believer's spirit is the place where, by means of God's own Spirit, the human and the divine interface in the believer's life' (ibid., 25).
[294] 1 Cor 14:15.
[295] 1 Cor 2:13.
[296] 1 Cor 2:12. See also Rom 14:17.
[297] Eph 5:18.
[298] 2 Tim 1:7.
[299] See Yong, *Spirit-Word-Community*, 106, for a list of the vast range of theological anthropological polarities that the Spirit helps to bridge.
[300] *We Believe in the Holy Spirit - a Report by the Doctrine Commission of the General Synod of the Church of England* (London: Church House Publishing, 1991), 124.
[301] Ibid.

cite as an example how the arguments in the Corinthian church ultimately led to a more developed understanding of the theology of the Lord's supper, the Christian ministry, and the relation between wisdom and the cross, as expressed in Paul's New Testament letter, 1 Corinthians.[302]

For a specific linking of the Spirit's help in coming to an accord, we could also mention Phil 2:1–2, noting the progression from 'participation in the Spirit' (κοινωνία πνεύματος v. 1) to 'being of one mind' (ἵνα τὸ αὐτὸ φρονῆτε lit. 'in order that the same thing you think' v. 2). Paul's great concern that the Philippians develop a common Christian mind-set,[303] was, then, combined with recognition that this could only be achieved with pneumatological assistance. Not that this entailed complete uniformity of thought. As Marshall says:

> It is perfectly possible for people to think independently and creatively in harmony with one another. It should be equally possible for them to have genuine differences of opinion as to the right way to proceed and yet to come to one mind in the end.[304]

We shall see a New Testament example of this when we consider the deliberations of the Council of Jerusalem as recorded in Acts 15, deliberations that centred around a Spirit-given reading of the Old Testament by the debating community.[305]

## (iii) Historical Conflicts: Creeds, Councils and Canon

The above references to 1 Corinthians and Philippians 2 illustrate just how much Pauline teaching could be read as a response to problems and conflicts within the early church. As doctrinal and theological disputes continued in subsequent centuries, they gave rise to the early ecumenical councils[306] and later conferences and conventions that went on to produce many great confessions of faith. Thus it can be seen that 'the creeds took the form they did *in response* to the situation in which they arose, that the selection of details related to the *challenges* presented to the Christian account of things.'[307] Both Pauline theology and Christian credal formulations can therefore be seen as a key way in which the Spirit guided the community to a deeper appreciation of scriptural truth as a result of the forces of disagreement, opposition, and even heresy.[308] This fact

---

[302] Ibid., 124–125.
[303] Marshall, *The Epistle to the Philippians*, 13, notes the frequency of the verb 'to think' – in 2:2a, 2b, 5; 3:15a, 15b, 19; 4:2, 10a, 10b.
[304] Ibid., 45.
[305] See pages 173–179.
[306] The first of these being the Council of Nicea in AD 325.
[307] Frances Young, *The Making of the Creeds* (London: SCM, 1991),6. Italics mine. Young goes on to say, however, that 'the common "catch phrases" are deeply traditional in oral confession material predating the formation of the creeds' (ibid., 6).
[308] A similar process can be traced in the history of church denominations and movements generally. As Grant Osborne has observed, 'it is a humbling experience to realize that one's church tradition does not go back to the apostles themselves (no matter what creative reasoning may be behind the claim) and arose due to church conflict rather than to pure theological reasoning'. *The Hermeneutical Spiral* (Downers Grove, IL: IVP, 1991), 291.

should perhaps help us to see that real interpretive fruit can and still does come out of conflicts within both the local and wider church, painful though the particular communal disputations may be at the time.[309]

It is not only Pauline and credal confessions that can be seen as a result of the Spirit's dialectical workings to produce a deeper community understanding of the Scriptural teaching. The very idea of the canon[310] of Scripture may be understood as a consequence of the Spirit's guidance of the community as not just interpreter but more fundamentally as custodian of Scripture.

It is thought that it was not until the late fourth century that the final canon of both the Old Testament and the New Testament was generally recognised as such.[311] The historical details of how this came about are sketchy, but that the process of canonisation took place against the background of debate and disagreement seems clear. Eusebius, writing in the early fourth century, refers to the last remaining books to be incorporated in the New Testament canon as the '*antilegomena*' or books 'spoken against'.[312] Gerald Bray says that 'the main spur towards developing a written New Testament canon seems to have come from the rise of competing groups which either disputed the authority of certain books or offered additional literature as authoritative Scripture.'[313] Even if details of the dialectics of canonisation have now been lost, 'that it transpired under the influence of the Spirit of God is commonly accepted among Christian people.'[314] Only the Spirit could have enabled the collocation of literature that constitutes the New Testament, in all its exegetically challenging unity and diversity. And as we shall see later, it is in the ongoing task of interpreting this in the variegated contexts of church life today that the Spirit is ever at work to guide and direct.

To summarise this section, then, I have been attempting to see how the Spirit uses the dynamics of dialogue to produce various forms of community interpretation of Scripture. Yong graphically speaks of a 'pneumatological "engine" which drives, incessantly, the dialectic of thought and reality.'[315] Underlying this is the basic 'two-stroke engine' of the Word/Spirit dynamic that is primary amongst the various Pauline antitheses. As the Spirit highlights

---

[309] Current ecclesiastical debates over homosexuality issues being a particularly poignant case in point.
[310] From the Gk. κανών – rod, rule, measure or standard and 'thus a criterion [which] (together with its cognates 'canonical' and 'canonize') began to be applied by Christian writers of the late 4$^{th}$ century to the correct collection and list of the Scriptures,' Roger Beckwith, 'The Canon of Scripture' in *New Dictionary of Biblical Theology*, eds. T. Desmond Alexander and B. S. Rosner (Leicester: IVP, 2000), 27.
[311] 'The earliest list of NT books containing only our twenty-seven appeared in AD 367 in a letter of Athanasius, Bishop of Alexandria.' J. R. McRay, 'Canon of Bible' in *Evangelical Dictionary of Theology*, ed.W. A. Elwell (Carlisle: Paternoster, 1984), 141.
[312] As opposed to those which were agreed (*homologoumena*). The disputed books were especially James, 2 Peter, 2 and 3 John, Jude and Revelation.
[313] Gerald Bray, *Biblical Interpretation - Past and Present* (Leicester: Apollos, 1996), 30.
[314] J. R. McRay, 'Canon of Bible,' 140.
[315] Yong, *Spirit-Word-Community*, 106, though he also goes on to say 'the result is better conceived as a hermeneutical *trialectic*' (ibid., 109, italics mine) in terms of his overall thesis of the need for a Word-Spirit-Community hermeneutic.

points of tension, so he acts in the resolution thereof. Pauline theology, credal formulations, and indeed the very canon of Scripture can all be seen as the product of the Spirit's superintendence of conflict to produce a deeper understanding of Scriptural truth through κοινωνία.

As I have been considering the dialogical role of the Spirit, I have not yet mentioned the two fundamental *temporal* dimensions that the Spirit embraces. Scripture testifies to his unique ability to produce a κοινωνία with both past and future for the people of God. I will turn to each of these in our remaining two sections.

## Historical

'He will teach you all things, and bring *to your remembrance (ὑπομνήσει)* all that I have said to you' (John 14:26). Of these words, J. C. Ryle writes:

> To my eyes they seem a general promise, primarily, no doubt, applying specially to the eleven,[316] but after them belonging also to all believers in every age. As a matter of experience, I believe that the awakening of the memories of true Christians is one of the peculiar works of the Holy Ghost on their souls.[317]

More recently, J. D. G. Dunn, in *Jesus Remembered*, has drawn attention to the key place that the original, transformative 'remembrance' of Jesus played in the formation of early Christian tradition and its inscripturation. We quote two of his summary propositions:

> The Jesus tradition shows us *how* Jesus was remembered; its character strongly suggests again and again a tradition given its essential shape by regular use and reuse in oral mode.... This suggests in turn that that essential shape was given by the original and immediate *impact made by Jesus* as that was first put into words by and among those involved as eyewitnesses of what Jesus said and did. In that key sense, the Jesus tradition *is* Jesus remembered.[318]

These assertions do seem to separate the 'Jesus of history' from the 'Christ of faith', but Dunn's emphasis upon the vital role of oral tradition—presumably with Spirit-assisted 'remembrance'—is being increasingly recognised as a primary factor in the transmission, recording, and interpretation of the Christian story.

---

[316] John 2:22 and 12:16.
[317] J. C. Ryle, *Expository Thoughts on the Gospels - St John Vol. 111* (Cambridge & London: James Clark & Co, 1969 reprint), 96.
[318] J. D. G. Dunn, *Jesus Remembered: Christianity in the Making, Vol. 1* (Grand Rapids, MI; Cambridge: Eerdmans, 2003), 882 (italics the author's).

'Remembrance' and the related notion of 'tradition' are both biblical categories about which much has indeed been written, not only from theological but also psychological and sociological standpoints. Our brief here is hermeneutical—to highlight the way in which the Spirit guides and has guided the community in its custodianship and interpretation of Scripture through the creation of a κοινωνία with believers and their beliefs across and down the ages. As C. H. Dodd has written, 'when once the corporate factor in Christian experience is admitted, the factor of historical tradition cannot be excluded.'[319]

In the previous section, I referred to the creeds and confessions which are an important part of this tradition. In this section my discussion will go on to compare contemporary and biblical perspectives, survey differing ecclesiastical outlooks and refer to Gadamer's notion of being part of a historic interpreting community. Underlying this discussion is the conviction that 'contrary to the way we often act, the Holy Spirit did not begin his illuminating work in our generation. He has always taught the church.'[320]

*(i) Contemporary Attitudes in Perspective*

'My infatuation with the past puts me at odds with my generation,' writes Jemima Lewis in a recent newspaper article where she speaks of a general 'disdain of tradition' that 'horrifies me.'[321] In Western society, the relentless tide of evolutionary theory, scientific rationalism, materialism, and pluralism has watered down and often washed away the remaining deposits of a shared Christian historical viewpoint.[322] Walter Brueggemann has written of how 'our society is ... increasingly *thinned* of memory, ethics, and hope,' in contrast to the '*thickness*' offered by participation in the rich world of biblical understanding with its 'many readings, many hearings, many interpretations, and many acts of faithful imagination.'[323] Such a heritage is now alien to the thought life of the average secularised and individualised inhabitant of the West.

---

[319] C. H. Dodd, *The Authority of the Bible* (London: Nisbet & Co., 1938), 299 (where he prefaces this statement with the assertion that 'an irresponsible individualism in religion is not Christian'). Conversely, those who exclude the corporate factor can belittle the role of historical tradition, for example, the person Lundin describes as 'the allegorist' who treats it as subject to the transitoriness of the temporal consensus of the age, and 'the intentionalist' who regards it as 'a desert through which we must travel if we are to drink from the clear springs of the author's mind,' R. Lundin in *The Promise of Hermeneutics* by R. Lundin, C. Walhout & A. C. Thiselton (Cambridge: Paternoster, 1999), 55.

[320] Richard L. Pratt, *He gave us Stories –The Bible Students Guide to Interpreting OT Narratives*, (Phillipsburg, NJ: Presbyterian & Reformed Publishing Company, 1990), 70.

[321] *The Sunday Telegraph*, Dec. 7 2003, 29.

[322] Roger Lundin traces the origins of this tide to the Enlightenment thinking of Rene Descartes. 'Perhaps more than any other figure at the dawn of modernity, Descartes launched the tradition of living without tradition; he became the father of all who would seek to live in a parentless world. After Descartes, in the words of Gerald Burns, "we are always in the *post* position, primed and impatient to start history over again in an endless recuperation of the Cartesian moment of self fathering."' See Roger Lundin, 'Interpreting Orphans: Hermeneutics in the Cartesian Tradition' in Lundin, *The Promise of Hermeneutics*, 3. A Christian worldview, of course, challenges this by providing a Spirit-given eschatology—see later in this chapter.

[323] Walter Brueggemann, *Deep Memory, Exuberant Hope: Contested Truth in a Post-Modern World* (Minneapolis: Augsburg Fortress, 2000), xii, italics mine.

This is illustrated by much contemporary ignorance of the Bible,[324] an ignorance that would dismay the small army of Sunday School teachers that gave a scriptural education to such a large proportion of the population of Britain just a two generations ago.[325]

It is this lack of a common Christian perspective today that has contributed to a general distrust of all tradition, not just that of the Bible. The contrast is even greater when comparing with the early Christian centuries.[326] To quote Anthony Thiselton:

> Whereas in postmodernism the recurring patterns of tradition are viewed as objects of intense *suspicion*, as devices of power to sanction monarchical, feudal, or bourgeois socio-political values, in the pre-modern ecumenical Christian world the framework remains an object of *trust*, because it embodies the testimony of the community to the historic apostolic faith as definitively revealed in Christ. Irenaeus, Tertullian, Origen, and Augustine did not doubt that a wilful departure from the boundaries of that tradition projected the individual into a sea of unchartered relativism. Both a *hermeneutic of trust* and a *hermeneutic of suspicion* equally recognize, as modernist individualism does not, the importance of the trans-individual frame within which understanding and interpretation operate.[327]

*(ii) Entering into the Historical Biblical Worldview*

In contrast to much modern disdain of tradition, the Scriptures themselves are full of examples of this 'trans-individual', historical frame of understanding that stems from being part of the Bible's 'covenantal history' which Brueggemann claims to be 'the main theme of the Bible.'[328] As a key part in the shaping of such a biblical tradition, Brueggemann picks out 'primal narratives'[329] that formed what Gerhard Von Rad called the *credo* of Israel. Its whole existence as a covenant community stemmed from two fundamentals: the call of Abraham and the exodus from Egypt. The regular remembrance and recital of these great events formulated the collective *psyche* of the nation. It was with such a mindset

---

[324] For example, as displayed in many contemporary TV quiz shows.
[325] Sunday school attendance in the UK has dropped from fifty-five per cent in 1900 to only four per cent today, according to the Bishop of London, *Baptist Times* 20th May 2004, 10.
[326] In the early church, appeal to apostolic tradition and the 'rule of faith' was considered vital in settling interpretive disputes with heretical groups, see Vanhoozer, *Is there a meaning in this text?*, 411.
[327] Thiselton, *New Horizons in Hermeneutics*, 146, italics mine.
[328] Paul Hanson, *The Bible Makes Sense: The Growth of Community in the Bible* (Atlanta, GA: Westminster John Knox, 2001), 13.
[329] The three he posits are: Deut 26:5-9; 6:20-24 and Josh 24:1-13. These speak specifically of the 'handing on' of tradition, which elsewhere in the OT is commonly presupposed rather that explicitly enjoined. 'Remembrance' is a common theme in Deuteronomy whose primal status in biblical tradition is attested to by the fact that it is among the four most frequently quoted OT books referred to by NT writers, being found in 17 of the 27 books, some 80+ references altogether. Other writers have suggested Exod 15:1-18 as a possibly earlier 'primal narrative' in the OT.

that the apostle Paul articulated his theology: 'as a Jew, Paul could not think of salvation other than through the paradigm of the Exodus.'[330]

It is in Paul's writings (but not exclusively) that C. H. Dodd highlights what he regards as the essential *kerygma* of the New Testament. Now the focus shifts from the faith of Israel to its fulfilment in Christ, and he quotes 1 Cor 1:23, 3:11 and 15:3-8[331] as epitomising the Christ-centred *kerygma* that he identifies as being at the heart of the preaching of the early church.[332] It was indeed, Dodd claims, Christ himself who taught the Apostles and early church a way of reading the Old Testament that applied select passages to himself and which thereby became an essential part of the Christian tradition.[333]

Von Rad's *credo* and Dodd's *kerygma* are, says Brueggemann, simply ways of saying that there is an 'elemental and nonnegotiable story line that lies at the heart of biblical faith,'[334] a '*primal narrative*'[335] that has always been deeply embedded in the memory of the redeemed communities of both the Old and New Testament, and indeed defined their whole *raison d'être*.[336]

How has this 'primal narrative', and indeed all biblical narrative, been kept alive, preserved, and transmitted? What silver thread binds together the manifold layers of biblical tradition? We must say that it is the 'Spirit of truth,'[337] who first inspired it.[338] This follows from Jesus's promise to his disciples that it was the Spirit who would 'bring to your remembrance all that I have said to you'[339] and 'guide you into all truth.'[340] Similarly, Paul's command to Timothy to 'guard the deposit (παραθήκην) entrusted to you' is followed by the means by which this is effected, namely '*the Holy Spirit who dwells within us* (ἐν ἡμῖν).'[341] Believers thus have a corporate Spirit-enabled privilege and duty to guard and indeed 'contend

---

[330] Tom Holland, *Contours of Pauline Theology*, iii of preface of pre-publication copy, now published (Fearn: Christian Focus-Mentor, 2004).
[331] See Brueggemann, *The Bible Makes Sense*, 24 for a summary of this. This *kerygma*, says Dodd, runs through the NT, its essential elements being shared by Paul, the preaching in the early parts of Acts, as well as the gospels.
[332] C. H. Dodd, *The Apostolic Preaching and Its Developments* (London: Hodder & Stoughton, 1936). 'The general scheme of the *kerygma* ... begins by proclaiming that "this is that which was spoken by the prophets"; the age of fulfilment has dawned, and Christ is its Lord; it then proceeds to recall the historical facts, leading up to the resurrection and exaltation of Christ and the promise of His coming in glory; and it ends with the call to repentance and the offer of forgiveness', ibid., 105.
[333] See C. H. Dodd, *According to the Scriptures –The Substructure of New Testament Theology* (London: Nisbet, 1952). See pages 94–95 for a summary of the argument of this book.
[334] Brueggemann, *The Bible Makes Sense*, 23.
[335] Ibid., 23.
[336] To join such a community by an act of faith, then, is to enter a whole new world of significance where personal identity and meaning is no longer defined by reference to individualised and selfish conceptions of personhood, but by becoming part of a historic company of the redeemed, with a rich past, as well as a glorious future. C. H. Dodd speaks about 'turn[ing] away from the narrow scene of individual experience at the moment, to the spacious prospect we command in the Bible,' *The Authority of the Bible* (London: Nisbet, 1938), 298.
[337] John 16:13. See further, chapter 4.
[338] 2 Tim 3:16. See further, pages 237–239.
[339] John 14:26.
[340] John 16:13.
[341] 2 Tim 1:14. See also v. 12. See also pages 231–239 for more detail on this.

for the faith that was once for all delivered to the saints (ἅπαξ παραδοθείσῃ τοῖς ἁγίοις).'[342]

### (iii) Κοινωνία and the New Testament Language of Tradition

To quote Riesner, παράδοσις is 'the standard [New Testament] word for "tradition"'[343] as derived from Judaism.[344] Jesus used the term negatively in the Gospels,[345] when he warned the Pharisees how they were 'annulling the word of God by your tradition that you have handed down';[346] a perennial danger of tradition when it becomes man-made.[347] Paul, however, used the word positively in 1 Corinthians,[348] thus linking in traditions about Christ's life, death, and resurrection with Old Testament traditions which 'are both temporal-historical and corporate.'[349]

1 Cor 11:23 ('for I received') leads Paul into his narrative exposition of the Lord's supper, which links our discussion of memory ('remembrance'/ ἀνάμνησιν vv. 24–25[350]) and tradition (παρέδωκα v. 23) with our ongoing concern with κοινωνία. Κοινωνία has been translated as 'a participation' ('the communion' AV) in the body and blood of Christ in 1 Cor 10:16, describing a conjunction[351] that Calvin attributes to the Spirit:

> Even though it seems unbelievable that Christ's flesh, separated from us by such great distance, penetrates to us, so that it becomes our food, let us remember how far the secret power of the Holy Spirit towers above all our senses ... What, then, our mind does not comprehend, let faith conceive: that *the Spirit truly unites things separated in space.*[352]

Such language has been accused of being 'excessively material,'[353] but laying aside such discussion,[354] one can go on from Calvin to say that the Spirit does not just unite 'things separated in space', but also people separated in time.

---

[342] Jude v. 3.
[343] R. Riesner 'Tradition' in *New Dictionary of Biblical Theology*, ed. T. D. Alexander and B. S. Rosner (Leicester: IVP, 2000), 823.
[344] '[I]n 1 Corinthians 11:23 and 15:3 [Paul] used Jewish terminology for the "delivering" (*paradidomai*) and "receiving" (*paralambanein*) of a tradition, terminology found also in the Mishnah, the first official written collection of the rabbinic oral laws. This shows that with respect to their tradition, the early Christians used common Jewish methods, as Jesus had done,' ibid., 825.
[345] Matt 15:3 and Mark 7:9,13.
[346] Mark 7:13.
[347] Note Paul's warning in Col 2:8.
[348] 1 Cor 11:2, 23; 15:3.
[349] Thiselton, *New Horizons in Hermeneutics*, 149.
[350] Cf. ὑπομνήσει in John 14:26.
[351] The ontological nature of this conjunction has of course been theologically contested for centuries, with debates over 'transubstantiation', 'consubstantiation', 'real presence', and memorialist understandings.
[352] John Calvin, *Institutes of the Christian Religion*, ed. J. T. McNeill, tr. F. L. Battles (London: SCM; Philadelphia: Westminster, 1961), IV.17.4, as quoted in Ferguson, *The Holy Spirit*, 202. Italics mine.
[353] Ferguson, *The Holy Spirit*, 203.
[354] For further details, see Ferguson, op. cit., 200–205. For a Catholic discussion of the Holy Spirit's role in the Lord's Supper, see Congar, *I Believe in the Holy Spirit*, Vol. 3, 258–265.

This is illustrated by 1 John 1:3 where, as already mentioned, John states that the proclamation of the incarnation, presumably in the power of the Spirit,[355] leads to a 'fellowship with us' (κοινωνίαν ... μεθ' ἡμῶν), as well as with Father and Son. Carson comments, 'we cannot enter into fellowship with God and with his Son Jesus Christ without entering into fellowship with the apostles who were the first witnesses of the incarnation.'[356] It is certainly true that as one grapples with the words of the New Testament writers in Bible study, reflection, and sermon preparation, one is entering a dialogue with and even some kind of relationship with a Peter, Paul, or John. This can also be said of the Old Testament, whether the 'revivifying' encounter be through the medium of dramatic narratives about Elijah, real-to-life accounts of David's exploits, or musings on the 'heart-on-the-sleeve' lamentations of Jeremiah. Something akin to this 'fellowship with the Christian departed' can be experienced when taking or attending their funerals or reading their biographies. They, 'though [they] died, still speak.'[357]

Is this an aspect of what the Apostles' Creed[358] calls 'the communion of saints' (*communion sanctorum*)? 'This term ... has enjoyed great favour among Catholics' writes Yves Congar.[359] He speaks of it thus: 'the biblical Greek word *koinonia*, translated by the Latin *communio*, requires us to see the matter in this light—it means the participation in the good things of the community of salvation together with the other members of that community.... What is the principle of this participation? ... charity.'[360]

Few would dispute this basic principle, but Protestants would certainly object when the flow of 'charity' between the departed and living saints is stated to include reliance on the merits of the former by the latter or on the prayers of the latter by the former! This is but one illustration of how different ecclesiastical 'traditions' view the importance and relevance of 'tradition', its participants and constituents and the relationship of the Spirit thereto. To this I must now turn.

---

[355] Implied by 1 John 2:20; 3:24 and 4:13 and explicitly affirmed by John in Rev 1:10; 2:7, 11, 17, 29; 3:6, 13, 23. See further chapter 7 on 1 John.
[356] D. A. Carson, *For the Love of God: A Daily Companion for Discovering the Riches of God's Word*, Vol. 1, Dec. 2 (Leicester: IVP, 1998).
[357] Heb 11:4.
[358] Considered to date just before AD 400.
[359] *I Believe in the Holy Spirit*, Vol.11, 59. Congar's book represents a comprehensive modern Catholic pneumatology in which the communal ('persons in communion') dimension is prominent. Groppe's critique is sympathetic: 'Congar should ... be remembered as a theologian of the Holy Spirit ... who gave new life to a neglected tradition in which pneumatology, theological anthropology, and ecclesiology had been seamlessly united.' Elizabeth Teresa Groppe, *Yves Congar's Theology of the Holy Spirit* (Oxford: Oxford University Press, 2004), 12).
[360] Ibid., 59, quoting Rom 5:5 and John 17:26 to illustrate 'charity'. In their renderings of *communio sanctorum*, Catholics like Congar above speak of 'participation' in holy/good things (such as the Eucharist), whereas evangelicals speak of 'the fellowship of the saints.'

## (iv) Differing Ecclesiastical Attitudes to Tradition

The fact that our last-but-one sentence included two different uses of the word 'tradition' reveals something of its diversity of meaning.[361] I shall use the word in its more general sense as referring to 'the entire process by which normative religious truths are passed on from one generation to another.'[362] The extent to which this process is attributed to the Spirit and therefore invested with greater or lesser authority varies according to which of the three main Christian groupings one belongs.

The *Orthodox Church* affords the highest status to tradition. The words of the highly respected John of Damascus[363] sum it up: 'we do not change the everlasting boundaries which our fathers have set, but we keep the traditions just as we have received them.'[364] Such a view arguably holds the church in something of a time warp. This is nevertheless justified on the ground that tradition is equated with the life of the Spirit in the church.

Tradition *is* the witness of the Spirit ... the constant abiding of the Spirit and not only the memory of words. Tradition is a *charismatic*, not a historical, principle.[365]

The fact that there is only one 'holy tradition', which can be either written or unwritten,[366] has the effect of giving equal authority to both Scripture and tradition, although the former is regarded as 'primary.'[367] Underlying this viewpoint is this strongly pneumatic conception of the church and theological authority, as expressed by Alexei Khomiakov:

---

[361] See Telford Work, *Living and Active: Scripture in the Economy of Salvation* (Grand Rapids, MI: Eerdmans, 2002), 261 and Daniel B. Clendenin, *Eastern Orthodox Christianity: A Western Perspective* (Grand Rapids, MI: Baker, 1994), 96. Sylvia Keesmat brings out the element of continuous actualization of tradition in her definition: 'tradition is comprised of those events, stories, rituals and symbols that shape the collective identity of a community, that are passed down in a community from generation to generation and that are rooted in the foundational past of that community.' Sylvia Keesmat, *Paul and His Story: (Re)Interpreting the Exodus Tradition* (Sheffield: Sheffield Academic Press, 1999), 17.
[362] J. Van Engen, 'Tradition' in *Evangelical Dictionary of Theology*, 1104.
[363] AD 675–749.
[364] *On the Divine Images* 2:12, quoted in Clendenin, op. cit., 18.
[365] George Florovsky, *Bible, Church, Tradition* (Belmont, MA: Nordland, 1972), 46–47, quoted in Clendenin, op. cit., 107.
[366] Spirit-given tradition can be found in various external forms, of which 'Timothy Ware lists seven: Scripture, the seven ecumenical councils, later councils and their dogmatic statements (Orthodoxy's so-called symbolic books), the Fathers, liturgy, canon law, and icons' Clendenin, op. cit., 108.
[367] Ibid., 109. A more modified attitude toward the place of tradition is represented in contemporary Orthodox writers such as Demetrios Bathrellos, a Greek orthodox priest. 'The Orthodox Church is not at one with the Protestant doctrine of *sola Scriptura*. Many Orthodox theologians, however, are not happy with the 'two sources' (Scripture and tradition) theory either ... Tradition provides, however, the context within which Scripture is written, canonised, read, interpreted and preached. To have no tradition is perhaps as bad as to have false tradition. Without a proper context of tradition and church life the authentic biblical message cannot be properly received and is bound to be distorted and eventually lost.' See Demetrios Bathrellos, 'The Eastern Orthodox tradition for today' in, *The Bible in Pastoral Practice: Readings in the place and function of Scripture in the Church*, ed. Paul Ballard and Stephen Holmes (London: Darton Longman and Todd, 2005), 45.

> Neither individuals, nor a multitude of individuals within the church preserve tradition or write the Scriptures, but the Spirit of God which lives in the whole body of the church.[368]

Such an *internal* view of ecclesiastical authority, along with disagreement over *filioque*, led to the great schism with the Western Church in 1054, with Orthodoxy's rejection of the *external* authority of the Papacy.

The *Roman Catholic Church's* attitude to tradition is not uniform, but three typical statements may be quoted from a 1993 Pontifical Biblical Commission:

> What characterizes Catholic exegesis is that it deliberately places itself within the living tradition of the church whose first concern is fidelity to the revelation attested by the Bible.[369]

> In the last resort it is the magisterium which has the responsibility of guaranteeing the authenticity of interpretation ... It discharges this function within the *koinonia* of the body, expressing the faith of the church, as a service to the church ... to this end it consults theologians, exegetes, and other experts.[370]

The church, as the people of God, is aware that it is helped by the Holy Spirit in its understanding and interpretation of scripture.[371]

A stronger role for the Spirit seems to be envisaged in the more recent teaching document *The Gift of Scripture*[372] issued by the Catholic Bishops' Conference:

> Exploration of the human dimensions of the Scriptures allows us to discover the divine message. In so doing *we need to invoke the assistance of the Holy Spirit*, who inspired these writings.[373]

> In the continuing tradition, based on the Scriptures, God still speaks to the church today and the Holy Spirit of God leads us onwards on the way of truth (John 16:13, *Dei Verbum* 8).[374]

Catholicism thus has a very high regard for tradition, a tradition which is seen as Spirit-given. Historically, by the Council of Trent,[375] 'tradition was said to be

---

[368] Alexei Khomiakov, 'The Church is One' in W. J. Birkbeck, *Russia and the English Church* (London: SPCK, 1953), 198, quoted in Clendenin, op. cit., 98.

[369] J. L. Houlden, ed., *The Interpretation of the Bible in the Church*, Pontifical Biblical Commission 1993(London: SCM, 1995), 58.

[370] Ibid., 72.

[371] Ibid., 65.

[372] Catholic Bishops' Conference of England and Wales, and of Scotland, *The Gift of Scripture* (London: Catholic Truth Society, 2005). The document acknowledges that it 'make[s] extensive use of the Council document, *Dei Verbum*, published in 1965,' Dogmatic Constitution on Divine Revelation of the Second Vatican Council,12.

[373] *The Gift of Scripture*, 20, italics inserted. The Spirit is mentioned several times in the opening chapters in connection with the inspiration and interpretation of the Bible.

[374] Ibid., 15. Note the capitalisation, 'the Tradition', and how Scripture and an official Catholic teaching document are cited as joint authorities for the statement. See chapter 4 for more on John 16:13.

[375] 1545–1563, the 'official Roman Catholic response to the Lutheran Reformation'; F. S. Piggin, 'The Council of Trent' in *Evangelical Dictionary of Theology*, 1109.

equally authoritative with Scripture,'[376] and the contemporary view is still that 'Scripture and the living tradition are intimately related, coming "from the same divine source" and [needing to] be "accepted and honoured with equal devotion and reverence."'[377] Despite this, since Vatican II, Scripture has been granted an outwardly more normative role,[378] though still under the ultimate interpretive authority of the *magisterium*.[379] This, in turn, is grounded upon the primacy and infallibility of the papacy,[380] which is an anathema to Protestants.

Thirdly, for *the Protestant Church,* ultimate authority resides in the Scripture itself, for as Luther said, 'Scripture is its own interpreter,' ('*Scriptura sui ipsius interpres'*).[381] In this, the need of the Holy Spirit's help is readily acknowledged, but the principles of *sola Scriptura* and scriptural perspicuity necessarily entail a much more critical approach to tradition. Calvin, for instance, wrote about the 'tyranny of human tradition which is haughtily thrust upon us under the title of the church.'[382] This is historically understandable considering the abuses and heresies which were challenged by the Reformation[383] and still abound in various branches of the church today in many different forms.

Protestants, especially of the more 'reformed' variety, nevertheless value their heritage, and are sometimes accused by Pentecostal/charismatic groupings of being imprisoned by it. For them, it is the Spirit, not the word that must lord it over tradition, tradition which is often regarded as a stultifying rather than enriching. On the other hand, an over-preoccupation with contemporary experiences of the Spirit, alongside evangelical reductionism and other factors, has resulted in some deserting the evangelical/charismatic fold and taking refuge within the ancient, unchanging traditions of Orthodoxy that are said to link them more closely with the primitive church.[384]

---

[376] Ibid., 1110, but Clendenin, op. cit., 96, refers to the debate about the precise outcome of Trent on this point.
[377] *The Gift of Scripture*, 15, quoting from *Dei Verbum*, 9.
[378] 'Within Tradition the Scriptures occupy a unique and normative place and belong to what has been given once for all' *The Gift of Authority* (Agreed Statement by the Second Anglican-Roman Catholic Commission) 1999, as cited in *The Gift of Scripture*, 14. The latter document admits that 'since its (Dei Verbum's) promulgation Catholics have learnt more than ever to cherish the Bible. We have rediscovered the Bible as a precious treasure, both ancient and ever new' (p. 6). *The Gift of Scripture* certainly exhibits a high, Christological view of Scripture and a scholarly approach to its interpretation (never referred to as 'hermeneutics') that acknowledges the fruits of historical criticism (19) as well as the interpretive role of the Holy Spirit in the community of faith. Its sacramentalist emphases and occasionally dehistoricising remarks, however, would not be acceptable to many evangelicals.
[379] See, for instance, *The Gift of Scripture*, 16: 'the task of safeguarding the understanding of the word of God is given to the teaching authority of the church, the bishops in unions with the Pope.' It is noteworthy that all the authorities cited in the document consist of the official teaching documents of the church, with no reference to any particular individual theologians.
[380] Note, for instance, the frequency Papal reference in *The Gift of Scripture*.
[381] Clendenin, op. cit., 105.
[382] *Institutes* 4.19.18, cited in Clendenin, op. cit., 104.
[383] Martin Luther, for instance, wrote: 'Our opponents skipped faith altogether and taught human traditions and works not commanded by God but invented by them without and against the Word of God; these they have not only put on a par with the Word of God, but have raised far above it.' Martin Luther, 'Lectures on Galatians' in *Luther's Works*, 56 vols. St Louis Concordia 1958-74, 26:52, quoted in Clendenin, op. cit., 103.
[384] See Clendenin, op. cit., 13.

Orthodox, Catholic, and Protestant communities, therefore, each have their own distinctive understanding of tradition[385] and the way the Spirit uses it. Over the centuries, the fundamental tenets of these traditions have been enshrined in various forms of creeds and confessions which shape the way in which Scripture is upheld and interpreted.[386] The effectiveness of these varies according to the relevant church order or attitude towards tradition in each respective church community.[387]

Ideally, 'inspired tradition' is 'the mutual breathing of life between the Christian community and the Christian canon,'[388] but each of the three groupings under discussion needs to be aware of ways in which the Spirit's work in this realm can be quenched. Orthodox Christians should remember that the Spirit as well as vitalizing tradition sometimes needs to challenge and change it,[389] for the Spirit is not static and not all tradition is 'good', or appropriate for succeeding generations. There must be ways in which 'bad' or 'dated' tradition can be critiqued, remembering that antiquity is not a guarantee of veracity. Such points indeed are also relevant for Catholics and Protestants. Catholics certainly need to realise that a number of their traditions, such as Mariolatry and the worship of the saints, when tested against the word of God, lack scriptural authority. For Protestants, the Catholic view of apostolic authority as expressed in papal hegemony usurps the proper headship of Christ over the church, whilst the weight given to the teaching authority of the *magisterium* can undervalue the Spirit-given insights of 'ordinary believers'.[390] Protestants, for their part, need to be made aware that despite their avowed declaration that the word of God must always sit in judgement upon tradition, they nevertheless are all subject to their own traditions of interpretation. In the words of J. Van Engen:

> Preaching is in fact the chief Protestant form of perpetuating tradition, i.e., authoritative interpretations and applications of the word. Protestants should therefore, at the very least, come to some understanding of how particular traditions of preaching were formed,

---

[385] Summarised by R. C. Hanson: 'Tradition in [the Orthodox] view cannot either conflict with [so Protestant] or supplement [so Catholic] scripture, but must interpret it.' R. C. Hanson, 'Tradition', in Alan Richardson and John Bowden, eds., *The Westminster Dictionary of Christian Theology* (Philadelphia: Westminster, 1983), 575, quoted in Telford Work, *Living and Active*, 265.

[386] Examples would be Anglicanism's 39 articles, various Baptist Confessions of Faith, Vatican Councils and Papal Encyclicals.

[387] In more recent times, churches and other Christian groupings have complemented traditional statements of faith with more abbreviated forms of hermeneutical control by borrowing the concept of 'the mission statement' from the language of management-speak. These are intended to give the church a greater sense of purpose and direction, but can sometimes end up as rather glib reductions of Scriptural truth.

[388] Telford Work, *Living and Active*, 262. N. T. Wright speaks of 'The Place of Tradition' in terms of 'Living in Dialogue with Previous Readings' on page 86 of *Scripture and the Authority of God* (London: SPCK, 2005) in a useful section (86–87) thereon.

[389] As in 1 John 4:1-6 and 1 Thess 5:21.

[390] Although *The Gift of Scripture*, in its section 'Bible reading for all' (p. 56), welcomes the place of Bible study groups and acknowledges the debt owed by Catholics 'to other Christians and to Jewish scholars in relation to the progress of biblical scholarship over many decades' (p. 57).

and then proceed to consider devotional practices, church polities, and forms of worship.[391]

This need to acknowledge the historical conditioning and presuppositions of the interpretive community of which one is part has been particularly highlighted by Gadamer.

### (v) Gadamer and the Language of Tradition

Gadamer exposed the Enlightenment myth of an autonomous, prejudice-free interpretation, insisting that these very prejudices are a necessary part of the interpretive process. In *Truth and Method*,[392] he warns against, 'the tyranny of hidden prejudices that makes us deaf to the language that speaks to us in tradition.'[393] Therefore,

> The important thing is to be aware of one's own bias, so that the text may present itself in all its newness and thus be able to assert its own truth against one's own fore-meanings.[394]

These 'fore-meanings' are in large part determined by the traditions in which the interpreters are placed, traditions that inevitably separate them, because of temporal and historical 'distance' ('*Horizontsentfremdung*'), from those of the original authors. Such separation can only be overcome when there is a conscious effort to merge the cultural horizons of past and present ('*Horizontsverschmelzung*').

> Every encounter with tradition that takes place within historical consciousness involves the experience of the tension between text and present. The hermeneutic task consists in not covering up this tension by attempting a naïve assimilation but consciously bringing it out ... In the process of understanding there takes place a real fusing of horizons, which means that as the historical horizon is projected, it is simultaneously removed.[395]

Understanding is not to be thought of so much as an action of one's own subjectivity, but as the placing of oneself within a process of tradition, in which past and present are constantly fused.[396]

---

[391] J. Van Engen, 'Tradition' in *Evangelical Dictionary of Theology*, 1106.
[392] Hans-Georg Gadamer, *Truth and Method* (London: Sheed & Ward, 1975; J. C. B. Mohr, Tübingen 1960).
[393] Ibid., 239. 'History does not belong to us, but we belong to it. Long before we understand ourselves through the process of self-examination, we understand ourselves in a self-evident way in the family, society and state in which we live. The focus of subjectivity is a distorting mirror ... That is why the prejudices of the individual, far more than his judgments, constitute the historical reality of his being', ibid. 245.
[394] Ibid., 238.
[395] Ibid., 273.
[396] Ibid., 258.

One can agree with Gadamer that some sort of 'fusion of horizons' is often taking place when the interpretive process is operating,[397] but if this is the only way to establish meaning, then this leaves the outcome rather open ended.[398] It also underestimates the value of individual inspiration. And as Thiselton says, 'pre-understanding [only] *partly* depends on the theological tradition of the community', even if 'corrected understanding also depends on the theology of the community.'[399] Nevertheless, Gadamer's work has highlighted the fact, as Packer says, that we are all 'children of tradition, and hence are both their beneficiaries and their victims. They have opened our eyes to some things, and closed them to others.'[400] In as much as it is the Spirit that opens blind eyes, his assistance is constantly needed to test and check the traditional readings of the community, as well as its contemporary readings. More will be said on this in chapter 7.

To summarise this section, I first remarked upon the importance of Spirit inspired remembrance in the Bible, in contrast to much contemporary disdain of tradition. I then compared and critiqued different ecclesiastical attitudes to the place of tradition and role of the Spirit. I noted Gadamer's insistence that all interpretation necessarily reflected historical participation in a community of interpretation and the importance of acknowledging this. What this involves will be discussed at the end of this chapter.

## *Eschatological*

The κοινωνία of the Spirit has a prospective as well as a retrospective orientation. Indeed, Fee's synthesis of the Pauline pneumatology starts with the notion of 'The Spirit as Eschatological Fulfilment'[401] 'because apart from the eschatological dimension of "promise and fulfilment" and "already but not yet," neither Paul's own experience of the Spirit nor his perception of that experience are intelligible.'[402]

In this it reflects the overall theological tension found in the New Testament between the kingdom of God having arrived, and yet being still to come. Christians have to learn to live and apply Scripture with the understanding that

---

[397] As an example C. J. Scalise cites how a contemporary understanding of the ancient Israelite tradition of keeping the Sabbath would 'include the interpretive horizons of the early church (Sabbath as Sunday) and the Puritans (strict community-wide moral restrictions)'. C. J. Scalise *From Scripture to Theology: A Canonical Journey into Hermeneutics* (Downers Grove, IL: IVP, 1996), 62.

[398] Thus, to cite the criticism of Joel C. Weinsheimer regarding Gadamer's hermeneutics: 'there can be no determinate criterion for correct interpretation, nor any single, correct, canonical, interpretation.' *Gadamer, Hermeneutics, Tradition and Reason* (Cambridge: Polity, 1987), 111, cited in Thiselton, *New Horizons in Hermeneutics*, 320.

[399] A. C. Thiselton, *The Two Horizons: New Testament Hermeneutics and Philosophical Description* (Carlisle: Paternoster, 1980), 324, italics added.

[400] J. I. Packer, *Beyond the Battle for the Bible* (Westchester, IL: Cornerstone, 1980), 25.

[401] Fee, *God's Empowering Presence*, 803.

[402] Ibid., 805–806.

they are also those 'on whom the *end* (lit. 'ends') of the ages (τέλη τῶν αἰώνων) has come,'⁴⁰³ but for whom 'the end' has not yet arrived. In so far it was the coming of the Spirit at Pentecost that marked the arrival of 'these last days,'⁴⁰⁴ it is in κοινωνία with that same Spirit that a proper balance between the 'now' and 'not yet' can be maintained. As Ferguson points out, 'several descriptions of the Spirit's role as fellowship-partner of the Christian possess an inherently eschatological structure; by definition they further underline the already/not yet nature of all present experience in Christ.'⁴⁰⁵ They also underline the essentially corporate nature of the eschatological hope⁴⁰⁶ given by the Spirit.

Eph 1:13-14 is a typical Pauline passage:

> In him you also, when you heard the word of truth, the gospel of your salvation, and believed in him, were sealed with the promised Holy Spirit, who is the guarantee of our inheritance until we acquire possession of it, to the praise of his glory.

This passage mentions three of the five main eschatological/corporate categories/metaphors that Paul applies to the Spirit which need to be borne in mind when relating the Spirit to the task of biblical interpretation.⁴⁰⁷ These will now be surveyed.

(i) *The promissory* category.⁴⁰⁸ Although there is no special technical term in the Hebrew Old Testament for 'promise',⁴⁰⁹ the Holy Spirit's designation as 'the Spirit of the promise' (τῷ πνεύματι τῆς ἐπαγγελίας⁴¹⁰) clearly points us back to Old Testament prophecies.⁴¹¹ On the basis of these, it was recognised within the Judaism of Paul's day that an outpouring of the Spirit in a new and more general way would mark the beginning of the Messianic era within a restored Israel. This was being sorely awaited at the start of the New Testament era, for 'there seems to have been a widespread belief in Second Temple Judaism that the prophetic Spirit had been withdrawn from Israel, or at least that prophecy had ceased.'⁴¹² For the first Christians, the events of Pentecost signified that 'the drought of the Spirit had ended' and 'the longed for and expected new age had begun.'⁴¹³ Peter

---

⁴⁰³ 1 Cor 10:11.
⁴⁰⁴ Acts 2:17, quoting Joel 2:28.
⁴⁰⁵ S. Ferguson, *The Holy Spirit* (Leicester: IVP, 1996), 176.
⁴⁰⁶ Rom 15:13.
⁴⁰⁷ The Pauline antitheses mentioned in the previous section could also be seen in an eschatological context.
⁴⁰⁸ On 'promise' see *NIDNTT*, Vol. 3, 68–74 and *NBD* 963. For a speech-act analysis of 'promise', see Anthony Thiselton, 'Communicative Action and Promise in Interdisciplinary, Biblical, and Theological Hermeneutics' in R. Lundin, C. Walhout & A. C. Thiselton, *The Promise of Hermeneutics* (Grand Rapids, MI: Eerdmans & Cambridge: Paternoster, 1999), especially 223.
⁴⁰⁹ 'Hebrew simply states that someone said or spoke (*amar, dabar*) some word with future reference.' J. Hoad in *NBD*, 963.
⁴¹⁰ Eph 1:13.
⁴¹¹ Such as Isa 32:15; 44:3; Ezek 36:25–27; 37:1–14 and Joel 2:28. Common imagery is of a pouring out upon a dry and thirsty land. Jesus, of course, also made promises regarding the Spirit, such as recorded in John 14–16; Luke 24:49; Acts 1:4–5.
⁴¹² J. D. G. Dunn, *Theology of Paul*, 417.
⁴¹³ Ibid., 416.

struck the note of eschatological fulfilment in Acts 2 when he declared from Joel 'in these *last days* ... I will pour out my Spirit on *all flesh*' (v. 17). Hence the outflow of the Spirit initially upon the waiting group of disciples severally (v. 3), then jointly (v. 4), then upon the 'three thousand souls' (vv. 38–41), and finally when 'the gift of the Holy Spirit was poured out *even* on the Gentiles.'[414]

The wonder of their inclusion comes out in the 'you also' of our text in Eph 1:13. This also marked the ultimate fulfilment of the Abrahamic promise[415] which Paul in Gal 3:14 links again with 'the promised Spirit'.[416] The fact that Peter, at the end of his Pentecost sermon, having mentioned 'the gift of the Spirit' then says that 'the promise is for you and for your children and for all who are far off'[417] points forward to the progressive ingathering of a people from 'all flesh' recorded throughout Acts and on into the ensuing ages, of which the church of today is but a part, but whose completion awaits fulfilment.

(ii) The *legal* metaphor. 'You ... were *sealed* (ἐσφραγίσθητε)[418] with the promised Holy Spirit'. As a symbol of ownership and authenticity,[419] the seal does not have an inherently eschatological nature. Paul, however, so invests it by linking it with both the beginning ('heard ... believed ... sealed'[420]) and end ('until the day of redemption'[421]) of the Christian life. The assurance that is brought by the sealing of the Spirit between these times has been the occasion of much theological debate, concerning both its nature and timing.[422] That this has centred on individual experience has diverted attention from the original corporate context of a passage whose emphasis, as we have seen, is upon the inclusion of Gentiles within the gospel inheritance. Sealing is not just a mark of individual belonging, but also of a collective identity, the manifestation of which becomes of crucial eschatological importance in the book of Revelation.[423] In so far as the term for 'seal' was used in connection with an engagement ring, there may be a further link by way of betrothal/marriage imagery with the concept of the church as the bride of Christ as in Eph 5:23–32.

---

[414] Acts 10:45. See also 1 Cor 12:13c where Paul uses the same 'water' imagery.
[415] Gen 12:3.
[416] Fee points out that these two references (i.e. Eph 1:13 and Gal 3:14) relating to the inclusion of the Gentiles are the only two places where Paul equates the Spirit with the language of promise, thus highlighting this as a key feature of eschatological fulfilment and the Spirit's nature as 'fulfilled promise.' Fee, *God's Empowering Presence*, 811.
[417] Acts 2:38–39.
[418] The 'sealing' metaphor is used in Eph 1:13; 4:30 and 2 Cor 1:22, in the latter passage following references to 'the promises of God' (v. 20). As in law, these are duly 'signed, sealed and delivered', not by a document, but through the Spirit.
[419] In the ancient world (as indeed also today) owners often marked their goods, cattle or slaves to protect their rights of ownership, whilst legal documents were sealed as a mark of authenticity.
[420] Eph 1:13.
[421] Eph 4:30. The immediate context here also reminds us that the Spirit is 'grieved' by lack of truthfulness (vv. 25–28), unwholesome talk (v. 29), and wrath and slander (v. 31), a reminder of the ethical conditions needed in the fellowship for spiritual progress and understanding.
[422] See Ferguson, *The Holy Spirit*, 180–182. Historically, this sealing has been equated with water baptism, but 'Spirit' baptism would seem to be more appropriate if baptismal imagery is to be imported into exegesis.
[423] Rev 7:1–14; 9:4, cf. the 'mark of the beast' in 14:9, 11; 16:2; 19:20.

(iii) The *business* metaphor. Paul's identification of the Spirit as 'the guarantee (AV 'earnest') of our inheritance' (ἀρραβὼν[424] τῆς κληρονομίας) is exclusive to him in the New Testament.[425] The commercial background was the 'down-payment', which established the contractual obligation, acted as an initial instalment and a pledge of what was to come.[426] Here is another clear example of the now/not yet aspect of the Spirit's activity, a sure and actual deposit of all that God has for us in the future, 'the first instalment of the kingdom of God.'[427] Again, the stress is on the corporate rather than the personal: it relates to '*our* inheritance',[428] 'in the *saints.*'[429] The sheer magnitude of what this inheritance might be also comes across in the use of ἀρραβὼν, for this implies 'only a *small fraction* of the future endowment.'[430]

(iv) A similar idea is contained in Paul's use of the *agricultural* metaphor of 'firstfruits' in Romans 8:23.[431] Ἀπαρχή has a rich Old Testament background,[432] the pneumatological fulfilment of which was perhaps confirmed in Paul's mind by the Spirit's coming at the Feast of Weeks/Pentecost—the festival that marked the beginning of harvest. In the quaint language of Charles Hodge:

> Those influences of the Spirit which believers now enjoy are at once a pre-libation or antepast of future blessedness, the same in kind though immeasurably less in degree, and a pledge of the certain enjoyment of that blessedness; just as the first-fruits were a part of the harvest, and an earnest of its ingathering.[433]

Such a taste of the future, however, makes one painfully aware of the limitations of the present.

(v) The *family* category. Paul's description of the Spirit as the 'spirit of sonship' in Romans 8:12–21 is full of pneumatological insights that are relevant for hermeneutics, not least in underscoring the combined testimony of the spirit in believers and the Holy Spirit as a means of confirming truth.[434] For our immediate purposes, however, we must note the Spirit-driven eschatological progression (slavery ... adoption ... sons ... children ... heirs) that culminates in being 'glorified with him' of v. 17 is found within a community setting, as

---

[424] It was originally a Hebrew word that apparently came into Greek usage through traders from Phoenicia.
[425] Eph 1:14; also in 2 Cor 1:21–22 and 5:5.
[426] Much like the deposit paid on exchange of contracts for the purchase of a house in England and Wales.
[427] Dunn, *Theology of Paul*, 469. Also Fee: 'the Spirit is both the fulfilment of the eschatological promises of God and the down payment on our certain future. We are both already and not yet. The Spirit is the evidence of the one, the guarantee of the other.' Fee, *God's Empowering Presence*, 826.
[428] Eph 1:14.
[429] Eph 1:18.
[430] J. B. Lightfoot, *Notes on Epistles of St Paul* (London: Macmillan, 1895), 324, as quoted in J. W. R. Stott, *God's New Society: The Message of Ephesians* (Leicester: IVP, 1979), 49.
[431] See pages 218–226 for more on Romans 8.
[432] Exod 22:29; 23:19; Lev 2:12; 23:10; Num 15:20; 18:12, 30; Deut 26:2.
[433] Charles Hodge, *A Commentary on the Epistle to the Ephesians* (London: James Nisbet & Co, 1856), 35.
[434] Rom 8:15–17, cf. Gal 4:1–7 and Deut 19:15. For a full discussion of Romans 8, see pages 217–225.

symbolised by the frequent use of the compound συν.⁴³⁵ In the Pauline argument this leads into the new creation hope,⁴³⁶ wherein will be experienced 'the glorious liberty of the children of God',⁴³⁷ thus placing it in a cosmic family context which is infinitely broader and richer than the nuclear family of today.

To summarise this section, we have noted the 'now/not yet' nature of Pauline pneumatology. This comes out in the five Pauline metaphors relating to the Spirit—that of 'promise,' 'sealing,' 'guarantee,' 'firstfruits,' and 'sonship;' each with their own eschatological character. Hence there is a necessarily forward orientation involved in the κοινωνία of the Spirit. As Geerhardus Vos says, 'the Spirit's proper sphere is the future aeon; from thence he projects himself into the present, and becomes a prophecy of himself in his eschatological operations.'⁴³⁸

## Conclusion to and Summary of the Whole Section

I have been exploring the notion of the κοινωνία of the Holy Spirit as a basis for a Spirit-through-community hermeneutic in four different dimensions. First, the *Trinitarian* focus roots the fellowship of the Spirit within the triune Godhead itself. It thus involves an 'upward' look to God, but also entails a 'horizontal' dimension in so far as the Trinitarian relations provide a model and dynamic for fellowship between believers. Secondly, the Spirit also operates in judgment and challenge in a 'downward' dimension of *dialogical* encounter. Pauline antitheses, credal formulations, and the canon of Scripture itself illustrate the Spirit's superintendence of conflict to produce a deeper κοινωνία of understanding. Thirdly, as the Spirit of 'remembrance', the *historical* aspect of κοινωνία links our understanding to that of the saints down the ages. This backward look shows how tradition can warn and inform us in the present. Fourthly, the *eschatological* character of the Spirit anticipates the full fellowship into which it shall finally develop. This ultimately forward focus comes out in the Pauline metaphors for the Spirit, which reflect the 'now/not yet' tension inherent in New Testament teaching.⁴³⁹ This can all be expressed in a diagram:

---

⁴³⁵ 'Heirs together with, suffering together with and being glorified together with'.
⁴³⁶ Rom 8:18, as mentioned in the previous section.
⁴³⁷ Rom 8:21.
⁴³⁸ Geerhardus Vos, *The Pauline Eschatology* (Grand Rapids, MI: Eerdmans, 1952, 1930 repr.), 165, as quoted in Ferguson, *The Holy Spirit*, 178.
⁴³⁹ For a similar summary, relating to 'walking in the Spirit' as an 'essentially communal event', see Kärkkäinen, *Pneumatology*, 176.

## The Dimensions of Κοινωνία

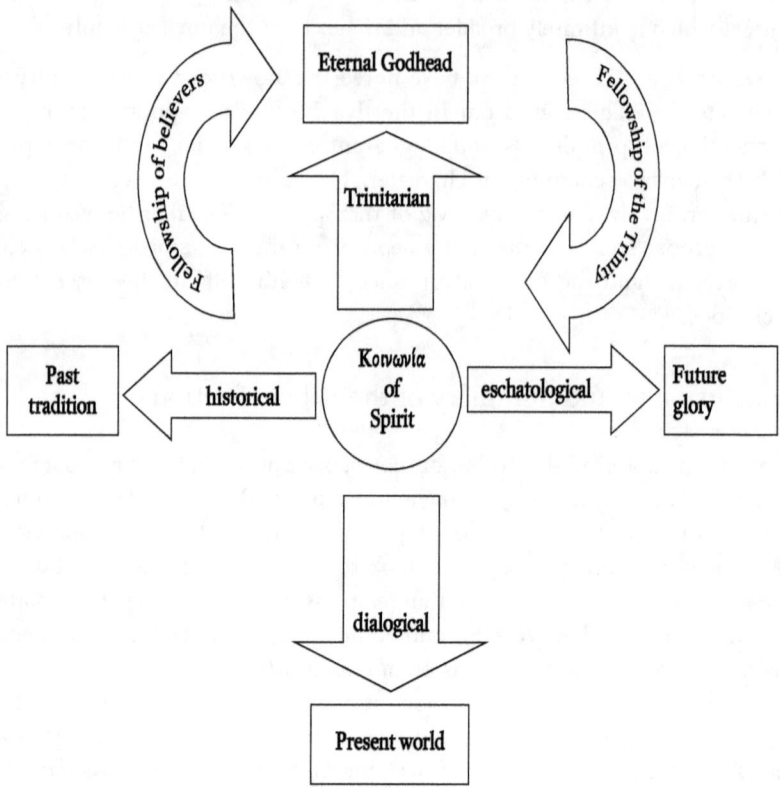

## Implications for Biblical Hermeneutics

Each of the four aspects of the κοινωνία of the Spirit explicated above carries implications for the theme of this book, with its concern to discover how the Spirit guides the community in the interpretation and custodianship of Scripture; and it is to an explanation of these implications that we now turn.

### (i) Trinitarian

I earlier remarked upon the Trinitarian presuppositions of Paul, shown by 2 Cor 13:14. Such presuppositions also need to be shared by contemporary interpreters, for fundamental interpretive errors have been made by what Vanhoozer has called 'non-Trinitarian'[440] views of God. Indeed, many heretical sects throughout Christian history have been spawned by a rejection of classic Trinitarianism. Considering this and other postmodern developments in

---

[440] Vanhoozer, *Is there a meaning in this text ?*, 456. He quotes Nietzsche as a prime example.

hermeneutical theory, Vanhoozer and Yong are examples of contemporary scholars[441] who vigorously argue for 'a robustly Trinitarian hermeneutic.'[442]

For Vanhoozer, Trinitarian theology, 'by specifying the ground and goal of interpretation ... offers to biblical interpreters a paradigm for ... hermeneutics.'[443] He conceptualises the Spirit as 'perlocutor' in his adaptation of Calvin's notion of the Spirit as the 'efficacy' of the Word to the tenets of speech act theory.

> Speech act theory serves as handmaiden to a Trinitarian theology of communication. If the Father is the locutor, the Son is his pre-eminent illocution. Christ is God's definitive Word, the substantive content of his message. And the Holy Spirit—the condition and power of receiving the sender's message—is God the perlocutor, the reason that his words do not return to him empty (Isa 55:11).[444]

Yong also argues the case for an essentially Trinitarian hermeneutic, although he seeks to 'supplement' what he sees as '[Vanhoozer's] emphasis on the Logos (the objectivity of the text) with emphases on Spirit (the subjectivity of the readers and doers) and Community (the contextuality of theological reflection).'[445] His concept of community is extracted from the Trinity:

> [T]he relationship of Father and Son is inseparable from, if not constitutive of the "community of the Holy Spirit" (2 Cor 13:13) ... [I]n the same way as the Father symbolizes the divine community, so community symbolizes the communal contexts of hermeneutical inquiry, interpretation, and discernment. At this theological level, community refers to the believing faithful ... at three levels: the immediate community of faith ... the larger community of faith ... and the historic Christian tradition itself.[446]

The Trinity thus affords Vanhoozer a model for 'communication' and Yong a model for 'community', both of which are key elements in the process of interpreting Scripture and for both of which the κοινωνία of the Spirit translates the model into a dynamic reality. In this connection, we can refer to Taylor's description of the Spirit as 'this current of communication, this invisible go-between'[447] linking Christians to the triune God and to each other. Not that Christians can ever emulate the perfect fellowship of the Trinity, but at least they can, as Gunton says, '*echo* the dynamic'[448] of Trinitarian relationship.

---

[441] Note also S. Grenz and J. R. Franke, *Beyond Foundationalism: Shaping Theology in a Postmodern Context* (Louisville, KY: Westminster John Knox, 2001), especially 169–202, 228.
[442] Yong, *Spirit-Word-Community*, 11.
[443] Ibid., 161.
[444] Ibid., 457.
[445] Yong, *Word-Spirit-Community*, 11.
[446] Ibid., 17.
[447] John V. Taylor, *The Go-Between God* (London: SCM, 2004), 17.
[448] C. E. Gunton, *The Promise of Trinitarian Theology* (Edinburgh: T&T Clark, 1991), 81, italics added.

And in the more specific area of biblical interpretation as it relates to pluralism, Vanhoozer has pointed out how 'as each person of the Trinity offers a different perspective on the one true God, so there may be a limited plurality of perspectives on meaning ... Trinitarian theology [thus] enables us to conceive of interpretive plurality in terms of harmony (three-in-one; one in three) rather than conflict.'[449]

There is thus a place for both individual and collective insights into the meaning of Scripture, reflecting both the personal and social aspects of human nature[450] that are derived from being created in the image of a triune God. This aspect of 'diversity within unity' is fully realised only when 'recreated' so as to become a part of the body of Christ, by the power of the Spirit. As Gunton says, '[The Spirit] ever and again incorporates people into Christ and in the same action brings them into and maintains them in community with one another.'[451]

Gunton here is expressing insights derived from Pauline teaching such as 1 Cor 12,[452] a chapter brimming with descriptions of the Trinitarian operations. As, later in this book, I explore examples of Spirit-led expositions of Scripture in the New Testament, we shall find that these too are careful to pay due deference to the several but complementary nature of the Trinitarian persons and operations. Lopsided theologies and lifestyles can result in interpretations that place an undue emphasis upon one person of the Trinity at the expense of the other, whether it be a traditional preoccupation with the Father by 'liberals', with the Son by evangelicals or with the Spirit by Pentecostals.

These, then, are but some of the ways in which a Trinitarian focus, as a product of the κοινωνία of the Spirit, should undergird the interpretive endeavours of the church, as it seeks to maintain its upward look to the triune God who communicates with his church within the 'communion' of the Holy Spirit. And it is within the 'horizontal' fellowship that ensues from this that his voice can be most clearly heard.

*(ii) Dialogical*

Sadly, however, such fellowship is not always what it should be. Sin and selfishness separates and causes dissension within the church, as well as in the world. Here again, however, we can see how the Spirit can and does use conflict and division within this fellowship to further understanding of Scripture.

In our previous section, I remarked how the Spirit used conflicts within the New Testament community and the early church to help shape the contents and canon of Scripture. This bigger picture of how the Spirit guides the church into

---

[449] K. J. Vanhoozer, *Is there a meaning in this text?*, 161.
[450] R.Martin, *The Family and the Fellowship: New Testament Images of the Church* (Exeter: Paternoster, 1979), 13.
[451] C. E. Gunton, *The Promise of Trinitarian Theology*, 82–83.
[452] Especially 12:13. Note also Phil 2:1 and Eph 4:3.

truth through the interface with difference and disagreement is repeated on a smaller scale every time God's people join together to learn, deliberate, and worship. The Spirit for ever operates as what Dunn has described as 'a centripetal force drawing believers together into the body of Christ,' whose constitution and continuance depends upon 'their common participation (*koinōnia*) in the one Spirit.'[453]

It is by this same Spirit that a disparate collection of people can come together and almost instantaneously offer up to God a united paean of praise in the opening songs of worship. The polyphonic aspect of music—with its blending together of different instruments and sounds into a melodious whole—is itself an appropriate analogy for the harmonising-through-difference of the Spirit's working. Ephesians 5:18-19 says that the filling of the Spirit should indeed issue in 'addressing one another in psalms and hymns and spiritual songs.'[454] Songs that express biblical truth afford another example of how the Spirit can guide the gathered Christian community in its interpretation and application of Scripture. In African Christian culture, singing operates as a particularly important medium for imbibing and expressing the truths of Scripture,[455] as well as operating as vital community imperative.[456]

The primary way in which the Spirit guides the community in the interpretation of Scripture, is, of course, in spoken form, as the word of God is read and preached in a corporate setting. When this is attended to with the anointing of the Spirit, one can witness what Lloyd-Jones describes as a congregation that is unitedly 'gripped ... convicted ... moved [and] humbled'[457] under the word that is 'piercing to the division of soul and spirit ...' (Heb 4:12b). This sifting and sharpening ministry of 'the sword of the Spirit, which is the word of God' (Eph 6:17b) also takes place in a more interactive way in the context of group Bible studies, ministers' fraternals, and church meetings, where readings of Scripture are challenged and reshaped in dialogical encounter.

---

[453] J. D. G. Dunn, 'Spirit' in *NIDNTT*, Vol. 3, 702, citing the Pauline conception of the Spirit in 1 Cor 12:13; 2 Cor 13:14; Eph 4:3f; Phil 1:27; 2:1.
[454] In Eph 5:19a, 'Paul is addressing a community setting in which believers *teach one another* with various kinds of songs,' Fee, *God's Empowering Presence*, 876.
[455] Services that my wife and I have attended in a village community church in Mozambique were marked by at least one hour's singing from different groupings from within the community (women, children, Bible college students, etc). These often included a dramatic acting out of the relevant Bible story in the act of singing, such as the story of Adam and Eve. An unforgettable sight was of men joined together and moving around in the form of a rugby scrum to illustrate Ps 133 ('how good and pleasant it is when brothers dwell in unity')!
[456] Pamela Couture in her chapter 'Bible music and pastoral theology' in Paul Ballard and Stephen Holmes, eds., *The Bible in Pastoral Practice: Readings in the Place and Function of Scripture in the Church* (London: Darton, Longman and Todd, 2005), writing from her experience of visiting the Democratic Republic of Congo and a Christian gathering of those torn apart by war says 'singing is a survival strategy for these Congolese Christians...' (p. 289). 'Biblical singing is an activity that helps to express, in a communal form, the mourning and the rejoicing that is shared in the community, and in so doing, helps build its life' (p. 290).
[457] D. Martyn Lloyd-Jones, *Preaching and Preachers* (London: Hodder & Stoughton, 1976), 324.

For all this to happen, then, the work of the Spirit in the community is vital. As Lesslie Newbigin has said:

> The *discernment* of the Spirit can only come by *living* in the Spirit ... all who have ever had any taste of His power to teach, convince, and subdue a gathering of Christians coming together with all their clashing wills and affections, know that this is true ... the church is a communion in the Holy Spirit [who] is no cipher, no abstract noun, but living Lord.[458]

And in this sovereign work, it is the Spirit that endues the church with both gifts (the χαρίσματα of 1 Cor 12:14-26[459]) and fruit (the καρπός of Gal 5:22-23) that build up the church in the spiritual maturity that is vital for the ongoing understanding of Scripture.

With 'love' (ἀγάπη) as the first mentioned fruit of the Spirit, it is not surprising that Stephen Fowl, following Augustine,[460] highlights the need for 'charity in interpretation,'[461] whose goals are 'to show points of agreement as a way of clarifying the disagreements, to maximise the rationality of those who hold different views, and to elaborate a position that recognises the strengths of opponent's views while avoiding their weaknesses.'[462] He pleads for 'vigilant communities and virtuous readers,'[463] where the regular practices of forgiveness, repentance, and reconciliation provide a suitable ethical and community context for ongoing biblical understanding. Besides charity, Vanhoozer also numbers wisdom, righteousness, and willingness to listen amongst 'the interpretive virtues', 'virtues that are best cultivated by the Spirit of understanding in the context of community.'[464] As Brown says, 'the interpretation of Scripture and the moral formation of reading communities are inextricably bound.'[465] This ongoing dialectic between Bible and behaviour is a continuous process, as the church, through its elders and teachers, with the help of the Spirit, constantly seeks to instruct, train, and disciple its members.

---

[458] Lesslie Newbigin, *The Household of God* (New York, NY: Friendship,1954), 107, as quoted in Telford Work, *Living and Active Scripture in the Economy of Salvation* (Grand Rapids, MI: Eerdmans, 2002), 254-255.
[459] Also Rom 12:4-8; 1 Cor 14:12, 26; Eph 4:11-16.
[460] Augustine's 'chief hermeneutic maxim is to "choose the interpretation that most fosters love of God and neighbour",' Vanhoozer, *Is there a meaning in this text?*, 32.
[461] Stephen Fowl, *Engaging Scripture* (Oxford: Blackwell, 1998), 86.
[462] Ibid., 92. Cf. the words of the Bishop of Oxford on recent discussions on sexuality issues within Anglicanism when presenting a discussion document to the General Synod: '[I]t was not designed to change Anglican policy on homosexuality, bisexuality or transgenderism, but to facilitate debate by presenting each view as sympathetically as possible ... Our hope is that "interpretive charity" ... will be an increasing feature of the debate on this issue' *Baptist Times*, Feb 19$^{th}$ 2004, 3.
[463] Ibid., 62.
[464] Ibid., 423-424.
[465] W.Brown, ed., *Character & Scripture: Moral Formation, Community, and Biblical Interpretation* (Grand Rapids, MI: Eerdmans, 2002), xi.

This work of Christian *formation* is also paralleled by the notion of *transformation* of the interpreter(s). Gary Nebeker, for instance, argues that 'because "truth" can be understood as that which is christocentric and transformational in character ... the Spirit's role—or goal—in interpretation is to allow the interpreter to understand the text in such a way that the text transforms the interpreter into the image of Christ,'[466] a process that is 'applicable not only *individually*, but also *corporately* as well.'[467] Thus congregations and individuals should aim to become epistles 'written ... with the Spirit of the living God ... to be known and read by all.'[468]

*(iii) Historical*

A vital imperative in apprehending the κοινωνία of the Spirit in its historical perspective must be a readiness to admit the factor of historical conditionedness, as Gadamer has insisted. We are all participants in a tradition, or traditions, of understanding. Barth likened the place of tradition to that of an 'elder brother',[469] a brother whose wisdom can certainly guide us but whose power, as Vanhoozer says, also 'occasionally ... bullies.'[470] This is where a group of Christians or sometimes an individual may have to stand up against the prevailing tradition of the community when it goes against the teaching of Scripture.

With such a caveat in mind, I will now explore some of the positive and practical ways in which the Spirit's activation of memory and interaction with tradition guides both the individual but especially the community in their custodianship and interpretation of Scripture. I will mention the contexts in which this can occur, working from the smallest to the largest groupings.

(a) The *individual's* interpretation of Scripture may have come about through Spirit-led understanding in private devotion and study. The use of biblical commentaries and other aids, however, represent a link with the wider community, as part of a complex web of community originated factors. These may date from the earlier nurture of a Christian family,[471] day or Sunday school, church-based children's or youth club. The long-term investment of such work has been proved time and time again when the Spirit has later in life brought back to mind a memory text, Bible story or truth learned in the past, but with a peculiar appropriateness for the present.

---

[466] Gary Nebeker, 'The Holy Spirit, Hermeneutics, and Transformation: From Present to Future Glory,' *Evangelical Review of Theology*, Vol.27 No.1 Jan 2003, 47. He bases his case on verses such as John 14:6, 2 Cor 3:18; Col 2:6–7; Luke 24:27.
[467] Ibid., 54. Italics mine.
[468] 2 Cor 3:2, 3; 2 Cor 3 will be explored more fully in chapter 6.
[469] Cited by Kevin J. Vanhoozer in 'The Spirit of Understanding: Special Revelation and General Hermeneutics' in *Disciplining Hermeneutics: Interpretation in Christian Perspective*, ed. Roger Lundin (Grand Rapids, MI: Eerdmans; Leicester: Apollos/IVP, 1997), 150.
[470] Ibid., 150.
[471] As in the case of Timothy: 2 Tim 1:5.

(b) On a *pastoral* level, then, every minister will be able to recount those memorable occasions in which the Spirit has evoked some Scripture when getting alongside another person or small group in the face of a crisis. As the words of Psalm 23 are read at the bedside of a dying person (as I have done), great comfort can, for instance, be brought out from the hermeneutical parallelism of verse one as it is read out to someone who may have been taught it many years before. If the Lord is *my* shepherd, then I will truly lack nothing—even in the face of death. Pastors can also experience triumphant hymn singing sessions around the deathbed of believers when one can only say that the Spirit takes hold of Scripture-based words, in a small community context, to bring the assurance of heaven. As I have already mentioned, singing is indeed one of the vital corporate ways in which the Spirit welds into the memory truths that will often resurface when confronted by a pastoral need or upon evocation of the relevant tune or a phrase.

(c) The small *cell/Bible-study group* provides many opportunities for Spirit enriched understanding through the recollections of the group. As the accumulated wisdom and experience of the older members of the group are interchanged with the enthusiasm and questions of the younger members within the body of Christ, so a group hermeneutic develops. This not only helps to build up the faith of believers, but also helps to produce it, for small groups have been the spiritual birthplace for many Christians. For them, the experience of the group's 'κοινωνία of the Spirit' has helped to draw them into enjoying the 'grace of our Lord Jesus Christ and the love of God' also.[472] Such groups need to be led by spiritually mature and accountable leaders, lest group fallibilities result in group deviation (i.e. from the beliefs and life of the church under whose auspices they are run).

(d) Coming, then, to *congregational* level, the centuries old architectural heritage of church buildings in Britain is in itself a testimony to the resilience of the Christian tradition. The story of each church is a fascinating record of how the Spirit has led a group of people to interpret the gospel in the formation of a Christian community. Sadly, the witness of many churches in Britain is at a low ebb, but the Spirit's word to the church to 'strengthen what remains'[473] is for ever relevant. What this might involve will vary according to one's theological tradition. The very word 'traditional', for instance, can be used to reassure ('our church maintains a traditional style of worship') or to criticise ('they are stuck in their past traditions!').

Every church, of course, has its traditions, especially in the realm of worship. 'Smells and bells', age-old or new liturgies, one-hour 'hymn sandwiches', two-hour charismatic 'happy-clappy' celebrations, services that centre on song or

---

[472] 2 Cor 13:14.
[473] Rev 3:2.

sermon—these are but some of the variegated ways claimed for 'worship in the Spirit'. All these need to be tested against the biblical criteria for worship: for example, that it should always be 'in spirit and truth,'[474] conducted 'decently and in order,'[475] and 'with reverence and awe.'[476]

Apart from these guidelines, one can point to many contemporary experiments for 'doing church' that are designed to reach out to today's unchurched. In these the concept of 'community' is frequently mentioned, usually in the context of the need to create community in a country where there is a distinct lack of it. An appeal to 'tradition' in this case may not sound so attractive or relevant. But if the Spirit who is the author of 'community' (Christian κοινωνία) is also the perpetuator of God-given tradition, then ways need to be found to introduce the rootless postmodern individual of today to the historically grounded faith of the ancient family of the church. This will include attempts to single out the essential message of the Bible from the cultural settings in which it has been originally and historically expressed so as to 'recontextualise' it for the needs of the present moment.[477]

And in the atheistic climate of the West today, Brueggemann sets out some challenges for preachers and Bible students:

> It is the preacher's primal responsibility to invite and empower and equip the community to reimagine the world as though Yahweh were a key and decisive player.[478]

> [This will involve] nurturing a historical imagination[479]... [which will mean that] we read the Bible as insiders.[480]

> The intent of [serious Bible study] is not to recover a museum piece as one might with an old Egyptian document...but to *get inside the confessions and traditions* that can still be energising for the church.[481]

> Let us give up thinking of [the Bible] as a "book" and regard it as a "tradition" that continues to be alive and surging among us ... [Whilst] we interpret the text ... we in turn are interpreted by the text.[482]

(e) Our discussion of the Spirit's use of tradition at the congregational level broadens out to wider questions concerning the *translocal* level. Denominations,

---

[474] John 4:24.
[475] 1 Cor 14:40.
[476] Heb 12:28.
[477] Paul's speech to the Athenians on Mars Hill in Acts 17:22–34 is often taken as a biblical paradigm for such an exercise.
[478] *Deep Memory, Exuberant Hope*, 2.
[479] W. Brueggemann, *The Bible Makes Sense: The Growth of Community in the Bible*, (Atlanta, GA: Westminster John Knox, 2001), 13.
[480] Ibid., 13.
[481] Ibid., 94.
[482] Ibid., 97.

theologically homogeneous movements, missionary societies, ecumenical bodies, evangelistic organisations, theological colleges, and many other groupings all have their own ethos that can only be understood historically. Often this is narrated as a story of a community led by the Spirit to a peculiar understanding of Scripture which has given rise to the body in question. Sometimes such language masks a story of painful splits and acrimonious disagreements that led to the birth of some new movement. This can indeed be a case of the Spirit's use of the dialectics of disagreement to bring to birth a new form of κοινωνία, as mentioned in the previous section. At other times, such disputes can lead to group defection, error and schism.[483]

That this can happen is a warning that the power of the group or the ecclesial body can be expressed in a hegemony that is heretical and unscriptural and which needs challenging, whether by groups loyal to Scripture or by godly individuals, as mentioned earlier. The bold outspokenness of the Old Testament prophets and Martin Luther's 'Here I stand!'[484] give eloquent testimony to this. To go against the prevailing interpretive tradition in this way is surely a prerogative of the Spirit in his desire to transform and make us conform more into the image of Christ.[485] To this end, 'the reformation motto of *Ecclesia Reformata Semper Reformanda* ("a church must be reformed and always reforming") needs to be taken seriously.'[486] The ongoing interpretive challenge is thus clear, for it is 'the tension between tradition as given and tradition as the process of traditioning [that] remains at the heart of theological interpretation.'[487] This interaction between past and present can only be safely negotiated with the help of the Spirit of truth, who also points forward to an ultimate resolution of all such tension in the future. To this I turn.

*(iv) Eschatological*

In the previous section, I noted the eschatological character of the Spirit, as derived from the Pauline categories/metaphors of 'promise', 'sealing', 'guarantee', 'firstfruits', and 'sonship'. The 'already/not yet' tension inherent in these categories needs to be reflected in interpretation that claims to be Spirit-led, alongside the primarily corporate nature of nature of the hope thereby engendered.

The 'already' element was inaugurated at Pentecost as the 'this is that'[488] motif in Peter's sermon highlighted the aspect of messianic fulfilment of the Old Testament prophecies in Christ, 'as uttered through the prophet Joel' (Acts 2:16)

---

[483] Such as many would claim is now happening in the contemporary debate over homosexuality - in the Anglican Church in particular.
[484] Vanhoozer, *Is There a Meaning in this Text?*, 466–467.
[485] 2 Cor 3:18.
[486] Yong, *Spirit-Word-Community*, 266.
[487] Ibid., 273.
[488] Acts 2:16.

and as 'David ... says' (2:25 and 2:34). We shall see several other examples of eschatological fulfilment in Part II of our book, as the New Testament writers interpreted Old Testament Scripture on the basis of its being realised in the coming of Jesus. Spirit-inspired interpretation should thus reflect this Christocentric fulfilment focus, alongside the urgency of the 'now' as 'the day of salvation' (2 Cor 6:2), as illustrated in many of the Acts sermons.

This salvation is, of course, not just for individuals, but also relates to the calling out of a people. In our previous section, we noted how the 'promise of the Spirit' needed to be read against the wider covenant promises of God concerning the restoration of Israel and the inclusion of the Gentiles into the one great community of the redeemed. As those who are still 'standing on the promises', Christians should be wary of narrowing down the corporate scope of these promises by over-individualisation, whether using the old fashioned 'promise boxes', modern 'text for the day' devotional aids, or personalised domestications of texts. Preachers for their part need to be aware of the dangers of textual preaching that privatizes great biblical promises that are made primarily to the church (as, for example, in 'prosperity' teaching), or that brings into the present that which is ultimately reserved for the eschaton.

This, then, is where the 'not yet' aspect of the Spirit's workings is relevant, as, for example, we have pointed out in relation to ἀπαρχή. 'First fruits' certainly implies that the lives of Christians, including their interpretations of Scripture, should be seasoned with the flavours of heaven. As Ferguson says, 'the Spirit enables believers to experience an overflow, as it were from that world.'[489] But alongside fruitfulness comes frustration. First fruits are not full fruits. Paul's use of ἀπαρχή ('firstfruits') in Romans 8:23 is linked with the consequence of 'groaning inwardly as we wait eagerly for adoption as sons.' Foretastes of glory afforded by the Spirit only serve to highlight the shortcomings of the present.

In terms of biblical interpretation, therefore, we need to be wary of over-realized or triumphalist readings that purport to be 'of the Spirit'. In this age of instant credit and impatience to wait for anything, the Spirit is indeed not infrequently regarded as the means of bringing all God's blessings into present enjoyment. Hence we have 'Spirit-given' readings of Scripture that 'claim' imminent healing, revival, fulfilment, victory, or whatever. That it can be said that these are usually found in the more 'charismatic' wing of the church shows how different eschatological emphases characterise, and indeed partly account for, the various traditions found within Christendom.[490]

---

[489] Ferguson, *The Holy Spirit*, 179.
[490] Note Telford Work's summary: 'How each party sees tradition depends on how each tradition sees the past, present, and future church in terms of God's eschatological *oikodome*. On the whole, Orthodox accounts of tradition are more *realized*, Catholic accounts more *inaugurated*, Lutherans and Reformed decidedly *futurist*, and radicals more *apocalyptic* or *dialectical*.' Telford Work, *Living and Active*, 290, italics mine. Vanhoozer cites the interesting observation of C. E. Gunton that 'nearly all the most discreditable actions of church institutions...flow

All sections of the Christian church, however, would subscribe to some notion of final judgment—that most ultimate of all events—which is proleptically anticipated by the work of the Spirit:[491]

> The Spirit brings the whole church to judgment in advance by bringing home where we need the Spirit's defending and supporting help, and where there are failures that need to be corrected.[492]

This convicting work of the Paraclete is described in John 16:8–11 and not infrequently takes place as the Spirit interprets and applies Scripture. The new life that follows the confession and conversion process again anticipates the fullness of the resurrection to come, the power for which is linked with the Spirit in Romans 8:11.

In 1 Cor 15:23, Paul uses ἀπαρχή ('firstfruits') not of the Spirit but of Christ's resurrection, which points forward not just to the individual resurrection of Christians but to a much wider event, heralded by the sounding of 'the last trumpet' (1 Cor 15:52). '[This] metaphor ... conveys the idea of a sleeping army jumping to its feet when the signal is given.'[493] The corporateness of this event is not always one that is sufficiently part of the Christian mindset.

In his book *In the end God* ... John Robinson rightly draws a contrast between western individualism which focuses hope on the hour of death and the expectation of immortality, and the wider cosmic perspective of the New Testament which focuses hope on the day of the Parousia, the reality of the last judgement, and the event of the general resurrection.[494]

Christians may enjoy their communal singing of 'We're marching to Zion!', but can still entertain rather individualistic and indeed rather selfish notions of 'a place in heaven for me when I die.'[495] Christian funeral services should not limit future reunion to 'a meeting up with my loved one in glory', but look forward to an ultimate gathering together with the whole company of the redeemed as described in 1 Thess 4:17 within the 'new heaven and the new earth.'[496]

The eschatological aspect of κοινωνία means, then, that Christians, as they read Scripture, need a Spirit-given perspective that embraces not only the individual but also the corporate and cosmic aspects of the Christian hope. It is a

---

from an improper anticipation of eschatology;' C. E. Gunton, *A Brief Theology of Revelation* (Edinburgh: T&T Clark, 1995), 97 n.19, cited by Vanhoover, *Is There a Meaning in this Text?*, 429.
[491] John 16:8–10 and Luke 3:16.
[492] General Synod, *We Believe in the Holy Spirit*, 182.
[493] Ibid., 182. For 'trumpet' imagery see 1 Cor 15:52 and 1 Thess 4:16. It can be traced back to the Pentateuch, the call of the trumpets being the means by which Moses summonsed Israel, for instance as in Numbers 10:2(NIV): 'use them for calling the community together...'
[494] Ibid., 179.
[495] Capitalized upon by the advert on a church noticeboard: 'Come to church and get an afterlife'!
[496] Rev 21:1.

perspective that should interpret the present in light of the future,[497] but also one that expresses the New Testament tension between the 'now' and 'not yet'. An over-realised and over-detailed eschatology is to be guarded against, for though 'we see', it is but 'through a glass, darkly.'[498] Only 'then' will it be 'face to face.'[499]

## Conclusion to the Chapter

The concept of 'pneumatological community' as a backdrop to biblical hermeneutics is a rich one. Paul's concept of the κοινωνία/fellowship of the Holy Spirit opens up wide vistas for the interpretive process. Sourced as it should be from the perichoretic life of the Trinity, Spirit-led interpretation draws upon the dynamic of *Trinitarian* relationship. This upward focus also has a horizontal dimension as it is pursued in κοινωνία with Christians in like fellowship with God. When this fellowship is absent or broken, the Spirit's ministry is again vital, this time in a downwards movement of conviction and judgment. Such a *dialogical* encounter can result ultimately in new forms of Scriptural understanding. Biblical interpretation also has to be pursued *historically* in conjunction with the saints of the past and an acknowledgment of our indebtedness to those who have taught and influenced us. This 'backward' link is also provided by the Spirit, as the Spirit of 'remembrance.' The provisionality of our understanding, however, is highlighted by the *eschatological* nature of the Spirit, which, whilst underlining present fulfilment in Christ, also points forwards to the fullness of understanding and fellowship that is yet to be realised in glory.

In view of the breadth of the communal focus afforded by these four dimensions, it could be claimed that for many Christians, at least in the Protestant tradition, the Spirit's role in biblical interpretation has often been conceived of too narrowly and too individualistically—helping 'the interpreter' in a present, illuminist type of understanding of the text that omits the wider parameters of κοινωνία. Of course, the Spirit does inspire individuals, as well as Christian communities, and gives them special interpretive insights that the Spirit uses to edify the church. But I have argued in this chapter that the study of the Scriptures, whether being undertaken individually or collectively, needs to be conducted within the context of the 'communion of the saints', in a prayerful dependence upon the κοινωνία of the Spirit that links Bible interpreters with God, his people, and his purposes in time and eternity. This was how the New Testament writers sought to interpret the Old Testament Scriptures in their day, as I shall explore in our next chapter.

---

[497] In contrast to the 'secular futurologist who speculates about the future on the basis of extrapolations from the present,' General Synod, *We Believe in the Holy Spirit*, 185.
[498] 1 Cor 13:12a (AV).
[499] 1 Cor 13:12b.

# CHAPTER THREE: THE SPIRIT AT THE INTERFACE OF THE OLD AND NEW TESTAMENTS

## Probing the Presuppositions of New Testament Exegesis

### Introduction

The New Testament (NT) breathes with the spirit of the Old Testament (OT).[500] Why? From a theological point of view, Christians believe it is because one and the same Spirit inspired both testaments.[501] From a human point of view, it was because the NT writers were immersed in the OT and could not help expressing themselves in its language and concepts. Direct quotations,[502] allusions,[503] echoes,[504] paraphrases, and stories from the OT—they are all there in the NT, and in abundance. Scholars vary in their precise estimates as to how many OT citations are found in the NT, but Earle Ellis estimates some 250 quotations and 2,500 allusions.[505] Such frequency, along with the fact that the verb used to introduce a quotation is often in the present tense,[506] bears witness to the continuing authority of the OT (as endorsed by the NT), the theological integrity of the Bible as a whole, and 'the eternal contemporaneity of Scripture.'[507] For A. T. Hanson, the NT writers have made it 'easier ... for us to understand the Old Testament ... [T]hey have in a sense done our homework for us: they have provided us with a Christian Bible which they did not have.'[508] Does this mean, then, that those early Christians who wrote the NT have provided us with models of interpretation that we can use today?

---

[500] From this point on I will use the abbreviations OT and NT to refer to the Old and New Testaments respectively.
[501] 2 Tim 3:16; 2 Pet 1:20–21.
[502] Such as Matthew's 'formula quotations': Matt 1:22; 2:5; 2:17; 3:3 and so on. Stendahl has likened the use of the OT quotations in Matthew to interpretations found in the Qumran Habbakuk commentary and claimed they represented the work of a Matthean 'school', thus constituting a kind of corporate study that developed in the early church: K. Stendahl, *The School of Matthew and its Use of the Old Testament*, 2nd ed (Philadelphia: Fortress, 1968). For appraisals of this theory, see D. Hill, *The Gospel of Matthew* (London: Marshall Morgan & Scott, 1972), 34–38 and I. Howard Marshall, 'Exegesis in the Dead Sea Scrolls' in *It is Written: Scripture Citing Scripture*, ed. D. A. Carson and H. G. M. Williamson (Cambridge: Cambridge University Press, 1988), 10–12.
[503] Intentional references to prior texts, e.g. Jude 11. The greatest frequency of these are in Revelation (estimates vary from 250 to 1,000!), a book thereby steeped in the OT yet without one direct quotation.
[504] Usually defined as unintentional references to prior texts.
[505] E. Earle Ellis, *The Old Testament in Early Christianity: Canon and Interpretation in the Light of Modern Research* (Grand Rapids, MI: Baker, 1991), 3. Nichole reckons that 'more than 10 per cent of the New Testament text is made up of citations or direct allusions to the Old Testament': see Roger Nichole, 'The New Testament Use of the Old Testament' in *The Right Doctrine from the Wrong Texts: Essays on the Use of the Old Testament in the New*, ed. G. K. Beale (Grand Rapids, MI: Baker, 1994), 14. Scholars have found OT allusions in all NT books except 2 & 3 John and Philemon.
[506] For example, Heb 10:15, prefacing a quotation from Jer 31:34 with 'The Holy Spirit also bears witness to us....'
[507] Nichole, *The Right Doctrine from the Wrong Texts*, 16.
[508] A. T. Hanson, *The Living Utterances of God* (London: Darton Longman & Todd, 1983), 189.

## The Spirit at the Interface of the Old and New Testaments 87

The problem here is that at times the NT writers use the OT in a way that most of us today would not dare to do, adjusting texts[509] and finding fulfilments[510] and applications[511] which at first glance seem somewhat strained. This has led to an 'ongoing debate between (a) those who argue that the NT writers usually respect the entire context of the OT texts they cite or to which they allude and (b) those who argue that the NT writers engage in a kind of "prooftexting" that takes OT passages out of their contexts so as to "prove" conclusions that belong to the commitments of NT Christianity but not to the antecedent Scriptures they cite.'[512]

Explanations for the various and distinctive ways the NT uses the OT have been sought by looking at parallels with the interpretive methodology of Jewish *midrash*[513] or Qumran *pesher*,[514] or by investigating their particular use of typology or allegory. Others have pointed out the frequent preference for quoting from the Septuagint (LXX) or similar Greek versions of the OT,[515] rather than the traditional Hebrew Masoretic text. There have also been interesting debates about the use of *testimonia* (portions of OT material) in the early church, and how far the use of these, and indeed the whole approach of the NT to the OT, was taught by Christ himself. More recently the concept of 'intertextuality' has brought a new element into the discussion from the realm of literary criticism.[516]

Underlying these debates are a number of highly involved matters, such as: the significance of the uneven spread[517] and different treatments of the OT in the NT;[518] methodological questions as to the use of 'inner-biblical' approaches that

---

[509] For instance, Matthew inserts οὐδαμῶς (by no means) into his quotation of Mic 5:2 in Matt 2:6 to emphasize the significance of Bethlehem as the place of Jesus's birth, thus reversing the emphasis of the original text.

[510] For example, where is the text from which Matthew quotes in Matt 2:23?

[511] For example, the use of Deut 24:14–15 in 1 Tim 5:18.

[512] G. K. Beale and D. A. Carson, eds. *Commentary on the New Testament Use of the Old Testament* (Grand Rapids, MI: Baker; Nottingham: Apollos, 2007), xxiii.

[513] Especially in Johannine and Pauline literature. Longenecker points out that 'the word [midrash] comes from the verb *derash* (to resort to, seek; figuratively, to read repeatedly, study, interpret), and ... denotes an interpretive exposition ... [that] contemporize[s] the revelation of God given earlier for the people of God living later in a different situation. What results may be characterised by the maxim': Richard Longenecker, 'That has Relevance for This,' in Beale, *The Right Doctrine from the Wrong Texts*, 381.

[514] Especially in Matthew, Paul, and Hebrews. '[T]he term "pesher" stems from the Aramaic word *pishar* meaning "solution" or "interpretation" ' and was used by the Qumran community to apply Scripture in a direct way to themselves as those who were 'living in the last days of "messianic travail" before the eschatological consummation,' Longenecker, *The Right Doctrine from the Wrong Texts*, 381. The hallmark of *pesher* was, then, eschatological fulfilment.

[515] It is commonly recognised that the LXX and other Greek versions, like all translations, contain interpretive elements that served the particular purposes of the NT writers. A modern parallel is the use of different biblical versions to suit the particular purposes of the preacher/expositor.

[516] See, for instance, Richard B. Hays, *Echoes of Scripture in the Letters of Paul* (New Haven, CT: Yale University Press, 1989). Intertextuality explores the dynamic of literary links (whether intentional or not, and whether by allusion or echo) between different texts.

[517] R. Longenecker, *Biblical Exegesis in the Apostolic Period*, 2nd ed. (Grand Rapids, MI: Eerdmans, 1999), xvii-xix. He points out, for instance, that of the 83 explicit OT quotations in the Pauline letters, 45 occur in Romans but none are found in Philippians.

[518] I. Howard Marshall has listed seven different 'types of use of the OT': Marshall, *It is Written: Scripture Citing Scripture*, 9–10.

confine investigation to literary and theological parallels between the two testaments, or 'extra biblical exegesis' that takes into account other interpretive methods found in the ancient world;[519] more generally, the ongoing question as to what is normative and what is descriptive in the NT;[520] and the complex relationship of continuity/discontinuity between the OT and NT.[521]

It is not the concern of this book to enter a detailed engagement with all these matters. The relevant issue for our purposes is to consider the extent to which the methods used by the NT writers, as they interpreted the OT, reveal ways in which they were guided as a community by the Spirit. Some questions relevant to our thesis have been summarised by G. K. Beale.

> If they [the New Testament writers] sometimes employed non-contextual interpretative procedures in using the Old Testament, did they err in doing so, or did the Holy Spirit guarantee the truth of their doctrinal conclusions for the church of following generations? Put another way, did Jesus and the apostles preach the right doctrine from the wrong Old Testament texts? If so, did apostolic inspiration make their exegetical methods unique and unrepeatable? Or did inspiration give the New Testament writers unique and greater epistemological certainty about their interpretative conclusions than twentieth-century interpreters could ever hope to attain concerning their interpretations?[522]

If one believes in the doctrine of the canon, there is undoubtedly an element of unrepeatability about the final text of Scripture. Yet if one takes the promise of Jesus in John 16:13 seriously, the same Spirit who led the NT writers to interpret as they did is still there to 'guide [us] into all truth.' This being the case, what lessons are to be learned concerning such guidance from the NT's use of the OT?

To explore such a question, I will first seek to look at some of the relevant presuppositions about the Spirit in contemporary second Temple Judaism that lay behind NT exegesis. Secondly, I shall investigate the way the use of OT portions or *testimonia* reveal a shared method of interpretation at work amongst the NT writers, relating it particularly to the theory of C. H. Dodd. Thirdly, I will look at how the 'man of the Spirit', Jesus himself, guided the disciples in the interpretation of Scripture. Fourthly, I make some concluding remarks concerning the Christian presuppositions of the NT writers and other relevant observations from the world of OT/NT studies.

---

[519] See Longenecker, *Biblical Exegesis*, xix–xxii.
[520] See G. K. Beale, *The Right Doctrine from the Wrong Texts*, 399–404.
[521] See, for instance, G. Goldsworthy 'Relationship of Old Testament and New Testament' in *New Dictionary of Biblical Theology* (Leicester: IVP, 2000), 81-89; N. T. Wright, *Scripture and the Authority of God* (London: SPCK, 2005), 41; Longenecker, *Biblical Exegesis*, xxxix–xli.
[522] Beale. *The Right Doctrine from the Wrong Texts*, 8.

## The Spirit in Contemporary Judaism

The Jewish writers of the NT inevitably brought with them certain understandings of the Spirit derived from the OT and other Jewish writings. The many different groups within Judaism present a complex and wide range of pneumatologies. In a recent study[523] John Levison concludes:

> Considering the diversity of conceptions that co-exist within the writings of individual first-century authors or within a single ancient document, it is ill-advised to attempt to ascertain for each first-century author one dominant conception of the spirit.[524]

It is, however, possible to isolate two strands of thought that run through many Jewish conceptions of the Spirit that are particularly relevant to this book.

### The 'Spirit of Prophecy'

Max Turner and other scholars have pointed out how the Spirit, especially in the Jewish Targums, was particularly identified (though not exclusively[525]) as 'the Spirit of prophecy.'[526] Many examples could be given from first-century Judaism.[527] From this, it must not be thought that 'the Spirit of prophecy' implied a role that was limited to the giving of 'prophecies'. As Turner points out, the term embraced much wider connotations 'as the organ of communication between God and a person.'[528] Turner goes on to cite examples from Jewish writings of how such an understanding recognised the Spirit as

---

[523] John R. Levison, *The Spirit in First-Century Judaism* (Leiden: Brill, 2002). His work concentrates on the writings of Philo Judaeus (c. 20/10 BCE to 50 CE), Josephus (37 CE to c.100 CE) and the anonymous first century CE Pseudo-Philo's *Liber Antiquitatum Biblicarum*.

[524] Levison, *The Spirit in First-Century Judaism*, 242. Thus he points out that besides being linked with prophetic inspiration (see above), the Spirit was also associated with creation, human purity and cleansing, community initiation (Qumran), entrance into a life of faith and purification (see 249–252).

[525] Archie Hui has cogently argued (*contra* E. Schweizer and R.Menzies) that the Spirit was not just associated with prophecy in first-century Judaism, but also with wisdom, power, righteousness, salvation, and life: Archie Hui, 'The Spirit of Prophecy and Pauline Pneumatology,' *Tyndale Bulletin* 50:1 (1999), 93–115.

[526] M. M. B. Turner, *The Holy Spirit and Spiritual Gifts* (Paternoster: Carlisle, 1996), 5–6. See also M. M.B.Turner 'The Holy Spirit' in Joel B. Green, Scot McKnight, I Howard Marshall, eds., *Dictionary of Jesus and the Gospels* (Leicester: IVP, 1992), 342. Also Levison: 'among the effects of the spirit prophecy is the most pervasive,' Levison, *The Spirit in First-Century Judaism*, 244. Hosea 9:7 provides an OT link between the prophet and the Spirit.

[527] To cite some from John Levison: 'For Philo, Balaam became possessed when "there fell upon him the truly prophetic spirit which banished utterly from his soul his art of wizardry" (*De vita Mosis* 1.277). "This is what regularly befalls the fellowship of the prophets. The mind is evicted at the arrival of the divine spirit, but when that departs the mind returns to its tenancy" (*Quis rerum divinarum heres* 265). Josephus, referring to 1 Sam16:13 relates that David "when the divine spirit had removed to him, began to prophesy" (*Antiquates Judaicae* 6:1). Pseudo Philo brings in an extra biblical insight to Judges 3:9–10 by inserting a reference to the spirit: "And when they had sat down, a holy spirit came upon Kenaz...and he began to prophesy" (*Liber Antiquitatum Biblicarum* 28:6)': Levision, *The Spirit in First-Century Judaism*, 244–245.

[528] Max Turner, *The Holy Spirit and Spiritual Gifts*, 6.

granting charismatic revelation, charismatic wisdom, invasive prophetic speech, and invasive charismatic praise.[529]

However, it was further held that the Spirit of prophecy, since the days of the last prophets, if not entirely withdrawn from Israel,[530] was certainly rare, because of the nation's sin. But based on such passages as Joel 2:28–32, it was anticipated 'that the Spirit of prophecy would be poured out on *all* of the restored Israel at the end.... This would bring Israel immediate knowledge of God and of his will, and thus promote ongoing obedience fulfilling the hope of Ezekiel 36:27.'[531] The community of Qumran certainly appear to have believed that their members were experiencing the realization of the eschatological gift of the Spirit that gave them special interpretive insight.[532]

Jewish eschatology also embraced a strong messianic hope. Amidst the variations of belief as to what this could involve, Turner has claimed:

> A major strand of Judaism anticipated a Messiah mightily endowed with the Spirit as *both* the Spirit of prophecy (affording unique wisdom and knowledge of the Lord as the basis of his dynamic righteousness and 'fear of the Lord') *and* the Spirit of power (i.e. of the 'might' by which he asserts liberating rule against opposition). The model is first David, then more especially the 'Davidic' figure of Isaiah 11:1–4 who would be endowed with the Spirit of wisdom, knowledge, and might.[533]

As we shall see later, this kind of background gives added significance to the announcement by Jesus in the synagogue of Nazareth as recorded in Luke 4:14–21.

## *Corporate Solidarity*

Conceptions of the Spirit that envisage his coming upon the prophets, the nation, and the Messiah, as outlined in the previous section, can (to the modern Western person) seem to be somewhat overlapping, coming as we do from an individualist mindset that tends to put rigid distinctions between such entities. But for the ancient Jew, all were vitally linked. The idea of 'corporate solidarity' has been defined as:

---

[529] Turner, *The Holy Spirit and Spiritual Gifts*, 6-12. Although Turner uses the word 'person' here, he does not intend to restrict the working of the Spirit to individuals, but also to the wider application of Israel as a nation. Levison remarks how 'the Israelite and early Jewish milieux exhibit ... a surprisingly refined conception of the spirit as the author of inspired exegesis': Levison, *The Spirit in First-Century Judaism*, 194.
[530] Note, for instance the Spirit's work in Zechariah, Simeon, and Anna (Luke 1–2).
[531] Turner, *The Holy Spirit and Spiritual Gifts*, 12.
[532] Turner, *The Holy Spirit and Spiritual Gifts*, 13, 15. Levison comments: 'Revealed interpretive insight lies at the heart of this desert community', and having surveyed several Qumran texts that identify the Spirit with revelation he concludes that 'for this community, it is not difficult to envisage that biblical interpretation by authorized, learned leaders was indeed attributed to the spirit.' Levison (*The Spirit in First-Century Judaism*, 200, 202.
[533] Turner, *The Holy Spirit and Spiritual Gifts*, 17.

that important Semitic complex of thought in which there is a constant oscillation between the individual and the group—family, tribe or nation—to which he belongs, so that the king or some other representative figure may be said to embody the group, or the group may be said to sum up the host of individuals.[534]

'Corporate solidarity' is not to be confused with 'corporate personality', a notion that derived from H. W. Robinson which has now been largely discredited by Rogerson and other scholars as 'an ambiguous term'[535] that is based upon outdated anthropological ideas, inappropriate legal and psychological analogies, and one that underrates the clear OT notion of individual responsibility.[536] Despite such criticisms, Rogerson credits Robinson with focussing attention upon the primary OT importance attached to group identity, including the notion of 'corporate representation.'[537] The latter is illustrated by 'the corporate "I" of the Psalms,'[538] the individual/collective aspects of the four Servant Songs in Isa 42–53, and the way in which individual leaders are considered to represent[539] or be responsible for the whole group. Jesus himself spoke about the responsibility of the Scribes and Pharisees in this way in Matt 23:35. More will be said about 'corporate solidarity' later in the chapter.[540]

---

[534] J. Reumann in his introduction to H. W. Robinson, *Corporate Personality in Ancient Israel* (Philadelphia: Fortress, 1964), cited in R. Longenecker, *Biblical Exegesis in the Apostolic Period*, 77. For example, in Lam 3 the use of the first person singular could be read as the lament of an individual (perhaps Jeremiah) or a representative of the nation over its exile. Son has further explored the OT conception of corporate solidarity which he says 'does not imply that individuality is absorbed or lost in the group or that the ancient Israelites could not recognize one's physical boundaries': Aaron Sang-Won Son, *Corporate Elements in Pauline Anthropology* (Rome: Editrice Pontificio Instituto Biblico-Roma, 2001), 78. On page 186 he separates out four essential aspects of the concept:
(1) *Identification* – the group (e.g., family, tribe and nation) is often identified with its leader (e.g. father, ancestor, and king)
(2) *Extension* – the individual man is thought of as extending himself beyond his individual existence to include those who belong to him. The father and the king, therefore, are understood as incorporating in themselves the household and the nation respectively.
(3) *Realism* – the corporate personality that the individual man forms with a group is regarded as an ontological reality. The act of the leader, therefore, often determines the destiny of the group that he represents.
(4) *Oscillation* – an oscillation or fluidity exists between the individual and the group.
The notion of corporate 'personality', as opposed to 'solidarity', however, is now seriously questioned.
[535] J. W. Rogerson, 'The Hebrew Conception of Corporate Personality: A Re-examination' *Journal of Theological Studies* Vol. XXI, 1970, 14. See also Rogerson, 'Corporate Responsibility' in. D. N. Freeman et al, eds, *Anchor Bible Dictionary* Vol. 1, (New York; London: Doubleday, 1992), 1156–1157.
[536] Ziesler (referring to the commonly quoted example of Achan's sin in Joshua 7) says 'without any dispute about the importance of solidarity, "corporate personality" as a Hebrew notion is now under grave question. The Achan case may be a matter of ritual or moral pollution rather than anything more abstruse. More important, while the Old Testament and later Judaism easily conceived of representative figures, it is not clear that they ever envisaged corporate figures, whether kings, patriarchs, Adam, or anyone else' John Ziesler, *Pauline Christianity*, rev. ed. (Oxford: Oxford University Press, 1990), 62.
[537] Rogerson, 'Corporate Personality', 1156.
[538] Rogerson, 'Corporate Personality', 1156, citing Ps 44:4–8 as an example.
[539] Notice the confessions in Ezra 9:7 and Neh 9:2, 34.
[540] See pages 107–108.

An appreciation of Jewish 'solidarity' notions and corporate thinking is not only vital for an understanding of NT Christology,[541] as is commonly noted,[542] but also of NT pneumatology. Rooted as it is in the OT, it brings with it this distinctively corporate perspective, as emphasized by W. D. Davies:

> [T]he Spirit in the Old Testament has a national reference. It is the possession of the Spirit that equips the national leaders, the judges (Judges 15:14; 6:34) and kings (1 Sam 10:6, 2 Sam 6:12f), for their functions. Moreover, prophecy, itself the activity of the Spirit *par excellence*, is directed always not to the individual but to the nation as a whole; the appeal of the prophets is invariably to 'the House of Israel' (Amos 3:1, Hos 4:1, Isa1:4, Jer1:4, Ezek 3:1 etc).[543]

Davies proceeds to refer to Ezek 37:11–14, Isa 44:3, and Joel 2:28–29, concluding that 'there is traceable in the Old Testament teaching on the Spirit a persistently communal reference.'[544] Such an understanding is obviously not so developed as Paul's later concept of the κοινωνία of the Spirit,[545] but it clearly undergirded the way in which the NT writers read the OT, operating as a Spirit-inspired community interpreting Spirit-given writings, as proclaimed to the nation via the words of the Torah and the company of the prophets.

As the NT writers sought to expound the Scriptures, they would do so with Jewish notions of corporate solidarity and covenant loyalty, which meant that great respect was indeed paid to the interpretations of past centuries. Yet alongside this was the aforementioned belief in the notion of Spirit-inspired exegesis for the present.[546]

Such a juxtaposition of ideas led to an inherent ambiguity within contemporary Judaism that has been highlighted by C. F. D. Moule in an assessment of 'two main attitudes' that were prevalent at the time. First there was:

> [an] attitude [that] attached a good deal of importance to the traditions of the great rabbis – to traditional interpretations of particular passages handed down communally ... [which helped] to prevent an irresponsible individualism in interpretation. [547]

---

[541] For instance, the Adam/Christ link in 1 Cor 15:22. See Son, *Corporate Elements in Pauline Anthropology*, 39–82.
[542] For example in Ellis, *The Old Testament in Early Christianity*, 110–112.
[543] W. D. Davies, *Paul and Rabbinic Judaism: Some Rabbinic Elements in Pauline Theology*, 3rd edition (London: SPCK, 1948, 1970), 203. Davies is arguing for a Jewish as against a Hellenistic background for Paul's pneumatology. 'For Rabbinic Judaism no individual in isolation, like the magician of the Hellenistic world, could receive the Spirit: it was necessary for him in order to do so to live in a particular milieu.' Hence 'it is doubtful if Paul would ever have claimed that he himself had the Spirit unless he had been convinced that he belonged to a peculiar community which was also experiencing the Spirit': ibid., 207.
[544] ibid., 204.
[545] See chapter 2.
[546] From a later NT perspective, one could view this tension as a precursor of the Spirit's work as the author of both unity and diversity within the body, as in 1 Cor 12.
[547] C. F. D. Moule, *The Birth of the New Testament*, 2nd ed. (London: Adam & Charles Black, 1966), 59.

> But second, there was another attitude to the text of the Torah [that] was essentially individualistic.... Viewing the actual written words as themselves a constant source of inspiration, it made it possible for any individual, provided only ... that he acknowledged his dependence upon God's grace, to expect direct divine guidance from his private study of them. [548]

Consequently:

> The former attitude tended to locate authoritative interpretation in the rabbinic leaders of learning and in the communally transmitted traditions of their wisdom; the latter in the individual's own use of the very words of Scripture (often, it must be confessed, in a wildly inaccurate Greek translation).[549]

Against such a background, one can understand that the NT writers, as they interpreted the OT, did so under the dual constraints of both tradition and Spirit. An overemphasis upon the 'leading of the Spirit' could have led to an individualistic, noncontextual use of Scripture, as indeed some have claimed. A. T. Hanson, for instance, says that 'since scripture was regarded as inspired by the Holy Spirit, the devout exegete has every reason for seeking as many meanings in any text as he thinks it can bear.'[550] However, there is good evidence to believe that this did not occur in the case of the NT writers, for there was another more influential community 'tradition' in biblical interpretation that had more recently developed that acted as a suitable corrective to individualistic interpretive deviancy and which had at its heart a Christological focus that was truly Spirit-inspired.

## The Use of Testimonia

The evidence for such a newer form of 'community' interpretation comes from the NT itself and the way in which it not only has a special method of dealing with OT texts, but also shows a distinct preference for the selection of such texts. Certain limited sections of the OT are much more commonly referred to than the rest of the OT. One explanation for this was offered by J. Rendall Harris,

---

[548] C. F. D. Moule, *The Birth of the New Testament*, 59.
[549] ibid., 59.
[550] Hanson, *The Living Utterances of God*, 25. Many OT/NT works refer to the extraordinary range of interpretations that could result from application of the so-called 'Seven Rules of Hillel' within rabbinic exegesis (see FN 91 of this chapter and also G. Bray, *Biblical Interpretation Past and Present* (Leicester: Apollos, 1996), 58-59 and E. Earle Ellis, *The Old Testament in Early Christianity*,87-88. Keesmat speaks of the great degree of 'flexibility' within first century Judaism as the various groups within it sought to interpret biblical texts in response to their particular cultural and historical situations. '[T]he biblical tradition was not recalled in any post-enlightenment 'literal' sense...there is a constant process of reinterpretation, transformation and recontextualization of the biblical material': Sylvia Keesmat, *Paul & His Story: (Re)Interpreting the Exodus tradition* (Sheffield: Sheffield Academic Press, 1999), 30.

who in 1916[551] suggested that such favourite portions[552] came from a 'Book of Testimonies' of OT texts which had been drawn by early Christians as 'an anti-Judaic polemic'[553] and upon which the NT writers later drew. This theory of a *written* collection of OT 'proof texts' was later challenged by C. H. Dodd in *According to the Scriptures* (1952).[554] In this important book, he argued that the commonality of OT references in the NT stemmed from an *oral* collection of *blocks* of OT material whose selection was originally inspired by Christ himself and later used by the NT writers. To summarise his argument in more detail:

1. The existence of fifteen or so texts[555] from the OT (mainly from Psalms, Isaiah, Jeremiah and certain minor prophets such as Hosea, Habakkuk and Joel) that are apparently cited independently of each other in diverse parts of the NT is evidence that there was a primitive *kerygma* in the early church, largely employed orally, but consisting of a body of texts that were recognised by the NT community as seen fulfilled in Christ, as per the OT messianic hope. They were used to bring out the significance of Christ's accomplishment.

2. These texts should be regarded as *testimonia* which, when cited, should be read by way of a reference to their whole context, rather than isolated 'proof texts' (as per Rendall Harris). Thus what may seem a rather unusual reference to Ps 69:25 in Acts 1:20 regarding a successor to Judas can only be appreciated in light of the overall context of Ps 69, as it was understood in relation to the sufferings of Christ. These larger contexts could in many ways be regarded as 'the Bible of the early church' (p. 61).

3. Such a body of material 'is common to all the main portions of the NT' (p. 127) and forms 'the substructure of all Christian theology and contains already its chief regulative ideas' (p. 127). Thus, for instance, a multiplicity of references to and reworkings of Isa 53 are used as a basis for formulating the NT's theology of atonement.

---

[551] J. R. Harris, *Testimonies*, I (1916), II (1920).
[552] As for instance those cited by Paul in Rom 3:10–18.
[553] R. Longenecker, *Biblical Exegesis*, 73. Lindars has argued that 'the use of Old Testament quotations belongs primarily to the apologetic element of the early preaching', and was particularly concerned to defend the truth of the resurrection (see also 51–59 for his relating of this to the gift of the Spirit). Barnabas Lindars, *New Testament Apologetic* (London: SCM, 1961), 19, I. Howard Marshall, however, argues that 'the field of use seems to be much wider than Lindars suggests', covering 'explanatory' and 'liturgical' uses alongside 'apologetic' and 'polemical' uses: see Beale, *The Right Doctrine from the Wrong Texts*, 204.
[554] C. H. Dodd, *According to the Scriptures: The Sub-structure of New Testament Theology* (London: Nisbett & Co, 1952). This work was also intended to counter arguments that Paul's theology of the OT was primarily influenced by his own religious experience or the concepts of Hellenism. 'In saying this Dodd was not arguing for an early church theology that was based on "the Word", but rather for one in which "the mighty acts of God" in history are understood in the context which is provided by the Old Testament,' I. Howard Marshall in Beale, *The Right Doctrine from the Wrong Texts*, 198.
[555] The complete list is: Gen 12:3; Deut 18:15, 19; Ps 2:7; 8:4–6; 110:1; 118:22–23; Isa 6:9–10; 28:16; 40:3–5; 53:1; 61:1–2; Jer 31:31–34; Joel 2:28–32; Hab 2:3; Zech 9:9.

4. This 'method' (p. 126) of interpretation that was employed by the early Christians seems to have been derived from Christ himself (p. 110), as illustrated in Lk. 24:25–27 & 24:44–46. It was his genius that must have been the source of applying such texts as Ps 110 and Dan 7 Son of Man terminology to himself. 'The NT itself avers that it was Jesus Christ Himself who first directed the minds of His followers to certain parts of the scriptures as those in which they might find illumination upon the meaning of His mission and destiny' (p. 110).
5. Christ is accordingly viewed as the representative head of the New Israel (74–88, 111–114) by which the new Christian community came to understand itself.
6. The existence of *testimonia* is also evidenced by the way Paul and Peter apply OT passages to Christ by way of *assumption* rather than *argument* (p. 19).
7. Acts 2 in its quotation of Joel 2 shows how the early church set out in a new and 'formidable task of biblical research' (13–14) which sought to interpret all that had recently happened as 'according to the determinate counsel and foreknowledge of God' (Acts 2:23). This was earnestly followed up by the church, as shown in various ensuing passages in Acts (p. 15).

Despite some criticisms of substance[556] and detail,[557] Dodd's theory has been generally accepted by scholars. In a later article, Dodd refers to the NT's use of the OT as:

> an intellectual achievement of remarkable originality, displaying meaning that lies beneath the surface of the text, and a power of synthesis which gathers apparently disparate elements into a many-sided whole, not unsuitable to convey some idea of "the manifold wisdom of God."[558]

In so far, however, as Dodd had earlier attributed the origin of this means of exegesis to Christ,[559] this wisdom can be surely be regarded as derived from the

---

[556] For a detailed critique, see Albert C. Sundberg, 'Response Against C. H. Dodd's View: On Testimonies,' in Beale, *The Right Doctrine from the Wrong Texts*, 182–193. He uses statistical arguments to argue for 'multiplicity rather than uniformity' in the NT's use of the OT and questions why, if there was an early collection of OT passages, it was omitted from the canon (188, 193). Cf. I. Howard Marshall's refutations of Sundberg, 'Counter-Response in Favor of C. H. Dodd's View' in Beale, *The Right Doctrine from the Wrong Texts*, 200–202. See also Beale, *The Right Doctrine from the Wrong Texts*, 390 fn. 9. For the view that 'general considerations make it rather unlikely that any very broad context would have been 'heard' by most readers/hearers in the first century' see Christopher Tuckett, 'Paul, Scripture and Ethics: Some Reflections' *New Testament Studies* Vol. 46 (2000), 403.

[557] Marshall suggests that Dodd's list is 'not ... wrong in principle but ... needs revision in detail' (ibid., 200). S. Moyise claims that the discovery of textual collections at Qumran has refuted Dodd's point against the use of written collections. 'Such collections *were* made and it is difficult to imagine Paul unrolling a 10 metre scroll every time he wanted to quote a particular verse from Genesis or Isaiah. He must surely have used notes of some kind,' S. Moyise, *The Old Testament in the New* (London: Continuum, 2001), 12–13.

[558] Dodd, 'The Old Testament in the New' in Beale, *The Right Doctrine from the Wrong Texts*, 181.

[559] See point 4 of the summary of *According to the Scriptures* above.

one whom Paul describes as 'the wisdom of God'.[560] And in so far as OT/Jewish thought viewed the Messiah as a man endowed *par excellence* with the Spirit of God, we can surely take this understanding to be Spirit-inspired. And in so far as Dodd points to the NT's use of the OT as primarily a function of 'oral tradition,'[561] this implies that the principal context of such instruction took place in a corporate setting. Moreover, the Jewish conception of the Spirit, as we have remarked, necessarily involved a corporate outlet for his operations. This, then, leads us into a discussion of some of the NT passages that demonstrate 'the man of the Spirit' teaching the group of his disciples by way of his own special interpretation of the OT.

## The Spirit-anointed Messianic Exegete

It is not difficult to spot many references to the OT in Jesus's teaching. Nevertheless, Hübner has observed that 'the question of Jesus's use of Scripture is one of the most disputed in exegetical scholarship.'[562] Did he abrogate or fulfil the Torah? Did his way of interpreting the OT inaugurate a completely new way of reading Scripture, or did it follow the methods of contemporary Judaism? What is the nature of the parallels with Qumran interpretation? Recent scholarship has generally approached the subject by 'viewing Jesus as a first-century Jew rather than the first Christian.'[563] Jesus's Jewishness certainly comes out in the way that he makes use of many of the OT texts and kingdom terminology that were prevalent in contemporary Jewish messianic thought. But he invests them with a new perspective that R. T. France describes as 'revolutionary', for 'Jesus's use of the Old Testament falls into one coherent scheme, with himself as the focus.'[564]

This comes out in the very first words recorded of his public ministry, as related in Luke 4:18–19. Jesus's quotation from Isa 61:1 in the Nazareth sermon has been described by Barrett as 'the most important OT citation in Luke.'[565] Significantly, the context of Jesus's inaugural use of the OT in Luke 4 reveals a strongly 'pneumatic emphasis [that] reflects Jesus's own experience of the Spirit in his life and ministry'[566] (note 'full of the Holy Spirit'—πλήρης πνεύματος ἁγίου—in 4:1). So Luke records how Spirit anoints (3:22), leads (4:1), and empowers (4:14) Jesus. Thus, 'full of the Holy Spirit' (4:1), Jesus quotes from

---

[560] 1 Cor 1:24.
[561] 'The early church was not ... a bookish community': Dodd, *According to the Scriptures*, 29.
[562] Hans Hübner, 'OT Quotations in the New Testament' in *Anchor Bible Dictionary*, Vol. 4, 1098.
[563] Steve Moyise 'Can we use the New Testament in the way the New Testament Authors used the Old Testament' *In die Skriflig* 2002, 643–660, as copied from last page of an article located at <www.ucc.ac.uk/theology/html/MoyiseCanWeUse.htm>.
[564] R. T. France, *Jesus and the Old Testament* (Grand Rapids, MI: Baker, 1971, 1982), 224. To this extent, there are parallels with the eschatologically-oriented interpretation of Qumran, though Jesus' focus is, of course, upon himself and what has happened, as opposed to the community focus of Qumran, and what is about to happen.
[565] C. K. Barrett, 'Luke/Acts' in *It is Written, Scripture Citing Scripture*, 231, along with Isa 53:12 in Luke 22:37.
[566] C. A. Evans, 'New Testament use of the Old Testament' in *New Dictionary of Biblical Theology*, 73.

Deuteronomy[567] and Psalms[568] to the devil, and from Isaiah to the Nazareth synagogue (cf. 'the law ... and the prophets and the Psalms' in Luke 24:44). This reading of Isaiah is 'of special programmatic significance.'[569]

'The Spirit of the Lord is upon me, because he has anointed me, to proclaim good news to the poor, He has sent me to proclaim liberty to the captives, And recovering of sight to the blind. To set at liberty those who are oppressed, to proclaim the year of the Lord's favour.'[570]

After handing back the scroll to the synagogue attendant in a gesture of self-embodiment, Jesus proclaims: 'Today this Scripture has been fulfilled in your hearing.'[571] Moyise points out that Jesus's quotation 'is not a reading from any known text of Isaiah 61 but a conflation of Isa 61:1–2 with a phrase from Isa 58:6'[572] and records Kimball's comment[573] that:

> In the linking of these texts, Jesus defined his ministry in terms of OT prophecy and fulfillment; he cited Isa 61:1–2 to claim that he was the herald who proclaimed the messianic release and inserted Isa 58:6d to emphasize that he was also the agent of this spiritual liberation.[574]

Hence from the very outset of his ministry, there are indications that Jesus's distinctive use of the OT was Spirit-led,[575] Christological, and eschatological. He was indeed fulfilling the mandate for a Spirit-anointed Messiah as anticipated not only by Isa 61:1–2 but also Isa 11:1–2.

How, then, was this interpretive methodology of Jesus, with these distinctive emphases, passed on to the community of his disciples and the writers of the NT? I shall look firstly at Jesus as a *model* and secondly as a *promiser of Spirit-inspired exegesis*.

---

[567] Deut 8:12 in Luke 4:4 and Deut 6:13 in Luke 4:8.
[568] Ps 91:11–12 in Luke 4:10–11.
[569] Hans Hübner, 'OT Quotations in the New Testament',1100. 'More than the other Synoptics, Luke submits the messianic ministry of the earthly Jesus to the prophetic promise', 1100–1101.
[570] Luke 4:18–19. I. Howard Marshall, *The Gospel of Luke* (Exeter: Paternoster, 1978), 183, points out that 'since the passage uses a language and style reminiscent of the earlier Servant passages [sic. in Isaiah] it may have been interpreted in terms of the Servant of Yahweh.' He refers (p. 183) to F. F. Bruce, *This is That* (Exeter: Paternoster, 1969), 90, who 'suggests that Isa 61 itself may be "the earliest interpretation of the Servant".' This raises the interesting question of the use of the OT within the OT (for another example, see the allusion to Hosea in Jeremiah 3) and the extent to which this influenced NT interpretive methods. Dodd numbers Isa 61 as amongst the *testimonia* of the early church: Dodd, *According to the Scriptures*, 94. Barrett says it was 'probably ... in familiar use' in the early church: Barrett, *It is Written, Scripture Citing Scripture*, 236.
[571] Luke 4:21.
[572] S. Moyise, *The Old Testament in the New: An Introduction* (London: Continuum, 2001), 51. He points out the omission of 'bind up the broken-hearted' and 'day of vengeance' ('perhaps deliberately so as to stress the grace of God': Marshall, *The Gospel of Luke*, 183) from Isa 61:1-2 and the insertion of 'let the oppressed go free' from Isa 58:6.
[573] Based on the assumption that these are the actual words Jesus used rather than Luke's theological reflections thereon.
[574] C. A. Kimball, *Jesus' Exposition of the Old Testament in Luke's Gospel* (Sheffield: JSOP Press, 1994), 110, as quoted in Moyise, *The Old Testament in the New*, 51.
[575] See also John 3:34.

## Jesus as a Model of Spirit-inspired Exegesis

The fact that Luke follows his record of the Nazareth reading of Isaiah with 'the eyes of all in the synagogue were upon him'[576] and that 'all ... marvelled at the gracious words ... coming from his mouth'[577] reminds us that Jesus's expositions took place before keenly attentive audiences. In the ensuing three years, his disciples would have heard many such expositions which would have indelibly shaped the way they understood Scripture. What would they have learned?

From the start, they would have seen Jesus making a selective and strategic use of particular Scriptures, of the kind highlighted by Dodd. The inaugural Nazareth synagogue incident illustrates this, with Jesus's Spirit-directed use of Isa 61:1–2 in a dynamic reading that was followed by a dialogical sermon in which he challenged his hearers regarding an ancient proverb ('physician heal yourself!'[578]), as well as a provocative reference to two OT stories that showed God's preference towards a poor woman and a rich Gentile (Luke 4:25–27).

Central to Jesus's teaching was the kingdom of God/heaven theme, again introduced in Mark 1:15 immediately following references to Jesus's being anointed (1:10) and directed (1:12) by the Spirit. In his ongoing ministry, Jesus reinterpreted a number of OT 'kingdom' passages so as to apply them to himself.[579] For example, in the parable of the tenants, as recorded in Matt 21:33–46, Ellis points out how Jesus does this in relation to his exposition of Isa 5.[580] He further suggests that 'memorized summaries of such expositions'[581] would have been taken out by the disciples in missions of the Twelve and the Seventy.[582] As Wright says, Jesus, by 'evoking and retelling this familiar story[line] [viz. of the 'reign' or 'kingdom' of Israel's God] in such a way as to subvert and redirect its normal plot,'[583] Jesus was formulating and indeed embodying the message that would constitute the gospel proclaimed by the early church. Thus, Acts begins with Jesus 'speaking about the kingdom of God' (1:3) to the apostles, continues with the record of a *kerygma* that Dodd says significantly 'follows the lines of the summary of the preaching of Jesus as given

---

[576] Luke 4:20.
[577] Luke 4:22. L. Morris points out that 'Luke speaks of astonishment, not admiration or appreciation': Leon Morris, *Luke* (Leicester: IVP, 1988), 117.
[578] Luke 4:23.
[579] Evans points out that the proclamation of the kingdom being at hand 'is drawn from passages in Isaiah (e.g. 40:9, 52:7 & 61:1), though the interpretive lens of the Aramaic synagogue: "the Kingdom of your God is revealed!" (*Targum of Isaiah* 40:9; 52:7).' See C. A. Evans, 'New Testament use of the Old Testament' in Desmond Alexander and Brian Rosner, eds., *New Dictionary of Biblical Theology* (Leicester: IVP, 2000), 77.
[580] Ellis, *The Old Testament in Early Christianity*, 135. Ellis shows how this parable in Matt 21 shows Jesus using 'a *proem*-type midrash' (commentary pattern) in his interpretation of Isa 5 in terms of 'the rejected stone' of Ps 118 and the 'crushing stone' of Daniel 2, both of which were interpreted messianically in contemporary Judaism, 135. By the use of such texts, Jesus is clearly warning the chief priests and Pharisees that there were biblical grounds for believing they would one day be usurped by the one they had rejected.
[581] Ellis, *The Old Testament in Early Christianity*, 135.
[582] As, for example, in Luke 9:2; 10:9, 11.
[583] N. T. Wright, *Jesus and the Victory of God* (London: SPCK, 1996), 199.

in Mark 1:14-15,'[584] and ends with Paul still 'proclaiming the kingdom of God' (28:31).

Associated with kingdom teaching went a number of other key OT concepts that Jesus developed and related to himself, such as 'the servant of Isaiah 40-55,'[585] Son of Man figure of Daniel 7,[586] various 'stone' passages,[587] portions from the Psalms[588] and so on. And after the resurrection, Luke concludes his gospel with Jesus telling his disciples: "...everything written about me in the Law of Moses and the Prophets and the Psalms must be fulfilled". Then he opened their minds to understand the Scriptures...' (Luke 24:44-45; cf. 24:27). As Evans says, 'Jesus's proclamation of the fulfilment of Scripture thus established the hermeneutical matrix, in the light of which the NT interprets and utilizes the OT.'[589]

Jesus's unique interpretive methodology did not mean he totally bypassed contemporary Jewish exegetical methods. Indeed, he made good use of them. This in itself is not, of course, a proof of Spirit inspiration, but does show how he purposefully participated in communally accepted interpretive practices. Bray has pointed out that Jesus does this particularly in *ad hominem* encounters with his Jewish critics in order 'to defeat them on their own ground.'[590] Hence his use of a literalistic approach similar to that of the Sadducees to show from Exod 3:6[591] that a relationship with God continues in the afterlife (Mark 12:26), and his use of the Hillel principle[592] of *qal wa-homer* (arguing from the lesser to the

---

[584] C. H. Dodd, *The Apostolic Preaching and Its Developments* (London: Hodder and Stoughton, 1936), 45. He equates 'kingdom of God' teaching with the *kerygma* of the early church whose basic elements he outlines as follows: 'It begins by proclaiming that "this is that which was spoken by the prophets"; the age of fulfilment has dawned, and Christ is its Lord; it then proceeds to recall the historical facts, leading up to the resurrection and exaltation of Christ and the promise of His coming in glory; and it ends with the call to repentance and the offer of forgiveness' (p. 105).
[585] For example, Isa 53:12 in Luke 22:37.
[586] For example, in Matt 19:28; 26:64.
[587] For example in Matt 21:42; cf. 1 Pet 2:4-8.
[588] Such as Ps 110 in Mark 12:36.
[589] C. A. Evans, 'New Testament use of the Old Testament', 77.
[590] Bray, *Biblical Interpretation - Past and Present*, 62-63.
[591] 'I am ... the God of Abraham, and the God of Isaac, and the God of Jacob.'
[592] The great Jewish teacher Hillel (died c. CE 10) is credited by the Talmud with establishing seven basic rules for rabbinic exegesis which would have been widely found in Jewish interpretation at the time of the New Testament. As recorded by Gerald Bray, these were:
1. *Qal wa-homer*: what applies in less important cases will apply in more important ones as well.
2. *Gezerah shawah*: the use of the same word in different contexts means that the same considerations apply to each context.
3. *Binyan ab mikathub 'ehad*: repetition of a phrase means that ideas associated with it are applicable in all contexts.
4. *Binyan ab mishene kethubim*: a principle can be established by relating two texts to each other; that principle can then be applied to other texts.
5. *Kelal upherat*: in certain cases, a general principle may be restricted in its application by certain qualifications placed upon it, and conversely, particular rules may be generalized for similar reasons.
6. *Kayoze bo bemaqom 'aher*: a difficulty in one text may be resolved by comparing it with another similar passage, though verbal correspondences are not required.
7. *Dabar halamed me 'inyano*: a meaning may be established by the context.
Bray further points out that 'these rules make more sense as they go along', for the last two would be generally accepted today, but not the first three. Bray, *Biblical Interpretation: Past and Present*, 59.
For specific examples of Jesus's possible use of the seven rules, see Ellis, *The Old Testament in Early Christianity*, 130-132.

greater) in arguments with the Pharisees about the use of the Sabbath in John 7:23 and about 'Son of God' terminology in his use of Psalm 82:6 in John 10:34–36.

Jesus was nevertheless no slave to current interpretive practices, bringing in his own unique form of OT reinterpretation: 'you have heard it said ... but I say to you.'[593] Nor was he averse to highlighting the interpretive misunderstanding and spiritual ineffectiveness of his Jewish contemporaries. In a discussion about the resurrection, for instance, he told the Sadducees, 'you are wrong, because you know neither the Scriptures nor the power of God!' (Mark 12:24)[594] In contrast to such spiritual ignorance and weakness, the powerful combination of Word and Spirit was always evident in Jesus, as recognized by the gospel writers. 'For he whom God has sent utters the words of God, for he gives the Spirit without measure' (John 3:34; cf. 6:63b).

John's testimony clearly reflects his own experience of Jesus as Spirit-anointed prophet and messiah, an outlook that coheres with similar emphases found in the synoptic writers. Here were men who recognized, as Moyise says, that 'at the heart of Christian exegesis is not a rule or principle but a person.'[595] I therefore agree with R. T. France's conclusion that 'the school in which the writers of the early church learned to use the OT was that of Jesus,'[596] a Jesus who was, throughout his ministry, anointed with the Spirit of God.

## *Jesus as a Promiser of Spirit-inspired Exegesis*

Scholars of the OT/NT relationship, as we have noted, frequently point out 'parallels with Qumran'. One such relevant parallel concerns one way of explaining the ongoing influence of Jesus's exegetical methodology. As Longenecker comments:

> It seems that the members of the Dead Sea community both passively retained interpretations of their Teacher on certain biblical portions and actively continued to study the Old Testament along lines stemming from him, either as directly laid out by him or as deduced from his practice.[597]

Such a statement could be made of the influence of any great teacher, of course, but the unique thing about Jesus, as indeed recognized by Longenecker, was that he bequeathed an interpretive legacy that had far greater power than the model

---

[593] Matt 5:21, 27
[594] Mark 12:24.
[595] Steve Moyise, *In die Skriflig*, 3:1. Many Christian preachers begin (and sometimes continue) their ministry by modelling their preaching on those by whom they have most been influenced.
[596] France, *Jesus and the Old Testament*, 225.
[597] Longenecker, *Biblical Exegesis*, 61–62.

of any human teacher. The Holy Spirit himself was given to the disciples that they might continue to benefit from having the mind of Christ as their guide.

Before he died, Jesus had told these disciples 'I still have many things to say to you, but you cannot bear them now.'[598] There was indeed a limit to what they could understand before the events of Christ's death, resurrection, and ascension. But '[w]hen the Spirit of truth comes, he will guide you into all the truth.'[599] As 'another comforter' (ἄλλον παράκλητον),[600] the Spirit would take the place of Jesus in drawing alongside them 'on the way'[601] in explaining and applying Scripture. Longenecker points out that this ongoing ministry of the Spirit 'was understood by the earliest believers to include advances in the interpretation of Scripture [which are] suggested in at least three places in John's gospel.'[602] He mentions 2:17 (cleansing of Temple/'zeal for thy house'), 2:22 ('temple of his body'/resurrection) and 12:16 (triumphal entry) where it is stated in all three instances that only later did they 'remember'(τότε ἐμνήσθησαν) and appreciate the significance of the events in question.[603] 'In each case there is a kind of delayed-action response to Jesus and understanding of Scripture, which ultimately found their source in Jesus himself but immediately resulted from the ministry of the Holy Spirit.'[604]

Spiritual understanding is indeed progressive and is frequently triggered off by the force of subsequent events. The Acts of the Apostles[605] gives a number of examples of 'advances of interpretation' afforded by the powerful arrival of the Spirit, the events of Pentecost, and their sequel.[606] In Acts 2, the coming of the Spirit upon the waiting church enabled Peter to make a *pesher*-like 'this is that' application of OT scripture from Joel 2 and Ps 16, as well as a *midrash* like (analogy/*gezerah shawah*) approach to Ps 16 and Ps 110 to argue the case for the resurrection on the basis of the common use of the phrase 'at my right hand.'[607] OT Scripture was subsequently used on many other occasions in speeches and debates in the defense and proclamation of the gospel, as well as in resolving issues within the church (as, for example, in Acts 15, where the Spirit's help is explicitly acknowledged in v. 28).

---

[598] John 16:12a. For a more detailed examination of the 'paraclete' passages in John 14–16, see chapter 4 'The Promise of the Paraclete.'
[599] John 16:12b.
[600] John 14:16.
[601] Luke 24:35 NIV, cf. Luke 24:32.
[602] Longenecker, *Biblical Exegesis*, 59.
[603] See John 12:16.
[604] Longenecker, *Biblical Exegesis*, 60. See also Longenecker's comment at xxx–xxi ('The Christocentric Nature and Pneumatic Quality of New Testament Exegesis').
[605] See chapter 5 for more detailed treatment of Acts.
[606] Hull makes the link between the promises of John and their fulfilment in Acts: 'If the Fourth Gospel claimed that the Spirit would call to mind all that Christ had said (14:21), it also claimed that the Spirit would guide into all truth (16:13). And in Acts we see this second promise being fulfilled as the Spirit leads the church into all the truth, of which understanding of Scripture formed a vital part', J. H. E. Hull, *The Holy Spirit in the Acts of the Apostles* (London: Lutterworth, 1967), 132–133.
[607] Acts 2:25, 34.

C. A. Evans believes that these constant references to the OT show that 'it is probable that the Lukan evangelist understood the story of Jesus (the Gospel) and the early church (the book of Acts) as the continuation of the biblical story.'[608] All that Jesus had accomplished for the church and the world was in fulfilment of the true destiny of Israel.

This narrative link with the OT concludes at the end of Acts with Paul's house church ministry in Rome with Paul 'testifying to the kingdom of God and trying to convince [his hearers] about Jesus both from the Law of Moses and from the Prophets.'[609] It is interesting to note that the Apostle follows this with a reference to 'the Holy Spirit ... saying ... through Isaiah ... "Go to this people, and say, you will indeed hear but never understand."'[610] This shows that the Spirit's leading does not guarantee a receptive audience,[611] and is therefore a timely reminder against an overly-triumphalist agenda for the Spirit, such as could be gleaned from a reading limited to the beginning of Acts.

Turning from Acts to the rest of the NT corpus,[612] we find a number of different ways in which the OT is cited and used. Matthew frequently likens the historical experience of Israel as a nation to the life of Jesus in a typological way and has a habit of using 'formula quotations' (for example, Matt 2:15b: 'This was to fulfil what the Lord had spoken by the prophet...'). These are not found so frequently in John, though he is partial to the use of typology, especially in linking the events of Jesus's life with Jewish festivals such as the Passover.[613] Both of these evangelists provide evidence of a strongly *pesher*-like fulfilment approach, which is not so prominent in the other two evangelists.[614] Mark, for his part, sets the beginning of Jesus' ministry in terms of a 'voice crying in the wilderness' that echoes from the chamber of a triple OT context,[615] whilst Luke's birth narratives

---

[608] *New Dictionary of Biblical Theology*, 78. For a detailed narrative hermeneutical approach to the New Testament, see N. T. Wright, *The New Testament and the People of God* (London: SPCK, 1992).
[609] Acts 28:23.
[610] Acts 28:25-26, citing Isa 6:9-10. Ezekiel's call also consisted of a Spirit-inspired warning concerning the rebelliousness of his hearers: Ezek 2:1-5.
[611] See also Acts 16:7 for the preventative guidance of the Spirit.
[612] For a summary of how each of the NT books uses the OT, see . D. A. Carson and H. G. M. Williamson, eds., *It is Written: Scripture Citing Scripture* (Cambridge: Cambridge University Press, 1988), 193-336.
[613] As in John 6, where 'bread of heaven'/manna terminology shows an Exodus motif at work. See Moyise, *The Old Testament in the New*, 73, for a summary of John's use of the OT.
[614] This, says Bray 'raises the interesting question of the author's relationship to Jesus. Both Matthew and John were his disciples, while Mark and Luke were not, which may be further evidence of the historical likelihood that Jesus' own method of biblical interpretation was dominated by the *pesher* mode, as applied directly to himself', Bray, *Biblical Interpretation*, 69.
[615] Mark 1:2-3, a composite quotation of Mal 3:1, Exod 23:20 and Isa 40:3. Marcus says that Isaiah is cited not as a proof text for the location of John's ministry (wilderness) nor to clarify his relationship with Jesus (forerunner) but 'it is quoted because the restoration promised in Isaiah is being fulfilled. Isaiah looked forward to the time when the heavens would be rent (64:1), the Spirit poured out (61:1), good news would be proclaimed (40:9-10) and God would come in power (40:10). Hence Mark speaks of heavens torn open 1:10, the Spirit descending on Jesus 1:10, the good news proclaimed in Galilee 1:14 and the dawn of the kingdom of God 1:15.' Joel Marcus, *The Way of the Lord. Christological Exegesis of the OT in the Gospel of Mark* (Edinburgh: T&T Clark, 1992), as cited by Moyise, *The Old Testament in the New*, 22, This use of an OT text to evoke the connotations of the great context fits well into Dodd's theory mentioned earlier.

are full of OT concepts and imagery, often upon the lips of the likes of Mary,[616] Zechariah,[617] and Simeon.[618] *Pesher* is not so characteristic of Paul's exegesis of the OT, although he uses a number of other interpretive methods, such as literalistic[619] and midrashic exegesis, the latter 'often in the form of "pearl-stringing", i.e. collecting passages from different portions of Scripture in support of a particular argument, and thereby demonstrating the essential unity of the biblical text.'[620] He also uses allegory twice.[621] Paul's and Peter's indebtedness to Jewish apocalyptic comes out in their concept of Scripture as sometimes containing hidden wisdom or mystery that needs an act of revelation or 'charismatic exegesis' to interpret it.[622] Hebrews has its own unique form of typology that frequently argues from the lesser to the greater, and includes a unique exploration of the mysterious king-priest Melchizedek,[623] who is also a key figure in the Qumran literature. In Revelation, with its multiple collections of OT allusions, '*pesher* exegesis reaches its ultimate stage of development in that the whole of the Old Testament becomes a type of the future life in heaven.'[624] The 'intertextual' link with Ezekiel in particular has been noted so that 'henceforth readers cannot read Ezekiel without thinking of Revelation or Revelation without thinking of Ezekiel.'[625] Particularly relevant for the purpose of this book is the ecclesial/pneumatological hermeneutic suggested by the phrase repeated in each of the letters to the seven churches: 'He who has an ear, let him hear what the Spirit says to the churches.'[626]

This brief survey,[627] then, reveals 'the astonishing variety of ways in which the various NT authors make reference to the OT.'[628] As Longenecker says:

> The first Christian preachers ... seem to have made no distinctions between a literalist treatment of the text, a midrashic analysis, a pesher interpretation, and the application of a generally accepted prophecy. All these exegetical methods come to expression in their recorded sermons, and at times there appears a blending and interweaving of these methods. What these preachers were conscious of, however, was interpreting the Scriptures from a christocentric perspective, in

---

[616] Luke 1:46–55.
[617] Luke 1:67–79.
[618] Luke 2:29–32.
[619] That is the use of direct quotations, such as in Rom 7:7/Exod 20:12–17; 1 Cor 6:16/Gen 2:24.
[620] Bray, *Biblical Interpretation*, 66. He quotes examples from Rom 3:10–18; 9:12–19; 10:18–21 and Gal 3:10–13. For more detail on Paul's use of the OT, see chapter 6.
[621] 1 Cor 9:9 and Gal 4:21–31.
[622] See pages 105–107 for more detail on 'charismatic exegesis.'
[623] From Gen 14 and Ps 110.
[624] Bray, *Biblical Interpretation*, 69.
[625] Moyise, *The Old Testament in the New*, 127.
[626] Rev 2:7. A comparison here can be made with Hebrews, where Hans Hübner notes that 'in quotations with a paraenetic purpose the Holy Spirit is introduced as speaker (3:7–11; 10:15–17). Thus God speaks as the Father to the Son (and vice versa) and God as the Holy Spirit to the church,' 'OT quotations in the New Testament,' *ABD*, 1103.
[627] See further Longenecker, *Biblical Exegesis*, xvii–xix.
[628] Beale and Carson, *Commentary on the New Testament Use of the Old Testament*, xxvi.

conformity with the exegetical teaching and example of Jesus, and along christological lines. In their exegesis there is the interplay of Jewish presuppositions and practices, on the one hand, and Christian commitments and perspectives on the other, which produced a distinctive interpretation of the Old Testament.[629]

This summary, however, does not refer to the role of the Holy Spirit in helping to produce such a 'distinctive interpretation'. Could we say that the differing approaches to interpretation found in the NT are a reflection of the 'diversity of operations'[630] of the Spirit?

One way of giving an overall explanation for the pneumatic component has been in the context of discussions concerning the so-called *sensus plenior* of texts. To quote Snodgrass's résumé of this Catholic originated notion: 'it refers to the "fuller sense" God intended for a text beyond the human author's intention. The New Testament writers are viewed as inspired by the Spirit to understand and apply this fuller sense.'[631] The debates that surround *sensus plenior* cannot be investigated here.[632] But a case can certainly be made for the NT writers, following Jesus' promise in John 16:13, being enabled by the Spirit to interpret the OT by way of what Beale calls 'an expansion [that] does not contravene the integrity of the earlier texts but rather develops them in a way which is consistent with the Old Testament author's understanding of the way in which God interacts with his people—which is the unifying factor between the testaments.'[633] We have already noted some such 'advances of interpretation' earlier that would have been appropriate to the new NT context.

Despite all that has been said, we do nevertheless need to recognise here that the number of *explicit* references to the Holy Spirit's interpretive help in actual citations of the OT by the NT is sparse. It seems clear that the Spirit's assistance and inspiration is often assumed rather than stated.[634] As Dodd has said, '[I]n Acts and epistles it is clear that the fact of life in the Spirit is presupposed.'[635] This, then, leads us to consider what kind of relevant presuppositions lay behind NT exegesis of the OT.

---

[629] Longenecker, *Biblical Exegesis*, 86–87. His words are particularly directed to the preaching of Acts, but could also be said of the NT as a whole. A. T. Hanson highlights Jesus's references to the suffering Servant passages in Isaiah, his teaching about the Kingdom and stress on God's mercy and concludes that 'we can reasonably claim that Jesus did present a certain interpretation of scripture which was normative for the early church': Hanson, *The Living Utterances of God*, 32.
[630] 1 Cor 12:6.
[631] K. Snodgrass, *The Right Doctrine from the Wrong Texts*, 34.
[632] For further reference, see *The Right Doctrine from the Wrong Texts*, 34, 49, 79, 110, 392–93.
[633] Beale, *The Right Doctrine from the Wrong Texts*, 392–393.
[634] It is interesting to note that in the three places in Hebrews where the same verse from Ps 95 (vv. 7-8) is quoted, it is prefaced by 'as the Holy Spirit says' in 3:7, 'as it is said' in 3:15 and 'saying through David' in 4:7, showing that Spirit-given inspiration, if not interpretation, is not always stated but invariably assumed, as is human mediation.
[635] C. H. Dodd, *The Apostolic Preaching and Its Development*, 135. He continues: 'The primitive church, in proclaiming its Gospel to the world, offered its own fellowship and experience as the realization of the Gospel.'

## Presuppositions of NT Writers

Various scholars have attempted to distil the underlying presuppositions and perspectives of the NT writers as they expounded the OT.[636] I shall highlight five:

(a) Charismatic exegesis

(b) Corporate solidarity

(c) Typology and correspondences in history

(d) Eschatological fulfilment

(e) Messianic presence, or Christocentricity

It is true that 'such a precise demarcation of categories would have seemed to [the early Christians] overly pedantic,'[637] but I shall attempt to explain such categories which sound strange to modern ears. In relation to the general theme of this book, the first section is of special relevance to the Spirit's guidance in interpretation, and subsequent sections to the components that make up the NT community's common hermeneutic. The section on typology will also include a discussion of the modern literary concept of 'intertextuality'.

### Charismatic Exegesis

Earlier in this chapter,[638] I referred to an underlying NT assumption that derived from Judaism which identified the Spirit as 'the Spirit of prophecy' that granted charismatic revelation and wisdom. This was particularly relevant to the understanding of the OT, for, as Earle Ellis points out, the NT, especially in the Gospels and Paul, often 'represent the Old Testament as a hidden word of God, a divine mystery whose interpretation is itself a divine gift ($\chi\acute{\alpha}\rho\iota\sigma\mu\alpha$) and act of revelation.'[639] He highlights such an emphasis in the teaching of Jesus.[640] This did not mean that he neglected contemporary exegetical methods in his expositions. But he regarded these as insufficient for understanding unless his hearers also had 'ears to hear',[641] especially his parables.[642] His description of

---

[636] For instance: Longenecker, *Biblical Exegesis*, 76-79; Hanson, *The Living Utterances of God*, 41-42; Beale, *The Right Doctrine from the Wrong Texts*, 392; and Ellis, *The Old Testament in Early Christianity*, 101-120.

[637] Richard Longenecker, 'Who is the Prophet Talking About? Some Reflections on the New Testament's Use of the Old' in Beale, *The Right Doctrine from the Wrong Texts*, 379. These 'presuppositions' can often be found in the same verse, for example in Matt 2:15's use of Hos 11:1, as mentioned in the next paragraph.

[638] See pages 89-90.

[639] *The Old Testament in Early Christianity*, 116. Beale and Carson point to the 'twenty-seven or twenty-eight' instances in the NT of 'the Greek word *mysterion*', saying the concept is much more common than the instances of the actual word suggest. 'Galatians and John, for example, are replete with the theological notion of "mystery" without the word "mystery" being present.' *Commentary on the New Testament Use of the Old Testament*, xxvii.

[640] For instance, in Matt 11:25; 16:17; cf. Luke 24:32.

[641] Matt 11:15; 13:43.

[642] Matt 13:10-17.

these as 'mysteries' (μυστήρια[643]) that need divine unlocking is paralleled in the writings of the Dead Sea community. Its wise teachers or *maskilim* likened their role to that of Daniel with his gift of wisdom and understanding.[644] 'They confess to God that "by your Holy Spirit" you opened knowledge "in the mystery (רז) of your wisdom" (שׂכל).'[645] The gift of revealing mysteries was regarded as the special endowment of the Teacher of Righteousness.[646]

Ellis regards this interpretive emphasis of Jesus and Qumran, namely 'the perception of Scripture as hidden wisdom requiring a charismatic, revelatory exposition',[647] as 'significant antecedents for Paul's thought.'[648] He refers to 'revelation of the mystery' passages like Rom 16:25–26 and Eph 3:3–6, the unveiling/Spirit liberating theme of 2 Cor 3:7–18[649] and the 'pneumatic interpreters'[650] (πνευματικοί) in 1 Cor 2:6–16[651] and 1 Cor 12–14, along with similar conceptions found in the Pastorals[652] and 1 Peter.[653]

Pauline teaching will be discussed in detail in chapter 6, but we will comment here on 1 Pet 1:10–12, particularly as it relates to the Spirit's interpretive role in the OT/NT relationship. Peter declares that it was 'the Spirit of Christ' within the OT prophets who gave them an anticipation of the 'sufferings of Christ and subsequent glories' (v. 11) and 'the Holy Spirit sent from heaven' (v. 12) who enabled the NT preachers to make a proclamation of the events that constituted the evangel. This double reference to the Spirit is significant. As Marshall says, 'the activity of the Spirit thus creates the connection between the giving of prophecy in the past and the interpretation of prophecy now.'[654] Here, then, Peter is articulating a NT assumption concerning the pneumatological functioning that is needed to explain 'the good news' (v. 12) of Christ that unites the focus of both OT and NT.[655] This must be preached [ἐν][656] πνεύματι ἁγίῳ — '"in (the power and character of)" or "by means of"' the Holy Spirit'.[657] According to Ramsey Michaels, 'the dative is not strictly instrumental in the sense that the proclaimers "use" the Spirit as a power under their control but rather "associative" in that it more loosely designates "the accompanying circumstances and manner" ... of the proclamation.'[658] The divine initiative in all the

---

[643] Matt 13:11, esp. ὑμῖν δέδοται γνῶναι τὰ μυστήρια τῆς βασιλείας.
[644] Dan 1:17; 2:47; 5:12; 12:9–10.
[645] Ellis, *The Old Testament in Early Christianity*, 120, quoting from Dead Sea Scroll 1QH 12:12f.
[646] Ibid., 120.
[647] Ellis, *The Old Testament in Early Christianity*, 119.
[648] Ibid, 119.
[649] See chapter 6.
[650] Ellis, *The Old Testament in Early Christianity*, 119.
[651] See chapter 6.
[652] 2 Tim 1:9; Tit 1:2.
[653] 1 Pet 1:11, 20; cf. 2 Pet 3:15.
[654] I. Howard Marshall, *1 Peter* (Leicester: IVP, 1991), 47.
[655] cf. 2 Pet 1:20–21.
[656] Michaels says that 'the simple dative is probably original': J. Ramsey Michaels, *1 Peter:Word Biblical Commentary* (Waco, TX: Word, 1988), 38.
[657] W.A. Grudem, *The First Epistle of Peter* (Leicester: IVP, 1988), 72.
[658] Michaels, *1 Peter*, 47.

'charismatic activity'[659] described in vv. 10–12 is reinforced by the use of passives in v. 12: ἀπεκαλύφθη ('it was revealed'), a verb always used in the NT with reference to divine and never human communication;[660] and ἀποσταλέντι ἀπ' οὐρανοῦ ('sent from heaven'), an expression that recollects the Spirit's coming at Pentecost and that emphasizes the divine authority of the message.

Ellis's concluding summary is fitting:

> The early Christian prophets and teachers explain the Old Testament by what may be called *charismatic exegesis*, or in the words of L. Cerfaux, "spiritual interpretation". Like the teachers of Qumran, they proceed from the conviction that the meaning of the Old Testament is a "mystery" whose "interpretation" can be given not by human reason but only by the Holy Spirit…. This view of their task does not preclude the New Testament writers from using logic or hermeneutical rules and methods. However, it does disclose where the ultimate appeal and authority of their interpretation lie.[661]

## *Corporate Solidarity*

This OT notion was previously discussed[662] in terms of Jewish presuppositions which were shared by the Jewish writers of the NT, so we will not add much more this point. The key development that explains much NT exegesis of the OT is that the early Christians applied corporate solidarity notions to link Israel first with Christ and then with those who belong to him, so that Christ and his church are now viewed as the true Israel, as opposed to Israel according to the flesh. This explains how Matthew, for instance, can apply a verse like Hos 11:1 ('out of Egypt I called my Son') to Jesus in Matt 2:15 to show how the original exodus of the nation found its ultimate realization in Christ.[663]

A corporate solidarity outlook also forms the basis of key elements of Pauline theology, such as his 'in Adam/in Christ' notion of federality and his concept of the church. Sang-Won (Aaron) Son has investigated the possible derivation for Paul's frequent designation of the church as the body of Christ[664] and links it to corporate notions found in the OT.[665] Similarly, the related conceptions of the

---

[659] Michaels, *1 Peter*, 46. 'The whole passage is bound together … by the repeated use of relative pronouns' (37) and verbs of prophetic searching and announcement.
[660] Grudem, *The First Epistle of Peter*, 71.
[661] E. Earle Ellis, 'How the New Testament uses the Old' in *New Testament Interpretation: Essays on Principles and Methods*, ed. I. Howard Marshall (Exeter: Paternoster, 1979), 214.
[662] See pages 90–93.
[663] For further examples of Matthew using events of the nation's history to prefigure Christ, see Matt 2:17–18's quoting Jer 31:15 and Matt 4:14–16 quoting Isa 9:1–2.
[664] 1 Cor 12:27; Eph 1:22–23; 5:30; Col 1:24; Rom 12:5. For the background to 'the body of Christ' concept, see Son, *Corporate Elements in Pauline Anthropology*, 11-117. Also J. D. G. Dunn, *The Theology of Paul the Apostle* (Edinburgh: T&T Clark, 1998), 551.
[665] Son, *Corporate Elements*, 120.

church as the people of God (λαός ... θεοῦ),[666] the temple (ναός),[667] household (οἶκος)[668] and building (οἰκοδομή)[669] all have their own specific OT connotations.[670] In so far as Paul argues that 'in one Spirit we were all baptized into one body,'[671] we can affirm an essential pneumatological condition for incorporation into the Christian church, a church which Paul likens to the true Israel,[672] an Israel that has come into being through a 'new exodus' accomplished through Christ. For Paul, not only Christ but also his church were accordingly Abraham's 'seed'.[673] Paul's understanding of ecclesiology and salvation thus issues from corporate understandings derived from the OT, as enabled by the Spirit who, as the Spirit of unity, links solidarity notions from both OT and NT into a rich and diverse whole.

## Typology, Correspondences in History and Intertextuality

Paul's Adam/Christ link[674] is not just an example of corporate solidarity but it also brings us to the related notion of typology, which, in theological thought, has centred upon the ideas of 'prefigurement'[675] and more recently 'correspondence.' To quote some examples given by Moyise:

> Thus eating and drinking in the wilderness corresponds to participation in the Christian Eucharist (both bring "types" of life). The lifting up of the serpent corresponds to the crucifixion (both bring "types" of healing). The crossing of the Red Sea corresponds to Christian baptism (both bring "types" of deliverance).[676]

David L. Baker has offered the following definitions:

- a *type* is a biblical event, person or institution which serves as an example or pattern for other events, persons or institutions;

---

[666] 2 Cor 6:16; Rom 9:25-26. For a discussion of this and other Pauline images of the church, see Longenecker, 'Paul's Vision of the Church and Community Formation' in *Community Formation in the Early Church and in the Church Today*, ed. R. N. Longenecker (Peabody, MA: Hendrikson, 2002), 75-80. Interestingly Longenecker includes 'The Community of the Spirit' as an important, albeit implied, Pauline image of the church, based on such verses as Gal 3:2, 5 and 1 Thess 4:8; 5:19 and 2 Thess 2:13-14.
[667] 1 Cor 3:16-17, 2 Cor 6:16.
[668] 1 Tim 3:15; cf. 'household of faith' (Gal 6:10) and 'household of God' (Eph 2:19).
[669] 1 Cor 3:9; Eph 2:21; 2 Cor 5:1-2.
[670] Especially, of course, the people of God and the temple. Such metaphors are also found in Qumran.
[671] 1 Cor 12:13. cf. also 1 Cor 3:16; 6:19-20.
[672] Gal 6:16, although some see a reference here to historical Israel rather than the Christian church as a whole. See W. R. Campbell, 'Israel,' in *Dictionary of Paul and His Letters*, ed. Gerald F. Hawthorne, Ralph Martin and Daniel G. Reid (Leicester: IVP, 1993), 441-442.
[673] Gal 3:16, 29. See also Rom 2 and 4.
[674] Rom 5:14 refers to Adam as 'a type of the one who was to come.'
[675] Stemming mainly from the early part of the 20th century: see David L. Baker, *Two Testaments, One Bible*. 2nd ed. (Leicester: Apollos, 1991), 180.
[676] Moyise, *The Old Testament in the New*, 129, referring to 1 Cor 10 and John 3.

- *typology* is the study of types and the historical and theological correspondences between them.⁶⁷⁷

For the NT writers, Christ had many OT individual counterparts whose life and work foreshadowed that of their greater successor.⁶⁷⁸ On a corporate level, Israel itself is seen as a type of Christ, who recapitulates and fulfils the history of Israel, as for instance, portrayed in the temptation narratives.⁶⁷⁹ Paul, as we have just seen, also draws many parallels between the OT and NT church.

This is not the place to enter into discussion with the considerable body of literature written on typology,⁶⁸⁰ but as a general statement it can be said that 'the basis of typology is God's consistent activity in the history of his chosen people.'⁶⁸¹ Ellis distinguishes between two basic types: 'creation typology' (which 'depicts the Messiah and his people as the head of a new creation in which, with a change of key, the original purposes of God are met'⁶⁸²) and 'covenant typology' (in which 'various persons, events and institutions of Old Testament Israel are viewed as prophetic prefigurements of New Testament realities'⁶⁸³). Thus Paul sees the Exodus events as 'types for us' (τύποι ἡμῶν)⁶⁸⁴ and 'were written down for our admonition upon whom the ends of the ages (τὰ τέλη τῶν αἰώνων) have come.'⁶⁸⁵ Such a statement reminds us that the element of historical correspondence in typology is also usually accompanied by an 'escalation or "heightening" (*Steigerung*), by which the divinely ordered prefiguration finds a complement in the subsequent and greater event.'⁶⁸⁶ The ultimate climax of the OT salvation-history of Israel, as typologically retold and reworked in the story of the NT redemption, is portrayed in the heavenly vision of Revelation when 'those who had conquered the beast and its image ... sing the song of Moses, the servant of God, and the song of the Lamb.'⁶⁸⁷

The frequency of typology in the NT leads Ellis, citing Kümmel, to say that '[t]ypological interpretation expresses most clearly "the basic attitude of primitive Christianity toward the Old Testament."'⁶⁸⁸ 'It is not so much a system of interpretation as ... a "spiritual perspective" from which the early Christian

---

⁶⁷⁷ Baker, *Two Testaments, One Bible*, 195.
⁶⁷⁸ See R. T. France, *Jesus and the Old Testament*, 43–50, listing characters such as Jonah, Solomon, David, and Elisha.
⁶⁷⁹ See Matt 4:1–11; Luke 4:1–13. France deduces three implications from Jesus' typology: Jesus is in line with the OT; superior to the OT; and the fulfilment of the OT: France, *Jesus and the Old Testament*, 50–52, 78–79.
⁶⁸⁰ See David L. Baker, *Two Testaments, One Bible*, 179–202.
⁶⁸¹ Baker, *Two Testaments, One Bible*, 195.
⁶⁸² Ellis, *The Old Testament in Early Christianity*, 107. Thus in Rom 5:14, Adam is portrayed as a type of Christ.
⁶⁸³ *The Old Testament in Early Christianity*, 107.
⁶⁸⁴ 1 Cor 10:6.
⁶⁸⁵ 1 Cor 10:11.
⁶⁸⁶ Ellis, *The Old Testament in Early Christianity*, 62–63, citing Leonhard Goppelt: *Typos: The Typological Interpretation of the Old Testament in the New* (Grand Rapids, MI: Eerdmans, 1982), 198–202.
⁶⁸⁷ Rev 15:2, 3.
⁶⁸⁸ E. Earle Ellis, 'How the New Testament uses the Old' in *New Testament Interpretation: Essays on Principles and Methods*, ed. I. Howard Marshall (Exeter: Paternoster, 1979), 210, quoting from W. G. Kümmel's 'Schriftauslengung,' RGG V, 1519.

community viewed itself.'[689] Such an approach enabled the NT community, according to Fishbane, to '"read" one historical moment in terms of another, and thereby project the powerful associations of the past into future images of longing and hope.'[690]

These kind of associative links lie behind the modern literary concept of 'intertextuality' mentioned earlier, although the interaction highlighted here is not so much typological but textual. Intertextuality[691] explores the dynamics of the relationships and meanings derived from words and phrases 'when the "textual matrix" is disturbed by a new text.'[692] As an example, Moyise mentions 'catch-word links'[693] that are exploited by Paul, such as his use of 'reckon' in Rom 4,[694] 'curse' in Gal 3[695] and various 'stone' passages scattered through the NT.[696]

Amongst the many recent scholars who have sought to adapt literary theories of intertextuality to the interpretation of scripture, whether by the original author or the subsequent readers, Richard Hays is regarded as the principal pioneer.[697] For him, 'categories such as midrash, typology, and allegory offer insufficient power of discrimination to probe the distinctive properties of Paul's interpretations.'[698] His influential work *Echoes of Scripture in the Letters of Paul* makes use of literary theories[699] to construct a new 'analytic framework'[700] for reading Paul, whose 'message is rooted in intertextual reflection.'[701] Hays seeks to show how Paul is constantly echoing words and phrases from Israel's Scriptures and investing them with new significations that are particularly relevant to the 'eschatological community'[702] which is the church.[703] Hays

---

[689] Ellis, 'How the New Testament uses the Old', 210–211, quoting from L. Goppelt, *Typos: die typologische Deutung des Alten Testaments im Neuen* (Darmstadt: Wissenschaftliche Buchgesellschaft,1969), 183, 243.

[690] M. Fishbane, *Biblical Interpretation in Ancient Israel* (Oxford: Clarendon, 1985), 371, as quoted in Moyise, *The Old Testament in the New*, 129.

[691] For a discussion of various conceptions of 'intertextuality' in the context of the 'The Scriptures and the Sufficiency of the Canon': see Timothy Ward, *Word and Supplement: Speech Acts, Biblical Texts, and the Sufficiency of Scripture* (Oxford: Oxford University Press, 2002), 210–223.

[692] Moyise, *The Old Testament in the New*, 136.

[693] Moyise, *The Old Testament in the New*, 129.

[694] Where Paul explicates Gen 15:6 ('the Lord reckoned it to him as righteousness') by reference to Ps 32:1–2 ('blessed is the one against whom the Lord will not reckon sin').

[695] Where Paul's use of Deut 21:23 and 27:26 'is not only an interpretation ... [but] also does something to the word 'curse', so that even historically unrelated writings are affected': Moyise, *The Old Testament in the New*, 136.

[696] Such as in Mark 12:10–11; Luke 20:18; Rom 9:33; 1 Pet 2:6–8.

[697] See Samuel Emedi, 'Intertextuality in New Testament Scholarship: Significance, Criteria and the Art of Intertextual Reading,' *Currents in Biblical Research* Vol 14:1 (2015), 8–23.

[698] Hays, *Echoes of Scripture in the Letters of Paul* (New Haven, CT: Yale University Press, 1989), 173. See Hays' explanation of his methodology at xi–xii of the Preface.

[699] Ibid., 173. The appropriateness of using contemporary literary theories to ancient biblical literature has, however, been questioned. For example, Christopher Tuckett, 'Paul, Scripture and Ethics: Some Reflections,' *New Testament Studies* Vol. 46 (2000), 409, fn. 22, says 'I find it difficult to accept that the use of allusive 'echoes' in English poetry is necessarily a good parallel to use for illuminating the way in which Paul's letters might have been read in the first century.'

[700] Hays, *Echoes*, 173.

[701] Ibid., 176.

[702] Ibid., 87.

[703] For example, he refers to 2 Cor 4:6 and detects intertextual echoes from Gen 1:3–4 and Isa 9:2 (9:1 LXX) and concludes that 'Paul's words, quoting neither of these texts but echoing both, fuse Israel's confession of God as

believes that 'we can learn from Paul's example how to read Scripture faithfully'[704] and imaginatively.

Above all, Paul provides us with a model of hermeneutical freedom [by which] we learn to appreciate the metaphorical relation between the text and our own reading of it. Thus, we would begin to cherish the poetics of interpretation, allowing rhetoric to lie down peacefully with grammar and logic. In our own proclamation of the word, we would grant a broad space for the play of echo and allusion, for figurative intertextual conjunctions.[705]

For this to happen, Hays highlights the ecclesial context with an application that is pertinent to the theme of this book:

> The story that Paul finds in Scripture is an account of God's dealing with a people. Consequently, *if we learned from Paul how to read Scripture, we would read it ecclesiocentrically,* as a word for and about the community of faith. Scripture discloses its sense only as the text is brought into correlation with living communities where the Holy Spirit is at work.[706]

Criteria for discerning such pneumatic activity are said to include: 'the obedience of faith'[707] on the part of the reading communities who 'under the guidance of the Spirit ... discover the operation of God's grace among [them] to be prefigured in Scripture';[708] the recognition that the 'original and proper *Sitz im Leben*'[709] for biblical interpretation is 'preaching or (as in Paul's letters) pastoral counsel' that 'thrusts the text's word directly into our faces';[710] the need for 'the community, under the guidance of the Spirit ... to remain open to fresh readings of the same text, through which God will continue to speak';[711] the realization that 'the word that is merely *written* is lifeless until it becomes enfleshed in the community that is being transformed into the image of Christ'[712] by the power of the Spirit;[713] and underlying all this, 'a hermeneutic of trust'[714] (as opposed

---

creator with Israel's hope of a messianic deliverer, thereby implicitly declaring the present illumination of Paul's faith community to be the action of the God who is both creator and redeemer': Hays, *Echoes*, 153.

[704] R. B. Hays, *The Conversion of the Imagination: Paul as Interpreter of Israel's Scripture* (Grand Rapids, MI: Eerdmans, 2005), viii.

[705] Hays, *Echoes*, 186.

[706] Hays, *Echoes*, 184. This conclusion comes partly as a result of his earlier exegesis of 2 Cor 3:6 at 130–131. See chapter 6 for further comment on 2 Cor 3.

[707] Ibid., 184.

[708] Ibid., 184

[709] Ibid., 184

[710] Ibid., 184.

[711] Ibid., 186–187, a deduction that Hays makes from 'recognizing the metaphorical character of intertextual relation [which] prevents us from literalizing or absolutizing Paul's reading', 186.

[712] From Hays's summary of chapter four of *Echoes* in R. B. Hays, 'Echoes and Intertextuality: On the Role of Scripture in Paul's Theology' in *Paul and the Scriptures of Israel*, ed. C. A. Evans and J. A. Sanders (Sheffield: Sheffield Academic Press, 1993), 45.

[713] Hays derives this point from 2 Cor 3, which he also uses to elucidate a key 'hermeneutical constraint' to operate as a 'check against arbitrariness and error': 'no reading of Scripture can be legitimate ... if it fails to shape the readers into a community that embodies the love of God as shown forth in Christ' *Echoes*, 191.

[714] Hays, *The Conversion of the Imagination*, 197.

to one of 'suspicion') that does not nevertheless exclude critical enquiry but recognizes that fallen minds need constant powerful transformation 'through reading Scripture receptively and trustingly with the aid of the Holy Spirit.'[715]

These are challenging points for every preacher and congregation, particularly the emphasis upon the Christ-shaping role of the Spirit in the interpreting community. Hays' ecclesiocentric reading of Paul has, however, been criticized for an over-emphasis upon the imaginative interpretive role of the readers that detracts from notions of textual objectivity.[716] Beker, for instance, detects a tendency towards the fusion of Word and Spirit: 'does this mean that the Word has now lost its critical function because it has reached its true fulfilment in a transformed church—a church which embodies the Spirit completely?'[717] Hays' homing in on Paul's evocative use of words and literary links, however, even if at times overstated,[718] gives a useful new dimension to OT/NT studies, and in particular 'the signifying power of intertextual figuration.'[719]

Speaking in more general terms of biblical interpretive approaches that centre on verbal and other correspondences, believers would say that it is a peculiar prerogative of the Spirit to direct the use of literary techniques such as pun, imitation, echo, allusion, and word play into analogies and meanings that are both edifying and truthful. Such methods are regularly used by preachers,[720] prayer-warriors,[721] and hymn writers,[722] alongside typological and allegorical approaches.

These can operate as an effective and enlightening form of 'spiritual shorthand'. If overused or misused, however, they can degenerate into a jargon that ceases to move the believer or mystifies the average biblically illiterate person of today. And the dangers of 'over-spiritualization' are ever real.[723]

---

[715] Ibid.,198.
[716] For example: 'texts have meaning only as they are read and used by communities of readers': Hays, *Echoes*, 189.
[717] J. C. Beker, 'Echoes and Intertextuality: On the Role of Scripture in Paul's Theology' in *Paul and the Scriptures of Israel*, 69. This book contains a detailed summary and critique of Hay's *Echoes* at 42–96. Hays accepts some of the criticisms of his original thesis, for example that Paul's hermeneutic can be considered just as much 'theocentric' as it is 'ecclesiocentric' (77–78). Hays, *The Conversion of the Imagination*, 163–189, reprints pages 70–96 of this book.
[718] As Longenecker says, following J. C. Beker's critique, 'which [echoes of the OT] were in the mind of Paul himself? Which did the apostle presuppose were also in the minds of his readers? And which could be said to be only in the mind of Professor Hays...?' *Biblical Exegesis*, xv. Longenecker himself prefers to focus on explicit OT quotations for his primary material rather than the more open ended 'allusions' the choice and supposed meaning of which lack necessary controls. Tuckett, in 'Paul, Scripture and Ethics: Some Reflections', 403–424, shows also how arguments that appeal for a meaning that depend on the larger context can be overplayed, especially if the initial readers of, say, the relevant letter of Paul, were Gentiles not familiar with Jewish Scriptures.
[719] Hays, *Paul and the Scriptures of Israel*, 43.
[720] As a list of many sermon titles will show!
[721] Such as 'Send the mercy drops, Lord!', or 'cover them with the blood!'
[722] Such as William Cowper's: 'There is a fountain filled with blood, Drawn from Immanuel's veins, And sinners, plunged beneath that flood, Lose all their guilty stains' *Christian Hymns* (Bridgend: Evangelical Movement of Wales, 1977), No. 198.
[723] David L. Baker says that 'perhaps the most common misuse of typology is to find correspondences in trivial details. Rahab's scarlet cord has been said to be a type of the death of Christ and the axe Elisha retrieved from the

## Eschatological Fulfilment

As already noted, Paul typologically refers to the events of the Exodus in 1 Cor 10:1–10 ('and the Rock was Christ'[724]) and concludes that 'they were written down for our instruction, on whom the end of the ages has come.'[725] This shows us that the implicit element of 'heightening' in typology leads logically into a conviction about eschatology. The NT writers, as they referred back to the events, promises, and prophecies of the OT, wrote as those who were acutely conscious that they were living in the age of fulfilment: 'but *in these last days* he has spoken to us *by his Son*.'(Heb 1:2a). With the coming of Jesus as Messiah 'the decisive event had occurred, and, in a sense, all else was epilogue.'[726]

As the Spirit came at Pentecost, Peter was able to declare[727] that 'the last days' had arrived, as per Joel's prophecy. And it was this decisive *experience* of the Spirit as an 'eschatological reality'[728] that caused the early church continually to turn to the OT to interpret their experience. Hence Fee's point in relation to Paul:

> Thus for Paul the line is not from the Old Testament to the New, but from his experience of the Spirit as the empowering presence of God back to the Old.... The lavish outpouring of the Spirit on him and his churches was the evidence for Paul that the end had begun. Thus Paul's understanding is not influenced by the literature of the period; it is primarily influenced by the experience itself.[729]

Not everyone would downplay the influence of contemporary literature and thinking upon Paul's thought forms quite so much as this. Indeed, the NT writers did share a number of eschatological convictions with contemporary apocalyptic Judaism, especially as expressed by the communities of Qumran and John the Baptist.[730] But NT eschatology radically departed from contemporary Jewish conceptions in the belief that the kingdom of God had already arrived, as opposed to its being imminently anticipated, and also in the notion of a 'two-stage consummation.'[731] And the period between the first and second comings was regarded pre-eminently as the age of the Spirit in which 'everyone who calls on the Lord shall be saved.'[732]

---

river, a type of Jesus' cross (1 Clement 12: Justin, *Dialogue*,86), but there is no historical or theological correspondence between these things,' *Two Testaments, One Bible*, 193.

[724] 1 Cor 10:4.
[725] 1 Cor 10:11.
[726] Longenecker, *Biblical Exegesis*, 79.
[727] Acts 2:16, citing Joel 2:2832.
[728] G. D. Fee, *God's Empowering Presence* (Peabody, MA: Hendricksen, 1994), 913. For more on the eschatological aspect of the Spirit's operations, see chapter 2 of this book.
[729] *God's Empowering Presence*, 915.
[730] These are listed in Ellis, *The Old Testament in Early Christianity*, 102.
[731] Ellis, *The Old Testament in Early Christianity*, 103. See 103-105 for his summary of 'Christian Distinctives'.
[732] Peter in Acts 2:21, quoting from Joel 2:32.

The prospect of final judgment, 'existentially "near" but chronologically indefinite,'[733] gave an urgent emphasis in Paul and the NT writers upon the 'now' as 'the day of salvation', as well as upon the need to be ethically ready as the great 'day of the Lord' approached, along with the renewal of the whole of creation.[734] Such a perspective that stretches from the soteriological immediacy of the present to the glorious transformation of the ultimate future shaped the whole interpretive outlook of the NT writers as they read Scripture with the aid of the same Spirit who empowers the whole redemptive and recreative process. Hays puts the ensuing challenge to us:

> *If we learned from Paul how to read Scripture, we would read as participants in the eschatological drama of redemption....* Can we join with Paul in regarding ourselves as people of the endtime? ... [For our] consciousness of temporality will shape the way in which the text is read.[735]

Such a reading is profoundly corporate in its essential nature.

## *Messianic Presence, or Christocentricity*

The Christocentric lens through which the NT writers interpreted the OT has been mentioned several times in this chapter. Jesus himself inspired and taught such a focus, as we have seen.[736] Once again the pneumatic element was a vital element for 'the living presence of Christ, through his Spirit, was considered to be a determining factor in all their [viz. the earliest believers'] biblical exegesis.'[737] As they sat down to write what later came to be known as the New Testament, the Apostles would no doubt have had in their minds the promise and purpose of the *Paraclete*, as foretold by Jesus: 'he will glorify me, for he will take what is mine and declare it to you.'[738]

Such guidance was exegetically vital if the Scriptures were to be interpreted aright. For as A. T. Hanson has pointed out, 'everyone in the Jewish world agreed that it was a pious and profitable occupation to "search the scriptures"':[739] Pharisees to find applications of the Torah; Qumran sectaries to identify prophecies about their destiny; Philo in his search for allegorical expressions of truth; and so on. But as John indicates, such searching was misdirected, unless it had Christ as its end. For, as Jesus said of his Jewish contemporaries, 'You search the Scriptures because you think that in them you have eternal life; and it is they that bear witness to me (καὶ ἐκεῖναί εἰσιν αἱ μαρτυροῦσαι περὶ ἐμοῦ), yet

---

[733] Ellis, *The Old Testament in Early Christianity*, 103.
[734] Rom 8:18-25.
[735] Hays, *Echoes*, 185 [italics his].
[736] See pages 96-104 and verses like Luke 24:27, 45-46; cf. Acts 8:34-35.
[737] Longenecker, *Biblical Exegesis*, 79.
[738] John 16:14 NIV.
[739] Hanson, *The Living Utterances of God*, 42.

you refuse to come to me to have life.'[740] Enshrined in this verse, says Carson, is 'a comprehensive hermeneutical key. By predictive prophecy, by type, by revelatory event and by anticipatory statute, what we call the Old Testament is understood to point to Christ, his ministry, his teaching, his death and resurrection.'[741]

## Conclusion to the Chapter

In this chapter I have sought to investigate how the NT writers were guided by the Spirit as a community to interpret Scripture. '[T]he character of the NT activity,' says Marshall, 'suggests the development of communally known and practised methods of understanding....'[742] We began to explore this activity by seeing how contemporary Jewish conceptions of the Spirit as the 'Spirit of prophecy', linked in with 'corporate solidarity' notions, would have shaped the interpretive endeavours of the NT writers. The commonality of their approach was further suggested by Dodd's *testimonia* thesis, namely their preference for distinct exegetical 'textual "fields"',[743] the choice of which can be traced back to the one who was 'full of the Spirit.' Jesus modeled and taught his disciples Spirit-inspired exegesis of Scripture in a unique way that both embraced and challenged contemporary Jewish methods, as exemplified in his teaching concerning the kingdom. His promised legacy of the Holy Spirit enabled the NT community to make 'advances in the interpretation of Scripture',[744] achieving what could also be described as a *sensus plenior* of the texts.

Further understanding of NT writers' exegesis of the OT can be gained by an appreciation of their interpretive presuppositions. Of these, 'charismatic exegesis' demonstrated a fundamental reliance upon the enlightenment of the Spirit, which is assumed if not always expressed. 'Corporate solidarity' helped explain the oscillation of application between individuals and groups and is relevant to those of us who live in a society dominated by Western individualism. The note of eschatological fulfilment afforded by the arrival of the Spirit produced an exegesis in the atmosphere of the 'endtimes'—again, relevant for a contemporary society bent on the materialistic enjoyment of the present. Intertextual analysis evinced what Hays calls an 'ecclesiocentric' hermeneutic that highlights the role of the Spirit in the interpreting community. The Christocentric emphasis points to the one of whom the Scriptures chiefly speak. All this means that the NT interpreters continue to provide us with a common Spirit-given framework with which to interpret Scripture, both OT and NT.

---

[740] John 5:39–40.
[741] D. A. Carson, *The Gospel According to John* (Leicester: IVP, 1991), 263.
[742] I. Howard Marshall, a remark made in relation to his discussion of Stendhal's *School of St Matthew*, 2nd ed. (XXX: XXX, 1968) in *It is Written: Scripture Citing Scripture*, 11.
[743] I. Howard Marshall, 'An Assessment of Recent Developments' in *It is Written: Scripture Citing Scripture*, 5.
[744] Longenecker, *Biblical Exegesis*, 59.

In matters of more detail, however, there will always be room for differences on just how far the methods of the NT interpreters provide us with a model to follow. On the one hand, there are those like Longenecker who argue that the peculiar first-century Jewish-based exegetical methodology of the NT writers is not generally appropriate for today.

> What the New Testament presents to us in setting out the exegetical practices of the early Christians is how the gospel was contextualized in that day and for those audiences. We can appreciate something of how appropriate such methods were for the conveyance of the gospel then ... and we can learn from their exegetical methods how to contextualize that same gospel in our own day. But let us admit that we cannot possibly reproduce the revelatory stance of pesher interpretation, nor the atomistic manipulations of midrash, nor the circumstantial or *ad hominem* thrusts of a particular polemic of that day—nor should we try.[745]

On the other hand, others argue that the Christocentric and Spirit-inspired hermeneutic of the NT radically differentiated it from the contemporary Judaism and gives it a timeless applicability. Beale,[746] for instance, argues that the NT only rarely cites the OT in non-contextual ways,[747] if one looks at the larger OT context from which the relevant text is quoted; the wider and 'unparalleled redemptive-historical perspective on the OT that Jesus and the apostles [had] in relation to their own situation'[748] ('as unified by an omnipotent and wise design'[749]); and the above-mentioned presuppositions shared by the NT writers. Thus he concludes:

> If the contemporary church cannot exegete and do theology like the apostles did, how can it feel corporately at one with them in the theological process? Furthermore, if Jesus and the apostles were impoverished in their exegetical and theological method and only divine inspiration salvaged their conclusions, then the intellectual and apologetic foundation of our faith is seriously eroded.[750]

Where one strikes the balance between the historical contingency and eternal relevance of Scripture and its interpretive methods will always be a matter for debate. Some of the OT applications made by the NT apostolic writers under the

---

[745] Longenecker, 'Who is the Prophet talking about?' in *The Right Doctrine from the Wrong Texts*, 385. See also Longenecker's *Biblical Exegesis*, xxxiv–xxxviii. Here, under the heading, 'Can we Reproduce the Exegesis of the New Testament?' Longenecker, *contra* Hays, argues for cultural conditionedness of Scripture and the need to 'recontextualise' its essential message.

[746] Beale, 'Did Jesus and His Followers Preach the Right Doctrine from the Wrong Texts? An examination of the Presuppositions of Jesus' and the Apostles' Exegetical Method' in *The Right Doctrine from the Wrong Texts*, 387–405.

[747] Ibid., , 389.

[748] Ibid., 391.

[749] Ibid., 394. He goes on to mention the typological perspective of the NT writers (p. 395).

[750] Ibid., *The Right Doctrine from the Wrong Texts*, 404.

inspiration of the Spirit within living tradition of the words and example of Jesus himself undoubtedly go beyond what most of us would dare to do today. In any event, the completed word of the canon means that 'we also have a more sure word of prophecy'[751] from which we have an adequate OT dispensary chosen by the NT writers from which to form our theology. We therefore, need to be wary of digging out further OT texts to demonstrate typological, allegorical, or prophetic links with Christ, the Christian message and its contemporary application in ways that the NT writers would never have envisaged.

This is not to say that the Spirit will not yet throw ever new light on old truth, filling out the essential meaning of Scripture in ways that are appropriate for the context and culture in which it is being used. Also, the way in which the NT writers constantly expressed themselves in OT concepts and phraseology reminds us of the need to think in the challenging categories of Scripture, to be constantly 'transformed by the renewing of our minds', in a spirit of non-conformity with the world.[752] The Holy Spirit is frequently in dialectical confrontation with the self-centred, restless spirit of this age; but through the alternative community which is the church, Christians, with the Spirit's help, can find a way of interpreting Scripture, history and reality that forms an integrated and meaningful whole, and one that finds its beginning and ending in Christ.

---

[751] 2 Pet 1:19a AV.
[752] Rom 12:2.

# PART 2

## THE PNEUMATOLOGICAL HERMENEUTICS OF THE NEW TESTAMENT COMMUNITY

*WITH SPECIAL REFERENCE TO THE JOHANNINE, LUKAN AND PAULINE LITERATURE.*

# INTRODUCTION TO PART 2

In Part I, 'Pneumatology, Hermeneutics and Koinonia', I sought to establish a theological basis for our study. Chapter 1, 'The Holy Spirit in Biblical Interpretation', argued that the role assigned to the Spirit in traditional thought has too often excluded a corporate perspective and in modern hermeneutics has often been marginalized. Having given some definitions of terms, I then highlighted some trends to individualism in biblical interpretation and outlined the case for a more corporate approach, along with some necessary caveats. Chapter 2, 'The *Koinonia* of the Spirit', explored the Pauline concept of the χοινωνία/fellowship of the Holy Spirit as a basis for biblical interpretation in four dimensions: the *trinitarian* that connects it with the dynamic of trinitarian relationship; the *dialogical* that can create a *koinonia* of understanding through conflict and judgment; the *historical* that links it with the saints of the past; and the *eschatological* which underlines present fulfilment in Christ in tension with ultimate understanding in glory. Chapter 3, 'The Spirit at the Interface of the Old Testament and the New Testament', argued that the way the New Testament writers interpreted the Old Testament revealed communal methods of interpretation that were informed by Jewish pneumatic and solidarity notions and shaped by Jesus' own Spirit-given example and his Holy Spirit legacy. Further weight for this came from Dodd's *testimonia* thesis and a consideration of the presuppositions of the New Testament interpretive community, which include 'charismatic exegesis.' I argued that the New Testament interpreters continue to provide a model of a common Spirit-given framework within which to interpret Scripture, although there was understandable debate as to how far all the details of their approach can still be followed today.

Here in Part 2, I embark on a more specific and detailed study of passages within the New Testament that reveal this 'Spirit through community' hermeneutic at work. Representative samples will be taken from John, Luke/Acts and Paul, following Turner's view that they 'provide the most profound theologies of the Spirit in the NT.'[753] The specific passages from these three corpora have been chosen either (a) because they contain specific examples of how Old Testament Scripture is being interpreted by members of the New Testament community, with the Spirit's help, or (b) because they speak of the Spirit's work of revelation/interpretation in a more general way, or because of a combination of both (a) and (b).

I will not seek to engage in a full discussion as to the theology or provenance of the biblical literature chosen. Critical scholarship has commonly attributed authorship or editing of Scripture to the various sections of the early Christian community, a possibility which could provide one a way into our study. Rather

---

[753] M. M. B. Turner, 'Holy Spirit' in T. Desmond Alexander et al, eds., *New Dictionary of Biblical Theology* (Leicester: IVP, 2000), 557.

than adopt this rather speculative approach, however, I will make a working assumption of apostolic authorship, taking the writers as representatives of the New Testament community.

A number of the verses from the passages chosen have already been referred to in Part 1. In the more detailed analysis I adopt in Part 2, I will at times supplement the traditional historical-grammatico approach by making use of more 'synchronic' methods of exegesis, such as found in 'intertextual', rhetorical and narrative approaches. I will also sometimes refer to the four dimensions of the *koinonia* of the Spirit (trinitarian, dialogical, historical and eschatological) that were suggested in chapter 2. My biblical exegesis, however, will not be comprehensive, but seek only to extract those elements that are particularly pertinent to our theme. In what ways do the writings of these three very different types of New Testament literature show the Holy Spirit guiding the Christian community in its custodianship and interpretation of Scripture?

In chapter 4, I will begin our journey in the Upper Room in the last week of Jesus' earthly ministry, looking at verses in John 14-16 that narrate Jesus' promise of the Spirit, or more accurately the Paraclete, to his troubled disciples following his departure. In subsequent chapters, the New Testament passages I look at can be read as a description of the fulfilment of this promise of the Paraclete being worked out in the life and Scriptural interpretations of the early Church. Hence Acts describes the Spirit-driven hermeneutics of the first Christian community (chapter 5). This will be followed by an investigation to see how Paul demonstrates a 'Spirit through community' hermeneutic in selected passages from his letters (chapter 6). The end of the Pauline section will include a section on the Pastoral letters. Their authorship is disputed in scholarly circles, but as one of the later New Testament writings the Pastorals can be linked with 1 John, the subject of chapter 7, to illustrate more particularly the 'custodianship' aspect of the Spirit's work in relation to Scripture. Chapter 8 will conclude the book with a summary of its arguments and some suggestions for their implications, not just for biblical hermeneutics, but also for the doctrine, use and custodianship of Scripture in the life and witness of the Church today.

# CHAPTER FOUR: THE PROMISE OF THE PARACLETE (JOHN 14–16)

## Introduction

Shortly before he died, Jesus reassured his troubled disciples that he would not leave them on their own, but would bequeath to them a precious legacy—the Holy Spirit, described in John 14–16 as ὁ παράκλητος (the Paraclete). Before I explore the hermeneutical relevance of this promise, I need to explain my approach to the communal aspect of this promise. This is because I am writing upon the assumption that the gospel was written by the Apostle John, the son of Zebedee, and not by some 'Johannine community.'

### *Methodological Approach to 'Community'*

As a prelude to my examination of John 14–16, I need, then, to mention what could have been one route into the way the 'community' aspect of the gospel material is handled, in light of the various viewpoints upon the relationship between the gospels and the communites in which they were formed and read. According to Richard Bauckham, the 'consensus'[754] of critical scholarship over the last century has been that the four canonical gospels were written for, and shaped by, the needs of (if not the hands of) specific early Christian communities—Matthean, Markan, Lukan, and Johannine. Elaborate reconstructions have been made of such communities,[755] and such reconstructions could well have been used in this chapter as a basis for an examination of a 'community-based' hermeneutic.

This critical consensus, however, has been fundamentally challenged by Bauckham and others who claim that 'the Gospels were written for general circulation around the churches and so envisaged a very general Christian audience.'[756] Without going into the details of the debate, it is interesting that even supporters of the critical approach have stated that their community reconstructions need to be regarded in terms of 'conjecture or historical imagination.'[757] Against these, Bauckham speaks of 'the early Christian

---

[754] R. Bauckham in R. Bauckham, ed., *The Gospels for All Christians: Rethinking the Gospel Audiences* (Edinburgh: T&T Clark, 1998), 1.

[755] See, for example, Culpepper's designation of 'The Gospel and Letters as the Literature of a Community': R. Alan Culpepper, *The Gospel and Letters of John* (Nashville, TN: Abingdon, 1998), 42. In this chapter he proposes a reconstruction of the 'Johannine community' divided into five periods, centered around developments that issued from rejection from the Jewish synagogue, the 'death of the Beloved Disciple' and subsequent doctrinal schism in the second generation church.

[756] R. Bauckham, *The Gospels for All Christians: Rethinking the Gospel Audiences*, 1. For some counter-arguments, see David C. Sim, 'The Gospel for All Christians? A Response to Richard Bauckham', *JSNT* 84 (2001), 3–27.

[757] To quote Culpepper, an actual proponent of the Johannine community: Culpepper, *The Gospel and Letters of John*, 54.

movement as a network of communities in constant communication'[758] in what Thompson calls 'the Holy Internet'.[759] In further support of Bauckham, Burridge argues that the literary genre of the Gospels is that of ancient biography (βίος[760]) which should accordingly be read primarily with reference to a person (Jesus) rather than a community,[761] whilst Watson contends that to read the Gospels purely as narratives concerning a community is to practise 'an allegorical reading strategy ... that systematically downplays and circumvents the literal sense of the text.'[762]

It is this literal concern with the text and its Christocentric focus that shall inform my approach to the text. At the same time I shall take care not to deny that the gospels do indeed reflect community problems and traditions.[763]

## Relevance of John 14–16 to the Subject of this Book

Eschewing, then, hypothetical reconstructions of a 'Johannine community',[764] I shall investigate another kind of 'community' focus brought out in the gospel of John which is derived from the very words of Jesus himself, as recorded in chapters 14–16. His promises concerning the Spirit, here distinctively called the Paraclete (ὁ παράκλητος), were made to the group of his disciples, rather than any one individual. The disciples were in a state of distress in view of the imminent departure of their Master and Teacher. Jesus's 'Farewell Discourse(s)' to them contain some reassuring and distinctive Johannine material concerning Christ's legacy of the Holy Spirit to the church.[765]

These promises were originally given to the disciples in an oral rather than written form and were related by Jesus, *inter alia*, to the remembrance (14:26) and understanding (16:13) of his teaching. To that extent, they logically and temporally precede the subject matter of this book with its concern that the interpretation of Scripture should be attempted only with the help of the Spirit.

---

[758] Bauckham, *The Gospel for All Christians*, 43.
[759] M. B. Thompson, *The Gospel for All Christians*, 49.
[760] R. A. Burridge, *What are the Gospels? A Comparison with Graeco-Roman Biography* (Cambridge: Cambridge University Press, 1992), 258.
[761] R. A. Burridge, 'About People, by People, for People: Gospel Genre and Audiences' in Bauckham, ed., *The Gospel for All Christians*, 113–145. The gospels were 'written to explain the person of Jesus to individuals and groups in many places, rather than just one specific sectarian community in one city', 144.
[762] F. Watson, as cited in *The Gospel for All Christians*, 7.
[763] Burridge, *The Gospel for All Christians*, 144.
[764] This is not to deny that there were in all probability communities of Christians in close association with the Johannine writer.
[765] There is, of course, teaching about the Spirit in other parts of John's Gospel, when the Spirit is referred to as πνεῦμα rather than παράκλητος (for example, John 3:4–5; 7:37–38 and 20:22). Felix Porsch, however, has convincingly argued that the two conceptions of the Spirit are essentially homogeneous ('*eine einheitliche Vorstellung*', in *Pneuma und Wort: Ein exegetischer Beitrag zur Pneumatologie des Johannesevangeliums* (Frankfurt, 1974), 3, as referred to in J. Ashton *Understanding the Fourth Gospel* (Oxford: Clarendon, 1993), 420. Moreover, the Paraclete passages represent the most relevant pneumatological passages of John for the purpose of this book.

But they have fundamental and foundational relevance nevertheless. For, as Jackman says, 'the major part of the fulfilment of [these promises] lay in the Spirit's inspiration of the apostles as they wrote the New Testament Scriptures'[766] (cf. John 20:30–31). But then 'they also have a continuing, subsidiary fulfilment in the work of the Spirit teaching every generation of believers the truth.'[767] For us, this continuing aspect is of perennial importance. It will be pursued in this chapter as I seek to extend the application of these verses to the Spirit's help to the church in the custodianship and interpretation of the truth of scripture—the scripture in which Jesus's promise of the Paraclete is now enshrined.

## Spirit, Individual and Community in John

In earlier chapters of the gospel, John has spoken of the ministry of the Spirit in the life of the individual believer—in regeneration ('unless one is born of water and the Spirit'[768]) and renewal ('out of his heart will flow rivers of living water'[769]). As Thompson says, 'certainly the Gospel of John emphasizes the necessity of the individual appropriation of faith in God through Jesus Christ.'[770] There is, indeed, a special emphasis in John concerning Jesus's encounters with individuals.[771] His portrayal of the Christian life, however, is far from individualistic, as is sometimes claimed.

To quote Thompson again, 'one cannot ... speak of the role of the Paraclete without also turning to the Gospel's vision of the community in which the Paraclete plays such a central role.'[772] Hence from the beginning, Nathanael recognises Jesus as 'the King of Israel',[773] and John subsequently in his gospel develops Old Testament imagery to describe that fellowship of believers which constitutes the church:[774] the new temple,[775] the new Israel,[776] the flock of the good shepherd[777] and the branches of the true vine.[778] Each of these metaphors

---

[766] D. Jackman, *Spirit of Truth: Unlocking the Bible's Teaching on the Holy Spirit* (Fearn: Christian Focus, 2006), 57. He is referring specifically to the 'guide you into all truth' promise in John 16:13, but, of course, the 'bring to your remembrance' promise of 14:26 is equally relevant.
[767] Ibid., 57.
[768] John 3:4–5.
[769] John 7:37–38.
[770] M. M. Thompson, 'Gospel of John', section 4:4 'The Community and the Paraclete' in J. B. Green, S. McKnight & I. Howard Marshall, eds., *Dictionary of Jesus and the Gospels* (Leicester: IVP, 1992), 382.
[771] Stephen Smalley, for instance, refers to Jesus's sayings in John 4:13f, 5:25–29 and 6:43–51 and to the fact that four of the seven Johannine signs involve individual people: chapter 4 (official's son), chapter 5 (the sick man), chapter 9 (the blind man) and chapter 11 (Lazarus): Stephen Smalley, *John: Evangelist and Interpreter* (Exeter: Paternoster, 1978), 234.
[772] Thompson, 'The Community and the Paraclete', 382.
[773] John 1:49.
[774] Though John never uses the term 'church' (ἐκκλησία) as such.
[775] John 2:13–22; cf. Ezek 37:27f.
[776] John 8:31–58; cf. Isa 63:16 (children of Abraham).
[777] John 10:14–16; cf. Ps 80:1 and Ezek 34.
[778] John 15:1, 5; cf. Ps 80:8–19 and Isa 5:1–7.

contains both the individual and corporate aspects involved in belonging both to Christ and his people. Thus Smalley concludes:

> the theology of the church in John is nicely balanced between the one and the many.... This theme is focussed in the Twelve, who appear under that title on only two occasions in John (6:67, 70 and 20:24), but are present throughout as the seminal nucleus of the new community. The disciples are called to follow Jesus individually; yet they believe in him together, and after the resurrection experience corporately the indwelling and activity of the Spirit-Paraclete.[779]

## The Paraclete Sayings

This, then, brings us to the subject of the Paraclete sayings in John 14–16 which, as Barrett rightly says, have as '[their] *Sitz im Leben* ... the church.'[780] Here, indeed, are pneumatological promises that are primarily corporate in nature, being made to the group of disciples (addressed in the plural form of 'you') that constituted the embryonic Christian church. Here are the five relevant sayings:

### John 14:15–18

[15] If you love me, you will keep my commandments. [16] And I will ask the Father, and he will give you another Helper, to be with you forever, [17] even the Spirit of truth, whom the world cannot receive, because it neither sees him nor knows him. You know him, for he dwells with you and will be in you. [18] I will not leave you desolate as orphans; I will come to you.

### John 14:25–26

[25] These things I have spoken to you while I am still with you. [26] But the Helper, the Holy Spirit, whom the Father will send in my name, he will teach you all things, and bring to your remembrance all that I have said to you.

### John 15:26–27

[26] But when the Helper comes, whom I will send to you from the Father, the Spirit of truth, who proceeds from the Father, he will bear witness about me. [27] And you also will bear witness, because you have been with me from the beginning.

### John 16:7–11

[7] Nevertheless I tell you the truth: it is to your advantage that I go away, for if I do not go away, the Helper will not come to you. But if I go, I will send him to

---

[779] Smalley, *John: Evangelist and Interpreter*, 234.
[780] C. K. Barrett, *The Gospel According to St John: An Introduction with Commentary and Notes on the Greek Text* (London: SPCK, 1978), 90.

you. ⁸ And when he comes, he will convict the world concerning sin and righteousness and judgment: ⁹ concerning sin, because they do not believe in me; ¹⁰ concerning righteousness, because I go to the Father, and you will see me no longer; ¹¹ concerning judgment, because the ruler of this world is judged.

## John 16:12–15

¹² I still have many things to say to you, but you cannot bear them now. ¹³ When the Spirit of truth comes, he will guide you into all the truth, for he will not speak on his own authority, but whatever he hears he will speak, and he will declare to you the things that are to come. ¹⁴ He will glorify me, for he will take what is mine and declare it to you. ¹⁵ All that the Father has is mine; therefore I said that he will take what is mine and declare it to you.

Before embarking on a study of these passages, I will first make a number of general points concerning the Spirit's special designation as 'Paraclete' here.

## The Nature of the Paraclete

The Paraclete, ὁ παράκλητος—a passive verbal adjective, lit. 'one called alongside' [i.e. to help]—is a word found only in the Johannine literature in the New Testament, and is used four times of the Holy Spirit in the gospel (14:16,26; 15:26; 16:7) and once of Jesus in the epistle (1 John 2:1).[781] Jackman says that the literal meaning of the term Paraclete 'corresponds exactly to the Latin *advocatus*.'[782] This claim will now be elaborated upon in the first of five points which I shall make concerning the meaning and use of the term.

### (a) The Legal Aspect as 'Advocate'

From the numerous studies that have been made of the word 'Paraclete' (παράκλητος),[783] the general consensus seems to be that it has a primarily, but not exclusively, legal connotation, for which the most appropriate English translation would be 'advocate.'[784] Hence Lochlan Shelfer's conclusion, having surveyed the use of παράκλητος in the Greek/Roman background of the New Testament era: 'the term is a precise calque for the Latin legal term *advocatus*, meaning a person of high social standing who speaks on behalf of a defendant

---

[781] Here, the term relates to Jesus' heavenly intercession for sinners.
[782] D. Jackman, *Spirit of Truth*, 130.
[783] See, for instance, R. E. Brown, *The Gospel According to John* Volume 2 (xiii–xxi) (London: Geoffrey Chapman, 1966), Appendix V, 1135–1144; Johannes Behm, 'Παράκλητος' in Vol. V of Kittel's *Theological Dictionary of the New Testament*, 800–814; Gary M. Burge, *The Anointed Community: The Holy Spirit in the Johannine Tradition* (Grand Rapids, MI: Eerdmans, 1987), 1–41; various works cited in Tricia Gates Brown, *Spirit in the Writings of John* (London/New York: T&T Clark, 2003).
[784] 'The primary meaning of the Greek word is "legal assistant, advocate"': Barrett, *The Gospel According to St John*, 462. Such person would help someone in court, if not as an advocate, then as a witness or representative.

in a court of law before a judge.'[785] This, however, should not cause us to limit his role to one which is akin to that of a professional legal representative today, for the *advocatus*, as is reflected in intertestamental Judaism, was 'a very nuanced figure,'[786] and so the word has other connotations.[787] Indeed, Tricia Gates Brown has recently claimed that the Paraclete's role is better conceived not in terms of forensic categories, but more generally in terms of the anthropological model of the ancient Mediterranean 'broker' who 'mediated between higher and lower orders while maintaining their separateness, bringing the more and less powerful into contact for personal benefit.'[788]

Whether this figure was in the back of the evangelist's mind or not, the difficulty of an adequate translation for παράκλητος is reflected in the different Bible versions: 'comforter' (AV), 'helper' (GNB, ESB), or 'counsellor' (NIV); 'exhorter' and 'encourager' have also been suggested.[789] None of these English terms, however, adequately accounts for Jesus's use of the term in John's Gospel, which extends to didactic, revelatory, and interpretive functions, as shall be seen later. In so far, however, as these were and are frequently carried out against the backdrop of a hostile world, as Jesus's words declare[790] and the background to the gospel suggests,[791] I would concur with Turner that the word 'advocate' 'is probably the most secure rendering.'[792]

## (b) The Paraclete as the Alter Ego[793] ('Other I') of Jesus[794]

Jesus, in his very first reference to the Spirit as the Paraclete, spoke of him in 14:16 as 'another Paraclete' (ἄλλον παράκλητον) with the necessary implication that he himself was the first Paraclete. Turner points out that 'the Greek *allos* regularly (not always) means "another (of the *same* kind)", in contrast to *heteros*

---

[785] Lochlan Shelfer, 'The Legal Precision of the Term "παράκλητος"' *JSNT* 32.2 (2009), 131.

[786] Burge, *Anointed Community*, 223.

[787] 'The puzzle of the combination of the kerygmatic and forensic features in the picture of the Spirit-Paraclete is solved if we trace back the tradition historically to the OT and Jewish idea of advocate in which there is reference already to an advocacy of the divine Spirit for man in the here and now of his earthly life.': J. Behm 'Παράκλητος' in Kittel *TDNT*, Vol. V., 813.

[788] Brown's study represents a 'social-scientific' approach to Johannine pneumatology that uses sociological, anthropological, psychological and other such insights. 'The Spirit-Paraclete brokers truth by providing access to Jesus, the truth', 'as well as in characterizing the Paraclete as the way to the Father, with both figures bridging the divide between disparate spheres'. Her work challenges religious-historical studies on Johannine pneumatology: Tricia Gates Brown, *Spirit in the Writings of John*, 28. 28, 231, 234.

[789] See Max Turner, *The Holy Spirit and Spiritual Gifts* (Carlisle: Paternoster, 1996), 77–79 and D. A. Carson, *The Gospel According to John* (Leicester: IVP, 1991), 499 for assessments of the various translations.

[790] John 15:18–27.

[791] 'The Fourth Evangelist and his community experienced intense conflict with the Jews and the world, and this conflict led them to elevate the traditional "persecution" context to the level of a literary motif: Jesus was presented as if on trial and the church was commissioned as his agents to carry on this lawsuit. Thus in the church's witness, the term *Paraclete* was employed to serve this juridical backdrop': Burge, *Anointed Community*, 221.

[792] Turner, *The Holy Spirit and Spiritual Gifts*, 79.

[793] A Latin expression used by several commentators, for example Smalley, *John: Evangelist and Interpreter*, 232.

[794] Another Latin expression is used by Luther who spoke of the Paraclete as *alter Christus*—another Christ.

"another (different)"'.[795] Jesus further says that the Father will send the Holy Spirit 'in my name',[796] also denoting a very close association. Indeed, many of the commentators point out how the promised functions of the Paraclete after Jesus's departure exactly parallel and continue the work of Jesus whilst he was here on earth.[797] Both, for instance, are stated by John to come forth from God into the world,[798] to remain with the disciples,[799] teaching[800] and witnessing[801] in a world that sadly does not want to receive either Jesus[802] or his Spirit.[803] Shillington points out how the promise of the Paraclete would have brought comfort to the initial recipients of the gospel in the face of hostility from Roman, Jewish and incipient gnostic groupings, bringing 'Jesus to life in the thought and activity of the threatened community.'[804] Witherington describes the Paraclete as 'Jesus'[s] agent on earth, just as Jesus had been the Father's agent.'[805] Dunn says that 'the Spirit is the Spirit of Jesus,'[806] Jesus's presence in his absence, his *alter ego*. Such a coincidence of person and purpose leads Burge to conclude that 'the single most important feature of the Johannine Paraclete is its christological concentration.'[807] Thus we should beware of creating false dichotomies between Jesus and his Spirit, whilst also not 'confounding the persons'.[808]

## (c) The 'Personal' Paraclete

This very close link between the Paraclete and Jesus leads us to think of him in particularly personal terms,[809] an emphasis which is perhaps not surprising if the gospel was written by 'the beloved disciple.' This helps to explain why the Paraclete is referred to in the masculine form παράκλητος,[810] as opposed to neuter

---

[795] Turner, *The Holy Spirit and Spiritual Gifts*, 79.
[796] John 14:26. Barrett suggests this phrase means "'because I ask" or "to act in relation to me, in my place, with my authority'": Barrett, *The Gospel According to St John*, 467.
[797] See for instance R. E. Brown, 'The Paraclete in the Fourth Gospel', *New Testament Studies* 13 (1966–67), 113–32.
[798] John 15:26a; 16:28.
[799] John 14:17; 15:4.
[800] John 7:14–17; 14:26.
[801] John 8:17–18; 15:26b.
[802] John 1:11.
[803] John 14:17a.
[804] V. George Shillington 'The Spirit-Paraclete as Jesus' alter ego in the Fourth Gospel (John 14–16)' *Vision* 13:1 (2012), 38.
[805] B. Witherington, *John's Wisdom: A Commentary on the Fourth Gospel* (Cambridge: Lutterworth, 1995), 252.
[806] J. D. G. Dunn, *Jesus and the Spirit*, 350. The actual expression is used by Paul in Phil1:19, though not by John himself.
[807] Burge, *Anointed Community*, 41.
[808] Tricia Gates Brown, in *Spirit in the Writings of John* accuses Burge and others of doing just this, i.e. of 'blur[ring] the distinction between Jesus and the Spirit', 263, (see also 233), although she acknowledges a 'functional unity', 265, between Jesus and the Spirit. For her, 'the Paraclete continues Jesus' presence and work not as Jesus' alter ego, but as broker', 262.
[809] This point has been disputed by some in light of the impersonal connotations contained in the idea of the Holy Spirit as 'power', but this latter aspect is not prominent in John.
[810] Also note the personal pronouns ἐκεῖνος and αὐτὸς in 14:26; 15:26; 16:7, 8, 13, 14.

form πνεῦμα.⁸¹¹ Further intimacy and closeness is suggested by Jesus's telling the disciples in John 14:17 that in future, the Spirit would not just 'dwell with you' (παρ' ὑμῖν μένει) but also 'will be in you' (καὶ ἐν ὑμῖν ἔσται), paralleled by the comforting (and amazing) promise in 14:23 that Father and Son would 'make [their] home' (μονὴν παρ' αὐτῷ ποιησόμεθα) with 'anyone [who] loves [him]' (τις ἀγαπᾷ με).⁸¹² Jesus's own love for his disciples is shown by his desire that they would not be left 'as orphans'⁸¹³ and his reassurance 'I will come to you.'⁸¹⁴ Through the Paraclete he would indeed be 'with [them] for ever' (μεθ' ὑμῶν⁸¹⁵ εἰς τὸν αἰῶνα 14:16c). In his summary of the distinctiveness of the pneumatology of the Fourth Gospel, Dodd highlights this personal aspect:

> the gift of the Spirit to the church is represented, not as if it were a separate outpouring of divine power under the forms of wind and fire (as in Acts), but as the ultimate climax of the personal relations between Jesus and his disciples: ἐνεφύσησεν καὶ λέγει αὐτοῖς, Λάβετε πνεῦμα ἅγιον ['he breathed on them and said to them "Receive the Holy Spirit"'] (John xx.22).⁸¹⁶

That this post-resurrection breathing out of the Spirit was made in the context of the disciples being commissioned to take out the message of forgiveness⁸¹⁷ brings us back to consider another aspect of the Paraclete's identity relating to the communication of that message.

## (d) The Spirit of Truth

Three times in Jesus's farewell discourse, the Paraclete is designated 'the Spirit of truth' (τὸ πνεῦμα τῆς ἀληθείας).⁸¹⁸ In contemporary Judaism this expression was used as parallel to 'the spirit of perversity', which fought against 'the spirit of truth' in every human being. Carson, however, argues against such a dualistic reading in John,⁸¹⁹ and prefers to link its meaning with John's earlier references

---

[811] Turner, however, points out that 'the masculine pronoun was virtually forced on the writer to agree in gender with *ho paracletos*, a masculine noun. And in 14:17 the *neuter* pronoun is used, not the masculine.' Turner, *The Holy Spirit and Spiritual Gifts*, 179. Granted this, the personal aspect of the Paraclete does not, as the rest of this paragraph argues, rest solely on arguments based upon the use of the relevant personal pronoun.
[812] Note John's balance between individual and corporate indwelling.
[813] John 14:18a 'Οὐκ ἀφήσω ὑμᾶς ὀρφανούς'. Barrett points out that ὀρφανούς was not just used of children left without a parent but also of disciples left without a master: Barrett, *The Gospel According to St John*, 463.
[814] 14:18b. Most seem to think this is a reference to Jesus's coming to his disciples after the Resurrection rather than a reference to the coming of the Spirit, though a Johannine 'double-reference' could be intended.
[815] Cf. μεθ' ἡμῶν in John 16:4b used of Jesus's presence with his disciples in his earthly ministry.
[816] C. H. Dodd, *The Interpretation of the Fourth Gospel* (Cambridge: Cambridge University Press, 1953), 227.
[817] John 22:21–23.
[818] John 14:17; 15:26 and 16:13. Ashton points out that 'De La Potterie (1977) has shown conclusively that Dodd is wrong to think of Johannine truth as Platonic and that Bultmann is wrong to think of it as quasi-Gnostic': Ashton, *Understanding the Fourth Gospel* (Oxford: Clarendon), 423.
[819] Carson, *The Gospel According to John*, 500.

to the Spirit.[820] From this he concludes that 'the Paraclete is the Spirit of truth primarily because he *communicates* the truth.'[821] Ashton also links the Paraclete sayings with earlier references[822] and makes the point that 'in the body of the Gospel the Spirit is scarcely ever mentioned without some specific association with the word.'[823] Although the λόγος (word) is never equated with the πνεῦμα (spirit) the latter is always needed to give life to the former, whether it be (in the particular passages under consideration) in guiding Christians into the truth (16:13), or in convicting the world of its sin (16:7-11). In both these cases, as Barrett emphasizes, the vital medium through which such communication is effected is the church.

> [T]rue notions are not projected upon space. They are made known within the church, the proper sphere of the Spirit's activity (14:17). The Spirit thus relates the church positively to the truth upon which it stands, and by so doing reacts negatively upon the world, which is judged.[824]

It is of course by reference to Christ that the New Testament as a whole proclaims that one stands or falls,[825] and John's particular christocentric focus on truth is maintained throughout the gospel,[826] particularly at 14:6 which links us in close textual proximity with the first reference to the 'Spirit of truth' in 14:17.

## (e) The Didactic Spirit

A major role attributed to the Paraclete in these passages is one of teaching, as in 14:26 'he shall teach you all things' (ἐκεῖνος ὑμᾶς διδάξει πάντα) and 16:13 'he shall guide you into all truth' (ὁδηγήσει[827] ὑμᾶς ἐν τῇ ἀληθείᾳ πάσῃ·). One thesis on the function of the Paraclete in John encapsulates this in its title: *Revelation Taught*.[828] In another recent work, the pneumatically cooperative outworking of this in the life of the early church is postulated by Morgan-Wynne in the role of its teachers and preachers. 'There would be a mutual interplay between Spirit-guided teachers and the Spirit-indwelt congregation, and the result would be

---

[820] Such as John 1:32-33; 3:5-8; 4:23-24; 6:63 and 7:37-39. Despite Carson's comment, note the frequent use of contrasts and opposites in Johannine literature, including one between 'the Spirit of truth and the spirit of error' in 1 John 4:6.
[821] Carson, *The Gospel According to John*, 500, following Barrett, *The Gospel According to St John*, 463. Italics mine.
[822] Specifically John 3:34 and 6:63.
[823] Ashton, *Understanding the Fourth Gospel*, 420.
[824] Barrett, *The Gospel According to St John*, 91.
[825] For instance as in 1 Pet 2:4-8.
[826] As, for example, at John 8:32-33 and 18:37-38. Ashton points to John's particular use of irony in these references to truth: Ashton, *Understanding the Fourth Gospel*, 423.
[827] Note the link with Christ as 'the way' (ὁδός) in John 14:6.
[828] E. Franck, *Revelation Taught: The Paraclete in the Gospel of John* (Lund: Gleerup, 1985), referred to in Turner, *The Holy Spirit and Spiritual Gifts*, 82.

that the whole community would be led into, and built up in, the truth that is in Jesus.'[829] For Hoeck, 'one could ... argue that the Spirit as Teacher will simply complete the apostles' education.'[830] Away from the world of contemporary studies, it is interesting that a primary didactic connection with the Holy Spirit has long been recognised in the Anglican Book of Common Prayer (1552) in its Collect for Whit-Sunday.

> God, who as at this time didst *teach* the hearts of thy faithful people, by the sending to them the light of thy Holy Spirit; Grant us by the same Spirit to have a right judgement in all things, and evermore to rejoice in his holy comfort; through the merits of Christ Jesus our Saviour, who liveth and reigneth with thee, in the unity of the same Spirit, one God, world without end. *Amen*

With that prayer in mind, I shall now embark on a more specific examination of the Paraclete passages, particularly as they relate to the Christian community's understanding and application of Christian truth, as now found in Scripture. As I describe the function of the Paraclete in this connection, I shall trace the historical, dialogical/dialectical, eschatological, and Trinitarian aspects that were highlighted in my exploration of the *koinonia* of the Spirit in chapter 2. Alongside these, I shall point out other characteristics of the Paraclete's workings, not least in light of what has already been said in relation to his roles as advocate, the *alter ego* of Jesus, the personal Spirit who is also the Spirit of truth, and the didactic Spirit.

## The Hermeneutical Functions of the Paraclete

I shall list the five sayings under four main categorisations that describe his hermeneutical operations, beginning with the second of the Paraclete sayings (the first saying being linked together with the fifth under my fourth categorisation).

### Historical and Didactic (14:25–26)

'[He] ... will bring to your remembrance all that I have said to you' (v. 26d). Burge remarks that '[t]he primary importance of 14:26 is that it affirms a definite historicizing work of the Spirit.'[831] The wider parameters of such a historicizing work have already been discussed in chapter 2, but limiting ourselves to what

---

[829] John Eifion Morgan-Wynne, *Holy Spirit and Religious Experience in Christian Writings, ca. AD 90–200*, Studies in Christian History and Thought (Carlisle: Paternoster, 2006), 34.
[830] A. Hoeck, 'The Johannine Paraclete: Herald of the Eschaton,' *Journal of Biblical and Pneumatological Research*, Vol. 4 (Sept 2012), 34.
[831] Burge, *Anointed Community*, 212–213.

John has to say here, I shall select points that highlight the interpretive work of the Spirit in the life of the Christian community.

(i) 'But the Paraclete, the Holy Spirit' (ὁ δὲ παράκλητος, τὸ πνεῦμα τὸ ἅγιον), 14:26a. Westcott points out that this is the only time in the gospel where 'the full emphatic title'[832] of the Spirit is mentioned, underlining the focus on 'holy'. The resultant ethical imperative for the interpretive community is clear: 'the moral character of the Spirit as fashioning the life of the church is added to the teaching power of the Spirit (vv. 16, 17) as the Revealer [sic] of the Truth.'[833] A proper understanding of the truth is then closely linked with the practical obedience of those being taught.

(ii) 'Whom the Father will send in my name, he will teach you'. As the personal emissary of the Father and Son, the Spirit will establish a pupil/teacher relationship with those first disciples who heard these words from Jesus, to whom the primary reference for this promise must be made. Most commentators, however, recognize a secondary application to succeeding generations of Christians. The Paraclete is indeed earlier promised 'to be with you for ever'[834] (εἰς τὸν αἰῶνα) in 14:16—a loyal teacher for the church with a ministry that is both perpetual and peripatetic (in the widest sense).

(iii) 'Will ... bring to your remembrance' (καὶ ὑπομνήσει ὑμᾶς). Evidence for the initial, primary fulfilment of this promise can be seen in 'the disciples ... remembered' of 2:22 and 12:16[835] (cf. 13:7). Hence 'remembering' did not just consist of a process of mental recollection but of the greater spiritual understanding facilitated by the Paraclete in the light of Jesus's subsequent death and resurrection. Hoskyns extends the application of the verse to the ongoing work of exposition. 'His [the Paraclete's] work is more than a reminiscence of the *ipsissima verba* of the Son of God: it is a living representation of all that He had once spoken of to His disciples, a creative exposition of the Gospel.'[836] We live with the benefit of having had two thousand years of such 'creative expositions', some more profitable than others. A key criterion relating to this is brought out by the next point.

(iv) 'Shall teach you all things, and bring to your remembrance all that I have said to you.'

---

[832] B. F. Westcott, *The Gospel According to St. John* (London: John Murray, 1903), 209. Because it is the only such reference, some commentators think the expression may have been introduced in subsequent editing of a passage that originally referred only to the Paraclete: see R. E. Brown, *The Gospel According to John* Volume 2 (xiii–xxi) (London: Geoffrey Chapman, 1966), 650.
[833] Ibid.,209.
[834] John 14:16.
[835] For more on these verses in the OT/NT context, see chapter 3.
[836] Edwyn C. Hoskyns, *The Fourth Gospel* (London: Faber and Faber, 1948), 461.

These parallel expressions[837] and in particular the two 'alls' (πάντα) clearly need to be held together here, for the subsequent understanding gleaned from ὑμᾶς διδάξει πάντα καὶ ὑπομνήσει ὑμᾶς ('shall teach you all things and bring to your remembrance') must never be divorced from the original teaching of Jesus: πάντα ἃ εἶπον ὑμῖν [ἐγώ] ('all that I have said to you'). Dunn accordingly points out that the teaching function of the Spirit for John, whilst not limited merely to a recalling of the actual words of Jesus, is neither to produce fresh revelation that:

> portray[s] a Jesus who is not in substantial continuity with the once incarnate Jesus. There is *both freedom and control*—liberty to reinterpret and remould the original kerygma, but also the original kerygma remains as a check and restraint.[838]

Affirming this statement (apart from the ambivalence of 'remould'), I would want to underwrite the more unambiguously conservative summary given by Carson: 'The Spirit's ministry in this respect was not to bring qualitatively new revelation, but to complete, to fill out, the revelation brought by Jesus himself.'[839] Such a 'filling out' of the revelation has been enabled by the Spirit as the church has continually sought to (re)contextualise and apply the message to its particular situation down the ages and in differing cultures.[840] Maybe this is something of what Gadamer meant when he wrote of the 'merging of horizons' of original writers and subsequent interpreters in order to create a meaningful application.[841]

More will be said on this aspect when 16:13, a closely related passage, is discussed. Suffice it to say for now that this ever present dynamic/tension—between the original teaching of Jesus and its contemporary re-appropriation by the Spirit; between past tradition and present inspiration; between the word as given and the word as interpreted—can also be expressed in the language of dialectic, a special feature of Johannine style. I will now turn to look at a particular aspect of this dialectic that is found in the next Paraclete saying, a dialectic that is there expressed not in terms of 'past v. present', but as 'church v. the world'.

---

[837] On the assumption that the καὶ that joins them is epexegetic, the second expression explaining the first.
[838] Dunn, *Jesus and the Spirit*, 352.
[839] Carson, *The Gospel According to John*, 505. Also note R. E. Brown's comment on what he renders as 'will teach you everything': 'The "everything" sets up a contrast with the "this" ("these things") of 25, but not necessarily in the sense that the Paraclete will teach more quantitatively than Jesus during his ministry. Rather, as we gather from xvi 13, the Paraclete will enable the disciples to see the *full meaning* of Jesus' words,' citing further 1 John 2:27 and 2 John 9: Brown, *The Gospel According to John* Volume 2 (xiii–xxi) (London: Geoffrey Chapman, 1966), 650.
[840] Fowl links this hermeneutical task with words from the earlier part of John 15. 'The Spirit's role is to guide and direct this process of continual change in order to enable communities of Christians to "abide in the true vine" in the various contexts in which they find themselves.' Stephen Fowl, *Engaging Scripture* (Oxford: Blackwell, 1998), 101.
[841] See chapter 2, pages 68–69.

## Dialectical and Convictional (15:26-27; 16:7-11)

The third Paraclete saying[842] comes hard on the heels of 15:18-25—a passage which warns of the world's hatred of Jesus and his servants—and is followed by 16:1-4, that speaks of their being killed. It has already been noted that a number of the commentators speak of this persecution/ 'law-suit' background to John's Gospel.[843] Against such an adversarial context, the Paraclete's succour for the church as 'advocate' takes on a particular relevance, in both this third and also the fourth set of Paraclete sayings.[844] As Burge comments, 'the power of the Spirit would appear most clearly in duress.'[845] A communal aspect is inherent in the two aspects of the juridical motif that characterizes both these passages.

### (i) The Co-witness of Paraclete and Church (15:26-27)

The witness/testimony theme that runs through John's Gospel[846] is brought to something of a head here as the effectual, joint witness of 'the Spirit of truth' and church is explicated. On the one hand, it is the Paraclete, as commissioned by the Father, who will be a personal witness to Christ: 'he will bear witness about me' (ἐκεῖνος μαρτυρήσει [future tense] περὶ ἐμοῦ), v. 26d. As Morris says, 'the Spirit, so to speak, conducts Christ's case for Him before the world.'[847] On the other hand, this witness seems to be inseparably linked with, if not dependent upon, the ongoing witness of the church[848]: 'and you also will bear witness' (καὶ ὑμεῖς δὲ μαρτυρεῖτε [present indicative or imperative]), v. 27a. Though this verse primarily had application to the first disciples, as those who had been with him 'from the beginning',[849] the derivative application to subsequent generations is no less important, and is indeed absolutely vital.[850] In this, the cooperation between Paraclete and people is both essential and effective. As Bultmann puts it:

> The word μαρτυρήσει indicates that the Spirit is the power of proclamation in the community, and this is made fully clear by the

---

[842] John 15:26-27.
[843] See Turner, *The Holy Spirit and Spiritual Gifts*, 85.
[844] John 16:7-11.
[845] Gary Burge, 'The Gospel of John', in T.J. Burke & K. Warrington, eds., *A Biblical Theology of the Holy Spirit* (Eugene, OR; Cascade Books, under license from SPCK, 2014), 114.
[846] For example, at 1:7, 8, 3:26, 28, 5:31-37, 8:18. 10:25.
[847] L. Morris, *The Gospel According to John* (London: Marshall Morgan & Scott, 1971), 684.
[848] Cf. Acts 5:32. S. Escobar says: 'there is a connection between the testimony of the Spirit to the church and the testimony of the church to the world. The presence of the Spirit among the disciples, in the church, is what makes the church different from the world. The willingness to be filled and guided by the Spirit comes from God himself to the church (14:15-17).' S. Escobar, *A Time for Mission: The Challenge for Global Christianity* (Leicester: IVP, 2003), 123. M. Turner: 'John knows of no witness by the Spirit that is not witness through the church' 'The Holy Spirit in John' in J. B. Green, S. McKnight, I. Howard Marshall, eds., *Dictionary of Jesus and the Gospels* (Leicester: IVP, 1992), 350.
[849] ἀπ' ἀρχῆς, another favourite Johannine expression that speaks of authentic, first-hand witness. Thus the experience of Jesus to which the disciples were to bear witness was historical, not mystical.
[850] It has been remarked that the church is never less than two generations away from extinction, if the second generation fails in its mandate of bearing witness to the truth.

juxtaposition of the disciples' witness and that of the Spirit: καὶ ὑμεῖς δὲ μαρτυρεῖτε (v. 27).[851]

*(ii) The Paraclete as Cosmic Prosecutor (16:7–11)*

If 15:25–27 portrays more of a defensive aspect[852] to the work of 'the Spirit of truth' (hence 'Counsellor' in NIV), this next section pictures the advocate as 'counsel for the prosecution.' The Spirit is often, rightly, thought of in terms of his role of 'convicting the sinner', but John here uses wider terminology: 'he will convince *the world*' (ἐκεῖνος ἐλέγξει τὸν κόσμον[853]). Thus, in contrast to the frequent contemporary individualisations of the Spirit as 'the one who helps me in my Christian life and witness'[854] (although that is a role the Spirit certainly does fulfil), we are presented with the one who is, literally, a 'cosmic' prosecutor. To quote Newbigin, 'the Spirit is not the domesticated auxiliary of the church, he is the powerful advocate who goes before the church to bring the world under conviction.'[855] Thus the very work of conviction ('shaming the world and convincing it of its guilt, thus calling it to repentance'[856]) is spoken of in terms of a great work within the global community.[857] This occurs when it is confronted by the witness of that other community which is the church, to whom Jesus sends the Paraclete (v. 7c). Hence Burge's comment:

> As the community stands on trial for Christ, the Spirit will turn the tables (as in reality Christ had already done in his "trial") and address the world through the church with the veracity of its own Christ-centred message.[858]

This is, of course, not to deny the absolute necessity of a work of the Spirit in convicting and regenerating the *individual*, as, for instance, in John 3:5–6. But this must be seen as taking place within the wider framework of the Spirit's ministry through the church to the world.[859]

---

[851] R. Bultmann, *The Gospel of John: A Commentary*, trans. G. R. Beasley-Murray (Oxford: Blackwell, 1971), 553–554.

[852] This is not to deny the essentially positive, indeed proactive aspect of 'bearing witness'. Smalley makes the point that 'the only defence he [the Paraclete] makes (in the sense of 'witness') is of Jesus and not of the disciples.' Smalley, *John: Evangelist and Interpreter*, 230.

[853] Κόσμος is a typically Johannine word commonly used to express the world of people living in active rebellion against God (as opposed to the created world), but also a world which God came to save. See Barrett, *The Gospel According to St John*, 161–162.

[854] A glance at many contemporary 'worship songs' relating to the Spirit will show this.

[855] L. Newbigin, *The Light Has Come* (Grand Rapids, MI: Eerdmans, 1982), 211, as cited in B. Milne, *The Message of John* (Leicester: IVP, 1993), 231.

[856] Carson, *The Gospel According to John*, 537.

[857] This, of course, is seen in particular prominence when whole communities come under conviction in times of revival.

[858] Burge, *Anointed Community*, 210.

[859] Morris balances the global and the individual: 'The world is guilty, but it requires the Spirit to sheet this home. The Spirit convicts the world in two senses. In the first place He "shows the world to be guilty", i.e. He secures a verdict of "Guilty" against the world. But in the second place we should take the words to mean also that the Spirit

The first instance of the Paraclete's role of convicting the world of 'sin, righteousness, and judgment' came, of course, on the day of Pentecost itself, as Peter preached the gospel of Christ in the power of the Spirit.[860] The response of corporate and individual repentance ('repent ... every one of you'[861]) that followed has been repeated on countless occasions and in varying degrees throughout the history of Christian proclamation. To the extent that such a convicting work anticipates that final day when the secrets of every heart will be exposed,[862] one can agree with Barrett that 'the Spirit ... places the world in the position which it will occupy at the last judgement.'[863] This language brings us into the realm of eschatology, to which, *inter alia*, I now turn.

## *Eschatological and Interpretive (16:12–15)*

Extending the idea expressed in the last quotation, Barrett remarks that, 'The Spirit is ... the eschatological *continuum* in which the work of Christ, initiated in his ministry and awaiting its termination at his return, is wrought out.'[864] This *continuum* began to operate when the anticipated coming of the Paraclete, following Jesus's rich string of promises—that the Paraclete '*will* teach (διδάξει)[865] ... bring to your remembrance (ὑπομνήσει)[866] ... bear witness (μαρτυρήσει)[867] ... convict (ἐλέγξει)[868] ... guide (ὁδηγήσει)[869] ... glorify (δοξάσει)[870] and declare (ἀναγγελεῖ)'[871]—started to become a present reality in the ministry of the disciples following Pentecost. Having considered the first four in this list, we now turn to the fifth: 'when the Spirit of truth comes, he will guide you (note ὑμᾶς plural) into all truth' (16:13). This fifth and last of the Paraclete sayings (i.e. John 16:12–15) is one that is particularly relevant to the subject of this book. We shall work our way through the relevant verses.

(a) v. 12 'you cannot bear (οὐ δύνασθε βαστάζειν) them now'. This is an uncommon use of βαστάζειν ('to endure', 'support'[872]), which speaks of the inability of Jesus's disciples to take on board all that Jesus would share with

---

brings the world's guilt home to itself. The Spirit convicts the individual sinner's conscience. Otherwise men would never be convicted of their sin.' Morris, *The Gospel According to John*, 698.
[860] See Acts 2:14–41, and especially vv. 22, 24, 36, 37.
[861] Acts 2:38.
[862] To revert to Pauline terminology, for instance as in Rom 2:16; 1 Cor 4:5; cf. 1 Cor 14:25, where Paul anticipates this happening as the unbeliever comes into the fellowship of those who are prophesying.
[863] Barrett, *The Gospel According to St John*, 90.
[864] Ibid., 90.
[865] John 14:26.
[866] John 14:26.
[867] John 15:26.
[868] John 16:8.
[869] John 16:13.
[870] John 16:14.
[871] John 16:14, 15.
[872] Being the only occasion in the New Testament where the thought is that of bearing words. See Morris, *The Gospel According to John*, 699 fn. 25, and Barrett, *The Gospel According to St. John*, 489, citing also its use in other ways in Acts 15:10; Gal 5:10 and Rev 2:2.

them, owing, perhaps, to their pre-crucifixion limitations (of time and understanding), but also to his kindness and perception. Spiritual understanding is a function of spiritual maturity as well as the chronology of divine disclosure. Jesus knows what we can take![873]

(b) 'The Spirit of truth will *guide*'. Here, the verb used is ὁδηγέω, literally 'to lead the way', hence R. E. Brown's rendering: 'he will guide you along the way of all truth.'[874] Hoskyns points out that 'the Greek word recalls the story in the LXX of God's leading of His children in the desert and the language of the Psalms *Guide me in thy truth*.'[875] This Old Testament context suggests a 'step by step' impartation of truth, just as the people of Israel were guided a step at a time on their pilgrimage through the wilderness.[876]

In the New Testament the word is not common, the only other significant reference for our purposes being Acts 8:31 when the Ethiopian eunuch, in response to Philip's question as to his understanding of Isaiah, replies 'how can I, unless someone guides me (μή τις ὁδηγήσει με)?' Philip's help shows the Spirit's use of a human intermediary in biblical comprehension (the Spirit having directed Philip to the Ethiopian's chariot[877]). But the fact that the Eunuch's enquiry led Philip to answer in terms of 'good news about Jesus' (v. 35) brings us back to the Johannine link with Jesus as 'the way and the truth' (ἡ ὁδὸς καὶ ἡ ἀλήθεια) earlier on in John 14:6. He indeed epitomises the truth into which the disciples must be guided by the Spirit of truth. Lindars says that 'John thinks of the Spirit's guidance exactly in the same way as he thinks of the teaching of Jesus.'[878]

This terminology of 'guiding/leading the way' suggests that the leading of the Spirit involves gracious help and direction, being a far cry from the language of manipulation or control. It also implies the need for willing cooperation, effort and discernment on the part of those being so led.

(c) 'Will guide you into all truth' (ὁδηγήσει ὑμᾶς ἐν τῇ ἀληθείᾳ πάσῃ). There is much discussion in the commentaries as to whether this could include the impartation of 'new revelation' by the Spirit. Such discussion is sometimes compounded by different understandings attached to 'new'. The discovery of

---

[873] Cf. Matt 11:28–30, which, interestingly, is preceded by vv. 25–27 that relate to Jesus's revelation of truth to his disciples.

[874] R. E. Brown, *The Gospel According to John* Volume 2 (xiii–xxi), 703. He points out that 'the verb [*hodegein*] is used in Rev vii:17 to describe how the Lamb leads the saints to living water,' 707.

[875] Hoskyns, *The Fourth Gospel*, 485. G. Ebel says that ὁδηγέω is found 42 times in the LXX of the Old Testament and is 'universally used with reference to God' in C. Brown, ed., *New International Dictionary of New Testament Theology*, (Exeter: Paternoster, 1978), Vol. 3, 937, see, e.g. Ps 25:5 (of God) and Ps 143:10 (of the Spirit). In the New Testament, note ὁδηγέω in Matt 15:14; Luke 6:39 (blind *leading* the blind); Acts 8:31 (see above) and Rev 7:17 (the Lamb *will guide* them to springs of living water).

[876] As, for instance in Num 9:15–23. Notice also the step by step teaching approach of the Old Testament prophets, as in Isa 28:10, 13.

[877] Acts 8:31.

[878] Barnabas Lindars, *The Gospel of John* (London: Marshall, Morgan & Scott, 1987), 505.

'new truth' or 'fresh revelation' has certainly been claimed by many groups down the ages, ranging from the heretical to the radical and the charismatic. However, most commentators think it is better to understand Jesus's promise in terms of the Paraclete leading the disciples into a deeper and fuller knowledge and understanding of the truth which had already been 'principally disclosed'[879] in and through himself, for reasons such as:

1. Contextually, the need to tie the verse in with its counterpart in 14:26 (in particular 'all that *I* have said to you') and also 16:14 ('take what is *mine* and declare it to you'), as well as the fact that the Spirit is stated 'not to speak on his own authority' (16:13) but only what he hears from Father and Son (16:14–15), thus excluding 'independent' revelation.

2. Linguistically, the use of

- ἐν (in) rather than εἰς (into).[880] As R. C. H. Lenski says, '"Into" would mean entrance, while "in" assumes that the entrance has already been made and that all that is needed it to explore what lies within the circle of the truth.'[881]
- ἀναγγελεῖ for 'declare' in 16:13 and 16:14, the prefix ἀνά- giving the idea of reiterative announcement.[882]

3. Generally, New Testament teaching concerning the finality of revelation in Jesus Christ.[883]

As R. E. Brown comments: 'It is unlikely that in Johannine thought there was any concept of further revelation after the ministry of Jesus, for Jesus is *the* revelation of the Father, the Word of God.'[884]

'All truth' implies the all-sufficiency of the Spirit's work in its revelation to the church[885] as he makes the truth of Scripture accessible and applicable. As Felix Porsch puts it, 'Jesus brings the truth, and makes it present through his coming

---

[879] Carson, *The Gospel According to John*, 539. See also R. H. Lightfoot, *St John's Gospel* (Oxford: Clarendon, 1956), 287–288. Catholics like to refer to the *sensus plenior* ('fuller sense') of Scripture on the basis 'that the text itself is often richer than the author's intention and contains potentialities which the Holy Spirit actuates in the course of history,' Catholic Bishops' Conference of England and Wales, and of Scotland, *The Gift of Scripture* (London: Catholic Truth Society, 2005), 21.

[880] Assuming this is the better reading.

[881] R. C. H. Lenski, *The Interpretation of St John's Gospel* (Minneapolis: Augsburg, 1943), 1090.

[882] See R. E. Brown, *The Gospel According to John*, 708. Ashton interestingly points out that 'the emphatic repetition of the verb ἀναγγελλεῖ, used in this concluding summary in its technical, apocalyptic sense ... confirms that his role is that of the *angelus interpres*. He is sent from heaven to clarify what could not be fully comprehended without him; he completes a revelation that was previously partial and obscure': Ashton, *Understanding the Fourth Gospel*, 423. In doing this, the Spirit thus completes the chain of biblical revelation: from prophets to Son to Spirit to church.

[883] For instance, 2 Pet 1:3-4; Heb 1:1–2a ('in these last days he has spoken to us *by his Son*'). See Carson, *The Gospel According to John*, 539.

[884] Brown, *The Gospel According to John*, 714.

[885] 'No part of this blessed domain of truth is foreign to this guide [sic. the Spirit of truth], and he will withhold no part from the disciples': Lenski, *The Interpretation of St John's Gospel*, 1090.

into the world; the Spirit-Paraclete opens up this truth and creates the entrance into it for believers.'[886]

(d) 'He will declare to you the things that are to come' (καὶ τὰ ἐρχόμενα ἀναγγελεῖ ὑμῖν). The expression 'things that are to come' (τὰ ἐρχόμενα) has been taken to refer to the events of both the imminent future (the passion) and the ultimate future[887] (the apocalypse), but many commentators see this to be a reference primarily to all that happens between these two pivotal points in eschatology,[888] i.e. the age of the church, when it is constantly in need of the Spirit's help in interpreting and applying truth to present and 'coming' situations, working out 'the *consequences* of the Christ-event'[889] in its life and teaching. The effectiveness of the Paraclete's help in this connection can be initially seen in the completion of John's Gospel itself,[890] in the subsequent compilation of the canon of the whole of Scripture, and in the central and determinative place accorded to Scriptural interpretation and application in the Christian church living 'in these last days.'[891]

## *Trinitarian and Exegetical (14:16; 16:13–15 and previous verses)*

Barrett has said of John in his gospel that 'more than any other New Testament writer he lays the foundations for a doctrine of a co-equal Trinity.'[892] The Paraclete sayings themselves conclude on an explicitly Trinitarian note, a note which has been frequently sounded throughout the five sayings and indeed the whole of the farewell discourse(s). The blessed Trinity, that heavenly 'community of communities,' encompasses all aspects of the Spirit's work of revelation. Truth is not the product of a unifocal human mind, but of the trifocal operations of Father, Son, and Holy Spirit.[893] A scan of the divine movements between the three persons and their relating to the church in the Johannine verses under discussion produces a picture of intense dynamic activity and

---

[886] Felix Porsch, *Pneuma und Wort: Ein exegetischer Beitrag zur Pneumatologie des Johannesevangeliums* (Frankfurt am Main: Knecht, 1974), 300, as quoted in Turner, *The Holy Spirit and Spiritual Gifts*, 84. See also '"He will Lead you into all Truth" ': On the Relationship between Christology and Pneumatology' by Eberhard Hahn in *European Journal of Theology* (1996) 5:2, 93-103 for a discussion of this and other New Testament verses on a similar theme.

[887] Such a reference point would not fit in naturally with the general eschatology of the gospel, which is generally considered to be more 'realised' than 'futurist'.

[888] Carson, *The Gospel According to John*, 540. Barnabas Lindars writes of 'the whole range of eschatological events, which have been anticipated in Jesus, and remain to be worked out through time in the life of the church': Lindars, *The Gospel of John*, 495.

[889] Turner, *The Holy Spirit and Spiritual Gifts*, 84.

[890] See Burge, *Anointed Community*, 217; R. Alan Culpepper, *The Gospel and Letters of John*, 217-218; and Dunn, *Jesus and the Spirit*, 352: 'John would undoubtedly regard his own gospel as the product of this inspiring Spirit ... indeed these very [Paraclete] promises may constitute an implicit apologia for his gospel.'

[891] Heb 1:2a.

[892] Barrett, *The Gospel According to John*, 92. Note also Turner, *The Holy Spirit and Spiritual Gifts*, 178-180 for a discussion of the parameters of a Trinitarian pneumatology in John 14-16.

[893] Cf. Jeremiah's critique of the false prophets: 'they speak visions of their own minds.... who among them has stood in the council of the LORD ...?' Jer 23:16, 18.

interchange which is to be reflected in the church. By way of a brief threefold summary of this activity we can say that as to the:

- *sending* of the Spirit. In response to the prayer of the Son, the Father gives (δώσει) the Paraclete (14:16), whom Jesus says 'the Father will send (πέμψει) in my name' (14:26) but also 'whom I shall send to you (ὃν ἐγὼ πέμψω ὑμῖν) from the Father'(15:26), but who also 'proceeds[894] (ἐκπορεύεται) from the Father'(15:26). The three verbs used seem to have much the same meaning in this context. Their use illustrates the complete duality of operation of Father and Son in the giving of the Spirit, who has himself recently been described as 'The Giving Gift.'[895]

- *substance* of what is shared. Jesus says of the Spirit of truth that 'whatever he hears he will speak' (16:13) and that 'he will take what is mine and declare it to you' (16:14). But whence does this derive? 'All that the Father has is mine' (16:15a)[896]. And the wonder of it is that this rich divine treasury is opened up through the work of the Paraclete to his disciples: 'he will take what is mine and declare it to you'! (16:15c).[897]

- *sequel* of all this. It is that the Spirit of truth focuses all the gaze upon Jesus: 'he will bear witness to me' (15:26c) and 'he will glorify me' (ἐκεῖνος ἐμὲ δοξάσει 16:14a). In so far as the δόξα ('glory') word group in the Bible has been defined as having reference to 'the luminous manifestation of [God's] person, his glorious revelation of himself,'[898] further light is thrown upon the Spirit's epistemological role here as he 'shows off' Christ. Moreover, in John, the work of glorification is always reciprocated between Father and Son.[899] 'Just as the Spirit is concerned to set forward the things of Christ so is He concerned to set forward the things of the Father.'[900]

In this connection, Morgan-Wynne has remarked that 'as Jesus is the "exegete" of the Father (1.18), so the Paraclete-Spirit is the "exegete" of the Son.'[901] And as the truth of the Father became incarnate in Jesus, so now it is to be incarnated in the life of the church through the work of the Paraclete as he seeks to appropriate and apply the message of Jesus. As Smail puts it, 'the Spirit is the artist who shapes his people into countless creative portrayals of the risen

---

[894] From the language of 'proceeding' has, of course, come the centuries old debate about the 'procession' of the Spirit and the *filioque* controversy. See Carson, *The Gospel According to John*, 528–529.
[895] Tom Smail, *The Giving Gift* (London: Hodder and Stoughton, 1988; repr. Darton Longman and Todd, 1994)
[896] Cf. John 5:19–20.
[897] Cf. John 15:15c.
[898] S. Aalen, 'Glory, Honour' in *New International Dictionary of New Testament Theology*, Vol. 2, 45.
[899] Cf. John 13:31 and 14:13b 'that the Father may be glorified in the Son.'
[900] Morris, *The Gospel According to John*, 701.
[901] John Eifion Morgan-Wynne, *Holy Spirit and Religious Experience in Christian Writings, ca. AD 90–200* (Studies in Christian History and Thought) (Carlisle: Paternoster, 2006), 30.

Lord.'[902] This can only happen when his people seek to partake in and imitate, albeit imperfectly and infinitesimally, the living fellowship of the Trinity, from the intimacy of that 'ἐν' ('in') relationship[903] with the Godhead of which John loves to speak. This, in turn, requires a life of obedience in which the interpretation consequently provided by the Spirit, as per John 14:15–16, is not pursued as an end in itself, but as a means of providing an effective, corporate, and loving witness to the world.[904]

## Conclusion to the Chapter

Jesus's teaching about the person and work of the Paraclete, as recorded in John 14–16, provides us with some distinctive[905] insights into the way the Spirit guides the Christian community in its remembrance of, and understanding of, the words and truth of Jesus—a truth which for Christians is now enshrined in Scripture. The Paraclete's role as 'advocate' or 'counsellor' highlights his help in drawing alongside God's people in defence of this truth against the hostility of the world. As the *alter ego* of Jesus, his ministry mirrors and extends all that the Saviour did for and with his disciples whilst on earth. Here indeed is assistance that is truly personal, as is epitomised in his role as 'the Spirit of truth', teaching and guiding the church into all truth. This help, of course, is available to all Christians individually as well as collectively, but the concern of this chapter has been to underline the wider corporate context in which all this should take place, as per the corporate context in which the Paraclete promises were originally given to the apostolic group.

From my perusal of the relevant verses, I have therefore sought to outline four different corporate dimensions that explicate the Paraclete's hermeneutical functions: firstly, a historical and didactical dimension (14:25–26) that brings out the meaning of Jesus's original teaching for the subsequent church; secondly, a dialectical and convictional dimension (15:26–27; 16:7–11) that links Paraclete and church in confronting the world in witness and judgment; thirdly, an eschatological and interpretive dimension (16:12–15) in which the church is for ever being guided into all truth on its journey to the *eschaton*; and fourthly, a Trinitarian and exegetical dimension (14:16; 16:13–15 and previous verses) in which all that the church shares and communicates is to be a reflection of the fellowship of the Trinity.

---

[902] Smai, *The Giving Gift*, 180.
[903] Such as in the 'abiding in' language of the vine imagery of John 15.
[904] For more on this line of thinking, see Paul Brown, *The Holy Spirit and the Bible: The Spirit's Interpreting Role in Relation to Biblical Hermeneutics* (Fearn: Christian Focus, 2002), 72.
[905] This is not to suggest that the Johannine Paraclete teaching contradicts other pneumatological teaching in the New Testament. Indeed Johannes Behm points out that 'the idea of the Spirit as παράκλητος is not unfamiliar to the rest of the NT even if the word is not used', citing, *inter alia*, Rom 8:26f and Mark 13:11, 'Παράκλητος' in Kittel, *TDNT*, 813.

Each of these four areas brings with it both encouragements and warnings for the church in its use of Scripture. In relation to the first, the assurance of an ever-present teacher bringing ever deeper understanding is matched by an underlining of the ethical requirements of a *Holy* Spirit (cf. 'keep my commandments' 14:15) in which not just mental 'remembrance' but also moral activation is expected. As to the second, the power of the advocate in witness needs to be accompanied by a spirit of constant cooperation, not just between Paraclete and people but also between Christians working together. As to the third, the gradual, ongoing guidance of the 'Spirit of truth' in helping Christians apply Scripture to ever new situations needs to be combined with a wariness concerning claims of 'new revelation' that deny the sufficiency of the Jesus revelation and thus create a dichotomy between word and Spirit. As to the fourth, the revelatory dynamic provided by the workings of the Trinity can only be activated in the life of a fellowship that ever abides in and displays the life of the Trinity in a manner that brings glory to Jesus.

The working out of these insights is illustrated time and time again in the history of the church, starting with the early stages of its story as recorded in Acts, to which I now turn in the next chapter.

# CHAPTER FIVE: SPIRIT AND HERMENEUTICS IN THE FIRST CHRISTIAN COMMUNITY

## Acts 1–15 (Selected Passages)

## Introduction

Acts is a unique and exciting book. Luke's record of the birth and growth of the Christian church has inspired church life and missionary endeavour down the ages. It also constitutes a story from which we can 'learn theological interpretation.'[906] For as has been emphasized by Stronstad and others, Luke was not just writing as a historian, simply describing events. He also constructed his narrative as a theologian, indebted to the Old Testament and Jewish (particularly Septuagintal) historiographical tradition, and inspired by the Spirit of God.[907]

My approach in this chapter is to explore the interpretive dynamic created by the interrelationship between three key players in the Lukan narrative. First, the Spirit, which is promised in Acts 1:4, 8 and 'poured out' in chapter 2. Second, the Scriptures, which are so commonly referred to in the speeches of those first intrepid Christian preachers. Third, the Christian community, which is no longer just a group of disciples, but now becomes the 'church' (ἐκκλησία).[908]

In this connection, the first section in this chapter will make some preliminary comments on Lukan pneumatology, on the speeches and their use of Scripture, and on issues of community that arise from the nature of the narrative. Following this, in the second major section, I will consider five key passages (Acts 1:15–26; 2; 4:23–31; 6–7; 15) which reveal ways in which the primitive church was guided by the Spirit in its custodianship and interpretation of Scripture. These passages have been singled out because they present a variety of community contexts in which Old Testament Scripture is being interpreted with the Spirit's help.[909] During the chapter, reference will also be made to verses in the Gospel of Luke where there are relevant links.

---

[906] Joel B. Green, 'Learning Theological Interpretation from Luke' in C. Bartholomew et al., eds., *Reading Luke: Interpretation, Reflection, Formation*, Scripture and Hermeneutics Series Vol. 6 (Milton Keynes: Paternoster, 2005), 55. He asserts this over against 'the common assumption ... in some parts of the church ... that narrative is not a good source for theology', 56.
[907] Roger Stronstad, *The Charismatic Theology of St. Luke* (Grand Rapids: Baker Academic, 2012), 5-14.
[908] Acts 5:13; 7:38; 8:1-3.
[909] There is, of course, much more material relevant to the thesis of this book in Acts where Scripture is being cited or alluded to.

## Spirit, Scripture and Community

### Lukan Pneumatology

*(i) Critical Approaches to Acts and their Relevance to Pneumatology*

The Holy Spirit plays a very prominent role in Acts, with πνεῦμα in relation to the divine spirit occurring some 57 times.[910] The nature of this role has been variously described, according to the manner of approach taken to the book. According to I. Howard Marshall, this has passed through three main phases.[911]

Traditionally, Acts has been regarded simply as a *historical* record of the early church written by Luke, the companion of Paul.[912] This viewpoint has been vulnerable to critical attack,[913] but in this perspective, the Holy Spirit is the prime mover for and enabler of the first missionary advance. Hence its popular designation as 'the Acts of the Holy Spirit'.[914]

In the last fifty years or so, more attention has been paid to the *theological* emphases that lie behind Acts. The programmatic role for the Spirit, as first recorded in Acts 1:8,[915] as the one who empowers witness and directs mission has been duly affirmed.[916] Others have also highlighted his consequent role in Christian conversion,[917] assurance,[918] and authentication.[919] In connection with this, the concerns of the charismatic movement have fuelled debates about the point and purpose of the reception of the Spirit, especially in Luke-Acts.[920] The

---

[910] Making a total of a quarter of the references for the whole of the New Testament. For a scholarly treatment of Lukan pneumatology in recent times, see M. Turner, 'Luke and the Spirit: Renewing Theological Interpretation of Biblical Pneumatology' in C. Bartholomew et al., eds., *Reading Luke: Interpretation, Reflection, Formation*, Scripture and Hermeneutics Series Vol. 6 (Milton Keynes: Paternoster, 2005), 267–293.

[911] I. Howard Marshall, *The Acts of the Apostles*, NT Guides (Sheffield: Sheffield Academic Press, 1992), 14–15. For a recent review of scholarship on Acts, see Todd Penner, 'Madness in the Method? The Acts of Apostles in Current Study' in *Currents in Biblical Research* (Continuum Publishing), Vol. 2:2, April 2004, arguing for a greater methodological and ideological awareness amidst the contemporary multiplicity of approaches.

[912] Col 4:14; 2 Tim 4:11.

[913] Traditionally from the nineteenth century advent of critical studies, especially F.C. Baur (Acts the product of the early church's desire to create an 'early catholicism'), and later E. Haenchen (Acts largely the product of the author's mind) and H. Conzelmann (the presence of the Holy Spirit in Acts the church's substitute for a delayed parousia). For a response to the historical scepticism expressed by those operating from a 'hermeneutic of suspicion', see Howard Marshall, *The Acts of the Apostles* (1992), 98.

[914] Kistemaker objects to this expression in view of the emphasis in Acts 1:1: 'all that *Jesus* began to do', S. Kistemaker *Exposition of the Acts of the Apostles* (Grand Rapids: Baker, 1990), 3.

[915] Acts 1:8 provides a narrative structure for Acts: growth in Jerusalem (chapters 1–7); in Judea and Samaria (chapters 8–12); and to the ends of the earth (chapters 13–28). Note the Spirit's leading in mission positively in Acts 8:29, 10:19, 13:2 and 20:23, and negatively in 16:6–7.

[916] See, for instance James B. Shelton, *Mighty in Word and Deed: The Role of the Holy Spirit in Luke-Acts* (Peabody, MA: Hendrickson, 1991).

[917] As in Acts 2:38.

[918] As in Acts 8:14–19, 10:44–47, 11:15–16. Hence Marshall's comment: 'a view which confines the experience of the Spirit in the theology of Acts to empowerment for witness and direction for mission is too narrow. The gift of the Spirit plays an important role in Christian assurance, just as it does in Paul' *The Acts of the Apostles* (1992), 69.

[919] As in Acts 15:8.

[920] Ju Hur, for instance, in *A Dynamic Reading of the Holy Spirit in Luke-Acts* (Sheffield: Sheffield Academic Press: 2001), 14–21, records the different views of J. D. G. Dunn (who sees it as part of Christian conversion/initiation),

Spirit is also portrayed in Acts as having an ongoing role in corporate encouragement[921] and prophetic utterance.[922] More recently, Stronstad has claimed that 'for Luke, the Holy Spirit relates not to salvation or to sanctification ... but exclusively to a third dimension of Christian life – service ... [that is] a charismatic rather than a soteriological theology of the Holy Spirit.'[923] Wenk, further, has argued 'that the underlying motif for Luke's pneumatology is his eschatological vision of the renewed people of God, including those who were traditionally marginalized or had no power in society and comprising both Jews and Gentiles.'[924] From such varied and sometimes overlapping pneumatological descriptions, we can agree with Marshall that 'the Spirit's working is not something that can be neatly categorised in a rational way but retains an element of the mysterious.'[925]

More recently, the significant turn from historical-critical methodology towards *literary* criticism[926] in biblical studies has emphasized the narrative aspect of Luke-Acts (cf. 'narrative' [διήγησις] in Luke 1:1[927]). Thus, attention has been focused upon the 'narrative function' of the Holy Spirit in the story-line or 'plot'[928] of Acts. In this capacity, he has, for instance, been described by W. H. Shepherd as 'God's onstage representative'[929] and 'the character [that] signals narrative reliability.'[930] Ju Hur has developed further literary categories to define his narrative character: 'christocentric mission director';[931] 'reliable revealer';[932] 'reliable Scripture commentator';[933] and 'God's verifier'[934] (confirming the acceptance of certain groups as God's people, notably the Gentiles[935]). This

---

R. Menzies (a Pentecostal scholar who links it with the Jewish 'spirit of prophecy' and sees it as a *donum superadditum* for Christian service) and Max Turner (who, *contra* Menzies, sees it not just as empowerment for mission, but as the *sine qua non* of the Christian life). Turner argues his case in *Power from High: The Spirit in Israel's Restoration and Witness* (Sheffield: Sheffield Academic Press, 1996), chapter 2 of which has a useful summary of 'Diverging Explanations of the Essential Character of the Gift of the Spirit', 38–78.

[921] Acts 9:31; 11:24.

[922] See, for instance, Acts 2:10 if one uses 'prophetic' in the 'telling forth' sense and in Acts 11:28 and 21:11 if one uses 'prophetic' in the 'foretelling' sense.

[923] Stronstad, *The Charismatic Theology of St. Luke*, 14.

[924] Matthias Wenk, 'Acts' in Trevor J. Burke and Keith Warrington, eds., *A Biblical Theology of the Holy Spirit* (London: SPCK; Cascade, 2014), 116. He is arguing this *contra* scholars who claim that the Spirit in Acts is principally related to inspired or prophetic speech, citing J. R. Levison as a recent exponent of this view.

[925] Marshall, *The Acts of the Apostles*, 69.

[926] For a discussion of the literary genre of Acts, see T. E. Phillips. 'The Genre of Acts: Moving Toward a Consensus' in *Currents in Biblical Research*, Vol. 4.3, June 2006, 365–396.

[927] Some question whether διήγησις can be applied to Acts as well as the gospel of Luke. See Paul Elbert 'Spirit, Scripture and Theology Through a Lukan Lens: a review article' in *Journal of Pentecostal Theology* 13 (1998), 62.

[928] For Hur, '*the plot of Luke-Acts is the way of witness, in seeking and saving God's people, engendered by Jesus* (in the Gospel) *and his witnesses* (in Acts), *through the power and guidance of the Holy Spirit in accordance with the plan of God*'. Hur, *A Dynamic Reading*, 185–186, italics the author's.

[929] Hur, *A Dynamic Reading*, 30, summarising W. H. Shepherd's view.

[930] An expression of W. H. Shepherd in *The Narrative Function of the Holy Spirit as a Character in Luke-Acts* (Atlanta: Scholars, 1994), 101, as quoted in Hur, *A Dynamic Reading*, 30.

[931] Hur, *A Dynamic Reading*, 151.

[932] Ibid., 151.

[933] Ibid., 151.

[934] Ibid., 255.

[935] Acts 10:44–48.

verification role is particularly pertinent in relation to Scripture. Thus J. A. Darr avers from his reading of Acts that 'The scriptures alone are not sufficient to legitimate anything; they too must be accredited in each case by the Spirit, or by a figure who has the Spirit's sanction.'[936] Recent rhetorical approaches have further emphasized the role of the anticipated hearing community in the understanding of the book.[937]

In this chapter, I shall seek to combine insights from all three of these approaches (historical, theological, and literary) as we investigate the hermeneutical role of the Spirit in Acts in relation to the Christian community's understanding of Scripture.

### (ii) The Spirit as the 'Spirit of Prophecy'

Hur refers to the Old Testament background as an essential part of the 'literary repertoire'[938] of the Spirit. 'Scholars ... have by and large agreed that the Lukan pneumatology is strongly indebted to the Jewish tradition or understanding of the Spirit: the Spirit of prophecy.'[939] Significantly, the very first outpouring of the Spirit at Pentecost is associated with utterance: 'they were all filled with the Holy Spirit and began to speak' (Acts 2:4). Barrett remarks, 'speech is in Acts the characteristic mark of the Spirit's presence, sometimes in glossolalia (2:4; 10:46; 19:6), sometimes in prophecy (2:17,18; 11:27; 13:1–3; 21:4, 9, 10, 11), sometimes in proclamation (4:31).'[940] To such a statement, we would wish to add the importance of Scriptural citation and exposition in such proclamations, not least in the Pentecost sermon itself.

---

[936] J. A. Darr, *On Character Building: The Reader and the Rhetoric of Characterization in Luke-Acts* (Louisville: Westminster John Knox, 1992), 53, quoted approvingly by Hur, *A Dynamic Reading*, 100.

[937] 'it was a document written to be read aloud, and the author attended to his writing so that what he had written could be rhetorically effective when read and heard by the first listener or listeners.' Ben Witherington III, *Acts of the Apostles: A Socio-Rhetorical Commentary* (Grand Rapids: Eerdmans; Carlisle: Paternoster, 1998), Foreword, x.

[938] Defined by Hur as 'the references to God's spirit in the Jewish Bible that are often explicitly cited and/or implicitly embedded in Luke-Acts', *A Dynamic Reading*, 33, fn. 62.

[939] Ibid., 25.

[940] C. K. Barrett, *The Acts of the Apostles* (ICC commentary), Vol. II (Edinburgh: T&T Clark, 1998), Introduction, lxxxiv. In terms of relative importance, I would wish to reverse the order of these three things and challenge the view that Acts 2 relates to glossolalia as opposed to speaking in foreign languages.

## The Use of Scripture in Speeches

With one exception,[941] all the Old Testament citations in Acts[942] appear in the speeches of individuals. Speeches[943] or discourse make up approximately one third of Acts[944] and thus constitute a substantive part of the overall message of the book. The historical accuracy of these speeches has been questioned,[945] but F. F. Bruce endorses F. J. Foakes-Jackson's assessment: 'Luke seems to have been able to give us an extraordinarily accurate picture of the undeveloped theology of the earliest Christians, and to enable us to determine the character of the most primitive presentation of the gospel.'[946]

Although these speeches, then, were of necessity made by individuals, we can view them in terms of their representing the primitive *kerygma* of the early church, to use Dodd's terminology.[947] Hans F. Bayer has argued this in relation to Peter's early speeches.

> According to Luke ... we are not so much to identify idiomatic Petrine elements in the initial Petrine speeches and statements in Acts 1–9:32 as much as we are to view them as collective, apostolic witness establishing the foundation for the rest of Acts.[948]

Foundational speeches were, of course, made not only by Peter but also later by Paul,[949] the two names that dominate the first (chapters 1–12) and second (chapters 13–26) halves of Acts respectively. As our sample passages in this chapter will be taken from the first half, we shall concentrate on the speeches of Peter (1:15–26; 2), along with those of Stephen (chapters 6–7) and the contributors to the Council of Jerusalem (chapter 15), all of which are pregnant with Old Testament reference.[950]

---

[941] Acts 8:32–33.

[942] For the full list, see Hur, *A Dynamic Reading*, 108, showing how heavily Luke relies on the LXX rather than the MT. Witherington says that Luke thus sees himself as writing a continuation of biblical history 'modelling his work to some extent on the style and tenor of the LXX, but if so it is a new sort of Scripture, a Scripture that focuses on fulfilment and the completion of God's providential salvation plan.' *The Acts of the Apostles: A Socio-Rhetorical Commentary*, 124.

[943] J. A. Fitzmyer underlines their literary importance: 'speeches are a subform found in ancient Greek historiography, used to produce a dramatic effect and often serving to aid the author's purpose in writing' *The Acts of the Apostles: The Anchor Bible* (New York: Doubleday, 1998), 105.

[944] Scholars estimate between 24 to 28 such speeches, taking up about 295 of 1,000 or so verses.

[945] Notably since H. J. Cadbury and M. Dibelius in the 1920s likened them to the more imaginative/literary inventions of the ancient Greek historian, Thucydides, R. Longenecker, *Acts*, Expositor's Bible Commentary (Grand Rapids: Zondervan, 1995), 25–26. For a defence of the authenticity of the speeches see J. R. W. Stott, *The Message of Acts* (Leicester: IVP, 1990), 69–72.

[946] F. J. Foakes-Jackson, *The Acts of the Apostles* MNTC (London: Hodder and Stoughton, 1931), xvi., as quoted by F. F. Bruce, *The Acts of the Apostles* 3rd ed. (Leicester: Apollos, 1990), 39.

[947] C. H. Dodd, *The Apostolic Preaching and its Developments* (London: Hodder and Stoughton, 1936), 28.

[948] Hans F. Bayer, 'The Preaching of Peter in Acts' in I. Howard Marshall and David Peterson, eds., *Witness to the Gospel: The Theology of Acts* (Grand Rapids: Eerdmans, 1998), 262, in a section headed 'The Portrait of Peter as spokesman of the collective, apostolic witness.'

[949] Note the close parallels between Peter's Pentecost speech (2:13–36) and Paul's speech at Pisidian Antioch (13:16–41).

[950] I shall also be looking at the use of Scripture in the prayer meeting recorded in 4:23–31.

According to Darrell Bock, the use of Scripture in Acts comprises five basic themes: covenant and promise; Christology; community mission or community guidance; commission to the Gentiles; challenge and warning to Israel.[951] Such scriptural usage 'support[ed] the new community's claim to the heritage of God as revealed in Moses and the prophets.'[952] Green spells this out:

> Within the speeches of Acts, Jewish people might hear the familiar stories borrowed from their Scriptures ... cast in ways that advocate a reading of that history that underscores the fundamental continuity between the ancient story of Israel, the story of Jesus, and the story of the Way. Israel's past (and present) ... is understood ... in relation to the redemptive purpose (βουλή) of God ... [which] can be understood only in the light of Jesus's ministry, crucifixion, and exaltation, and through exegetes operating in the sphere of the Holy Spirit.[953]

Such an *apologetic* use of the Old Testament, then, entailed a 'promise and fulfilment' approach to Scripture which centred upon Jesus as the promised Messiah and the inclusion of the Gentiles within God's plan of salvation (thus also describable as a '*salvation history*' use.[954]) Recent intertextual approaches have introduced further subtleties. As Koptak says:

> The older paradigms of promise-fulfilment and salvation history are enriched by the recognition that the biblical writers stood in dialectical relationship with their own written tradition. Simply put, interpreters will not only look for what is old in the new; they will also see how the new sheds light on the old.[955]

In such a rich use of the Old Testament, the Spirit's authenticating, guiding, interpreting, and reinterpreting role is regarded in Acts as a vital accompaniment. This follows on from the fulfilment of Joel's universal promise of the Spirit being poured out 'upon all flesh' with the result that 'your sons and daughters shall prophesy' (Acts 2:17). Thus, before they speak, Peter (Acts 2), Stephen (6:5, 10), and Philip (8:29) are clearly understood to be endowed with the Spirit.

---

[951] D. Bock, 'Scripture and the Realisation of God's promises' in Howard Marshall and Peterson, eds., *Witness to the Gospel*, 41–62. See also Hur, *A Dynamic* Reading, 109, for another summary of the purpose of Old Testament citations.
[952] Bock, in Marshall and Peterson, eds., *Witness to the Gospel*, 41.
[953] J. Green, 'Learning Theological Interpretation from Luke,' in *Reading Luke: Interpretation, Reflection, Formation*, 72.
[954] S. Moyise, *The Old Testament in the New. An Introduction* (London; New York: Continuum, 2001), 61. This 'salvation-history' categorization fits in with the general understanding of the nature of the book of Acts by the scholars who contributed to Howard Marshal and Peterson, eds., *Witness to the Gospel, 16*: 'We believe that Acts is primarily about God's action in offering salvation through Jesus Christ to both Jews and Gentiles and thereby creating a new people'.
[955] E. Koptak, 'Intertextuality' in K. J. Vanhoozer, ed. et al., *Dictionary for Theological Interpretation of the Bible* (Grand Rapids: Baker, 2005), 334.

Such an endowment, however, is not always specifically expressed in the Lukan narrative. As Dodd has pointed out, 'in Acts and epistles it is clear that the fact of life in the Spirit is *presupposed*. The primitive church, in proclaiming its Gospel to the world, offered its own fellowship and experience as the realization of the Gospel.'[956] This, then, brings us to some comments regarding the role and relevance of community.

## Spirit, Word and Community

It is self-evident that the speeches in Acts took place in the various kinds of 'community' contexts as the forum in which the Spirit took hold of the words of the Spirit-anointed servants of God. Consequently, 'the word of God continued to increase, and the number of the disciples multiplied greatly' (6:7). Besides the great unnamed host of 'three thousand souls' (2:41) on the day of Pentecost, many individual conversions are recorded, several by name.[957] Thus 'slowly, the story of individuals becomes the narrative of the church.'[958] The Spirit who called individuals also formed them into communities (cf. Acts 2:42–47; 4:32–35; 5:12–16). Indeed, Bock avers that 'Luke emphasizes what the Spirit does for the community more than what the Spirit does in each believer.'[959] The 'community-forming power'[960] of the Holy Spirit is particularly highlighted by Matthias Wenk. Citing the programmatic role of the Spirit, as per the Old Testament quotations used by Jesus in Luke 4:16–30 and Peter in Acts 2:14–41, he argues that 'Luke expects the fulfilment of the eschatological renewal of God's people to be of pneumatic origin and with social-ethical consequences.'[961] Recalling, inter alia, the Spirit's role in the conversions of Samaritans[962] and the Gentile Cornelius,[963] as well as in the deliberations of the Jerusalem Council,[964] he concludes that the Spirit's main task is to enable and 'certify the universal and inclusive character of the community.'[965]

---

[956] C. H. Dodd, *The Apostolic Preaching and its Developments*, 135, italics added. Cf. I. Howard Marshall: 'the Spirit ... is throughout Acts the guide of the church in its decisions and actions,' *The Acts of the Apostles* (Leicester, IVP: 1980), 255.

[957] For example Paul (chapter 9), the Ethiopian Eunuch (chapter 8), Cornelius (chapter 10), Lydia (chapter 16).

[958] Luke Timothy Johnson, *Scripture and Discernment: Decision Making in the Church* (Nashville: Abingdon, 1996),107.

[959] Darrell L. Bock, *Acts* (Grand Rapids: Baker, 2007), 37.

[960] M. Wenk, *Community-Forming Power: The Socio-Ethical Role of the Spirit in Luke-Acts* (Sheffield: Sheffield Academic Press, 2000).

[961] Wenk, *Acts*, in Trevor J. Burke and Keith Warrington, eds., *A Biblical Theology of the Holy Spirit*, 117.

[962] Acts 8:4–25.

[963] Acts 10:1–11:18.

[964] Acts 15:8, 28.

[965] Wenk, *Acts*, in Burke and Warrington, eds., *A Biblical Theology of the Holy Spirit*, 126. 'Any limitation of Luke's pneumatology either to an individualised conversion-initiation paradigm or to inspired speech falls short of his vision of a universal and reconciled people of God who by the presence of the Spirit becomes the continuation of Jesus's liberating and restoring ministry and thereby reflects the characteristics of the kingdom of God in this world.' Ibid., 128.

In describing the development of this Christian community, Luke singles out many advances that were indeed initiated by the Spirit, frequently following the exposition of Scripture. These range from the first expression of κοινωνία after Pentecost (note κοινωνία ('fellowship') immediately following διδαχή ('teaching') in Acts 2:42), to the great extension that the conversion of the Gentiles brought to the fellowship of the church.[966] And the Spirit that facilitated such advances was also instrumental in resolving the problems that accompanied them.[967]

In one of the early incidents that arose from the communal sharing of goods, F. F. Bruce draws attention to the grounds on which Peter challenges the deceit of Ananias and Sapphira: 'How is it that you have agreed together to test the Spirit of the Lord?' (Acts 5:9):

> This implies an association of the Spirit with the community amounting in some sense to identity: it is the Spirit that informs and animates the community, which indeed, apart from the Spirit, would not be a community but an aggregate of individuals.[968]

This is where Acts has valuable lessons for us in the realm of hermeneutics. The close association between Spirit and community needs to be maintained not just in the sharing of physical goods and bread but also in the appropriation of spiritual truth and bread. In the light of this, I shall now proceed to my main section, selecting key parts of the Lukan narrative where Scripture is being interpreted in various kinds of community contexts, under the guidance of the Spirit.

## The Spirit-enabled Hermeneutics of the Early Christian Community

I shall begin our five-stage journey at a post-ascension meeting of the disciples (1:15–26); proceed to the great gathering on the day of Pentecost (chapter 2); join the more intimate group of believers at prayer (4:23–31); listen to Stephen speaking to an antagonistic Sanhedrin (chapters 6–7); and finally attend the proceedings at the Council of Jerusalem (chapter 15). In these diverse communal settings, what kind of Spirit-assisted understanding of Scripture do we find at work?

---

[966] Acts 10:45.
[967] For instance in Acts 6:3 where men 'full of the Spirit' were chosen to help in the dispute over the distribution to the widows, and in Acts 15:28 ('it seemed good to the Holy Spirit and us') in the debate over Gentile inclusion.
[968] F. F. Bruce, 'The Holy Spirit in Acts of the Apostles', *Interpretation* 27:2 April 1973, 173.

## Acts 1: 15-26 The Election of Matthias: Reconstitution of the Apostolic Group

The events recorded here take place in the ten-day interval between the Ascension and Pentecost and thus, of course, precede the full endowment of Spirit-given κοινωνία. A prayerful, group dynamic is nevertheless evidently at work amongst the disciples (1:14). They would have had plenty of recent exegetical instruction from Jesus, not just in his pre-resurrection Spirit-anointed person but in his post-resurrection glory.[969] This surely would have left a lasting and unforgettable impact on the way they understood and applied Scripture.

The importance of deliberation around Scripture in relation to the replacement for Judas is shown by the detail in which it is recorded: Luke devotes as much of his narrative to this in his first chapter of Acts (vv. 15-26) as he does to the last days of Jesus on earth (vv. 1-11). The record of Peter's address begins with a statement that highlights the inevitability of Scriptural fulfilment: ἔδει πληρωθῆναι τὴν γραφὴν ('Scripture had to be fulfilled' v. 16a) as its starting point, along with a recognition of Holy Spirit authorship: ἣν προεῖπεν τὸ πνεῦμα τὸ ἅγιον ('which the Holy Spirit spoke' v. 16b), and is set in the context of the gathered Christian company: ἐν μέσῳ τῶν ἀδελφῶν ('in the midst of the brothers' v. 15—note this first reference to Christians as 'brothers').

The importance of the community element is further stressed by the reference to the number of the assembled company in the parenthesis of v. 15—important because 'in Jewish law a minimum of 120 Jewish men was required to establish a community with its own council'[970]—along with a recognition that Judas's sin was not just a great 'wickedness' (ἀδικίας, v. 18) but more particularly here a betrayal of the privileged group of Twelve of which he was a member: ὅτι κατηριθμημένος ἦν ἐν ἡμῖν ('for he was numbered among us', v. 17a).

For Luke, 'the apostles' were a key and primary group in the fulfilment of God's purposes for the early church.[971] He thus stresses how imperative it was that the eleven, dutifully listed in v. 13, be augmented to form the apostolic complement. 'The apostasy of Judas is significant because it broke the symbolic circle of the Twelve, who represent the restored Israel upon which the Spirit is to fall.'[972] Such a restoration would begin with the Spirit-anointed proclamation of

---

[969] Luke 24:25-27, 32, 44-47; Acts 1:2, 3, 6, 7.
[970] I. Howard Marshall, *The Acts of the Apostles* (TNTC) (Leicester: IVP, 1980), 64. To conclude the quote: 'in Jewish terms the disciples were a body of sufficient size to form a new community.'
[971] See Andrew C. Clark, 'The Role of the Apostles', chapter 9 in *Witness to the Gospel: The Theology of Acts*, eds. I. Howard Marshall and D. Peterson, 169-185. He notes that whereas '"the apostles"' is 'only used once in Matthew (10:2), and once or twice in Mark (3:14; 6:30), it occurs six times in Luke's Gospel and twenty eight times in Acts ... for Luke the term is always used in the plural', 170. He sees their strategic collective role in terms of: the nucleus of a restored Israel; witnesses to Jesus' resurrection; authoritative teachers; and missionaries to Israel, 173-185.
[972] Luke Timothy Johnson, *Scripture and Discernment: Decision Making in the Church* (Nashville: Abingdon, 1996), 83, noting also their future judgment role in Luke 22:30.

Pentecost for which 'the Twelve' were such a vital part in 'confront[ing] Israel assembled in Jerusalem.'[973]

From the deliberations concerning the selection of the twelfth apostle in Acts 1:15–25, I wish to underline seven special features that attended the community's understanding of Scripture, as expounded by Peter.

(i) The context of *prayer*. The appointment of Matthias that follows the exposition of Scripture is preceded generally by a spirit of communal prayer that is united: ὁμοθυμαδόν ('with one accord', v.14) and persistent (v. 14), and specifically by prayer to the Lord who is the 'heart knower' of all (Σὺ κύριε καρδιογνῶστα πάντων, v. 24). Maybe the church was following the cue of the very same Psalm from which Peter was about to quote: 'but I give myself to prayer' (Ps 109:4b). 'The nascent church is showing some of its most fundamental characteristics: gathered, seeking the Lord's will with one mind in prayer, and assembled to carry out God's mission.'[974]

(ii) The sense of '*divine necessity*'[975] implied by the double 'must' (ἔδει) of vv. 16 and 21–22. The choice of Matthias was thus driven not just by a community need but also by an imperative felt by Peter and those with him arising from their belief in a sovereign purpose at work.

(iii) This imperative derived in no small measure from an *interpretation of Scripture* that highlighted divine fulfilment and thus justified Peter's action. In 1:20 he focuses upon two Psalms attributed to David that spoke of the suffering and vindication of the righteous. Peter individualizes the judgment of Ps 69:25 ('may *his* camp become desolate') to apply it to Judas. The use of Ps 109:8 to refer to 'another tak[ing] his office' (τὴν ἐπισκοπὴν αὐτοῦ in the LXX from which Peter quotes) might have been influenced by the later use of ἐπίσκοπος ('overseer') for the role of leadership in passages such as 1 Tim 3:1. The employment of Jewish midrashic exegesis could also help explain other links that were made.[976] However, as Ps 69 is referred to four other times in the New Testament,[977] it seems more likely that its specific use derived from the fact that it formed part of the early church's emerging block of *testimonia* (as per C. H. Dodd[978]) from which they commonly drew a messianic application. As has been

---

[973] Fitzmyer, *The Acts of the Apostles*, 221. Note 'Peter, standing with the eleven' in Acts 2:14.
[974] Bock, *Acts*, 78.
[975] Richard N. Longenecker, *Acts*, Expositor's Bible Commentary (Grand Rapids: Zondervan, 1995), 61.
[976] Longenecker, for instance, says that 'Peter ... cite[s] Psalm 109:8 on the Jewish exegetical principle of analogous subject [Hillel's sixth exegetical rule] in order to defend the legitimacy of replacing a member of the apostolic band,' Ibid., 60–61.
[977] Verse 4 is quoted by Jesus himself in John 15:25, verse 9 by his disciples in John 2:17 and Paul refers to the Psalm in Rom 11:9–10 and 15:3.
[978] C. H. Dodd, *According to the Scriptures: The Substructure of New Testament Theology* (London: Nisbet, 1952), 57–59, 96–97.

seen, Dodd and others have argued that the ultimate inspiration for such a use of these passages would have derived from Jesus himself.[979]

(iv) Luke Timothy Johnson highlights the part played by the use of *narrative* as an accompaniment to interpretation.

> Peter's narrative dominates the passage.... He tells how Scripture 'had to be fulfilled' ... by telling the story of Judas' defection.... The narrative does not baldly recite facts, but interprets the very psalm verses it invokes for authority ... psalms which are found together only here in the New Testament. We see narrative and scriptural interpretation interpenetrate.... The decision to replace Judas is based on a theological interpretation of the event of his betrayal.[980]

In the midst of Peter's narration, Luke inserts a parenthetic one of his own, concerning Judas's grisly end (vv. 18–19). R. L. Brawley, writing from an 'intertextual' perspective, picks up on the way this account of a 'grotesque evisceration'[981] is set off against the choice of the new apostle who would become 'a witness of the resurrection' (v. 22).

> Acts 1:15–26 employs the carnivalesque in concert with the voices of Scripture in order to reduce Judas to utter absurdity. This contrasts Judas with Jesus, who is vindicated from the degradation of the crucifixion by the resurrection. ...[982]

> The choice of Matthias is the positive affirmation of the development of a community founded on a construct of world that centers on the God of Israel who raised Jesus from the dead.... They come to their understanding ... through interpretation of scripture.[983]

An interpretive element within the narrative also comes out in the community's prayer at the end of our passage ('from which Judas turned aside to go to his own place', v. 25c), which could have been influenced by the logic of the thought flow arising from Peter's use of Ps 69:25 concerning Judas's ultimate destination.

(v) Stott also points to the community's use of '*common sense*'[984] in choosing a substitute for Judas who had 'the same qualifications, including an eyewitness experience of Jesus and a personal appointment by him.'[985] Such a person could

---

[979] David Gooding, *True to the Faith: A Fresh Approach to the Acts of the Apostles* (London: Hodder & Stoughton, 1990), 45, says that it is 'unthinkable' that Jesus (in Luke 24:27, 44–47) would not have made reference to David as a messianic 'prototype king' as in the Psalms.
[980] Luke Timothy Johnson, *Scripture and Discernment*, 83–84.
[981] Robert L. Brawley, *Text to Text Pours Forth Speech: Voices of Scripture in Luke-Acts* (Bloomington: Indiana University Press, 1995), 63.
[982] Ibid., preface x. Brawley also reckons that 'the astute reader who knows the Septuagint may pick up allusions to scripture in the figure of Judas', 71, i.e., in Gen 38. 'Just as Judas the patriarch sets off Joseph to advantage, so Judas the betrayer sets off Jesus to advantage', 73–74.
[983] Ibid., 74.
[984] J. R. W. Stott, *The Message of Acts,* BST (Leicester: IVP, 1990), 58.
[985] Ibid., 58.

help act as a guarantor of the gospel tradition with the authority of direct personal experience 'from the beginning.'[986]

(vi) Overall, although the community played such an important part in the decision-making process, the choice of Matthias, being narrated as a result of Scriptural warrant, prayer, and the casting of lots (v. 26)[987] is thereby recorded as a result of *divine appointment* rather than 'democratic election.'[988]

(vii) Although *the Holy Spirit* is only explicitly mentioned in terms of the Davidic authorship of the relevant Psalms (v. 16), David Gooding makes an interesting, albeit speculative, suggestion that links the work of the Spirit with the 'law court' scenario of the second mentioned Psalm from which Peter quotes. In a section entitled '*History's cause célèbre*',[989] he reads Psalm 109 as 'prototypical' of what Jesus suffered at the hands of the Jewish religious establishment and highlights the Psalm's adversarial language[990] along with its call for judgment upon the guilty.

> In a few days' time [viz. at Pentecost] the Holy Spirit would come to promulgate the verdict of the High Court (John 16:8–11) … [Judas'] defection, fulfilling Scripture as it did, was one more piece of evidence in favour of the Holy Spirit's case.[991]

To conclude this section, this record of the church's inaugural use of Scripture demonstrates that deliberation around Scripture played a determinative role in the life of the church from the start. A community setting is evident in both Scripture's use (amongst the group of 120) and its purpose (to complete the apostolic group), though its interpretation was mediated through the narrative exposition of the community's acknowledged leader, Peter. His emphasis upon God's purpose, alongside 'the brothers'' use of prayer and lots, however, shows that the community was seeking to rely not upon human insight but upon divine help to interpret and apply Scripture. This task would be greatly facilitated by the coming of the Spirit, as described in the next chapter.

## Acts 2 Pentecost: Spirit, Scripture and the Birth of the Church

According to Witherington, 'no text in Acts has received closer scrutiny than Acts 2. Whole theologies and denominations have been built up around the Acts 2 accounts.'[992] My own investigation of the chapter will be limited to underlining the communal dimensions of the Spirit's interpretive and constitutive work,

---

[986] Acts 1:21–22.
[987] Cf. Prov 16:33. Many commentators point out that this is the last recorded use of the Old Testament system of lots for discerning the divine will, since after the events of Acts 2 the Holy Spirit is given as guide for the church.
[988] Fitzmyer, *The Acts of the Apostles*, 228. See also his comments at 220.
[989] Gooding, *True to the Faith*, 50.
[990] Especially vv. 4–7 and vv. 25–31.
[991] Gooding, *True to the Faith*, 50.
[992] Witherington, *Acts of the Apostles*, 128.

particularly in relation to the Old Testament Scriptures referred to in Peter's explanation of the Pentecost event. I will make five sets of observations, mainly in the order in which we find them surfacing in the chapter.

*(i) Pentecost as the Great Communal Event that Constituted the Church*

All the foundational events in the life of the Christian church had Old Testament counterparts. Thus, the Old Testament feast of the Passover prefigured Christ's passion and New Testament soteriology.[993] And the Feast of Weeks that came fifty days later (hence 'Pentecost'), celebrating the beginning of the grain harvest,[994] foreshadowed the great spiritual harvest that would follow the coming of the Holy Spirit after Christ's departure.[995] Not that Luke himself makes such an explicit link, although the language of Acts 2:1 highlights a distinct fulfilment aspect. Fitzmyer captures the force of συμπληροῦσθαι ('arrived'): 'in the coming of the fiftieth day to full number.'[996] This may be a reference to the Jewish tradition that the giving of the law at Sinai also took place at the same time as Pentecost. Hence Thomas Aquinas's comment that 'the feast of Pentecost, when the Old Law was given, has been succeeded by the Pentecost in which was given the law of the Spirit of life.'[997] Luke himself, however, does not explicitly parallel the giving of the Torah and giving of the Spirit,[998] although links with Exodus terminology could be read from the account. These include references to 'fire' in v. 3 and 'blood, fire and smoke' in v. 19,[999] whilst 'poured out' as used of the Spirit in v. 33 could be paralleling Ps 68:19 with the idea of the law coming down from Mount Sinai.[1000]

The great festivals of Judaism[1001] were naturally great communal events that marked their identity as the people of God. By the new Pentecost, the Spirit of God was to constitute the new Christian community. To use Paul's language, 'in one Spirit we were all baptized into one body' (1 Cor 12:13).

---

[993] cf. 1 Cor 5:7.
[994] Exod 23:16; Lev 23:15–21; Deut 16:9–12. Fitzmyer (*The Acts of the Apostles*, 235–236) claims three Pentecostal feasts were celebrated by the Jews, including the 'Feast of New Wine', which could help to explain 'not drunk' in Acts 2:15.
[995] J. H. E. Hull, *The Holy Spirit in the Acts of the Apostles* (London: Lutterworth, 1967), 51, says that 'Pentecost was also known as the Day of the First Fruits' and that 'no reader of the New Testament would find it hard to discern divine symbolism in the choice of the Day of First Fruits for the imparting of the Spirit', referring to 'firstfruits' in Rom 8:23, 11:16, 16:5, James 1:18 and Rev 14:4.
[996] Fitzmyer, *The Acts of the Apostles*, 237.
[997] *Summa Theologiae* I–II, q.103, a.3. ad 4, as quoted by Fitzmyer, *The Acts of the Apostles*, 237.
[998] As does Paul, for instance in 2 Cor 3 (see chapter 6, section 5).
[999] Exod 3:2–5; 13:21; 19:16–18; 24:17; 40:38. See C. A. Evans and J. A. Sanders, *Luke and Scripture: The Function of Sacred Tradition in Luke-Acts* (Minneapolis: Fortress, 1993), 214, fn. 5 re the debated Sinai/Pentecost link.
[1000] Ps 68:19 is reflected in Eph 4:8 and may be behind the wording used in Acts 2:33. There was apparently a rabbinic tradition that Ps 68:19 alluded to Moses's ascent of Mt Sinai. This could then be paralleling Jesus ascending to receive the Spirit that he then pours down.
[1001] Notably Passover, Pentecost, and Tabernacles.

## (ii) Significant Pneumatological Terms

The language of 'fire' does not just derive from the Old Testament, but was also used by John the Baptist. 'I baptize you with water, but ... he will baptize you with the Holy Spirit and with fire' (Luke 3:16). Luke adopts this contrast in Acts 1:5 which Longenecker sees as making another link.

> So Luke brings John's baptism of Jesus in the Jordan and the Spirit's baptism of assembled believers at Pentecost into a parallel in which each event is seen as the final constitutive factor for all that follows in the ministry of Jesus (cf. Luke's Gospel) and the mission of the early church (cf. Acts).[1002]

As the church was about to embark on this mission, the 'tongues as of fire' (2:3) would not just have evoked recollections of the divine presence as in Exodus. The 'sound like a mighty wind'[1003] also symbolized divine power, as earlier manifested on Mount Sinai and later prophesied in Ezek 37:9–14, a passage understood in Judaism as referring to events that would '[usher] in the final Messianic Age.'[1004] Most commentators reckon that the tongues themselves represent the ability to communicate in the different languages represented by the international crowd of 2:5–11,[1005] rather than ecstatic speech. A 'deliberate and dramatic reversal of the curse of Babel'[1006] has often understandably been suggested, though this is not a deduction that is made explicit in the passage itself. What is clear is that 'the Spirit [who] gave them utterance' (ἀποφθέγγεσθαι v. 4c) afforded the same help to Peter as he shortly afterwards 'addressed' (ἀπεφθέγξατο v. 14c) the multitude. Fitzmyer says that the verb in question (ἀποφθέγγομαι) means 'to speak out, declare boldly and loudly,'[1007] an ability that flows from being 'filled with' (ἐπλήσθησαν v. 4) the Holy Spirit.

This language of being 'filled with'/'full of' is a typically Lukan expression for Spirit-endowment.[1008] As used here in 2:4 (also in 4:8, 31), the phrase 'filled with the Spirit' has reference to the immediate and special inspiration of the Spirit for speaking the authoritative words of God.[1009] It 'always describes a specific,

---

[1002] Longenecker, *Acts*, 64.
[1003] The Greek term *pneuma* and the Hebrew *ruach* can mean either wind or spirit according to the context.
[1004] Longenecker, *Acts*, 66. Note other Old Testament theophanies using similar 'wind' imagery: 2 Sam 22:16; Job 37:10; Ezek 13:13.
[1005] Note especially v. 11b 'telling in our own tongues the mighty works of God.'
[1006] Stott, *The Message of Acts*, 68.
[1007] Fitzmyer, *The Acts of the Apostles*, 239.
[1008] Turner says there are twenty-seven occurrences in Luke-Acts, fourteen of which pertain to the Spirit. M. Turner, *Power from on High – the Spirit in Israel's Restoration and Witness in Luke-Acts* (Sheffield: Sheffield Academic Press, 1996), 165. Paul, by contrast, only uses the expression five times. See Turner, *Power from on High*, 165–169 and Hurr, *A Dynamic Reading of the Holy Spirit in Luke-Acts*, 165–171 for a fuller account of Lukan 'filled with'/ 'full of' vocabulary.
[1009] 'The phrase "to be filled with the Holy Spirit" is *not always*, *but often* tied with narrative contexts in which characters are presented as giving inspired speeches. Through their prophetic or inspired utterances, these characters act as witnesses to Jesus: Luke1:42; 1:67; Acts 2:4; 4:8a; 4:31; 13:10a': Hurr, *A Dynamic Reading*, 168.

though potentially repetitive, act of prophetic inspiration.'[1010] When people are said to be 'full of the Spirit' (πλήρεις πνεύματος), however, as for instance of those 'seven men of good repute' in 6:3 and that 'good man' Barnabas in 11:14, the reference is to the state of persons 'whose lives are particularly marked by the work of the Spirit from ordinary Christians.'[1011] The importance of this distinction between 'filled with' and 'full of' is stressed by Turner:

> Once we observe that in Luke-Acts the words 'filled with the Holy Spirit' usually designate short outbursts of spiritual power/inspiration, rather than the inception of long-term endowments of the Spirit, we need not agonize with, for example J. E. Hull over the question why the disciples who were 'filled' with the Spirit at Pentecost (Acts 2:4) needed to be 'filled' again with the Spirit at 4:8, 31, etc. The Lukan use of these expressions allows that a person might on many occasions be 'filled with the Holy Spirit' while nevertheless remaining 'full' of the Spirit: the two types of metaphor make different but complementary assertions.[1012]

Despite this semantic differentiation, Marshall observes a certain degree of commonality in Acts concerning the verb used regarding Spirit endowment.

> It is ... important to observe that what is here [sic. in Acts 2:4] called a 'filling' is called a 'baptizing' (1:5 and 11:16), a 'pouring out' (2:17f; 10:45), and a 'receiving' (10:47). The basic act of receiving the Spirit can be described as being baptized or filled, but the verb 'baptize' is not used for subsequent experiences. A good deal of theological confusion would be avoided if we were careful to use these terms in the biblical manner.[1013]

Pentecostal theologians would not necessarily agree with Marshall here, but his point acts as a general warning against the dangers of building dogmatic theologies upon decontextualized individual words. Not that this prevents us from drawing significance from the nuances of terms, such as, indeed, 'pouring out'.

This brings us to Acts 2:17 where Peter, quoting from Joel 2, refers to the promise to 'pour out' the Spirit in 2:17 (cf. 2:33). Of this Stott says:

---

[1010] Stronstad, *The Charismatic Theology of St. Luke*, 61: pointing out that 'being filled with the Spirit is both an individual [e.g. Peter and Paul] and collective [e.g. Jerusalem and Iconium disciples] experience', 60.
[1011] Turner, *Power from on High*, 169.
[1012] Turner, *Power from on High*, 169, referring to J. H. E. Hull, *The Holy Spirit in the Acts of the Apostles*. Roger Stronstrad makes a slightly different deduction from the Lukan terminology, saying that 'full of the Holy Spirit' 'describes enabling for ministry', whilst 'filled with the Holy Spirit' 'describes prophetic office and potentially repetitive experience' *Spirit, Scripture and Theology: A Pentecostal Perspective* (Baguio City: Asian Pacific Theological Seminary, 1995), as summarized by Paul Elbert in 'Spirit, Scripture and Theology Through a Lukan Lens', *Journal of Pentecostal Theology* 13 (1998),61.
[1013] I. Howard Marshall, *The Acts of the Apostles* (Leicester: IVP, 1980), 69. He points out that 'the noun-phrase "*baptism* with the Spirit" does not occur in the New Testament' fn., 69.

> The picture is of a heavy tropical rainstorm, and seems to illustrate the generosity of God's gift (neither a drizzle nor even a shower but a downpour), its finality (for what is 'poured out' cannot be gathered again) and its universality (widely distributed among the different groupings).[1014]

Haenchen further notes that 'I will pour out *from* my Spirit' (ἐκχεῶ ἀπὸ τοῦ πνεύματός μου) 'indicates that the fullness of the Spirit remains with God and that man only partakes of it.'[1015]

### (iii) The Old Testament Interpretive Context

As Peter commences the first recorded sermon[1016] of the Christian church, he is described as 'standing with the eleven' (v. 14) and is thus represented as 'spokesman for the collective.'[1017] I will here proceed on the assumption that the speech is authentic to Peter rather than a Lukan fiction,[1018] although the account in 2:14–40 is clearly a highly compressed and structured Lukan summary of the 'many ... words' (v. 40) that he spoke. The elements of apologetic thrust, theological depth, Scriptural and prophetic fulfilment, Christological focus and evangelistic challenge that we find in the sermon, coming from one who is later described as 'unlearned and ignorant',[1019] can surely only be fully explained by reference to its Spirit-inspired endowment.[1020]

As such, it is impregnated with Old Testament allusions and quotations, the latter primarily from Joel 2, Psalms 16 and 110. These three passages between them take up over half of the recorded part of the sermon and are numbered by Dodd as amongst the *testimonia* of the early church.[1021] Thus Peter's hermeneutic is driven by an understanding of Scripture and its fulfilment that was shared in the primitive Christian community. And in so far as Peter's words were addressed principally to a congregation of Jews (2:14, 22), the use of Scripture was a vital means of apologetic. As A. Weiser has said (doubtless bearing in mind the largely biblically illiterate and multi-cultural society of today):

> Such a 'proof from Scripture' is strange to our way of thinking and does not satisfy us; but for the early church it was of fundamental importance

---

[1014] Stott, *The Message of Acts*, 73–74.
[1015] Ernst Haenchen, *The Acts of the Apostles: A Commentary* (Oxford: Blackwell, 1971), 179.
[1016] Earlier sermons (sermonettes?) were clearly spoken by the initial recipients of the Spirit as they declared 'the mighty works of God' 2:11 to the 'devout men from every nation' (2:5) gathered in Jerusalem.
[1017] Hans F. Bayer, 'The Preaching of Peter in Acts' in I. Howard Marshall and David Peterson., eds, *Witness to the Gospel: The Theology of Acts*, eds. (Grand Rapids: Eerdmans, 1998), 262.
[1018] As for example, claimed by E. Haenchen, *The Acts of the Apostles*, 185.
[1019] Acts 4:13 (AV).
[1020] Implied from Acts 2:4, 17 and expressed relating to Peter's speech in Acts 4:8.
[1021] Dodd points out how the quotation of Joel by Peter ends at Acts 2:21 in the middle of Joel 2:32, but the latter part of v. 32 ('those whom the Lord has called') 'crops up at Acts 2:39 in a way that shows that the whole passage was in mind.', Dodd, *According to the Scriptures*, 47, fn. 1.

that what had happened to Jesus had to be brought into harmony with the OT, because that was the Jews' book of belief.[1022]

A detailed analysis of the interpretive process exhibited in the Lukan account is a complex matter that is beyond the scope of this book, but I will seek to make some comments thereon that are pertinent to this book's theme.

As to the use of Joel generally, C. A. Evans claims that 'Luke's setting for Peter's sermon is laced throughout with language from the Greek version of Joel',[1023] detecting many allusions to it in Acts 2 apart from the actual verses directly quoted by Peter, leading up to the final call to repent.[1024] He also refers to the prophetic expectations that had arisen from Joel and other traditions that were associated with God's speaking at Sinai (and in many languages according to some), such prophetic speaking which would again sound forth at the coming of the Spirit.

> The Lukan narrative illustrates and testifies how these prophetic traditions had come to be experienced in the Christian community. Acts 2 certainly tells us something about how Joel is interpreted (or appropriated) from a Christian point of view, but the real issue is how Christian history and experience are understood from a scriptural point of view. It is Joel that informs Luke's community, and it is Joel that 'rewrites' the history and experience of this community.[1025]

Such a comment generally serves to remind us that Christian experience (notably, as here, that of the Spirit, as in 2:1-13) needs to be interpreted by Scriptural truth and that Scriptural truth (as here in 2:14-36) should be interpreted through Christian experience of the Spirit.

It was the Pentecostal, individual-yet-also-communal experience of the Spirit which, Vanhoozer insists, enabled Peter specifically to say 'this is that' of the Joel prophecy as he saw it coming to pass in the very birth of the church. 'Such an interpretation is not merely Peter's human projection but a product of the Spirit's guidance. Only his sharing in the life of the believing community, however, allowed Peter to see "this" as "that".'[1026]

Peter's τοῦτό ἐστιν τὸ in relation to Joel 2 in 2:16 introduces his sermon and evidences a *pesher*/fulfilment approach to OT Scripture, pointed up by the addition of the words 'and they shall prophesy' in v. 18 and some other

---

[1022] A. Weiser "Die Pfingstpredigt des Lukas" *BibLeb 14* (1973):1-12: as cited in Fitzmyer, *The Acts of the Apostles*, 257.
[1023] 'The Prophetic Setting of the Pentecost Sermon' in Evans and Sanders, eds., *Luke and Scripture*, 215-216, he lists 'approximately twenty words' in Acts 2:2-15 that can be traced back to Joel, for instance: οὐρανός (Acts 2:2; Joel 2:10,30); πῦρ (Acts 2:3; Joel 1:19, 20; 2:3, 5, 30); and πίμπλημι (Acts 2:4; Joel 2:24).
[1024] Μετανοήσατε (Acts 2:38; Joel 2:13,14).
[1025] Ibid., 224. Evans claims that 'the use of Joel ... plays a major role in Luke's theology of universal salvation', 212, and that 'Joel's prophecy is not only foundational to Luke's pneumatology but serves as a major contributing element to the evangelist's understanding of the Gospel itself': ibid., 220.
[1026] K. J. Vanhoozer, *Is there a Meaning in this Text?* (Leicester: Apollos; IVP: 1998), 410.

variations.[1027] The return of the 'Spirit of prophecy', as we have seen, was considered to mark the beginning of 'the "last days" of God's redemptive program.'[1028] The Spirit's interpretive help is reflected in Brawley's observation that Peter's use of Joel exhibits more of a 'hermeneutical' rather than a 'prophetic prediction' use[1029] of the OT in so far as it is employed to *explain* the events of Pentecost. After an 'intertextual' exploration, Brawley concludes:

> The revisionary and reciprocal relationship between Acts 2 and Joel corresponds to what Bloom calls "tessura"—a relationship of completion—like particles of a shattered piece of pottery patched together to restore its wholeness. On their own Joel 3 LXX and Acts 2 are fragments. Apart from Joel, Pentecost is incomprehensible. Apart from Acts, Joel is an antiquated poet.[1030]

This may be overstating the case, but such a comment highlights the way in which the Spirit enabled Peter and the early church to understand the epoch-making events going on around them in what Thiselton elsewhere refers to as the 'selected or privileged frame of reference'[1031] of the Old Testament.

As Peter goes on in his sermon in 2:25–35 to quote from Ps 16:8–11 to support what he has said in v. 24 concerning the resurrection, and from Ps 110:1 in relation to Christ's Lordship, it seems clear that he is using the midrashic rule of 'verbal analogy'[1032] to link together the implications of the expression 'at my right hand' that appears in both Psalms. Jesus himself is reported in all three synoptic gospels as applying the messianic application to Ps 110:1 to his own person,[1033] and its frequent citation in other parts of the NT leads Dodd to say that it was 'one of the fundamental texts of the *kerygma*.'[1034] Thus Peter can proclaim Jesus 'as both Lord and Christ' (v. 36) on the basis of OT Scripture. To quote Longenecker's summary, 'it is an argument based on the exegetical precedent set by Jesus, inspired by the church's postresurrection perspective,

---

[1027] Amongst variations from the text of the LXX that Peter's recorded speech contains, Fitzmyer points out how the repetition in v. 18 of v. 17b includes the 'Lucan addition of "my" [which] changes the male and female "slaves" of the original into "servants" and "handmaids" of God. All human beings, male and female, young and old, free and slave, are to be affected by God's Spirit on the day of such a visitation.' Fitzmyer *The Acts of the Apostles*, 253,
[1028] Longenecker, *Acts*, 71.
[1029] Brawley, 'Hermeneutical Voices of Scripture in Acts 2' in R. L. Brawley, *Text to Text Pours Forth Speech: Voices of Scripture in Luke-Acts* (Bloomington: Indiana University Press, 1995), 78-79. As an example of 'prophetic prediction', Brawley cites how John the Baptist's prediction in Luke 3:16 is fulfilled by Pentecost and Mic 5:2 is fulfilled in Matt 2:6.
[1030] Brawley, ibid., 89, referring to the use of the term 'tessura' in H. Bloom's works such as *The Anxiety of Influence* (New York: Oxford University Press, 1973).
[1031] A. C. Thiselton, *New Horizons in Hermeneutics: The Theory and Practice of Transforming Biblical Reading* (London: Harper Collins, 1992), 148.
[1032] See Longenecker, *Acts*, 75: where he refers to the second of the so-called midrashic exegetical rules attributed to Rabbi Hillel: 'where the same words appear in two separate passages, the same considerations apply to both.'
[1033] Mark 12:35–37 and parallels.
[1034] 'underlying almost all the various developments of it, and cited independently in Mark, Acts, Paul, Hebrews and 1 Peter': Dodd, *According to the Scriptures*, 35.

and worked out along the lines of the commonly accepted midrashic principles of the day.'[1035]

*(iv) The Kerygmatic Core*

For Dodd, Peter's speech constitutes 'the first rendering of the apostolic *kerygma* in the Acts, presented as a kind of programme of the Christian mission.'[1036] Dodd highlights the main features of this early *kerygma* as it is recorded in the ongoing account of sermons in Acts, emphasizing divine fulfilment through Christ's ministry, death and resurrection, his exaltation, the Holy Spirit in the church, the return of Christ and the consequent call for repentance.[1037] The existence of such common features clearly demonstrates a common set of understandings and beliefs in the early church which, as has been seen, can be argued to stem back to Christ himself.[1038]

The strong dominical influence is reflected in the line of argument of Peter's sermon which, following on from the prophetic explanation for the Spirit's coming, turns the focus, as indeed the Spirit does, wholly to Christ from the opening 'Jesus of Nazareth' (v. 22) to the great Christological climax in v. 36. Peter's argument, besides being based upon the Old Testament, explicates a Christology that Longenecker calls 'functional ... rather than philosophical,'[1039] concluding the story of Jesus's 'mighty works' with the final affirmation that 'God has made him both Lord and Christ' (καὶ κύριον αὐτὸν καὶ Χριστὸν ἐποίησεν ὁ θεός v. 36). As Bruce says, 'the first Christian sermon culminates in the first Christian "creed".'[1040] This, then, involved acclaiming Jesus as both κύριος, ('Lord') a title used of Yahweh by contemporary Jews, and Χριστός ('Christ'), a term used in Judaism for God's anointed agent, the Messiah.

The magnitude of the crime ('this Jesus whom you crucified' v. 36c) is only matched by the grace offered to his killers as Peter concludes his sermon with the offer of forgiveness to those who repent (v. 38), echoing again the ideas and

---

[1035] Longenecker, *Acts*, 76. I have not sought to list all the other possible Old Testament references in Peter's sermon.

[1036] Dodd, *According to the Scriptures*, 47. See pages 61 and 93–96 for Dodd's use of *kerygma* to describe the primitive preaching of the early church.

[1037] C. H. Dodd, *The Apostolic Preaching and Its Developments* (London: Hodder & Stoughton, 1936), 38–45. For a similar analysis of the *kerygma* as observable from the recorded speech of Peter in Acts 2 and subsequent sermons, see F. F. Bruce, *The Acts of the Apostle: The Greek Text with Introduction and Commentary* 3rd ed. (Leicester: Apollos 1990), 120: 'substantially the same pattern can be traced in the kerygmatic speeches of 3:12–26; 5:30–32; 10:36–43; 13:16–41.'

[1038] Peter and the early Christians, then, had the benefit of a first-hand 'interpretive grid' supplied by Christ himself. Over the centuries other 'interpretive grids' have developed which can press the Christian message into moulds that 'gridlock' the distinctive thrusts of Scripture (for example, the 'five points' of Calvinism, the demands of Pentecostal experience or liberationist theology, the presumptions of liberalism or dispensationalism, or the reader's personal needs).

[1039] Longenecker, *Acts*, 74.

[1040] F. F. Bruce, *The Acts of the Apostles,* The Greek Text with Introduction and Commentary (London: Tyndale Press, 1951), 96, referring also to similar Christological confessions in Rom 10:9; 1 Cor 12:3 and Phil 2:11.

words of Joel (such as 'return to me with all your heart' in Joel 2:12). Fitzmyer has described this as a 'benevolent ... thrust',[1041] an understatement compensated for by Gooding's comment concerning the whole event.

> those tongues of fire came to announce to the murderers of Jesus ... that pardon and forgiveness were offered to them and to all mankind, together with a hitherto unparallel gift of new life and of a new relationship with God.[1042]

Maybe at the back of Peter's mind also was his own experience of Christ's forgiveness and restoration,[1043] another possible example, then, of Christian experience shaping one's hermeneutic.

*(v) The κοινωνία of the Spirit*

In Acts 2, we can detect the four characteristics that we noted in chapter 2 in relation to the κοινωνία operations of the Spirit.

First, from the *historical* perspective, the consequence of the Spirit coming upon Peter and the disciples is a 'bringing to remembrance' of Old Testament Scriptures along with Christ's own treatment thereof. Peter's Spirit-given re-reading of scriptural history involves him in referring to David as 'a prophet' (2:30) and giving a messianic reference point to Psalms that formerly centred on David.

Secondly, the *eschatological* note is also immediately sounded as Peter changes Joel's 'afterward' to the portentous 'in the last days' (2:17). Clearly he has a Spirit-given conviction that the end times had now arrived, indeed the age of the Spirit in which 'everyone who calls upon the name of the Lord shall be saved' (2:21). The passage in Joel from which Peter quotes contains apocalyptic language ('wonders in heaven' 2:19), which could be taken as referring backward to the crucifixion[1044] or forward to 'the day of the Lord' or read more symbolically as eschatological terminology.

Thirdly, a great *Trinitarian* operation runs through the whole of Acts 2 which would repay detailed examination. Suffice it to say here that despite the surging flood of the *Holy Spirit* that sweeps through the chapter ('filling' vv. 2, 4, giving utterance vv. 6ff, being 'poured out' vv. 17, 33, being a 'promise' v. 33 and a 'gift' v. 38), Peter's sermon focuses upon *Christ* (his earthly ministry v. 22, crucifixion v. 23, resurrection vv. 24–32, and exaltation v. 33). And yet again Peter's ultimately causatory emphasis falls upon *God's* sovereignty ('God declares' v. 17, 'God did through him' v. 22, 'the foreknowledge of God' v. 23, 'God raised him

---

[1041] Fitzmyer, *The Acts of the Apostles*, 248.
[1042] Gooding, *True to the Faith*, 53.
[1043] Luke 22:31; John 21:15–19.
[1044] Luke 23:44ff.

up' vv. 24, 32, 'God made him Lord and Christ' v. 36 and so on).[1045] This theocentric weighting comes out in the Trinitarian focal point in v. 33,[1046] where it is said of Jesus that 'having received from the Father the promise of the Holy Spirit, he has poured out this that you yourselves are seeing and hearing.' To use Trinitarian language, an economic subordination of the Son to the Father is thus implied by reference to the procession of the Spirit from Father to Son to people.[1047]

Fourthly, the *dialogical* aspects of the Spirit's workings are highlighted in the response to Peter's sermon when it is said of his hearers that 'they were cut to the heart' (v. 37).[1048] This radical change of attitude indeed is but one instance of the 'tables being turned around' by the Spirit. Brawley indeed draws attention to many 'antitheses'[1049] that are described in the text which 'give readers, as it were, two sides of a triangle from which they may infer the third.'[1050] He refers to the many contrasts found in Acts 2 such as 'empty/full, earth/heaven ... lawless/devout ... separation/unity'[1051] and comments:

> The Spirit which fills the messianists internally gives external indicators (a sound and tongues as of fire) that move the messianists from inside to outside, from tarrying to proclaiming. Joel's prophecy from the past gives meaning to the present. This prophecy links with the story of Jesus, who is the site of conjunction of death and life, in order to make an audience of outsiders, who do not comprehend, capable of understanding and capable of becoming insiders.[1052]

This aspect of the Spirit's bringing in and blending together is encapsulated in Luke's closing cameo of the fellowship of the early church in vv. 42–47. Peter's Spirit-given message was followed by a Spirit-driven progression from conviction (v. 37) to conversion (v. 41) to κοινωνία (v. 42). Thus, a Holy Spirit hermeneutic produces holistic results in so far as the combination of Word and Spirit creates a united community out of those who were once separated by language, ethnicity, and individuality. From the diversity, and indeed

---

[1045] 'Though Christology influences the use of scripture in Acts 2, it does not control it. Rather, God's performance dominates. The spring out of which the eschatological, ecclesiastical, *and christological* currents flow is God': Brawley, *Text to Text Pours Forth Speech*, 86.
[1046] Some commentators detect an allusion to Ps 68:18 in this verse.
[1047] See further M. M. B. Turner, 'The Outpouring of the Spirit as Trinitarian Disclosure' in *The Holy Spirit and Spiritual Gifts*, 172–178. '[As] we go through Acts it appears that the Spirit is the self-manifesting and empowering presence of both the Father and the Son', 174.
[1048] Words also found in Ps 109:16 LXX.
[1049] Brawley, *Text to Text Pours Forth Speech*, 82.
[1050] Ibid., 82–83.
[1051] Ibid., 83.
[1052] Ibid., 83. Brawley here is drawing on a theory of literary communication which describes the way in which texts can build up a series of antitheses in order to produce a non-verbalized meaning for the reader ('the symbolic voice', Roland Barthes). A textual/stylistic device may also, it is submitted, be a reflection of a spiritual reality.

universality, represented in 2:8–11 Pentecost gives birth to one people with a shared faith and a common spiritual language and lifestyle.[1053]

As then we conclude this section on Acts 2, we have noted that Peter's Pentecostal message, albeit from the lips of an individual, in no way portrays an 'individualistic' hermeneutic. 'Standing with the eleven' (2:14), he is representing the apostolic group, with a 'this is that' message that is rooted in Old Testament Scripture and encapsulates the *kerygma* of the early church. His scriptural interpretation is influenced partly by Jewish midrash, determinatively by Jesus's own exegesis and embodiment, and decisively by the experience of the Pentecostal Spirit, both by himself and the Christian community. The κοινωνία operations of the Spirit are all to be found, embryonically, in the Acts 2 account. The Spirit, who is so generously 'poured out', 'fills' not only Peter and the apostles, but 'all' the disciples (2:4) and is promised to 'everyone' who repents (2:38). This leads Turner to say that for Luke, 'as indeed Joel promised, the gift of the Spirit is *essentially* the Spirit of prophecy and it is for *all* God's people'.[1054] As I now proceed to explore further passages in Acts, I shall seek to show how the Spirit's hermeneutical operations are seen to be extending far beyond that of Peter and the original group of disciples to embrace the whole Christian community.

### Acts 4:23–31 Scripture in the Prayer Meeting

In this passage, we have a very different kind of community context for the interpretation of Scripture. From the pre-Pentecost congregation of one hundred and twenty to whom Peter spoke in 1:15–26 and the great public crowd addressed in chapter 2, we now find ourselves in the more intimate scenario of the believers at prayer. It is occasioned by the report of Peter and John following their release by the religious authorities after their hostile response to Peter's defiant speech before the Sanhedrin (4:8–22) consequent upon the healing of the cripple at the Beautiful Gate.[1055] As 'they went to their friends (τοὺς ἰδίους, lit. 'their own') and reported' (4:23), their verbal report of recent events gave rise to a prayerful narration/petition couched in the language of Scripture which set these events against a much wider backcloth, as prayer can and should do.

Thus the attempted muzzling (4:17) and threatening (4:21) of the apostles is countered by a prayer whose opening (4:24) could have been inspired by

---

[1053] See A. Yong, 'As the Spirit gives Utterance: Pentecost, Intra-Christian Ecumenism and the Wider Oikoumene' in *International Review of Mission*, Vol. xcii No. 366, July 2003. 'The Holy Spirit is the ground of identity in diversity, and of unity in plurality,' 303.

[1054] Turner, 'Luke and the Spirit' in *Reading Luke*, 289. Stronstad notes that 'it is of tremendous significance for the interpretation of the gift of the Spirit on the day of Pentecost that Peter does *not* appeal to Isaiah and Ezekiel, who announce the inward renewal of the Spirit, but rather appeals to Joel, who announces the prophetic activity of the Spirit ... [thus showing] that Pentecost stands in continuity with the charismatic activity of the Spirit in the Old Testament times and in the ministry of Jesus.' Stronstad, *The Charismatic Theology of St. Luke*, 63.

[1055] Acts 3:1–10.

Hezekiah's prayer in Isa 37:16–20, that is theologically grounded in Gen 1:1 ('who made the heaven and the earth') at 4:24, that prophetically interprets Psalm 2 at 4:25–26, and, temporally speaking, recalls Luke 23 ('Herod and Pontius Pilate') at 4:27. Following this recital, the substance of the prayer is not for vengeance or protection but for boldness in speaking the word (v. 29), a boldness (μετὰ παρρησίας v. 31) that was answered with their all being filled 'again'[1056] with the Holy Spirit (ἐπλήσθησαν ἅπαντες, 'they were all filled', v. 31),[1057] soon to be demonstrated in practice (καὶ δυνάμει μεγάλῃ, 'and with great power', in v. 33).

This leads to the first of my two comments.

### (i) The Linking of Word and Spirit

The ascription of Psalm 2 to David, even if the introduction to it in v. 25a is in somewhat garbled Greek in the original,[1058] clearly attributes its ultimate inspiration to the Holy Spirit, with consequent implications of divine authority and contemporary relevance. Hence the community's use of it 'as a blow by blow account of the passion of Jesus.'[1059] The actual process of interpretation is not expressly attributed to the Spirit in this passage, but we can reiterate Dodd's comment that in Acts, life in the Spirit is 'presupposed,'[1060] a life that for the early church would have included the ongoing, 'formidable task of biblical research'[1061] to see how God's plan in Scripture applied to recent events.

Before they 'lifted their voices together to God' (v. 24), then, they may have been lifting them to one another, discussing relevant passages that were then to be recited corporately in prayer. I. Howard Marshall's suggestion can be noted:

> Although the prayer is ascribed to the church as a whole, it is hard to believe that a whole group could speak together in this way without some form of written prayer available for them all to read simultaneously or without a common form of words being learned off by heart previously; the view that the Spirit inspired each member to say exactly the same words reflects an impossibly mechanical view of the Spirit's working. It is, therefore, more likely that one person spoke in the name of the whole company.[1062]

---

[1056] J. W. R. Stott, *The Message of Acts*, 100.

[1057] Note the progression from Peter being filled in 4:8 to all the community being filled here.

[1058] 'It is recognized that there is a primitive error in the text in the first half of ver. 25; it is impossible to construe it as it stands.' R.A. Marshall, *The R.S.V. Interlinear Greek-English New Testament*, 3rd ed. (London: Samuel Bagster and Sons Limited, 1975), 478.

[1059] Brawley, *Text to Text Pours Forth Speech*, 102.

[1060] Dodd, *The Apostolic Preaching and its Developments*, 135.

[1061] Dodd, *According to the Scriptures*, 14.

[1062] Howard Marshall, *The Acts of the Apostles* (1980), 103. He further suggests, 103, fn. 1, that 'possibly early Christian congregations repeated prayers a phrase at a time after a "precentor".'

However their collective voice was articulated, the assembling of the believers together for prayer not only evoked Scripture, but also resulted in the aforesaid powerful manifestation of the Spirit. The shaking or quaking of the place referred to in v. 31 links it with Yahweh's speaking at Sinai (Exod 19:18) and the prophet's in Isa 6:4. It also augurs the power that will attend the future preaching of 'the word of God' (τὸν λόγον τοῦ θεοῦ v. 31), a designation that Luke uses regularly from now on[1063] and that embraces the wider implications[1064] of the message of Jesus Christ for the world. The sequel to our passage relates the preaching of this word with such power and signs following (4:32–5:16) that the Sanhedrin are unable to prevent the further spread of the gospel (5:17–42). 'The faithful community "gathered together" in the dynamic presence of the Holy Spirit, on the one side, proves to be much more than the political and religious rulers "gathered together" against them, on the other side, can constrain.'[1065]

## (ii) The Use of Psalm 2 and its Extended Application

According to Longenecker, Psalm 2 was beginning to be used as a messianic psalm in Jewish nonconformist circles just before the Christian period.[1066] Dodd includes it amongst the *testimonia* collection of the early church,[1067] verse 7 ('thou art my Son') being especially commonly quoted or alluded to in the New Testament in relation to Christ.[1068] And if Dodd's theory as to whole contexts being brought to mind is correct,[1069] then maybe the 'nations your heritage/ends of the earth' promise of Ps 2:8[1070] would have been particularly encouraging to the Acts community as they had begun to face persecution.

The interest of the verses quoted in Acts 4 (i.e. Ps 2:1, 2), however, lies in the way the Christian community saw it as a mirror of their own situation. A Psalm that, if the ascription to David is correct,[1071] has an original setting of opposition to an ancient king, is first applied to the one who is regarded as the Messiah (v. 26, note the ready made link of '*mesiho*'/'anointed' in Ps 2:2c). As the community begins to recite Ps 2:1-2 (vv. 25–26), they abruptly break off with a *pesher* application (vv. 27–28) that next links 'kings of the earth' with Herod, 'rulers' with Pilate, 'nations' with the Gentile authorities and 'people' with Israel. But

---

[1063] See, for instance, at 6:2, 7; 8:14; 11:1; 12:24; 13:5, 7 and so on.
[1064] Fitzmyer, *The Acts of the Apostles*, 311.
[1065] F. S. Spencer, *Acts* (Sheffield: Sheffield Academic Press, 1997), 55, as quoted in David G. Peterson, *The Acts of the Apostles* (Grand Rapids; Cambridge: Eerdmans, 2009), 202–203.
[1066] Longenecker, *Acts*, 104: 'Psalm 2:1-2 has been found as a messianic testimonia portion in the DSS 4QFlorilegium, in connection with 2 Samuel 7:10-14 and Psalm 1:1.'
[1067] Dodd, *According to the Scriptures*, 31–32 and 104–105, with the necessary implication that the use of the Psalm would have been taught to the disciples by Jesus himself.
[1068] Matt 3:17 and 17:5; Acts 13:33; Rom 1:4; and Heb 1:5. Ps 2:9 is referred to in Rev 12:5; 19:15; and 2:27, of which Dodd remarks that it is 'a significant example of the transference of attributes between Christ and the church, which we note in many places': Dodd, *According to the Scriptures*, 105.
[1069] Affirmed here by R. Brawley: 'Readers who know this Psalm peruse the quotation but hear the aggregate-tessura-fragments forming a whole' *Text to Text Pours Forth Speech*, 107.
[1070] Cf. 'end of the earth' in Acts 1:8.
[1071] Or at least a king from the Davidic dynasty.

then the application is taken a stage further as the opposition prophetically pitted against Christ is now also seen as pitted against his servants (v. 29). This is particularly so as the thrust of the Lukan account, according to Fitzmyer, is that 'Peter and John have not been acting on their own, but rather as God's agents on behalf of the rest of Jerusalem Christians.'[1072]

This passage in Acts 4, then, demonstrates the great sense of solidarity experienced amongst the early Christians, with Scripture being used in prayer that unites them with one another and with the cause of the Lord's anointed down the ages. That this solidarity could be regarded as an expression of the κοινωνία of the Spirit is suggested by the immediate sequel, in which the explicit reference to their being filled again by the Holy Spirit (v. 33) is followed by a reference to the believers having 'everything in common' (v. 32), in a passage (4:32–37) reminiscent of the Pentecostal κοινωνία of 2:42–47.

The community of God's servants[1073] that is expressed in 4:23–31, however, finds itself increasingly opposed by the official Jewish community represented by the Sanhedrin.[1074] This comes to a climax when Stephen enters the Lukan account. His death as the first Christian martyr comes about as a direct consequence of a Spirit-given reading of the Old Testament before the hostile court of the Sanhedrin, as recorded for us in Acts 7. Thus as opposed to the sympathetic gathering that constituted the community context for the interpretation of Scripture in Acts 4, we now have an example of a more polemical use of Scripture employed in an adversarial setting. To this I now turn.

## Acts 6–7 The Spirit's Witness through Stephen and the Old Testament Before the Sanhedrin

The figure of Stephen and the nature and purpose of his speech, the longest in Acts, have been the subject of considerable theological debate.[1075] Few, however, would disagree that Luke's detailed account in Acts 6 and 7 underlines the crucial role attributed to Stephen's Spirit-anointed words and works in the narrative of the early church. His speech, which criticized the Jews for repeatedly rejecting God's deliverers and prophets, led to 'his execution ... and ... a great persecution against the church' (Acts 8:1), spearheaded initially by Saul.[1076] The resultant scattering of believers in fact only led to a further spreading of the gospel (8:4ff.),

---

[1072] Fitzmyer, *The Acts of the Apostles*, 306.
[1073] Note the common servanthood theme (under the 'Sovereign Lord'/Δέσποτα of v. 24): David (παιδός σου, v. 25); believers (τοῖς δούλοις σου, v. 29); and Jesus as 'your holy servant' (τὸν ἅγιον παῖδά σου, vv. 27, 30).
[1074] Brawley, *Text to Text Pours Forth Speech*, 104, highlights the contrast in the Acts account between 'the community of messianists in the venerable line of Israel's tradition' and 'the council [viz. Sanhedrin], the presumed purveyors of sociocultural norms.'
[1075] See, for instance, Fitzmyer, *The Acts of the Apostles*, 386–388, and Heinz-Werner Neudorfer 'The Speech of Stephen', chapter 14 in I. Howard Marshall and D. Peterson, eds., *Witness to the Gospel: The Theology of Acts*, 277, fn. 4.
[1076] Stephen's martyrdom is often considered an important factor in Saul's subsequent conversion.

ultimately to the Gentiles. To this end, some scholars have detected a missionary motif running through Stephen's speech.[1077]

Mission has a vital link with the Spirit in Acts, as has already been already noted,[1078] and I shall shortly consider the pneumatic element lying behind Stephen's exegesis, as well as the speech itself as an example of Spirit-given historiography and Old Testament interpretation. Before that, however, as this book concerns the 'community' element in interpretation, I will look at Stephen as a representative of a wider group.

*(i) Stephen as a Representative Figure*

Jesus included 'those ... with them' (Luke 24:33), i.e. the original apostles, amongst the community of his witnesses.[1079] From these, it would seem, comes Stephen, chosen by the disciples at the instigation of 'the Twelve' (Acts 6:2) initially to be part of a team of seven who were to sort out the problem of food distribution between the 'Hellenists' and 'Hebrews' (6:1). The Greek names of all those chosen suggests that they all came from the former group, of which the seven were possibly numbered amongst its leaders.[1080] Of these, Stephen (Στέφανος: 'crown, wreath') emerges as the principal character in the ensuing clash with the Jewish authorities.

It is not clear how strong or distinctive a group the Hellenists were in the early Christian community,[1081] but it is safe to conclude with Fitzmyer that the record of Stephen's speech constitutes 'an invaluable first-century testimony'[1082] as to 'how *some* Jewish Christians were trying to interpret the Christ-event in light of their traditional biblical religion and esteem for the law of Moses.'[1083] This 'some' must have been representative if the detailed Lukan account is anything to go by. From this, Andrew C. Clark has argued that Stephen fits squarely into a 'prophetic paradigm [which] stresses above all the theme of continuity, a prophetic continuity which links the key figures in Luke-Acts with one another, with the Old Testament prophets, and supremely with Jesus, the "prophet like

---

[1077] Heinz-Werner Neudorfer, 'The Speech of Stephen' chapter 14 in *Witness to the Gospel: The Theology of Acts*, for instance, points out how Stephen's speech follows the Lukan emphasis upon the gospel prompting people to 'become mobile', 279, as illustrated by the portrayal of the true Israel as a pilgrim people (noting the frequent use of verbs of movement) and the portrayal of 'the "diaspora" as an opportunity to live and die with God,' 284.

[1078] See page 144. The Lukan account frequently emphasizes the role of the Spirit in gospel advance, for instance at Acts 1:8; 2:38; 8:15–18, 29, 39; 9:17; 10:19, 44–47.

[1079] Luke 24:47–48. See Fitzmyer, *The Acts of the Apostles*, 390

[1080] Cf. Longenecker: 'we may say that in some way Stephen, Philip, and perhaps others of the appointed seven may well have been to the Hellenistic believers what the apostles were to the native-born Christians,' Longenecker, *Acts*, 131.

[1081] Witherington says that Luke uses the term in Acts 6 and 9 to refer to Diaspora Jews living in and around Jerusalem for whom Greek was their spoken language, some of whom had become Christians. He dismisses the earlier view that the Hellenist Christians (Acts 6:1) were doctrinally distinctive from the Hebrew Christians. Witherington (*The Acts of the Apostles*, 242. (cf. Bruce, *The Book of Acts*, 143, Neudorfer, *Witness to the Gospel*, 290, who claim that the distinction was primarily linguistic (see also ibid., 240–242).

[1082] Fitzmyer, *The Acts of the Apostles*, 367.

[1083] Ibid., 367–368. Italics mine.

Moses".'[1084] And as to the sequel of events that follows, Fitzmyer reckons that Stephen 'becomes, by his speech and martyr's death, the faithful devotee of the God of [Israel's] ancestors. What he stands for is only the outgrowth of all that God has achieved in the past through Abraham, Joseph and Moses.'[1085]

*(ii) The Pneumatic Framework of the Speech*

The qualification for membership of the seven men chosen in Acts 6:3 was, literally, 'being witnessed to ... as full of Spirit and wisdom' (μαρτυρουμένους ... πλήρεις πνεύματος καὶ σοφίας). Such a noticeable characteristic receives further emphasis in the references to Stephen, as 'a man full of faith and of the Holy Spirit' (6:5), 'full of God's grace and power' (6:8) and one who could not be argued against because of 'the wisdom and the Spirit with which he was speaking' (6:10). As with Peter before him (Acts 2) and Philip afterwards (8:29, 39), the fullness of the Spirit evidently endowed Stephen with eloquence, power and insight. This was manifested in his monumental speech before the council of the Sanhedrin.

The council strongly reacts against Stephen's inspired Old Testament exposition and indictment, with their hostility being linked by Stephen to the corporate rejection of the message of God's servants by Israel down the ages. This rejection of the prophetic word is interpreted as an attitude of 'resisting' or 'opposing' of the Holy Spirit (7:51,[1086] echoing Isa 63:10), thus affording an illuminating equation between Word and Spirit (cf. Acts 6:10). Having delivered his fateful sermon, Stephen is filled again with the Spirit (7:55a), after which 'he gazed into heaven and saw the glory of God' (7:55b, cf. the suggestive parallel with the radiance of Moses as he brought down God's law from Sinai[1087]). Stephen himself had an angelic countenance even before he began his sermon (6:15). Since his time, the church has been graced with the shining faces of many Spirit-filled Bible expositors and martyrs. And that same Spirit that used Stephen to bring conviction to his killers (cf. John 16:8–11) also enabled him to show mercy to them (Acts 7:60).

*(iii) The Historiographical Character of the Speech*

Considering the charges made against Stephen that he was blaspheming the law of Moses, the temple and indeed God himself (Acts 6:11–15), Stephen's speech, at first reading, with all its OT narrative detail and concluding vitriol against his accusers, seems a far cry from being an effective defence. Indeed, Dibelius

---

[1084] Andrew C. Clark, *Parallel Lives: The Relation of Paul to the Apostles in the Lucan Perspective* (Carlisle: Paternoster, 2001), 279.
[1085] Fitzmyer, *The Acts of the Apostles*, 364.
[1086] 7:51: 'you always resist the Holy Spirit' (ὑμεῖς ἀεὶ τῷ πνεύματι τῷ ἁγίῳ ἀντιπίπτετε).
[1087] Exod 34:29–35; 2 Cor 3:7–18.

claimed that 'the most striking feature of this speech is the irrelevance of its main section.'[1088]

Such a comment overlooks the fact that the speech was intended as much more than a personal defence, as well as failing to consider the type of historiography that was common in the ancient world. Neudorfer, for instance, draws attention to the record of Josephus's first speech made in front of the besieged Jerusalem when he provides an in-depth historical analysis that includes a particular ethical understanding of the threatening situation.[1089] More relevantly, the Bible itself contains a good number of parallel literary pieces that provide a special type of 'historical review'[1090] of Israel's situation in ways that show both a solidarity with but also critique of Israel in its frequent faithlessness in the face of God's faithfulness: for example, in Psalms 78 and 106, and Ezekiel 20.[1091] This so-called 'pattern of contrasts' ('you Jews have ... but God has')[1092] is found not only in Stephen's speech[1093] but in other parts of Acts.[1094] Thus Stephen, by choosing to reply in the way he did, was conforming to an Old Testament genre, and one that Paul similarly employed in his speech in Antioch of Pisidia (Acts 13:16b–41).

Stephen's speech can also be analysed in terms of contemporary rhetoric. Witherington argues that in view of his hostile audience, Stephen needed to adopt 'the indirect route of *insinuatio*.'[1095] Thus he began his speech with a longish *narratio* to establish common ground with his hearers before he launched his attack. Witherington offers a full rhetorical analysis of the speech as propounded by J. Dupont.[1096]

### (iv) Stephen's Purposeful use of the Old Testament

Stephen's speech consists almost wholly of a polemical exposition of the Old Testament in which the LXX, and perhaps another version of the Old Testament, are continuously quoted or alluded to. But as F. F. Bruce says, 'the speech is no mere catena of quotations, studiously put together; the way in which they are introduced suggests that the author has the OT narrative at his finger-tips and

---

[1088] M. Dibelius, *Studies in the Acts of the Apostles*, ed. H. Greeven (London: SCM, 1956),169: quoted by Longenecker, *Acts*, 134.
[1089] Neudorfer , 'The Speech of Stephen' in *Witness to the Gospel: The Theology of Acts*, 282.
[1090] Ibid., 281.
[1091] Other historical reviews, sometimes referred to as the Deuteronomic view of history, can be found in passages such as Deut 26, 2 Kgs 17:7–20, Josh 24 and Neh 9.
[1092] Neudorfer, 'The Speech of Stephen' in *Witness to the Gospel: The Theology of Acts*, 288.
[1093] Joseph was 'sold' to Egypt, but God was with him (7:9); Moses was 'disowned' by Israel, but God sent him as a ruler and deliverer (7:35).
[1094] For example, in Acts 2:36; 5:30; 10:39.
[1095] Witherington, *Acts*, 260.
[1096] '1. *exordium* (v. 2a –very brief); 2. *narratio* (vv. 2b–34); 3. transition/*propositio* (v. 35); 4. *argumentatio* (vv. 36–50); 5. *peroratio* (vv. 51–53).' J. Dupont 'La structure oratoire du discours d'Etienne (Actes 7)' *Bib. 66* (1985), 153-67, as quoted in Witherington, *Acts*, 260-261. Witherington says: 'I would not rule out that Stephen was rhetorically adept, especially since there is evidence of the teaching OT Greek rhetoric in Jerusalem during this era,' 261, fn. 271.

can use it with a striking freshness and freedom.'[1097] With the Spirit's help, Stephen retells the whole Old Testament story to the Sanhedrin with a remarkable 'degree of compression'[1098] and so 'as to draw lessons from it which they had never learned or even noticed.'[1099]

Hence a variety of approaches to the Old Testament that includes:

- A selective summarising and paraphrasing of Pentateuchal history that highlights the stories of Abraham, Joseph, and Moses, drawing out the themes of pilgrimage (i.e. God's presence not confined to the Temple), the goodness of the law as 'living words' (7:38), but also the persistent rejection of God's messengers. The account does include some difficulties of chronology[1100] and detail[1101] that Longenecker attributes to 'the conflations and inexactitude of popular Judaism.'[1102]

- A use of typological exegesis relating to Joseph and Moses whose saving role and yet rejection by their own people is an antitype of Christ, the ultimate redeemer, 'ruler and deliverer' (ἄρχων καὶ λυτρωτής[1103] in 7:35).

- A pesher treatment in 7:37 ('this is' οὗτός[1104] ἐστιν) of Deut 18:15[1105] that looks beyond Moses to *the* prophet to come, followed by a reference to the 'church in the wilderness' (7:38), ἐκκλησία[1106] possibly suggesting a parallel between Moses and Christ in accompanying the pilgrim people of God.

- Another pesher type use of Amos 5:25-27 in 7:41-43, suitably adapted to apply to a Judean audience[1107] and confirming the prophet's indictment of the people's perpetual apostasy. Longenecker points out a similarity with Qumran usage here.[1108]

- Use of Jewish tradition that the law was mediated through angels (7:53).[1109]

---

[1097] Bruce, *The Book of the Acts*, 146.
[1098] Peterson, *The Acts of the Apostles*, 271.
[1099] Stott, *The Message of Acts*, 130.
[1100] For instance, 7:3 suggests God's word came to Abraham in Mesopotamia whereas the context of Gen 12:1 suggests it came to him in Haran.
[1101] For instance, 7:14 records the number of 75 going down to Egypt whereas Gen 46:27 (MT) mentions 70.
[1102] Longenecker, *Acts*, 136.
[1103] Neudorfer points out the Christological significance of λυτρωτής (redeemer) from its use in Luke 1:68, 2:38 and 24:21: 'The Speech of Stephen' in *Witness to the Gospel: The Theology of Acts*, 287.
[1104] Note the frequency of οὗτός ἐστιν in vv. 35-39.
[1105] Following Peter's reference to Deut 18:15 in his address in the temple court in 3:22.
[1106] Following its use in Deut 18:16 LXX.
[1107] The original reference in Amos to Damascus being changed to Babylon.
[1108] Longenecker, *Acts*, 140.
[1109] Angels are not mentioned in the OT account of Mount Sinai except in the LXX of Deut 33:2. The contemporary belief that the law was given to Moses through angels is also reflected in Gal 3:19 and Heb 2:2.

- A following of the prophetic line of Isa 66:1-2a in 7:49-50 against the localization of God's presence, and leaving an inference of the part of the verse not quoted.[1110]

- The employment of 'stiff-necked'[1111] and 'uncircumcised'[1112] vocabulary that echoes prophetic denouncements of old (7:51).

- Following a further reference to the fullness of the Spirit, Stephen's vision of 'the Son of Man standing at the right hand of God' (7:56) evokes Jesus's words before the same court of the Sanhedrin (Mark 14:62). The 'Son of Man' terminology derived from Dan 7:13ff was used 'almost exclusively on the lips of Jesus himself,'[1113] bringing with it many associations, including that of ultimate vindication and universal rule. The changing of Ps 110:1 from sitting to 'standing'[1114] envisions Jesus 'as advocate to plead Stephen's cause before God and to welcome him into God's presence.'[1115]

- Amongst the many parallels between Stephen's martyrdom and Christ's passion,[1116] the words of his final committal are notable: 'Lord Jesus, receive my spirit' (7:59, cf. Luke 23:46). 'As he dies, he utters a traditional evening prayer, based on Ps 31: [5].'[1117]

This rich tapestry of Old Testament usage not only defended Stephen's stand on matters relating to the law and the temple, but more significantly acted as a fundamental indictment against the Jewish establishment for their refusal to accept the prophets sent to them throughout their history, culminating in the killing of 'the Righteous One' whom the prophets had predicted (7:52). Stephen's argument, leading to the insistence that 'the Most High does not dwell in houses made by hands' (7:48), constituted a significant criticism of the temple cult. To quote Tannehill, 'this declaration of God's independence of the Jerusalem temple is also a declaration of God's availability to all with or without the temple.'[1118] As has been seen, this paved the way for mission to the Gentiles which was such an anathema to Jewish particularism.

---

[1110] 'But this is the one to whom I will look: he who is humble and contrite in spirit and trembles at my word' Isa 66:2b.
[1111] Exod 33:5; Deut 9:13.
[1112] Lev 26:41; Deut 10:16; Jer 4:4; 9:29.
[1113] I. Howard Marshall, *The Acts of the Apostles* (1980), 149.
[1114] Doubly emphasized in 7:55, 56.
[1115] Marshall, ibid., 149.
[1116] Witherington enumerates ten: trial before high priest/Sanhedrin (Mark 14:53/Acts 6:12; 7:1); false witnesses (Mark 14:56-57/Acts 6:13); testimony concerning destruction of the temple (Mark 14:58/Acts 6:14); temple 'not made with hands' (Mark 14:58/Acts 7:48); Son of Man saying (Mark 14:62/Acts 7:56); charge of blasphemy (Mark 14:64/Acts 6:11); High priest's question (Mark 14:61/Acts 7:1); committal of spirit (Luke 23:46/Acts 7:59); cry out with a loud voice (Mark 15:34/Acts 7:60); intercession for enemies forgiveness (Luke 23:34/Acts 7:60). Witherington, *Acts*, 253.
[1117] Fitzmyer, *The Acts of the Apostles*, 394, where he refers to 'Ps 31:6.'
[1118] R. Tannehill, *The Narrative Unity of Luke-Acts: A Literary Interpretation* Vol. 2 (Minneapolis: Fortress, 1986, 1990), 93, quoted in Witherington, *Acts*, 264.

## (v) Concluding Remarks

If we want to employ our fourfold classification of the Spirit's κοινωνία operations, we can clearly discern in Stephen's speech an *historical* reading of Scripture that retells the story of God's people in a *dialogical/dialectical* fashion that challenges Israel's disobedience. This comes out in the increasingly accusatory tone, culminating in the 'suddenness of ... invective'[1119] in 7:51, symbolized in the change from 'we/our' to 'you/your' in vv. 51-53. An *eschatological* note is struck in the implied pesher/fulfilment motifs noted above, whilst a *Trinitarian* reference is epitomized in Stephen as one who was evidently 'full of the Spirit' and his power (6:3-15; 7:51, 55), full of God and his ways (7:1-50), and full of Christ and his glory (7:52-59).

This Trinitarian accompaniment therefore portrays Stephen as a representative of a God and a defender of 'pure Christianity,'[1120] rather than of personal self-interest. This comes out in his Spirit-assisted reading of Scripture, which boldly challenged the misinterpretations and Spirit-resistance of Judaism which had culminated in the murder of 'the Righteous One' (7:52). Thus, he is shown 'to be the precursor of the later Christian apologists,'[1121] apologists who would time and again prove Jesus's promise to those brought before the authorities for his sake: 'for the Holy Spirit will teach you in that very hour what you ought to say' (Luke 12:12). Stephen's words and martyrdom were also to operate as a true catalyst for the growth of the new ἐκκλησία (church), whose widening out to include Gentiles provided the opportunity for another vital development in the life of the early church that was facilitated by a Spirit-given understanding of Scripture, as we shall now see.

## Acts 15: Spirit and Scripture at the Council of Jerusalem

Haenchen rightly asserts that chapter 15 constitutes a 'watershed'[1122] in the story of Acts. The decision of the Council of Jerusalem 'liberated the gospel from its Jewish swaddling clothes into being God's message for all humankind.'[1123] This key development was facilitated by Spirit-assisted reading of events and Scripture which many scholars see epitomized in 15:28a: 'it has seemed good to the Holy Spirit and to us'. The significance of this statement and the chapter have been vigorously debated.[1124] Further questions have arisen as to the relation

---

[1119] F. F. Bruce, *The Book of The Acts*, 161.
[1120] Bruce, *The Book of The Acts*, 141.
[1121] Ibid.,141.
[1122] Haenchen, *The Acts of the Apostles*,461.
[1123] Stott, *The Message of Acts*, 241.
[1124] Timothy Wiarda, 'The Jerusalem Council and the Theological Task', *Journal of the Evangelical Theological Society*, Vol. 46, No.2, June 2003, 233, lists the numerous issues for which the record of the Jerusalem Council has been taken as a theological paradigm.

174      *Reading Scripture in the Fellowship of the Spirit*

of the events recorded here with those in Galatians 2:1–10,[1125] as well as the extent to which Acts 15 is regarded as a Lukan composition.

I cannot pursue all the issues here, but need to emphasize that in the obviously selective Lukan account of the ground-breaking[1126] inclusion of the Gentiles within the church as recorded in Acts 10 to 15, the Holy Spirit is portrayed as playing a leading role. To quote Turner:

> For Luke, 'Holy Spirit' is not a *theologoumenon* for rubber-stamping merely human or ecclesial decisions (even at 15:28). For him, the Spirit takes the initiative … and the church follows. The movement to the Gentiles provides the most startling series of instances, commencing with the puzzling vision to Peter, and the instructions of the Spirit to accompany Cornelius' messengers (10:19; 11:12), moving to the remarkable outpouring of the Spirit in 10:44, which commits the church to accepting the Gentile household without Judaizing (10:45, 47; 11:15–18), but then also following through in the dramatic call of Barnabas and Saul (13:2, 4), to a mission which brings more Gentiles to faith. All this stands behind James's assertion 'it seems good to the Spirit and to us', that is, the will of the Spirit had been made manifest.[1127]

The particular issue that gave rise to the deliberations recorded in Acts 15 was, of course, the problem caused by certain Judaizers' insistence that the new Gentile converts needed to be circumcised to be saved.[1128] This kind of problem is not faced by many Christian congregations today, but the way that the early church dealt with it, under the implicit guidance of the Spirit, reveals several perennially important hermeneutical factors at work. These led them to interpret Scripture and God's leading in a way that resulted in Christians agreeing (Acts 15:25) and rejoicing (15:31), and more Gentiles being saved (Acts 16).[1129] What then were these factors? I shall now seek to isolate seven key ones: narrative, rhetorical, consensual, corporate, apostolic, theological, scriptural, and Spirit.

*(i) Narrative*

Turner (as in the quotation above) and other scholars trace the chain of events relating to Gentile inclusion as recorded in Acts 10–15,[1130] leading up to narrations concerning the God's work among the Gentiles by Peter (15:7–11, as

---

[1125] For a summary of the issues, see I. Howard Marshall, *The Acts of the Apostles* (Sheffield: Sheffield Academic Press, 1992), 94–95 (who sees a possible reference to two events) and Barrett, *The Acts of the Apostles*, 710–711 (who sees a probable reference to a single event).

[1126] Jervell points out how the Spirit had been regarded as the exclusive preserve of Israel. But now 'the Gentiles receive the Spirit which is the property of Israel and so they share the promises to the people of God': Jacob Jervell, *The Theology of the Acts of the Apostles* (Cambridge University Press, 1996), 45. See also Stott, *The Message of Acts*, 241.

[1127] Turner, *Power from on High*, 440.

[1128] Acts 15:1, 5.

[1129] Lydia, the slave girl, and the Philippian jailor.

[1130] See also, for example, Stephen Fowl, 'The Spirit at Work: Acts 10–15' in *Engaging Scripture* (Oxford: Blackwell, 1998), 101–113,

endorsed by James, 15:14) and by Barnabas and Paul (15:4, 12). Luke Timothy Johnson thus concludes that 'Acts 15 witnesses to the church concerning the way it reaches decisions, not by prescription, but way of a paradigmatic story.'[1131]

Story telling is, of course, prone to individual subjectivities and biases, but the objective side is stressed by the speakers here as together they emphasize that it is a story initiated by 'God [who] made choice' (15:7), 'bore witness to ... by the Holy Spirit' (15:8), and 'with this the words of the prophet agree' (15:15).

*(ii) Rhetorical*

According to Witherington, the community response to the 'dissension' (στάσις 15:2) caused by the circumcisers followed a familiar pattern.

The main way to resolve such conflict in antiquity was to call a meeting of the ἐκκλησία, the assembly of the people (cf. vv. 12, 22), and listen to and consider speeches following the conventions of deliberative rhetoric, the aim of which speeches was to overcome στάσις and produce concord or unity.[1132]

The speeches of Peter and James are accordingly analysed in this light,[1133] highlighting the standard *exordium* ('men, brothers' Ἄνδρες ἀδελφοί 15:7, 13) and *narratio*, followed by their arguments to the assembly.[1134]

Church meetings down the ages have often followed a similar, if not identical procedure. Many of them would have been more agreeable if endowed with the kind of periods of silence and attentiveness as recorded in 15:12.[1135]

*(iii) Consensual*

Vanhoozer claims that 'the Jerusalem Council must surely rank as the high-water mark in the history of church consensus.'[1136] The 'no small dissension and debate' that started in Antioch (15:2) was repeated in Jerusalem (15:7). Barrett says 'πολλῆς δὲ ζητήσεως γενομένης' ('after there had been much debate') in 15:7 'means search ... for truth through public inquiry and debate.'[1137] The rest of Acts 15 records how this duly took place, eventually resulting in the 'one accord'

---

[1131] Luke Timothy Johnson, *Scripture and Discernment: Decision Making in the Church*, 78-79.
[1132] Witherington, *The Acts of the Apostles*, 450.
[1133] Ibid., 450.
[1134] 'Theophilus would have recognised the appropriateness of this procedure': Witherington, ibid., 451.
[1135] John Howard Yoder, *Body Politics: Five Practices of the Christian community Before the Watching World* (Scottdale, PA: Herald Press, 1992, 2001), 68, links this, inter alia, with the Quaker practice of maintaining silence in their meetings until everyone led to speak by the Spirit has had the opportunity of doing so and a common mind thus reached by listening to the Spirit through each other.
[1136] K. J. Vanhoozer, 'The Promise of Consensus: Towards a Communicative Hermeneutic', *TransMission* Spring 2001, 6. Yoder traces how the Christian church has historically sought to follow the decision-making process of the Jerusalem Council in Acts 15: Yoder, *Body Politics*, 62-70. Linking it also with 1 Cor 14, he concludes: 'Because God the Spirit speaks in meeting, conversation is the setting for truth-finding. That is true in the local assembly and in wider assemblies, in the faith community and in wider groups', *Body Politics*, 70.
[1137] Barrett, *The Acts of the Apostles*, 713.

of 15:25. Barrett says of ὁμοθυμαδὸν that it denotes not only 'unanimity' but also 'physical assembly' in which 'even the extremists agreed.'[1138]

The highly compressed Lukan account of how such agreement finally came about masks what must have been a lengthy and painful process. We can see this as an example of how the Spirit creates κοινωνία out of conflict. Fowl argues[1139] that the main purpose of the "burdens" placed on the Gentiles by the Council was to enable table fellowship between Jews and Gentiles, and so promote good relationships in which 'the voice of the Spirit' could be heard between 'Christians with differing convictions.'[1140]

> Rushing into judgments risks lapsing into patterns of discrimination characterised in Acts by the use of διακρίνω as opposed to the κρίνω offered by James which "seems good to the Holy Spirit and to us". It is only within communities which sustain and nurture certain types of friendship and exhibit patience in discernment that we will find the sort of consensus emerging that is narrated in Acts.[1141]

The fruit of this consensus is seen in the great expansion of the church that followed the Council's decision as recorded in the remainder of Acts.

*(iv) Corporate*

The 'us' of 15:28 indicates the decision was a corporate one, though as the account is read there are evidently different levels of corporateness at work. Because of the initial circumcision problem in the local church at Antioch, 'Paul and Barnabas and some of the others' (15:2) were 'sent on their way by the church' (προπεμφθέντες ὑπὸ τῆς ἐκκλησίας 15:3) to the Jerusalem 'HQ'. There they were to consult with 'the apostles and elders' (15:2), although when they arrived it is stated that they were welcomed 'by the church' (ἀπὸ τῆς ἐκκλησίας) and the apostles and the elders' (15:4). The actual debate is recorded as being conducted exclusively between 'the apostles and elders' (15:6, with only the contributions of named individuals being thereafter recorded), although they are once again bracketed with 'the whole church' when men are delegated to take the result to Antioch (15:22). Yet again, 'the rank and file Christians have disappeared in the next verse [15:23] ... and are given no share in the writing of the Council's letter.'[1142] This letter is conveyed by Judas and Silas (15:22, 27, renowned for their prophetic gifting 15:32), along with Paul and Barnabas (15:22, 25, renowned for their sacrificial service 15:26). Having 'gathered the congregation together' (συναγαγόντες τὸ πλῆθος 15:30) at Antioch, they read it out, generating a corporate response of joy (15:31).

---

[1138] Ibid., 742.
[1139] Fowl, *Engaging Scripture*, 118.
[1140] Ibid., 118.
[1141] Ibid., 119.
[1142] Barrett, *The Acts of the Apostles*, 738.

From the account as we have it, then, the process was a joint/collective one throughout, but conducted on the different kind of levels that are determined by calling and gifting, and with no vote as such being mentioned by Luke. A neatly organised corporate pattern is not easy to discern. As Barrett says:

> The representation of monarchical, oligarchical, and democratic elements in the NT church needs ... qualification; categorization in such ready-made terms is dangerous ... Luke is in any case not thinking in terms of legal validity; what was important was the claim (v. 28) that the Holy Spirit had directed the proceedings.[1143]

### (v) Apostolic

Despite the broad level of corporateness in Acts 15, it is noticeable that special weight *is* given in the account to the authority of the apostles or those with similar standing, whilst none of the opponent's contributions are even mentioned. Peter's speech clearly stands out as primary in the wake of the debate (15:7-11)[1144] after which 'the assembly fell silent' (v. 12), and no more discussion is recorded. His speech is followed by speeches from the only other named participants. These are Barnabas and Paul (15:12) and, notably, James (15:13-21), brother of Jesus, who, by now, Longenecker reckons to be 'the chief figure in the Jerusalem church'[1145] and consequently the likely chairman of the proceedings. Timothy Wiarda considers that Peter, Barnabas, Paul, and James are 'uniquely authoritative figures ... something other than typical Christians.'[1146] Bruce, however, generalises from James's 'summing up' that 'the direction of the Spirit may be received through the judgment of wise leaders as well as by unpremeditated utterances of prophets.'[1147]

### (vi) Theological

'Peter's last words recorded by Luke in Acts'[1148] express a fundamental article of faith that is evidently common to all the Council members, and later stressed by Paul and the New Testament generally: 'we believe that we will be saved[1149] *through the grace* of the Lord Jesus, just as they will' (15:11). On this basis, then, circumcision was totally unnecessary for the salvation of Gentiles and constituted an unbearable 'yoke' (15:10).

---

[1143] Ibid., 738.
[1144] Fitzmyer points out that 'MSS D*, 257, and 614 read "Peter arose in the Spirit and said",' thus giving added authority to his words, *The Acts of the Apostles*, 546.
[1145] Longenecker, *The Acts of the Apostles*, 240.
[1146] Wiarda, 'The Jerusalem Council and the Theological Task', 238-239.
[1147] Bruce, 'The Holy Spirit in the Acts of the Apostles', *Interpretation* 27:2 (April 1973), 174.
[1148] Simon J. Kistemaker, *Exposition of the Acts of the Apostles*, 546.
[1149] 'Luke uses the timeless aor. inf. *sothenai*, to express "salvation" in the eschatological sense. The Lucan Peter thus sums up the essence of the Christian gospel: salvation comes to human beings by the grace that God has accorded them': Fitzmyer, *The Acts of the Apostles*, 548.

## (vii) Scriptural

It is arguable that an appreciation of grace was also a strong factor in James's choice of the text from the Old Testament in relation to God's promise 'to rebuild the tent of David that is fallen' (15:16).[1150] The passage, mainly from Amos 9:11–12,[1151] which constitutes the major basis for his argument (15:16–17), is quoted from the LXX.[1152] This, *inter alia*,[1153] substitutes *adam* for *edom*, and thus explicitly widened the text to include the whole of humanity in the restored Israel. Hence the interpretation reaches out to 'the other' (i.e. non-Jews), very different from the rather self-centred ways in which texts are sometimes read in today's individualistic society.[1154] Consideration for the 'other' in terms of Jewish sensibilities can also be read from the extra conditions for Gentiles that James goes on to propose in 15:20, which seem to be based on certain scriptural traditions.[1155] Such an 'altruistic' approach to Scripture and tradition therefore had the effect of removing barriers to salvation for Gentiles and barriers to fellowship for Jews, thus cohering with other subsequent Scriptural teaching on such matters.[1156]

Although James speaks in terms of 'my judgement' (ἐγὼ κρίνω 15:19), the wording and context suggests this is not his own autocratic ruling,[1157] but rather a conviction he has which is later stated to have been shared by the Holy Spirit and the rest of the Council (15:28a). James's prior reference to 'the words of the prophets' (15:15) also shows that he is basing his overall case not just on Amos but upon the eschatological hope of the Old Testament as a whole.[1158] From this Stott rightly deduces that 'councils have no authority in the church unless it can be shown that their conclusions are in accord with Scripture.'[1159]

Johnson refers to the testimonies of Peter, Barnabas, and Paul that preceded James's scriptural exposition and concludes that 'the text is confirmed by the

---

[1150] Amos 9:11.
[1151] Witherington also detects other OT allusions in the quoted text, for example, re the building of the eschatological temple (Hos 3:4–5; Jer 12:15–16) and the conversion of the nations (Jer 12:15–16; Zech 8:22; Isa 45:20–23): Witherington, *Acts of the Apostles*, 459.
[1152] Possibly based upon a Hebrew text which was different from the MT. It is probable that James spoke Greek which also may have been the language used in the Council. The predominantly oral culture of the time also gave more scope for interpretive renderings – see chapter 6, section 3 (c).
[1153] For the textual issues involved in the quotation, see Longenecker, *Acts*, 243, and Barrett, *The Acts of the Apostles*, 725–729.
[1154] 'The decree of the council in Jerusalem was prompted out of a concern for precisely those who were "other": non-Jews, non-Christians. If anything, the apostles interpreted the prophets *against* their own interests', K. Vanhoozer 'The Promise of Consensus', 6. See also Fowl, *Engaging Scripture*, 116.
[1155] Barrett, *The Acts of the Apostles*, 733–734, mentions the regulations in Lev 17 and 18 for Gentiles living among Jews, and other possibilities for the background/origin of these conditions.
[1156] For instance, 1 Cor 10:23–33 and Rom 14.
[1157] Stott says of κρίνω that the context suggests a meaning 'stronger than "opinion" and weaker than "decree", perhaps "conviction", since James was making a firm proposal, which in fact the other leaders endorsed, so that the decision was unanimous': Stott, *The Message of Acts*, 248.
[1158] Longenecker says that 'James' major contribution to the decision of the council was to shift the discussion of the conversion of Gentiles from a proselyte model to an eschatological one.' Longenecker, *Acts*, 242.
[1159] Stott, *The Message of Acts*, 247.

narrative, not the narrative by the Scripture'[1160] (cf. 15:15). And in the proper discernment of understanding that flows from the dynamic between experience and Scripture, the role of the Spirit is crucial. This brings us, then, to the last determinative and authenticating operant we see in this chapter.

## (viii) Spirit

By 'it has seemed good to the Holy Spirit and to us' (15:28a), the Council clearly regards its proceedings to have been superintended by the Spirit, here 'characterized as God's reliable and authoritative decision-maker.'[1161] Yong comments upon the threefold dynamic: 'here one finds the hermeneutical trialectic clearly at work in the convergence of Spirit and Word within community of faith.'[1162] The Spirit's earlier mention in 15:8 provides a link with his leading in all the preceding events concerning Gentile inclusion. Suggit reads 15:28a in a rather *subjective* way, deducing the essential 'provisionality' of decisions made between the church and Spirit.[1163] This would certainly be the case in relation to transient contemporary issues, such as the circumcision problem here.[1164] From another angle, McIntosh has argued that in Acts 15, 'the Spirit's determination [was] based on a *threefold*, collectively incontrovertible, *objective* testimony of the Holy Spirit',[1165] as recorded in the earlier part of the Council's debate. The translation of ἔδοξεν[1166] as 'it has *seemed* good' does betray the stronger connotations of the word which was commonly used in ancient Greek of the promulgation of official decrees. Its import for the Council then, says Calvin, was that:

> the Holy Ghost was their captain, guide and governor, and that they did set down, and decreed that which they write as he did indite it to them. For this manner of speech is used commonly in Scripture, to give ministers the second place after that the name of God is once expressed.[1167]

---

[1160] Johnson, *Scripture and Discernment*, 105. He continues, 'As Peter had come to a new understanding of Jesus' words because of the gift of the Spirit, so here the Old Testament is illuminated and interpreted by the narrative of God's activity in the present'.

[1161] Ju Hur, *A Dynamic Reading of the Holy Spirit in Luke-Acts*, 256.

[1162] Yong, *Spirit-Word-Community*, 270.

[1163] J. N. Suggit: 'A resolution taken under the direction of the Spirit may not necessarily be binding in later ages. So, there is a certain provisionality both in the resolutions adopted by the church and in its structures and institutions.' "The Holy Spirit and We resolved..." (Acts 15:28) in *Journal of Theology for Southern Africa* 79:1, June 1992, 45.

[1164] Stott, *The Message of Acts*, 255.

[1165] John McIntosh, 'For it seemed good to the Holy Spirit' Acts 15:28. How did the members of the Jerusalem Council *know* this?' *The Reformed Theological Review* 61:3 (December 2002), 133, 'objective' italicised. The 'threefold ... objective testimony' is said to consist of:
(i) the witness of Peter concerning the conversion of the household of Cornelius (15:8-9);
(ii) the account by Paul and Barnabas of their missionary journey (15:12; cf. also v.4b); and
(iii) James's citation of scriptural support (15:16-18).

[1166] Also used of the decision of the Council in vv. 22 and 25.

[1167] John Calvin, *Commentary upon the Acts of the Apostles*, Vol. 2. (Edinburgh: Calvin Translation Society, 1844), 77.

To conclude this section on Acts 15, I have argued that as the Christian community sought to take 'second place' to God in its deliberations, they were influenced by several interacting factors. We have mentioned narrative 'shaping', the use of rhetoric, consensual and corporate workings, apostolic leading, theological dogma, scriptural grounding, and Spirit-directing. Acts 15:28a certainly evidences a church that was 'entirely intimate in its relationship with the Spirit,'[1168] a fact which reassured them whilst the Gentiles were brought into the fold, as the record of their discussions and use of the Old Testament, makes clear. From this, Fowl concludes that 'experience of the Spirit shapes the reading of Scripture, but Scripture most often provides the lenses through which the Spirit's work is perceived and acted upon.'[1169] Once again, we can discern a fourfold pattern of the Spirit's κοινωνία operations at work: the *dialogical* context created by the circumcision issue (which is resolved into consensus); the *historical* focus given by the testimonies given in the speeches; the *Trinitarian* affirmations (especially in 15:7–11); and the *eschatological* note afforded by the Old Testament fulfilment citation (15:16–17). The net result was that the mission to the Gentiles could now proceed unabated, to which the conversions recorded in Acts 16 testify.

## Conclusion to the Chapter

This selection of passages from the first part of Acts has sought to demonstrate how the interrelationship between the Spirit, the Scriptures, and the community provided a vital hermeneutic in the primitive church. Even before Pentecost, we saw in Acts 1 the importance of the Christian community's deliberation, under God, around Scripture, albeit expounded through Peter. His sermon at the great assembly of Pentecost in chapter 2 is presented in terms of his representing the apostolic group, with a 'this is that' message that is rooted in Old Testament Scripture and that encapsulates the *kerygma* of the early church. His scriptural interpretation is influenced partly by Jewish midrash, determinatively by Jesus's own exegesis and embodiment, and decisively by the experience of Pentecostal Spirit, both by himself and in the Christian community. These three key interpretive factors can also be seen in Stephen's polemical address before the Sanhedrin in Acts 7, and thus reveal a hermeneutic that is not 'individualistic' but one that is inspired by the κοινωνία operations of the Spirit, whose characteristics (Trinitarian, dialogical, eschatological, and historical) can be detected in both Peter's and Stephen's Old Testament expositions. A more obviously communal dimension to biblical interpretation is displayed in Acts 4:23–31 in the context of a believers' prayer meeting that used Scripture to create a link with both current events and the cause of the Lord's anointed down the

---

[1168] Mun Hong Choi, *The Personality of the Holy Spirit in the New Testament with special reference to Luke-Acts* Ph.D. thesis University of Wales, Lampeter/Evangelical Theological College of Wales, Bridgend, 1999, 192.
[1169] Fowl, *Engaging Scripture*, 114.

ages. The implied link with the Spirit in Acts 4 becomes more explicit in Acts 15 in relation to the proceedings of the Council of Jerusalem, which, besides some key apostolic contributions, demonstrated a number of corporate interpretive factors at work, epitomized in 'it has seemed good to the Holy Spirit and to us' in 15:28. The combination of Scripture and the κοινωνία of the Spirit in the early Christian community resulted in an interpretive dynamic that truly speeded the mission of the church. Thus we can concur with F. F. Bruce's reading from Acts and its conclusion that 'the future belongs to the Spirit, and thanks to him, the gospel cannot be stopped.'[1170]

---

[1170] 'The Holy Spirit in Acts of the Apostles', *Interpretation* 27:2, April 1973, 183.

# CHAPTER SIX: SPIRIT, COMMUNITY AND HERMENEUTICS IN PAUL

## (1 Cor 2; 2 Cor 3; Rom 8 and the Pastorals)

## Introduction

'Be filled with the Spirit,'[1171] Paul commanded the Ephesian church—and hence us! As Fee says, 'for Paul the Spirit, as an experienced and living reality, was the crucial matter for the Christian life, from beginning to end.'[1172] And as Whiteley asserts, 'the Spirit plays a dominant part in his teaching.'[1173] To explore how this influenced Paul's 'Spirit through community' hermeneutic, I shall first make some general comments about the apostle's pneumatological and corporate outlook. I will then recapitulate on material on Paul in previous chapters and look at the Jewish (Old Testament) background for his pneumatology, as shaped by his Christological experience. Lastly I will carry out a detailed examination of some relevant passages in his epistles.

### The Flow of the Spirit

The 'rivers of living water' promised by Jesus (John 7:38) burst forth at Pentecost and surged through the early church. Thus, both Acts and Paul exult in the 'pouring out' of the Spirit,[1174] and both acclaim the work of the Spirit at the start of the Christian life,[1175] in the inclusion of the Gentiles,[1176] the granting of spiritual sight,[1177] as well as in the authentication of ministry.[1178] Compared with the narrative structure of Acts, however, Paul writes within a more conceptual framework which results in a more developed pneumatology. Not that he was a *systematic* theologian, in our modern sense of the word, for the content and nature of his writings were inevitably influenced by the church situation he was addressing. Such an occasional and epistolary genre provides its own exegetical challenges. Indeed, it could be said that it is just as hard to categorise Pauline thought as it is to categorise the work and person of the Spirit.

Theologians nevertheless have repeatedly attempted to define the 'centre' of Pauline theology, such as the traditional Protestant 'justification by faith', to

---

[1171] Eph 5:18b.
[1172] G. D. Fee, *God's Empowering Presence: The Holy Spirit in the Letters of Paul* (Peabody, MA: Hendrickson, 1994), 1.
[1173] D. E. H. Whiteley, *The Theology of St. Paul* (Oxford: Blackwell, 1974), 124.
[1174] Rom 5:5; cf. Acts 2:17. Johannes Behm referring to the New Testament use of ἐκχέω speaks of 'the idea of outpouring, of the streaming down from above of a power hitherto withheld': Kittel, *Theological Dictionary of the New Testament* Vol. II, 468.
[1175] Gal 3:2-3; cf. Acts 2:38.
[1176] Rom 15:16; Gal 3:14; cf. Acts 10:45, 15:8.
[1177] 2 Cor 3:16; cf. Acts 9:17.
[1178] 2 Cor 3:3; cf. Acts 6:3.

which others have responded with the 'mystical experience of being *in Christ*.'[1179] Both of these can be criticised for being 'too narrow,'[1180] just as Plevnik's 'the whole Christ' is obviously "too wide".'[1181] Martin opts for 'reconciliation,'[1182] whilst Beker highlights Paul's 'apocalyptic substratum.'[1183] All such summaries are inevitably reductionist[1184] and many of them miss out on what Fee sees as the key role of the Spirit in Paul.

> There is no aspect of [Paul's] theology—at least what is fundamental to his theology—in which the Spirit does not play a leading role. To be sure, the Spirit is not *the* center for Paul—Christ is, ever and always—but the Spirit stands very close to the center, as the crucial ingredient of all genuinely Christian life and experience.[1185]

Thus πνεῦμα (spirit) with reference to God's Spirit occurs frequently in Paul, with some 112–115 references.[1186] Also significant is his use of related pneumatological expressions, such as 'in the Spirit' (ἐν πνεύματι), a phrase with a generally corporate reference[1187] that occurs some seventeen times.[1188]

And undergirding all Christian understanding, there needs to be a pneumatological hermeneutic: 'no one comprehends the thoughts of God except the Spirit of God. Now we have received not the spirit of the world, but the Spirit who is from God that we might understand the things freely given us by God' (1 Cor 2:11b–12). I shall explore this verse later.

---

[1179] A. Deissmann, *Die neutestamentliche Formel "in Christo Jesu"* (Marburg: N. G. Elwert, 1892), as cited by G. D. Fee in *God's Empowering Presence*, 12.
[1180] R.Martin, 'Center of Paul's Theology' in G. F. Hawthorne et al., eds., *Dictionary of Paul and His Letters* (Leicester: IVP, 1993), 92.
[1181] Ibid., 92–93.
[1182] Ibid., 94.
[1183] J. Christiaan Beker, *The Triumph of God: The Essence of Paul's Thought* (Fortress Press, Minneapolis, 1990), 62. He 'prefer[s] the flexible term "coherence" to the rigid term "center" or "core",' 62.
[1184] Both Martin ('Center of Paul's Theology', 93) and Fee (*God's Empowering Presence*, 12) refer to *several* key theological elements in Pauline theology. Fee's summary of Pauline (and New Testament) thought: 'Through the death and resurrection of his Son Jesus, our Lord, a gracious and loving God has effected eschatological salvation for his new covenant people, the church, who now, as they await Christ's coming, live the life of the future by the power of the Spirit,' Ibid., 13.
[1185] Fee, *God's Empowering Presence*, 896–897.
[1186] See T. Paige, 'Holy Spirit' in *Dictionary of Paul and His Letters*, 405, comparing this with only 100 or so times in the whole of the LXX.
[1187] Son, comparing Paul's use of ἐν πνεύματι with ἐν Χριστῷ, says: 'Unlike his use of the ἐν Χριστῷ formula, Paul rarely speaks of the believer's indwelling or state/status in the Spirit. Only in Rom 8:9 does he possibly refer to a personal indwelling in the Spirit. He frequently refers, however, to the Spirit's indwelling in believers' [Rom 8:9, 11; 1 Cor 3:16, 6:19; 2 Tim 1:14]: Sang-Won (Aaron) Son, *Corporate Elements in Pauline Anthropology* (Editrice Pontificio Istitituto Biblico: Rome, 2001), 20. See also Richard L. Jeske, 'Spirit and Community in the Johannine Apocalypse' in *New Testament Studies* Vol. 31 1985, 452–466, for an argument for a communal rather than a private understanding of ἐν πνεύματι, in both Revelation and Paul.
[1188] See K. H. Easley, 'The Pauline Usage of *Pneumati* as a Reference to the Spirit of God' in *Journal of the Evangelical Theological Society* 27/3 (1984), 299–313 for a comprehensive survey.

## Corporate Terminology in Paul

As shall be seen, much of Paul's thinking can only be understood in the light of the Old Testament. There, God's priority was not just to save individuals, but more particularly to create *a people* for his name.[1189] Holland has highlighted the fundamental importance of the new exodus and Passover motifs in Pauline thought, alongside their essentially corporate/covenantal categories.[1190] Dunn draws attention to the Hebrew notion of 'assembly' (*qahal*) lying behind Paul's most common designation for groups of Christians meeting in the name of Christ: ἐκκλησία ('church').[1191] Fee points to the '"people" language' Paul uses for Christians[1192] and the essentially corporate nature of his 'major images'[1193] for the church—family,[1194] temple,[1195] and body[1196]—in which the Spirit plays a central role.[1197] Moreover, 'most of [Paul's] indicatives and imperatives are in the second person plural with the whole church in purview ... even though they must be responded to at the individual level.'[1198] Of the plural imperatives, the command to 'be filled with the Spirit' (πληροῦσθε ἐν πνεύματι) in Eph 5:18 is a significant example.[1199] Fee also points to the common, but 'frequently overlooked,'[1200] use of 'one another'/'each other' in Pauline exhortations. '*Everything* is done ἀλλήλων ... [for we] ... are members of one another' (Rom 12:5), who are to build up *one another* (1 Thess 5:11)'.[1201]

Another important corporate indicator is Paul's use of σύν, which expresses 'being or acting together and sharing a common task ... supporting or helping one another.'[1202] From the basic 'with Christ' concept, Dunn refers to Paul's development of an extensive and distinctive vocabulary of some forty συν-compounds that 'describe the common privilege, experience and task of believers.'[1203] Significant nouns relating to corporate discipleship include συνεργός ('fellow worker', 1 Cor 3:9), συγκοινωνός ('partaker'/'partner', Phil 1:7) and σύμψυχος ('united in spirit', Phil 2:2). Significant verbal uses relating to the Spirit include Rom 8:16 ('the Spirit himself bears witness [συμμαρτυρεῖ] with our

---

[1189] Fee, *God's Empowering Presence*, 870.
[1190] Tom Holland, *Contours of Pauline Theology: A Radical New Survey of the Influences on Paul's Biblical Writings* (Fearn: Christian Focus-Mentor, 2004).
[1191] J. D.G. Dunn, *The Theology of Paul the Apostle* (Edinburgh: T&T Clark, 1998) 2003 edition, 537–538, where he refers to the 62 occurrences of ἐκκλησία in the Pauline corpus, and the link with the c. 100 occurrences of ἐκκλησία in the LXX, usually translating the Hebrew *qahal* (assembly).
[1192] God's 'people' (λαός), 'saints' (ἅγιοι), 'elect' (ἐκλεκτός). Fee, *God's Empowering Presence*, 870.
[1193] Ibid., 873.
[1194] Eph 2:19; 1 Tim 3:15.
[1195] 1 Cor 3:16–17; 2 Cor 6:16; Eph 2:19–22; 1 Tim 3:15–16.
[1196] 1 Cor 10:16–17; 11:29; 12:12–27; Rom 12:4–5; Col 1:18; 3:15; Eph 1:23; 2:16; 4:3–16; 5:23.
[1197] Fee, *God's Empowering Presence*, 873–876.
[1198] Ibid., 876. See also page 32.
[1199] Ibid., 876.
[1200] Ibid., 871.
[1201] Fee, *God's Empowering Presence*, 871, citing also Rom 13:8; Eph 4:25; 1 Thess 5:15; Gal 6:2 and so on.
[1202] G. Kittel, *TDNT*, one vol. abridgement by G. W. Bromiley, (Grand Rapids: Eerdmans, 1985), 1103.
[1203] Dunn, *The Theology of Paul the Apostle*, 402, and listed in fns. 62 and 63, 402–403. See also W. Grundmann, 'σὺν-μετά' in Kittel, *TDNT*, Vol. 7, 786–794.

spirit') and Rom 8:26 ('the Spirit helps /takes part with [συναντιλαμβάνεται] us in our weakness').[1204] Romans 8 also illustrates the eschatological[1205] dynamic that is not infrequently included in corporate aspects of συν- compounds (particularly in vv. 17, 22, 29). Dunn concludes that 'Paul's language indicates ... a profound sense of participation with others in a great and cosmic movement of God centred on Christ and effected through his Spirit.'[1206]

I have already explored the Spirit's role as the agent of κοινωνία,[1207] another vital Pauline corporate word, but I will now summarise our earlier findings in relation to the theme of this book.

## Recapitulation

In chapter 2, I sought to apply Paul's concept of the κοινωνία of the Spirit in 2 Cor 13:14 and related verses to the work of Spirit-led interpretation. I argued that this should be sourced, firstly, from the perichoretic dynamic of *Trinitarian* relationship, thus involving a primary 'upward' look to God, but also a secondary 'horizontal' dimension as it is pursued in fellowship with other believers. Secondly, I extrapolated a *dialogical* dimension in the Spirit's work, characterised by a 'downward' movement of conviction and judgment, and illustrated by the Pauline pneumatological antitheses. Such dialogical encounters between God and his people could result in new depths of Scriptural understanding. This was further enriched, thirdly, by a *historical* ('backward') dimension afforded by the Spirit of remembrance, linking us with the insights of the saints of the past. This was illustrated by Paul's references in 1 Corinthians to the traditions handed down to him.[1208] Fourthly, I noted the *eschatological* character of the 'Spirit of promise'. As 'firstfruits' (ἀπαρχή) and 'guarantee/earnest' (ἀρραβών), the Spirit thereby affords a 'future' dimension to understanding that also reflects the 'now–not yet' tension inherent in New Testament teaching.

This fourfold categorisation—Trinitarian, dialogical, historical, and eschatological—is intended neither be exclusive nor exhaustive, but nevertheless provides some key hallmarks of a 'Spirit through community' hermeneutic, with essentially Pauline roots, which I will refer to again in some of the passages discussed in this chapter.

In chapter 3, it was seen how Paul's use of Scripture could be understood as a function of his sharing a number of presuppositions of the New Testament community in their treatment of the Old Testament. These included charismatic

---

[1204] The clustering of συν- compounds in Romans 8 will be noted later in this chapter.
[1205] See W. Grundmann, *TDNT*, Vol. 7, 787-794.
[1206] Dunn, *The Theology of Paul the Apostle*, 404.
[1207] See chapter 2.
[1208] For example, at 1 Cor 11:23 and 15:3.

exegesis, corporate solidarity, typology and 'intertextual' Old Testament echoes, eschatological fulfilment and messianic presence or Christocentricity.[1209]

## Foreword

Against this background, I will now seek to elaborate on some of the key factors that shaped Paul's pneumatology and hence the hermeneutic that flowed from it. This will be followed by further consideration of Paul's particular use of the Old Testament. I will then undertake a detailed analysis of three passages that help to illustrate the communal dimensions of Paul's 'hermeneutic of the Spirit': 1 Corinthians 2, 2 Corinthians 3 and Romans 8. I will conclude with a brief look at the Pastoral Epistles, which, whether written by Paul or not, show how the later New Testament writings reveal an increasing concern for the preservation of the gospel 'deposit', but again with a pneumatic emphasis. The methodology I use will involve not just looking at what precious little Paul himself has to say about his hermeneutics on the surface of the text but also, more deductively, seeking to look beneath that surface to see how he has interpreted and used the Old Testament, within a corporate/pneumatic context.

## Sources of Paul's Pneumatology

Paul, as one who wrote Scripture under the inspiration of the Holy Spirit,[1210] was evidently given direct assistance from *the* source (i.e. the Spirit) as he wrote about the work of the Spirit. But three factors that contributed to his pneumatological understanding can be especially noted: Paul's identity as a Jew; the Old Testament Scriptures; and the Jesus encounter/tradition.

### Paul as a Jew

Here I would like to draw attention to three influences from Judaism upon Paul: first, his Hebrew background; second, his theological presuppositions; and third, more speculatively, the Qumran community.

*(i) Paul's Hebrew Background*

Paul's birth in the Greek city of Tarsus (Acts 22:3) led scholars of the last century, such as Bultmann, to understand Paul as a Hellenized syncretistic Jew of the Diaspora. One can certainly detect the influence of Greco-Roman culture in some of the ways in which Paul expressed himself, such as the rhetoric illustrated in his speech to the Athenians in Acts 17 and also in some of his letters. At heart, however, Paul was a Hebrew, schooled in the Old Testament tradition. As Stegner says, 'today... NT scholarship finds *more* evidence for the

---

[1209] See pages 105–115.
[1210] 2 Tim 3:16.

Jewishness of Paul's life and thought.'[1211] It takes seriously Paul's autobiographical statements in Phil 3:3-4 ('a Hebrew born of Hebrews; as to the Law a Pharisee'), and his claim to have been brought up in Jerusalem and trained under Gamaliel (Acts 22:3). The latter was probably the son or grandson of the famous Hillel, whose midrashic rules of exegesis[1212] would in all probability have been taught to Paul, as shown by his likely use of them in Romans 9.[1213] Paul also made use of contemporary Jewish exegetical traditions, such as his statement in 1 Cor 10:4 about the mobile rock in the wilderness.[1214]

This Jewish background meant that Paul shared a number of Jewish presuppositions that are reflected in his pneumatology. These presuppositions have already been discussed generally in chapter 3,[1215] but I will now enlarge on two of them in relation to the Pauline concept of the Spirit.

*(ii) Jewish Presuppositions*

Paul, first, would have shared in viewing the Spirit, although not exclusively, as *'the Spirit of prophecy'*.[1216] I have noted Turner's comments that the Jewish concept of 'prophecy' was not limited to the giving of prophecies, but had wider connotations that extended right up to the conception of the Spirit as 'the organ of communication between God and a person.'[1217] These more flexible contours of the Spirit's prophetic role are also found in Paul. Thus Archie Hui points out how it is not always clear whether 'Paul is thinking primarily of immediate Spirit-inspired utterance or of non-charismatic communication-report of revelation previously given by the Spirit.'[1218] The former is probably in view in 1 Cor 14, and the latter in 1 Cor 2:10-16 and Eph 1:17 as 'the Spirit of wisdom and revelation'. Hui further says that Paul probably saw some of his own 'visions' and 'revelations'[1219] and 'mysteries'[1220] as 'part and parcel of the Spirit's revelatory work,'[1221] for which there are 'indications'[1222] that Paul was linking

---

[1211] W. R. Stegner, 'Paul, the Jew' in *Dictionary of Paul and His Letters*, 503, italics mine. According to Prof. Morna Hooker, Paul remained 'a Jew to his fingertips' and wrote as a Jew from the perspective of current debates in Judaism. Lecture given in the Theological Public Lecture series, Swansea University, 4th March 2004.
[1212] See page 99, fn. 592.
[1213] See Stegner, 'Paul, the Jew' in *Dictionary of Paul and His Letters*, 505.
[1214] Ibid., 505, referring to Conzelmann's view that Paul derived this from a Jewish haggadic tradition that appears in later Jewish writings.
[1215] See pages 89-93.
[1216] 1 Cor 12:10, 14:1-5, 39 and 1 Thess 5:19-20. 'There is little question that, like Judaism, Paul views the Spirit as the Spirit of prophecy': Archie Hui, 'The Spirit of Prophecy and Pauline Pneumatology' in *Tyndale Bulletin* Tyndale House, Cambridge 50:1 (1999), 105.
[1217] M. M. B. Turner, *The Holy Spirit and Spiritual Gifts* (Carlisle: Paternoster, 1996), 6.
[1218] Hui, 'The Spirit of Prophecy and Pauline Pneumatology', 105, following a distinction previously discussed by Max Turner.
[1219] 1 Cor 9:1; 15:8; 2 Cor 4:6; 12:1,7; Gal 1:12, 16; 2:2.
[1220] Rom 11:25; 1 Cor 4:1; 15:51; Eph 3:9; 5:32; 6:19; Col 1:26-27; 4:3.
[1221] Hui, 'The Spirit of Prophecy and Pauline Pneumatology', 106.
[1222] Ibid., 106.

with Joel's promise to pour out the Spirit upon the eschatological people of God granting them 'visions' and 'dreams'.[1223]

As has been seen, for Jews the return of the 'Spirit of prophecy' was indeed regarded as signalling the beginning of the new age, as per the Old Testament hope, now being fulfilled in those 'on whom the end of the ages has come.'[1224] The role of the Spirit in bringing this about is demonstrated by the eschatological language Paul uses of the Spirit[1225] with their Old Testament roots. From this, Fee concludes that 'the Spirit is the evidence that the *eschatological promises of Paul's Jewish heritage have been fulfilled.*'[1226] Now both Jews and Gentiles would be incorporated into the church, which is the body of Christ (1 Cor 12:13).

This leads us, secondly, to another presupposition derived from Judaism, the notion of *corporate solidarity*. I discussed this in chapter 3,[1227] but here will mention again the corporate notions of 'in Adam'/'in Christ' in Rom 5 and 1 Cor 15, and the metaphor of the church as the body of Christ. From 1 Cor 12, Fee points out that 'the need for unity *and* for diversity in the believing community ... are [represented as] the work of the "one and the same Spirit" (1 Cor 12:11).'[1228] That the Spirit is given 'to each' (v. 7) as well as to 'all' (v. 13) indicates he is the author of the best kind of 'individualism'—individual gifting that is intended to enrich, not to divide, the whole. Thus the role of the prophet in 1 Cor 14 was repeatedly defined in terms of corporate rather than self-edification,[1229] as well as being under the control of the wider prophetic community: for 'the spirits of prophets are subject to prophets.'[1230]

### (iii) Qumran

The Jewish hope of the return of the Spirit in the Messianic Age is evidenced in literature of the Intertestamental period (when the designation 'Holy' was more commonly used of the Spirit), and particularly in the literature of the Qumran community. Their writings, as we have seen,[1231] contain a strong note of eschatological fulfilment as well as pneumatic enlightenment. Geza Vermes has noted how:

Convinced that they belonged to a Community which alone interpreted the Holy Scriptures correctly, theirs was the "last interpretation of the Law" (4Q266 fr.11; 270 fr.7), and they devoted their exile in the wilderness to the study of the Bible.

---

[1223] Rom 5:5; Titus 3:6; cf. LXX Joel 3:1–2; Acts 2:17–18.33; 10:45.
[1224] 1 Cor 10:11b.
[1225] Down-payment/promise/inheritance (2 Cor 1:21–22; 5:5; Eph 1:14); firstfruits (Rom 8:23); seal (2 Cor 1:21–22; Eph 1:13; 4:30). See pages 70–73 for an elaboration of these terms.
[1226] Fee, *God's Empowering Presence*, 808.
[1227] See pages 90–93 and 107–108.
[1228] Fee, *God's Empowering Presence*, 874.
[1229] 1 Cor 14:3, 5, 12, 26 and 31.
[1230] 1 Cor 14:32.
[1231] See pages 89–90 and 105–107.

Their intention was to do according to all that had been "revealed from age to age, and as the prophets had revealed by His Holy Spirit" (1QS 8.14–16; cf.4Q265 fr.7).[1232]

Hui says that:

> The Teacher of Righteousness ... believed himself to be endowed with the Spirit of wisdom and revelation in order that he might instruct and so lead the Qumran community (cf. 1QH 9:30–32; 12:11–13; 14:12–13:25; 16:6–7:11–12; 1QS 4:18–22).[1233]

The extent to which this kind of Qumran thinking influenced the New Testament writers is still a matter of considerable debate. The fact that Scripture, interpretation within the eschatological community and the Spirit's illumination played such a key role in both Qumran and Christian literature at least shows how important these three factors were considered to be in certain sectors of first century Judaistic thought, and indeed well before the writing of the New Testament.[1234] It does not of itself, however, prove dependence either way, although Vermes believes that 'the parallelism between Paul's theology and that of Qumran is too pronounced to be no more than a coincidence.'[1235] He goes on to make a case for Essene ideas of community organization having had some influence on the early Christians,[1236] but much in this realm remains speculative.[1237]

Pauline pneumatology has more obvious links with the Old Testament canon itself, however, to which I now turn.

## The Old Testament

As Holland has emphasized, 'Paul was a Jew who lived in the full flow of Old Testament promises and expectations. In order to read him correctly, we have to immerse all his arguments back into the Old Testament, allowing its themes and patterns of thought to control how we read his writings.'[1238] Various Old

---

[1232] Geza Vermes, *An Introduction to the Complete Dead Sea Scrolls* (Minneapolis: Fortress, 1999), 147.

[1233] Hui, 'The Spirit of Prophecy and Pauline Pneumatology', 108.

[1234] Wright has argued that 'a Spirit-led' hermeneutic existed within Judaism at least two centuries prior to the emergence of Christianity.' Archie T. Wright, 'Second Temple Period Jewish Biblical Interpretation: An Early Pneumatic Hermeneutic' in Kevin L. Spawn and Archie T. Wright, eds., *Spirit & Scripture: Exploring a Pneumatic Hermeneutic* (London: Bloomsbury T&T Clark, 2013), 74. See his discussion of Qumran interpretation, 77–93. Besides unearthing evidence of ' "a pneumatic hermeneutic" in both Jewish literature from the 2TP [Second Temple Period] and the New Testament', 97, he also points out that whereas 'the texts of Qumran are looking forward to the eschaton with their Old Testament interpretations ... the New Testament passages are looking back to the Old Testament to understand the ministry of Jesus and his fulfilment of the role of Messiah,' 98.

[1235] Vermes, *An Introduction to the Complete Dead Sea Scrolls*, 189. He claims that 'it is probable that he [Paul] was acquainted with Qumran Temple symbolism and adapted it in shaping his own teaching on spiritual worship.'

[1236] Ibid., 189.

[1237] As J. A. Fitzmyer says, 'Where and how would he [Paul] have come into contact with this non-Pharisaic Palestinian Judaism, which some of the items in his theological teaching echo?' *According to Paul: Studies in the Theology of the Apostle* (Mahwah, NJ: Paulist Press, 1993), 35.

[1238] Tom Holland, *Hope for the Nations: Paul's Letter to the Romans* (London: Apostolos, 2015), 40.

Testament links with Paul's pneumatology have been traced, such as one highlighted by Paige:

> OT roots are evident in the fact that for Paul the Spirit is singular and unique. To speak of the Spirit is to speak of God's presence and power (Isa 31:3; 34:16; 40:13). As God is one, so there is only one Spirit of God (1 Cor 12:4–6, 11, 13; Eph 4:4–6).... This singularity of the Spirit can be used as a theological argument for the unity of the church (1 Cor 12:13).[1239]

Another link comes from Paul's description of the Spirit as 'the Holy Spirit of promise'[1240] i.e. promised to Israel. This underlines the strong eschatological perspective that, as we have seen, governed much of his pneumatology.[1241] This perspective extended beyond the Joel 2 prophecy quoted by Peter at Pentecost in Acts 2 to embrace the fuller hope of the Old Testament which shaped so much of Paul's thinking. In relation to this hope, Fee has indeed pinpointed 'three related OT realities that Paul sees "fulfilled" by the coming of the Spirit':[1242]

(i) His association of the Spirit with the *new covenant*. Hence Ezekiel's promise of a 'new heart ... and a new spirit within you' (36:26–27; 37:14 and 27 'I will dwell among them'), a promise that in Jer 31:31, 33 is specifically directed to 'the house of Israel', and is taken up by Paul in 2 Cor 3:1–6.[1243]

(ii) This Old Testament language of *'indwelling'* in speaking of the Spirit, for example, being 'in the hearts' of the believers (2 Cor 1:22) and 'dwelling in' them (Rom 8:9–11).[1244] In 1 Cor 14:24–25 (citing Isa 45:14, 'surely God is among you') Paul cites an Old Testament text that speaks of God's dwelling in the midst of his people now being attributed to the presence of the Spirit.

(iii) This is also the case in Paul's collocation of the Spirit with the imagery of the *temple* (1 Cor 3:16, 2 Cor 6:16, citing Ezek 37:27). Whereas in Old Testament times, the distinctive presence of God among his people was symbolised by the Tabernacle/Temple, it is now symbolized, and actualized, by the Spirit. Hence Paul's description of the church as "a holy temple in the Lord. In him you also are being built together into a dwelling place for God by the Spirit" (Eph 2:21–22).

It will be noted that in all three cases, the application is primarily corporate in nature, being made to a specific people. Fee also points out that when in Eph 4:30 the church is told 'not to grieve the Spirit':

---

[1239] T. Paige, 'Holy Spirit' in *Dictionary of Paul and His Letters*, 404–405.
[1240] Eph 1:13. See also Gal 3:14.
[1241] See pages 69–73. For a fuller treatment of 'The Spirit as Eschatological Fulfilment', see Fee, *God's Empowering Presence*, 803–826.
[1242] Ibid.,843.
[1243] For more detail on 2 Cor 3, see next section. Note also that 1 Thess 4:8 also reflects Ezek 36–37.
[1244] See also 1 Thess 4:18; 1 Cor 3:16; 6:19; 14:24–25; 2 Cor 1:22; 3:3; 6:16; Gal 4:6; Rom 2:29, 5:5.

Paul uses the language of Isa 63:10, the one certain place in the Old Testament where the concept of divine presence with Israel in the tabernacle and temple is specifically equated with "the Holy Spirit of Yahweh." This equation is the presupposition behind Paul's own prohibition. The divine presence ... journeyed with God's people in the desert. By the Holy Spirit God's presence has now returned to his people, to indwell them corporately and individually so that they might walk in his ways (hence the significance in Paul of "being led by the Spirit").[1245]

Old Testament concepts and terminology, then, clearly informed Paul's pneumatology. But I must now mention an even more decisive influence.

## *The Jesus Encounter and Tradition*

As Paige points out, 'one notable aspect of Paul's teaching on the Spirit which distinguishes it from Israelite and Jewish faith is the intimate association of the Spirit with the risen Lord Jesus, the "Jesus character" of the Spirit.'[1246] To discover why this is so, I will adopt Seyoon Kim's postulation of a basic 'double origin'[1247] for Paul's gospel (i.e. including the role of the Spirit in it): 'the Damascus revelation[1248] and the Jesus tradition.'[1249] In relation to the Damascus Road encounter with the risen Lord Jesus, Kim speaks of an 'overwhelming experience of the Spirit at [Paul's] conversion and call,'[1250] referring to Acts 9:17-18 ("filled with the Holy Spirit") This experience, says Kim, is reflected in the prominence given to the Spirit in his theology.[1251] Thus in Gal 3:2-5, Paul 'define[s] the beginning of his converts' life also in terms of the reception of the Spirit' (Gal 3:2-5) and in 2 Cor 3 the life giving role of the Spirit in new covenant ministry is highlighted, being read as a fulfilment of God's promises in Ezek 36-37 and Jer 31.[1252] Amongst other Old Testament connections, Kim particularly

---

[1245] Fee, *God's Empowering Presence*, 845.
[1246] T. Paige, 'Holy Spirit' in *Dictionary of Paul and His Letters*, 406-407. See also 404-405 regarding the sources of Paul's concept of the Spirit.
[1247] Seyoon Kim, *Paul and the New Perspective: Second Thoughts on the Origin of Paul's Gospel* (Grand Rapids: Eerdmans, 2000), Introduction, xv.
[1248] The constituent elements of this were, according to Kim, ibid., 295:
1) the revelation of the gospel of the Son of God, the Lord over all, and of justification *sola gratia/fide*
2) the apostolic call to the Gentiles
3) the endowment of the Holy Spirit; and
4) the revelation of the "mystery" of Rom 11:25-26.
[1249] Ibid., Introduction, xv. He argues this position against those who view Paul's theology as, for example, a product of his debates with the Judaizers.
[1250] Ibid., 158. Note also 'Spirit' references in Acts 13:2-4. As to the debate over whether the Damascus Road experience should be called a 'conversion' and/or a 'call'. See J. M. Everts, 'Conversion and Call of Paul' in *Dictionary of Paul and his Letters*, 156-163; S. Chester, *Conversion at Corinth: Perspectives on Conversion in Paul's Theology and the Corinthian Church* (London: T&T Clark, 2003).
[1251] Kim cites 2 Cor 21-22 and 2 Cor 3:16-18 as examples, ibid., 117-122.
[1252] Ibid., 158.

homes in on Isa 42, which, inter alia,[1253] he sees alluded to in Gal 1:15-17,[1254] helping to show how Paul interpreted his call to ministry with his being 'conscious of having been commissioned as an apostle *with the endowment of the Holy Spirit.*'[1255]

Isa 42 provides one of the links between Paul and the Jesus tradition,[1256] in which the passage plays an important role, not least in the Spirit endowment emphasized at Jesus's baptism[1257] and during his ministry.[1258] Citing these and other references to Isaiah in Paul, Kim argues that Paul saw himself as carrying on the work of Christ in terms of 'the Ebed role',[1259] recalling his words in Rom 15:18-19: "Christ worked through me ... by the power of the Holy Spirit."[1260]

Such pneumatic assistance, then, helped to provide the close identification that Paul obviously felt with Jesus. It contrasts with the more indirect way he describes having 'received' the Christological tradition in 1 Cor 15:3. Here is a reference to the input supplied by 'the early church kerygma,'[1261] which Dodd has described,[1262] and with which Paul probably first became familiar through his encounters with key Christian witnesses such as Stephen,[1263] Peter,[1264] and Barnabas.[1265]

The experiences that these and many other early Christians had of the Spirit's power, wisdom and direction, as recorded in Acts and the epistles, must also have played their part in helping to formulate Paul's concept of the Spirit.[1266] His knowledge of and references to the vibrant 'charismatic' communities at Corinth[1267] and Thessalonica[1268] can be mentioned here, serving to illustrate the perpetual mutual interplay between experience (here, that of Paul and his churches) and theology.

---

[1253] Kim notes the recognized allusions to Isa 49:1,6 and Jer 1:5: ibid., 101.
[1254] Ibid., 101. He argues this from the connections between Isa 42 and 2 Cor 4:4-6 and other Pauline passages.
[1255] Ibid., 126: noting especially Isa 42:1c 'I have put my Spirit upon him'.
[1256] The relationship between Paul and the Jesus tradition is hotly debated. Links noted by Kim in *Paul and the New Perspective*, 289, include 'over twenty-five instances where Paul certainly or probably makes reference or allusion to a saying of Jesus' and 'over forty possible echoes of a saying of Jesus.' See also J. M. G. Barclay, 'Jesus and Paul' in *Dictionary of Paul and His Letters*, 492-502 and D. Wenham, *Paul: Follower of Jesus or Founder of Christianity?* (Grand Rapids: Eerdmans, 1995).
[1257] Matt 3:17 and parallels, echoing Isa 42:1.
[1258] Matt 12:17-21: citing Isa 42:1-3.
[1259] Kim, *Paul and the New Perspective*, 127.
[1260] See also Rom 8:9; 2 Cor 3:17 and Phil 1:19 for further linking by Paul of the Christ with the Spirit. Ziesler has written of 'the equivalence of being in Christ and being in the Spirit, which emerges from passages like Rom 8 and 1 Cor 15:45b', J. Ziesler, *Pauline Christianity* (Oxford University Press, 1990), 63.
[1261] Kim, *Paul and the New Perspective*, 296.
[1262] See references to Dodd's *According to the Scriptures* and *The Apostolic Preaching and Its Development* in chapter 3.
[1263] Acts 6-7. Paul's witnessing of Stephen's Spirit-filled martyrdom must have left a lasting impression.
[1264] Gal 1:18.
[1265] Acts 9:27; Gal 2:1.
[1266] T. Paige, 'Holy Spirit' in *Dictionary of Paul and His Letters*, 405.
[1267] For example, in 1 Cor 2, 12 and 14.
[1268] For example, in 1 Thess 1:4-6; 5:19.

This experience of the Spirit in the churches, then, must be reckoned alongside Paul's personal 'help [from] the Spirit of Jesus Christ' (Phil 1:19) and his knowledge of the Jesus tradition as informing his doctrine of the Spirit. This, as has been seen earlier in this section, also needs to be understood in terms of Paul's Jewish background and presuppositions, including his use and adaptation of Old Testament concepts and terminology.

The Old Testament, of course, was used by Paul not just in relation to his pneumatology, but in relation to all of this theology. I now need to make some further comments upon this, before embarking on our exegetical study.

## Paul's Use of the Old Testament

In chapter 3, I noted some of the ways in which the authors of the New Testament made extensive use of the Old Testament, which we must believe took place under the guidance of the Holy Spirit, even though not expressly stated as such. Here I shall highlight four characteristics of Paul's use:

### Source of Authority

Silva has listed 107 times in which the Apostle directly quotes the Old Testament.[1269] One of the explanations for the special density of these in Romans, 1–2 Corinthians and Galatians is that 'in [such] polemical contexts he explicitly invokes the OT as the final court of appeal; such is in fact the point of the introductory formulas—to say "as it is written" [γέγραπται], in effect settles the argument.'[1270] The Old Testament, then, operated as a definitive source of authority for Paul, and not just in the face of his critics but for himself personally. As Hooker says, 'Paul's arguments have validity for him only because they rest on Scripture.'[1271]

### Influence of Allusions

The Pauline Old Testament allusions far outnumber the direct quotations and permeate his writings. They demonstrate how Paul 'lived in the Bible'[1272] and articulated much of his theology. For example, in Philippians, a book devoid of

---

[1269] 42 of these are said to follow both MT and LXX, 7 the MT rather than LXX, 17 the LXX rather than the MT, 31 neither the LXX nor MT, and 10 are disputed: M. Silva, 'Old Testament in Paul' in *Dictionary of Paul and His Letters*, 631.

[1270] Ibid., 638. C. D. Stanley, in *Paul and the Language of Scripture: Citation Technique in the Pauline Epistles and Contemporary Literature* (Cambridge University Press, 1992), 339, remarks how 'Paul's frequent use of γράφειν to introduce his quotations is without parallel in any of the materials examined here [from Qumran and contemporary Greco-Roman literature]', with similar concentrations of γράφειν forms found throughout the New Testament, which 'locates Paul squarely in the mainstream of early Christian biblical interpretation', 348.

[1271] Morna Hooker, in a review of C. D. Stanley's *Arguing with Scripture: The Rhetoric of Quotations in the Letters of Paul* (T&T Clark International: London, 2004) in *Journal of Theological Studies*, Vol. 57, April 2006, 270.

[1272] Silva, 'Old Testament in Paul', 635.

direct Old Testament quotations, he uses 'fragrant offering' terminology from the Old Testament to foster the notion of Christian service in terms of priestly ministry.[1273] The associations arising from such Old Testament phraseology, such as 'fragrant offering' or 'Abraham's seed', have been the subject of modern literary theories of 'intertexuality'.[1274] These explore how these Pauline citations might have generated further meaning for the original readers/hearers, particularly as they linked them with the wider connotations of their original context: 'the signifying power of intertextual figuration,'[1275] to quote Hays. We shall see examples later in the chapter. This 'signifying power' can, however, be overestimated, as Stanley has recently argued,[1276] especially in the case of Gentile readers who would not have been familiar with the Old Testament, even though they may have respected Paul's appeal to 'authority'.

From the Old Testament corpus, Psalms and Isaiah feature prominently in Paul. Stanley notes Paul's detailed treatment of such texts: 'such close attention to the implications of every word is at least consistent with the suggestion that Paul drew his quotations from a personal collection of excerpts to which he resorted for meditation and study when he was travelling or otherwise denied access to a written copy of the Scriptures.'[1277] Maybe his selection was determined in part by the kind of New Testament *testimonia* collection proposed by Dodd.

## Jewish and Contemporary Interpretation

I have already remarked that in the absence of any sustained explanation of his hermeneutics,[1278] we have to make deductions from Paul's writings. From his Jewish heritage, we can, as noted above,[1279] detect the influences of the interpretive traditions of the Greek LXX,[1280] the Aramaic interpretive renderings of the MT used in the synagogues (the targums),[1281] as well as links with Qumran[1282] and rabbinic exegesis, such as the 'Hillel' rules of interpretation.[1283]

---

[1273] Phil 4:18; cf. Ex. 29:18. See Silva,'Old Testament in Paul', 634–635.
[1274] See also pages 110–112.
[1275] As cited in C. A. Evans and James A. Sanders, eds., *Paul and the Scriptures of Israel* (Sheffield Academic Press, 1993), 43.
[1276] C. D. Stanley, *Arguing with Scripture: The Rhetoric of Quotations in the Letters of Paul* (T & T Clark International: London, 2004). See also chapter 3, fn. 718 for more criticism of Hays' 'intertextual' arguments.
[1277] Stanley, *Paul and the Language of Scripture*, 349.
[1278] M. Silva ,'Old Testament in Paul', 639; Stanley, *Paul and the Language of Scripture*, 359, notes that 'only in 2 Cor 3:7–18 and such isolated verses as Rom 4:23–4, 15:4 and 1 Cor 9:10, 10:11 does Paul offer any hint as to the principles that guided his "Christian" reading of the Jewish Scriptures'.
[1279] See also chapter 3.
[1280] For instance in 1 Cor 2:16 where Paul uses the LXX's 'mind' (*nous*) in Isa 40:13a instead of the MT's "spirit" (*ruach*).
[1281] For instance in Eph 4:8, Ps 68:18 is quoted with the Targum rendering of "gave" instead of the LXX and MT's "took".
[1282] Noll notes that amongst the 'closest parallels' between Paul's and Qumran's use of Scripture are 'the [Qumran] rules [which] demonstrate an eclectic use of Scripture, including quotation, allusion and paraphrase in the context of pastoral exhortation,' S. F. Noll 'Qumran and Paul' in *Dictionary of Paul and His Letters*, 780. Paul did not, however, employ the Qumran technique of a detailed verse by verse recital of Scripture with commentary.
[1283] See page 99, fn. 592.

Precise parallels in this realm, however, are difficult to draw, partly because of problems of chronology and variety in the Jewish sources.[1284]

What can be said with confidence, however, is that in the Jewish, and indeed Greco-Roman, literature of the time, "interpretive renderings"[1285] of texts, whether of the Torah or of Homer, were considered, in varying degrees, to be an acceptable and indeed normal convention.[1286] Scribes copying manuscripts did not always resist the temptation of inserting their own interpolations.[1287] And in the days before the fixity of the canon and the standardization afforded by modern mass printing, the predominantly oral and rhetorical renderings of written texts gave further scope for interpretive renderings.

When, then, Paul, and indeed the other New Testament writers, came to use and reinterpret Scripture, the conventions of the day may have helped them to feel a greater degree of interpretive liberty, as shown by the not infrequent number of times in which their renderings followed neither the MT nor the LXX. This is not something that should necessarily alarm us. As Rosner has claimed:

> The concern for 'dead-accurate' quotation is not only a modern invention, but it is limited to the academic context. Paul's practice is closer to the citation technique of a sermon than a scholarly monograph. And we all know that despite free quotation sermons often maintain a higher view of Scripture than scholarly monographs.[1288]

Despite this last comment, I would argue that a scholarly, and indeed evangelistic, concern to maintain the integrity and relevance of the text *does* lie behind many present-day attempts to paraphrase or provide 'dynamic equivalents' of Scripture for contemporary readers, which maybe provides another analogy to what Paul was seeking to do for the readership of his day.

## *Christian Convictions and Ecclesial Concerns*

Paul's own 'interpretive freedom' was certainly not uncontrolled, but rather one which in 2 Cor 3:17 he links with 'the Spirit of the Lord' (cf. 1 Cor 2:10 'revealed ... through the Spirit'), as I shall investigate in more detail shortly. Convictions as to pneumatology and Christology, then, acted as a sure control over Pauline exegesis, alongside the other Christian theological convictions and presuppositions that he shared with the New Testament writers, as noted in chapter 3. These would have included his belief in a church that comprised both Gentiles and Jews, for whom the God of Abraham was also the Father of our

---

[1284] Silva says that most of the rabbinic literature that remains dates back only to the beginning of the third century. M. Silva, ' Old Testament in Paul', 637.
[1285] Stanley, *Paul and the Language of Scripture*, 352.
[1286] Ibid., 348.
[1287] Ibid., 354.
[1288] B. Rosner, '"Written for Us": Paul's View of Scripture' in E. Satterthwaite & D. F.Wright, eds., *A Pathway to the Holy Place* (Grand Rapids: Eerdmans, 1994), 97.

Lord Jesus Christ, and whose Old Testament Scriptures therefore continued to be 'the oracles of God' (Rom 3:2) that were 'written for our instruction' (Rom 15:4).[1289]

The fact that most of Paul's writings were addressed to pockets of new Christians in various locations and with different types of problems also helps to explain his shaping of Scripture. Texts were interpreted and sometimes adapted to suit the needs of the local congregation, just as indeed preachers still do today. This also demonstrates once again the corporate context in which Paul's epistles must be understood. 'Paul's letters were more than personal reminiscences; they represented his presence in the community and were meant to be read again and again in the worship service.'[1290] This doubtless involved constant reinterpretations by the Spirit, inhabiting his people as 'the temple of the living God' (2 Cor 6:16) and, hopefully, transforming them more and more into the image of the Lord (2 Cor 3:18).

To recap this section, Paul's use of the Old Testament reveals his submission to the authority of Scripture, his interpretation of that Scripture through the lens of Jewish and Christian presuppositions, his dependence upon the Spirit, and his angling of it to the church situation he was addressing.

These, of course, include Paul's letters to the churches in Corinth and Rome, some of which literature I will now explore. I have chosen passages from 1 Corinthians 2 and 2 Corinthians 3, as well as Romans 8, because these are prime locations that contain overt references to the Spirit's interpretive work in a general sense, as well as specific examples of Paul's own use of the Old Testament, and all in a community setting.[1291] I will then take a look at what the Pastoral Epistles (and, in particular, verses from 2 Tim 2 and 3) have to tell us, particularly relating to the way in which the Spirit acts as custodian, as well as an interpreter, of Scripture. It is hoped that an in-depth study of these various passages will be more profitable than a more cursory glance at the many other Pauline passages that refer to the Spirit's work in understanding and interpretation, whether explicitly or implicitly.

## 1 Corinthians 2:6–16: The Spirit of Understanding

This passage is full of the wonder of the Spirit's ἀποκάλυψις (revelation).[1292] Yet, as Fee notes, it 'has endured a most unfortunate history of application in the

---

[1289] See also 1 Cor 10:11 and Paul's testimony in Acts 26:22.
[1290] G. R. Osbourne, 'Hermeneutics/Interpreting Paul' in *Dictionary of Paul and His Letters*, 391.
[1291] Amongst the many other Pauline passages that speak of the Spirit's work through community, we could cite 1 Cor 12 and 14, explored by John Howard Yoder in *Body Politics: Five Practices of the Christian Community Before the Watching World* (Scottdale, PA: Herald, 1992; 2001), 61-70. One of his key points: 'God's will is known by the Spirit working in the meeting,' 67.
[1292] Noun taken from the verb used in 2:10 and usually translated as 'revelation' or 'unveiling'.

church.'[1293] The very arguments used by Paul to counter spiritual elitism have been (mis)used to promote it.[1294] One reason for this arises from a failure to read the passage in its 'crucial' context: the Spirit of God always has to operate within the shadow of the cross, as the repeated emphasis upon 'the word of the cross' from 1 Cor 1:18–2:4 demonstrates.[1295] Another reason is a literalistic reading of language that Paul himself in 2:6–16 was more probably employing in what Hays describes as 'ironic mode'.[1296] Thiselton refers to Paul's use of some of 'the major catchwords'[1297] of the Corinthians, such as 'wisdom' (σοφία)[1298] and 'the mature' (τέλειοι) in 2:6, and 'in mystery' (ἐν μυστηρίῳ) in 2:7.[1299] By redefining these concepts in gospel terms and arguing with scriptural support, Paul demonstrates how all true Christians, not just a select few, possess the Spirit. The common spiritual comprehension thereby afforded to the Christian community is then contrasted with the common spiritual incomprehensibility of the non-Christian community.

My exploration of the passage will begin with some general comments upon these communal dimensions, followed by some more detailed lessons that can be derived from the verses concerning Spirit-led hermeneutics.

*The Communal Dimensions*

Paul's arguments in this passage bring out three different dimensions of 'community.'

*(i) Paul's Concern for the Christian Community*

Pursuant to Paul's primary concern in 1 Corinthians for 'the common life of the congregation,'[1300] the apostle's main purpose in 1 Cor 2 was not to give lessons in biblical interpretation, but to address the root causes of the division that had sprung up in the 'lively charismatic' church at Corinth. Hence our passage comes between references to 'quarrelling' (ἔριδες) in 1:11 and 'jealousy and strife' (ζῆλος καὶ ἔρις) in 3:3. This strife flowed from the influence of worldly thinking, as it often does. Against the background of a Greek culture that judged character by

---

[1293] Gordon D. Fee, *The First Epistle to the Corinthians* (Grand Rapids: Eerdmans, 1987), 120. For a history of the interpretation of this text, see Anthony Thiselton, *The First Epistle to the Corinthians: A Commentary on the Greek Text* (Grand Rapids: Eerdmans; Carlisle: Paternoster: 2000), 276–286.
[1294] Fee, *The First Epistle to the* Corinthians, 120.
[1295] See D. A. Carson, 'The Cross and the Holy Spirit' in *The Cross and Christian Ministry: An Exposition of Passages from 1 Corinthians* (Grand Rapids: Baker; Leicester: IVP, 1993), 43–66.
[1296] Richard B. Hays, *First Corinthians* (Louisville: John Knox Press, 1997), 39.
[1297] Thiselton, *The First Epistle to the Corinthians*, 224.
[1298] Used seventeen times in 1 Cor, more than the cumulative total of references in other Pauline letters.
[1299] Earlier commentators thought the use of these kind of terms showed the influence of Graeco-Roman mystery religions, but this theory is now less favoured as these are 'general terms used within a variety of religious outlooks': Thiselton, *The First Epistle to the Corinthians*, 226. Paul's frame of reference was primarily that of the Old Testament.
[1300] I. Howard Marshall, *New Testament Theology: Many Witnesses, One Gospel* (Downers Grove, IL: IVP, 2004), 274. Note, for instance, Paul's corporate metaphors for the church: God's field and building (3:9), temple (3:16–17) and Christ's body (ch. 12).

rhetorical ability[1301] and placed great emphasis upon an esoteric kind of 'wisdom', the unity of the church was being disturbed by the claims of various elitist groups vaunting their favourite 'celebrity' preachers (1:10–12). For some, then, this excluded a Paul who came among them 'in weakness and in ... much trembling' (2:3), and whose preaching was not 'with lofty speech or wisdom' (2:1). But when Paul said 'I decided to know nothing among you except Jesus Christ and him crucified' (2:2), he was declaring a message that by its very nature should exclude all self-promotion and factionalism, and one that could only be properly proclaimed (v. 4) and understood (v. 12) by the power of the Holy Spirit, rather than by the force of human rhetoric.

*(ii) Paul's Plural Terminology*

As Paul proceeds to elaborate on this theme in 2:6–16, he enunciates principles which give an insight into his own particular brand of a 'Spirit through community' hermeneutic. The change from the 'I' of 1:1–2:5 to the 'we' of 2:6–16 and the reversion to 'I' in 3:1 would seem to be particularly significant here. The 'we' is arguably much more than a 'common editorial "we"',[1302] referring more generally to 'Paul and his fellow believers'.[1303] As Barrett remarks on v. 6, '"we speak *among*" implies that all may speak.'[1304] For Schrage and Collins, 'we' denotes 'a common activity within the community.'[1305] 'The use of the first person plural ... suggests that the *locus operandi* of the Spirit is the fellowship of the Christian community.'[1306] This communal forum, of course, embraces the perceptions of the individual believer, as Blomberg's application notes:

> Paul shares with the most immature Corinthian that which all Christians today therefore share: an ability to commune with God, understand his will, and make sense of the foundational truths of Scripture.[1307]

Hence the note of amazement implied by the emphatic ἡμῖν placed at the beginning of 2:10 ('*to us* God has revealed through the Spirit!')[1308] and similarly in ἡμεῖς δὲ[1309] at the start of 2:16a ('*but we* have the mind of Christ'). And in so

---

[1301] Ben Witherington, *Conflict and Community in Corinth: A Socio-Rhetorical Commentary on 1 and 2 Corinthians* (Grand Rapids: Eerdmans; Carlisle: Paternoster: 1995), 121–124.
[1302] Fee, *The First Epistle to the Corinthians*, 101, fn. 13.
[1303] Thiselton, *The First Epistle to the Corinthians*, 230.
[1304] C. K. Barrett, *First Epistle to the Corinthians* (London: A & C Black, 2nd ed. 1971), 69.
[1305] W. Schrage, *Der Erste Brief an die Korinther* (Neukirchen-Vluy: Benziger Verlag, 1991), 1:248, as cited by Thiselton, *The First Epistle to the Corinthians*, 229.
[1306] W. F. Orr and J. A. Walther, *1 Corinthians*, AB 32 (Garden City, N. Y.: Doubleday, 1976), 166, as cited by Thiselton, *The First Epistle to the Corinthians*, 229.
[1307] Craig Blomberg, *1 Corinthians: NIV Life Application Commentary* (Grand Rapids: Zondervan, 1994), 70. Note also the wider application by Garland: 'although Paul primarily has his own preaching in mind, all who proclaim the gospel speak this wisdom,' David E. Garland, *1 Corinthians* (Grand Rapids: Baker 2003), 91.
[1308] My own exclamation mark. Cf. 'you *all* have knowledge' in 1 John 2:20, see chapter 7.
[1309] 'The emphatic ἡμεῖς [in v.16] ... serves to associate all πνευματικοί with the Apostle, and also all his readers, so far as they are, as they ought to be, among οἱ σωζόμενοι (i.18).' A. Robertson and A. Plummer, *First Epistle of St Paul to the Corinthians* (Edinburgh: T&T Clark, 1914), 51.

far as such a mindset is 'cruciform'[1310] and self-sacrificial, this, in Paul's argument, should serve to quench the party spirit amongst the Corinthians. As Prior says, 'we must link closely with our fellow-believers in the body of Christ, because to have the mind of Christ [2:16] is essentially a corporate experience,'[1311] an experience which, if it follows that of Christ's, should, metaphorically speaking, be one of self-crucifixion. There is, therefore, no room for individualistic expressions of human allegiance (cf. '"I follow Paul" ... " I follow Apollos"' 3:4), for 'we are God's fellow workers' (θεοῦ γάρ ἐσμεν συνεργοί[1312] 3:9a).

*(iii) Community Conflicts*

These verses are characterized by the use of contrasts and opposites: 'Antitheses expressed in "not/but" statements pervade Paul's argument.'[1313] Underlying such polarities lies conflict between two sets of communities:

### The Spiritual 'Elitists' v. the 'Ordinary' Christians

As we have seen, Paul was especially targeting the elitist group in his letter, whose profession of spiritual superiority[1314] was in fact a form of immaturity (3:1, 14:20). In spite of the clear teaching of this letter, groups and individuals exhibiting childish behaviour have frequently spoiled the concord and spirituality of many church fellowships.

### The 'natural person' (ψυχικὸς ἄνθρωπος, v. 14) v. the 'spiritual person' (ὁ πνευματικός, v. 15).

ψυχικός is used appositionally here of those who do not have the Spirit, the 'person who lives on an entirely human level' (Thiselton)[1315], in contrast to the πνευματικός, a reference not to a spiritual 'superman', but to the ordinary Christian who, in Paul's understanding, possesses the Spirit.[1316] Despite the individual terminology, these two terms clearly represent the two fundamental communities in his thought. Amongst the former group ('the natural person'), Paul identifies in this passage an important subset[1317] which was responsible for the crucifixion: 'the rulers of this age' (οἱ ἄρχοντες τοῦ αἰῶνος τούτου, 2:6 & 2:8). Commentators are divided as to whether this has a political reference (for

---

[1310] 1 Cor 1:23; 2:2; cf. Phil 2:5-8.
[1311] David Prior, *The Message of 1 Corinthians* BST series (Leicester: IVP, 1985), 54.
[1312] Note the συν- compound.
[1313] Garland, *1 Corinthians*, 90.
[1314] Cf. also the elitism of the secessionists referred to in 1 John, see chapter 7.
[1315] Thiselton, *The First Epistle to the Corinthians*, 268. cf. L. Morris: 'the man whose horizon is bounded by the things of this life', *The First Epistle of Paul to the Corinthians* (Leicester: IVP, 1991), 60.
[1316] See Thiselton, *The First Epistle to the Corinthians*, 267-270 for a discussion of these two terms. Bruce, considering also 1 Cor 15:44-46, concludes: 'Everything that belongs to our heritage from the first Adam, the father of our mortal humanity, is ... *psychikon*; everything which we derive from union with the exalted Christ, the head of the new creation, is *pneumatikon*, the more so as it is conveyed to us by the Spirit': F. F. Bruce, *1 and 2 Corinthians* (London: Oliphants; Marshall, Morgan and Scott, 1971), 41.
[1317] Other subsets are mentioned in 1:20 and 1:26.

instance, to Herod or Pilate) or a spiritual one, i.e. to demonic powers.[1318] Garland combines elements of both, saying that the expression 'represents a collective evil that transcends individuals and their acts.'[1319] The defeat of such a cosmic body of wickedness[1320] is now represented by the coming into being of the counter-community implied by 1 Cor 2, the community of the cross under which 'all [Christians] must stand together.'[1321] This community, consisting of the totality of the πνευματικόι ('the spiritual person[s]') of v. 15, is also identified as the 'mature'[1322] of v. 6, who alone can discern 'the secret and hidden wisdom of God' (v. 7). Indeed, it is interesting to note in these verses how Paul repeatedly and singularly defines the two groups, i.e. the πνευματικός ('spiritual person') and the ψυχικός ('natural person'), in terms of their ability to understand/not understand the 'things' of God. The ultimate indictment against 'the natural man' is that for him these things are but 'folly' (μωρία v. 14). To use Calvin's rather uncomplimentary but graphic metaphor, as cited in Garland, '"Faced with God's revelation, the unbeliever is like an ass at a concert." It is completely uninterested in the music and disturbs the concert with an irritating commotion'![1323]

## Spirit-led Hermeneutics

Such 'commotion' can only be translated into concord by the Spirit, mentioned no less than six times in vv. 10–14. As Fee says of 1 Cor 2:6–16, for Paul 'the Spirit is ... the key to everything—Paul's preaching (vv. 4–5, 13), their conversion (vv. 4–5, 12), and especially their understanding of the content of his preaching as the true wisdom of God' (vv. 6–13).'[1324] Fee's heading for the passage is accordingly 'God's Wisdom: Revealed by the Spirit.'[1325] This, then, does not entirely cohere with this book's concern with 'the Spirit's guidance of the community in the interpretation of Scripture.' Nevertheless, Paul's sandwiching of his assertions in vv. 9–16 between two references to Old Testament Scripture—with Isaiah being cited in vv. 9 and 16—shows the importance he attaches to the authority of Scripture. As Hays says, 'Paul is trying to remake the minds of his readers by teaching them to interpret their lives in light of an

---

[1318] Garland, *1 Corinthians*, 92–93.
[1319] Ibid., 94.
[1320] Cf. Col 1:15.
[1321] Garland, *1 Corinthians*, 93. The full quote: 'The wisdom of this age creates a stratified society of elites and inferiors. By contrast, the wisdom of the cross emphasizes human solidarity. Under the cross, all must stand together.'
[1322] Paul is probably adapting the τελείοι word from Corinthian vocabulary so as to refer not to a more 'advanced' Christians but rather 'to all Christians, who cherish the message of the cross, over against the world that rejects the message of the cross': D. A. Carson, *The Cross and Christian Ministry: An Exposition of Passages from 1 Corinthians* (Grand Rapids: Baker; Leicester: IVP, 1993), 46.
[1323] Garland, *1 Corinthians*, 100.
[1324] Fee, *The First Epistle to the Corinthians*, 114.
[1325] Ibid., 97.

eschatologically interpreted Scripture'[1326]—as indeed Bible expositors still do today.[1327] And in so far as Paul's arguments speak of the indispensability of the Spirit as the only way of understanding the 'secret and hidden wisdom of God' (v. 7), I feel justified in using this passage to extract some basic lessons concerning Spirit-led hermeneutics in relation to Scripture, which, for us as Christians, records this wisdom.

Against the background of Paul's concern for the corporate vitality of the Corinthian church, I will seek to describe Spirit-led hermeneutics in eight conceptualizations extracted from the verses.

*(i) As 'Mystery' (v. 7) to be 'Revealed' (v. 10)*

The designation of God's wisdom in terms of μυστήριον (v. 7) is an example of Paul's redefinition of a Corinthian catchphrase. Hence Hays's assertion that 'mystery' has no connection with Hellenistic mystery religion, but is a term rooted in Jewish apocalyptic,[1328] that Paul uses to encompasses the content of the gospel.[1329] Conzelmann says 'a constitutive element of the "mystery" is its unveiling.'[1330] Here in 1 Cor 2:12, the 'mystery', in terms of 'what God has prepared' (v. 9d), is said to be 'revealed to us through *the Spirit*' (v. 10).[1331] One way of reading the aorist ἀπεκάλυψεν for 'revealed' ('uncovered', 'disclosed') is that the moment of revelation stems from conversion and is thus available to all Christians.[1332] This universal aspect is emphasized by Bruce, who, despite the difficulty of the syntactical link between v. 9 and v. 10,[1333] declares 'the wonderful mysteries "which God has prepared for those who love him" are accessible "through to the Spirit" to all believers. This is no esoteric knowledge, confined to an inner ring of select initiates.'[1334]

*(ii) As eschatological truth to be realised (vv. 6b–9)*

Here we find highly eschatological/apocalyptic language typically associated with the Spirit. That the 'rulers of this age' are doomed to pass away' (v. 6d) reminds Witherington that 'the things of the end time have already broken into human history and have relativized all purely human values, wisdom, and

---

[1326] Richard B. Hays, *The Conversion of the Imagination: Paul as Interpreter of Israel's Scripture* (Grand Rapids: Eerdmans, 2005), 18.

[1327] Fee notes the 'piling up of γάρ's' in the passage, *God's Empowering Presence,*100, fn. 57, with the 'explanatory "for"', 99, in vv. 10, 11, 14, 16, ibid., 99–110.

[1328] Hays, *First Corinthians*, 43, citing Dan 2:27-28.

[1329] See, for instance, Eph 3:9-10; Rom 16:25-26.

[1330] H. Conzelmann, *1 Corinthians* (Philadelphia: Fortress, 1975 English Translation), 62.

[1331] Cf. Rom 16:25-26, where Paul says 'the revelation of the mystery (ἀποκάλυψιν μυστηρίου) ... has been disclosed (φανερωθέντος) ... through *the prophetic writings*,' affording an interesting Word/Spirit link in the work of revelation.

[1332] Other readings include 'the entry of the gospel into the world': Robertson and Plummer, *First Epistle of St Paul to the Corinthians*, 43, or an event of special revelation to Paul and/or the Apostles.

[1333] Fee, *The First Epistle to the Corinthians*, 109–110. Fee argues for an explanatory 'for' (γάρ) that links v. 10 with the last line of v. 9, rather than an adversative 'but' (δέ) that creates a contrast with the first three lines of v. 9.

[1334] F. F. Bruce, *1 and 2 Corinthians* (London: Marshall, Morgan and Scott, 1971), 39.

structures.'¹³³⁵ Now, the future belongs to the people of God: God's 'secret and hidden wisdom' is, remarkably and 'moving[ly]',¹³³⁶ destined 'for *our* glory' (v. 7c). The inexplicability of this to 'the rulers of this age' is backed up by the καθὼς γέγραπται ('as it is written') citation in v. 9. The form and origin of the composite Old Testament quotation is debated,¹³³⁷ but Thiselton concludes that it is '"a pastiche of biblical allusions",'¹³³⁸ including the LXX of Isa 64:4¹³³⁹ and Isa 65:16.¹³⁴⁰

Such a 'pastiche' was, apparently, a popular citation in apocalyptic Judaism¹³⁴¹ and thus represents the use by Paul of a common hermeneutic. Hence also Horsley's comment on 'what God has prepared for those *who love him*' (ἀγαπῶσιν αὐτόν, v. 9d, possibly alluding to Isa 64:4d): 'the similarity of the ... phrase to Paul's expression "those who love God" in a similarly dramatic crescendo in Rom 8:28 suggests that such language was standard in Jewish apocalyptic circles.'¹³⁴² Barrett's application is pertinent for those who are the privileged recipients of the Spirit's revelation: 'not *gnosis* but love is the touchstone of Christian maturity and spirituality.'¹³⁴³

Horsley's linking of this passage with Rom 8 (esp. vv. 27–30)¹³⁴⁴ points to one ultimate explication of the 'mystery' in terms of the glory of being conformed to the image of the Son in the κοινωνία of the heavenly inheritance.¹³⁴⁵

*(iii) As the 'depths of God' to be explored (v. 10b)*

Barrett translates ἐραυνᾷ as 'searches out'.¹³⁴⁶ For Stott, it portrays the Spirit's work 'as a restlessly inquisitive researcher, even a deep sea diver, seeking to fathom the deepest depths of the being of God.'¹³⁴⁷ Thiselton speaks of the Spirit's 'exploring God's purposes thoroughly in order to reveal them.'¹³⁴⁸ The emphasis, then, is 'not to do with "deeper truths" available only to "insiders", but with the formerly hidden wisdom of God now revealed as such through the

---

¹³³⁵ Witherington, *Conflict and Community in Corinth*, 127.
¹³³⁶ Thiselton, *The First Epistle to the Corinthians*, 242.
¹³³⁷ Ibid., 248–252.
¹³³⁸ Ibid., 252, citing R. F. Collins, *First Corinthians*, SacPag 7 (Collegeville, MN: Glazier; Liturgical Press, 1999), 132.
¹³³⁹ But note Stanley: 'even here the resemblance is quite loose': C. Stanley, *Paul and the Language of Scripture: Citation Technique in the Pauline Epistles and Contemporary Literature* (Cambridge: Cambridge University Press, 1992), 188 and fn. 16.
¹³⁴⁰ See Fee, *The First Epistle to the Corinthians*, 108–109.
¹³⁴¹ Fee, ibid.,109, referring to its use in 'the Ascension of Isaiah.'
¹³⁴² R. A. Horsley, *1 Corinthians* (Abingdon Press, Nashville, 1998), 60.
¹³⁴³ Barrett, *First Epistle to the Corinthians*, 73. Note also 1 Cor 13:1–2.
¹³⁴⁴ Note also the 'search' motif in Rom 8:27 and 1 Cor 2:10 and the 'glory' motif in Rom 8:30 and 1 Cor 2:7.
¹³⁴⁵ Cf. Eph 3:4–6, where the 'mystery of Christ' refers to the incorporation of both Gentiles and Jews into Christ's body.
¹³⁴⁶ Barrett, *First Epistle to the Corinthians*, 67.
¹³⁴⁷ J. W. R. Stott, *Calling Christian Leaders: Biblical Models of Church, Gospel and Ministry* (Leicester: IVP, 2002), 70. He says that τὰ βάθη later became a favourite term of the Gnostics.
¹³⁴⁸ Thiselton, *The First Epistle to the Corinthians*, 256.

Spirit.'[1349] Wright notes that in using concepts of 'mystery' and 'deep things' being revealed by the Spirit, Paul is using 'language ... very similar to what is found in the *pesharim* of Qumran.'[1350]

*(iv) As divine truth to be disclosed exclusively by divine means (v. 11)*

In the words of Barth, 'God is known through God alone,'[1351] or those of Veenhof, 'This object remains always subject.'[1352] Paul argues this point by the use of his spirit of man/spirit of God analogy, based upon an unusual use by him of what Fee describes as 'the Greek philosophical principle of "like is known only by like".'[1353] As Atkinson puts it, 'God's Spirit is understood as the only competent reader of God's innermost being.'[1354] Paul's chain of thought here may also have been 'influenced by the OT motif that no one has ever seen God.'[1355] The initiative in revelation must always come from him.

Verses 11 and 12 have also been used as the basis for arguments concerning the essential difference between divine and human discourse and their interpretation. As Ingraffa and Pickett have said, 'the spirit of the human author does not indwell us as the Holy Spirit indwells the believing reader of Scripture,'[1356] Scripture that was originally written by the inspiration of the very same Spirit ('an astounding claim').[1357]

*(v) As transcendental truth to be received as 'gift' (v. 12)*

The ἡμεῖς ('now we') placed at the start of this verse again emphasizes the primacy and privilege of revelation to the Christian community. Thiselton highlights the importance of πνεῦμα τὸ ἐκ τοῦ θεοῦ ('the Spirit who is from God') in v.12, which he sees as a direct challenge to prevailing Stoic conceptions of πνεῦμα ('spirit')[1358] (possibly included in Paul's 'the spirit of the world' v. 12) and, maybe we could add, to 'New Age' type thinking of today:

---

[1349] Fee, *God's Empowering Presence*, 100.

[1350] Wright, 'Second Temple Period Jewish Biblical Interpretation,' 97. But note that Pauline interpretation democratizes the promises of such revelation to all believers, not just a select few members of a group.

[1351] *CD*, 2/1, sect 27, 179, as quoted in Thiselton, *The First Epistle to the Corinthians*, 258.

[1352] Jan Veenhof, 'The Holy Spirit and Hermeneutics' in *Scottish Bulletin of Evangelical Theology*, Vol. 5 No. 1 (1987), 117, following the view that 'the central moment in this passage is the '*homoion*-thesis, which has been proposed from ancient times until now: the equal can only be known and understood by the equal, *simile simile cognosci*, 116–117.

[1353] Ibid., 110.

[1354] William Atkinson, '1 Corinthians' in Trevor J. Burke & Keith Warrington., eds., *A Biblical Theology of the Holy Spirit* (London: SPCK, 2014), 149. He makes the further interesting point from vv. 10–11 and related verses that 'the Spirit too, clearly, has access to the (otherwise?) depths of the human—certainly any human who has acknowledged the lordship of Christ,' 159.

[1355] Veenhof, 'The Holy Spirit and Hermeneutics', 111.

[1356] Brian D. Ingraffa and Todd E. Pickett, 'Reviving the Power of Biblical Language' in C. Bartholomew, C. Greene, and C. Moller, eds., *After Pentecost: Language and Biblical Interpretation*, Scripture and Hermeneutics Series, Vol. 2 (Carlisle: Paternoster, 2001), 247, discussing whether the Bible can be read 'like any other text,' 245.

[1357] Ibid., 247, referring to 1 Cor 2:12.

[1358] 'In all strands [of Stoic thought] the world is conceived of as an organic whole, animated by a rational force called πνεῦμα or *spiritus*,' Thiselton, *The First Epistle to the Corinthians*, 261.

As against immanental notions of "spirituality" as qualities of human religiosity generated by attention to the inner human spirit, true "spirituality" is a creation by the agency of God's *transcendent Holy Spirit who is Other and comes from* (ἐκ) *God alone.*[1359]

'Freely given to us', χαρισθέντα (passive participle)[1360] ἡμῖν, emphasizes the gracious generosity of God's revelation to his people, which in turn needs be passed on by them, as the next verse literally says : 'which things also we speak' v. 13a. The Spirit, to quote Smail's language, is for ever 'The Giving Gift'[1361] to be shared with others. Indeed, Robertson and Plummer consider λαλοῦμεν ('we speak/impart') to be 'the dominant verb of the whole passage.'[1362]

*(vi) As verbalized wisdom to be taught (v. 13a)*

Bruce points out that the conceptualisation by the Spirit of God's wisdom into 'words' reminds us that the Spirit 'supplies the language as well as the substance of revelation.'[1363] Accordingly, the language used of 'spiritual' wisdom should be different to that used of 'worldly' wisdom and conveyed in a didactic manner ('taught'=διδακτοῖς). Maybe this is a warning against using some less worthy aspects of popular speech or rhetoric in our preaching.

*(vii) As spiritual truth to be interpreted only by spiritual people (vv. 13b–15)*

The expression πνευματικοῖς πνευματικὰ συγκρίνοντες ('interpreting spiritual truths to those who are spiritual') in v. 13b is capable of a number of alternative translations.[1364] If the verbal participle συγκρίνοντες means 'comparing' (as opposed to 'interpreting'), then it refers to a similar activity Paul is undertaking in this very passage (in his use of 'not ... but' argumentation) and which also frequently takes place in any group discussion. If it is translated as 'bringing together' in the sense of 'matching' or 'fixing', it implies the need to adapt the revelatory content to what Thiselton refers to as 'what they [the hearers] are ready to take.... Every pastor knows the crucial importance of *pastoral timing* (not only *what* to say but also *when* to say it) and matching a mode of discourse to the situation (not just *what* to say, but also *how* to say it).'[1365]

If, however, the primary meaning is indeed 'interpreting', as most commentators seem to think, then it has reference to the wider explanatory role that is facilitated by the Spirit. As to the nouns, πνευματικοῖς πνευματικὰ, they could be

---

[1359] Ibid., 225.
[1360] Strictly speaking a 'neuter plural aorist passive participle of the deponent form χαρίζομαι', Thiselton op. cit., 263. Note Barrett's comment: 'the tense is important because it shows that in verse 9, and in the passage generally, Paul is not speaking only of the future but also of the present life of Christians,' Barrett, *First Epistle to the Corinthians*, 75.
[1361] Tom Smail, *The Giving Gift* (London: Darton, Longman & Todd), 1994.
[1362] Robertson and Plummer *The First Epistle of St Paul to the Corinthians*, 46. Hence their rendering: 'Which are the very things that we do utter.'
[1363] F. F. Bruce, *1 and 2 Corinthians*, 40.
[1364] Thiselton, *The First Epistle to the Corinthians*, 264–265.
[1365] Ibid., 266–267.

neuter ('spiritual things/words/truths') or masculine ('spiritual people'). Out of the various possibilities that this creates, something like 'interpreting spiritual truths to spiritual people' seems near the mark. The emphasis then is on the need for the interpreters to be mature people of the Spirit, in contrast to the 'infantile attitudes and behaviour'[1366] exhibited by the Corinthian Christians (1 Cor 3:1-4). This also links in with the contrast Paul makes in the next two verses.

On the one hand there is the ψυχικός ('natural person') of v. 14 who can neither receive/welcome (δέχεται) or know (γνῶναι) the 'things of the Spirit'—'like a child incapable of communicating with a parent, unable to understand the parent's mind or intentions'.[1367] On the other hand, there is the πνευματικός ('the spiritual person') of v.15 who 'judges/discerns/investigates all things' (ἀνακρίνει [τὰ] πάντα) but is himself judged by no one.' Taken at face value, this text could be (and has been)[1368] taken as a manifesto for the 'spiritually' arrogant who wish to rid themselves of any form of community censure. In response to this, a number of commentators think this may be an example of Paul making an ironic use of a Corinthian saying. This is now to be understood as a comment upon the spiritual depths which the πνευματικός can plumb (as opposed to the ψυχικός), rather than as a claim that they can be immune to criticism or correction.

As additional arguments against the egotistical spiritual elitism that can arise from a misconstruction of the verse, one can cite Thiselton,[1369] who draws attention to the passage's Christian community setting, out of which any kind of spiritual 'judgments' should take place. Also Bruce, who emphasizes that 'by "all things" we should understand 'the gifts bestowed on us by God' (verse 12),'[1370] i.e. as endowments of grace rather than merit. As Bruce goes on to say (also referring to 1 Cor 4:3-4):

> it is plain throughout that [Paul] recognizes the value of self-judgment (11:31), constructive criticism (11:17ff.) and community discipline (5:3ff.); but ultimately the man of God is answerable to God alone, and in any case he cannot be assessed at all by those who have not the same Spirit as he has received.[1371]

*(viii) As Christological access to the thoughts of God (v. 16)*

Paul concludes his reasoning with a γάρ ('for') that buttresses his case with a final appeal to Old Testament Scripture, such appeals in both 1 and 2

---

[1366] Atkinson, '1 Corinthians', 156.
[1367] Roy E. Ciampa & Brian S. Rosner, *The Letter to the Corinthians* (Grand Rapids: Eerdmans; Nottingham: Apollos, 2010), 136.
[1368] See ibid., 272 for examples in the 'posthistory' of the text.
[1369] Ibid., 273-274, following Kistemaker.
[1370] Bruce, *1 and 2 Corinthians*, 41.
[1371] Ibid., 41. See also 1 Cor 14:29 for another example of testing by the community. Barrett's rendering of the verse gives further elucidation: 'The spiritual man, however, investigates all things, but he himself is not open to comparable investigation on the part of anyone,' Barrett, *First Epistle to the Corinthians*, 77.

Corinthians viewable as 'attempt[s] to ground the experientially oriented Corinthians more completely in the Word.'[1372] His reference to Isaiah 40 recalls a chapter whose evocation of the unfathomable greatness of God ('to whom then will you compare me?' v. 25) links in with Paul's 'depths of God' in 1 Cor 2:10, thus adding to the sense of amazement that mere mortals can actually know something of these depths by the Spirit, via the very mind of Christ in which they are privileged to share.

Paul's citation from the LXX of Isa 40:13 entails a substitution of 'mind of the Lord' (νοῦν κυρίου) in place of the MT's 'Spirit (Heb *ruach*) of the Lord'. Silva sees this as deliberate: 'what the apostle means is "We have the Spirit of Christ and therefore we really know Christ,"'[1373]—and therefore develop his way of thinking. It also constitutes a challenge to the rigid dichotomy often made between 'mind' and 'spirit.' Paul further substitutes 'Christ' for 'Lord' in the very last phrase. This Trinitarian interchange serves to reinforce the Trinitarian dynamic that permeates the whole chapter:[1374] the Spirit sent from God should lead to Christ, and in particular a Christ who was crucified (2:2). As Ciampa and Rosner affirm, 'the Spirit and the cross go together.'[1375] The realization of such a Trinitarian and cross-centred dynamic in the church at Corinth would promote the kind of fellowship that Paul was longing to see there as together they possessed the 'mind of Christ', with its concomitant self-humbling. For as Willis says, '"to have the mind of Christ" does not mean to think Christ's thoughts after him, nor to have ecstatic experiences, nor knowing proper dogma. The 'mind of Christ' is not focussed upon special wisdom or experiences, but on community life.'[1376] Preachers can sometimes sense such a mindset when the congregation evidences a humble and affirmatory receptivity to the word of God.

Such a communal mindset and understanding is fostered when Christians appreciate that it is 'we' rather than 'I' who have the mind of the Christ, who, on the cross,[1377] gave up all he had for the sake of others (cf. Phil 2:5ff.: 'have this mind among you').[1378]

## Conclusion to 1 Corinthians 2

A Christ-like, self-sacrificial mind-set, then, should be the hallmark of a community that is led by the Spirit. The Corinthian Christians needed to learn this, attracted as they were by the kind of individualistic personality cults (1:12; 3:4) and worldly wisdom of the times (1:18), as Christians still can be. 1 Cor

---

[1372] Witherington, *Conflict and Community in Corinth*, 129.
[1373] M. Silva, 'Old Testament in Paul' in *Dictionary of Paul and His Letters*, 634. Put another way, perhaps we can see this as another example of the closest of communion with Christ that is enabled by the Holy Spirit.
[1374] For Prior, this 'is a chapter explicit with the doctrine of the Trinity': Prior, *The Message of 1 Corinthians*, 49.
[1375] Ciampa & Rosner, *The First Letter to the Corinthians*, 139.
[1376] Willis 1989, as quoted in Garland, *1 Corinthians*, 102.
[1377] Note again the contextual emphasis upon the Cross in 1:18–2:2.
[1378] Note Phil 2:1–8 and 2 Cor 5:15.

2:6–16 is a strong rebuttal of all such forms of spiritual elitism[1379] and an impassioned plea that all Christians have the Spirit and should therefore be able to understand—in measure—the true wisdom of God, as demonstrated by the cross and now recorded in Scripture. Not that this understanding is a simple thing, for as we have seen, Paul describes the mechanics of Spirit-led interpretation in multi-dimensional terms, as: 'mystery' to be revealed; eschatological truth to be realized; the 'depths of God' to be explored; divine truth to be disclosed by divine means; transcendental truth to be received as 'gift'; verbalized wisdom to be taught; spiritual truth to be interpreted by spiritual people; and Christological access to the thoughts of God. Such full and diverse interpretive endeavour can only be accomplished within the wider parameters of the Christian community, as the prevalence of communal/'we' terminology in the passage makes clear, an insight reinforced by the contrasting incomprehensibility of the non-Christian community. Individuals as well as groups, of course, play their part in the hermeneutical task, but always within the context of their dependence upon and accountability to the pneumatic community, which is the church (cf. 1 Cor 12). To go about the task with an arrogant, party spirit is to revert to the kind of individualism which Paul so strongly rebuked.

## 2 Corinthians 3: The Spirit of Glory

'The letter kills, but the Spirit gives life' (2 Cor 3:6d), declares Paul in a chapter in which the Spirit plays a leading role, being mentioned seven times. Hubbard interestingly points out that 'while elsewhere Paul describes his mission as the proclamation of the gospel (Rom 1:1), or the cross (1 Cor 2), in this passage he defines it as "the ministry of the Spirit" (3.8).'[1380] Such a pneumatological undergirding was obviously vital for the apostle in his polemics with his critics, but is also of perpetual relevance for all who seek to be 'ministers of [the] new covenant' (3:6).

Not that all the complexities of 2 Cor 3 are easily interpreted, as shown by the way the chapter has been variously read by church and academy down the years. Historically, it has been misapplied by those seeking a pretext for extracting esoteric 'spiritual' meanings supposedly lying behind the 'letter' of the law.[1381] Others have isolated v. 18 from the rest of the chapter and pursued a mystical quest of 'transfiguration by vision.' More recently, scholarly studies have sought

---

[1379] See further, Fee *God's Empowering Presence*, 112; T. Paige 'Holy Spirit' in *Dictionary of Paul and His Letters*, 406.
[1380] M. Hubbard, '2 Corinthians' in Trevor J. Burke & Keith Warrington, eds., *A Biblical Theology of the Holy Spirit* (London: SPCK, 2014), 165.
[1381] Origen is generally attributed with inspiring such an allegorical approach to Scripture (severely criticized by Calvin). See page 23 and also Paul Brown, *The Holy Spirit and the Bible* (Fearn: Mentor; Christian Focus, 2002), 105, 229 (fn. 10).

to examine 2 Cor 3 as a 'Christian midrash',[1382] or 'as an apologetic letter of the sort derived from forensic rhetoric.'[1383]

The theme of apostolic defence clearly *does* motivate this chapter: 'to counter any suggestion that an itinerant preacher with a poor speaking style and a prison record is not fit to be an apostle of the Lord of glory.'[1384] Paul seeks to refute such criticism from his Jewish opponents,[1385] who championed the Mosaic covenant, first by pointing to the changed lives of the Corinthians as living proof of the authenticity of his ministry (vv. 1–3), and secondly by moving on to a detailed argument for the superiority of the new covenant (of which he was a minister) over the old (vv. 4–18).

As with 1 Cor 2, then, the prime purpose of the chapter is not instruction about scriptural interpretation, though as Hays says, the text is 'laden with hermeneutical implications.'[1386] This is so because Paul's assertions in 2 Cor 3 necessarily entail a 'new form of reader competence'[1387] that is a direct result of the new covenant. And in so far as this is sourced by 'the Spirit' who is so frequently mentioned[1388] in this chapter, a chapter that progresses from a personal 'we' in v. 1 to the universal 'we' of v. 18, we have here material that is highly pertinent to the main theme of this book. I will endeavour to learn not just from what Paul has to say about the nature of Spirit-led interpretation, or more precisely 'unveiling', but also from how he himself demonstrates it in practice by the way he uses the Old Testament in his arguments. As these unfold, I will seek to abstract and categorize six aspects of Christian experience and understanding that have implications for Spirit-led hermeneutics: incarnation; disjunction; liberation; contemplation; transformation; and glorification.

## Incarnation

> you show [being manifested (φανερούμενοι)] that you are a letter of Christ ... written ... by the Spirit ... on tablets of human [fleshly (σαρκίναις)][1389] hearts (v. 3)

---

[1382] i.e. one based upon a Jewish '*Moses-Doxa*' tradition, but with distinctive Pauline elements. See Linda L. Belleville, 'Tradition or Creation? Paul's Use of the Exodus 34 Tradition in 2 Corinthians 3:7-18' in C. A. Evans and J. A. Sanders, eds., *Paul and the Scriptures of Israel* (Sheffield: Shefield Academic Press, 1993), 165-186.
[1383] B. Witherington, *A Socio-Rhetorical Commentary on 1 & 2 Corinthians* (Carlisle: Paternoster, 1995), 376.
[1384] N. T. Wright, *The Climax of the Covenant: Christ and the Law in Pauline Theology* (London: T&T Clark, 1991), 177.
[1385] The exact nature of Paul's opponents (usually implied from 3:1-8; 11:4 and 11:22-23) in 2 Corinthians is debated. If they were not Galatian type 'Judaizers', they certainly believed in promoting their Jewish heritage, including participation in the Sinai covenant.
[1386] Hays, *Echoes of Scripture*, 146.
[1387] Ibid., 123.
[1388] Not referred to as the 'Holy' Spirit in the chapter but generally understood as such.
[1389] As to φανερούμενοι and σαρκίναις, the same root words are used of Christ's incarnation in 1 Tim 3:16: "Ὃς ἐφανερώθη ἐν σαρκί.'

Paul pleads that his credibility does not rest on written letters of recommendation but from the living letters constituted by the changed lives of the Corinthians themselves. They were to be both 'known' and 'read' by all men (v. 2), as emphasized in the progression of the participles, γινωσκομένη καὶ ἀναγινωσκομένη ('read and recognized'), leading to the universal ὑπὸ πάντων ἀνθρώπων ('by all men'):[1390] 'a communication from Christ to the world.'[1391] The power for such an integrated witness of inward inscription (v. 3) and outward manifestation (v. 2) lay in the engraving (ἐγγεγραμμένη v. 3) work of the Spirit. This is further illuminated by the Exodus allusion in v. 3 ('stone tablets, written with the finger of God' Exod 31:18 LXX), as commented upon by Martin: 'the most striking change is that "with the finger of God" becomes "by the Spirit of the living God", in turn an exceptional title—found only here in the Bible—for the Holy Spirit.'[1392]

In fact, the language of Paul in vv. 1–6 echoes several words from Exodus, Jeremiah, and Ezekiel: v. 2 'engraved on the heart'[1393]; v. 3 'stone tablets'[1394]; v. 3 'hearts of flesh'[1395]; v. 6 'new covenant'.[1396] Hays claims that these 'echoes' could generate further resonances of meaning:

> The reader who follows these echoes will be led back into a thesaurus of narrative and promise; only there, in the company of Moses, Jeremiah, and Ezekiel, does Paul's metaphor of the Corinthians as a 'letter from Christ' disclose its true wealth.[1397]

Carol Stockhausen also reflects intertextually, especially upon Paul's use of γράφω (write), λίθος (stone), διαθήκη (covenant) and πνεῦμα (Spirit) in 2 Cor 3[1398] and notes how 'the Torah narrative is brought into Paul's contemporary world in such a way that Paul can pass critical judgment on it on the basis of other scriptural passages and accepted interpretive procedures.'[1399]

At the same time, he can give positive endorsement to the experience of the Corinthians as the fulfilment of the prophetic hope. The ἐν Χριστῷ ('in Christ')

---

[1390] Thrall comments that this expression 'may be somewhat exaggerated, but Corinth was an important city and commercial centre, and it might be reasonable to suppose that information about the Christian church there would spread to other cities and regions': Margaret E. Thrall *The Second Epistle to the Corinthians* Vol. 1 (Edinburgh: T&T Clark, 1994), 223.
[1391] C. K. Barrett, *A Commentary on the Second Epistle to the Corinthians*, 2nd ed. (London: A&C Black, 1973), 108.
[1392] Ralph Martin, *2 Corinthians,* Word Biblical Commentary (Milton Keynes: Word, 1991), 52.
[1393] ἐγγεγραμμένη ἐν ταῖς καρδίαις : Jer 38:31–34 (LXX)
[1394] πλαξὶν λιθίναις: Exod 34:1–4, 27–28.
[1395] καρδίαις σαρκίναις: Ezek 11:19 and 36:26.
[1396] καινῆς διαθήκης: Jer 38:31–34 (LXX).
[1397] Hays, *Echoes of Scripture*, 127–128.
[1398] Carol Stockhausen, '2 Corinthians and the Principles of Pauline Exegesis' in Craig A. Evans and James A. Sanders, eds., *Paul and the Scriptures of Israel,* (Sheffield: Sheffield Academic Press, 1993), 144. Her comments also relate to Exod 34, as used later in 2 Cor 3. She asserts that 'narrative texts from the Pentateuch are usually (perhaps always) at the core of [Paul's] arguments' but that Paul commonly 'appl[ies] prophetic and occasionally sapiential texts to bring the Torah into contemporary focus.'
[1399] Ibid., 158.

of v. 14 and ἡμεῖς δὲ πάντες ('but we all') of v. 18 then link their experience with that of all other Christians who can and should always be encouraged to read their Christian experience as a realization of Scripture, as effected by the Spirit. This, in turn, has implications for Christian witness. As Hays concludes from Paul's 'intertextual trope' (esp. in vv. 1–3): 'in the new covenant, incarnation eclipses inscription.'[1400] Sermons become more effectual when congregationally fleshed out in Christlike, Spirit-empowered lives which by their very nature proclaim the gospel in the community.

## Disjunction

### not on tablets of stone but on tablets of human hearts (v. 3)

The 'not ... but' (οὐ ... ἀλλά) terminology and motif of v. 3 continues throughout this chapter. The contrast between the *old* covenant (uniquely and thus pointedly described here as παλαιᾶς διαθήκης v.14)[1401] and the *new* covenant[1402] is vividly portrayed in a complex web of *a minore ad maius* argumentation,[1403] particularly from vv. 7–18. Not that all was 'bad' in the old covenant days. Indeed the law came 'with glory' and Moses himself was able to have access to God 'with unveiled face'. But there were inherent deficiencies.

Stockhausen says that 'a favourite occupation of Paul's in relation to Scripture, in particular the Torah, is the location and solution of contradictions or uneasily reconciled passages.'[1404] She follows Dahl and Beker in asserting 'there is a strong element of discontinuity in Pauline thought.'[1405] Here, this comes out in the extended *dissimile* ('not like Moses' v. 13) which Paul elaborates in this chapter.[1406] I have already noted in our journey through other Scriptures the dialogical/dialectical operations of the Spirit.[1407] Good hermeneutics often turns upon the drawing up of suitable sets of opposites/parallels, as employed here: stone/heart, Old/New covenant, Moses/Paul, fading/ever-increasing glory, letter/spirit. That these contrasts need to be rightly understood and applied is

---

[1400] Hays, *Echoes of Scripture*, 129.

[1401] Naylor says that 'because the expression 'old covenant' occurs nowhere else in the New Testament it must have a pointed meaning': Naylor, *A Study Commentary on 2 Corinthians* Vol. 1 (Darlington: Evangelical Press, 2002), 158.

[1402] Old covenant features: 'The letter kills' v. 6, 'ministry of death' v. 7, 'condemnation' v. 9, 'once had glory' v. 10, 'being brought to an end' vv. 7 & 13. Cf. New covenant features: 'the Spirit gives life' v. 6, 'even more glory' v. 8, 'ministry of righteousness' v. 9, 'what is permanent' v. 11.

[1403] i.e., *qal wahomer* in Jewish exegesis, an argument from the lesser to the greater (*a fortiori*). Witherington says '[Paul's] argument is in essence that one good thing is simply eclipsed by something better': Witherington, *A Social-Rhetorical Commentary on 1 and 2 Corinthians*, 376.

[1404] Stockhausen, '2 Corinthians and the Principles of Pauline Exegesis', 145.

[1405] Ibid., 145.

[1406] Although, as Hays points out, 'in the end, the dissimile collapses into a positive metaphor and Moses becomes a figure for the Christian community that stands with unveiled face before the Lord and thus undergoes transformation': Hays, *Paul and the Scriptures of Israel*, 45.

[1407] See also pages 53–58.

shown by the way in which the last mentioned pair has been frequently misunderstood.

As Hays says, 'When Paul contrasts Spirit to *gramma*, he is not opposing the *basic intent* of Scripture to its *specific wording*, as in our familiar distinction between "the spirit and the letter of the law." Nor is he thinking, like Philo or Origen, about a mystical latent sense concealed beneath the text's external form.'[1408] Such allegorizing tendencies have been seen throughout interpretive history right up to the subjectivisms of today's post-modernism.[1409] Rather the contrast is between the 'writtenness' of the law of the Old Testament covenant, 'lacking the power to effect the obedience that it demands,'[1410] and the enabling, transforming power of new covenant's 'Holy Spirit, who is palpably present in the community as an experienced reality.'[1411]

This contrast is not just a feature of pneumatically assisted scriptural interpretation, but also has ecclesiastical and evangelistic implications, as the church seeks the Spirit's help in becoming a visible, dialectical, alternative community for people whom Paul later describes as, by nature, 'perishing ... blinded ... by the god of this world' (2 Cor 4:3, 4).

## Liberation

### where the Spirit of the Lord is, there is freedom (v. 17)

Release from being 'blinded by the god of this world' is also what Paul is explaining here in 3:17. The word ἐλευθερία ('freedom') in Paul is variously used to describe freedom from death,[1412] sin,[1413] the law,[1414] and condemnation.[1415] A number of commentators import such meanings into its use in v. 17. But surely Linda Belleville is right in saying that 'here it means to be free of barriers that would impede spiritual understanding. It is the work of the Spirit to remove such spiritual impediments.'[1416] This fits into the context of a discussion in which Paul has been lamenting the spiritual dullness of the Israelites under the old

---

[1408] Hays, *Echoes of Scripture*, 150. Italics added.
[1409] Note Hafemann's comment: 'Under the influence of postmodernism, the supposedly true, spiritual meaning of the text is once again being determined not by the author's statements read within their own context, but by one's own spiritual, ethnic, gender, or socio-political experience,' Scott J. Hafemann, *2 Corinthians NIV Application Commentary* (Grand Rapids: Zondervan, 2000), 168.
[1410] Hays, *Echoes of Scripture*, 131.
[1411] Ibid.,150. The conclusions that Hays draws from this (for example his comment that 'Paul's ministry of the new covenant ... centers not on *texts* but on the Spirit-empowered transformation of human community' [130], have been criticized by J. C. Beker: 'does this mean that the Word has now lost its critical function, because it has reached its true fulfilment in a transformed church—a church that embodies the Spirit completely?': Beker, *Paul and the Scriptures of Israel*, 69. In response, Hays claims that 'Paul conceives of the word as alive and dangerous, always at work to shape and transform the community in ways that could not have been predicted', ibid., 95.
[1412] Rom 8:2.
[1413] Rom 6:18, 22.
[1414] Gal 5:1–3.
[1415] Rom 8:1–2.
[1416] Linda L. Belleville, *2 Corinthians*, NT Commentary Series (Leicester: IVP, 1996), 111.

covenant, which had persisted 'to this day' (vv. 14–15). This discussion, in vv. 13–17, takes the form of a complex exegesis and commentary on Exod 34:29–35, maybe fuelled by Paul's knowledge of Jewish *haggadah*.[1417]

In this discussion, the key metaphor he uses is that of the 'veil' (κάλυμμα v. 14) and unveiling. Fitzmyer sees Paul's use of this metaphor as part of what he is doing in the chapter as a whole, i.e. employing a 'free association of ideas ... caused by catchword bonding, in which one sense of a term suggests another.'[1418] Thus in the case of 'veil', 'what began as an instrument to conceal the glory of Yahweh from frightened Israelites has become an instrument that prevents Israelites from understanding Moses, as they read him.'[1419] The notion of the fading of the glory from Moses's face is not found in the Exodus account, but is introduced by Paul as a figurative portrayal of the impermanence of the old covenant, which could not be discerned by the Israelites because of their spiritual dullness.

Such a veil of incomprehensibility can, writes Paul, only be removed 'in Christ' in whom 'it is being abolished'[1420] (καταργεῖται, v. 14). It is 'taken away' (περιαιρεῖται v. 16) whenever anyone 'turns to the Lord' (ἐπιστρέψῃ πρὸς κύριον, v. 16) 'who is the Spirit' (v. 17). This is not the place to discuss all the complex issues arising from these and other terms used here, but it is possible to discern five progressive stages in spiritual comprehension in vv. 14–17, ending with the glorious cry of freedom of v. 17:

*(i) hardened minds (ἐπωρώθη τὰ νοήματα αὐτῶν v. 14)*

ἐπωρώθη (v. 14a) can be translated 'made obtuse, dull', the passive aorist implying a settled condition of spiritual sluggishness for which they were responsible but for which there was also 'an external hardening agent (God),'[1421] whilst the plural νοήματα ('thoughts, minds'[1422]) speaks of a common mindset. Such hardening and spiritual miscomprehension was also exhibited elsewhere in the New Testament on the part of disciples[1423] as well as the Jewish crowds.[1424]

---

[1417] Belleville's analysis (ibid., 103): '(1) verses 12–13a: opening statement, (2) verses 13b–14a: Exodus 34:33, (3) verses 14b–15: commentary, (4) verse 16: Exodus 34:34, (5) verse 17: commentary and (6) verse 18: Exodus 34:35 and commentary intermixed.'

[1418] J. A. Fitzmyer, 'Glory reflected on the Face of Christ' in *According to Paul: Studies in the Theology of the Apostle* (Mahwah, NJ: Paulist Press, 1993), 68. He traces six sets of such associations that run through the apostles' argument, revolving around different connotations suggested by terms such as 'letter', 'glory', 'veil' and 'Moses'.

[1419] Ibid., 72.

[1420] Barrett, *The Second Epistle to the Corinthians*, 110, cf. Naylor, *2 Corinthians*, 158: 'being discontinued'.

[1421] Naylor, *2 Corinthians*, 157. Thrall's comment: 'Rom 11:7 where the verb ἐπωρώθησαν occurs, is immediately followed (v. 8) by allusions to Isa 29.10 and 6.9f, where it is God who is the agent of hardening, and the same thought is doubtless present in 2 Cor 3:14a, although this does not ... wholly absolve Moses from responsibility': M. E. Thrall, *The Second Epistle to the Corinthians*, 262.

[1422] See also 2 Cor 2:11; 4:4; 10:5; 11:3; Phil 4:7.

[1423] Mark 6:52 and 8:17–18 (referring to Isa 6:9–10 and Jer 5:21).

[1424] John 12:40, citing Isa 6:10.

'Hardening' also implies that spiritual incomprehension often has moral rather than intellectual causes.

## (ii) veiled understanding (v. 15)

The reference to the reading of Moses in the synagogue indicates a public, community setting. Belleville remarks: 'the plural *their hearts* is to be noted. It is corporate darkness that is in view here.'[1425] Naylor comments: 'The attentive congregation is impervious to the built-in inadequacies of the Sinai arrangement.'[1426] Preachers, evangelists and youth workers can sometimes discern such a spirit of communal incomprehension amongst their non-hearers—an incomprehension in which they themselves can also share.

## (iii) turning to the Lord (v. 16)

This is the only way by which the spiritual cataract[1427] can be removed (περιαιρεῖται: 'is taken away'). The indefinite, subjectless ἡνίκα δὲ ἐὰν ἐπιστρέψῃ πρὸς κύριον is capable of various translations,[1428] but the thrust seems to be upon the universal offer of grace: 'whenever anyone turns to the Lord.' 'Turn' (ἐπιστρέφω) is commonly used in the New Testament of Christian conversion,[1429] indicating that repentance is a *sine qua non* for interpretive freedom. Although conversion for the Christian is initially a personal matter, there is also a communal dimension, as the call of the Old Testament prophets for Israel as a whole to repent reminds us. The converse to a veiled understanding within the reading of the Israelite community is surely an unveiled understanding within the reading of the Christian community. Moreover, 'we all, with unveiled face' (ἡμεῖς δὲ πάντες ἀνακεκαλυμμένῳ[1430] προσώπῳ) in v. 18a speaks not only of a communal act, but also of a completed one. The cataract operation should not, ideally, need repeating!

## (iv) boldness of expression (vv. 12, 18)

Bruce points out that by the use of 'unveiled face' 'Paul may also have in mind the Semitic idiom in which "to uncover the face (head)" means 'to behave boldly (frankly)." If so, then "with unveiled face" has practically the same meaning as "with boldness" (Gk *parrhesia*) and may help to explain Paul's use of the latter expression in verse 12.'[1431]

In contrast to the restrictions of the old covenant, Paul insists that the New Testament hope means that he can speak πολλῇ παρρησίᾳ ('with much boldness')

---

[1425] Belleville, *2 Corinthians*, 107.
[1426] Naylor, *2 Corinthians*, 159.
[1427] One of the root meanings of ἐπωρώθη is 'to cause a stone or callus to form': Belleville, *2 Corinthians*, 104.
[1428] Thrall, *The Second Epistle to the Corinthians*, 268–271, outlines six possibilities, opting for the sixth: 'the subject is Moses, but Moses seen as a type of the Christian convert', 271.
[1429] Acts 3:19; 1 Thess 1:9; 1 Pet 2:25.
[1430] Perfect participle.
[1431] Bruce, *1& 2 Corinthians*, 193.

(v. 12) as he addresses the Corinthians. This is what N. T. Wright sees as constituting the 'freedom' of v. 17b: 'freedom in the sense of freedom of speech, boldness, openness and honesty in proclaiming and defending the gospel (cf. 2.17, 4.1f.).'[1432]

*(v) freedom (v. 17b)*

A 'freedom', then, which begins with a correct understanding of Scripture should result in freedom in proclaiming the gospel. This should encourage Christian preachers in a pluralistic society that often derides 'preaching'. On another point, maybe the impassioned plea of James Denney a century ago contains something of an answer to Gadamer's later worries concerning the 'fore-meanings'[1433] of interpreters.

> Turn to Jesus Christ, as Moses turned to God, with face uncovered; put down prejudice, preconceptions, pride, the disposition to make demands; only look stedfastly till you see what He is, and all that perplexes you will pass away, or appear in a new light, and serve a new and spiritual purpose.[1434]

There may be some triumphalism here, but the last point at least brings us back to the pneumatological functioning that lies at the heart of the Pauline hermeneutic. True interpretive freedom is genuinely, but only achieved when there is a turning to 'the Lord [who] is Spirit' (ὁ δὲ κύριος τὸ πνεῦμά ἐστιν), v. 17a. This expression has been the subject of much debate, not least over what could superficially be construed as a binitarian confusion of Christ and the Spirit. However, the better reading seems to be that the κύριος ('Lord') of v. 17 is a reference back to the κύριος of v. 16,[1435] thus referring to the Yahweh of Exod 34:34.[1436] The point Paul is making is therefore functional rather than ontological, namely that, whereas under the old covenant Moses turned to Yahweh to remove the veil, believers under the new covenant now turn to the help of the Spirit. He alone can lift the veil of spiritual blindness and release them into an interpretive freedom that is part of 'the glorious liberty of the children of God' (Rom 8:21 RSV).

---

[1432] N. T. Wright, *The Climax of the Covenant: Christ and the Law in Pauline Theology* (London: T&T Clark, 1991), 179.

[1433] See pages 68–69.

[1434] James Denney *The Second Epistle to the Corinthians,* Expositors Bible 5th ed. (London: Hodder and Stoughton, 1917), 136–137.

[1435] Following Barrett's view (*The Second Epistle to the Corinthians,* 122) that 'the article with Lord (ὁ κύριος) is anaphoric..., and directs the reader's attention to *the Lord* in verse 16.' Thrall says from v. 17b that 'this is the only occasion when [Paul] designates the Spirit as πνεῦμα κυρίου, and the designation indicates that he still has the OT background in mind, since πνεῦμα κυρίου occurs frequently in the LXX as the rendering of *ruah yhwh*, the Spirit of Yahweh': Thrall, *The Second Epistle to the Corinthians,* 274.

[1436] 'Against the backdrop of Exodus 34, the "Lord" (*kyrios*) in view in verse 16 is not Christ, *in whom* the veil of hard-heartedness is taken away (2 Cor 3:14b), but Yahweh, *to whom* one turns once the veil has been removed,' Hafemann, *2 Corinthians,* 160.

## Contemplation

*but we all, with unveiled face, beholding the glory of the Lord (v. 18a)*

In contrast to Paul's use of simple first person plurals in preceding verses, he now uses the emphatic ἡμεῖς δὲ πάντες ('but we all'). According to Hughes, this 'expression ... signifies all Christians without exception,'[1437] in contrast to the exclusive experience of Moses under the old covenant. Héring's reading—'every Christian has become a Moses'[1438]—is understandable but sounds somewhat individualistic. A more 'mutual' aspect comes out from N. T. Wright's interesting suggestion from the translation of κατοπτριζόμενοι as 'beholding as in a mirror':

> The 'mirror' in which Christians see reflected the glory of the Lord is not ... the gospel itself, nor even Jesus Christ. *It is one another.* At the climax of Paul's whole argument, he makes ... the astonishing claim that those who belong to the new covenant are, by the Spirit, being changed into the glory of the Lord: *when they come face to face with one another* they are beholding, as in a mirror, the glory itself...This is the final proof that the Corinthians themselves are Paul's "letter of recommendation".... It is a peculiar glory of the Spirit that is seen when one looks at one's fellow-Christians.[1439]

This may not, of course, always be the case in practice, but the 'enfleshment' of the Spirit's working in people's lives (cf. vv. 2–3) certainly includes a horizontal dimension that also comes out in the alternative[1440] translation of κατοπτριζόμενοι as 'reflecting.' Reflecting on and upon the glory of the Lord will necessarily involve reflecting him out to others.[1441]

This should not, however, be seen as a replacement for the essentially vertical dimension implicit in 'beholding' ('gazing intently on')[1442]—contemplative thought and prayer centering around δόξα κυρίου ('the glory of the Lord', for instance, as explicated further in 2 Cor 4:3–6) should precede our interpretive endeavours. In the busy world of today, there is indeed a wider recognition of the place of contemplative and meditative approaches to the Bible.[1443] Such

---

[1437] E. Hughes, *The Second Epistle to the Corinthians* (Grand Rapids: Eerdmans, 1962), 117.

[1438] Cited by R.Martin in *2 Corinthians Word Biblical Commentary* (Milton Keynes: Word, 1991), 71.

[1439] Wright, *The Climax of the Covenant*, 185–186, second italics mine. As to the use of 'mirror' imagery, Fee says 'this usage is a clear case of Paul's "contextualizing", since Corinth was famous throughout the Greco-Roman antiquity for the superior quality of its bronze mirrors': Fee, *God's Empowering Presence*, 316.

[1440] Though less favoured by contemporary commentators.

[1441] Cf. Stephen's face in Acts 6:15, 7:55. See also Matt 5:14; Phil 2:15.

[1442] Witherington, *A Socio-Rhetorical Commentary on 1 and 2 Corinthians*, 382.

[1443] 'Gradually it is being recognized that the interpretation of the Bible is not exclusively a matter of scholarship and analysis; there is also a place for meditative and creative approaches': Helmut Gabel, 'Ignatian Contemplation and Modern Biblical Studies' in *The Way: a Review of Spirituality Published by the British Jesuits* April 2005, Vol. 44, No. 2., 37. He classes the Ignatian contemplative method amongst 'reader-centred' method, but claims that it is not 'in any way individualistic, for all that its primarily done by an individual in personal relationship to God. There is always a social connection present, through the contact with the one giving the Exercises, or with a faith-

approaches maybe also challenge some of the 'wordiness' of contemporary evangelical spirituality. 'As in a mirror' further evokes thoughts of Christ as the image of God,[1444] but also of the partiality of all human understanding ('now we see through a glass, darkly').[1445]

## Transformation

> are being transformed into the same image τὴν αὐτὴν εἰκόνα μεταμορφούμεθα (v. 18b)

Fitzmyer suggests that Paul has borrowed the *metamorphosis* concept from the classical mythology of the time, which regularly recorded tales of amazing transformations, and has thus 'suffused the Graco-Roman image with Jewish, Old Testament, and Palestinian motifs.'[1446] The present tense/indicative μεταμορφούμεθα speaks of a process that is both ongoing—the mirror needs 'continual polishing'[1447]—as well as thorough, for it involves a change of the μορφή ('real/essential being').[1448] The goal is a restoration of the *imago Deo*,[1449] εἰκών ('image') having nothing to do with any kind of contemporary 'ikon', but rather evoking the primeval εἰκών of Gen 1:26–27,[1450] a motif which is also found in the next chapter,[1451] and developed into the 'new creation' of 5:17. Applied to the Christian interpretive community, this means the end result of their work should be moral transfiguration[1452]—into the likeness of Christ. To quote Hays: 'Thus, true reading produces the transformation of the readers. Consequently, there can be no dichotomy between hermeneutics and ethics.'[1453] It should therefore help promote holiness in the life of the congregation or community in which such reading of Scripture takes place.

---

community,' (44). Endean claims that a greater scope for the Spirit's workings is afforded by the more limited role for the spiritual director whom Ignatius instructs to go 'over the Points with only a short or summary development ... for it is not the knowing of much that contents and satisfies the soul, but the feeling and relish for things from inside.' 'Ignatius Loyola, prayer and Scripture' in Ballard & S. Holmes, eds., *The Bible in Pastoral Practice: Readings in the Place and Function of Scripture in the Church* (London: Darton Longman and Todd, 2005), 278–279.

[1444] Col 1:15; Heb 1:3.
[1445] 1 Cor 13:12a, AV.
[1446] Fitzmyer, *According to Paul*, 66. Fitzmyer also refers to parallels in Qumran literature where 'we read about God illumining the face of the Teacher of Righteousness or of the priests of the community, and about him/them, in turn, illumining the face of the Many in the community,' ibid., 74–75.
[1447] Belleville, *2 Corinthians*, 112.
[1448] Hughes, *The Second Epistle to the Corinthians*, 118, fn. 18.
[1449] Already seen in Christ 2 Cor 4:4. The Greek fathers extended the idea to embrace the divinisation of believers.
[1450] Barrett, however, suggests the 'looking-glass' imagery is inspired by the literature of wisdom speculation, such as Wisdom vii.26. Barrett, *A Commentary on the Second Epistle to the Corinthians*, 125
[1451] 2 Cor 4:4–6.
[1452] 'Paul's argument from the Scriptures as common ground with his opponents assumes that the role of the Holy Spirit in biblical interpretation is not to provide God's people with hidden information or insights into the Scriptures, but to change their moral disposition': Hafemann, *2 Corinthians*, 170.
[1453] Hays, *Paul and the Scriptures of Israel*, 45.

## Glorification

*from one degree of glory to another'* ἀπὸ δόξης εἰς δόξαν *(v. 18c)*

'With this sentence we reach the heights.'[1454] Compared with the fading glory of Moses, that which belongs to the new covenant community is 'ever-increasing'.[1455] Its grandiose sweep stretches from the historical ἀπὸ δόξης ('from glory') to the eschatological εἰς δόξαν ('to glory'),[1456] when words of interpretation will no longer be required. As Wesley's hymn puts it:

> *Changed from glory into glory*
> *Till in heaven we take our place*
> *Till we cast our crowns before Thee*
> *Lost in wonder, love, and praise.*[1457]

Paul concludes this glorious end to the chapter by bringing us back to its pneumatic starting point: 'for this comes from the Lord who is the Spirit' v. 18d, a translation that seems to be the most straightforward translation of the rather cryptic καθάπερ ἀπὸ κυρίου πνεύματος.[1458] From beginning to end, the process of *metamorphosis* is a divine work, as effected by the Spirit.

## Conclusion to 2 Corinthians 3

This Pauline exposition of life under the new, as opposed to the old, covenant continues to present its interpretive challenge to us, as Richardson notes:

(i) We are faced by the nature of the interpretive task with a written text (*gramma*) which for most people is just as lifeless as ever the law of Moses was for Jews contemporary with Paul.

(ii) The goal of interpretation is understanding: removing the veil, softening what has become hard, writing on the heart.

(iii) The newness of the new covenant in Christ has for most people today become existentially meaningless.[1459]

This challenge is pointed up by the TV culture of the West that manifestly depends on 'image' rather than 'word', an influence that has not escaped the church.[1460] Paul, in 2 Cor 3, shows how the Spirit helps us to 'image' (cf. v. 18

---

[1454] Fee, *God's Empowering Presence*, 314, referring to the whole of verse 18.
[1455] From NIV of v. 18.
[1456] Rom 8:17, 29, 30.
[1457] From Charles Wesley's hymn, 'Love Divine, All Loves Excelling.'
[1458] Following Barrett, *The Second Epistle to the Corinthians*, 126, who sees the two nouns as appositional. For other suggested translations, see R. Martin, *2 Corinthians*, 72.
[1459] Peter Richardson 'Spirit and Letter: A Foundation for Hermeneutics' in *Evangelical Quarterly*, Vol. XLV No. 4, (1973), 213.
[1460] D. Bebbington, 'Evangelicals and Public Worship, 1965-2005' in *Evangelical Quarterly* 79.1 (2007), 22, argues that 'the logocentricity of earlier times [has been] drastically modified by the rise of the visual.'

εἰκών) *the* Word. Through the Spirit's provision of a 'hermeneutic of the heart,'[1461] the Word can indeed become vitalized and visible in the understanding and witness of both Christian individuals and communities. The communal aspect, however, seems to be the emphasis of this chapter, as evidenced by its plural terminology and the contrast with Old Testament Israel. Now the whole Christian community is pictured as being able to enjoy the Mosaic access to and reflection of God: '*we all*, with unveiled face' (v. 18). This latter expression, says Scott, 'most naturally includes Paul and all other believers, another aspect of the mutuality to which Paul has repeatedly brought attention in the letter.'[1462]

Hence Paul shows how the Spirit helps the Christian community to flesh out the gospel in the form of 'living epistles', for in the new covenant '*incarnation* eclipses inscription.'[1463] Such a *disjunction* from the old covenant marks out the Christian faith as the only alternative for those whose minds are spiritually hardened. Their *liberation* can only come about through an 'unveiling' when they turn to the Lord, for repentance is a *sine qua non* for interpretive freedom, i.e. for spiritual understanding. This understanding increases with further *contemplation* on the glory of the Lord that will in turn reflect him out to others. The ongoing *transformation* of the reading community into the likeness of Christ reminds us of the link with ethics and the ultimate goal of interpretation, issuing in a work of *glorification* whose ultimate realization will make hermeneutics redundant. From beginning to end, it is all a work of the Spirit, the hallmarks of whose operations are evidenced in this chapter, brimming, as it is, with '*Trinitarian* presuppositions,'[1464] *historical* reference (Exod 34), *dialectical/dialogical* contrasts (old v. new covenant) and *eschatological* denouement ('from glory to glory'). These multi-faceted operations of the Spirit[1465] are all part of the κοινωνία τοῦ ἁγίου πνεύματος ('the fellowship of the Holy Spirit'), which forms the very last part of the apostle's closing prayer for the Corinthian church (2 Cor 13:14).

## Romans 8: The Spirit of Sonship

The glorious negatives of 'no condemnation' (v. 1) and 'no separation' (v. 39)[1466] frame this great chapter. Its light and hope are warmly welcomed by readers of the previous chapters (i.e. Rom 1-7), dominated as they are by what Dunn describes as 'the fearful triumvirate (sin, death, and law as used by sin).'[1467] The

---

[1461] Hafemann, *2 Corinthians*, 164.
[1462] J. M. Scott, *2 Corinthians* (Peabody, MA: Hendrickson, 1998), 82, referring also to 2 Cor 3:1:1-2, 3-11, 24; 2:2.
[1463] Hays, *Echoes of Scripture*, 129, italics added.
[1464] See Fee, *God's Empowering Presence*, 320 (italics added) where he unfolds the 'thoroughgoing ... Trinitarian implications' of the chapter.
[1465] See chapter 2.
[1466] J. R. W. Stott, *The Message of Romans* (Leicester: IVP, 1994), 217.
[1467] J. D. G. Dunn, *The Theology of Paul the Apostle* (Edinburgh: T&T Clark, 1998), 423.

main reason for this dramatic change of atmosphere is the shining forth of 'the Spirit of life' (8:2), largely hidden in chapters 1 to 6, glimpsed in 7:6, but fully blazing in chapter 8, where he is mentioned no less than nineteen times in vv. 1–27. My study will be focussed on these verses, containing as they do, the greatest intensity of pneumatic reference in the Pauline corpus: 'unquestionably the high point of Paul's theology of the Spirit.'[1468]

As Paul expounds the monumental consequences of how 'the law of the Spirit of life has set you[1469] free in Christ Jesus from the law of sin and death' (8:2), he is not *prima facie* giving lessons on Spirit-led hermeneutics. Nevertheless, I would argue that the command to 'walk ... according to the Spirit' (v. 4) includes vital lessons for biblical interpreters in the context of a discipleship that is largely corporate. This is shown by Paul's use of 'we/you (plural)' language, the frequency of συν- compounds and the family metaphor he uses in the chapter. Underlying these concepts is what Holland describes as an 'argument ... driven by the new exodus theme', along with its 'pilgrimage imagery.'[1470] The use of corporate Old Testament motifs, as reflected for instance in 'all who are led by the Spirit of God are sons of God' (v. 14), is indeed illuminating, as has been seen in the previous studies from 1 Cor 2 and 2 Cor 3. This latter chapter and Rom 8 both describe a process of pneumatic activity within the Christian community that results in freedom[1471] and glory.[1472]

Here, I will seek to extract five aspects of this activity that bear on the subject of our book: the life-giving Spirit; the spiritual mindset; the family setting;[1473] eschatological tension/'groaning'; and support in weakness.

### The Life-giving Spirit (τοῦ πνεύματος τῆς ζωῆς[1474] in v. 2 and ζωή in vv. 6, 10, 11)

According to Fee, 'the phrase "the Spirit of life" ... is perhaps the single most significant designation of the Spirit in the Pauline corpus,'[1475] identifying him with 'the living God' of the Old Testament who is the exclusive source of all life. He is indeed 'the Lord, the giver of life', as the Nicene Creed puts it. The Old

---

[1468] Ibid., 423.
[1469] Some Mss. have 'me' instead of 'you': J. A. Fitzmyer, *Romans*, The Anchor Bible (London: Doubleday; Geoffrey Chapman, 1992), 483. However, the rest of the pronouns in the chapter are unambiguously plural when referring to Christians.
[1470] Tom Holland, *Romans: The Divine Marriage – A Biblical Theological Commentary* (Eugene, OR: Pickwick, 2011), 294.
[1471] 2 Cor 3:17; Rom 8:2. Stuhlmacher points to the Old Testament link: 'it is natural to interpret Rom 8:2–7 against the background of Jer 31:31ff.; Ezek 36:27; and the early Jewish expectation that the end-times people of God, in fulfilment of the promise of a son from 2 Sam7:12–14, will be led into the perfect obedience of the "sons of God",'Stuhlmacher *Paul's Letter to the Romans* (Edinburgh: T&T Clark, 1994), 118.
[1472] 2 Cor 3:18; Rom 8:30.
[1473] This constitutes our major section, hence our heading for Rom 8 as 'the Spirit of Sonship'.
[1474] Fitzmyer, *Romans*, 482, notes that the genitive 'indicates that which the Spirit guarantees (compare 6:4 and 7:6).'
[1475] Fee, *God's Empowering Presence*, 525.

Testament background is also highlighted by Stuhlmacher: 'the formulation "Spirit of life" is Semitic and, as Ezek 37:5f. and above all 1 Enoch 61:7 show by way of example, refers to the Spirit of God which fills the eschatological people of God with new life and the knowledge of God.'[1476] Fitzmyer describes 'the law of the Spirit' v. 2 as 'the dynamic "principle" ... supplying the very vitality that the Mosaic law could not give.'[1477] The discontinuity with the Old Testament suggested by Paul's πνεῦμα v. νόμος/σάρξ (spirit v. law/flesh) antitheses in vv. 2–13, however, is modified in vv. 14–16, which, arguably, constitutes a reanimation of the Exodus tradition, reworking and 'pneumatologising' themes such as freedom from slavery, being 'led' and sonship (vv. 14–16), as shall be seen later.

The 'life' of the Spirit, further, is linked with 'peace' in v. 6 and 'resurrection' in v. 11. As to v. 6, Sanday and Headlam say εἰρήνη ('peace') refers to both 'the state of reconciliation with God' and 'the sense of reconciliation which diffuses a feeling of harmony and tranquillity over the whole man.'[1478] Spirit-directed apprehension and appropriation should ultimately lead to peace with God and peace within (cf. Rom 5:1). In v. 11, Paul assures his readers there that '...he who raised Christ Jesus from the dead will also give life to your mortal bodies *through his Spirit* who dwells in you (note plural: ἐν ὑμῖν).' Such a quickening, then, links Christians with the power of the risen Christ and thus should enable them to speak with the life-giving vitality of the one whose words were 'spirit and life' (John 6:63). Their service, then, should always aim to be in 'newness of Spirit and not in oldness of letter' (ἐν καινότητι πνεύματος καὶ οὐ παλαιότητι γράμματος, Rom 7:6).

## The Spiritual Mindset (vv. 4–13)

Paul in v. 5 contrasts two natures: of 'those who live according to the flesh' (κατὰ σάρκα)[1479] and of 'those who live according to the Spirit' (κατὰ πνεῦμα). These two natures issue in two contrasting 'mindsets':[1480] 'set their minds (φρονοῦσιν) on the things of the flesh ... [or] of the Spirit' (v. 5). These in turn bear two very different kinds of fruit: 'death' (v. 6) and enmity to God (vv. 7–8) or 'life and peace' (v. 6).[1481] Commentators differ as to whether the distinction between the

---

[1476] Stuhlmacher, *Paul's Letter to the Romans*, 118. Schreiner also links 'Spirit of life' with Ezek 37 as 'one of the antecedents for the Pauline expression', thus underlining its wider corporate context in relation to the resurrection of Israel. T. R. Schreiner, *Romans* (Grand Rapids: Baker, 1998), 415.

[1477] Fitzmyer, *Romans*, 482–483. As to Paul's word-play on νόμος in v. 2 he comments that 'Paul indulges in oxymoron as he now applies *nomos* to the Spirit, which is anything but "law" ', 482.

[1478] W. Sanday and A. C. Headlam, *The Epistle to Romans*, ICC (Edinburgh: T&T Clark, 1898), 196.

[1479] Stott's definition: 'by *sarx* (flesh) Paul means neither ... soft muscular tissue ... nor our bodily ... appetites, but rather the whole of our humanness viewed as corrupt and unredeemed, "our fallen, ego-centric human nature" [Cranfield], or more briefly "the sin-dominated self [Ziesler]" Stott, *The Message of Romans*, 222. The precise meaning of σάρξ, however, depends on the context.

[1480] 'Mind-set' is used by the commentators for Paul's φρόνημα (vv. 6 and 7). Moo defines it as 'our fundamental orientation, the convictions and heart attitude that steers the course of our life' D. J. Moo, *Romans (Life Application Commentary)* (Grand Rapids: Zondervan, 2000), 257.

[1481] Cf. Gal 5:16–26. Paul's life/death language reflects Old Testament passages such as Deut 30:15–20.

two natures is an absolute one (describing the unregenerate and the regenerate),[1482] or more a designation of '"ideal types" [on the basis that] human beings partake in different measures of the two types.'[1483]

Christian experience endorses this latter point. We do not always 'walk in the Spirit', as Paul implies by the verbal indicatives of vv. 4–17,[1484] and commands by the verbal imperative of Gal 5:25. To that extent, we can see again that there is an ethical conditioning for a spiritual mindset, for walking κατὰ πνεῦμα involves a life of righteousness (v. 4) and mortification (v. 13b). Hence Burke's emphasis on how the guidance of the Spirit promised in v. 14 'is *moral* and involves "putting to death the misdeeds of the body" (v.13b).'[1485] This necessarily involves 'the daily responsibility to kill off sin in its various forms (thoughts, habits and attitudes, 1.26,31; 3:13–17)),'[1486] which can only be done with 'the divine energy and dynamic power' of the Spirit.'[1487] As applied to the task and aim of interpretation, self-pleasing should give way to 'pleas[ing] God' (v. 8), who truly 'knows what is the mind (φρόνημα) of the Spirit' (v. 27).[1488]

The spiritual mind-set also requires that 'the Spirit of God *dwells in* you' (v. 9). As to οἰκεῖ ἐν, Sanday and Headlam say it 'denotes a settled permanent penetrative influence,'[1489] implying that constant indwelling is needed for consistent hermeneutics. More actively, it also involves being 'led by the Spirit' (v. 14). As to πνεύματι θεοῦ ἄγονται, Käsemann interprets the verb in light of charismatic enthusiasts: 'driven by the Spirit'[1490] (cf. Dunn's 'constrained by a compelling force'[1491]), an experience to which some Old Testament prophets and New Testament exegetes could certainly testify. Stott, however, says that ἄγω does 'not necessarily or normally imply the use of force', favouring a more moderate rendering along the lines of Lloyd Jones's language of the Spirit's 'enlightening' and 'persuading,'[1492] which is surely the more usual experience for contemporary exegetes. Murray's 'governed by the Spirit'[1493] represents a middle position. The manner of the Spirit's leading is indeed not always easy to define or delineate. It can easily be over-subjectivised ('I was led by the Spirit') in a way that does not do justice to the corporate context of its use here.

---

[1482] Cf. Stott, *The Message of Romans*, 224, and Fee's reference to '*two different* groups of people—flesh" people and Spirit people,' *God's Empowering Presence*, 540.
[1483] Dunn, *The Theology of Paul*, 478, cf. Nygren's reference to Paul's 'dualism' in Rom 7 and 8: 'the Christian is *simul justus et peccator*, he is righteous and a sinner at the same time' A. Nygren, *Commentary on Romans* (Philadelphia: Fortress, 1949), 322.
[1484] Bornkamm notes that Romans 8 'contains not a single verb in the imperative' G. Bornkamm, *Paul* (London: Hodder & Stoughton, 1971), 156.
[1485] Trevor J. Burke, 'Romans' in Burke & Warrington, eds., *A Biblical Theology of the Holy Spirit*, 136.
[1486] Ibid., 137.
[1487] Ibid., 137.
[1488] Cf. 1 Cor 2:16: 'the mind (νοῦν) of Christ'.
[1489] Sanday and Headlam *The Epistle to Romans*, 196.
[1490] Ernst Käsemann, *Commentary on Romans* (London: SCM; Eerdmans, 1973), 226.
[1491] J. D. G. Dunn, *Romans*, Word Biblical Commentary No. 38 (Dallas: Word, 1988), 456.
[1492] As referred to in J. R. W. Stott, *Romans*, 231. Cf. Ps 32:8–9.
[1493] John Murray, *The Epistle to the Romans* (Grand Rapids: Eerdmans, 1968), 295.

This corporate aspect is underlined by Holland, who links v.14 with the way God has led his people by his Spirit 'throughout the ages'—as demonstrated in the Old Testament stories of Abraham journeying to the land of promise, and of Israel later being led out of slavery from Egypt and subsequently out of exile from Babylon.[1494] Sylvia Keesmat also points to the passage's Old Testament associations.[1495] In a detailed exploration of the 'intertextual matrix of ideas'[1496] underlying Rom 8:14–39, she exposes many echoes of the Exodus story which might have resounded with readers from a Jewish background. She recalls many Old Testament passages where the LXX uses ἄγω of God leading Israel out of Egypt and through the wilderness, and how they were employed 'as a basis for assurance for God's continued faithfulness to Israel,'[1497] as well as for 'pleas for God's *future* salvation.'[1498]

As contemporary interpreters trek through the wilderness of current secularism, they too can look to the Spirit to lead them on, especially if they seek to do so as constituents of the journeying people of God. For as Paul reminds us, such leading brings with it a special status: 'for all who are led by the Spirit of God are *sons of God*' (v. 14), a privileged status which we will now explore.

### The Family Setting (vv. 14–17)

Burke notes 'the heavy preponderance of filial language' in these verses.[1499] Sonship, of course, is another concept with deep Old Testament roots, with Israel commonly referred to as a son of God.[1500] Keesmat points out how ἄγω ('lead') and υἱός ('son') regularly occur together in the Song of Moses in Deut 32, of which there are 'abundant ... echoes' in Romans 8.[1501] She also sees allusions to Jer 31:8, 9 ('I will lead them' ... 'father to Israel' ... 'firstborn') and Isa 63:7–19, which includes references to the Exodus leading of the Holy Spirit (vv. 10–12) and God as Father as the basis for a plea for help (vv. 15ff): 'a progression echoed in Rom 8:14–15.'[1502] The 'Abba' cry (Rom 8:15), then, reflects the cry of a people,[1503] whose 'adoption as sons' is not so much to be understood against the background of Greco-Roman law, but rather of Israel's adoption as a nation by Yahweh, which is closely linked with the Spirit in Ezek 36:24–28. Keesmat traces

---

[1494] Holland, *Romans: The Divine Marriage*, 268–269. 'The leading of the Spirit is essentially a corporate experience, when the covenant community is guided on its pilgrimage to the New Jerusalem (Acts15:28; 16:7–10),' 269.
[1495] Sylvia C. Keesmat, *Paul and His Story:(Re)Interpreting the Exodus Tradition* (Sheffield: Sheffield Academic Press, 1999), 56.
[1496] Ibid., 59.
[1497] Ibid., 59, having referred to passages such as Exod 15:13, Ps 104:37 and 77:14, 52, 54 (LXX).
[1498] Ibid., 59, referring to Ps 30:4 (LXX).
[1499] Burke, 'Romans', 137, mentioning 'sons' v.14, 'slaves' v.15a, 'adopted son' v.15b, 'children' v.16, 'heirs' v.16.
[1500] For example, Exod 4:22; Deut 14:1, 32:6; Hos 2:2 (LXX) Isa 1:2, 4. See Keesmat, *Paul and His Story* 60, for an exploration of 'Leading and Sonship' as the Old Testament background for Rom 8:14–17.
[1501] For instance from Deut 32:5, 6, 12, 19, 20: Keesmat, *Paul and His Story*, 61.
[1502] Ibid., 63.
[1503] Ibid., 77.

further exodus motifs in the language of 'slavery/fear' of v. 15,[1504] 'witness' in v. 16[1505] and 'inheritance'[1506] and 'glory'[1507] of v. 17. She concludes from all this that 'the community of believers has already experienced the new exodus event, they are already sons, they are no longer in bondage, they are already witnesses', and are thus 'part of the eschatological restoration,'[1508] although its completion is still awaited (vv. 18–25).

If Keesmat's intertextual analysis is correct, then Paul's reshaping of the Exodus tradition so as to broaden it out from Israel to embrace the wider family of the Christian church affords an interesting illustration of how he sought to expound that to which 'the Law and the Prophets bear witness' (Rom 3:21), or, in the language of modern hermeneutics, to 'read Scripture ... as story and as prophecy.'[1509] As those who represent the continuation of that story, Christians are likewise called upon to retell it for today in ways enabled by the Spirit, with the kind of prophetic insight he still provides. And since it is he 'who bears witness with (συμμαρτυρεῖ) our spirit that we are the children of God' (v. 16), the category of 'family' presents us with another Spirit-created context for the interpretation of Scripture in a corporate setting. I venture to apply this context on two levels.

On the 'horizontal' level, the family model implies the need for a fraternal spirit of openness and sharing between biblical interpreters. Disagreement must be faced with constructive criticism, and opposing views respected rather than 'rubbished'. Claims to have the discernment of the Spirit should be matched by a display of the fruit of the Spirit.[1510] The '*many* brothers' of 8:29 also indicates the breadth of the interpretive task, ideally crossing boundaries of time, culture, theology, and denomination in engagement with the wider parameters of the Christian family.

On the 'vertical' level, that Christians can come to Scripture as 'sons of God' (v. 14) signifies a relationship of intimacy and respectful familiarity with their Creator that should prevent them from treating hermeneutics as a purely intellectual exercise. Burke has drawn attention to the highly personal language used of the verbs to describe the Spirit's activities in Romans 8, making him 'a relational Spirit for a relational community.'[1511] He is 'not only God's empowering presence ... but *God's personified presence* at work in a number of vital ways within the community of God's people, of *desiring, leading,*

---

[1504] Ibid., 66.
[1505] Ibid., 77. Keesmat sees in 'witness' a wider concept than a merely juridical one, referring to passages that speak of Israel as a witness to Yahweh's saving deeds, such as Isa 55:4-5.
[1506] Ibid., 81.
[1507] Ibid., 84.
[1508] Ibid., 96.
[1509] Ibid., 231.
[1510] Gal 5:22-26 (also noting v. 26a AV: 'let us not be desirous of vain glory').
[1511] Burke, 'Romans', 139.

*indwelling, witnessing* and *interceding*.'[1512] Such a personal ministry requires a personal response from us, as sons and daughters of God's family. As Dodd says, 'the idea of sonship connotes loyalty, obedience, imitation and responsive love.'[1513] Such responsiveness is characterized by the Spirit-enabled 'Abba Father' (v. 15) cry[1514] uttered by needy Christians, not least as biblical interpreters. Barth indeed avers that 'all that occurs to us and in us can be *no more than an answer* to what the Spirit Himself says.'[1515]

## Eschatological Tension/'Groaning' (vv. 17–25)

That being 'children of God' (v. 16) makes us also 'heirs of God and fellow heirs with Christ' (v. 17, noting 'the piling up of the συν- compounds')[1516] not only 'staggers the imagination,'[1517] but also assures us of ultimate explanation. The eschatological tension in the waiting period between present 'suffering' and future 'glory' (v. 18) is inaugurated by the Spirit who is the 'firstfruits' (ἀπαρχή v. 23)[1518] of the new order. In this already/not yet age, the Spirit is, then, the source of both 'longing and hope,'[1519] reminding us of the partiality[1520] and provisionality inherent in the Christian life. We are not alone in this, for there is a communion of 'groanings' that is shared between creation (v. 22),[1521] Christians (v. 23), and the Spirit himself (v. 26). This communion should help biblical interpreters to share in the world's pain, frustration, and incompleteness and to guard against triumphalism, superficiality, and glibness.

## Support in Weakness (vv. 26–27)

A comforting 'likewise' (Ὡσαύτως v. 26a) introduces us to a further ministry of the Spirit, who 'helps us in our weakness' (v. 26b). Here is another 'συν- compound' verb, συναντιλαμβάνεται[1522] 'takes hold of a thing with another, takes

---

[1512] Ibid., 141.
[1513] C. H. Dodd, *The Epistle of Paul to the Romans* (London: Hodder and Stoughton, 1932), 131.
[1514] Dunn points out that 'the use of the same phrase in Gal 4:6 clearly indicates that it was an established formula in the churches known to Paul ... [and] ... evidently taken up by the first followers of Jesus, no doubt in imitation of Jesus, and most likely at his direct instruction (Luke 11:2),' Dunn, *Romans*, 461. Cf. Mark 14:36.
[1515] As cited (with italics inserted) from his comments on 'the Spirit beareth witness': 'Ecstasies and illuminations, inspirations and intuitions are not necessary. Happy are they who are worthy to receive them! But woe be to us if we wait anxiously for them! Woe be to us, if we fail to recognize that they are patchwork by-products! All that occurs to us and in us can be no more than an answer to what the Spirit Himself says': Karl Barth, *The Epistle to the Romans* (Oxford: Oxford University Press, 1968), 298.
[1516] Dunn, *Romans*, 447: συγκληρονόμοι (joint heirs) ... συμπάσχομεν (suffer with) ... συνδοξασθῶμεν (we may be glorified with).
[1517] Fee, *God's Empowering Presence*, 569.
[1518] See chapter 2, section 2 (d) (iv) for more on ἀπαρχή.
[1519] Dunn, *Theology of Paul*, 437.
[1520] 'The Christian life is never more than partial in this life': Nygren, *Commentary on Romans*, 324.
[1521] Note again the συν- compounds: συστενάζει (groans together) καὶ συνωδίνει (travails together).
[1522] Cranfield points out that the verb occurs in the LXX in Exod 18:22 and Num 17:17 (thus evidencing another Exodus background), as well as Ps 89:21 (LXX: 88:22) and the more practical Mary/Martha context of Luke 10:40: Cranfield, *The Epistle to the Romans*, 421.

a share in,' as of someone sharing in the carrying of a weighty plank or log.[1523] Such assurance brings encouragement to those bearing the heavy responsibility of biblical interpretation, with the primary focus of the Spirit's help here being in the realm of prayer: 'we do not know what to pray for ... but the Spirit himself intercedes for us with *groanings too deep for words* (στεναγμοῖς ἀλαλήτοις).' (v.26b). As Dunn says, 'this is an astonishing feature of Paul's pneumatology: the Spirit experienced not in power, but in weakness; the Spirit experienced not in articulate speech but through "inarticulate groans".'[1524] This mysterious, wordless supplication[1525] for the saints ensures their pleas are articulated to God in accordance with his will (v. 27): 'the groanings of believers are overridden by the intercessions of the Spirit.'[1526] Not only, then, does the Spirit interpret *God* to *us* (considered to be his more usual role), but he also interprets *us* to *God*. He is thus the great facilitator in the 'toing and froing' of the hermeneutical process in the context of Spirit-assisted prayer.

## *Conclusion to Romans 8*

As with 1 Cor 2 and 2 Cor 3, Rom 8:1–27 is not a passage whose express purpose is to give instruction in Spirit-led biblical hermeneutics for the people of God. But its dense pneumatological reference[1527] points to several relevant implications for biblical hermeneutics in the context of a discipleship that has a corporate emphasis, as illuminated by the Exodus background,[1528] use of plural terminology and συν- compounds. Christians, as biblical interpreters as much as anything else, need *the 'life-giving Spirit'*, who authors words that quicken the dead and exude 'newness'. They should also cultivate a *spiritual mindset* that requires moral obedience and the constant indwelling and leading of the Spirit. The Pauline link with the Old Testament people of God being led through the wilderness evokes a corporate context and suggests a method of reading Scripture 'as story and prophecy.'[1529] Being led as 'sons of God' further speaks of

---

[1523] Martyn Lloyd-Jones, *Romans, Exposition of Chapter 8:17–39* (Edinburgh: Banner of Trust, 1975), 134. The συν- prefix also points to the fact that 'the verb is probably intensive, indicating not merely that the Spirit joins in helping but also that the Spirit himself and alone renders the assistance believers need': Schreiner, *Romans*, 442. Cf Holland's comment: 'The Spirit does not come to the church's aid to boost her strength; he comes to her aid when strength is completely gone': Holland, *Romans: The Divine Marriage*, 279.

[1524] Dunn, *Theology of Paul*, 438–439.

[1525] 'The children of God have two divine-intercessors. Christ is their intercessor in the court of heaven (*cf.* v. 34; Heb 7:25; 1 John 2:1). The Holy Spirit is their intercessor in the theatre of their own hearts (*cf.* John 14:16, 17)': Murray, *The Epistle to the Romans*, 311.

[1526] Arland J. Hultgren, *Paul's Letter to the Romans* (Grand Rapids: Eerdmans, 2011), 325. Further, Hodge: 'The Holy Spirit dictates those petitions and excites those desires which are consistent with the divine purposes, and which are directed towards the blessings best suited to our wants': C. Hodge, *A Commentary on Romans* (Edinburgh: Banner of Truth, 1972), 280.

[1527] We can trace our fourfold κοινωνία patterning in the chapter with its '*Trinitarian* presuppositions' (Fee, *God's Empowering Presence*, 538, e.g. 'sons of God' and 'led by the Spirit' [v. 14], 'heirs with Christ' [v. 17]); *dialogical* aspect (πνεῦμα v. νόμος/σάρξ); Exodus *historical* allusion; and *eschatological* 'groanings').

[1528] 'In a context of *extreme individualism* which has led to heightened personal alienation and loneliness, the exodus story as told by Paul reminds us that in Christ we are *called to be a community* with a common identity and a common calling': Keesmat, *Paul and his Story: (Re)telling the Exodus Tradition*, 236.

[1529] Keesmat, *Paul and His Story: (Re)Interpreting the Exodus Tradition*, 231.

a *family setting* and therefore of the fraternal spirit in which biblical interpretation should take place, as well as the 'Abba Father' relationship enabled by the Spirit. That interpretation is carried out against the background of *eschatological tension/'groaning'*, itself inaugurated by the Spirit, helps us share in the realities of this present world, and is thus a check against triumphalism and glibness. The Spirit's *support in weakness* in the form of 'inarticulate groans' in prayer shows us how the Spirit interprets *us* to *God*, as well as interpreting *God* to *us*.

## The Pastoral Epistles: The Spirit and Tradition

The collective designation of 1 and 2 Timothy and Titus as 'the Pastoral epistles'[1530] ('PE') is a recognition of their common practical relevance, in Aquinas's language, as 'a rule, so to speak, for pastors.'[1531] As such, their thought pattern is quite different from that which has been seen earlier in this chapter in the letters Paul wrote to the churches in Rome and Corinth. Instead of a tightly packed flow of argument pregnant with Old Testament and pneumatological reference, we find a more diffuse form of argumentation,[1532] including lists of 'rules', in which the Old Testament background is not so pronounced, the Spirit is rarely mentioned and in which there is an emphasis upon maintaining 'sound doctrine,'[1533] godly leadership and a more 'structured ministry'[1534] (described by some as 'early catholic'[1535]). This, along with their distinctive vocabulary[1536] and theological emphases,[1537] has led many to date their origin to a period of later church development in the post-Apostolic era, possibly at the transition from second to third generation Christianity, a period that reflects a greater concern

---

[1530] Designated as such by eighteenth-century scholars, see J. A. Fitzmyer, 'The Structured Ministry of the Church in the Pastoral Epistles' in *Catholic Biblical Quarterly*, Vol. 66 No. 4 (2004), 582.

[1531] Cited by Jerome Quinn and William C. Wacker, *The First and Second Letters to Timothy* (Grand Rapids: Eerdmans, 2000), 1.

[1532] Often by way of categorical statement, example (sometimes negative) or deduction. There seems to be little agreement amongst the commentators about the structure of the PE (i.e. Pastoral Epistles).

[1533] 1 Tim 1:10 (ὑγιαινούσῃ διδασκαλίᾳ); Titus 1:9.

[1534] J. Fitzmyer, 'The Structured Ministry of the Church in the Pastoral Epistles', *Catholic Biblical Quarterly* Vol. 66 No. 4 (Oct. 2004), 582–595, an article elaborating on four titles: ἐπίσκοπος ('bishop', 'overseer'), πρεσβύτερος ('presbyter', 'elder'), διάκονος ('deacon', 'minister') and χήρα ('widow').

[1535] For example, by Dunn: 'here [in the PE] we probably see the merging of Jewish Christian church order with the more formal order which emerged in the Pauline churches in the early Catholicism of second and third generation Christianity': J. Dunn, *Jesus and the Spirit: A Study of the Religious and Charismatic Experience of Jesus and the First Christians as Reflected in the New Testament* (London: SCM, 1975), 347. For a discussion of the 'early Catholic' interpretation, see I. Howard Marshall in collaboration with Philip H. Towner, *The Pastoral Epistles*, A Critical and Exegetical Commentary (Edinburgh: T & T Clark, 1999), 512–514. They, however, conclude that 'what dominates the PE is not "the principle of office" but "the principle of tradition"', 514.

[1536] Quinn and Wacker estimate that one third of the words in the PE do not appear in the other Paulines and almost one fifth do not appear elsewhere in the NT: Quinn and Wacker, *The First and Second Letters to Timothy*, 14.

[1537] For instance, familiar Pauline themes ('flesh', 'body', God as Father, 'in Christ') are missing, whereas a new vocabulary of ethical instruction ('piety', 'self-control' and 'conscience') appears, whilst the church as the 'body of Christ' has given way to a 'household' conception. See I. Howard Marshall, 'Recent Study of the Pastoral Epistles' in *Themelios*, Vol. 23 No. 1 (1997), 12 & 19.

with the preservation of the faith, 'order' and 'office.'[1538] Fitzmyer has claimed that 'today the majority of NT interpreters regard the Pastoral Letters as pseudepigraphical writings within the Pauline corpus,'[1539] doubtless containing genuine Pauline 'fragments' but also other material from the early church, and subsequently put together by a 'pseudo-Paul' or some sort of Pauline school, perhaps for the training of pastors.[1540] The latter is a suggestion of James Miller who has generally argued that:

> The diversity of literary forms within these letters, the variations in content, the traditional character of much of the material, all converge to suggest that these documents are *composite* works, consisting of gathered collections of community traditions.[1541]

If this were the case, it might be possible to address the principal question of our book by attempting a reconstruction of the methods of the community in shaping and reinterpreting Christian tradition, for instance by the application of redaction criticism to the letters.[1542] But this would involve embarking on a route that is essentially speculative and one that has proved less than productive.

Philip Towner has, moreover, argued that 'unnecessary methodological assumptions'[1543] lie behind a post-Pauline (early second-century) dating. 'It is more likely that the Pastoral Epistles develop Pauline theology at the juncture of first and second generation Christianity.'[1544] Many other scholars would support such a view, arguing that the difference of style and approach found in the PE is not necessarily the result of subsequent development in a later generation, but quite possibly in the apostle's thought itself. As E. K. Simpson has said 'great souls are not their own mimes,'[1545] and even lesser mortals such as 'ordinary' pastors are aware of 'development' in their preaching style and content from

---

[1538] i.e. around 100 CE or 'in the first decades of the second century': G. Bornkamm, *Paul* (London: Hodder & Stoughton, 1971) 242. Hence Miller's conclusion: 'on literary, stylistic, historical, and linguistic grounds, the acceptance of the Pauline authorship of the Pastorals seems untenable': J. Miller, *The Pastoral Letters as Composite Documents* (Cambridge: Cambridge University Press, 1997), 10.

[1539] Fitzmyer, 'The Structured Ministry of the Church in the Pastoral Epistles', 582. For the attribution of the PE to a 'pseudo-Paul', see M. Dibelius and H. Conzelman, *The Pastoral Epistles* (Philadelphia: Fortress, 1972), 5-8. Pseudonymity to modern ears might imply deception, but it was a more acceptable form of literary device in the ancient world. More conservative scholars who hold to Pauline authorship sometimes attribute the differences from the earlier Paul in style and content to the work of an amanuensis or secretary.

[1540] Miller, *The Pastoral Letters as Composite Documents*, 157.

[1541] Ibid., 138, italics mine.

[1542] Miller admits that his attempts to identify the community apparently lying behind the PE entailed 'rely[ing] heavily upon historical imagination and plausible conjecture' and concludes that 'the origins of the Pastorals remain shrouded in mystery': Miller, *The Pastoral Letters as Composite Documents*, 156, 158.

[1543] See Philip H. Towner 'Pauline Theology or Pauline Tradition in the Pastoral Epistles: The Question of Method', *Tyndale Bulletin*, 46:2 (1995), 287. Towner challenges F. C. Baur who 'endowed New Testament scholarship with a rigid dialectical paradigm, whereby early, genuine Paul could be identified primarily by the Jew/Gentile debate, and later writings by its resolution (or absence) and by "early catholic" tendencies' thus setting 'the Pastoral Epistles into the second century, as if in concrete.' He challenges those who follow this late dating and asks: 'why would a third generation writer produce the Pastorals?': ibid., 311.

[1544] Ibid., 287.

[1545] E. K. Simpson, *The Pastoral Epistles* (London: Tyndale Press, 1954), 15, as cited by J. R.W. Stott in *Guard the Gospel: The Message of 2 Timothy* (Leicester: IVP, 1973), 15.

their earlier sermonic productions. In Paul's case, the reflections of his latter years and concern for the church's ongoing ministry in view of his own impending death, especially as Christianity faced increasing threats from false teaching,[1546] might well have necessitated new formulations of the faith and order, not only grounded in the church's own traditional expressions of worship and belief, but arguably also led by the Spirit (note 1 Tim 4:1: '*the Spirit* expressly says that in later times).

Working, then, upon the assumption of Pauline authorship, how can we use letters from an apostle, ostensibly written to two individuals, Timothy and Titus, in such personal terms, to illustrate our investigation into the Spirit's guidance of the *community* as custodian and interpreter of Scripture? I shall look at the communal dimensions suggested: firstly, by the epistolary form and secondly by the theological make up of the Epistles. I shall then investigate the pneumatology that undergirds them, and finally seek to extract some guidance for interpreters. Considerations of space prohibit the kind of detailed textual investigation undertaken earlier in the chapter.

## The Epistolary Form

Quinn and Wacker, assuming a second-century dating, identify the PE as fitting into a contemporary classical literary genre that afforded collections of letters, written by or in the name of a notable person, a wider representative significance than that suggested by the individual names of its recipients:

> [R]ecent studies have specified the *parenetic*—in other words, hortatory—character of the PE as the ancient world understood parenesis…, namely, as traditional ethical exhortation, universally applicable to individual persons, addressed to an audience that is paradigmatic and typical rather than genuinely individual and historical, and often an admonition that does not envision or admit contradiction.[1547]

If, however, the Pastorals are what they purport to be, it seems clear that they, like the rest of the Pauline corpus, were—despite being addressed to named individuals—intended to be read aloud in public[1548] and applied in a genuinely

---

[1546] See Oskar Skarsaune, 'Heresy and the Pastoral Epistles' in *Themelios*, Vol. 20, No.1 (1994), 9–13, where he deduces from verses that mention the heretics (1 Tim 1:4; 1:7; 4:3; 4:7; 4:8; 6:20; 2 Tim 2:18; Titus 1:10; 1:14; 3:9) that their doctrines involved speculative interpretations of the law, a negative attitude to the created order and a spiritualised conception of resurrection: 'most commentators conclude that the adversaries were Judaizing Christians with a Gnostic leaning, or gnosticizing Christians with a Judaizing tendency', ibid., 9.
[1547] Quinn & Wacker, *The First and Second Letters to Timothy*, 9, italics mine. Also Bassler: 'the letters are … essentially hortatory documents, not polemical ones … the author's major goal was to exhort the community, various groups within it, and the leaders of it to embrace or continue in certain modes of behaviour and to avoid other modes': J. M. Bassler, *1 Timothy, 2 Timothy, Titus* (Nashville: Abingdon, 1996), 22.
[1548] Cf. Col 4:16 and 1 Thess 5:27.

historical[1549] but also corporate context. Note, for instance, 'if you put these things before the brothers' (1 Tim 4:6) and also the plural form of benediction that concludes each letter: 'ἡ χάρις μεθ' ὑμῶν' ('grace be with you').[1550] In Guthrie's words, 'much of the material appears to be designed for the communities to which Timothy and Titus were ministering.'[1551] He accordingly describes the epistles as 'quasi-public',[1552] otherwise designated by Fee as 'third-party documents'[1553] whose reading by the community would help them appreciate the nature of the pastoral function and the gospel mandate.[1554]

We now read the letters two thousand years later as a part of the innumerable host who constitute the successors to the initial 'third-party' hearers, the ongoing Christian community that needs to be perpetually reminded of the responsibilities and privileges that issue from belonging to 'the household of God, which is the church of the living God, a pillar and buttress of truth' (1 Tim 3:15).

## Use of Theological Concepts, Sources and Traditions

This latter verse is sometimes used as an example of an evolution of thought away from the more dynamic Pauline concept of the church as the 'body of Christ' to one that implies a more 'fixed' understanding of the church. It could be argued, however, that Paul's use of household imagery[1555] in the PE shows a sensitivity to the behavioural expectations that accompanied 'the social institution of the οἶκος'[1556] in the ancient world, as well as a readiness to use terms that would be more readily understandable to 'a predominantly Gentile readership.'[1557] They would also better understand the distinctive vocabulary of ethical instruction with the use of words such as εὐσέβεια ('piety/godliness'),[1558] σωφρονισμός ('self-control'),[1559] and συνείδησις ('conscience').[1560] Towner argues that many such terms were probably derived from the Hellenistic ethicists[1561] of the day, but adapted to fit in with the Hebrew concept of the 'fear of the Lord'.

---

[1549] Hence Timothy is told to 'remain at Ephesus' (1 Tim 3:3) and Titus has been 'left in Crete' (Titus 1:5).
[1550] 1 Tim 6:21 and 2 Tim 4:22. ἡ χάρις μετὰ πάντων ὑμῶν in Titus 3:15c.
[1551] D. Guthrie, *The Pastoral Epistles* (Leicester: IVP, 1957), 11.
[1552] Ibid.,11.
[1553] Fee, *God's Empowering Presence*, 794.
[1554] We can apply this to the relevance of church constitutions, articles of faith and mission statements which help the whole congregation to understand its ethos and support one another in their respective roles.
[1555] See 1 Tim 3:5, 12; 2 Tim 2:20; Titus 1:7.
[1556] Marshall refers to the 'household codes' in Titus 2–3; Col 3:18–4:1 and Eph 5:21–6:9; and the 'station code' in 1 Pet 2:13–3:7. Marshall, 'Household Codes and Station Codes', 231–236.
[1557] Towner, 'Pauline Theology or Pauline Tradition in the Pastoral Epistles: The Question of Method', 309, arguing that household imagery would be more relevant to them than temple imagery (e.g. as in 2 Cor 6:16). Early Christians, of course, often met in homes.
[1558] 1 Tim 2:2; 3:16; 4:7; 4:8; 6:3, 5, 6, 11; 2 Tim 3:5; Titus 3:5. Marshall describes this as 'a fresh term with a history in Judaism and in the Hellenistic world': Marshall, 'Household Codes and Station Codes', 104.
[1559] 2 Tim 1:7.
[1560] 1 Tim 1:5; 1:19; 3:9; 4:2; 2 Tim 1:3; Titus 1:15.
[1561] Towner says that 'Titus 2:12, in describing the new Christian life, makes use of three of the Greek cardinal virtues: "self-controlled, upright and godly"': H. Towner, *1 Timothy & Titus* (Leicester: IVP, 1994), 28.

The description of Christ's first and second advents in terms of ἐπιφάνεια ('appearing')[1562] also exemplifies 'old wine ... being preserved in new skin.'[1563] These are but some of the examples of the flexible use of concepts that make up the Pastorals, along with their highly variegated use of sources.

It is not feasible to enter detailed discussion of these sources here, but it can be noted how the PE contain snatches of personal testimony alongside a sizeable use of traditional material, with the one often used to complement the other. Thus, there is no disparity between individual and collective truth. So Paul's personal confession that he was 'chief of sinners' (1 Tim 1:15) comes in the midst of one of the five distinctive 'faithful sayings' (πιστὸς ὁ λόγος),[1564] a Hellenistic 'turn of phrase'[1565] used to confirm the truth of a commonly accepted statement, and employed in the Pastorals with reference to its soteriological claims.[1566] According to Hendriksen, 'the saying is the testimony of Christian experience, and is now also the utterance of the Holy Spirit.'[1567] Paul's personal experience of God's mercy (1 Tim 1:16) similarly leads into a doxology ('to the King of ages')[1568] whose phraseology reflects Jewish tradition. Liturgical material also appears in the form of credal statements (2 Tim 2:11–13), prayers (2 Tim 1:15–18; 4:22) and hymnic confessions (1 Tim 3:1; 2 Tim 1:9–10), the latter also being combined with a 'midrash' on the Old Testament in Titus 3:3–7.

Other Old Testament material appears in the form of Old Testament allusions that evoke larger 'echoes' (such as Titus 2:14 which 'invites the readers to understand the death of Christ as the outworking of God's faithfulness to his covenant promises')[1569] and two specific Old Testament quotations at 1 Tim 5:18–19 and 2 Tim 2:19.[1570] The former text, relating to the support of elders, quotes Deut 25:4 ('do not muzzle an ox') followed by a saying of Jesus ('the labourer deserves his wages,' Luke 10:7, alluding to Num 18:31), a combination of texts also seen in more expanded form in 1 Cor 9:9–14. This constitutes an interesting use of the Jesus tradition in which 'the apostle brings together the relevant, authoritative OT text and the Lord's authoritative expansion, and reinforces them with his own apostolic authority.'[1571] The Corinthian reference also points to the fact that the author of the Pastorals, in Bassler's words, 'was

---

[1562] 1 Tim 6:14; 2 Tim 1:10; 4:1, 8; Titus 2:13.
[1563] I. Howard Marshall, 'Recent Study of the Pastorals', *Themelios* Vol. 23:1 (1997), 20.
[1564] 1 Tim 1:15; 3:1; 4:9; 2 Tim 2:11; Titus 3:8. See Marshall, 'Household Codes and Station Codes', 326–330 on 'The trustworthy sayings.'
[1565] Following Marshall, 'Household Codes and Station Codes', 327. Ellis, however, says that 'the formula ... apparently had its origin among Jewish apocalyptic prophets or at Qumran': E. E. Ellis, 'Pastoral Letters' in *Dictionary of Paul and His Letters*, 664.
[1566] Except for 1 Tim 3:1, where it is used of the one desiring the office of overseer/bishop.
[1567] W. Hendriksen, *1 & 2 Timothy and Titus* (Edinburgh: Banner of Truth, 1957), 76.
[1568] 1 Tim 1:17.
[1569] See H. Towner, 'The Pastoral Epistles' in the *New Dictionary of Biblical Theology* (Leicester: IVP 2000), 335, which lists the other Old Testament allusions.
[1570] Quoting from Num 16:5 and 16:26, with a possible reference also to the LXX of Isa 52:11, which uses the same word for 'depart' (*aphistemi*).
[1571] Towner, 'The Pastoral Epistles,' 335.

# Spirit, Community and Hermeneutics in Paul    231

familiar with a number of Pauline letters; certainly, Romans and 1 Corinthians and Philippians,'[1572] a fact which would not be surprising if he actually wrote them!

Besides scriptural citation, Paul employs predictive prophecy (1 Tim 4:1-4), an uncomplimentary quote concerning Cretans from a pagan poet[1573] (Titus 1:12) and an apocryphal composition about Jannes and Jambres in 2 Tim 3:8. He also makes use of what Quinn and Wacker refer to as 'sources ... that were in more plastic forms, relatively open to redactional activity,'[1574] such as the lists relating to order in worship (1 Tim 2), ministerial qualities (1 Tim 3:1-12), household/domestic codes (1 Tim 1-2; 6:1-2; Titus 2:2-10), and vice lists (1 Tim 1:9-10; 2 Tim 3:2-5) which 'appear to use more archaic catechetical materials.'[1575]

Reviewing such a large miscellany of sources, E. E. Ellis concludes that '*preformed* materials make up about forty-three percent of 1 Timothy, sixteen percent of 2 Timothy and forty-six percent of Titus.'[1576] Such precision may be questionable,[1577] but the quantity and variety of traditional material used in the Pastorals undoubtedly reveal a complex, multi-sourced community hermeneutic in operation. Here can be found samples from Old Testament, Jewish and Jesus traditions together with material from the life and worship of the early church and its cultural setting, all blended together in what Marshall has described as an example of the way in which 'the early church ... developed its theology in various ways.'[1578] Dibelius and Conzelmann's statement, then, that 'the traditional material is not interpreted ... [and] remains fixed'[1579] seems the very opposite of the case. It would, consequently, seem that the gospel 'deposit' spoken of in 2 Tim 1:14, although doubtless containing a non-negotiable 'core', consisted of a veritable treasury of truths that could be expressed and applied in a multiplicity of ways that were arguably inspired by 'the Holy Spirit who dwells within us.'[1580]

---

[1572] J. Bassler, *1 Timothy, 2 Timothy, Titus*, 23. 'He was also probably familiar with Acts', citing the 'things that happened to me in Antioch, Iconium and Lystra' (2 Tim 3:11, cf. Acts 13-14) and points out similarities with a second century apocryphal document *The Acts of Paul* to argue that the 'same oral legends' were being relied upon, 24.
[1573] Epimenides (c. 600 BCE), per Fee, *God's Empowering Presence*, 777.
[1574] Quinn & Wacker, *The First and Second Letters to Timothy*, 10.
[1575] Ibid., 10.
[1576] E. E. Ellis, 'The Pastoral Letters' in *Dictionary of Paul and His Letters*, 665. Italics mine.
[1577] Marshall says that 'the tests which [Ellis] proposes for the presence of tradition are not altogether convincing' and that 'the style of the epistles is remarkably uniform, even in the passages which are allegedly based on tradition,' 'Recent Study of the Pastoral Epistles' *Themelios* (1997), 13. In discussing A. T. Hanson's analysis of preformed sources, Marshall also claims 'we should attribute more to the creative powers of the author than to the use of pre-formed material': Marshall, 'Household Codes and Station Codes', 16.
[1578] I. Howard Marshall, *Beyond the Bible: Moving from Scripture to Theology* (Milton Keynes: Paternoster; Grand Rapids: Baker, 2004), 52. He concludes: 'Whether the author was Paul or a disciple is immaterial to the issue. Whoever wrote the letters did not feel tied to the manner of expression of the earlier Paul,' 53.
[1579] Dibelius & Conzelmann, *The Pastoral Epistles*, 9.
[1580] 2 Tim 1:14.

## The Pneumatological Undergirding

The aforementioned reference to the Spirit comes from 2 Tim 1:14, which contains one of the five likely references[1581] to the Holy Spirit in the Pastorals. The relative paucity of such references has been used as one of the arguments against Pauline authorship. Such arguments from silence, however, are not convincing.[1582] Schweizer has further argued that 'πνεῦμα occurs in the Pastorals ... in a way which is quite un-Pauline'[1583] and Dunn has claimed that in the (late-dated)[1584] epistles, 'Spirit and charisma have become in effect subordinate to office, to ritual, to tradition.'[1585]

Such an 'imprisoned' view of the Spirit, however, has been countered by Michael Haykin who argues for a 'vibrant pneumatology'[1586] as shown by: the high regard given to the Spirit of prophecy;[1587] the fact that the Spirit of ministry, although stated as equipping Timothy for his work,[1588] is nevertheless 'poured out richly on *us*', i.e. the whole church, in Tit 3:5; this passage[1589] also speaking of the more general and dynamic work of the Spirit in 'regeneration and renewal', rather than being confined to 'the rites and institutions of the church.'[1590]

'Fan [fully] into flame'[1591] certainly portrays an active Spirit given not just to Timothy but also *to us* (ἔδωκεν ἡμῖν 2 Tim 1:7a), i.e. all believers, whose possession of 'a spirit not of *fear* but of power' provides a direct link with Rom 8:15.[1592] The corporate nature of the Spirit's working is also demonstrated by reference to 'the presbyteral college'[1593] who laid hands upon Timothy (1 Tim 4:14) 'in the context of the believing community.'[1594] Without detailing further debate on the pneumatology of the Pastorals, it seems not unreasonable to conclude with Towner that they 'emit an understanding of the Holy Spirit that

---

[1581] 1 Tim 3:16; 4:1; 2 Tim 1:7, 14; Titus 3:5. 1 Tim 3:16 and 2 Tim 1:7 are debated. See H. Towner, *The Structure of Theology and Ethics in the Pastoral Epistles* (Sheffield: Sheffield Academic Press, 1989), 56–59.
[1582] Fee, *God's Empowering Presence*, 756, pointing out that Philippians has a similar proportion of references to the Spirit, and Philemon none.
[1583] E. Schweizer, 'πνεῦμα' in G. Kittel and G. Friedrich, eds., *Theological Dictionary of the New Testament* (Grand Rapids: Eerdmans, 1967), 445. 'Un-pauline' is not defined.
[1584] Dunn attributes them to 'the early Catholicism of second and third generation Christianity': Dunn, *Jesus and the Spirit*, 347.
[1585] Ibid., 349. In italics in the original.
[1586] M. A. G. Haykin, 'The Fading Vision? The Spirit and Freedom in the Pastoral Epistles' in *Evangelical Quarterly*, Vol. LVII No. 4 (1985), 294.
[1587] 1 Tim 1:18; 4:14.
[1588] 2 Tim 1:6–8, 13–14.
[1589] Along with 1 Tim 4:14 and 2 Tim 1:6.
[1590] Ibid., 304. Haykin concludes that 'the Pastoral Epistles reiterate the frequent concern of Paul to strike a balance between barren orthodoxy and unbridled enthusiasm', 305.
[1591] 2 Tim 1:6; cf. 1 Thess 5:19 for the same imagery: Marshall, 'Household Codes and Station Codes', 696.
[1592] This link reinforces the view that 'the gift of God' in 2 Tim 1:6 relates to the gift of the Holy Spirit.
[1593] Fitzmyer, 'The Structured Ministry of the Church in the Pastoral Epistles', 594, saying that the expression in 1 Tim 4:14 'denotes the collectivity of πρεσβυτεροι.'
[1594] Fee, *God's Empowering Presence*, 775.

is fairly consistent with (if not as complete as) that found in the undisputed Paul.'[1595]

For our purposes, the most significant pneumatological passage is 2 Tim 1:13–14, which relates to the role of the Spirit in guiding the community in its 'custodianship' (as opposed to the 'interpretation') of Scripture. Admittedly, it is the gospel as taught by Paul rather than Scripture as such which is in view here, but its subsequent inscripturation surely gives us some justification for relating Paul's twofold description of the gospel to our investigation.

First, then, v. 13a: 'follow the *pattern* of the sound words.' With ὑποτύπωσιν ('pattern')[1596] starting the sentence, the emphasis lies on the standard or example of 'healthy' (ὑγιαινόντων 'sound', ESB) teaching to which Timothy must hold fast (ἔχε). Quinn and Wacker render v. 13a 'stick to the model of the wholesome words,'[1597] as first heard in the public teaching of the Apostle in the assembly of believers, and now being committed to writing.[1598] An alternative (though now generally less favoured) translation of ὑποτύπωσις as an 'outline sketch' as used by an artist (i.e. which subsequently needs filling out) is advocated by Kelly,[1599] suggesting that while Timothy is to be loyal to the message 'he should be free to interpret or expound it in his own way.'[1600] Such 'freedom', however, if that is what is implied, would be qualified by the concluding 'in the faith and love that are in Christ Jesus' (v. 13b), a 'formulaic phrase'[1601] which implies that right interpretation can only issue out of a right relationship with Christ and others. The way orthodoxy is to be kept is just as important as the orthodoxy itself. Hermeneutics and ethics, again, need to cohere.

Following 'pattern' in 2 Tim 2:13, the second description of the gospel, in v. 14, is that of the 'good/beautiful deposit'[1602] (καλὴν παραθήκην).[1603] The powerful legal metaphor is 'drawn from one of the truly sacred trusts of the ancient world'[1604] implying the need for absolute 'trustworthiness and faithfulness on

---

[1595] H. Towner, *The Structure of Theology and Ethics in the Pastoral Epistles*, 58. For a similar viewpoint see Marshall, 'Household Codes and Station Codes', 105 & 519 and Fee, *God's Empowering Presence*, 756–757. Fee's conclusion: 'What emerges in these final Pauline letters ... is exactly what emerges elsewhere in Paul: The Spirit plays the crucial role in Christian conversion and ongoing Christian life; the Spirit is the key to Christian ministry; the Spirit is perceived in terms of power; and the Spirit is present in the church partly through gifts experienced by individuals within a community context,' 757.

[1596] ὑποτύπωσις is also used in 1 Tim 1:16 of Paul's conversion as a pattern/example of what Christ can do for sinners.

[1597] Towner, *The First and Second Letters to Timothy*, 606.

[1598] Ibid.,607, linking it with the 'many witnesses' of 2 Tim 2:2.

[1599] Also Guthrie, *The Pastoral Epistles*, 132, citing N. White (*The Pastoral Epistles*: Expositor's Greek Testament, 1910) regarding 'outline sketch': 'it happily suggests the power of expansion latent in the simplest and most primitive dogmatic formulas of the Christian faith.'

[1600] J. N. D. Kelly, *Pastoral Epistles* (London: Black, 1963), 166. Also Guthrie, *The Pastoral Epistles*, 132.

[1601] R. F. Collins, *1 & 11 Timothy and Titus* (London; Louisville: Westminster John Knox Press, 2002), 213, referring to the same expression in 1 Tim 1:14: 'a succinct description of the Christian way of life.'

[1602] Παραθήκη is also used in 1 Tim 6:20 and 2 Tim 1:12.

[1603] 'In the context of the PE ... καλός has the distinct sense of what is good because it is approved by God,' Marshall, 'Household Codes and Station Codes', 714.

[1604] Fee, *God's Empowering Presence*, 791.

the part of the recipient.'¹⁶⁰⁵ This, then, involves not just preserving it, as per v. 13, but actively protecting it in light of the risk of it being lost or damaged by the dangerous effects of false teachers whose 'talk will spread like gangrene' (2 Tim 2:17). Calvin warns how 'it is exceedingly harmful to corrupt doctrine even in the smallest degree.'¹⁶⁰⁶ More recently, Clark notes how 'there is a tendency in the Christian community to be attracted away from genuine operations of the Holy Spirit towards revelations and demonstrations of false spirits and charlatans.'¹⁶⁰⁷ Hence the perpetual importance of the Pastorals' imperative φύλαξον—keep guard!—whether it be against gossips and heretics (1 Tim 6:20–21), or defectors (2 Tim 1:15). As Schutz has commented, 'the future of the church depends on the disciples of the apostles guarding, working out, making real the inheritance from the apostles.'¹⁶⁰⁸ To use Paul's language, 'what you have heard from me in the presence of *many witnesses* entrust (παράθου) to faithful men who will be able to teach others also' (2 Tim 2:2). The apostolic deposit that was first given in a public, corporate setting must be passed on in the ever-greater corporate setting of successive generations.¹⁶⁰⁹ And as Stott says, 'it is to be a succession of apostolic tradition rather than of apostolic ministry, authority or order.'¹⁶¹⁰

This heavy responsibility can only be discharged 'by the Holy Spirit who dwells in us' (διὰ πνεύματος ἁγίου τοῦ ἐνοικοῦντος [lit. 'makes his home'] ἐν ἡμῖν (v. 14b). According to Marshall,¹⁶¹¹ 'διὰ πνεύματος is a Pauline phrase…¹⁶¹² as is the use of ἐνοικέω … for the presence of the Spirit in God's people'¹⁶¹³ (cf. Rom 8:9). Such a common expression therefore would have evoked other connotations of pneumatological support. The use of παραθήκη ('deposit') would have evoked further connotations, this time of Christological support (cf. παραθήκην in v. 12), in the guarding of the deposit first entrusted to Paul. As Quinn and Wacker put it, 'the same Spirit dwells in both the apostle and his co-worker, empowering each for his role in visibly transmitting (hence [καλὴν]) what Christ invisibly is sustaining and protecting.'¹⁶¹⁴ Not that such an endowment was theirs alone, for as Marshall says, 'in us' (ἐν ἡμῖν) should be thought of here in the 'universal'¹⁶¹⁵

---

¹⁶⁰⁵ Marshall, 'Household Codes and Station Codes', 675.
¹⁶⁰⁶ As quoted by Nick Needham in 'Tradition in 2 Timothy' in *Evangel* 17:1 (1999), 7.
¹⁶⁰⁷ M. Clark, 'The Pastoral Epistles,' in Burke and Warrington, *A Biblical Theology of the Holy Spirit*, 225.
¹⁶⁰⁸ H. G. Schütz, 'Guard, Keep, Watch'/ φυλάσσω in C. Brown, ed., *New International Dictionary of New Testament Theology*, Vol. 2 (Exeter: Paternoster, 1976), 135.
¹⁶⁰⁹ Stott points that 2 Tim 2:2, relating to the open sharing of the whole of apostolic doctrine (whose authenticity could be tested in the public arena ['many witnesses']), became especially relevant in the subsequent second-century spread of Gnosticism with its emphasis upon private revelations and secret traditions. Stott, *Guard the Gospel*, 50–51.
¹⁶¹⁰ Ibid., 52.
¹⁶¹¹ Marshall, 'Household Codes and Station Codes', 715.
¹⁶¹² Citing Rom 5:5; 8:11; 2 Cor 6:16.
¹⁶¹³ Citing Rom 8:11; 2 Cor 6:16; Col 3:16.
¹⁶¹⁴ Quinn & Wacker, *The First and Second Letters to Timothy*, 608.
¹⁶¹⁵ Marshall, 'Household Codes and Station Codes', 715.

sense, and not limited to Paul and Timothy. Christians, both individually and especially collectively, have a Spirit-enabled duty to be ever 'on doctrinal watch'.

The idea, then, that 'guarding a deposit' in 2 Timothy implies something essentially 'static', as some have claimed, seems unsupportable. As Fee says, 'guarding ... does not mean to "sit on it", but to stay loyal to it, even to the extent of taking [one's] share in the suffering'[1616] (2 Tim 1:8), as many martyrs and saints have done through the ages, and still do. Nor, however, does it mean keeping it in some sort of theological straightjacket. As we have shown from the PE themselves, the theological development they evidence from the earlier Paul shows that their teaching 'goes beyond the "deposit" and expresses the faith in new ways.'[1617] Not that this means an end to written creeds and confessions, for they, along with the regular oral preaching of the church from generation to generation, are an essential means of handing on and indeed 'contend[ing] for the faith once delivered unto the saints' (Jude 3). But as this brief survey of the Pastorals has shown, the lively operations of the Holy Spirit will often involve a rewording and reworking, though not a revision or reinvention, of scriptural truth, to make it relevant and applicable to the situation of the hearers/readers.

As a postscript to this section, it can be noted that, as in some of my other New Testament investigations, it is possible to identify four characteristics of the Spirit's κοινωνία workings: Tit 3:4–6 encompasses a *Trinitarian* formulation grounded in God's 'mercy', the Spirit's 'washing'[1618] and Christ's 'grace'; in 2 Tim 1:6–7 the appeal to Timothy to 'fan into flame the gift of God' is set in the context of a *historical* recollection ('God has not given us a Spirit of fear') and of a thanksgiving that is 'full of "memory" words'[1619] (cf. vv. 3–5); whilst in 1 Tim 4:1 ('the Spirit says that later times') we have an *eschatological*/apocalyptic motif that also constitutes a *dialogical* confrontation with the 'deceitful spirits and teachings of demons (διδασκαλίαις[1620] δαιμονίων).' Warnings against heresy are indeed frequent in the Pastorals and, as we have mentioned, provide an incentive for revised formulations of the faith.

## Guidance for Interpreters

I have already sought to investigate something of the hermeneutical process that lay behind the composition of the Pastorals. Their content is admittedly more concerned with the urgency of 'preaching the word' (1 Tim 4:2) than 'interpreting Scripture'. Nevertheless, some implications for the responsibility,

---

[1616] Fee, *God's Empowering Presence*, 791. See also Luke Timothy Johnson, *The First and Second Letters to Timothy* (New York: Doubleday, 2001), 356–7, for arguments for a 'dynamic' rather than 'static' concept of 'guarding the deposit.'
[1617] I. Howard Marshall, *Beyond the Bible*, 53.
[1618] Fee sees an allusion to Ezek 36:25–27 (LXX). Fee, *God's Empowering Presence*, 782.
[1619] Ibid., 785.
[1620] Note the frequency of διδάσκω and related words in the Pastorals, especially considering the New Testament's common association of the Spirit's work with teaching.

task, and purpose of such interpretation can be deduced from what they have to say regarding the teaching and preservation of the gospel tradition and the nature and role of the 'sacred writings' (2 Tim 3:15).

*(i) The Responsibility for Interpretation*

The principal addressees of the Pastorals are church leaders, especially overseers/elders, who are needed to counter the 'vain babblings'[1621] of heretics with 'sound doctrine.'[1622] From this, many scholars have assumed that the PE advocate a so-called teaching '"office"' in a way that reduced the congregation to "mere hearers and doers" of the word.'[1623] In response to this, I would rather go along with Marshall's reading that both the 'concept [of] office'[1624] and 'the antithesis between the congregations and their (local) leaders'[1625] is missing from the Pastorals. A teaching, and therefore interpretive, role that extends beyond church leaders, is, *inter alia*, implied by 'if anyone teaches' of 1 Tim 6:3, the family context of 2 Tim 1:5 and the 'faithful men'[1626] teachers of 2 Tim 2:2. And I have already noted the PE's instruction concerning the Spirit's activation of and within the congregation, including the task of guarding the gospel 'deposit' (2 Tim 2:14), which applies both individually and collectively. Nevertheless, the Pastorals certainly do stress the importance of a special teaching role that is vested in church leaders who are 'apt to teach'[1627] and whose credentials stem not just from the laying on of hands[1628] but more especially from their character traits[1629] and Spirit-engifting.[1630] As Clark says, '[the] emphasis upon the charismatic endowment of a local Christian leader robustly subverts any notion of an indispensable *ex officio* basis for the exercise of power or authority.'[1631]

*(ii) The Task of Interpretation*

This emphasis upon the character of teachers is complemented by a passage that speaks of the nature of their task: 2 Tim 2:15. 'Do your best to present yourself to God as one approved, a worker who has no need to be ashamed' (v.15a). This

---

[1621] 1 Tim 6:20 and 2 Tim 2:16 (AV).
[1622] Titus 2:2.
[1623] Marshall, 'Household Codes and Station Codes', 516.
[1624] Ibid., 520.
[1625] Ibid., 517. See also 521.
[1626] Whether and how the Pastorals might prohibit a teaching role for women is, of course, a highly debated issue. Suffice it to say that the teaching role of women to children (2 Tim 1:5) and of older women to younger women (Titus 2:3–4) 'may suggest that the ban in 1 Tim 2 is not as total as is generally maintained and was particularly linked to heresy and to something about the form of teaching which infringed unacceptably upon the social position of men': Marshall, 'Household Codes and Station Codes', 521.
[1627] 1 Tim 3:3. See also 1 Tim 1:17.
[1628] 1 Tim 4:14.
[1629] Note especially 1 Tim 3 and Titus 3.
[1630] 1 Tim 4:14–15; 2 Tim 1:6–7
[1631] Mathew Clark, 'The Pastoral Epistles' in Burke and Warrington, *A Biblical Theology of the Holy Spirit*, 218. But note one of his balanced conclusions from the Pastorals: 'the powerfully charismatic element, so crucial to Christian leadership and ministry, is to be demonstrated in a context of both personal gentleness and of sound knowledge of Scripture and doctrine': ibid., 225.

suggests a double context for hermeneutics: ultimate heavenly accountability[1632] (cf. 'the Lord's servant' 2:24), along with present earthly endeavour as a 'workman' (ἐργάτης, also in 1 Tim 5:18: 'the *labourer* deserves his wages'). That this labour should be directed into 'rightly handling (ὀρθοτομοῦντα) the word of truth'[1633] (v. 15b) speaks, more literally, of a process not so much of 'cutting up',[1634] but rather 'cutting straight', the verb ὀρθοτομέω having a background in Hebrew wisdom literature in relation to the cutting of a path or road through obstacles in a straight direction.[1635] So there is to be no diversion into the 'thoroughly useless word-battles'[1636] (λογομαχεῖν) of 2:14, for the Timothy-type leader should be 'a *workman*, not a *quibbler*.'[1637] This suggests that interpretive complexity must at some point be resolved into proclamatory clarity. The messages of preachers should be for the renewal rather than 'for the ruin of the hearers' (2:14) (ἐπὶ καταστροφῇ τῶν ἀκουόντων—a warning against 'catastrophic' sermons!)

*(iii) The Purpose of Interpretation*

The 'perspiration' involved in such a task should be relieved by an appreciation of the 'inspiration' (or rather 'expiration') that lies behind the Scriptures, as per 2 Tim 3:15b–16:[1638] 'all Scripture is breathed out[1639] by God and profitable for' (v. 16a). This text has been much discussed in debates on 'inspiration' and 'inerrancy.'[1640] The original reference here, of course, is to the Jewish Scriptures, but it is generally agreed that 'the extension of applying the text to apply to the NT is fully justified.'[1641] Verse 16a points to Scripture's divine origin (θεόπνευστος, 'God breathed') and practical outcome (καὶ ὠφέλιμος πρὸς ... 'and

---

[1632] Also 2 Tim 4:1.

[1633] Quinn and Wacker comment that 'the PE contains nearly half as many uses of [ἀλήθεια] as the rest of the Paulines (fourteen to thirty-three), wherein the meaning entails "the *opening up* of the divine world and its claim" ... and not simply knowledge in the generic sense': Qinn & Wacker, *The First and Second Letters to Timothy*, 658, italics mine.

[1634] As per the AV's 'rightly dividing', i.e. 'not as a sacrificial victim to be cut into pieces': Stott, *Guard the Gospel*, 67.

[1635] Marshall, 'Household Codes and Station Codes', 748, referring to Prov 3:6 and 11:5.

[1636] Hendriksen's rendering of 2:24 in *1 & 2 Timothy*, 261.

[1637] Hendriksen, ibid., 262, noting the context of the verse.

[1638] As to the 'multitude of exegetical issues' in v. 16, see W. D. Mounce, *Pastoral Epistles* (Nashville, TN: Thomas Nelson, 2000), 565–571.

[1639] The ESB translation reflects Warfield's concern that θεόπνευστος does not mean '"breathed *into* by God" ... but breathed *out* by God ... the product of the creative breath of God.... What is declared by this... passage is simply that the Scriptures are a Divine product, without any indication of how God has operated in producing them': B. B. Warfield, *The Inspiration and Authority of the Bible* (Philadelphia: Presbyterian and Reformed Publishing Company, 1948), 133, italics mine.

[1640] Along with 2 Pet 2:21. Barr has criticized 'the fundamentalist use', of these two texts in their argument for the verbal inspiration of Scripture, preferring 'a modern view of inspiration which [sees it] as part of the total movement of tradition out of which the Bible came .... In this sense it is not the beginning of the church's thinking about the Bible, rather it is its ending; it is not the source from which authority is derived': James Barr, in *Fundamentalism* (London: SCM, 1981), 79, 298, 299. For a reply to Barr, seeR. Wells, *James Barr and the Bible: Critique of a New Liberalism* (Phillipsburg, New Jersey: Presbyterian and Reformed Publishing Company), 1980.

[1641] I. Howard Marshall, '2 Timothy' in K. J. Vanhoozer et al, eds., *Dictionary for Theological Interpretation of the Bible* (SPCK; Baker Academic: Grand Rapids, 2005), 806, adding that 'there is at least the possibility that some early Christian writings were being regarded as Scripture by this date.'

profitable for'). These two ends of the Scriptural spectrum therefore do not explicitly mention the mechanics of the interpretive *process* that link the one to the other, but they do nevertheless speak about interpretive *purpose*. For as Dibelius and Conzelmann have rightly pointed out, 'the emphasis ... lies, not on the concept of inspiration, but on the *usefulness* of the inspired scriptures'[1642] which arises in consequence of their status as 'enspirited by God'[1643] (θεόπνευστος, the second part of this compound noun affording a link with the Holy Spirit). The two main uses of Scripture are contained in the words that frame v. 16a, and in both cases a communal reference can be traced.

The first use comes in v. 15b: the 'sacred writings ... are able to make you wise for *salvation*.' The priority of σωτηρία is a regular concern of the Pastorals[1644] and the means through which it is to be effected are the 'sacred letters' (ἱερὰ[1645] γράμματα) of the Old Testament scriptures, with the implied aid of a Christian interpretation ('through faith in Christ Jesus' v. 15d). Biblical hermeneutics, therefore, should have a soteriological orientation. Scripture's description as kind of 'handbook of salvation', moreover, makes an ongoing link with the community of Christians down the ages who have similarly so regarded and experienced it. For Kern Trembath, discussing 'Biblical Inspiration and the Believing Community':[1646]

> The material distinctiveness of biblical inspiration is seen in the church's claim that its salvation, its being located in a process of transcendence, is both initiated by God *and* congruent with the experience of salvation enjoyed by apostolic generations of Christians to which we have access in the Bible.[1647]

The second use, in vv. 16b–17 ('profitable for'), is for *sanctification*: 'of supreme value for all holy purposes,' as Warfield says.[1648] The fourfold teaching–education and conviction–correction chiastic sequence therein described,[1649] culminates in the 'high point'[1650] of 'training in righteousness' (πρὸς παιδείαν τὴν ἐν δικαιοσύνῃ). Παιδεία ('training') recalls the educational and religious

---

[1642] Dibelius and Conzelmann, *The Pastoral Epistles*, 120, my italics. Also R. Collins: 'the many citations of 2 Tim 3:16 in the patristic era ... emphasize the usefulness of the Scriptures far more than they do their inspiration' R. Collins, *1 & 11 Timothy* (Louisville: Westminster John Knox, 2002), 264.
[1643] Quinn & Wacker, *The First and Second Letters to Timothy*, 762.
[1644] σωτηρία in 2 Tim 2:10; 3:15; σῴζω in 1 Tim 2:4,15; σωτήρ in 1 Tim 1:1; 2:3; 4:10; 2 Tim 1:10; Titus 1:3,4; 2:10,13; 3:4,6.
[1645] The only time in the New Testament when it is used of Scripture, also rare in the LXX, but more commonly found in Hellenistic Judaism: Marshall, 'Household Codes and Station Codes', 789.
[1646] K. R. Trembath, 'Biblical Inspiration and the Believing Community' in *The Evangelical Quarterly*, Vol. LVIII, No. 3 (1986), 245-256.
[1647] Ibid., 254-255.
[1648] The fuller quote from Warfield: 'what the apostle asserts is that the Sacred Scriptures, in their every several passage—for it is just "passage of Scripture" which "Scripture" in this distributive use of it signifies—is the product of the creative breath of God, and because of this its Divine origination, is of supreme value for all holy purposes': B. B. Warfield, *The Inspiration and Authority of the Bible*, 134.
[1649] Marshall, 'Household Codes and Station Codes', 795.
[1650] Collins, *1 & 11 Timothy*, 264, reading it as the rhetorical technique of climax.

instruction that was traditionally given in the communal context of the family, not the state, in ancient Hebrew culture[1651] (cf. 3:15 'from childhood' and 2 Tim 1:5), the kind of commonality also stressed in the Pastorals' depiction of the church as a 'household.' Again, then, we have the family context for biblical interpretation that is found in Romans 8. And the result of such training through Scripture should be that 'the man of God may be competent, equipped for every good work' (v. 17). Good hermeneutics should result in good deeds. Proclamation without praxis is useless.[1652]

*Conclusion to the Pastoral Epistles*

The epistolary form of the Pastorals shows that they were intended not just for Timothy and Titus but for wider use within 'the household of God'. Their theological make-up reveals that the author used traditional, communal material from Jewish, Christian and contemporary sources that expressed the gospel 'deposit' in a variety of ways, arguably all inspired by the Spirit. A lively pneumatically-driven hermeneutic is thus seen at work not only in the composition of the Pastorals, but also in the role they assign to the help of the Spirit in the active preservation and empowered preaching of the gospel deposit—hence the title of this section: 'The Spirit and Tradition'. The pneumatological endowment is not restricted to Christian leaders but 'poured out' on the whole Christian community. They together share a Spirit-enabled duty to guard and hand on the apostolic tradition, with a godliness of lifestyle and appropriate manner of speech, although the emphasis of the Pastorals is upon the teaching and consequent interpretive role of church leaders. The God-breathed nature of Scripture provides an authoritative foundation for such a hermeneutic worked out within the Christian community for salvation and sanctification.

## Conclusion to the Chapter

In this chapter, I have attempted to investigate some of the riches of Paul's hermeneutical approach, exposing its pneumatic and corporate veins. To do this, it was necessary to look not only *at*, but also *beneath* the surface of the text, as Paul rarely gives explicit explanations of his interpretive methods. I therefore began by highlighting the prominence of Spirit reference and corporate terminology in Paul. It was suggested that the distinctive features of Paul's pneumatology derived from his Jewish background, with its emphasis upon 'the Spirit of prophecy' and Old Testament notions of corporateness, along with the pneumatic components of the Jesus encounter and tradition. I then looked at

---

[1651] See Quinn & Wacker, *The First and Second Letters to Timothy*, 765–766, and Collins, *1 & 11 Timothy*, 265, for the Jewish scriptural programme of training in righteousness.
[1652] Cf. James 4:26.

some of the factors that determined Paul's use of the Old Testament as a source of authority, including his use of allusion and the interpretive conventions of his Jewish heritage, as shaped by his Christian convictions, Spirit dependence, and ecclesial concerns.

I next sought to explore Paul's methods of interpretation, whether explicitly or implicitly demonstrated, in four New Testament passages where the rich pneumatological seam that runs through his epistles surfaces, noting the communal and corporate dimensions of his hermeneutics. Full summaries of my findings for each passage will be found at the end of each relevant section.

Suffice it to say here that in 1 Cor 2, I highlighted the role of the Spirit of *understanding* by whom 'God has revealed [these things] *to us*' (v. 10), the Christian community, as opposed to the incomprehensibility of the non-Christian community. In 2 Cor 3, I noted the contrast between hardened Old Testament Israel and the repenting, liberated New Testament community as it enjoyed the Spirit of *glory* by whom '*we all*, with unveiled face, behold the glory of the Lord' (v. 18), a contemplation resulting in transformation. In Rom 8, the Spirit of *sonship* by whom we can utter the 'Abba, Father' family cry, evoked a family context for hermeneutics, again with Old Testament parallels concerning obedience and pilgrimage. The use of communal material and flexible terminology in the Pastoral Epistles reveal a lively pneumatically-driven hermeneutic that illustrates how the *tradition* of the 'good deposit'[1653] is to be guarded and expressed by the 'household of God,'[1654] a common Christian duty for which church leaders nevertheless have special responsibilities.

In my exegesis of these four passages, I noted the Trinitarian, dialogical, historical, eschatological, and other characteristics that illustrate the communal dimensions of Paul's multi-faceted, pneumatically-driven hermeneutic at work. From this, I tried to spell out several implications for the ongoing interpretation and custodianship of Scripture by the Christian community. Through all the complexities involved in this process, the basic promise of 1 Cor 2:12 continues to sustain us: 'Now we have received not the spirit of the world, but the Spirit who is from God, that we might understand the things freely given us by God.'

---

[1653] 2 Tim 1:14.
[1654] 1 Tim 3:15.

# CHAPTER SEVEN: SPIRIT AND HERMENEUTICS IN THE JOHANNINE COMMUNITY

## Κοινωνία and Truth in 1 John

## Introduction

I am returning to the Johannine corpus, and in particular the first letter of John, for my final exegetical chapter because 1 John arguably shows a 'development and fulfilment'[1655] of the pneumatological promises given by Jesus to his disciples as recorded in the gospel of John. Accordingly, the letter affirms the universal endowment of the Spirit to all Christians ('you have been anointed ... and you *all* have knowledge' 2:20), but also along with the community imperative to 'test the spirits' (4:1–6.). First John, as one of the later New Testament writings,[1656] like the Pastorals, illustrates a concern for the Spirit's 'custodianship' role in relation to the truths now found in Scripture, in the face of the increasing threat of heterodoxy that emerged towards the end of the first century.

Not that this 'custodianship' was explicitly of 'scriptural' truth as such, because at the time of the writing of 1 John, the New Testament canon had obviously not been settled. And, unlike the Pauline writings investigated in the previous chapter, we do not find in the letter such an abundant use of Old Testament quotation and allusion that gives clues as to the way the New Testament writers were interpreting the Old Testament Scriptures.[1657] Nevertheless, the Johannine teaching surrounding its strong antithesis between 'the Spirit of truth'[1658] and 'the spirit of error' (4:6) offers us some hermeneutical guidelines that are especially relevant in discerning deviations from what Christians have long since regarded as the truth that is inscribed in the biblical canon.

The initial readers/hearers of the letter had evidently been unsettled by false prophets/secessionists who had seemingly invoked some kind of 'Spirit authority'[1659] for their wayward beliefs and behaviour, stemming from what

---

[1655] Ezra Sang-beop Shim, 'The Holy Spirit in 1 John in the Light of Structural Analysis' in *ChongShim Theological Journal 2* (1997), 111. For John 14–16, see chapter 4 and the relationship between the Johannine gospel and the letters, see fn. 7 in this chapter.

[1656] Commonly dated c. 90–110 CE, although Burge claims that 'a date between 70 and 90 is not unreasonable,' Gary Burge, *Letters of John*, Life Application Commentary (Grand Rapids: Zondervan, 1996), 40.

[1657] Lieu highlights just one 'explicit reference' from the Old Testament in the mention of Cain in 3:12 (which Cain narrative she says '[leaves] its mark' on 3:8–3:21) as well as a small number of other Old Testament Scriptures which are echoed. Judith Lieu, *I, II & III John* (Louisville, Westminster John Knox, 2008), 16–17.

[1658] ἀλήθεια occurs nine times in 1 John, often in an antithetical context.

[1659] Implied from 1 John 2:19–20 and 4:1. They denied that Jesus was the Christ (2:22), denied the Son (2:23), and rejected the incarnation (4:2–3).

Burge describes as a 'faulty christology [that] spilled into unethical conduct.'[1660] He construes such unorthodox belief and practice as 'an abuse of the Paraclete's revelatory work,'[1661] resulting from an overstretching of the pneumatological promises,[1662] such as John 14:26 ('teach you all things') and 16:13 ('guide you into all truth').[1663] This abuse may account for a deliberate avoidance of παράκλητος[1664] motifs in 1 John.[1665] Church history abounds with examples of similar unorthodox splinter groups, claiming 'the leading of the Spirit' for their particular wayward beliefs. In response to the 'antichrists' (2:18) of the early Christian era, 1 John reasserts what had been heard 'from the beginning', centering upon an incarnate Christ, as confirmed by a Spirit-enabled hermeneutic. Schweizer has written of the epistle:

> Nowhere else in the NT is there so strong an emphasis as here on trust in the *pneuma* who works in the community, who needs no official authorisation, who bears witness, not by bringing new and unheard of revelations, but by bringing the old message.[1666]

In this chapter, I will start with some remarks concerning the corporate context of the epistle, along with its pneumatology. This will be followed by a detailed study of 1 John 2:20–27, concerning the gift of the Spirit 'to all', followed by a review of the communal operation of 'testing the spirits' in 4:1–6, the two passages in 1 John that are arguably most relevant to the hermeneutical theme of this book. The discussion on 4:1–6 will also include a more general comment on 'testing the spirits' from a wider biblical and historical perspective.

---

[1660] G. Burge, *Letters of John*, 31. Cf. Tricia Gates Brown: 'evidently the community behind 1 John were being faced with a choice of brokers: either the spirit or Jesus. The opponents apparently taught that the spirit provided them with direct access to God.... The author in response ... strives to teach his followers of the indispensability of Jesus' life and death ... [but also] fashions a theology according to which the significance of the spirit lies in its work of affirming the Jesus traditions,' Tricia Gates Brown, *Spirit in the Writings of John* (London/New York: T&T Clark, 2003), 267. For Gates Brown's concept of the Spirit/paraclete as 'broker', see page 127.

[1661] G. Burge, *The Anointed Community* (Grand Rapids: Eerdmans, 1987), 224, also 218–221, following R. E. Brown.

[1662] Following the commonly accepted assumption that 1 John was written after and developed from the Gospel of John. For the 'similarities' between 1 John and the Gospel, see R. E. Brown, *The Epistles of John*, Anchor Bible (New York: Doubleday, 1982), 757–759. For links with the 'Farewell Discourse' in John 14–17, see Stephen Smalley, *1, 2, 3 John* (Milton Keynes: Word, 1991), xxix–xxx. Smalley describes 1 John as 'a "paper", which sets out to expound Johannine teaching and ideas, now preserved in the tradition and theology of the Fourth Gospel, for the benefit of heterodox members of John's community who were also indebted to the teaching of the Gospel, but who were understanding it differently,' xxvii.

[1663] See also D. Rensberger, 'Conflict and Community in the Johannine Letters', *Interpretation*, July 2006, Vol. 60, No. 3, 283.

[1664] The singular occurrence of παράκλητος in 1 John refers to Christ (2:1), and not to the Holy Spirit (παράκλητος in John 14:16; 14:26; 15:26; 16:7). As the Spirit is παράκλητος/advocate for Jesus through Christians in the world, so Jesus himself is our παράκλητος/advocate with the Father in heaven.

[1665] Burge, *Anointed Community*, 219. Lieu, however, claims that the paucity of Spirit reference represents a '"thin" area in its theology,' Judith Lieu, *The Theology of the Johannine Epistles* (Cambridge: Cambridge University Press, 1991), 105.

[1666] E. Schweizer, 'πνεῦμα' in Kittel, *TDNT*, Vol. 3, 449.

## Corporateness and Pneumatology in 1 John

As we enter the world of 1 John we find our initial encounter is not with the authorship of a named individual but the declaration of a corporate experience to an unnamed community that produces κοινωνία: 'that which ... *we* have heard ... seen ... touched ... *we* proclaim to you (ἀπαγγέλλομεν ὑμῖν) so that you ... may have fellowship with us (ἵνα καὶ ὑμεῖς κοινωνίαν ἔχητε μεθ' ἡμῶν)' (1:1–3). Judith Lieu has highlighted the pervasive community element that characterizes the Epistle:

> 1 John is guided less by argument than by its use of "you" (plural) and even more of "we" (which appears more times in 1 John than any other NT letter of comparable length). This, the author and the community, his use of "we" and "you", offers a starting point for 1 John's theology.[1667]

Such a 'starting point', however, has been pursued in differing interpretive directions, not least with regard to the meaning of the aforesaid opening 'we'.[1668] R. E. Brown, for instance, sees it as a reference to 'the Johannine community'[1669] which he and many others consider to be largely responsible for the final production of the epistle: 'the tradition-bearers and the interpreters who stand in a special relationship to the Beloved Disciple in their attempt to preserve his witness.'[1670] More conservative scholars who favour direct apostolic authorship see it as a reference to John and his fellow apostles who had been with Jesus 'from the beginning', to echo a favourite Johannine expression (normally used

---

[1667] Judith Lieu, *The Theology of the Johannine Epistles*, 23. Rensberger says 1 John 'resembles ancient demonstrative rhetoric', 'Conflict and Community in the Johannine Letters,' 279.

[1668] Lieu eschews apostolic authorship, arguing that that purpose of the opening 'we' is to 'to deflect attention away from the author ... [and to] create a sense of corporate unity and of continuity reaching beyond the present situation and player' Judith Lieu, *I, II & III John*, 39. Other suggestions include an authorial/editorial 'we'; an authoritative (royal like) 'we'; and a universal 'we' (referring to the whole church in its solidarity with the first eyewitnesses). For further discussion, see R. E. Brown, *The Epistles of John*, 158-161; S. J. Kistemaker, *James, Epistles of John, Peter and Jude* (Grand Rapids: Baker, 1996), 204-205; J. R. W. Stott, *Epistles of John* (Leicester: IVP, 1964), 26-34; I. Howard Marshall, *The Epistles of John* (Grand Rapids: Eerdmans, 1978), 106-107; Judith Lieu, *I, II & III John*, 15-16.

[1669] The community is said to have consisted of several churches in Asia Minor (distinct from the Jerusalem/Judean churches, and those created through Paul's missions) and whose experiences and problems accounted for the distinctive Johannine literature (notably the gospel and letters) and maybe was responsible for it. See R. E. Brown, *The Epistles of John*, xi-xii, xv, 29-35, 103-115; C. Kruse, *The Letters of John*, 1-7; R. Alan Culpepper, *The Gospel and Letters of John* (Nashville: Abingdon, 1998), 42-61; and Stephen Smalley *1,2,3 John*, xxiii-xxxii. The intimate language of 1 John certainly indicates that the writer, if he was an individual, had a close connection with his readers, but does not actually refer to a particular community. This suggests it was initially sent out as a circular letter to a group of churches. Kruse's working assumption is that the author's community is 'simply a group of loosely related churches operating in fellowship with one another and with the author' (Kruse, *The Letters of John*, 5). In any event, Lieu cogently argues that any 'exercise of reconstructing a situation for the letters and then interpreting them in its light involves a degree of circularity that may prove sterile ... [T]he letters are best understood as far as possible in their own terms with minimal reference to any proposed setting,' Lieu, *I, II & III John*, 29.

[1670] R. E. Brown, *The Epistles of John*, 95.

to point his readers 'back to their traditional basis'[1671]). In this case the 'we' functions as what Bruce calls an '*exclusive* we' ('we and not you')[1672] marking off the unique experience and authoritative pronouncements of the apostles (as in 1:1–5 and 4:14), as opposed to the '*inclusive* we'[1673] ('the community together with the author'[1674]), more generally found in the Epistle, that has reference to the common experience of the Johannine community and indeed of all Christians.[1675] According to Stott, as the letter progresses, the exclusive 'we/I-you' mode of address is frequently employed when authoritative apostolic teaching is at stake,[1676] whereas an inclusive 'we' is used especially where universally shared ethical responsibility is involved.[1677] Such a combination is sometimes found in the same verse, for instance 3:11: 'this is the message *you* have heard ... that *we* should love one another.' Both messenger and recipients stand under the authority of the same word, not least in their common duty: 'that we should love one another' (ἵνα ἀγαπῶμεν ἀλλήλους) (3:11c).

This concern for mutual love in the fellowship is exhibited by the use of corporate language that is often of an intimate, familial nature—'beloved' (Ἀγαπητοί),[1678] 'my little children' (Τεκνία μου),[1679] 'brothers' (ἀδελφοί)[1680]—all of which is expressed as an outworking of the more fundamental 'fellowship with the Father and with his Son Jesus Christ' of 1:3.[1681] The four occurrences of κοινωνία[1682] at the outset of the epistle (1:3–7) help T. Griffith to claim[1683] that the main reference point of the letter is one of an 'intimate circle of fellowship.'[1684] He argues that it accordingly has a primarily *pastoral* purpose

---

[1671] Burge, *Anointed Community*, 219, pointing out the frequency of ἀπ' ἀρχῆς (1:1; 2:7,13,14; 3:8,11).

[1672] F. F. Bruce, *The Epistles of John* (Grand Rapids: Eerdmans, 1979), 38.

[1673] i.e. 'you and I' or 'you and we', ibid., 38.

[1674] Lieu, *The Theology of the Johannine Epistles*, 26.

[1675] For example, at 1:6, 7–10; 2:1–3, 5, 28; 3:1–2; 4:9–13; 5:2–3, 18–20. The reference to 'we' in 4:6 is debated—see later. See also, Kruse, *The Letters of John*, 150–151. Cf. Stott's comment: 'In one sense, associated with his fellow-apostles, [John] was unique; in another sense, associated with his readers, he was just a common Christian,' Stott, *Epistles of John*, 32–33.

[1676] Stott, *Epistles of John*, 33.

[1677] Ibid., 33.

[1678] 2:7; 3:2, 21; 4:1, 7, 11.

[1679] 2:1; see also 2:12, 28; 4:4. Note also the groups mentioned in 2:12–14.

[1680] 3:13, see also 3:14, 17; 5:16.

[1681] Notice how καὶ ὑμεῖς κοινωνίαν ἔχητε μεθ' ἡμῶν is immediately followed by καὶ ἡ κοινωνία δὲ ἡ ἡμετέρα μετὰ τοῦ πατρὸς καὶ μετὰ τοῦ υἱοῦ αὐτοῦ Ἰησοῦ Χριστοῦ in 1:3.

[1682] Κοινωνία may have been a word used by the secessionists (2:19) who still claimed to have fellowship with God despite no longer having it with other believers. Smalley says that 'the phrase κοινωνίαν ἔχειν, "to have fellowship", not the verb κοινωνεῖν ("to fellowship", see 2 John 11) ... expresses not only the *fact*, but also the conscious *enjoyment*, of fellowship in Christ,' Smalley, *1,2,3 John*, 12.

[1683] T. Griffith, 'A Non-Polemical Reading of 1 John: Sin, Christology and the Limits of Johannine Christology,' *Tyndale Bulletin* 49:2, 1998, 253–276.

[1684] Ibid., 261. He argues that the 'if we say/claim' (ἐὰν εἴπωμεν) statements in 1:6–10 must be read 'as a *pluralis sociativus*, which was widely used in Greek literature,' 256, to incorporate the readers or hearers into the action of the writer or speaker. They are therefore not to be regarded as quotations from schismatic opponents (as commonly supposed) but as 'rhetorical devices, that reinforce commonly-held beliefs and values, and promote his stated aim "that you also may have fellowship with us" (1:3),' 257.

('to secure the boundaries of the community against further losses')[1685] by recalling it to 'right confession' and 'right conduct'),[1686] rather than the *polemical* purpose that is more commonly predicated of it[1687] (i.e. as a letter designed to refute 'gnosticising or docetic-like opponents').[1688] It is not difficult to argue, of course, that the epistle contains a mix of both the pastoral and the polemical.[1689] However we read the *rationale* of the Epistle, there can be little doubt that it exudes with expressions of a deep seated κοινωνία that was not only the reflection of the closest bond between author(s) and readers/hearers abiding in Christ (cf. John 15:1-10), a bond that stood in need of protection, but, one is tempted to say, was also the result of a work of the Spirit.

Not that the Spirit is explicitly linked with the κοινωνία of chapter 1 (vv. 3, 6, 7), although the first explicit mention of πνεῦμα (Spirit)[1690] in 3:24 (cf. also 4:13) says that believers can know they abide in Christ and he in them 'by the Spirit whom he has given *to us*' (ἡμῖν ἔδωκεν—a corporate endowment).[1691] Such a relatively late appearance of the word 'Spirit' in the Epistle masks the fact that a pneumatological undercurrent can nevertheless be detected running through each of its chapters. Although lying beneath the surface of the text as the implied enabler of κοινωνία in 1:3-7, a strong case can be made for a reference to the Spirit in the 'anointing' (χρῖσμα) of 2:20 and 2:27[1692] and the 'seed' (σπέρμα) of 3:9,[1693] two terms which Edwards says 'suggest a vital role for the Spirit.'[1694] The Spirit's assurance of the indwelling in believers of Christ in 3:24 and of God in 4:13 sandwich the key passage of 4:1-6,[1695] in which the Spirit is stated as having a crucial role in the discerning of truth and error, particularly relating to the incarnate Christ. The last chapter of the Epistle speaks of a more objective work of the Spirit in not only testifying to the truth (5:6-8), but being equated with it

---

[1685] Ibid., 275. For Griffith, these are 'Jewish Christians returning to Judaism,' 275.

[1686] Ibid., 253.

[1687] Ibid., 253. Such divergent readings of the Epistle are a good example of how assumptions relating to the *Sitz in Leben* of Scripture can radically affect its interpretation.

[1688] Other suggestions for 'the opponents' in 1 John include lapsed Jewish Christians, Jews who opposed the Messiah, charismatics and Cerinthians. Ruth B. Edwards, *The Johannine Epistles* (Sheffield: Sheffield Academic Press, 1996), 60-67 concludes that 'none of these identifications is fully convincing,' 67. See also R. E. Brown, *The Epistles of John*, 49-68.

[1689] Hence R. B. Edwards' conclusion: 'The Epistle combines encouragement, warning and polemic,' *The Johannine Epistles*, 81.

[1690] i.e. as a reference to the Spirit of God. He is never referred to as 'the Holy Spirit' in 1 John.

[1691] Brown points out that κοινωνία never appears in the Gospel of John but says that 'κοινωνία can service as a nominal expression for what [the Gospel] covers by verbs of indwelling,' Brown, *The Epistles of John*, 186.

[1692] See pages 247-249.

[1693] Shim says of 3:9: 'the *sperma* phrase stands exactly at the center of the passage', and noting the links between the Spirit and divine birth/regeneration in John: 3:5-8, concludes that '*sperma* denotes the agent of life rather than life itself [and] is best understood as the Holy Spirit or the Spirit working in conjunction with God's word.' 'The Holy Spirit in 1 John in the Light of Structural Analysis,' 114 & 116. See also Kruse on *sperma* in *The Letters of John*, 124-125.

[1694] Edwards, *The Johannine Epistles*, 81.

[1695] See pages 253-264 below.

('the Spirit is the truth'—τὸ πνεῦμά ἐστιν ἡ ἀλήθεια 5:6c). Such a strong[1696] external witness thus supplements the internal witness of 3:24 and 4:13.

From her reading of these verses, Lieu asserts that the essential characteristic of the Spirit in 1 John is confessional rather than 'charismatic',[1697] such a role necessitating a communal context: 'the spirit is experienced within the community, for it is there that confession is made and tested.'[1698] External confession, however, can only truly emanate from internal assurance. As Shim points out, 'the reference to the Holy Spirit is often related with the verbs, γινώσκω or οἶδα.'[1699] He concludes that 'the Holy Spirit has the important function and role of supporting the certainty of faith which is the central message of 1 John.'[1700] Such 'certainty' was needed by the Johannine community in the face of the danger of their being 'led astray'[1701] (2:26) by false teaching which apparently claimed to have a pneumatological basis, as shall be seen from an exploration of the first of our two selected passages.

## χρῖσμα and Community in 1 John 2:20 and 27

Chapter 2:18–27 is addressed to 'children' (Παιδία[1702]) and contains instruction on what we, two millennia later, might describe as 'the hermeneutic of the "pneumatic community" ' (Burge[1703]). My discussion of the passage will be focussed upon the χρῖσμα ('anointing') verses (vv. 20 and 27) and around four key 'A's: antichrists, anointing, all and abiding.

### (a) Antichrists (2:18–19)

The context of the Johannine teaching here in 2:18 is one of eschatological imminence ('the last hour'[1704]) characterized by the coming of 'many antichrists'

---

[1696] Shim points out that 'the verb μαρτυρέω and the noun μαρτυρία occur ten times in this section [viz.5:6–12],' 'The Holy Spirit in 1 John in the Light of Structural Analysis,' 121.

[1697] Lieu: 'The only mark of the spirit and the only concern of the author is true confession.... The focus is on the spirit present in the community rather than in the hearts of individual believers, and it is the community rather than the individual which provides the battlefield,' *The Theology of the Johannine Epistles*, 46–47.

[1698] Ibid., 47.

[1699] Ibid., 110, referring to 2:20; 3:24; 4:2; 4:6; 4:13.

[1700] Ibid., 110–111. Shim's summary: 'according to 1 John ... true orthodoxy (sound confession) and true orthopraxy (holiness and life of love) through the ministry of the Spirit meet and complement each other in full harmony,' Shim, 'The Holy Spirit in 1 John in the Light of Structural Analysis,' 122.

[1701] 2:26 uses πλανάω (to seduce, lead astray, deceive) of the false teachers.

[1702] From the diminutive of *pais* ('boy, son'): 'the plurals of *teknion* and *paidion* are used as direct address for the readers who are clearly Christians of the author's own community,' Brown, *The Epistles of John*, 214.

[1703] A common description of the Johannine community by Burge, see for example his comment: 'the Johannine community was a vital, pneumatic community, but ... its pneumatology was entirely Christocentric,' Burge, *Anointed Community*, 45.

[1704] Note the twofold reference to ἐσχάτη ὥρα at the beginning and end of 2:18.

whose claims[1705] and denials[1706] are echoed in 1 John. The term ἀντίχριστος ('antichrist') is unique to the Johannine Epistles,[1707] although the idea is found elsewhere in Scripture.[1708] The 'anti' prefix highlights the error of christology perpetrated by the false teachers in terms of their opposition to, and maybe also counterfeiting of, true christology.[1709] Such doctrinal defection eventually manifested itself in physical departure: 'they went out from us (ἐξ ἡμῶν ἐξῆλθαν), but they were not of us' (2:19). Strecker comments that 'not all who count themselves as members of the community really belong to it.'[1710] Smalley points out how 'the "withdrawal" of [the] heretics [in 1 John] is anticipated by Judas Iscariot, who "went out" (ἐξῆλθεν) from the company of Jesus and the disciples (John 13:30a).'[1711] In 1 John 2:19, the corporate nature of the particular secession there is underlined by the plural genitive ἡμῶν ('of us'), which, as Brown says, 'is used 5 times in the 6 lines of this verse.'[1712] The turmoil to the Johannine community that such a rupture of fellowship caused evinced a proclamation ('but you' 2:20) that has brought consolation to all groups who have suffered similar defections from those claiming 'higher forms' of Christianity.

## (b) Anointing (2:20, 27)

The reassuringly adversative καί that introduces this verse is followed by the emphatic plural ὑμεῖς ('but *you*'): as against those who had left the fellowship, they, the Johannine community as a whole, could lay claim to an 'anointing' (χρῖσμα) which was their 'protection'[1713] against the 'antichrists' (v.18 ἀντίχριστοι—note the probable wordplay, with the further connection to χριστός).

The meaning and significance of the cognate noun χρῖσμα ('anointing'), found in the New Testament only here in 2:20 and 2:27, is debated.[1714] As to the Old Testament background, the LXX uses the verb χρίω ('to anoint') not only in the literal sense of the oil used for purposes of consecration,[1715] but also in a more figurative sense, symbolizing the outpouring of the Spirit upon David as king (1 Sam 16:13) and upon the Servant of Yahweh as the coming Messiah/Lord's

---

[1705] For example, at 1:6, 8; 2:9.
[1706] For example, at 2:2; 4:3.
[1707] 1 John 2:18, 22; 4:3; 2 John 7.
[1708] Especially in 2 Thess 2:1-12.
[1709] See Stott, *Epistles of John*, 104-105.
[1710] Georg Strecker, *The Johannine Letters* (Minneapolis: Fortress Press, 1996), 64. Some commentators see the doctrines of the 'visible'/'invisible' church and the perseverance of the saints here.
[1711] Smalley, *1,2,3 John*, 102: 'like the schismatics he was not "walking in the light" (1:7a; cf. John 13:30*b*, when Judas left "it was night" (John13:30b).' He regards Judas in the gospel as an antichrist figure, ibid., 219.
[1712] Brown, *The Epistles of John*, 338, four of which are found in the expression ἐξ ἡμῶν. Smalley highlights the wordplay set off by the ambivalence of the preposition 'from' (ἐξ) 'signifying both "out of" (membership) and "part of" (origin).' Smalley, *1,2,3 John*, 102.
[1713] Stott, *Epistles of John*, p. 106.
[1714] See Strecker, *The Johannine Letters*, 65-66; Stott, *Epistles of John*, 109-110; Brown, *The Epistles of John*, 341-348; Kruse, *The Letters of John*, 109-110; Smalley, *1,2,3 John*, 105-107; Lieu, *I, II & III John*, 102-104.
[1715] For example in Ex. 29:7; 30:25; 40:15.

anointed (Isa 61:1). This latter verse is taken up by Jesus in Luke 4:18, with further linking of χρίω with the Spirit to Jesus in Acts 4:27, 10:38 and Heb 1:9, and to Christians in 2 Cor 1:21–22. Such New Testament usage points to a primary reference also being to the Holy Spirit in 1 John 2:20, also suggested by the parallels between the 'anointing' in 1 John and the ministry of the παράκλητος in the John 14–16. As Thomas points out, 'both are spoken of as being "received by" (John 14:17; 1 John 2:27), "abiding in" (John 14:17; 1 John 2:27)), and "teaching all things to" (John 14:26, 1 John 2:20, 27) the believers.'[1716]

Some, however, see in 'the anointing' a reference to the word (or gospel) of God,[1717] or, as seems quite possible, some sort of combination of both word and Spirit. Stott, for instance, connects with 'what you have heard from the beginning' (2:24) and concludes: '[h]ere, then, are the two safeguards against error—the apostolic word and the anointing Spirit (cf. Isa 59:21).'[1718] For Burge, 'the anointing stands apart from the word as independent but finds its primary function in confirming the word and applying it in the present schism.'[1719]

Further debate concerns whether the source of the anointing—'by the Holy One' (ἀπὸ τοῦ ἁγίου 2:20b)—is a reference to God the Father[1720] or Jesus. The majority opinion seems to favour Jesus, as the 'Holy One of God'[1721] and giver of the Spirit.[1722] As to the time of reception of the anointing, this is not mentioned in 1 John 2:20, although Smalley comments on 2:27 ('the anointing you have received' [ἐλάβετε—aorist]) that it 'relates to a particular moment of spiritual experience but this need not be linked exclusively to the rite of baptism,'[1723] despite the obvious association of 'anointing' with baptism in the case of Jesus's 'anointing' with the Holy Spirit.[1724] Thomas says that 'received' in v. 27 points to 'the readers ... being reminded of their Spirit baptism',[1725] whereas Brown speaks in more general terms of 'a conversion/initiation/baptismal background for the author's ideas,'[1726] claiming that more scholars favour a 'figurative

---

[1716] John Christopher Thomas, 'The Johannine Epistles' in Trevor J. Burke & Keith Warrington.,eds., *A Biblical Theology of the Holy Spirit* (London: SPCK, 2014), 251. Note also further parallels with John 15:26 and John 16:13.
[1717] Brown, *The Epistles of John*, 345-346. Lieu views the 'anointing' not in terms of the Spirit but as referring to 'the readers' possession of true understanding, an internalization of the teaching that had transformed and shaped them,' J. Lieu, *I, II, & III John*, 103. Tricia Gates Brown claims that the author may be deliberately 'avoid[ing] spirit-language that could be used as fodder for the opponent's position, while still confirming that his own group is divinely anointed,' Tricia Gates Brown, *Spirit in the Writings of John*, 241.
[1718] Stott, *Epistles of John*, 114. Also note Marshall's comment: 'the antidote to false teaching is the inward reception of the Word of God, administered and confirmed by the work of the Spirit,' Marshall, *The Epistles of John*, 155.
[1719] Burge, *Anointed Community*, 175.
[1720] 'God the holy': Isa 5:16; Hos 11:9. 'The Holy One of Israel': Isa 1:4; Ps 71:22.
[1721] Mark 1:24; Luke 4:34; John 6:69. Cf. also 'the Holy One' in Acts 3:14; Rev 3:7.
[1722] John 15:26; 16:7; Acts 2:33.
[1723] Smalley, *1,2,3 John*, 124.
[1724] Matt 3:16; Acts 10:38. See R. E. Brown, *The Epistles of John*, 370.
[1725] Thomas, 'The Johannine Epistles', 251–252.
[1726] Brown, *The Epistles of John*, 343.

anointing' rather than 'an initiatory ritual anointing.'[1727] Whatever the connotations, the anointing must relate to some specific point of entrance of the Johannine readers into the Christian community and its beliefs.

Stott, along with many of the commentators, says that 'it is probable that [the secessionists] used the word *chrisma* as a technical term for initiation into a special *gnōsis*.'[1728] If this is the case, then the Johannine author is directly contradicting their claim to such elitism ('the seductiveness of "the inner circle"'[1729]) by insisting that the whole community has received the χρῖσμα. This is reinforced by the implication of the opening καὶ ὑμεῖς[1730] ('you, no less than they, are among the initiated' NEB), as well as by the consequence spelt out in the second half of 2:20: 'and you *all* have knowledge,' which leads us to our third 'A'.

*(c) All (2:20c)*

The translation just cited follows the rendering καὶ οἴδατε πάντες (lit. 'you all know'). An equally attested textual variant that replaces the nominative subject πάντες with a neuter accusative πάντα gives another meaning: 'and you (plural) know all things,' a reading preferred by some commentators. Of the alternative readings,[1731] πάντες best fits the context, following Brooke:

> Under the new dispensation the special gift, which in old times was bestowed on the few, is the common possession of all. Cf. Joel ii. 28 (iii.1); Ac. ii.... The true text emphasizes the universality of the possession among Christians (οἴδατε πάντες), and not of the knowledge which it conveys (πάντα). The possession by all of them of the knowledge which *enables them to discern*, and not the extent of their knowledge, is the ground of the writer's appeal.[1732]

Bruce concurs, linking it with the thought of following verse: 'They know the difference [between truth and falsehood] ... not because they have explored the mazes of falsehood but because they "know the truth"'[1733] (2:21).

---

[1727] Ibid., 343-344.
[1728] Stott, *Epistles of John*, 107.
[1729] Bruce, *The Epistles of John*, 70, quoting from C. S. Lewis's 'The Inner Ring' in *Transposition and Other Addresses* (London, 1965), 55.
[1730] Smalley says that 'the force of the conjunction καί ("and") in this phrase is certainly adversative (= "but"). It also carries here ... the significance of "moreover",' Smalley, *1,2,3 John*, 105.
[1731] Discussed in R. E. Brown, *The Epistles of John*, 348-349.
[1732] A. E. Brooke, *A Critical and Exegetical Commentary on the Johannine Epistles* (Edinburgh: T&T Clark, 1912), 56, my italics. Brown defines 'the few' who 'were anointed and given the spirit of wisdom' in the OT era as 'kings, prophets [and] priests.' Brown, *The Epistles of John*, 370.
[1733] F. F. Bruce, *The Epistles of John*, 72.

Another relevant Old Testament passage, which Brown claims 'is very much in [the author's] mind,'[1734] is Jer 31:34: 'they shall all (πάντες) know me, from the least of them to the greatest.' This prophesied democratization of the knowledge of God was the peculiar prerogative of the Spirit who was subsequently 'poured out' upon 'all flesh' (Acts 2:17)[1735]—'irrespective of gender, age, race or social status—and upon them permanently.'[1736] Such a generous endowment, such a 'χρῖσμα' in the terms of 1 John 2, leads Stott to say that 'there is a sense in which every Christian is a true "Christ", having received the same spiritual "chrism" as He received.'[1737]

Genuine spiritual illumination is thereby afforded to 'ordinary' Christians, and is demonstrated to pastors and teachers whenever a member of their congregation or Bible study group comes out with a seemingly 'instant' or intuitive spiritual insight that they themselves may have taken hours pouring over commentaries to attain![1738] The hermeneutical role of such 'ordinary theologians' (as opposed to academic ones) that constitute the major part of the Christian Church is increasingly being investigated and analysed under the rubric of 'ordinary theology'[1739]—the 'reflective practice of non-academic and non-clerical Christians.'[1740] Their reflective (and 'non-reflective'!) insights can, not infrequently, act as a stimulus, or even a corrective, to those academically trained. But they can also, of course, be erroneous and need checking by the relevant bible study leader and/or the group (whether this be in a smaller or larger setting). Indeed, the main emphasis of this passage seems to be upon the

---

[1734] Brown, *The Epistles of John*, 349.

[1735] Acts 2:17, citing Joel 2:28-32. Note also Moses' yearning in Num 11:29b.

[1736] G. F. Hawthorne, 'Holy Spirit' in *Dictionary of the Later New Testament and its Developments*, eds. R. P. Martin and P. H. Davids (Leicester: IVP), 489, referring to Acts 2:4,17-20.

[1737] Stott, *Epistles of John*, 106, citing 2 Cor 1:21,22. For the parallel with Jesus, see Brown, *The Epistles of John*, 370, concluding that 'Christians who have been anointed or consecrated in truth have the privileges of God's consecrated Son because their anointing was through his Spirit.'

[1738] Note also the apostolic example of Peter and John, 'unschooled, ordinary men' (Acts 4:13 NIV), who were 'filled with the Holy Spirit' (Acts 4:8). This raises an important contemporary question: why is it that Christianity is currently thriving in cultures that are generally less literate than the rich West? This in turn is linked with the perennial question articulated by Christopher Lewis: 'How can the Bible be used and understood by people other than scholars?' 'The Bible and Ordinary People' in Dan Cohn-Sherbok, ed., *Using the Bible Today: Contemporary Interpretations of Scripture* (London: Bellen, 1991), 94. See also: Peter van Inwagen, 'Do You Want Us to Listen to You?' in Craig Bartholomew, Stephen Evans, Mary Healy and Murray Rose, eds., *'Behind' the Text: History and Biblical Interpretation* Scripture and Hermeneutics Series Vol. 4 (Carlisle: Paternoster, 2003), 101–129; F. D. Macchia, 'Pentecostal Theology' in S. M. Burgess & E. M. Van Der Maas, eds., *New International Dictionary of Pentecostal and Charismatic Movements* (Grand Rapids: Zondervan, 2002), 1120 ('The Significance of Nonacademic Theology'); and J. B. Thomson, 'Time for Church? Evangelicals, Scripture and Conversational Hermeneutics' in *Anvil*, Vol. 21, No. 4, 2004, 257.

[1739] This term, coined by Jeff Astley, has been defined more fully by him as 'the theological beliefs and processes of believing that find expression in the God-talk of those believers who have received no scholarly theological education.' Jeff Astley 'The Analysis, Investigation and Application of Ordinary Theology' in Jeff Astley and Leslie J. Francis, eds., *Exploring Ordinary Theology* (Farnham: Ashgate, 2013), 1.

[1740] Nicholas M. Healey, 'Ordinary Theology, Theological Method and Constructive Ecclesiology' in Astley and Francis, eds., *Exploring Ordinary Theology*, 14.

corporate insight of the community (the 'all')[1741] rather than individual perspective (the 'every'). In this respect, many examples could be given of relatively uneducated communities who have exhibited great spiritual understanding because they have seemingly been taught directly by the Spirit in group encounter.[1742]

Is this, then, what is meant when 2:27 says 'you have no need that anyone teach you' for 'his anointing teaches you about everything'? Such statements nevertheless need to be understood against the background of the false teachers who were 'trying to deceive' (2:26) the Johannine readers. They certainly did not need *their* teaching if they had the very Spirit of truth abiding in them. He was their ultimate teacher (cf. 1 Cor 2:6–16), although of course he used human vessels through which to teach (not least the Johannine author).[1743] As Augustine said of his own teaching ministry, 'the sound of my voice strikes your ears, but the real Teacher is within.'[1744] Not that such an explicit exterior/interior distinction is explicitly being made here, although links with the Johannine Gospel's emphasis upon the Spirit teaching 'all things' (John 14:25) and 'guid[ing] into all truth' (16:13) are more obvious. In this, the corporate note is again underlined by Strecker, pointing to the emphatic καὶ ὑμεῖς ('but ... you') at the start of 2:27 and emphasizing that 'the spirit of truth, *being given to the community*, leads them—like the Paraclete in the Fourth Gospel—to knowledge of the truth.'[1745] Bruce also stresses the 'fellowship' aspect of the verse, commenting on the 'no need of any teacher' part:

> It is not to be taken as absolute affirmation that the experience of the Spirit in personal life carries with it independence of the ministry of teaching in the church.... But [this] ministry ... must be exercised by men who themselves share 'the anointing' of which John speaks, men who themselves remain in the fellowship of the Spirit.... It is within the fellowship that the Spirit operates.... So Paul prays that those who are inwardly strengthened by the Spirit "may have power to comprehend

---

[1741] '[A]nointing is attributed only to the true community,' Strecker, *The Johannine Letters*, 65.

[1742] For one published example, see Ernesto Cardenal, *The Gospel in Solentiname* (London: Search, 1977), recording the bible discussions (in place of a sermon) of '*campesinos*' (farm workers and fishermen) during and after their Sunday Mass, sometimes in church and sometimes in a hut opposite the church around a communal lunch. Cardenal claims that 'the commentaries of the *campesinos* are usually of greater profundity than that of many theologians, but of a simplicity like that of the Gospel itself,' vii. 'The author of this book are these people ... I am wrong. The true author is the Spirit that has inspired these commentaries', x. Chapter 1, 1–12, contains a detailed dialogue on John 1:1–18.

[1743] The highly didactic nature of 1 John itself is often noted. Brown refers to 'the Johannine *School* which has a special place in the Johannine community. Their authority is not as teachers but as witnesses who are vehicles of the Paraclete, the only teacher,' Brown, *The Epistles of John*, 96.

[1744] *In Epistolam* 3:13; SC 75,210, as quoted in Brown, *The Epistles of John*, 376.

[1745] Strecker, *The Johannine Letters*, 77.

*with all the saints* what is the breadth and length and height and depth" (Eph 3:18).[1746]

Shim comments: 'under the teaching ministry of the Spirit, Christians give one another mutual instruction, without which no single individual can appreciate the whole of God's truth.'[1747]

As in 2:20, the 'all things/everything' (πάντων) of 2:27, is hardly likely to imply 'omniscience'[1748] but rather an *adequacy* of knowledge. As Marshall says, 'we may legitimately take "all things" to mean "all that you need to know",'[1749] or, as John Owen puts it, 'all things necessary unto our ingrafting into and continuance in Christ.'[1750] For the original recipients of the letter, it particularly related to the Johannine community's understanding of the Son whose essential nature had been denied by the heretics (2:22–23). For Christians, the Spirit's anointing affords an all sufficient knowledge of Christ, beyond which they need not go. The trouble with the Johannine heretics was that they tried to do just this, which brings us to our last 'A.'

## (d) Abiding (2:19, 24, 27)

Instead of abiding in the truth, they had left it behind, as symbolized in their physical departure from the community. If they had truly been 'of us, they would have continued with us' (μεμενήκεισαν ἂν μεθ' ἡμῶν 2:19b). The importance of this Johannine 'abiding/remaining/continuing' concept to our particular hermeneutical theme is demonstrated by the fact that there are no less than six occurrences of words with the μένω root in 2:19–27. After 2:19, we find the next two references in 2:24, both concerning the need to abide in what the community had heard 'from the beginning.' The common Johannine ἀπ' ἀρχῆς ('from the beginning')[1751] speaks of the need to ground all Spirit-led understanding upon the original gospel message, centering on the Jesus, especially as recorded in the Fourth Gospel—whose christology is also driven by a foundational 'in the beginning' (John 1:1–2). What Burge calls a 'Christocentric pneumatology'[1752] can therefore be deduced from this passage, which can also be seen in the ensuing flow of the Johannine argument: ('then you too will abide in the Son' 2:24c). The vital necessity of believers remaining in personal fellowship with

---

[1746] Bruce, *The Epistles of John*, 76, italics the author's, further pointing out the essentially oral context of pre-canonical Christianity.
[1747] Shim, 'The Holy Spirit in 1 John in the Light of Structural Analysis,' 113.
[1748] Marshall, *The Epistles of John*, 163.
[1749] Ibid., 163.
[1750] John Owen, *The Causes, Ways, and Means of Understanding the Mind of God as Revealed in His Word, With Assurance therein* (1678), as cited in J. Owen, *The Works of John Owen* (Edinburgh: Banner of Truth, 1967), Vol. IV, 146.
[1751] Also in 1:1; 2:7, 13, 14; 3:8, 11; 2 John 5, 6.
[1752] 'We need to cultivate a *Christocentric pneumatology* that at once joins our view of Christ as Lord and our experience of Spirit as his powerful presence,' Burge, *Letters of John*, 139.

God by his Spirit (cf. 4:13), as well as each other (3:23-24), is reinforced by the final 'abide in him' (μένετε ἐν αὐτῷ, 2:27), which can be read as a collective imperative.[1753] Its address is to each and to all, for as Lieu has shown from the epistle, '"abiding" is both an individual experience (3:6, 4:15,16b) and a corporate one ... (4:13 ... 2:24, 27-28).'[1754] Strecker concludes: 'the call to believers to abide "in him" (or: "it," i.e., the anointing) expresses a challenge to realize anew, at all times, the truth that is the gift of the Spirit.'[1755]

To summarise this section on 1 John 2:18-27, I have highlighted some features that characterized the hermeneutic of the Johannine 'pneumatic community'. The context for this was the eschatological 'last hour', marked by the arrival and defection of 'many *antichrists*' (2:18). The community's reassurance in the face of such brazen heresy lay in its *anointing* by the Spirit, a χρῖσμα received by *all* Christians. The faculty of spiritual discernment is thus assured and adequate for every Christian, but always to be exercised within the context of the 'fellowship of the Spirit.' The constant imperative of *abiding* therein was a vital ingredient in the hermeneutics of the Johannine community and not to be divorced from what they had heard ἀπ' ἀρχῆς ('from the beginning'), for 'both apostolic teaching and the Heavenly Teacher are necessary for continuance in the truth.'[1756] And not only continuance in but also contending for this truth is also required, as can be seen from our next passage from 1 John.

## Testing the Spirits in 1 John 4:1-6

It is a sad fact of Christian experience that the claims of 'prophetic' groups and individuals to be 'anointed' with the Spirit are sometimes spurious. Such was the case with the false prophets who were troubling the Johannine community with what Rensberger has described as 'an individualistic and spiritualized Christianity.'[1757] And so in 4:1, the *community* is encouraged to '*test* the spirits to see whether they are from God.' Thomas says that this command can be read as '"Do not keep believing every spirit", perhaps suggesting a situation where believing every spirit was common.'[1758] In the face of such potential gullibility, 1 John stresses the importance of discerning or testing these spirits. Indeed, Robert Law in his classic study 'The Tests of Life' has claimed that the whole of 1 John can be read in terms of an exposition of three basic tests:

> The key to the interpretation of the Epistle is the fact that it is an apparatus of *tests*; that its definite object is to furnish its readers with

---

[1753] Following Strecker: 'the verb is probably not an indicative ... but rather an imperative, as one can see from the subsequent v. 28,' Strecker, *The Johannine Letters*, 77.
[1754] Lieu, *The Theology of the Johannine Epistles*, 43.
[1755] Strecker, *The Johannine Letters*, 77.
[1756] Stott, *Epistles of John*, 115.
[1757] D. Rensberger, 'Conflict and Community in the Johannine Letters,' 284.
[1758] Thomas, 'The Johannine Epistles,' 253.

an adequate set of criteria by which they may satisfy themselves of their being "begotten of God." "These things I write unto you, that ye may know that ye have eternal life" (5:13). And throughout the Epistle these tests are definitely, inevitably, and inseparably: doing righteousness; loving one another; and believing that Jesus is the Christ, come in the flesh, sent by the Father to be the Saviour of the world.[1759]

Following Law, Stott[1760] categorizes these three 'tests', respectively, as 'moral', 'social' and 'theological'. If we adopt this analysis, we can say that it is primarily a 'theological' testing that is being employed in 4:1–6 (though shading into a more 'practical' emphasis in the second half, paving the way for a 'social' test of love in 4:7–21).

Before I embark on a more detailed exegesis of 4:1–6, I shall explore its corporate and pneumatological context. In the light of its general relevance to our book the 'corporate context' will be extended to include a perspective that is wider than 1 John.

*(a) The Corporate and Pneumatological Context*

(i) Corporate Context

a. *The Wider Biblical and Ecclesial Perspective*

'Testing the spirits' in 1 John 4 belongs to the biblical vocabulary of spiritual discernment which Amos Yong describes as 'wide ranging and ... complex,'[1761] and is 'understood as a hermeneutics of life that is both a divine gift and a human activity aimed at reading correctly the inner processes of all things.'[1762] He demonstrates this from a discussion of *nākar* ('discern', 'recognize') and *bînâ* (discernment, insight, perception) in the Old Testament and *krinō* (judge, select, assess) and *dokimazō* ('prove', 'test', 'approve', 'examine') and cognates in the New Testament.[1763] The discernment of spirits in both testaments includes a number of tests for false prophets.

In the Old Testament, these are highlighted in Deut 13:1–5 ('if he tries to lead his hearers astray to serve other gods') and 18:22 ('if the word does not come to pass'[1764]). The pertinence of such 'reality' tests was demonstrated in Elijah's contest with the prophets of Baal (1 Kgs 18) and in Jeremiah's tirades against those who were 'saying, "Peace, peace, when there is no peace"' (8:11)– prophesying 'smooth things'[1765] rather than true things. Ezekiel spoke out

---

[1759] Robert Law, *The Tests of Life* (Grand Rapids: Baker, 1979, copy of 3rd edition of 1914), 4–5.
[1760] Stott, Epistles *of John*, 53–55.
[1761] Amos Yong, *Beyond the Impasse: Toward a Pneumatological Theology of Religions* (Carlisle: Paternoster, 2003), 145.
[1762] Ibid., 130.
[1763] Ibid, 139–149, using his transliterated terms.
[1764] See also 1 Kgs 22:28.
[1765] Bruce, *The Epistles of John*, 103.

against 'foolish prophets who follow their own spirit' (13:3) and 'shepherds who [only] fed themselves' (34:8), whilst Micah exposed 'prophets [who] practise divination for money' (3:11).

In the New Testament, Jesus regularly denounced hypocrisy,[1766] saying of false prophets: 'you will recognize them by their fruits' (Matt 7:16a), which is not so far from 1 John's insistence on the need for 'righteousness' (3:10) and 'love' (4:7–21.). Besides such tests of outward morality, Paul spoke about inward prophetic motivation (2 Cor 2:17 'men of sincerity' and 4:2 'renounced ... underhanded ways'), as well as oral christological confession ('no one can say "Jesus is Lord" except by the Holy Spirit' 1 Cor 12:3). And as Martin points out from both Paul and John, 'there is no confession of Jesus Christ that divides the earthly, lowly Jesus from the exalted, regal Lord.'[1767]

Paul's call to 'not quench the Spirit ... but test (δοκιμάζετε) everything' (1 Thess 5:19–20) is echoed by the Pastorals' concern for 'sound doctrine' and many other New Testament passages.[1768] These all show, according to Marshall, that 'by ... the late first century church there was a consciousness of the distinction between orthodoxy and heresy'[1769] (i.e., presumably, in more refined form than in the Old Testament). Such a distinction was also sharply acknowledged in the language of Qumran dualism, although parallels with New Testament thought in general and Johannine dualism are not straightforward.[1770]

In response to early heresies, Christian literature continued to advocate the exercise of spiritual discernment. For instance, *Didache* 12:1 uses similar vocabulary to 1 John when it insists: 'Receive everyone who comes in the name of the Lord; then by testing [*dokimazein*] you will come to know him, for you will have the wisdom to distinguish between right and left.'[1771] The vast numbers of Christian creeds, confessions, theological writings and ecclesiastical movements that follow down the centuries exhibit an ongoing concern to spell out the implications of what is included in the 'right' and the 'left.'

Skating across the centuries to 1741, we note Jonathan Edwards's classic essay, 'The Distinguishing Marks of a Work of the Spirit of God', based on 1 John 4.[1772]

---

[1766] Matt 6:2, 5, 16; 7:5; 15:7; 23:13–36.
[1767] R. P. Martin, *The Family and the Fellowship: New Testament Images of the Church* (Exeter: Paternoster, 1977), 50, citing 2 Cor 4:11, 12, 17; John 13:1–20; 1 John 4:11.
[1768] For example, Matt 24:24; Mark 13:22, 23; Acts 20:28–30; 2 Cor 11:4, 12–15; 1 Tim 4:1; 2 Pet 2:1 (cf. 2 Pet 1:20–21); Rev 2:14, 20.
[1769] I. Howard Marshall, 'Orthodoxy and Heresy in Earlier Christianity' in *Themelios*, Sept. 1976, 9. '[T]eaching regarded by [the NT writers] as false was extremely common,' 12.
[1770] Both Lieu (*The Theology of the Johannine, Epistles*, 82–83) and Smalley (*1,2,3 John*, 231), for instance, view the dualism of 1 John in ethical rather than cosmic terms.
[1771] Quoted in Brown, *The Epistles of John*, 506, citing also the second-century *Hermes Man*.11:7: "You shall test [*dokimazein*] the prophet and the false prophet: test by his way of life the man who has the divine Spirit."
[1772] These (to be applied initially to manifestations of spiritual revival in New England) are:
  1. 'When the operation is such as to raise their esteem of that *Jesus* who was born of the Virgin, and was crucified without the gates of Jerusalem' (vv. 2 and 3).

Edwards' fifth 'mark'—'if the spirit that is at work among a people operates as a spirit of *love* to God and man' (vv. 6–21)—underlines 1 John's strong overall 'stress on the need for love in practical ways [as] a flank on [the writer's] opponents.'[1773] It ties in with similar teaching in Paul from which Hays deduces a key 'hermeneutical constraint'[1774] that operates as 'the most powerful check against arbitrariness and error':[1775] 'no reading of Scripture can be legitimate … if it fails to shape the readers into a community that embodies the love of God as shown forth in Christ.'[1776]

Such attempts to synthesize and apply Scriptural teaching regarding interpretive orthodoxy are continually needed, for as Jackman comments, 'the world has never been without all sorts of fantastic religious notions and cults and the truth of God's revelation has always been counterfeited by false prophets.'[1777] In the face of this, the literature of the church, then, witnesses an overall corporate concern for the testing of spirits, as mirrored in the narrower context of the community (or communities) addressed by 1 John.

### b. *The Specific Johannine Perspective*

The fact that 1 John 4 begins with a fatherly, affectionate appeal to 'beloved' (Ἀγαπητοί v.1), also called 'little children' (τεκνία) in v. 4, help to show that 'this section is … conceived as an address to the community.'[1778] Burge further notes that 'throughout 4:1-6 [the] verbs are plural ("together all of you test the spirits"), implying that this spiritual discernment is an obligation of the gathered body and its leadership.'[1779] Stott's talk of 'the right of private judgment'[1780] therefore seems somewhat misplaced here, for as Thompson says, 'we are called as a *corporate community* to *test the spirits*.'[1781] Not that this excludes the need

---

2. 'When the spirit that is at work operates against the interests of *Satan's kingdom*' (vv. 4 and 5).
3. 'The spirit that operates in such a manner, as to cause in men a greater regard to the *Holy Scriptures*, and establishes them more in their truth and divinity' (v. 6).
4. 'It operates as a spirit of *truth*, leading persons to truth and convincing them of those things that are true' (v. 6).
5. 'If the spirit that is at work among a people operates as a spirit of *love* to God and man' (vv. 6–21).

Jonathan Edwards, *The Distinguishing Marks of a Work of the Spirit of God*, 1741 in *The Works of Jonathan Edwards* Vol. 2 (Edinburgh: Banner of Truth Trust, 1974), 266-268, italics added. For an application to a contemporary phenomenon, see Gary Benfold, 'Jonathan Edwards and the "Toronto blessing"' in *Evangelicals Now*, Oct. 1994, 8–9.

[1773] I. Howard Marshall, 'Orthodoxy and Heresy in Earlier Christianity,' 9. On the primacy of the 'love' concept in 1 John, see also I. Howard Marshall, *New Testament Theology* (Downers Grove: IVP, 2004), 538-540.
[1774] Hays, *Echoes of Scripture*, 191.
[1775] Ibid., 191.
[1776] Ibid., 191, along with two other 'hermeneutical constraints': 'no reading of Scripture can be legitimate if it denies the faithfulness of Israel's God to his covenant promises' or 'if it fails to acknowledge the death and resurrection of Jesus as the climactic manifestation of God's righteousness.'
[1777] David Jackman, *The Message of John's Letters* (Leicester: IVP, 1988), 110.
[1778] Strecker, *The Johannine Letters*, 131, noting μὴ … πιστεύετε and δοκιμάζετε in 4:1.
[1779] Burge, *Letters of John*, 179.
[1780] Stott, *Epistles of John*, 153.
[1781] Thompson, *1–3 John* (Leicester: IVP, 1992), 118, italics the author's.

for individual discernment within such a context, nor that it implies a simplistic understanding of the 'communal' perspective, which is variously expressed in 1 John 4. Smalley, for instance, draws attention to the 'interesting alternation in vv. 2–6 between the third person singular (vv. 2*b*, 3, 6*a*), the second and third persons plural (vv. 2*a*, 4, 5), and the first person plural (v. 6*b*).'[1782] The significance of this, as we shall see, seems more than stylistic, constituting a possible example of the multi-directional pointing of the finger of the Spirit, whose leading role in this passage I now explore.

(ii) Pneumatological Context

His 'cue' comes at the end of the previous chapter, the first explicit mention of πνεῦμα regarding the Spirit of God in 1 John: 'by this we know that he abides in us, by the Spirit whom he has given us' (3:24). This follows the command to '*believe* (πιστεύσωμεν) in the name of ... Jesus Christ' (3:23), which is more fully explicated in 4:1–6,[1783] following the corresponding rubric *not to believe* (μὴ ... πιστεύετε) every spirit (v. 1). And so the writer proceeds to define his tests, 'By this you know the Spirit of God' (v. 2a), finishing it with a summary 'by this we know the Spirit of truth and the spirit of error' (4:6). Such a Spirit-encased beginning and ending mark a passage (4:1–6) characterized not only by the notion of πνεῦμα (mentioned seven times[1784]) but also by what some have labelled a 'chiastic' pattern (abc[d]c`b`a`).[1785] Its centrepiece, fittingly, is the triumphal assertion 'you ... have overcome[1786] them, for he who is in you[1787] is greater than he who is in the world' (v. 4). So encompassed and indwelt by the Holy Spirit, the Christian community is thus assured of victory over every deceiving spirit.

Not that this victory is achieved without considerable pneumatologically directed activity. Besides the alternation between the different persons used of

---

[1782] Smalley, *1, 2, 3 John*, 216.

[1783] The second part of the commandment in 3:23 ('love one another') is explicated in 4:7 to 5:4a.

[1784] Twice in v.1, twice in v. 2, once in v. 3, and twice in v. 6, although only τὸ πνεῦμα τοῦ θεοῦ in 4:2 and arguably τὸ πνεῦμα τῆς ἀληθείας in 4:6 refer to the Holy Spirit, the other πνεῦμα references being to what could be described as the 'spirit of man' (Shim, 'The Holy Spirit in 1 John,' 118–119).

[1785] Brown, *The Epistles of John*, 502; Smalley, *1, 2, 3 John*, 216; E.S. Shim, 'The Holy Spirit in 1 John', 119, offers the following chiastic outline:

    A. By this you know the Spirit of God (v. 2a)
        B. the spirit who is of God—confession of Jesus (v. 2bcd)
            C. the spirit not of God—not confession of Jesus (v. 3c)
                D. you who are of God overcome them because of the One in you (v. 4)
            C`. they are of the world—the world listens to them (v. 5)
        B`. we are of God—the one who knows God listens to us 9 (v. 6abc)
    A`. By this we know the spirit of truth (6d).

[1786] L. Morris notes that 'this short letter has the verb 'to overcome' six times ... more than any other NT book other than Revelation ... the perfect tense [showing] that the victory is more than a passing phrase; it is decisive and continuing.' '1 John' in D. A. Carson et al, eds., *New Bible Commentary 21st Century Edition* (Leicester: IVP, 1994), 1406.

[1787] Assuming this refers to the Holy Spirit—see comment on this in later exegesis of the verse.

the verbs mentioned above, note also the variety of actual verbs used in the passage: 'do not believe', 'test' (v. 1), 'know' (vv. 2, 6), 'confess' (vv. 2, 3), 'overcome' (v. 4), 'speak' (vv. 5, 6), 'listen' (v. 5, 6). These belong to the vocabulary of spiritual discernment. In the process, several contrasts are also made: of God/not of God; of God/of the world; you/they; we or us/they or them; false prophets/little children; speak/listen; Spirit of truth/error.

Besides being typical examples of Johannine antitheses, these polarities can also be read as illustrations of the *dialogical* workings of the Spirit. If placed alongside the *trinitarian* operations ('know the Spirit of God ... confesses ... Jesus Christ ... from God') and *historical* perspective ('has come in the flesh') of v. 2, as well as the *eschatological* note of v. 3d ('in the world already', cf. 'last hour' 2:18), one can detect the same fourfold patterning of the Spirit's κοινωνία that has been highlighted in previous chapters.

### (b) The Christological (4: 1–3) and 'Hearing' (4: 4–6) Tests

As I turn to a more detailed exegesis of the passage, the links with and progression from 2:18–27 need to be noted. Besides the evident pneumatological connection, the description of 'antichrists' (2:18) who 'went out' (ἐξῆλθαν) in 2:19 parallels 'the false prophets [who] have gone out (ἐξεληλύθασιν) into the world' in 4:1—'like Christian missionaries (2 John 7).'[1788] The potential danger of their influence is underlined by the essential orality of the first-century culture, when, in the days before the establishment of the New Testament canon and formal creeds, the church often relied on travelling emissaries, initially sent out by John, Paul[1789] or the other apostles, to communicate between one Christian community and another. This made the groups of believers, who often 'met in houses in groups of about twenty to thirty people,'[1790] vulnerable to intrusion by non-accountable itinerants with less worthy credentials, a problem that is greatly exaggerated in the global internet/television culture of today.

In the face of the 'false prophets' (ψευδοπροφῆται, v. 1) troubling the Johannine community in the Asia Minor of the first century with their erroneous teaching, maybe of an incipient Gnostic/docetic kind, the Johannine 'tests' ('field marks'[1791]), though not comprehensive,[1792] were doubtless sufficient for the situation being addressed then and at many other times in Christian history. They boil down to two: the christological (theological) in vv. 1–3 and 'hearing'

---

[1788] Marshall, *The Epistles of John*, 204. Other links between 2:18–27 and 4:1–6 include the nature of christological confession and lying/deceit.
[1789] See 3 John 3–8 for a Johannine example, and 1 Cor 4:17 and Phil 2:19 for Pauline examples.
[1790] Thompson, *1–3 John*, 112.
[1791] Ibid., 111, using an ornithological analogy.
[1792] Howard Marshall says that 'the tests in 1 John, though they are an advance on 1 Cor 12, are not infallible.... There is a trajectory here that entitles us to establish even more stringent tests. The later development of creeds and systematic theology is a continuation of this process that can never come to an end ... for ... one cannot make a body of doctrine heresy-proof, because heretics are so ingenious,' I. Howard Marshall, *Beyond the Bible: Moving from Scripture to Theology* (Grand Rapids: Baker, 2004), 72.

(practical) tests in vv. 4–6, both in the Johannine argument, requiring a pneumatological functioning.

(i) Christological (vv. 1–3)

Central to all Christian orthodoxy is the question of christology, which here is approached from three angles:

a. *Pneumatological Derivation* (v. 1)

The fact that the false prophets are initially described in v. 1 as πνεύματα ('spirits') follows the reference to πνεῦμα in 3:24 and suggests that they were claiming 'Spirit' authority for their teaching. It also coheres with the Johannine notion[1793] that 'behind every prophet is a spirit, and behind each spirit either God or the devil.'[1794] The importance of origin comes out in the significant formula εἶναι ἐκ ('to be from', with τοῦ θεοῦ ('God') in vv. 1, 2, 3, 4, 6, and with τοῦ κόσμου ('of the world') [twice] in v. 5), which, as Smalley points out, expresses notions of 'origin and ... essence ... is characteristically Johannine ... and often occurs in antithetical statements contrasting what is of divine derivation with what is not.'[1795] Hence the vital importance of 'testing' the Spirits: 'put these Spirits to a test to see which belongs to God.'[1796] The use of δοκιμάζειν ('to test, tempt, experiment with,'[1797] 'examine'[1798]), is the only Johannine example of the use of a verb that is mostly found in Paul.[1799] The present, plural imperative employed here (δοκιμάζετε) implies the need for continuous, perpetual testing, in view of there being πολλοί ψευδοπροφῆται ('*many* false prophets)'. Their description as 'false prophets' rather than 'false teachers' suggests they were claiming some sort of link with the Old Testament prophetic community that had helped them to attain a following. Such 'prophets' therefore stood ever in need of being tested, not only by the Johannine community but also, by applicatory extension, by the Christian community as a whole as an ongoing exercise.

---

[1793] Cf. 1 John 3:10; 4:4; 5:19.

[1794] Stott, *Epistles of John*, 153. Smalley, *1, 2, 3 John*, 218, speaks of 'a possible background in Qumran to the idea, present throughout this section, of two contrasting "spirits" (the spirit of truth and the spirit of falsehood, corresponding to the two spheres of light and darkness; cf.1 QS 3:18; 4:23).'

[1795] Smalley, *1, 2, 3 John*, 218, citing also 2:21; 3:19; 4:5 and John 3:31.

[1796] Brown, *The Epistles of John*, 485. He contrasts this testing of (good or evil) spirits, a Spirit-enabled gift of every Christian in 1 John, with the discernment of (good) spirits in 1 Cor 12:10, a 'charism ... given only to some' (503–504).

[1797] Brown, ibid., 488, also paralleling the notion of 'testing the spirits' with Deut 13 and 18 and Qumran.

[1798] Smalley, *1, 2, 3 John*, 218.

[1799] δοκιμάζειν is used in Rom 2:18; 1 Cor 3:13, 11:28; Eph 5:10; 1 Thess 5:21, and twenty-two times in the New Testament as a whole.

b. *Incarnational Confession* (vv. 2–3)

'By this' (ἐν τούτῳ) anticipates the way in which the Johannine community was to 'know'/ 'recognize' (γινώσκετε[1800]) the 'Spirit of God' (τὸ πνεῦμα τοῦ θεοῦ—unique in the Johannine literature[1801]). It was to publicly confess, in worship and witness, 'Jesus Christ', ὁμολογεῖν ('to acknowledge, confess') signifying 'both a recognition of his true identity ... and an open proclamation of faith in him,'[1802] or to use Edwards' warmer terminology, 'declaring [him] with manifestation of esteem and affection.'[1803] The precise significance of the confession, that 'Jesus Christ has come in the flesh' (Ἰησοῦν Χριστὸν ἐν σαρκὶ ἐληλυθότα) is debated.[1804] It seems clear, however, that against the background of those who in some way challenged the incarnation, John was using traditional terminology[1805] to reassert the reality of Jesus' humanity—'his career in the flesh.'[1806] Bound up with such a confession would be further assumptions concerning his divinity and pre-existence, as well as the efficacy of the atonement and the continuing significance of the incarnation, arising from the perfect tense of ἐληλυθότα ('has come').

As opposed to the fuller doctrinal content of the confession in v. 2, it is interesting that v. 3, in reiterating the confession, simply states 'does not confess Jesus.'[1807] For Marshall, this 'abbreviated form ... indicates that *personal allegiance to Jesus* is what is at stake.'[1808] Indeed Thomas emphasizes that the confession required in both verses 2 and 3 'is not simply a doctrinal confession' but one that is generated by the Spirit of God 'in the believer as a result of and growing out of one's experiential relationship to Jesus in the various dimensions of his person' and work.[1809] Failure to make such an acknowledgement of Jesus, then, both in terms of a creed and a personal relationship, is severely censured as 'the spirit of antichrist' (τὸ τοῦ ἀντιχρίστου, v. 3).[1810] Burge notes that 'in all five uses of "antichrist" in the Johannine letters, such a denial of Jesus Christ is

---

[1800] An indicative rather than an imperative, Brown, *The Epistles of John*, 491, implying that 'John is appealing to his orthodox readers' knowledge and experience here ... rather than issuing a new command,' Smalley, *1, 2, 3 John*, 220.

[1801] Brown points out that 'the epistles never speak of "the Holy Spirit"': Brown, *The Epistles of John*, 491.

[1802] Smalley, *1, 2, 3 John*, 221, referring also to John 20:29.

[1803] Jonathan Edwards, *Distinguishing Marks of a Work of the Spirit of God*, 266, also citing Matt 10:32; Rom 15:9; Phil 2:11; 1 John 5:1 and 1 Cor 12:3.

[1804] See Thompson, *1–3 John*, 113, fn. on 4:2; Smalley, *1, 2, 3 John*, 222–223 and Brown, *The Epistles of John*, 492–493.

[1805] Cf. John 1:14; 6:51–55.

[1806] Brown, *The Epistles of John*, 493.

[1807] The insertion of 'is come in the flesh' into v. 3 (AV), is now considered to be a later scribal addition.

[1808] Marshall, *Epistles of John*, 206, italics added.

[1809] Thomas, 'The Johannine Epistles', 253, referring the confession as a 'shorthand for a whole matrix of beliefs about and experiences with Jesus', including those described in 1:3, 1:7, 2:1, 2:2, 2:6, 2:12, 2:14, 2:28–29, 3:2–3, 3:5–6 and 3:7.

[1810] Some commentators think the omission of 'spirit' (πνεῦμα) here is deliberate, to avoid any comparison which might suggest equality between the Spirit of God and the spirit of antichrist.

the antichrist's principal interest.'[1811] An ancient variant reading—'every spirit that annuls (λύει) Jesus is not from God'—may be the result of a 'sharpening of the text of 1 John for controversy,'[1812] perhaps in the face of subsequent Gnostic debate, but this reading is not followed by most Bible translations.[1813]

This christological concentration that predominates the Johannine 'testing of the spirits' is consistent with the New Testament's emphasis that the Spirit's work is to glorify Christ.[1814] It also highlights a fundamental priority that must not be lost amongst the many things that can distract the church from its main task of 'confessing' Jesus Christ. Burge says of 4:1–6 generally, using the imagery of modern technology:

> The Johannine call here is to build a Christian maturity that can use theological radar to spot intruders who want to upend the church's beliefs. This is a high-tech radar that can tell the difference between pleasure aircraft and lethal bombers, between minor issues and colossal errors that deserve a fierce struggle.[1815]

c. *Eschatological Imminence* (v. 3d)

John was certainly aware of such a 'fierce struggle', as the dramatic ending to v. 3 makes clear with its reference to the 'spirit of antichrist' not only 'coming', but 'now in the world *already*' (ἤδη, emphatically placed at the end). As observed in 2:18, 'antichrist' is associated in Johannine thinking with 'the last hour'. The note of eschatological imminence/realization is underlined by Strecker.

> In contrast to the idea of history as a linear time sequence, the end has already become a dangerous present in the persons of the false teachers. The dialectic of "already-not yet," which also marks the appearance of the Revealer in the Fourth Gospel, can thus be experienced in negative form within the life of the community. The apocalyptic phenomenon of the antichrist has become a historical fact through the appearance of the false prophets.[1816]

This, then, adds a 'crisis' dynamic to the community imperative to test the spirits.

(ii) The 'Hearing' Test (vv. 4–6)

Lest the community be overwhelmed by such a task, v. 4 comes as a much-needed assurance. This is initiated by the opening plural ὑμεῖς ('now as for you'),

---

[1811] Burge, *Letters of John*, 175, citing 1 John 2:18–22; 4:3 and 2 John 7.
[1812] Marshall, *The Epistles of John*, 208, fn. 11.
[1813] Though favored by Brown who translates it 'everyone who negates the importance of Jesus reflects a Spirit which does not belong to God,' Brown, *The Epistles of John*, 494–496.
[1814] John 15:26; 16:13–15; 1 Cor 12:1–3.
[1815] Burge, *Letters of John*, 179.
[1816] Strecker, *The Johannine Letters*, 136, citing John 4:23; 5:25; 12:31; 13:31.

an 'emphatic pronoun [which] separates the readers from the false teachers,'[1817] as followed by the ἐκ τοῦ θεοῦ (εἶναι) ('of God') construction noted above, which reinforces the distinctiveness of their divine origin and belonging. This verse has already been commented upon in terms of its central place within both the chiastic and pneumatological framework of vv. 1–6. In view of this, the 'he who is in you' (ὁ ἐν ὑμῖν) would seem to be a clear reference to the Holy Spirit.[1818] Through him, the community is assured of a decisive and continuing victory (note νενικήκατε [perfect tense], 'have overcome') over the power of 'he who is in the world', an expression which parallels 'the spirit of antichrist' in v. 3 and 'the spirit of error' in v. 6. To quote F. F. Bruce, the community's 'built-in spiritual instinct'[1819] (cf. 2:20; 3:24) gave them the knowledge to define and resist error. 'John's readers were not more learned, more skilled in philosophical debate, than the false teachers; yet by refusing to be persuaded by the false teachers they had overcome them.'[1820]

From such a reassurance, the Johannine author proceeds to enunciate the second of the two tests given for the discernment of spirits. Having first spoken of the character of Christ (vv. 2–3), he now speaks of the character of the audience that is willing to listen to the Christian message through the community (vv. 5–6), and in so doing moves from a theological to an empirical approach. This consists of sharply contrasting two audiences, the world and the church, both in their speaking and in their listening.

a. *The World's Closed Mind* (v. 5)

The nominative plural αὐτοί ('They' v. 5a)[1821] sets the heretical community against the ὑμεῖς ('you', v. 4a) and ἡμεῖς ('we', v. 6a) of the Christian community. What distinguishes the heretical community is its origin from and allegiance to 'the world' (ἐκ τοῦ κόσμου), described graphically in 2:15–17 and succinctly by Marshall: 'both mankind united in opposition to God and the evil characteristic of such people.'[1822] The repetitive beating out of κόσμος ('world') in 2:15–17 (six times) and here in 4:3–5 (five times)[1823] symbolizes the rut into which the world has put itself, for ever 'speaking' and 'listening' to itself (4:5). This was the closed system inhabited by the heretics who, like all worldly speakers, received a ready hearing from those who were also of 'the world', since '*akouein*, "to hear", with the genitive, implies audition with acceptance.'[1824] This, then, suggests that the

---

[1817] Brooke, *The Johannine Epistles*, 115.
[1818] Although some see a reference to 'God', or 'God in Christ', or even 'an allusion to God as Father, Son *and* Spirit', Smalley, *1,2, 3 John*, 227.
[1819] Bruce, *The Epistles of John*, 106.
[1820] Ibid., 106.
[1821] 'Found only here in the Johannine letters,' Smalley, *1,2, 3 John*, 228.
[1822] Marshall, *The Epistles of John*, 209.
[1823] Twenty-four times in the Johannine letters.
[1824] Brown, *The Epistles of John*, 498, cf. Brooke, *The Johannine Epistles*, 114: 'like associates with like.' Also cf. John 3:31.

false teachers in John's day had indeed met with some success, though not in any great measure with the faithful community addressed by this letter, as the next verse confirms.

### b. *The Christian Community's Open Ear* (v. 6)

In contrast to the world's deafness to God, the church *does* listen to him—through the Christian community—because it belongs to him: 'we are from God' (ἡμεῖς ἐκ τοῦ θεοῦ ἐσμεν, v. 6a). Whether this ἡμεῖς is an exclusive 'we', i.e. referring to the apostles and their authorized teachers, or a more inclusive one that refers to the author and his readers, is debated.[1825] But even if the initial reference was to the message brought by the apostles and their delegates, the application is surely not limited to them or the Johannine community,[1826] but extends to the Christian community as a whole, which has an ongoing mandate both to listen to and to speak out the word of God.

The divine origin of the message is only recognized by 'whoever knows God' (v.6b), the present tense of ὁ γινώσκων suggesting 'a relationship with God which is continuous and growing.'[1827] Those who are so walking with him have a spiritual affinity with all others so doing, especially in the perception of the word. 'My sheep hear my voice', said Jesus,[1828] and the common recognition of the same evokes a harmony of correspondence[1829] between preachers, message, and hearers which, in the argument of 1 John 4:1–6, is inspired by the Spirit. On the other hand, 'whoever is not from God does not listen to us', a fact to which all open-air preachers and indeed all Christian witnesses can readily testify.

This sharp contrast between those who listen to and those who do not listen to God through his people is the marker by which to discern the spirits: 'by this we know (γινώσκομεν "we can distinguish"[1830]) the Spirit of truth and the spirit of error.'[1831] Smalley points out that τὸ πνεῦμα τῆς ἀληθείας ('the Spirit of truth') could be a reference to a person inspired by the Spirit rather than a reference to the Spirit himself.[1832] However, the identical expression ('the Spirit of truth'[1833]) in John 14:17, 15:26 and 16:13 makes an allusion to the Holy Spirit more probable. He stands over against the 'spirit of error/falsehood/deceit/deception', translating τὸ πνεῦμα τῆς πλάνης, an expression found only here in the New

---

[1825] See Brown, *The Epistles of John*, 498–499, 509–510; Smalley, *1, 2, 3 John*, 229; Strecker, *The Johannine Letters*, 139 and fn. 57.
[1826] *Contra* Brown, *The Epistles of John*, 509–510.
[1827] Smalley, *1, 2, 3 John*, 229.
[1828] John 10:27. Note also John 10:4, 5, 16 and 26.
[1829] Burge, *Letters of John*, 176.
[1830] Smalley, *1,2,3 John*, 230.
[1831] Assuming that the referent of ἐκ τούτου is v. 5 (Strecker, *The Johannine Letters*, 139–140), rather than 3:24c (Brown, *The Epistles of John*, 500).
[1832] Smalley, *1,2,3 John*, 230.
[1833] i.e. τὸ πνεῦμα τῆς ἀληθείας.

Testament. Commentators, however, point out parallels[1834] with 'the spirit of truth and falsehood' found in Qumran literature,[1835] although, as Smalley claims, 'John's dualism at this point is ethical, and not cosmological or thoroughgoing; for the victory is ultimately God's (v. 4).'[1836] He also links γινώσκομεν ('we know') with the 'all' of 2:20 and concludes that 'the ability to distinguish between truth and falsehood (v. 6) are gifts which belong to *any* genuine child of God, as well as to the orthodox community as a whole.'[1837]

True as this may be, the main emphasis of the passage seems to be upon the latter corporate aspect, as argued from the communal nature of the subjects and verbs employed in the section. As Lieu says, 'the testing of statements of faith in the light of tradition and experience is the task and responsibility of the whole community of faith.'[1838]

## Conclusion to the Chapter

I have sought to show how 1 John, as one of the later New Testament writings, demonstrates a vital hermeneutical connection between Spirit and community in the defence and custodianship of the apostolic tradition, which, for us as Christians is now enshrined in Scripture. The proclamation of 'that which was from the beginning' (1:1) emanates in a 'striking'[1839] spirit of κοινωνία (1:3) which permeates an epistle that assures the whole Johannine community of its common anointing (χρῖσμα) with the Spirit. The faculty of spiritual discernment is thus assured to all Christians, both individually and particularly collectively as they 'abide' in the original message and together 'abide in the Son and in the Father' (2:24), 'by the Spirit whom he has given us' (3:24). The Spirit's vital role, even if expressed in the less explicit terms of χρῖσμα ('anointing', 2:20, 27) and σπέρμα ('seed', 3:9), is portrayed 'primarily as a testimony to tradition, not as a source of new revelation.'[1840] In the face of 'tendencies which were more comfortable with Jesus' divinity than with his full participation in our common humanity,'[1841] this required a strong restatement of the incarnational nature of ὁ Χριστός ('the Christ'). Such theological testing for orthodoxy was to be supplemented by more practical tests concerning 'listening' (4:5-6), and 'loving' (4:7-21.).

---

[1834] As well as in 4:1–6 generally.
[1835] And Jewish intertestamental literature generally. See Smalley, *1,2,3 John*, 231; Kruse, *The Letters of John*, 150, referring to 1QS 3:18–19, 25; Strecker, *The Johannine Letters*, 140–141.
[1836] Smalley, *1,2,3 John*, 231.
[1837] Ibid., 230.
[1838] Lieu, *The Theology of the Johannine Epistles*, 117.
[1839] R. Edwards, *The Johannine Epistles*, 71.
[1840] Colin G. Kruse, *The Letters of John*, 155. Cf. Burge: 'in the Johannine hermeneutic the conservative, preserving emphasis had won out. Anamnesis had overtaken inspiration and no longer worked along with it,' Burge, *Anointed Community*, 220.
[1841] Lieu, *The Theology of the Johannine Epistles*, 116.

This command to 'test the spirits,' whilst incumbent upon every Christian, is an essentially corporate responsibility. As Burge concludes from 4:1–6, 'the *church* is the custodian of the truth, and my impulse to critique, to analyze, or to judge must be worked out in the community of the church's leadership.... This calls for a humility and courage that is willing to submit to the corporate voice while still retaining its passion and vision.'[1842] Unlike the Pastoral epistles, the ecclesiastical offices and structures for this exercise of discerning and upholding 'truth' are not elaborated upon in 1 John,[1843] although it is evident that the two fundamental 'christological' and 'hearing' Johannine tests are always to be worked out within the parameters of the 'pneumatic community'. And in the face of ever continuing heretical threats, this community has often had to devise other critical 'tests' and countering theologies, with the help of the same Holy Spirit who inspired the critical evaluations of 1 John.

---

[1842] Burge, *The Letters of John*, 180.
[1843] See C. Kruse's 'Note on the Teaching Authority of the Church,' in *The Letters of John*, 111–112. He concludes that in 1 John, 'the connection is not between the Holy Spirit and the teachers of the church but between the Holy Spirit and the gospel message as it was heard from the beginning,' 111–112. See also Lieu, *The Theology of the Johannine Epistles*, 109–110 regarding 'authority within the community.'

# CHAPTER EIGHT: READING SCRIPTURE IN THE FELLOWSHIP OF THE SPIRIT

## Implications of a Spirit through Community Hermeneutic

Following the outpouring of the Holy Spirit as recorded in Acts 2, we are told that that the early Christians 'continued steadfastly in the apostles' teaching and fellowship' (ἦσαν δὲ προσκαρτεροῦντες τῇ διδαχῇ τῶν ἀποστόλων καὶ τῇ κοινωνίᾳ) (Acts 2:42, RV). How are we to guard, interpret and apply the message of Scripture today, in the fellowship of the Holy Spirit? In this last chapter, I will first summarise the arguments of our chapters before spelling out some of their implications in terms of the hermeneutical task and the doctrine, use and custodianship of Scripture.

## Summary of Chapters

**Part I** of this book, entitled *'Pneumatology, Hermeneutics and Koinonia,'* explored the corporate dimensions of biblical interpretation opened by the Spirit in the face of historical and contemporary individualism.

In **chapter 1,** I argued that the *role assigned to the Holy Spirit in biblical interpretation* in traditional thought has too often excluded a corporate perspective and in modern hermeneutics has often been marginalized. Having giving some definitions of terms, I then highlighted some trends to individualism in biblical interpretation and outlined the case for a more corporate approach, along with some potential dangers, such as 'community absolutism' and the erosion of textual autonomy.

In **chapter 2,** I argued that the Pauline concept of the *'koinonia of the Spirit'* (2 Cor 13:14) opened wide vistas for the interpretive process. Sourced as it should be from the perichoretic life of the Trinity, Spirit-led interpretation draws, first, upon the dynamic of *Trinitarian* relationship. This 'upward' focus also has its 'horizontal' dimension as it is pursued in κοινωνία with Christians in like fellowship. Secondly, when this fellowship is absent or broken, the 'downward' movement of the Spirit, in conviction and judgment, can ultimately result in new forms of Scriptural understanding, as the Spirit works in *dialogical* encounter. Thirdly, biblical interpretation must be pursued *historically*, in conjunction with the insights of saints of the past. This 'backward' link is enabled by the Spirit of 'remembrance,' whose help is also needed for the revivifying of tradition. Fourthly, the provisionality and partiality of understanding is highlighted by the *eschatological* nature of the Spirit, which, whilst underlining present fulfilment in Christ, points 'forwards' to the fullness of understanding and fellowship in glory.

In **chapter 3**, I investigated whether *the Old Testament's use in the New Testament* could be considered under the rubric of a 'Spirit through community' hermeneutic. I argued that contemporary Jewish conceptions of the Spirit as 'the Spirit of prophecy', linked with 'corporate solidarity' notions, would have shaped the interpretive endeavours of the New Testament writers. Their commonality of approach was further suggested by Dodd's *testimonia* thesis that highlighted textual fields whose choice could be traced back to Christ, the one 'full of the Holy Spirit' (Luke 4:1). Jesus modelled and taught his disciples Spirit-inspired exegesis of Scripture in a unique way that both embraced and challenged contemporary Jewish methods. His legacy of the Holy Spirit enabled the New Testament community to make advances in the interpretation of Scripture. Their methods could be further understood by an appreciation of their common interpretive presuppositions. These included charismatic exegesis, corporate solidarity, typology and correspondences in history, eschatological fulfilment, and Christocentricity. 'Intertextual' analysis by scholars such as Hays also demonstrated an 'ecclesiocentric' hermeneutic highlighting the Spirit's role in the interpreting community. The perpetual tension between the *historical contingency* of the New Testament writers' use of Scripture, subject as they were to contemporary exegetical approaches, and the *enduring relevance* of their methods, driven as they were by a common Spirit-led hermeneutic that was taught by and pointed to Christ, provides a continual challenge to contemporary interpreters.

In **Part II** of this book, '*The Pneumatological Hermeneutics of the New Testament Community*', I embarked on a more exegetically-based study of certain New Testament passages that give evidence as to how the Spirit is seen to be guiding the community in its interpretation of Scripture, either explicitly or implicitly. I took sample passages from three different New Testament corpora, namely the *Johannine writings, Luke/Acts and Paul.*

In **chapter 4,** I looked at Jesus's *Promise of the Paraclete* in John 14–16, highlighting his role as 'advocate' and as 'the Spirit of truth', teaching and leading the church in truth which for Christians is now enshrined in Scripture. I outlined four different corporate dimensions that explicated the Paraclete's hermeneutical functions: first, a historical and didactical dimension (14:25–26) that brings out the meaning of Jesus's original teaching for the subsequent church, for which an ethical conditioning is required by the *Holy* Spirit; secondly, a dialectical and convictional dimension (15:26–27; 16:7–11) that links Paraclete and church as they cooperate together in confronting the world in witness and judgment; thirdly, an eschatological and interpretive dimension (16:12–15) in which the church is for ever being guided into all truth on its journey to the *eschaton*, whilst also guarding against claims of 'new revelation' that deny the sufficiency of the Jesus revelation; and fourthly, a Trinitarian and exegetical dimension (14:16; 16:13–15 and previous verses) in which all that the church shares and communicates is to be a reflection of the fellowship of the Trinity in which Christians are ever to abide.

In **chapter 5**, '*Acts, Spirit and Hermeneutics in the first Christian Community*', my selection of passages sought to demonstrate how the interrelationship between the Spirit, the Scriptures and the Christian community provided a vital hermeneutic in the primitive church. Even before Pentecost, Acts 1 revealed the importance of the Christian community's deliberation, under God, around Scripture, albeit expounded through Peter. His Pentecost sermon in Acts 2 was presented in terms of his representing the apostolic group, with a 'this is that' message that was rooted in Old Testament Scripture and which encapsulated the *kerygma* of the early church. His scriptural interpretation was influenced partly by Jewish midrash, determinatively by Jesus's own exegesis and embodiment, and decisively by the experience of Pentecostal Spirit, both by himself and in the Christian community. These three key interpretive factors could also be seen in Stephen's polemical address before the Sanhedrin in Acts 7, and thus revealed a hermeneutic that was not 'individualistic' but one that was inspired by the κοινωνία operations of the Spirit, whose characteristics (Trinitarian, dialogical, eschatological, and historical) could be detected in both Peter's and Stephen's Old Testament expositions. A more obviously communal dimension to biblical interpretation was displayed in Acts 4:23–31 in the context of a believers' prayer meeting that used Scripture to create a link with both current events and the cause of the Lord's anointed down the ages. The implied link with the Spirit in Acts 4 became more explicit in Acts 15 in relation to the proceedings of the Council of Jerusalem, which, besides some key apostolic contributions, demonstrated several corporate interpretive factors at work, epitomized in 'it has seemed good to the Holy Spirit and to us' in 15:28. The combination of Scripture and the κοινωνία of the Spirit in the early Christian community resulted in an interpretive dynamic that truly speeded the mission of the church.

In **chapter 6**, I turned from the narrative structure of Acts to the more conceptual approach of Paul in investigating '*Spirit, Community and Hermeneutics in Paul*'. I argued that some of the rich pneumatological and corporate emphases in his interpretive methodology derived from his Jewish background, with its emphasis upon 'the Spirit of prophecy' and Old Testament notions of corporateness, whilst other pneumatic components came from the Jesus encounter and tradition. Factors that determined Paul's use of the Old Testament as a source of authority included the interpretive conventions of his Jewish heritage, as shaped by his Christian convictions, Spirit dependence, and ecclesial concerns.

I then investigated four sample passages, using intertextual and other interpretive tools, to explore the corporate and pneumatological dynamics of his interpretive methodology. In 1 Cor 2, I highlighted the role of the Spirit of *understanding* by whom 'God has revealed [these things] *to us*' (v. 10), the Christian community, as opposed to the incomprehensibility of the non-Christian community. In 2 Cor 3, I noted the contrast between hardened Old Testament Israel and the repenting, liberated New Testament community as it enjoyed the Spirit of *glory* by whom '*we all*, with unveiled face, behold the glory of the Lord' (v. 18), a contemplation that should lead to transformation. In Rom 8, the Spirit of *sonship* by whom we can utter 'Abba, Father' evoked a family context for hermeneutics, again with Old Testament parallels concerning obedience and pilgrimage. The use of communal material and flexible terminology in the Pastoral Epistles reveal a lively pneumatically-driven hermeneutic that illustrates how the *tradition* of the 'good deposit'[1844] is to be guarded and expressed by the 'household of God,'[1845] a common Christian duty for which church leaders nevertheless have special responsibilities. In our exegesis of these New Testament passages, we noted the Trinitarian, historical, eschatological, dialogical, and other characteristics that illustrate the communal dimensions of Paul's multi-faceted, pneumatically-driven hermeneutic at work, alongside their ongoing implications for the Christian interpretive community.

Finally, **chapter 7**, marked a return to our Johannine starting point as I looked at '*Spirit and Hermeneutics in the Johannine Community*' as expressed in 1 John, which, as one of the later New Testament writings, arguably develops the παράκλητος promises of John 14–16, and is steeped in κοινωνία. The connection between this fellowship and the work of the Spirit in the preservation of the apostolic tradition was shown to be a vital hermeneutic for the Johannine community. Its common anointing (χρῖσμα) with the Spirit indicates that the faculty of spiritual discernment is available to all Christians, both individually and particularly collectively as they 'abide' in what they 'heard from the beginning ... and abide in the Son and in the Father' (2:24) ... 'by the Spirit' (3:24). The Spirit's role is portrayed 'primarily as a testimony to tradition, not as a source of new revelation.'[1846] In the context of 1 John, this required a strong restatement of the incarnational nature of ὁ Χριστός, although other tests for orthodoxy are found in both the Old Testament and New Testament, as well as in the history of the church as it relies on the Spirit's ongoing help to counter ongoing heresies. The command to 'test the spirits,' whilst incumbent upon every Christian, is an essentially corporate responsibility.

## Some Implications of a 'Spirit Through Community' Hermeneutic

In light of all this, what, then, are the implications of a hermeneutic that focuses upon the Spirit's guidance of the community as custodian and interpreter of Scripture? I have sought to spell these out throughout this book. Here I will elaborate upon four: the hermeneutical task, and the doctrine, use and custodianship of Scripture.

---

[1844] 2 Tim 1:14.
[1845] 1 Tim 3:15.
[1846] C. G. Kruse, *The Letters of John* (Leicester: Apollos, 2000), 155.

## For the Hermeneutical Task

Our sampling from three New Testament corpora revealed a hermeneutic rich in corporate and pneumatological emphases, commonly including, *inter alia*, Trinitarian, historical, dialogical, and eschatological dimensions. Not that this commonality represents uniformity, for different perspectives are afforded by different genres, whether that be the dualistic/dialectical patterning of Johannine literature, the conceptualisations of the Pauline epistles or the narrative framework of Luke–Acts. Despite these distinctives, it is evident that the New Testament writers read Scripture not in an individualistic way but as part of a wider community, as illustrated by their frequent use of the Scriptures of Israel, often sharing a preference for similar Old Testament selections. For them, then, the interpretive community was primarily a Jewish one, which in large part determined their presuppositions and practices, as transformed by the Christocentric and pneumatological imperatives of their newly acquired Christian heritage.

The New Testament was, of course, written against a background of the larger Greco-Roman civilisation whose philosophies had an important influence upon biblical interpretation, especially in the early Christian centuries. Today, we read the ancient Scriptures with two millennia of scriptural interpretations behind us, and many different communities, traditions and historical events affecting the way we understand Scripture. What, then, is involved in a 'Spirit through community' reading of Scripture today? I would argue that it is a case of rightfully balancing the influence of 'the one and the many'[1847] communities from whose perspective we understand the Bible, along with the vital superintendence of the Holy Spirit—not forgetting either the role of individual inspiration. As Lints, discussing the responsibilities of biblical interpreters in light of what he calls the contemporary 'turn to community,'[1848] says, 'living with the dialectic between unity and diversity and between communities and individuals requires the wisdom of the gospel.'[1849] Let us, then, explore briefly the basic components of a biblical hermeneutic that seeks to work out such a dialectic—as a reflection, maybe, of Paul's 'different kinds of gifts, but the same Spirit' (1 Cor 12:4).

---

[1847] Richard Lints sees analogies for balancing 'the one and the many'—unity and diversity—in the Trinity (three persons and one being), the Scripture (a single story with many episodes), and the church (one body, many members). Richard Lints, 'To Whom Does the Text Belong? Communities of Interpretation and the Interpretation of Communities,' in D. A. Carson, ed., *The Enduring Authority of The Christian Scriptures* (Apollos, London, 2016), 925–931.
[1848] Following what he calls 'the turn to the subject in the era of the Enlightenment' and 'the turn to language in early-twentieth-century philosophical circles': Lints, 'To Whom Does the Text Belong?' in Carson, *Enduring Authority*, 921.
[1849] Lints, 'To Whom Does the Text Belong?' in Carson, *Enduring Authority*, 920.

## (i) Diverse Communities

Taken, then, that we need to read Scripture with a critical, Spirit-assisted, and gospel-informed awareness of the interpretive communities of which we are necessarily a part, what sort of communities are we thinking about? In 'The Corporateness of Scriptural Interpretation,'[1850] John Goldingay enumerates five such communities, construed in the broader sense of that word. I shall provide some brief evaluative comments thereon, alongside those of Goldingay. The *Confessional Community*, first, reminds us that Scripture was originally written to and read by faith-communities, and therefore is to be understood with an appreciation of such a communal consciousness, rather than a purely individual existential self-awareness. As Goldingay says, 'the Bible was written for believing communities, not critics'.[1851] Nevertheless, there is, secondly, a role for the *Academic Community* which, over against the committed/confessional stance of the church, is in the position of being more 'distanced from the text.'[1852] It can thus provide critiques of dogmatic traditions, checks on misreadings as well as distinctive insights of its own, albeit sometimes propounding what Carson calls 'a hermeneutic of mistrust'.[1853] Goldingay also acknowledges that the readings of both confessional and academic communities can be adversely affected by vested interests, but they ought to 'complement each other even insofar as they stand in tension with each other.'[1854] Thirdly, reading the text from within *Society*, says Goldingay, provides a context for understanding that also takes into account the reality of the human situation and changing cultural conditions and norms. Such 'norms', we would have to say, might well be unbiblical and need confronting as part of the Holy Spirit's own critique of 'the world' (John 16:8). The standpoint of *the universal church*, fourthly, opens up a vast array of other perspectives, as Goldingay explains: 'interpretation is an inherently catholic enterprise. The whole church needs the ways into Scripture that the church's different parts can offer us: the Fathers and the Puritans, liberation theology and Western theology, the suburban church and the urban church, women and men, Jews and Christians.'[1855] Such critical engagement with traditions other than our own helps us avoid 'seeing our own face at the bottom of the hermeneutical well.'[1856] Fifthly, the *Universal human context* constitutes a final overarching 'community'. Despite the great gulf that separates the biblical

---

[1850] John Goldingay, *Models for Interpretation of Scripture* (Carlisle: Paternoster, 1995), 233–250.
[1851] Goldingay, *Models for Interpreting Scripture*, 235.
[1852] Goldingay, *Models for Interpreting Scripture*, 236–237.
[1853] D. A. Carson, 'The Many Facets of the Current Discussion' in Carson, *Enduring Authority*, 5, where the expression is being used of the kind of biblical hermeneutic taught by liberal scholars from German universities to many German pastors.
[1854] Goldingay, *Models for Interpreting Scripture*, 238. As Pietro Bolognesi has asserted, 'A theology that cannot be road tested on the church pews is of little value. Many of the issues dealt with by theologians are distant light years from the ecclesiastical life': Pietro Bolognesi, 'Is There An Evangelical Vision? Reflections from an Italian Perspective,' *European Journal of Theology* (2004) 13:2, 106. He pleads for a theology that is 'confessing', 'communal', and 'concrete.'
[1855] Goldingay, *Models for Interpreting Scripture*, 242.
[1856] Goldingay, *Models for Interpreting Scripture*, 247.

world from ours, from an anthropological viewpoint 'the links between cultures are often stronger than we imagine.'[1857] Thus we share 'a common humanity, a common language (in the broad sense), and a common experience of the same world'[1858] with the biblical writers.

I would agree with Goldingay that listening to the voices that come to us from each of these five key communities—and indeed of the myriads of sub-communities that come under them—should certainly enrich our interpretive endeavours. However, without the discernment afforded by the Holy Spirit, a wholesale submission to any 'community' reading would certainly lead to confusion and what Lints calls 'interpretive relativism'.[1859] I noted some of the dangers of 'community absolutism' in chapter 1.[1860] As Carson says, 'just because some interpretation or other is espoused and protected by a particular community, it does not follow that it is faithful to Scripture. And so we return to careful listening to others, and to rereading of the Bible, eager to be corrected if that means greater fidelity—and eager, too, not to stand over Scripture as if we are the final judges, when in reality Scripture must stand over us and be our judge.'[1861]

Goldingay's description of the necessary breadth of the corporate focus could also seem to be somewhat overwhelming to biblical interpreters, but against this Goldingay rightly underlines their vital link with the biblical writers. 'We are children of the same heavenly father, brothers and sisters of the same Christ, and partakers of the same Holy Spirit and therefore have more in common with scripture than with other ancient writings.'[1862]

*(ii) The One Christian Community*

The reality of this 'family' *unity* that exists between the Bible writers and Bible interpreters, as 'brothers and sisters of the same Christ,'[1863] (Goldingay's 'universal church') needs to be set off, then, against the aforesaid *diversity* of communities which frame the corporate hermeneutical task. The notion of the 'family' context for biblical interpretation was explored in my chapter on Pauline hermeneutics.[1864] And in so far as it is 'the Spirit himself who bears witness with our spirit that we are children of God' (Rom 8:16), we are reminded again of the necessity of a pneumatological functioning. In contrast to hermeneutical theories that can emphasize the gap or distance that separates us from the

---

[1857] Goldingay, *Models for Interpreting Scripture*, 249.
[1858] Goldingay, *Models for Interpreting Scripture*, 249.
[1859] Lints, 'To Whom Does the Text Belong?' in Carson, *Enduring Authority*, 927.
[1860] See pages 35–36.
[1861] Carson, 'Summarising FAQs' in Carson, *Enduring Authority*, 1175.
[1862] Goldingay, *Models for Interpreting Scripture*, 249.
[1863] Ibid.
[1864] See pages 222–224 on Rom 8:14–17 and pages 238–239 on 2 Tim 3:16–17.

biblical world, then, we can appeal to 'the *eternal* Spirit'[1865] who unites us with the great family of the church, in the past and the future as well as today. It expresses a 'hermeneutical principle' succinctly put by the narrative theologian James McClendon: '*shared awareness of the present Christian community as the primitive community and the eschatological community.* In a motto, the church now is the primitive church and the church on judgment day.'[1866]

Hence the value of reading Scripture in light of historical exegeses of particular passages, as Lints argues from an example he takes from the study of the rich Christological passage, Colossians 1:15–17. 'Reading ... Colossians with the aid of Chrysostom, Aquinas, Calvin, Wesley, J. B. Lightfoot, H. C. G. Moule, as well as contemporary interpreters in the West and among the majority world ... along with the community of interpreters across the ages and across the globe cannot but help us to see and hear more of the text than otherwise.'[1867] It is the privilege of those who have been theologically educated or similarly resourced to be able to benefit from such exegetical enrichment.

Lints, of course, acknowledges that those without such exegetical help can still '[hear] the text in part.'[1868] And as has been mentioned in our previous chapter on 1 John 2:20 ('you all have knowledge') and 1 John 2:27 ('you have no need that anyone should teach you'),[1869] increasing recognition and importance is being given today in theological circles to the insights of the 'ordinary theologians', that is 'those believers who have received no scholarly theological education'[1870] and who make up the vast bulk of the Christian church. Armstrong has made the point that such ordinary theologians, particularly those who 'demonstrate sufficient critical reflection ... and evidence of personal appropriation of [their] beliefs'[1871] have a 'key role'[1872] to play in the task of theological discernment. Using an analogy from the world of electrical engineering and 'the device used ... for the extraction of information from complex signals in the presence of noise,'[1873] he argues that ordinary theologians can act as 'signal processors of the Spirit'[1874] in the task of filtering and clarifying the voice of the Spirit. He writes this 'as a congregationalist [whose] basic

---

[1865] Heb 9:14. This verse is discussed in 'The Holy Spirit and Time in Contemporary Catholic and Protestant Theology' by Wolfgang Vondey in *Scottish Journal of Theology*, Vol. 58 No. 4, 2005, 393-409. 'A pneumatological approach to time suggests that eschatology is determined not only by the end and the consummation of the present in the future but also by the perpetuation of the present moment through the power of God unfolding in time in the operation of the Holy Spirit,' 393.
[1866] James Wm. McClendon, *Ethics: Systematic Theology* Vol. 1 (Nashville: Abingdon, 2nd ed., 2002), 30.
[1867] Lints, 'To Whom Does the Text Belong?' in *Enduring Authority*, 936.
[1868] Ibid., 936.
[1869] See pages 249–252.
[1870] Jeff Astley, *Ordinary Theology: Looking, Listening and Learning in Theology* (Aldershot: Ashgate), 1, as quoted in Jeff Astley and Leslie J. Francis, eds., 'The Analysis, Investigation and Application of Ordinary Theology' in *Exploring Ordinary Theology* (Farnham: Ashgate, 2013), 1.
[1871] Michael Armstrong, 'Ordinary Theologians as Signal Processors of the Spirit', in Astley and Francis, eds, *Exploring Ordinary Theology*, 65.
[1872] Ibid., 67.
[1873] Ibid., 67.
[1874] Ibid., 67.

assumption is that the community of believers is the place where God's guidance is sought and the promptings of the Spirit discerned.'[1875] Whilst acknowledging that this process is not always 'straightforward or foolproof',[1876] he claims that 'ordinary theologians are those best placed to notice when theology goes astray at a fundamental level, because they are the community of practice and belief where theology is accepted or rejected, tested and judged.'[1877]

This, of course, can happen in a broader church context when ordinary theologians challenge current theological deviations from orthodoxy.[1878] And at the local level, most pastors can give testimony to occasions when 'ordinary' members of their churches have given short shrift to expressions of 'theological claptrap' from the pulpit or to elaborations of theological 'niceties' that do not help with the practicalities of everyday Christian living.

*(iii) 'Good News for the Poor'*

As also mentioned in our exegesis of 1 John 2:20,[1879] the 'democratization' of the Spirit's endowment and enabling can be further illustrated by the profound spiritual insights and deep expressions of faith in Scriptural promises that have been revealed from studies of 'Basic Ecclesial Communities'. Christians in such communities in Brazil and Africa commonly read the gospel very literally as 'good news for the poor.'[1880] Their liberationist and practical insights may not always fit into the mould of 'historico-grammatical exegesis', but do express a hermeneutic that is intensely relevant to the needs of the present. This coheres with the insistence of Pentecostal hermeneutics that the deduced meaning of Scripture needs to be 'livable' by the community.[1881] Another example of this would be the Bible reading habits of African-American slaves, such as revealed in 'negro spirituals', with their 'pre-critical' approach to the Bible, including its ancient cosmology, in a way that has helped them to come to terms with their situation by entering into the exodus/liberationist expectations of the ancient

---

[1875] Ibid., 68.
[1876] Ibid., 68.
[1877] Ibid., 67.
[1878] Armstrong cites as a historical example Cardinal Newman's stress upon the *consensus fidelium* and his view that 'the Nicene dogma was maintained not by bishops, councils or Pope, but by the ordinary people of the church,' ibid., 68.
[1879] See pages 249–252 regarding 'all' in connection with the 'anointing' of 1 John 2:20. Note also 'all flesh' in Acts 2:17 - see page 148 - and 'we all' in 2 Cor 3 - see pages 215–216.
[1880] See Zoë Bennett and Christopher Rowland, 'Contextual and Advocacy Readings of the Bible' in Paul Ballard and Stephen Holmes, eds., *The Bible in Pastoral Practice: Readings in the Place and Function of Scripture in the Church* (London: Darton Longman & Todd, 2005), 177–178. They link such 'grassroots' scriptural reading with earlier examples from sixteenth-century Anabaptists,176–178, in their conviction that God spoke primarily through the Spirit's work in the gathered church of 'ordinary' Christians, revealing things that may be hidden from 'the wise and learned' (Matt 11:25). The contemporary study of 'ordinary' theology that surveys the insights of the poor and oppressed is developing. See, for instance, Gerald West, *The Academy of the Poor: Towards a Dialogical Reading of the Bible* and *The Biblical Hermeneutics of Liberation* (Sheffield Academic Press, 1999); Jeff Astley and Leslie J. Francis, eds., *Exploring Ordinary Theology* (Farnham: Ashgate, 2013).
[1881] Kenneth J. Archer, *A Pentecostal Hermeneutic for the Twenty-First Century: Spirit, Scripture and Community* (London: T&T Clark, 2004), 190.

people of God.[1882] These two examples from Brazil and African-America afford illustrations of the divergence of approach that can occur between the confessional and academic communities.

If we regard the insights of the uneducated poor with such value and respect, does this, then, mean that all academic study of the Bible is unnecessary? Can we simply rely upon the Spirit's guidance of the Christian community, in whatever form that may take for the biblical interpreters in question, as the main way of accessing the message of the Bible? For localized groups of Christians that have been or are unable to have the benefits of books, computers, education, and the internet, this, in the providence of God, may well be the case, especially if they lack trained leadership.

But the Spirit's promised help through community should afford no excuse for intellectual laziness.[1883] For those of us who have access to extra means of study, we can agree with Osborne that 'the hermeneutical tools all provide grist for the Spirit's will in the act of interpretation.'[1884] Not that such tools can be used unreservedly provided they are used in a community context, as has already been noted. To reiterate McClendon's point, ultimately authority belongs to God and the authority of the church community is therefore only permissible if 'it functions as a fellowship in the Spirit.'[1885] As emphasized in our discussion on 'testing the Spirits' in 1 John 4,[1886] his authenticating and authorizing stamp is required to produce right readings of Scripture in a world, and indeed a church, that is infested with many corrupt communities, 'pseudo-communities,'[1887] or communities too narrowly construed. Amongst the latter, we could mention the postmodern focus upon the *present* reading community, at the expense of the *past* reading community. And the reading community generally must also be linked with the original author(s) and texts in another kind of threefold 'community' that should be involved in a proper interpretation of the biblical text. This brings us to my last point under 'the hermeneutical task.'

*(iv) The 'Community' Between Author, Text, and Readers*

I cannot here enter into the complexities of hermeneutical debate concerning the respective roles of *author (or authorial/divine intention)*, *text*, and *readers* in the process of interpretation. Postmodern hermeneutical theories, as has been

---

[1882] I owe this insight to Edward Wimberly in a paper given to a conference on 'The Bible as Pastor' at Cardiff University, Sept. 2005, convened by the Bible Society and the Religious and Theological Studies Department of the University. Wimberly quotes from his *African American Pastoral Care* (Nashville: Abingdon Press, 1991), 13: 'The dominant plot that gives life meaning for the African American Christian is what I call an eschatological plot, one that envisions hope in the midst of suffering and oppression, because God is working out God's purposes in life on behalf of persons.' Cf. the chorus: 'This world is not my home/I'm just a-passing through/My treasures are laid up/Somewhere beyond the blue' *Youth Praise* (London: Falcon/Church Pastoral Aid Society, 1969), No. 136.
[1883] See J. R. W. Stott, *Christian Mission in the Modern World* (London: Falcon, 1975), 126–127.
[1884] G. R. Osborne, *The Hermeneutical Spiral* (Leicester: IVP, 1991), 340.
[1885] J. W. McClendon, *Systematic Theology: Doctrine* Vol. II (Nashville: Abingdon Press, 1994), 477.
[1886] See pages 253–264.
[1887] Pietro Bolognesi, 'Is There An Evangelical Vision?', 106.

seen,[1888] commonly over-favour the reader(s) at the expense of author and text. In response, it is submitted that a true balance can only be restored with the aid of a pneumatological functioning. The same Spirit that moved the author, inspired the text, and indwells the readers, is for ever needed to supply the necessary dialectic ('trialectic'?) between the three that produces meaning and transformation. He does, after all, operate as the 'go-between God'[1889] within the community of the Trinity,[1890] and he is needed for the performance of a similar role in the community between the writers, writings, and readers/receivers of the gospel message in Scripture when it is communicated 'not as the word of men but as ... the word [text] of God [author], which is at work in you believers [readers/hearers],' (1 Thess 2:13; cf. 1:5 'in power and in the Holy Spirit'). Sadly, the word of God is not always so regarded and communicated. This, then, leads us to another implication of a 'Spirit through community' hermeneutic: in helping to provide the basis for a right doctrine of Scripture.

## For the Doctrine of Scripture

The work of the Spirit operating 'in and through'[1891] Scripture has been theologically articulated in the doctrine of its 'inspiration,'[1892] as epitomized in Fee's expression *Listening to the Spirit in the Text*.[1893] Here I will mention contemporary reworkings of three other doctrines, prized especially by Protestants, concerning the 'clarity', 'sufficiency' and 'authority' of Scripture, and note how each of them can be seen to embrace both the ecclesial and pneumatological components that are central to this book.

### (i) The Clarity/Perspicuity of Scripture

Our previous discussion concerning the Spirit's interpretation to the poor and uneducated links us to the Reformation doctrine concerning the essential clarity of Scripture.[1894] *Claritas scripturae* was first formulated by the likes of Luther,

---

[1888] See pages 26–28 and 38–39.
[1889] John V. Taylor, *The Go-Between God* (London: SCM, 1972).
[1890] See pages 46–53 and 74–76.
[1891] K. J. Vanhoozer, 'On the Very Idea of a Theological System: An Essay in Aid of Triangulating Scripture, Church and Word' in A. T. B. McGowan, ed., *'Always Reforming': Explorations in Systematic Theology* (Leicester: IVP, 2006), 170, discussing the significance of the prepositions in terms of speech/act theory: 'the understanding that the Spirit's illumination brings about is the result of communicative rationality, not of causal coercion' (ibid.).
[1892] See pages 16 and 38.
[1893] G. D. Fee, *Listening to the Spirit in the Text* (Grand Rapids: Eerdmans, 2000). Related debates concern the 'inerrancy' and 'infallibility' of the Bible.
[1894] Note also Richard M. Edwards' thesis, 'Scriptural Perspicuity in the Early English Reformation' University of Wales, Lampeter/Evangelical Theological College of Wales, 2001. In contrast to the complexity of modern hermeneutical theories, Edwards makes a strong case for the Reformation doctrine of *perspicuity*, namely that 'Scripture is written in such a way that its teachings are able to be clearly understood by the reader' (p. 1). Such a doctrine rests upon the assumption of 'the Holy Spirit as author and interpreter of Scripture' (p. 1). He laments the fact that 'the role of the Holy Spirit has been denigrated since the Early English Reformation because of the lack of doctrinal unity, the rise of rationalism and empiricism disputing revelatory truth, and the tacit acceptance of the Schleiermacherian experiential hermeneutic that elevates Christian experience over the revelation given in Scripture and over doctrine, thereby seeding the ground on which the "reader response" and "reader oriented"

Zwingli, and Bullinger, but has subsequently suffered from a 'decline of confidence in [its] hermeneutical viability,' according to John Webster.[1895] Part of this he attributes to hermeneutical trends that have tended to secularize Scripture or devalue the church context.[1896] Accordingly he seeks to reformulate the doctrine in a way that restores a rightful role to the enlightening work of the Holy Spirit and the essential 'ecclesial nature of Holy Scripture.'[1897] Thus:

> The clarity of Scripture is the work which God performs in and through this creaturely servant [viz. Holy Scripture] as, in the power of the Holy Spirit, the Word of God illumines the communion of saints and enables them to see, love and live out the gospel's truth.[1898]

> To confess the clarity of Holy Scripture is to acknowledge the radiant presence of God, who through Holy Scripture sheds abroad the light of the knowledge of his reconciling works and ways in the communion of the saints, assembled by the Word of God and illuminated by the Spirit to hear the gospel with repentance and faith.[1899]

As Lints says more simply, 'the Scriptures in the power of the Spirit provoke the appropriate response that enables us to call them "clear".... Our trust in the clarity of Scripture ... is the trustworthiness of the Spirit.'[1900]

*(ii) The Sufficiency of Scripture*

This is closely related to 'clarity' and has recently been reworked by Timothy Ward.[1901] He asserts that '"the sufficiency of Scripture" is not a "self-sufficiency of Scripture"'[1902] and adopts the Derridean notion of 'supplementation' of

---

approaches to hermeneutics stand' (p. 323). Such approaches, he claims, 'tend to impose on the innately perspicuous Scripture external individualistic *Weltanschauungen*,' 314.

[1895] J. Webster, 'Biblical Theology and the Clarity of Scripture' in C. Bartholomew and others, eds., *Out of Egypt: Biblical Theology and Biblical Interpretation*, Scripture and Hermeneutics Series, Vol. 5 (Milton Keynes: Paternoster, 2004), 353.

[1896] The omission of the emphasis that 'scripture is clear in the gathering of the saints' is partly because 'in Reformation and post-Reformation polemic, *claritas* was a key weapon in protest against the authority of interpretive traditions and their agents,' ibid., 371.

[1897] Ibid., 369. 'Holy Scripture is an ecclesial reality ... not because Scripture is the church's invention ... [but] because the place of Scripture is in the economy of salvation, and the economy of salvation concerns the divine work of restoring fellowship through the gathering of the *sanctorum communion*,' 369-370. 'The churchly component [in *claritas scripturae*] must be articulated in such a way that its role is not one of presiding over or supplementing and so "clarifying" Scripture, but rather of receiving its inherent clarity in holy attentiveness,' ibid., 371.

[1898] Ibid., 353.

[1899] Ibid., 357.

[1900] Lints, 'To Whom Does the Text Belong' in Carson, *Enduring Authority*, 935. See also Mark Thompson, 'The Generous Gift of a Gracious Father: Toward a Theological Account of the Clarity of Scripture' in Carson, *Enduring Authority*, 615-643, especially 635-638: 'The Spirit's Enabling of the Clarity of Scripture.'

[1901] Timothy Ward, *Word and Supplement: Speech Acts, Biblical Texts, and the Sufficiency of Scripture* (Oxford University Press, 2002).

[1902] Ibid., 10.

texts[1903] in conjunction with the tenets of speech/act theory in the following restatement:

> This scriptural sufficiency can be described in terms of the action of the Holy Spirit.... The text itself cannot produce faithful response; it is sufficient for *notitia* ('intelligent cognition' of 'intelligible information'), but insufficient for the two stages of faithful response, for both of which the Holy Spirit is required: *assensus* ('cognition passed into conviction') ... and *fiducia* ('conviction passed into confidence').... The Spirit *is* therefore a kind of supplement to the text, but only in the sense that he brings the possibility of appropriate response to the text's illocutionary act.... Scripture is sufficient for the performance of the divine illocutionary act, which includes the conveying of its necessary propositional content, but insufficient to bring about the intended perlocutionary effect. For that, as ... the Westminster Confession acknowledges, the work of the Holy Spirit through the Word is required.[1904]

Our only critique of this otherwise helpful summary would be that 'complement' might better describe the Spirit's role vis-à-vis the Word rather than 'supplement'. What is notable, however, is the appropriateness of bringing in an essential pneumatological element in the formulation of a doctrine of Scriptural sufficiency.

*(iii) The Authority of Scripture*

Amongst the many contemporary discussions of this foundational doctrine,[1905] we could mention N. T. Wright's recent re-exploration.[1906] He asserts that '"authority of Scripture" is a shorthand for God's authority exercised *through* Scripture,'[1907] regards Scripture as God's speech/acts,[1908] and pleads for an integrated view of the Scriptures which 'highlights the role of the Spirit as the powerful, transformative agent.'[1909]

> [T]he shorthand phrase "the authority of scripture", when unpacked, offers a picture of God's sovereign and saving plan to the entire cosmos,

---

[1903] Ward quotes from Jacques Derrida's *Of Grammatology* on his title page: 'If the texts that interest us *mean* something, it is the engagement and the appurtenance that encompass existence and writing in the same *tissue*, the same *text*. The same here is called supplement.'
[1904] Ibid., 202–203, incorporating Latin terminology taken from John Murray, *Collected Writings of John Murray*, ii. *Systematic Theology* (Edinburgh: Banner of Truth, 1977), 257–258. Ward's reference to the Westminster Confession of Faith includes 1.10: 'The supreme Judge, by which all controversies of religion are to be determined, and all decrees of councils, opinions of ancient writers, doctrines of men, and private spirits, are to be examined, and in whose sentence we rest, can be no other but the Holy Spirit speaking in the Scripture.'
[1905] See Carson, *Enduring Authority*, and especially Carson's 'The Many Facets of the Current Discussion', 3–40, for a helpful summary of the contemporary debate.
[1906] N.T. Wright, *Scripture and the Authority of God* (London: SPCK, 2005).
[1907] Ibid., 17. But note Carson's criticism of Wright on this point in Carson, *Enduring Authority*, 13–14.
[1908] Ibid., 24.
[1909] Ibid., 84.

dramatically inaugurated by Jesus himself, and now to be implemented through the Spirit-led life of the church *precisely as the scripture-reading community.*[1910]

Here again is a restatement of 'the authority of Scripture' which rests on an assumption of the Spirit working through the Christian community.

These three recent reworkings of the doctrine of Scripture, then, reaffirm that its clarity, sufficiency and authority only become evident when Scripture is read with the help of the Spirit in the communal context. Not that this context guarantees an answer to every Scriptural difficulty, but, with notable exceptions, an understanding reached in the context of community under the Spirit is generally safer than one reached by an individual. As Robert Johnston has said:

> It is true that the formulation of all 'orthodox' beliefs remains fallible and thus may need revision, that all theological understanding remains partial and incomplete, and that even communities can get 'it' wrong. It is also tragically the case that communities can coerce individual members. But it is nonetheless true that one is more likely to get the truth right in community, for here are present other Christians illumined by the same Word and Spirit. To recognize the value of a theological community is important for all evangelicals where individualistic judgments are too often the rule rather than the exception.[1911]

It is evident that the evangelical constituency *is* increasingly recognising and valuing the 'interpretive community' and place of 'tradition' alongside *sola Scriptura*.[1912] But the need remains for a more thoroughgoing working out of a 'Spirit through community hermeneutic.' In the next section, I will suggest some of the ways that it should affect the use of Scripture in the life of the church.

## *For the Use of Scripture*

My comments here will in places overlap with some of the observations made in earlier chapters[1913] in relation to some of the more practical aspects of church life. Here I will seek to catalogue some of the areas for the outworking of a 'Spirit through community hermeneutic'—educationally, ethically, ecumenically, ecclesiologically, homiletically, pastorally, evangelistically and missiologically.

---

[1910] Ibid., 84.

[1911] Robert K. Johnston, 'Orthodoxy and Heresy: A Problem for Modern Evangelicalism' in *Evangelical Quarterly* 69:1 (1997), 29.

[1912] For example, N. Needham, 'Tradition in 2 Timothy' in *Evangel* 17:1 Spring 1999 pleads for Evangelicals to take a more active interest in the notion of tradition, based on 2 Tim 1:13 and 2 Tim 2:2, in contradiction to those who say 'I can sit down by myself with a Bible, and the Spirit will then teach me everything in splendid isolation,' 6–7. He emphasizes the interpretive grids we all have. S. Dray acknowledges the 'situatedness' of all interpreters, in 'Evangelical Tradition' in *Evangel*, 25:1, Spring 2007, 1 and the 'need to rediscover the benefits as well as the dangers of an interpretive community,' 2.

[1913] Especially chapter 2, but also throughout this book.

Each of these eight areas, of course, is immense and I can only make a few pertinent comments thereon in order to point to the large range of implications of this kind of hermeneutic.

## (i) Educationally

The communal context of Scriptural education 'from childhood' (2 Tim 3:15) has much biblical warrant.[1914] The 'family' setting for such instruction was supplemented by the Sunday 'school' movement pioneered in the UK from the 18th century.[1915] This has suffered a sad decline in a secularised Britain, although children and families are now being reached in other ways, such as through 'Messy Church.' Nevertheless, the 'congregational' environment of a Sunday service for those who do attend church continues to afford a vital educational role in the atmosphere of the gathered church family where the Spirit is at work. The stimulus of children's talks/young people's presentations, as complemented by the testimonies of older folk provide communal forums for Spirit-activated learning. Pastors and church leaders especially need the stimuli of fraternals, retreats, conferences, conventions, and continuing education to promote spiritual freshness and scriptural learning. This is particularly relevant for those from more 'independent' church settings that lack the input of a wider fellowship or denominational linking.

The fact that the main communal forum for biblical learning is the local church, rather than the academy, has fostered the recent development of so-called 'congregational hermeneutics.'[1916] This 'explores how people in churches, say, do and learn biblical hermeneutics' understood by Rogers in terms of 'how such Bible readers move between the text and their context.'[1917] His research, focussed upon 'two contrasting evangelical congregations' (one reformed and one charismatic), showed that such 'lived' hermeneutics were mainly 'implicit',[1918] although there were explicit convictions about wanting 'to hear God speak' through Scripture and how it 'should be relevant for life today.'[1919] There were, however, differences between the two churches on how these convictions were expressed.[1920]

The most common 'hermeneutical process'[1921] Rogers observed in both churches was 'text-linking', namely 'the cross-referencing and linking of biblical texts in

---

[1914] For example: Deut 6:7; Prov 22:6; 2 Tim 1:5.
[1915] Pioneers in the UK included Robert Raikes, Thomas Charles and John Wesley.
[1916] See Andrew Rogers, 'Congregational Hermeneutics: Towards Virtuous Apprenticeship', in Astley and Francis, eds., *Exploring Ordinary Theology*, 117, fn.1, where attributes the origin of the term to the Anabaptist theologian Stuart Murray.
[1917] Ibid., 117.
[1918] Ibid., 117–118.
[1919] Ibid., 119.
[1920] For instance, the reformed fellowship referred to 'Bible-centredness' and emphasised inerrancy whilst the charismatic fellowship spoke of 'Bible passion', was 'more activist than doctrinal' with less emphasis upon the doctrine of Scripture and openness to other ways of God speaking besides Scripture. Ibid., 119.
[1921] Ibid., 121.

songs and sermons,'[1922] a process which was carried out particularly well in small groups in the reformed church. He further noted how the 'configurations of congregational hermeneutics were carried by *mediators* ... such as sermons, liturgy, prayers, songs, house groups, congregants, Christian publications' but also, interestingly, through 'church interior layout, web site design, and hand-held microphones',[1923] to which we could add the requirements of PowerPoint presentations, when used. He observed that 'some congregants' had 'the courage' to challenge 'the hermeneutical practices of their congregation'[1924] as well as critique their own personal scripture reading habits. Hence one person who confessed to having 'read the Bible from a very me-centred perspective ... [and so] weakened [its] message.'[1925] But overall Rogers speaks of the need for congregations to be more critically aware of their hermeneutical horizons as well as cultivating the hermeneutical virtues.[1926]

In this regard, good pastors should act as a continuing model of hermeneutical practice. As Stott has said, 'we want to let the congregation into the secret as to how we have reached the conclusions we have reached as to what the Bible is actually saying.... And gradually, as you are doing this from the pulpit, the congregation is schooled not only in what the Bible teaches but in how we come to the conclusion as to what it teaches. So we have to show what our hermeneutical methods are.'[1927]

Turning from education in the local church to theological education for church leadership, there is a well-recognised need for a proper partnership between church and theological training institution in which the needs of the former are matched by the curriculum of the latter. The benefits of collegiate-based learning are manifold, especially where is a healthy interaction between staff and students, and between confessional and critical approaches. This kind of fellowship can be missing from 'distance learning' methods, although compensated for when students are gathered together in local learning communities.[1928] Internet connections and video conferencing also facilitate shared learning in a more personalised yet globalized κοινωνία. Electronic communications, however, are not a substitute for face to face encounters or for printed books, with their hugely seminal influence. Here, the contemporary penchant for theological dictionaries and compilations also testifies to the benefits of shared insights, which are enriched if pursued cross-culturally.

---

[1922] Ibid., 118.
[1923] Ibid., 118.
[1924] Ibid., 123.
[1925] Ibid., 122–123.
[1926] See sections (ii) and (iv) below.
[1927] John Stott, 'Rehabilitating Discipleship: An Interview with John Stott', *Prism*, July–August 1995, as cited in Timothy Dudley-Smith, *John Stott: A Global Ministry* (Leicester: IVP, 2001), 335.
[1928] As, for instance, developed by the Union School of Theology, Bridgend, South Wales where the author is a visiting lecturer.

The Levisons' *Return to Babel: Global Perspectives on the Bible*[1929] for instance, adopts such a cross-cultural approach by including ten interpretations of the same biblical texts from Latin American, African, and Asian perspectives, thus seeking to herald 'loosening of the hegemony of European and North American biblical interpretation.'[1930] Indeed, David Smith asserts that 'the most urgent challenge confronting the church worldwide, is that Christians in both North and South should listen to each other and, in fellowship together, hear what the Spirit is saying to them.'[1931] This process is facilitated when pastors and teachers from the northern and the southern hemispheres are able to traverse the equator to spend time experiencing the hermeneutical dynamics of the other culture.[1932]

The 'gross [socio-economic] imbalance'[1933] between the North and the South poses many challenges to the expression of κοινωνία in the realm of the theological education that is still needed particularly for the growing churches in the South. Noelliste's argument for a partnership in which the southern church takes the role of 'supportive ownership'[1934] in contextually relevant education whilst the northern church takes a 'collaborative and supportive'[1935] but 'not determinative'[1936] role represents one paradigm that is gradually being implemented.[1937]

*(ii) Ethically*

That the Spirit is the *Holy* Spirit alerts us to the ethical element inherent in all Spirit-led interpretation. My exegesis of the New Testament texts has noted this several times,[1938] with scholars today likewise recognising that 'the interpretation of Scripture and the moral formation of reading communities are inextricably bound.'[1939] Doriani pleads that as 'sinner[s] saved by grace ... we should approach every text penitently, *confessing* our need for its rebuke and

---

[1929] Pope-Levison and J. R. Levison, eds., *Return to Babel: Global Perspectives on the Bible* (Louisville, KT: Westminster John Knox, 1999).
[1930] Ibid., 2.
[1931] David W. Smith, *Against the Stream: Christianity and Mission in an Age of Globalization* (Leicester: IVP, 2003), 23. Cross-cultural differences can of course be overdone. Interestingly, Carson points out that the *Africa Bible Commentary*, ed. Tokunboh Adeyomo (Grand Rapids: Zondervan, 2006), although dealing in some detail with some questions particularly relating to African culture, nevertheless has '90 or 95 percent of its content [which] could be read and understood by, and could have been written by, believing Christians in virtually any part of the world.' See 'The Many Facets of the Current Discussion' in Carson, *Enduring Authority*, 12.
[1932] Cf John Stott's comment: 'all of us need to be delivered from the prison of our own culture': 'People in Close-up: John Capon Talks to John Stott (2),' *Crusade*, June 1974, as cited in Dudley-Smith, *John Stott: A Global Ministry*, 435.
[1933] Dieumeme Noelliste, 'Theological Education in the Context of Socio-Economic Deprivation,' *Evangelical Review of Theology* Vol. 29:3 (2005), 271.
[1934] Ibid., 276.
[1935] Ibid., 282.
[1936] Ibid., 282.
[1937] Ibid., 283.
[1938] For instance in relation to John 14:26 (chapter 4, page 132); 2 Cor 3:18 (chapter 6, page 215); Rom 8:4-13 (chapter 6, page 220); 1 John (chapter 7, page 220). See also chapter 2, page 78.
[1939] W. Brown, ed., *Character and Scripture: Moral Formation, Community, and Biblical Interpretation* (Grand Rapids: Eerdmans, 2002), Preface, xi.

correction, and *behaving* meekly as well.'[1940] He also points to what we can learn from both the ancient contemplative art of *lectio divina* and the modern literary discipline of speech-act theory concerning the inseparable connection between reading, meditating, and living.[1941] For this, the ongoing work of the fruit giving Spirit[1942] in the church is vital for what Vanhoozer calls 'cultivating the interpretive virtues,'[1943] 'relative to the sorts of life that bespeak sound biblical interpretation.'[1944] Rogers argues that such virtues should be learned by Christians 'through being apprenticed within their congregation.'[1945] In that context, 'growth in virtue should not only be the outcome of reading the Bible, but virtues should inform the reading itself—a truly virtuous circle.'[1946]

Some of these interpretive virtues were listed in chapter 2,[1947] including readiness to listen, charity and discernment.[1948] All who seek to interpret the truth of God's word need to be truthful and honest themselves. Augustine advocated interpreters whose prime goal was 'to engender the love of the Triune God and of the neighbour' along with 'a personal orientation towards holiness and the fear of God.'[1949] Vanhoozer highlights 'humility: the willingness to assume a lower status, to serve and attend others—authors [viz. divine and human]—as greater than oneself.'[1950] Lints points out how in the 'pluralistic interpretive square' that we inhabit today 'dealing with [such] diversity requires faith, hope and charity.'[1951] As Wright insists, 'integrity consists not of having no presuppositions but of being aware of what one's presuppositions are and of the obligation to listen to and interact with those who have different ones.'[1952] This then brings us more specifically, then, into the wider ecumenical realm in which this should take place, as we discuss another implication for the working out of a Spirit through community hermeneutic in the 'universal church.'

### (iii) Ecumenically

Earlier in this book, I referred to the vast range of pneumatologies on offer today.[1953] Several of these afford a strong role for the Holy Spirit in the

---

[1940] Daniel M. Doriani, 'Take Read', in Carson, *Enduring Authority*, 1145.
[1941] Ibid., 1132–1138.
[1942] Gal 5:22–23.
[1943] Vanhoozer, *Is there a Meaning in this Text?*, 430.
[1944] A. K. Adam, S. E. Fowl, K. J. Vanhoozer, and F. Watson, *Reading Scripture with the Church: Toward a Hermeneutic for Theological Interpretation* (Grand Rapids: Baker Academic, 2006), 11.
[1945] Rogers, 'Congregational Hermeneutics: Towards Virtuous Apprenticeship' in Astley and Francis, *Exploring Ordinary Theology*, 124, where he also enumerates various interpretive virtues listed by scholars.
[1946] Ibid., 123.
[1947] Page 78.
[1948] See also the discussion on 'testing the Spirits' in 1 John 4 in chapter 7, section 4.
[1949] From Augustine's *On Christian Doctrine*, as cited by F. Watson, 'Authors, Readers, Hermeneutics' in Adam et al, *Reading Scripture with the Church*, 120.
[1950] Vanhoozer, 'Imprisoned or Free? Text, Status, and Theological Interpretation in the Master/Slave Discourse of Philemon' in Adam et al, *Reading Scripture with the Church*, 92. Vanhoozer argues that biblical interpnreters should not see themselves as either masters or slaves of texts, but rather 'willing servant[s],' 91.
[1951] Lints, in Carson, *Enduring Authority*, 946–947.
[1952] Wright, *Scripture and the Authority of God*, 11.
[1953] See chapter 2, page 43.

hermeneutical process. As has been seen,[1954] illustrations could be cited from the Anabaptist, Reformed, Pentecostal and Orthodox traditions.

The very diversity of just these four traditions reminds us how Christians have frequently separated into different camps, including Anglican/free church, Protestant/Catholic, evangelical/liberal, charismatic/reformed, Eastern/Western traditions. Another distinction, already noted, is often made between the wealthier, but declining, churches in the northern hemisphere, and the poorer, but growing, churches of the southern hemisphere.[1955] In biblical interpretation, further distinctions are sometimes made between approaches that are 'pre-critical' and 'post-critical', or come from 'behind the text' or 'in front of the text.'[1956] And there are, of course, many other kinds of ecclesiastical and theological divides.

A hermeneutic that is rooted in the κοινωνία of the Spirit will certainly seek to cross many of these divides in dialogical interaction,[1957] although it will not wish to travel to those ends of ecumenical or postmodern thinking that want to blur all such distinctions. For underlying many of them are fundamental theological convictions that, for evangelicals at least, need always to be rooted in Scripture. For them, the combination of Word and Spirit is inseparable and forms the basis for their doctrine of the church, as I shall now mention.

*(iv) Ecclesiologically*

In Packer's words, the Bible's perpetual role, in a general sense, is both to 'form' and 'reform' the church.[1958] Grenz similarly refers to the 'ongoing activity of the Spirit'[1959] with regard to Scripture's 'constitutional role'[1960] in shaping the Christian community by supplying 'a set of categories'[1961] which nurture the self-identity of the people of God.[1962] These categories encompass past, present, and future orientations, as indeed were seen in our study of the early church's interpretation of Scripture in Acts 1–15.[1963] This threefold temporal span could also be defined in terms of the historical, dialogical, and eschatological

---

[1954] See chapter 1, pages 15–19 and chapter 2, pages 64–68.
[1955] Chapter 8, page 282. 'Researchers have estimated that presently some 62% of Christians live in the South and they expect this percentage to reach 70% by the year 2025,' Dieumeme Noelliste, 'Theological Education in the Context of Socio-Economic Deprivation,' 270.
[1956] The concept of Paul Ricoeur.
[1957] For one attempt in the subject realm of this book, see Ted M. Dorman 'Holy Spirit, History, Hermeneutics and Theology: Toward an Evangelical/Catholic Consensus,' *Journal of the Evangelical Theological Society* 41/3, Sept. 1998, 427–438.
[1958] J. I. Packer, *Beyond the Battle for the Bible* (Westchester, IL: Crossway, 1980), 122.
[1959] Stanley J. Grenz, *Theology for the Community of God* (Carlisle: Paternoster, 1994), 508.
[1960] Ibid., 508. Grenz here is using a concept developed by Francis Fiorenza.
[1961] Ibid., 508.
[1962] Ibid., 508–510, using insights from David H. Kelsey, *The Uses of Scripture in Recent Theology* (Philadelphia: Fortress Press, 1975), 214.
[1963] See chapter 5.

operations of the Spirit, with the ongoing and ultimate goal of transformation into the likeness of Christ.[1964]

For this to be achieved there is a perpetual need of Spirit assisted interpretations, whose characteristics have been summarized by Vanhoozer:

(1) faithfulness: interpretations that *extend* the meaning of the text into new situations;

(2) fruitfulness: interpretations that *enliven* the reader and show forth the Spirit's fruits;

(3) forcefulness: interpretations that *edify* the community, resolve problems, foster unity;

(4) fittingness: interpretations that *embody* the righteousness of God and contextualize Christ.

The testimony of the Spirit is not only to individuals but primarily to the church as a whole.[1965]

In view of the primacy of this church context, it is imperative that appropriate ecclesial structures are in place if such Spirit-led interpretations are to be facilitated. The claims of the institutional churches in this regard have not always been upheld in the face of criticisms that the work of the Spirit has been quenched, for instance, by rigidity of tradition, authoritarian leadership, or doctrinal compromise. This has led to many alternative models for 'doing church' which 'give the Spirit greater freedom.'

One such response has been the Pentecostal movement, described by Archer as a 'protest to modernistic Liberalism and ... Protestant cessationist orthodoxy.'[1966] For him, the vibrancy of Pentecostalism, with its scriptural readings that 'speak to the present eschatological community,'[1967] stem from 'a hermeneutical strategy [based upon] a narrative approach to interpretation that embraces a tridactic negotiation for meaning between the biblical text, Pentecostal community, and the Holy Spirit.'[1968]

Another kind of ecclesiastical model, based upon the Anabaptist tradition, has been propounded by Keith Jones who has 'argue[d] the case for gathering, intentional, convictional communities of radical believers.... The gathering *koinonia* will be communities of the street corners, of the side streets and apartment blocks, of the corner shop and the corner pub.'[1969] Such smaller

---

[1964] See the discussion on 2 Cor 3:18 in chapter 6, page 215.
[1965] Vanhoozer, *Is there a Meaning in This Text?*, 431.
[1966] Archer, *A Pentecostal Hermeneutic for the Twenty-First Century: Spirit, Scripture and Community*, 4.
[1967] Ibid., 195.
[1968] Ibid., 5.
[1969] Keith Jones, 'Towards a Model of Mission for Gathering, Intentional, Convictional *Koinonia*,' *Journal of European Baptist Studies*, Vol. 4 Jan. 2004, 5–13.

localised, committed, but non-institutionalized groupings would, it is claimed, be better able to model the life of the Spirit-led community for reading Scripture and witnessing within the individualistic culture of today. Others have argued that this can be achieved within the parameters of larger congregational structures by creating within them more flexible 'cell' like units that can foster κοινωνία. Experiments continue to be made along these and many other lines, demonstrating the more fluid patterns of ecclesiology that are deemed appropriate to postmodernism.[1970]

Tidball, however, has argued that evangelical churches are commonly undergirded by a spirituality that *does* foster an anti-individualistic κοινωνία through the threefold combination of 'the individual practice of personal devotion; the corporate study of the Bible in small groups and the exposition of Scripture through preaching in the church.'[1971] As to the first of these, the risk of individual aberrations[1972] could be diminished if a church could devise imaginative ways of individuals sharing and 'checking' the results of their 'quiet times' with one another. This could be especially illuminating if they were reading from the same texts, maybe as a congregational exercise with a biblical curriculum offered by the church leadership.[1973] As to the second, group Bible studies need to be directed by Spirit-led, church authorized leaders if they are not to 'degenerate into a sophisticated sharing of ignorance.'[1974] As to the third—preaching—see the next section.

A fuller understanding of the κοινωνία of the Spirit will also help individual congregations to value interdependency within rather than independence from the wider church, taking more seriously the concept of the church universal, as well as local. Such a vision needs to be communicated as part of the church's preaching mandate, to which I now turn.

*(v) Homiletically*

The misconception of the sermon as a monologue to a passive group betrays the corporate dynamic of preaching when undertaken in 'the unction and anointing of the Holy Spirit.'[1975] Such preaching should be vitally 'dialogical' in the sense of its creating a relationship of mutual challenge and response, under God, between preacher and congregation. Both parties have responsibilities which, if fulfilled, should facilitate a 'Spirit through community' hermeneutic.

---

[1970] Sometimes such experiments are accused of over-accommodation to contemporary culture. See D. Jackman, 'Next Step?' in *Evangelicals Now,* Nov. 2005, 13, reviewing D. A. Carson, *Becoming Conversant with the Emerging Church* (Grand Rapids: Zondervan, 2005).
[1971] D. Tidball, 'The Bible in Evangelical Spirituality' in Ballard and Holmes, *The Bible in Pastoral Practice*, 268.
[1972] Chapter 1, pages 27-28.
[1973] S. Winter, *More Light and Truth? Biblical Interpretation in Covenantal Perspective.* Whitley Lecture 2007 (Oxford: Whitely, 2007), 35.
[1974] Tidball, 'The Bible in Evangelical Spirituality,' 268.
[1975] D. Martyn Lloyd-Jones, *Preaching and Preachers* (London: Hodder & Stoughton, 1976), 304.

The preacher, for his part, should speak from a life that aims to 'keep in step with the Spirit,'[1976] seeking the Spirit's unction upon all sermon preparation and delivery. Such dependence acknowledges that the power and authority of the pulpit is God-given. It is not personal to the preacher, who should see his role as a servant of the Word,[1977] 'a voice'[1978] not 'a personality'. A 'come ... let us reason together' (Isa 1:18) style that draws the hearers in with questions, exhortations, and space for reflection aids congregational participation. Expository preaching still needs to be declaratory and authoritative, but not arrogantly authoritarian or focussed upon the wit or eloquence of the preacher.

Winter indeed mentions that 'in early Baptist worship there would often be more than one sermon *on the same text.*'[1979] The diverse insights afforded thereby would be one means of recognizing that 'the Lord has yet more light and truth to break forth from his Word.'[1980] Having more than one preacher in a service may not be a feasible or indeed a palatable option for many churches today. But it does cohere with an historic Anabaptist conviction that emphasizes the importance of interpreting Scripture in an essentially corporate context under the guidance of the Holy Spirit. Mennonite-Brethren worship today that is rooted in such Anabaptist principles continues to work this out, for example, by having three different preachers from the same fellowship expound Scripture in a service, though not necessarily on the same text. Such worship commonly includes space after the sermon for a corporate response in open prayer that applies the message of the sermon, as well as opportunities to testify to God's help in working out Scripture in everyday life.[1981] This is a challenge to what can seem to be the passivity of some church congregations.

Even in the more usual scenario of one preacher per service, it is important for the members of the congregation to take 'far more responsibility than they commonly recognise for the kind of ministry they receive,'[1982] and not just to 'sit together under the Word.' Stott mentions the need for congregations to encourage the pastor/preacher to expound Scripture, to come to church with 'a receptive and expectant mood,'[1983] and to take sermon notes. Azurdia says that 'the congregation must consciously refrain from any attitude or activity that might contribute to a withholding of the effects of the Holy Spirit',[1984] referring specifically to things that 'grieve' (Eph 4:29–30) or 'quench' (1 Thess 5:19) 'the

---

[1976] J. I. Packer, *Keep in Step with the Spirit* (Leicester: IVP, 1984), the title reflecting Gal 5:25.
[1977] 2 Tim 4:2.
[1978] Mark 1:3, citing Isa 40:3.
[1979] S. Winter, *More Light and Truth?*, 36.
[1980] Ibid., 6, citing some famous words from John Robinson, pastor of the Pilgrim Fathers, in a sermon preached on 21st July 1620 before the boarding of the Mayflower.
[1981] These observations were made by the writer in August 2016 after attending the services of Mennonite-Brethren churches in Albisheim and Frankenthal, Southern Germany.
[1982] J. R. W. Stott, *Understanding the Bible* (Milton Keynes: Scripture Union, 2003), 200.
[1983] Ibid.
[1984] Arturo G. Azurdia III, *Spirit Empowered Preaching: The Vitality of Holy Spirit in Preaching* (Fearn: Mentor, 1998), 153.

sensitive Spirit.'[1985] And following Paul's common requests for prayer for his preaching,[1986] Azurdia paraphrases a Dutch pastor's congregational plea: 'If you pray me full, I'll preach you full'![1987] Then after the sermon has been delivered, the congregation faces the more challenging ongoing task of working out its implications in practical living. As James says, 'be doers of the word, and not hearers only' (James 1:22).

Further communal participation in the preaching process has been suggested in the involvement of consultative groups to work with the preacher in the preparation for and/or feedback from the sermon.[1988] Such feedback can be given by way of written notes or text messages that can be responded to by the preacher even before the service finishes. If this is regarded as impractical or unnecessary, good preachers will nevertheless have their sermons informed by the communal experiences of their pastoral work and seek to pay more attention to the corporate as well as the individual application of texts. This leads us into our next point.

*(vi) Pastorally*

For the Bible to function pastorally, a 'Spirit through *community*' hermeneutic is highly relevant, for pastoral work is not, or never should be, the prerogative of one individual. Helpers are needed to act in conjunction with pastors/elders who themselves constantly need the Spirit's guidance in the use of Scripture in the varied and often demanding encounters of 'car[ing] for the church of God ... the flock of which the Holy Spirit has made [them] overseers.'[1989] These encounters invariably take place in a group context of two or more people, whether this is in the setting of a prayer meeting, a home visit, around a hospital bed, in a nursing home, in a wedding or funeral, during the laying on of hands, or other corporate occasion.

The dialectics of these occasions, as has been seen,[1990] can sometimes spark off surprisingly fitting applications of the Bible, whether quoted from specifically or alluded to more generally. Many pastors will have testimonies as to when 'a word in season' was brought to mind by the Spirit in a corporate setting. The cogency of these occasions may be reinforced by a κοινωνία that the Spirit can create through Scripture with the saints of old and their experiences, as recorded, for example, in the Psalms (a part of Scripture commonly used by those undertaking

---

[1985] Ibid., 149.
[1986] For example, 2 Thess 3:1; Col 4:2–4; Eph 6:19–20.
[1987] Azurdia, *Spirit Empowered Preaching*, 172.
[1988] Drew Gibson suggests that the use of such groups would constitute a 'people's hermeneutic', which, along with a more interactive homiletic, would 'seem to be consonant with both the method of Scripture itself and with contemporary western culture,' 'Evangelical Preaching in Northern Ireland: A Brainstorming Response,' *Evangel* 22:1 Spring 2004, 26. Michael Quicke, 'The Scriptures in Preaching' in Ballard and Holmes, *The Bible in Pastoral Practice*, 251 suggests similar methods. In response, many also would wish to reaffirm that preaching still needs to retain a clear declaratory element that differentiates it from discussional Bible studies.
[1989] Acts 20:28.
[1990] Chapter 2, pages 53–58 and 76–82.

pastoral visitation). As Epp says, 'sharing the wisdom of the sages ... keeps us linked to the community that passed this wisdom on. The treasure becomes part of the memory bank by which our lives are nurtured.'[1991] And the Spirit of remembrance who makes this possible is also the eschatological Spirit who gives a hope for the future, together 'with all the saints.'[1992]

In pastoral theology, there is much emphasis today upon the benefits of a *narrative* approach to Scripture.[1993] The grand storyline and myriad sub stories of the Bible contain many examples with which its readers can identify, negatively or positively. Space certainly needs to be created within the church's worship life and teaching programme where this interchange of biblical and readers' stories can regularly take place. But there are also, of course, other pastoral uses of Scripture that the Spirit can activate, whether it be through the genres of poetry,[1994] promise[1995] or even precept.[1996] I use the word 'even' because some biblical interpreters seek to play down the peremptory nature of the commands and prohibitions that are found in the biblical narrative. It is true that a number of these need to be regarded as culturally conditioned, but that should not diminish the force of the ethical absolutes that lie behind them.[1997] That said, the rigours of an authoritative text can be tempered by the ministry of an empathetic pastoral community that relies upon the Spirit's help to provide a compassionate application that does not nevertheless relativise the text.

And if, in this section, we adopt a wider definition of 'pastoral practice' to include 'the activity of Christians that nurtures flourishing in all areas of human life—individual, ecclesiastical and social,'[1998] the door is open to all kinds of imaginative uses of Scripture from many different kinds of Christian communities who certainly need the wisdom and guidance of the Spirit.

*(vii) Evangelistically*

The New Testament writings, as has been noted,[1999] are permeated with the use of Old Testament Scripture, the product of what in today's parlance might be called 'a Bible rich' culture. Many parts of Western society today are becoming increasingly 'Bible poor', with a consequent diminishing of the kind of community that stems from a shared worldview. Christian churches now have an opportunity and duty to offer authentic 'community' to a world that lacks it

---

[1991] Menno Epp, 'Using Scripture in Pastoral Care' in *Vision: A Journal for Church and Theology* (Institute of Mennonite Studies) Spring 2005, Vol. 6, No. 1, 66.
[1992] Eph 3:18.
[1993] See Ballard and Holmes, *The Bible in Pastoral Practice: Readings in the Place and Function of Scripture in the Church* (London: Darton Longman & Todd, 2005), for many examples, along with other approaches.
[1994] For example, Ps 61:2-3.
[1995] For example, Phil 4:19.
[1996] For example, 2 Cor 6:14.
[1997] For example, the requirements of the food laws in Deut 14:1-21 may no longer be relevant, but the ethical principle underlying them ('for you are a people holy to the Lord your God' v. 21) is.
[1998] Ballard and Holmes, *The Bible in Pastoral Practice*,vii, Series Preface.
[1999] See especially chapter 3.

as they seek to become Spirit-led communities that interpret and demonstrate the truths of Scripture in an attractive, welcoming way. 'Through the authority of the Spirit the church can become the sort of "hermeneutical community" in which the Word of God becomes embodied within the life and mission of the local community.'[2000] Such embodiment can take place when Christians, besides seeking to model κοινωνία in their own church activities, also seek to get involved, where feasible, in the ongoing life of that community, whether in the workplace, local schools, residents' groups, and other community groupings and ventures, and thereby seek to act as 'the salt of the earth.'[2001]

Sadly, this salt has lost a good deal of its savour in much of Western society as the forces of secularisation continue their insidious advance. In light of this, many in the church are praying for Spirit-given revival that makes the convicting power and 'fellowship of the Holy Ghost' an experiential, transforming reality in the wider community. For this, some take the monumental events of Acts 2[2002] as an authoritative, albeit unique, prototype.

In the absence of such a blessing, the effective presentation of the gospel today takes place within the confines of less dramatic expressions of the κοινωνία of the Spirit, in different kinds of settings. In the larger context of a traditional 'rally'/modern 'celebration', this may be manifested in preaching, singing and testimony gatherings, maybe supplemented by 'multi-media' elements,[2003] in which the unbeliever can sense that 'God is really among you!' (1 Cor 14:25). In the smaller 'cell' type context of an ongoing basics/nurture group, perhaps with a meal, developing relationships can provide another type of forum for a more intimate κοινωνία in which the Spirit gradually opens eyes to the truths of Scripture. In the context of a larger church mission, a κοινωνία atmosphere may be generated through friendly welcoming events and the compassion of a Spirit-anointed evangelist, as supported by a warm-hearted, prayerful mission team. Such a mission may take place in the setting of an inter-church, inter-denominational approach that can itself be a demonstration of the κοινωνία of the Spirit as Christians and churches are united through a common concern for the gospel and a commitment to Scripture.

Conversion to the Christian faith is personal in nature but communal in origin and outcome, for the focus of all good evangelism is 'from the church and into the church.' And the regenerative agent is, of course, always 'the Spirit who gives life' (John 6:63).

---

[2000] John A. Studebaker, Jr., 'The Authority of the Holy Spirit: The "Missing Link" in Our Contemporary Understanding of Divine Authority?' *Trinity Journal* 25.2 (2004), 234.
[2001] Matt 5:13.
[2002] See chapter 5, pages 154–164.
[2003] The place of the visual and dramatic arts in worship and evangelism is debated. For a sympathetic appreciation, see Gail Ricciuti, 'The Bible and the Arts' in Ballard and Holmes, *The Bible in Pastoral Practice*, 296–304. Others argue for the priority, if not exclusivity, of 'hearing' rather than 'seeing' (Rom 10:17).

## (viii) Missiologically

Here I briefly consider the wider evangelistic remit of the church more in terms of cross-cultural mission, for which the 'first missionary journey' in Acts records a leading role for the Spirit. 'While they were worshipping the Lord and fasting, the Holy Spirit said, "Set apart for me Barnabas and Saul for the work to which I have called them"' (Acts 13:2). Here again, then, the Spirit spoke the word through the community, as indeed is often recorded in Acts as the pneumatological mandate of 1:8 is fulfilled.[2004] The call of any individual(s) into the work of mission needs to be confirmed by the Christian community as the word of their testimony is tested by the spiritual discernment of the church. And it is to the church that those who are commissioned need to report back, as did Paul and Barnabas.[2005] Such 'reporting back' sessions can give rise to new communal understandings of Scripture, as was seen in our examination of Acts 4:23–31.[2006]

In this connection, Archer[2007] refers to the way that missionaries bring back to their sending communities hermeneutically enriching records of their experiences from 'outside of their cultural context and geographical locations.'[2008] Thus:

> engagement with other communal stories allows for openness to the voice of the Spirit to come to them from outside the community ... through missionaries, evangelists and recent converts. Once again, the community, Scripture, and Spirit are all necessary participants in the making of meaning with the community energized by the Spirit being the area in which the Scripture and the Spirit converge.[2009]

Churches need a continual missiological focus to bring healthy cross-cultural, global perspectives to their understanding of Scripture so as to prevent over-domesticated, parochialised readings. In this, the help of the Spirit of mission, so prominent has been noted from our chapter on Acts, is continually required.[2010]

Not that the Spirit is the only criterion, for mission and the hermeneutical process that undergirds it needs to take place within a *Trinitarian* context, as the great commission's 'in the name of the Father, Son and Holy Spirit' (Matt 28:19) insists; and as frequently pointed out in this book, it is within the dynamics of such Trinitarian fellowship, as mirrored within the church, that the Spirit

---

[2004] See chapter 5.
[2005] Acts 14:27.
[2006] See chapter 5, pages 164–167.
[2007] 'The Spirit's Voice Coming from Outside and yet Back through the Community' in Archer, *A Pentecostal Hermeneutic for the Twenty-First Century: Spirit, Scripture and Community*, 184.
[2008] Ibid., 184.
[2009] Ibid., 184.
[2010] For an example from an ecumenical perspective, see J. Matthey, ed., 'Come, Holy Spirit - Heal and Reconcile', in *International Review of Mission* Vol. 94, No. 372, Jan. 2005, 3.

operates, and within such a dynamic that the reading and spreading of Scripture's message is vitalized.

## For the Custodianship of Scripture

A 'Spirit through community hermeneutic,' then, carries with it far ranging implications—educationally, ethically, ecumenically, ecclesiologically, homiletically, pastorally, evangelistically, and missiologically. The use of Scripture in all these ways, however, must not result in its 'watering down'. Dissemination does not mean dissolution. The church is also entrusted with a 'custodial' role in relation thereto, for which this chapter has already spelt out various implications. Earlier chapters have also argued that the help of the Spirit in 'guiding ... into all truth' (John 16:13),[2011] 'guarding the good deposit' (2 Tim 1:14)[2012] and 'test[ing] the spirits' (1 John 4:1)[2013] should not involve a straightjacketing of 'the deposit' through preset interpretive grids, but rather an openness to exploring and expressing it in new ways, whilst remaining faithful to the gospel tradition now enshrined in Scripture. Hence the need to 'teach what accords with sound doctrine' (Titus 1:2) and defend it against heresies. My discussion on 1 John 4[2014] suggested that this could entail the Christian community's formulating new tests for biblical orthodoxy with the Spirit's help, as well as concerted action by the church leadership when aberrations occur.

The theological acumen needed to do this is fostered by the type of education mentioned earlier, including an appreciation of the original biblical languages, an essential for the understanding and preservation of Scripture. Its translation into the vernacular has historically been undertaken by many brave individuals, but that more recent translations have been generally undertaken by a panel is recognition of the value of the communal approach. As the Spirit works through a team of translators, so Scripture should hopefully be translated, or paraphrased, in ways that keep true to the original but also make it more contemporarily accessible, both to secularized westerners and unreached people groups throughout the world.

## Final Word

This book has attempted to underline the importance of working out and operating upon a hermeneutic that consists of the Spirit working through the community of God's people as custodians and interpreters of Scripture. Not that this should downplay the role of the interpretation by individuals or replace other hermeneutical strategies, but in one sense is one that ought to overarch all

---

[2011] Chapter 4, pages 136–139. Note also comments on page 133.
[2012] Chapter 6, pages 232–235.
[2013] Chapter 7, pages 253–264.
[2014] Ibid.

such efforts. For the Scriptures, as both a divine and human book, need an interpretive key that is both heavenly and human, that is supplied by God's person as well as God's people. The operational dynamic for this is supplied by the κοινωνία of the Spirit, which, *inter alia*, links us all together, in the Trinitarian, dialogical, historical and eschatological dimensions of the hermeneutical process. I have argued that it was fundamental to the way that the New Testament writers themselves interpreted and applied Scripture and needs to be given greater prominence in the hermeneutics of all who seek to follow their example, in response to their prayer: 'the grace of the Lord Jesus Christ, and the love of God and the fellowship of the Holy Spirit be with [us] all' (2 Cor 13:14).

# BIBLIOGRAPHY

Aalen, S. 'Glory, Honour.' Page 45 in *New International Dictionary of New Testament Theology*, Volume 2. Edited by C. Brown. Exeter: Paternoster, 1975.

Adam, A. K., S.E. Fowl, K. J. Vanhoozer, and F. Watson. *Reading Scripture with the Church: Toward a Hermeneutic for Theological Interpretation*. Grand Rapids: Baker Academic, 2006.

Alexander, T. D. and B. S. Rosner, eds. *New Dictionary of Biblical Theology*. Leicester: IVP, 2000.

Allert, C. D. 'What Are We Trying to Conserve? Evangelicalism and *Sola Scriptura*.' *Evangelical Quarterly* 76.4 (2004): 327–348.

Andre-Watson, C. Review of *Discerning the Spirit of the Age*, by Derek Tidball in Spurgeon's College's *The Record*, May 2003.

Archer, K. J. 'Pentecostal Hermeneutics: Retrospect and Prospect,' *Journal of Pentecostal Theology* 8 (1996): 63–81.

_____ *A Pentecostal Hermeneutic for the Twenty-First Century: Spirit, Scripture and Community*. London/New York: T&T Clark, 2004.

Arrington, F. L. 'The Use of the Bible by Pentecostals.' *Pneuma* Vol. 16 (1994):101–107.

Ashton, J. *Understanding the Fourth Gospel*. Oxford: Clarendon, 1993.

Astley, J and L. J. Francis, eds. *Exploring Ordinary Theology*. Farnham: Ashgate, 2013.

Aubrey, M. E., ed. *The Baptist Hymn Book*. London: Psalms and Hymns Trust, 1962.

Azurdia III, A. G. *Spirit Empowered Preaching: The Vitality of The Holy Spirit in Preaching*. Fearn: Mentor, 1998.

Baker, D. L. *Two Testaments, One Bible*. Leicester: Apollos, 1976. Repr., London: IVP, 1991.

Ballard, P. and S. Holmes, eds. *The Bible in Pastoral Practice: Readings in the Place and Function of Scripture in the Church*. London: Darton Longman and Todd, 2005.

Barclay, J. M. G., 'Jesus and Paul.' Pages 492-592 in *Dictionary of Paul and His Letters*. Edited by G. F. Hawthorne, Ralph P. Martin, and Daniel G. Reid, eds. Leicester: IVP, 1993.

Barnett, P. *The Message of 2 Corinthians*. Leicester: IVP, 1988.

Barr, J. *The Semantics of Biblical Language.* Oxford University Press, 1961.

_____ *Fundamentalism.* London: SCM, 1981.

Barrett, C. K. *First Epistle to the Corinthians.* Second Edition. London: A&C Black, 1971.

_____ *A Commentary on the Second Epistle to the Corinthians.* Second Edition. London: A&C Black, 1973.

_____ *The Gospel According to St John: An Introduction with Commentary and Notes on the Greek Text.* London: SPCK, 1978.

_____ *The Acts of the Apostles.* ICC. Edinburgh: T&T Clark, 1998.

Barth, K. *The Epistle to the Romans.* Trans. from 6th Edition by E. C. Hoskins. Oxford: Oxford University Press, 1968.

_____ *Church Dogmatics. Vol. 1.1. The Doctrine of the Word of God.* Edinburgh: T&T Clark, 1975.

Bartholomew, C., C. Greene and K. Moller, eds. *Renewing Biblical Interpretation*: Scripture and Hermeneutics Series. Vol. 1. Carlisle: Paternoster, 2000.

_____ *After Pentecost: Language and Biblical Interpretation.* Scripture and Hermeneutics Series. Vol. 2. Carlisle: Paternoster, 2001.

_____ *'Behind' the Text: History and Biblical Interpretation.* Scripture and Hermeneutics Series. Vol. 4. Carlisle: Paternoster, 2003.

_____ *Out of Egypt: Biblical Theology and Biblical Interpretation.* Scripture and Hermeneutics Series, Vol. 5. Milton Keynes: Paternoster, 2004.

_____ *Reading Luke: Interpretation, Reflection, Formation.* Scripture and Hermeneutics Series, Vol. 6. Milton Keynes: Paternoster, 2005.

Barton, S. 'The Communal Dimension of Earliest Christianity: A Critical Survey of the Field.' *Journal of Theological Studies* Vol. 43 Part 2 (1992): 399–427.

Bassler, J. M. *1 Timothy, 2 Timothy, Titus.* Nashville: Abingdon, 1996.

Bauckham, R., ed. *The Gospels for All Christians: Rethinking the Gospel Audiences.* Edinburgh: T&T Clark, 1998.

Beale, G. K., ed. *The Right Doctrine from the Wrong Texts: Essays on the Use of the Old Testament in the New.* Grand Rapids: Baker, 1994.

Beale, G. K. and D. A. Carson, eds. *Commentary on the New Testament Use of the Old Testament.* Grand Rapids: Baker; Nottingham: Apollos, 2007.

Bebbington, D. 'Evangelicals and Public Worship, 1965–2005.' *Evangelical Quarterly* 79.1 (2007): 3–22.

Beckwith, R. 'The Canon of Scripture.' Page 27 in *New Dictionary of Biblical Theology*. Edited by T. Desmond Alexander and B. S. Rosner. Leicester: IVP, 2000.

Behm, J. 'παράκλητος'. Pages 800–814 in G. Kittel and G. Friedrich, eds., *Theological Dictionary of the New Testament*. Volume V. Translated by G. W. Bromiley. Grand Rapids: Eerdmans, 1967.

Beker, J. C. *The Triumph of God: The Essence of Paul's Thought*. Fortress Press, Minneapolis, 1990.

Belleville, L. L. *2 Corinthians*. Leicester: IVP, 1996.

Benfold, G. 'Jonathan Edwards and the "Toronto blessing".' *Evangelicals Now* (Oct. 1994): 8–9.

Bennett, C. 'The Spirit in the Word - and Beyond?' *Foundations* No. 39 (1997): 10–20.

Best, T. F. and Gassman G. *'On the way to Fuller Koinonia.'* Faith and Order Paper No. 166. Geneva: WCC, 1993.

Bloesch, D. G. *The Holy Spirit Works and Gifts*. Downers Grove: IVP, 2000.

Blomberg, C. *1 Corinthians: NIV Life Application Commentary*. Grand Rapids: Zondervan, 1994.

Bock, Darrell L. *Acts*. Grand Rapids, Michigan, 2007.

Bockmuehl, M. *The Epistle to the Philippians*. London: A&C Black, 1997.

_____ *Seeing the Word: Refocusing New Testament Study*. Grand Rapids: Baker Academic, 2006.

Boff, L., *Trinity and Society*. Tunbridge Wells: Burns and Oates, 1988.

_____ *Holy Trinity, Perfect Trinity*. Maryknoll, NY: Orbis, 2000.

Bolognesi, P. 'Is There An Evangelical Vision? Reflections from an Italian Perspective.' *European Journal of Theology* 13:2 (2004): 103–109.

Bornkamm, G. *Paul*. London: Hodder & Stoughton, 1971.

Bouteneff, P. and Heller, D., eds. *Interpreting Together: Essays in Hermeneutics*. Geneva: WCC, 2001.

Brawley, R. L. *Text to Text Pours Forth Speech: Voices of Scripture in Luke-Acts*. Bloomington and Indianapolis: Indiana University Press, 1995

Bray, G. L. 'Hellenization of Christianity.' Page 290 in *New Dictionary of Theology*. Edited by S. B. Ferguson, D. F. Wright and J. I Packer. Leicester: IVP, 1988.

_____ *Biblical Interpretation - Past and Present*. Leicester: Apollos, 1996.

_____ Review of *The Trinity and Subordinationism: The Doctrine of God and the Contemporary Gender Debate*, by Kevin Giles. *The Churchman* (Autumn 2003): 267–272.

Briggs, R. '"Let the Reader Understand" The Role of the Reader in Biblical Interpretation,' *Evangel* (Autumn 1995): 72–78.

_____ 'Getting Involved: Speech Acts and Biblical Interpretation,' *Anvil* Vol. 20 No.1 (2003): 25–34.

_____ Review of *The Holy Spirit & The Bible*, by Paul E. Brown. *Anvil* Vol. 20 No. 4 (2003): 323

Brooke, A. E. *A Critical and Exegetical Commentary on the Johannine Epistles*. Edinburgh: T&T Clark, 1912.

Brown, C. 'The Enlightenment.' Page 355 in *Evangelical Dictionary of Theology*, ed. Walter A. Elwell. Grand Rapids: Baker Books; Carlisle: Paternoster, 1984.

_____ *Christianity and Western Thought*. Vol. 1. Leicester: Apollos, 1990.

Brown, C., ed. *New International Dictionary of New Testament Theology*. 3 Vols. Exeter: Paternoster, 1975.

Brown, P. *The Holy Spirit & The Bible: The Spirit's Interpreting Role in Relation to Biblical Hermeneutics*. Fearn, Ross-shire: Christian Focus, 2002.

Brown, R. E. 'The Paraclete in the Fourth Gospel.' *New Testament Studies* 13 (1966–67): 113–32.

_____ *The Gospel According to John*. 2 Vols. London: Geoffrey Chapman, 1966.

_____ *The Epistles of John*. Anchor Bible. New York: Doubleday, 1982.

Brown, T. Gates. *Spirit in the Writings of John*. London; New York: T&T Clark International, 2003.

Brown, W. P., ed. *Character and Scripture: Moral Formation, Community, and Biblical Interpretation*. Grand Rapids: Eerdmans, 2002.

Bruce, F. F. *This is That*. Exeter: Paternoster, 1969.

Bruce, F. F. *New Century Bible: 1 and 2 Corinthians*. London: Marshall Morgan and Scott, 1971.

_____ 'The Holy Spirit in Acts of the Apostles.' *Interpretation* 27:2 (1973): 166–183.

_____ *The Book of Acts.* London: Marshall, Morgan & Scott, 1977.

_____ *The Epistles of John.* Grand Rapids: Eerdmans, 1979.

_____ *The Acts of the Apostles: The Greek Text with Introduction and Commentary.* 3rd Edition. Leicester: Apollos, 1990.

Brueggemann, W. *The Prophetic Imagination.* Philadelphia: Fortress Press, 1978.

_____ *Deep Memory, Exuberant Hope: Contested Truth in a Post-Modern World.* Minneapolis: Augsburg Fortress Press, 2000.

_____ *Hopeful Imagination - Prophetic Voices in Exile.* Philadelphia: Fortress Press, 1986.

_____ *The Bible Makes Sense: The Growth of Community in the Bible.* Atlanta: Westminster John Knox, 2001.

Bultmann, R. *The Gospel of John: A Commentary.* Edited by Paul N. Anderson and R. Alan Culpepper. Translated by G. R. Beasley-Murray. Oxford: Blackwell, 1971.

Burge, G. M. *The Anointed Community: The Holy Spirit in the Johannine Tradition.* Grand Rapids: Eerdmans, 1987.

_____ *Interpreting the Gospel of John.* Grand Rapids: Baker, 1992.

_____ *Letters of John.* Life Application Commentary. Grand Rapids: Zondervan, 1996.

Burgess, S. M. and E. M. Van Der Maas, eds. *New International Dictionary of Pentecostal and Charismatic Movements.* Grand Rapids: Zondervan, 2002.

Burke, T. J. & K. Warrington, eds. *A Biblical Theology of the Holy Spirit.* Eugene, OR: Cascade: 2014.

Burnett, G. W. *Paul and the Salvation of the Individual.* Leiden: Brill, 2001.

Burridge, R. A. *What are the Gospels? A Comparison with Graeco-Roman Biography.* Cambridge University Press, 1992.

Calvin, J. *Calvin's Commentaries: The Acts of the Apostles 14–28.* Edited by D. W. Torrance and T. F. Torrance. Translated by J. W. Fraser. Grand Rapids: Eerdmans, 1979.

_____ *Commentary upon the Acts of the Apostles.* Vol. 2. Edited by Henry Beveridge. Translated by C. Fetherstone. Edinburgh: Calvin Translation Society, 1844.

Calvin, J. *Institutes of the Christian Religion.* Book 1. The Library of Christian Classics Vol. XX. Edited by John T. McNeill. Translated by F. L. Battles. Philadelphia: Westminster Press, 1960.

Campbell, W. S. 'Israel.' Pages 441–446 in *Dictionary of Paul and His Letters.* Edited by G. F. Hawthorne, Ralph P. Martin, and Daniel G. Reid, eds. Leicester: IVP, 1993.

Cardenal, E. *The Gospel in Solentiname.* Vols. 1 & 2. Translated by D. D. Walsh. London: Search Press, 1977.

Carson, D. A. *Exegetical Fallacies.* Grand Rapids: Baker, 1984.

_____ *The Gospel According to John.* Leicester: IVP, 1991.

_____ *The Cross and Christian Ministry: An Exposition of Passages from 1 Corinthians.* Leicester: IVP, 1993.

_____ 'How to Interpret the Bible.' Pages 10–19 in *New Bible Commentary.* 4$^{th}$ Edition. Edited by D. A. Carson, R. T. France, J. A. Motyer and G. J. Wenham. Leicester: IVP, 1994.

_____ *The Gagging of God: Christianity Confronts Pluralism.* Grand Rapids: Zondervan, 1996.

_____ *For the Love of God: A Daily Companion for Discovering the Riches of God's Word.* Vols. 1&2. Leicester: IVP, 1998; 1999.

Carson, D. A. and H. G. Williamson, eds. *It is Written: Scripture Citing Scripture.* Cambridge: Cambridge University Press, 1988.

Carson D. A. and J. D. Woodbridge, eds. *Scripture and Truth.* Leicester: IVP, 1983.

_____ *Hermeneutics, Authority and Canon.* Leicester: IVP, 1986.

Carson, D.A., ed. *The Enduring Authority of the Christian Scriptures.* London: Apollos, 2016.

Catholic Bishops' Conference of England and Wales, and of Scotland, *The Gift of Scripture: A Teaching Document.* London: Catholic Truth Society, 2005.

Chester, T. *Delighting in the Trinity.* Oxford: Monarch, 2005.

Childs, B. S. 'Speech-act Theory and Biblical Interpretation.' *Scottish Journal of Theology* Vol. 58 No. 4 (2005): 375–392.

Choi, Mun Hong. 'The Personality of the Holy Spirit in the NT with special reference to Luke-Acts.' PhD diss. University of Wales, Lampeter; Evangelical Theological College of Wales, Bridgend, 1999.

Church Pastoral Aid Society. *Youth Praise.* London: Falcon, 1969.

Ciampa, Roy E. and Brian S. Rosner. *The Letter to the Corinthians*, Grand Rapids: Eerdmans; Nottingham: Apollos, 2010

Clark, A. C. *Parallel Lives: The Relation of Paul to the Apostles in the Lucan Perspective.* Carlisle: Paternoster, 2001.

Clarke, G. W., ed. *The Hellenistic Inheritance and the English Imagination.* Cambridge: Cambridge University Press, 1989.

Clendenin, D. B. *Eastern Orthodox Christianity: A Western Perspective.* Grand Rapids: Baker, 1994.

Climenhaga, A. M. 'Mission and Neo-Universalism.' *Evangelical Review of Theology* 28:1 (2004): 4–20.

Cohn-Sherbok, D., ed. *Using the Bible Today: Contemporary Interpretations of Scripture.* London: Bellen Publishing, 1991.

Collins, R. F. *I & II Timothy and Titus.* London and Louisville: Westminster John Knox, 2002.

Congar, Yves M. J. *The Word and the Spirit.* London: Geoffrey Chapman, 1986.

_____ *I Believe in the Holy Spirit.* New York: Crossroad, 1997.

Conzelmann, H. *1 Corinthians.* Philadelphia: Fortress Press, 1975.

Cranfield, C. E. B. 'Fellowship, Communion.' Page 82 in *A Theological Word Book of the Bible.* Edited by Alan Richardson. London: SCM, 1950.

_____ *The Epistle to the Romans.* Vol. 1. Edinburgh: T&T Clark, 1975.

Culpepper, R. Alan. *The Gospel and Letters of John.* Nashville, TN: Abingdon, 1998,

Cunningham, D. *These Three are One: The Practice of Trinitarian Theology.* Massachusetts; Oxford: Blackwell, 1988.

Danielou, J. *Gospel Message and Hellenistic Culture.* London: Darton, Longman and Todd; Westminster Press, 1973.

Davies, W. D. *Paul and Rabbinic Judaism: Some Rabbinic Elements in Pauline Theology.* 3rd Edition. London: SPCK, 1970.

Davis, E. F. and R. B. Hays, eds. *The Art of Reading Scripture.* Grand Rapids: Eerdmans, 2003.

Denney, J. *The Second Epistle to the Corinthians.* Expositors Bible. 5th Edition. London: Hodder and Stoughton, 1917.

Dibelius, M. and H. Conzelman. *The Pastoral Epistles.* Philadelphia: Fortress, 1972.

Doctrine Commission of the General Synod of the Church of England Report, *We Believe in the Holy Spirit.* London: Church House, 1991.

Dodd, C. H. *The Epistle of Paul to the Romans.* London: Hodder and Stoughton, 1932.

_____ *The Apostolic Preaching and Its Developments.* London: Hodder and Stoughton, 1936.

_____ *The Authority of the Bible.* London: Nisbet, 1938.

_____ *According to the Scriptures: The Substructure of New Testament Theology.* London: Nisbet, 1952.

_____ *The Interpretation of the Fourth Gospel.* Cambridge: Cambridge University Press, 1953.

_____ *The Apostles.* London: Pickering & Inglis, 1975.

_____ 'The Old Testament in the New.' Pages 167–181 in *The Right Doctrine from the Wrong Texts: Essays on the Use of the Old Testament in the New.* Edited by G. K. Beale. Grand Rapids: Baker, 1994.

Dorman, T. M. 'Holy Spirit, History, Hermeneutics and Theology: Toward an Evangelical/Catholic Consensus.' *Journal of The Evangelical Theological Society* 41/3 (1998): 427–438.

Douglas, J. D., N. Hilyer and D. R. Wood, eds. *New Bible Dictionary.* 3rd Edition. Leicester: IVP, 1996.

Drane, J. *The McDonaldization of the Church: Spirituality, Creativity and the Future of the Church.* London: Darton, Longman and Todd, 2001.

Dray, S. 'Evangelical Tradition.' *Evangel*, 25:1 (2007): 1–2.

Dudley-Smith, Timothy. *John Stott: A Global Ministry.* Leicester: IVP, 2001.

Duncan, M. 'The Audience is Listening.' *Idea* (Nov/Dec 2004): 9.

Dunn, J. D. G. *Jesus and the Spirit: A Study of the Religious and Charismatic Experience of Jesus and the First Christians as Reflected in the New Testament.* London: SCM, 1975.

_____ *Romans.* Word Biblical Commentary. No. 38. Dallas: Word, 1988.

_____ 'Spirit, Holy Spirit.' Pages 689–707 in *NIDNTT*, Vol. 3.

_____ *The Theology of Paul the Apostle.* Edinburgh: T&T Clark, 1998.

_____ *Jesus Remembered: Christianity in the Making.* Vol. 1. Grand Rapids; Cambridge: Eerdmans, 2003.

———— 'On History, Memory and Eyewitness: In Response to Bengt Holmberg and Samuel Byskog.' *Journal for the Study of the New Testament* Vol. 26:4 (2004): 473–487.

Duvall, J. Scott and J. Daniel Hays. *Grasping God's Word: A Hands-On Approach to Reading, Interpreting and Applying the Bible.* Grand Rapids: Zondervan, 2001.

Easley, K. H. 'The Pauline Usage of *Pneumati* as a Reference to the Spirit of God.' *Journal of the Evangelical Theological Society* 27/3 (1984): 299–313.

Edwards, J. *The Works of Jonathan Edwards.* Vol. 2. Edinburgh: Banner of Truth, 1974.

Edwards, R. B. *The Johannine Epistles.* Sheffield: Sheffield Academic Press, 1996.

Edwards, R. M. 'Scriptural Perspicuity in the Early English Reformation.' PhD diss., University of Wales, Lampeter; Evangelical Theological College of Wales, Bridgend, 2001.

Elbert, P. 'Spirit, Scripture and Theology through a Lukan Lens: A Review Article.' *Journal of Pentecostal Theology* 13 (1998): 55–75.

Ellis, E. Earle. 'Pastoral Letters.' Pages 658–666 in *Dictionary of Paul and His Letters.* Edited by G. F. Hawthorne, Ralph P. Martin, and Daniel G. Reid, eds. Leicester: IVP, 1993.

———— *The Old Testament in Early Christianity: Canon and Interpretation in the Light of Modern Research.* Grand Rapids: Baker, 1991.

Elwell, W. A., ed. *Evangelical Dictionary of Theology.* Grand Rapids: Baker; Carlisle: Paternoster, 1984.

Emedi, Samuel. 'Intertextuality in New Testament Scholarship: Significance, Criteria and the Art of Intertextual Reading.' *Currents in Biblical Research* 2015 Vol. 14(1): 8–23.

English, D. *The Message of Mark.* Bible Speaks Today. Leicester: IVP, 1992.

Epp, M. 'Using Scripture in Pastoral Care.' *Vision: A Journal for Church and Theology*, Vol. 6 No.1 (2005): 63–69.

Escobar, S. *A Time for Mission: The Challenge for Global Christianity.* Leicester: IVP, 2003.

Evans, C. A. and S. E. Porter, eds. *Dictionary of New Testament Background.* Leicester: IVP, 2000.

Evans, C. A. and J. A. Sanders. *Luke and Scripture: The Function of Sacred Tradition in Luke-Acts.* Minneapolis: Fortress, 1993.

_____ eds. *Paul and the Scriptures of Israel.* Sheffield: Sheffield Academic Press, 1993.

Evans, C. A. 'New Testament use of the Old Testament.' Page 73 in *New Dictionary of Biblical Theology.* Edited by T. Desmond Alexander and B. S. Rosner. Leicester: IVP, 2000.

Everts, J. M. 'Conversion and Call of Paul.' Pages 156–163 in *Dictionary of Paul and His Letters.* Edited by G. F. Hawthorne, Ralph P. Martin, and Daniel G. Reid, eds. Leicester: IVP, 1993.

Fee, G. D. and D. Stuart. *How to Read the Bible for All Its Worth.* 2nd Edition. Bletchley: Scripture Union, 1994.

Fee, G. D. *The First Epistle to the Corinthians.* Grand Rapids: Eerdmans, 1987.

Fee, G. D. *God's Empowering Presence: The Holy Spirit in the Letters of Paul.* Peabody, MA: Hendrickson, 1994.

_____ *Paul's Letter to the Philippians.* Grand Rapids: Eerdmans, 1995.

_____ *Listening to the Spirit in the Text,* Grand Rapids: Eerdmans, 2000.

_____ 'Paul and the Spirit.' Lectures at Trinity College, Bristol, 26th Feb. 2004.

Ferdinando, K. *The Triumph of Christ in African Perspective.* Carlisle: Paternoster, 1999.

Ferguson, S. *The Holy Spirit.* Leicester: IVP, 1996.

Fiddes, P. *Participating in God: A Pastoral Doctrine of the Trinity.* London: Darton, Longman and Todd, 2000.

Fish, S. *Is There a Text in This Class? The Authority of Interpretive Communities.* Cambridge, MA: Harvard University Press, 1980.

Fishbane, M. *Biblical Interpretation in Ancient Israel.* Oxford: Clarendon, 1985.

Fitzmyer, J. A. *Romans.* Anchor Bible. New York: Doubleday; London: Geoffrey Chapman, 1992.

_____ *According to Paul: Studies in the Theology of the Apostle.* Mahwah, NJ: Paulist Press, 1993.

_____ *The Acts of the Apostles.* Anchor Bible. New York: Doubleday, 1998.

_____ 'The Structured Ministry of the Church in the Pastoral Epistles.' *Catholic Biblical Quarterly* Vol. 66 No. 4 (2004): 582–596.

Foakes-Jackson, F. J. *The Acts of the Apostles.* MNTC. London: Hodder and Stoughton, 1931.

Fowl, S., ed. *The Theological Interpretation of Scripture.* Oxford: Blackwell, 1997.

Fowl, S. *Engaging Scripture.* Oxford: Blackwell, 1998.

France, R. T. *Jesus and the Old Testament.* Grand Rapids: Baker, 1982.

Freedman, D. N. *Anchor Bible Dictionary.* 6 Vols. New York: Doubleday, 1992.

Gabel, H. 'Ignatian Contemplation and Modern Biblical Studies.' *The Way: A Review of Spirituality* Vol. 44 No. 2 (2005): 37–49

Gadamer, Hans-Georg, *Truth and Method.* London: Sheed and Ward, 1975.

Garland, D. E. *1 Corinthians.* Grand Rapids: Baker, 2003.

Gathercole, S. J. Review of *Conversion at Corinth: Perspectives on Conversion in Paul's Theology and the Corinthian Church* by Sephen Chester. *Journal for the Study of the New Testament* 26.2 (2003): 247.

Gibson, D. 'Evangelical Preaching in Northern Ireland: A Brainstorming Response.' *Evangel* 22:1 (2004): 21–26.

Goldingay, J. *Models for Interpretation of Scripture.* Carlisle: Paternoster, 1995.

Goldsworthy, G. 'Relationship of Old Testament and New Testament.' Pages 81-89 in *New Dictionary of Biblical Theology.* Edited by T. Desmond Alexander and B. S. Rosner. Leicester: IVP, 2000.

_____ *Gospel-Centred Hermeneutics.* Nottingham: Apollos/IVP, 2006.

Golligher, L. *The Fellowship of the King: The Quest for Community and Purpose.* Carlisle: Keswick Ministries and Authentic Lifestyle, 2003.

Gooding, D. *True to the Faith: A Fresh Approach to the Acts of the Apostles.* London: Hodder & Stoughton, 1990.

Goodliff, P. 'Recent Ecumenical Dialogue between Pentecostals and the World Council of Chruches.' *Baptist Times* 7th July 2005.

Green, J. B., S. McKnight and I. Howard Marshall, eds. *Dictionary of Jesus and the Gospels.* Leicester: IVP, 1992.

Green, J. 'Practicing the Gospel in a Post-Critical World: The Promise of Theological Exegesis.' *Journal of the Evangelical Theological Society* 47/3 (Sept. 2004): 387–397.

Green, M. *2 Peter and Jude.* London: IVP, 1968.

Greene, M. 'Can We Preach Today?' EG *Magazine of London Institute for Contemporary Christianity* (Dec. 2003): 7.

Grenz, S. *Theology for the Community of God.* Carlisle: Paternoster Press, 1994.

_____ *The Social God and the Relational Self: A Trinitarian Theology of the Imago Deo.* Louisville; London; Leiden: Westminster John Knox, 2001.

Grenz, S. and J. R. Franke. *Beyond Foundationalism: Shaping Theology in a Postmodern Context.* Louisville, KT: Westminster John Knox, 2001.

Griffith, T. 'A Non-Polemical Reading of 1 John: Sin, Christology and the Limits of Johannine Christology.' *Tyndale Bulletin* 49:2 (1998): 253–276.

Griffiths, M. *Cinderella with Amnesia: A Practical Discussion of the Relevance of the Church.* London: IVP, 1975.

Groppe, E. T. *Yves Congar's Theology of the Holy Spirit.* Oxford University Press, 2004.

Grudem, W. A. *The First Epistle of Peter.* Leicester: IVP, 1988.

Gunton, C. E. 'Eschatology and Elusiveness: Towards a Systematic Theology of the Holy Spirit.' Unpublished paper, copy held in library of Evangelical Theological College of Wales.

_____ 'The Spirit in the Trinity.' Page 123 in *The Forgotten Trinity: British Council of Churches Study Commission on Trinitarian Doctrine.* London: BCC, 1991.

_____ *The Promise of Trinitarian Theology.* Edinburgh: T&T Clark, 1991.

_____ *The One, The Three and the Many: God, Creation and the Culture of Modernity.* Cambridge University Press, 1993.

Guthrie, D. *The Pastoral Epistles.* Leicester: IVP, 1957.

Haenchen, E. *The Acts of the Apostles: A Commentary.* Oxford: Blackwell, 1971.

Hafemann, S. J. *2 Corinthians.* NIV Application Commentary. Grand Rapids: Zondervan, 2000.

Hahn, E. '"He will Lead you into all Truth"': On the Relationship between Christology and Pneumatology.' *European Journal of Theology* 5:2 (1996): 93–103.

Hanson, A. T. *The Living Utterances of God.* London: Darton Longman and Todd, 1983.

Hanson, P. 'Scripture, Community and Spirit: Biblical Theology's Contribution to a Contextualized Christian Theology.' *Journal of Pentecostal Theology* 6 (1995): 3–12.

Harrington, H. K. and R. Patten. 'Pentecostal Hermeneutics and Postmodern Literary Theory.' *Pneuma: The Journal of the Society for Pentecostal Studies* Vol. 16 No. 1 (Spring 1994): 109–114.

Harris, H. 'Hegel' Pages 288–289 in *New Dictionary of Theology.* Edited by S. B. Ferguson, D. F. Wright and J. I Packer. Leicester: IVP, 1988.

Harris, M. J. *The Second Epistle to the Corinthians: A Commentary on the Greek Text.* Milton Keynes: Paternoster, 2005.

Harvey, J. D. *Listening to the Text: Oral Patterning in Paul's Letters.* Leicester: Apollos, 1998.

Hawthorne, G. F., Ralph P. Martin, and Daniel G. Reid, eds. *Dictionary of Paul and His Letters.* Leicester: IVP, 1993.

Hawthorne, G. F. 'Holy Spirit.' Pages 489–99 in *Dictionary of the Later New Testament and its Developments.* Edited by R. P. Martin and P. H. Davids. Leicester: IVP, 1997.

Haykin, M. A. G. 'The Fading Vision? The Spirit and Freedom in the Pastoral Epistles.' *Evangelical Quarterly* Vol. LVII No. 4 (Oct. 1985): 291–305.

Hays, R. B. *Echoes of Scripture in the Letters of Paul.* New Haven: Yale University Press, 1989.

_____ *First Corinthians.* Louisville: John Knox, 1997.

_____ *The Conversion of the Imagination: Paul as Interpreter of Israel's Scripture.* Grand Rapids: Eerdmans, 2005.

Hendriksen, W. *1 & 2 Timothy and Titus.* Edinburgh: Banner of Truth, 1957.

_____ *The Gospel of John.* Edinburgh: Banner of Truth, 1959.

Heron, A. I. C., ed. *The Forgotten Trinity.* A Selection of Papers Presented to the B.C.C. Study Commission on Trinitarian Doctrine Today. London: BCC/CCBI, 1991.

Hill, D. *The Gospel of Matthew.* London: Marshall Morgan and Scott, 1972.

Hodge, C., *A Commentary on Romans* (Edinburgh: Banner of Truth, 1972, original ed. 1835)

_____ *A Commentary on the Epistle to the Ephesians.* London: James Nisbet and Co, 1856.

Hoeck, A. 'The Johannine Paraclete: Herald of the Eschaton,' *Journal of Biblical and Pneumatological Research.'* Vol. 4 (Sept 2012): 23–37.

Holland, T., 'Romans and the New Exodus: A Study in the Paschal New Exodus Theology of the Apostle Paul'. Ph.D. thesis, University of Wales, Lampeter, 1996

_____ *Contours of Pauline Theology: A Radical New Survey of the Influences on Paul's Biblical Writings.* Fearn: Christian Focus-Mentor, 2004.

_____ *Romans: The Divine Marriage – A Biblical Theological Commentary.* Eugene, OR: Pickwick, 2011.

_____ *Hope for the Nations. Paul's Letter to the Romans.* London: Apostolos 2015.

Homberg, B. and S. Byskog. Review of *Jesus Remembered: Christianity in the Making* Vol. 1 by J. D. G. Dunn. *Journal for the Study of the New Testament* Vol. 26:4 (June 2004): 445–471.

Horn, F. W. 'The Holy Spirit.' Pages 260–280 in *Anchor Bible Dictionary.* Vol. 3. Edited by D. N. Freedman. New York: Doubleday, 1992.

Horsley, R. H. *1 Corinthians.* Abingdon Press, Nashville, 1998.

Hoskyns, E. C. *The Fourth Gospel.* London: Faber and Faber, 1948.

Houlden, J. L. ed. *The Interpretation of the Bible in the Church.* Pontifical Biblical Commission 1993. London: SCM, 1995.

Hubner, H. 'OT Quotations in the New Testament.' Pages 1096–1103 in *Anchor Bible Dictionary.* Vol. 4. Edited by D. N. Freedman. New York: Doubleday, 1992.

Hudson, N. '"You'll Never Know your Future Until You Know Where your Past Is." British Pentecostalism's Development and Future Challenges.' *Evangel* 21:2 (Summer 2003): 37–40.

Hughes, P. E. *The Second Epistle to the Corinthians.* Grand Rapids: Eerdmans, 1962.

Hui, A. 'The Spirit of Prophecy and Pauline Pneumatology.' *Tyndale Bulletin* 50:1 (1999): 93–115.

_____ 'The Pneumatology of Watchman Nee: A New Testament Perspective.' *Evangelical Quarterly* 75:4 (2003): 3–29.

Hull, J. H. E. *The Holy Spirit in the Acts of the Apostles.* London: Lutterworth, 1967.

Hultgren, Arland J. *Paul's Letter to the Romans.* Grand Rapids: Eerdmans, 2011.

Hur, J. *A Dynamic Reading of the Holy Spirit in Luke-Acts.* Sheffield Academic Press, 2001.

Jackman, D. *The Message of John's Letters.* Leicester: IVP, 1988.

_____ 'Next Step?' reviewing *Becoming Conversant with the Emerging Church* by D. A. Carson. *Evangelicals Now* (Nov. 2005): 13.

_____ *Spirit of Truth: Unlocking the Bible's Teaching on the Holy Spirit.* Fearn: Christian Focus, 2006.

Jervell, J. *The Theology of the Acts of the Apostles.* Cambridge University Press, 1996.

Jeske, R. L. 'Spirit and Community in the Johannine Apocalypse.' *New Testament Studies* Vol. 31 (1985): 452–466.

Johnson, Luke Timothy. *Scripture and Discernment: Decision Making in the Church*. Nashville: Abingdon, 1996.

_____ *The First and Second Letters to Timothy*. New York: Doubleday, 2001.

Johnston, R. K. 'Orthodoxy and Heresy: A Problem for Modern Evangelicalism.' *Evangelical Quarterly* 69:1 (1997): 7–38.

Jones, K. G. *A Believing Church: Learning from Some Contemporary Anabaptist and Baptist Perspectives*. Didcot: Baptist Union of Great Britain, 1998.

Jones, K. 'Towards a Model of Mission for Gathering, Intentional, Convictional Koinonia.' *Journal of European Baptist Studies* Vol. 4 (Jan 2004): 5–13.

Kärkkäinen, Veli-Matti. 'Trinity, Spirit and Church.' *The Spirit and Church* 4:1 (May 2002): 9–26.

_____ *Pneumatology: The Holy Spirit in Ecumenical International and Contextual Perspective*. Grand Rapids: Baker Academic, 2002.

Karris, R. J. Review of *Mighty in Word and Deed: The Role of the Holy Spirit in Luke-Acts* James by B. Shelton in *The Catholic Biblical Quarterly* 55 (1993): 182–183.

Käsemann, E. *Commentary on Romans*. London: SCM, 1973.

Keesmat, S. C. *Paul and His Story: (Re)Interpreting the Exodus Tradition*. Sheffield Academic Press, 1999.

Kelly, J. N. D. *Pastoral Epistles*. London: A & C Black, 1963.

Kelsey, D. H. *The Uses of Scripture in Recent Theology*. Philadelphia: Fortress Press, 1975.

Kim, S. *Paul and the New Perspective: Second Thoughts on the Origin of Paul's Gospel*. Grand Rapids: Eerdmans, 2000.

King, U., ed. *Faith and Praxis in a Postmodern Age*. London: Cassell, 1998.

Kinnamon, M. *Truth and Community: Diversity and its Limits in the Ecumenical Movement*. Grand Rapids: Eerdmans; Geneva: WCC, 1988.

Kistemaker, S. J. *Exposition of the Acts of the Apostles*. Grand Rapids: Baker, 1990.

_____ *James, Epistles of John, Peter and Jude*. Grand Rapids: Baker, 1996.

Kittel, G. and G. Friedrich, eds. *Theological Dictionary of the New Testament*. 10 Volumes. Translated by G. W. Bromiley. Grand Rapids: Eerdmans, 1967.

Kostenberger, A. J. Review of *The Gospel of John: A Commentary* by Graig S. Keene in *Journal of the Evangelical Theological Society* Vol. 47 No. 2 (June 2004): 350–353.

Kraus, Hans-Joachim. *Heiliger Geist: Gottes befreiende Gegenwart.* Munich: Kosel-Verlag, 1986.

Kruse, C. G. *The Letters of John.* Leicester: Apollos, 2000.

Lampe, G. W. H. *God as Spirit.* London: SCM, 1977.

Lash, N. Public lecture 'The Christian Doctrine of God' at Theological Society of University of Wales, Swansea, 19th November 2003.

Law, R. *The Tests of Life.* Grand Rapids: Baker 1979.

Lenski, R. C. H. *The Interpretation of St John's Gospel.* Minneapolis: Augsburg, 1943.

Levison, J. R. *The Spirit in First Century Judaism.* Leiden: Brill, 2002.

Lewis, G. R. 'Is Propositional Revelation Essential to Evangelical Spiritual Formation?' *Journal of Evangelical Theological Society* Vol. 46 No. 2 (June 2003): 269–298.

Lewis, J. 'Tradition/history' in *The Sunday Telegraph*, Dec. 7 2003.

Lieu, J. *The Theology of the Johannine Epistles.* Cambridge: Cambridge University Press, 1991.

Lieu, J. *1, 11 & 111 John.* Louisville: Westminster John Knox, 2008.

Lightfoot, J. B. *Notes on Epistles of St Paul.* London: Macmillan, 1895.

Lindars, B. *The Gospel of John.* London: Marshall, Morgan and Scott, 1987.

Lloyd-Jones, D. Martyn. *Romans.* Vol. 7. Edinburgh: Banner of Truth, 1974.

_____ *Preaching and Preachers.* London: Hodder and Stoughton, 1976.

Longenecker, R. N. *Acts.* Expositor's Bible Commentary, Grand Rapids: Zondervan, 1995.

_____ *Biblical Exegesis in the Apostolic Period.* Grand Rapids: Eerdmans, 1999.

Longenecker, R. N., ed. *Community Formation in the Early Church and in the Church Today.* Peabody, MA: Hendrikson, 2002.

Longley, C. 'God Bless America?' An Extract from *Chosen People: The Big Idea that Shapes England and America* by C. Longley. EG *Magazine of London Institute of Contemporary Christianity* Edition 13 (March 2004): 3.

Lundin, R., ed. *Disciplining Hermeneutics: Interpretation in Christian Perspective.* Grand Rapids: Eerdmans; Leicester: Apollos/IVP, 1997.

Lundin, R., C. Walhout and A. C. Thiselton. *The Promise of Hermeneutics.* Carlisle: Paternoster, 1999.

Macchia, F. D. 'Pentecostal Theology.' Pages 1120–1140 in *New International Dictionary of Pentecostal and Charismatic Movements.* Edited by S. M. Burgess and E. M. Van Der Maas. Revised Edition. Grand Rapids: Zondervan, 2002.

MacCulloch, D. *Groundwork of Christian History.* London: Epworth, 1987.

Mackintosh, H. R. *Types of Modern Theology: Schleiermacher to Barth.* London: James Nisbet & Co., 1937.

Maclean, G. D. *'An Examination of the Characteristics of Short Term International Midwifery Consultants.'* PhD diss., University of Surrey, 1998.

Macleod, D. 'The New Perspective: Paul, Luther and Judaism.' *Scottish Bulletin of Evangelical Theology* Vol. 22 No. 1 (Spring 2004): 4–31.

Malina, B. *The New Testament World: Insights from Cultural Anthropology.* Louisville, KT: Westminster John Knox, 1993.

Marshall, I. Howard. 'Orthodoxy and Heresy in Earlier Christianity.' *Themelios* Vol. 2:1 (Sept. 1976): 5–14.

_____ *The Epistles of John.* New International Commentary on the New Testament. Grand Rapids: Eerdmans, 1978.

_____ *The Gospel of Luke.* Exeter: Paternoster, 1978.

_____ *The Acts of the Apostles.* TNTC, Leicester: IVP, 1980.

_____ *1 Peter.* Leicester: IVP, 1991.

_____ *The Acts of the Apostles.* NT Guides. Sheffield: Sheffield Academic Press, 1992.

_____ *The Epistle to the Philippians.* London: Epworth, 1992.

_____ 'Recent Study of the Pastoral Epistles.' *Themelios* Vol. 23:1 (Oct. 1997): 3–21.

_____ *Beyond the Bible: Moving from Scripture to Theology.* Milton Keynes: Paternoster; Grand Rapids: Baker, 2004.

_____ *New Testament Theology: Many Witnesses, One Gospel.* Downers Grove, IL: IVP, 2004.

Marshall, I. Howard, ed. *New Testament Interpretation: Essays on Principles and Methods.* Exeter: Paternoster, 1979.

Marshall, I. Howard and D. Peterson, eds. *Witness to the Gospel: The Theology of Acts.* Grand Rapids: Eerdmans, 1998.

Marshall, I. Howard and P. H. Towner. *The Pastoral Epistles.* Critical and Exegetical Commentary. Edinburgh: T&T Clark, 1999.

Marshall, M. *Joining the Dance: A Theology of the Spirit.* Valley Forge: Judson Press, 2003.

Marshall, R. A. *The R.S.V. Interlinear Greek-English New Testament.* 3rd Edition. London: Samuel Bagster and Sons Limited, 1975.

Martin, R. P. *The Epistle of Paul to the Philippians.* London: Tyndale, 1959.

_____ *The Family and the Fellowship: New Testament Images of the Church.* Exeter: Paternoster, 1979.

_____ *Philippians.* New Century. London: Marshall, Morgan & Scott, 1980.

_____ *2 Corinthians.* Word Biblical Commentary. Milton Keynes: Word, 1991.

Martin, R. P. and P. H. Davids, eds. *Dictionary of the Later New Testament and Its Developments.* Leicester: IVP, 1997.

Matheson, K. A. *The Shape of Sola Scriptura.* Moscow, ID: Canon Press, 2001.

Matthey, J., ed. 'Come, Holy Spirit: Heal and Reconcile.' Various articles in *International Review of Mission* Vol. 94 No. 372 (Jan 2005): 3ff.

May, R. J. 'The Role of the Holy Spirit in Biblical Hermeneutics.' http://www.biblicalstudies.org.uk/th_spirit_intro.html

McBain, D. *Fire Over the Waters-Renewal among Baptists and others from the 1960s to the 1990s.* London: Darton Longman and Todd, 1997.

McClendon, J. W. *Systematic Theology: Doctrine,* Vol. II. Nashville: Abingdon, 1994.

_____ *Ethics: Systematic Theology.* Vol. 1. 2nd Edition. Nashville: Abingdon, 2002.

McGowan, A. T. B., ed. *'"Always Reforming": Explorations in Systematic Theology.'* Leicester: IVP, 2006.

McGrath, A. *An Introduction to the History of Christian Thought.* Oxford: Blackwell, 1998.

McIntosh, J. '"For it Seemed Good to the Holy Spirit" Acts 15:28. How did the Members of the Jerusalem Council *Know* This?' *The Reformed Theological Review* 61: 3 (Dec. 2002): 131–147.

McIntyre, J. *The Shape of Pneumatology*. Edinburgh: T&T Clark, 1997.

McRay, J. R. 'Canon of Bible' Pages 140–141 in *Evangelical Dictionary of Theology*. Edited by W. A. Elwell. Grand Rapids: Baker; Carlisle: Paternoster, 1984.

Meadowcroft, T. 'Between Authorial Intent and Indeterminancy: The Incarnation as an Invitation to Human-divine Discourse.' *Scottish Journal of Theology* Vol. 58 No. 2 (2005): 199–218.

Means, J. E. B. *Leadership in Christian Ministry*. Grand Rapids: Baker, 1989.

Michaels, J. Ramsey. *1 Peter*. Word Biblical Commentary. Waco, TX: Word, 1988.

Miller, J. D. *The Pastoral Letters as Composite Documents*. Cambridge: Cambridge University Press, 1997.

Milne, B. *The Message of John*. Leicester: IVP, 1993.

Moltmann, J. *The Spirit of Life*. London: SCM Press, 1992.

Moo, D. J. *Romans*. Life Application Commentary. Grand Rapids: Zondervan, 2000.

Morgan-Wynne, J. E. *Holy Spirit and Religious Experience in Christian Writings, ca. AD 90–200*. Studies in Christian History and Thought. Carlisle: Paternoster, 2006.

Morris, L. *The First Epistle of Paul to the Corinthians*. TNTC. Leicester: IVP, 1958.

_____ *The Gospel According to John*. London: Marshall Morgan and Scott, 1971.

_____ *New Testament Theology*. Grand Rapids: Zondervan, 1986.

_____ *Luke*. TNTC. Leicester: IVP, 1988.

Motyer, J. A. Lecture at Trinity College, Bristol, 23.11.77

Moule, C. F. D. *The Birth of the New Testament*. 2nd Edition. London: Adam and Charles Black, 1966.

_____ *The Holy Spirit*. London: Mowbray, 1978.

Moule, C. F. D., ed. *Essays in New Testament Interpretation*. Cambridge: Cambridge University Press, 1982.

Moule, H. C. G. *Romans*. London: Hodder & Stoughton, 1992.

Mounce, W. D. *Pastoral Epistles*. Nashville: Thomas Nelson, 2000.

Moyise, S. *The Old Testament in the New: An Introduction*. London; New York: Continuum, 2001.

Moyise, S. 'Can We Use the New Testament in the Way the New Testament Authors used the Old Testament?' *In die Skriflig* (2002): 643–660. As copied from last page of an article located at www.ucc.ac.uk/theology/html/MoyiseCanWeUse.htm

Murray, J. *The Epistle to the Romans*. Grand Rapids: Eerdmans, 1968.

Naylor, P. *A Study Commentary on 2 Corinthians*. Vol. 1. Darlington: Evangelical Press, 2002.

Nebeker, G. 'The Holy Spirit, Hermeneutics, and Transformation: From Present to Future Glory.' *Evangelical Review of Theology* Vol. 27 No.1 (Jan. 2003): 47–54.

Needham, N. 'Tradition in 2 Timothy.' *Evangel* 17:1 (Spring 1999): 6–9.

Neudorfer, Heinz-Werner. 'The Speech of Stephen' Chapter 14 in *Witness to the Gospel: The Theology of Acts*. Edited by I. Howard Marshall and D. Peterson. Grand Rapids: Eerdmans, 1998.

Noble, P. R. *The Canonical Approach: A Critical Reconstruction of the Hermeneutics of Brevard S. Childs*. Leiden; New York; Koln: Brill, 1995.

Noelliste, D. 'Theological Education in the Context of Socio-Economic Deprivation.' *Evangelical Review of Theology* Vol. 29:3 (2005): 270–283.

Noll, S. F. 'Qumran and Paul.' Pages 777–783 in *Dictionary of Paul and His Letters*. Edited by G. F. Hawthorne, Ralph P. Martin, and Daniel G. Reid, eds. Leicester: IVP, 1993.

Nuffer, C. J. Review of *Theology, Music and Time* by Jeremy Begbie in *Dialog: A Journal of Theology* Vol. 44 No.1 (Spring 2005): 109.

Null, A. 'Understanding the Episcopal Church and Why They Consecrated a Gay Bishop.' *The Briefing* (Jan. 2004): 11–15.

Nygren, A. *Commentary on Romans*. Philadelphia: Fortress Press, 1949.

O'Brien, P. T. *The Epistle to the Philippians: A Commentary on the Greek Text*. Grand Rapids: Eerdmans, 1991.

Old, Graham. Letter about Report on Sunday School Attendance. *Baptist Times* 20.11 (2003): 10.

O'Murcho, D. 'Spirituality and the Holy Spirit.' *Retreats* 2004.

Osborne, G. R. *The Hermeneutical Spiral*. Leicester: IVP, 1991.

Owen, J. *The Works of John Owen*. Vol. IV. Edinburgh: Banner of Truth, 1967.

_____ *Communion with God*. Abridged Edition. Edinburgh: Banner of Truth, 1991.

Packer, J. I. *Beyond the Battle for the Bible.* Westchester, IL: Cornerstone, 1980.

_____ *Keep in Step with the Spirit.* Leicester: IVP, 1984.

_____ *Collected Shorter Writings of J. I. Packer.* Vol .3. Honouring the Written Word of God. Carlisle: Paternoster, 1999.

Paige, T. 'Holy Spirit.' Pages 104–405 in *Dictionary of Paul and His Letters.* Edited by G. F. Hawthorne, Ralph P. Martin, and Daniel G. Reid, eds. Leicester: IVP, 1993.

Parker, Kelly A. 'Josiah Royce.' *The Stanford Encyclopedia of Philosophy* (Summer 2005). Edited by Edward N. Zalta. <http://plato.stanford.edu/archives/sum2005/entries/royce/>

Pearse, M. 'Problem? What Problem? Personhood, Late Modern/Postmodern Rootlessness and Contemporary Identity Crisis.' *Evangelical Quarterly* 77.1 (2005): 5–12.

Penner, T. C. 'Madness in the Method? The Acts of Apostles in Current Study.' *Currents in Biblical Research* Vol. 2:2 (April 2004): 223–293.

Peterson, David G. *The Acts of the Apostles.* Grand Rapids; Cambridge: Eerdmans, 2009.

Phillips, T. E. 'The Genre of Acts: Moving Toward a Consensus.' *Currents in Biblical Research* Vol. 4.3 (June 2006): 365–396.

Piggin, F. S. 'Council of Trent.' Page 1109 in *Evangelical Dictionary of Theology.* Edited by W. A. Elwell. Grand Rapids: Baker, 1984.

Pinnock, C. 'The Work of the Holy Spirit in Hermeneutics.' *Journal of Pentecostal Theology* 2 (1993): 3–23.

Pope-Levison, P. and J. R. Levison, eds. *Return to Babel: Global Perspectives on the Bible.* Louisville, KT: Westminster John Knox, 1999.

Porter, S. E. and C. A. Evans, eds. *The Pauline Writings: A Sheffield Reader.* Sheffield: Sheffield Academic Press, 1995.

Pratt, R. L. *He Gave us Stories: The Bible Students Guide to Interpreting OT Narratives.* Phillisburg, NJ: Presbyterian and Reformed Publishing Company, 1990.

Prior, D. *The Message of 1 Corinthians.* BST. Leicester: IVP, 1985.

Purvis, J. *The Triune God and the Charismatic Movement: A Critical Appraisal from a Scottish Perspective.* Carlisle: Paternoster, 2004.

Quinn, J. and W. C. Wacker, *The First and Second Letters to Timothy.* Grand Rapids: Eerdmans, 2000.

Rensberger, D. 'Conflict and Community in the Johannine Letters.' *Interpretation* Vol. 60, No. 3 (July 2006): 278–279.

Richardson, A., and J. Bowden, eds. *The Westminster Dictionary of Christian Theology*. Philadelphia: Westminster, 1983.

Richardson, P. 'Spirit and Letter: A Foundation for Hermeneutics.' *Evangelical Quarterly* Vol. XLV No. 4 (Oct./Dec. 1973): 208–218.

Riesner, R. 'Tradition.' Pages 822–826 in *New Dictionary of Biblical Theology*. Edited by T. D. Alexander and B. S. Rosner. Leicester: IVP, 2000.

Ripken, N. 'Two Sides of Pentecost.' *Evangelical Missions Quarterly* Vol. 39 No. 2 (April 2003): 148–150.

Robertson, A. and A. Plummer, *First Epistle of St Paul to the Corinthians*. Edinburgh: T&T Clark, 1914.

Rogerson, J. W. 'The Hebrew Conception of Corporate Personality: A Re-examination.' *Journal of Theological Studies* Vol. XXI (1970): 1–16.

_____ 'Corporate Responsibility.' Pages 1156–1157 in *Anchor Bible Dictionary*. Vol. 1. Edited by D. N. Freeman. New York; London: Doubleday, 1992.

Royce, J. *The Problem of Christianity*. 2 Vols. New York: MacMillan, 1913.

Ryle, J. C. *Expository Thoughts on the Gospels: St John*. Vol. III. Cambridge; London: James Clark and Co., 1969 reprint.

Sacks, J. *Celebrating Life*. London: Continuum, 2003.

Salvation Army, *The Responsibility Gap-Individualism, Community and Responsibility in Britain*. As reported in *The Daily Telegraph,* Jan. 13$^{th}$ (2004): 8.

Sanday, W. and A. C. Headlam. *The Epistle to Romans*. ICC. Edinburgh: T&T Clark, 1898.

Sanders, J. A. *Canon and Community: A Guide to Canonical Criticism*. Philadelphia: Fortress, 1984.

Satterthwaite, P. E. and D. F. Wright, eds. *A Pathway to the Holy Place*. Grand Rapids: Eerdmans, 1994.

Scalise, C. J. *From Scripture to Theology: A Canonical Journey into Hermeneutics*. Downers Grove: IVP, 1996.

Schreiner, T. R. *Romans*. Grand Rapids: Baker, 1998.

Schütz, H.-G. 'Guard, Keep, Watch'/ φυλάσσω. Pages 132–133 in *New International Dictionary of New Testament Theology*. Vol. 2. Edited by Colin Brown. Exeter: Paternoster, 1976.

Schweizer, E. 'πνεῦμα.' TDNT 1:332–451.

Scirghi, T. J. 'The Trinity: A Model for Belonging in a Contemporary Society.' *Ecumenical Review* W.C.C. Vol. 54 No. 3 (July 2002): 333–342.

Scobie, C. H. H. 'The History of Biblical Theology.' Page 11 in *New Dictionary of Biblical Theology*. Edited by T. Desmond Alexander and B. S. Rosner. Leicester: IVP, 2000.

Scott, J. M. *2 Corinthians*. New International Commentary. Peabody, MA: Hendricksen, 1998.

Segner, W. R. 'Paul, the Jew.' Pages 503–511 in *Dictionary of Paul and His Letters*. Edited by G. F. Hawthorne, Ralph P. Martin, and Daniel G. Reid, eds. Leicester: IVP, 1993.

Seifrid, M. A. 'The "New Perspective on Paul" and its Problems.' *Themelios* Vol. 25:2 (Feb. 2000): 4–18.

Sentamu, J. Sermon preached at his inauguration as Archbishop of York 30th November 2005, www.cofe.anglican.org/news/pr9205.html

Schattenmann, J. 'Fellowship.' Pages 635–644 in *New International Dictionary of New Testament Theology*. Edited by C. Brown. Vol. 1. Exeter: Paternoster, 1975.

Shiel, J. *Greek Thought and the Rise of Christianity*. London; Harlow: Longmans, 1968.

Shim, E. S. 'The Holy Spirit in 1 John in the Light of Structural Analysis.' *Chongshin Theological Journal 2* (1997): 109–126.

Silva, M. 'Old Testament in Paul.' Pages 631–642 in *Dictionary of Paul and His Letters*. Edited by G. F. Hawthorne, Ralph P. Martin, and Daniel G. Reid, eds. Leicester: IVP, 1993.

Sim, D. C. 'The Gospel for All Christians? A Response to Richard Bauckham.' *JSNT* 84 (2001): 3–27.

Sine, T. W. 'Globalization, Creation of Global Culture of Consumption and the Impact on the Church and its Mission.' *Evangelical Review of Theology* Vol. 27 No. 4 (Oct. 2003): 353–370.

Skarsaune, O. 'Heresy and the Pastoral Epistles.' *Themelios* Vol. 20:1 (Oct 1994): 9–13.

Smail, T. *The Giving Gift*. London: Hodder and Stoughton, 1988. Reprint London: Darton Longman and Todd, 1994.

Smalley, S. *John: Evangelist and Interpreter*. Exeter: Paternoster, 1978.

_____ *1, 2, 3 John*. Milton Keynes: Word, 1991.

Smeaton, G. *The Doctrine of the Holy Spirit.* London: Banner of Truth, 1958.

Smith, D. W. *Against the Stream: Christianity and Mission in an Age of Globalization.* Leicester: IVP, 2003.

Son, Sang-Won Aaron. *Corporate Elements in Pauline Anthropology.* Rome: Editrice Pontificio Istituto Biblicio-Roma, 2001.

Spawn, K. L. and A. Wright, eds. *Spirit and Scripture: Exploring a Pneumatic Hermeneutic.* London: Bloomsbury T&T Clark, 2013.

Spencer, A. 'Culture, Community and Commitments: Stanley J. Grenz on Theological Method.' *Scottish Journal of Theology* Vol. 57 No. 3 (2004): 338–360.

Spencer, N. 'Choice.' *EG Magazine of the London Institute for Contemporary Christianity* 17 (Dec. 2005): 12.

Stanley, C. D. *Paul and the Language of Scripture: Citation Technique in the Pauline Epistles and Contemporary Literature.* Cambridge: Cambridge University Press, 1992.

_____ *Arguing with Scripture: The Rhetoric of Quotations in the Letters of Paul.* London: T&T Clark, 2004.

Shelfer, Lochlan 'The Legal Precision of the Term παράκλητος'.' *JSNT* 32.2 (2009): 131–150.

Shillington, V. George. 'The Spirit-Paraclete as Jesus' alter ego in the Fourth Gospel (John 14-16).' *Vision* 13:1 (2012): 31–39.

Stegner, W. R. 'Paul, the Jew.' Pages 503–511 in *Dictionary of Paul and His Letters.* Edited by G. F. Hawthorne, Ralph P. Martin, and Daniel G. Reid, eds. Leicester: IVP, 1993.

Stendahl, K. *The School of Matthew and its Use of the Old Testament.* 2nd Edition. Philadelphia: Fortress, 1968.

Stewart, K. S. 'A Bombshell of a Book: Gaussen's *Theopneustia* and its Influence on Subsequent Evangelical Theology.' *Evangelical Quarterly* Vol. LXXV No. 3 (July 2003): 215–237.

Stott, J. R. W. *Epistles of John.* Leicester: IVP, 1964.

_____ *Guard the Gospel: The Message of 2 Timothy.* Leicester: IVP, 1973.

_____ *Christian Mission in the Modern World.* London: Falcon, 1975.

_____ *God's New Society: The Message of Ephesians.* Leicester: IVP, 1979.

_____ *The Message of Acts.* Leicester: IVP, 1990.

_____ *The Message of Romans.* Leicester: IVP, 1994.

_____ *Calling Christian Leaders: Biblical Models of Church, Gospel and Ministry.* Leicester: IVP, 2002.

_____ *Understanding the Bible.* Milton Keynes: Scripture Union, 2003.

Strecker, G. *The Johannine Letters.* Minneapolis: Fortress Press, 1996.

Stronstad, Roger. *The Charismatic Theology of St. Luke.* Grand Rapids: Baker Academic, 2012.

Studebaker Jr., J. A. 'The Authority of the Holy Spirit: The "Missing Link" in Our Contemporary Understanding of Divine Authority?' *Trinity Journal* 25.2 (2004): 215-245.

Stuhlmacher, P. *Paul's Letter to the Romans.* Edinburgh: T&T Clark, 1994.

Sugden, C. 'Good News to the Poor and the Crisis in the Anglican Communion.' *Evangelicals Now* (Feb. 2007): 7.

Suggit, J. N. '"The Holy Spirit and We Resolved..." (Acts 15:28).' *Journal of Theology for Southern Africa* 79:1 (June 1992): 45.

Taylor, J. V. *The Go-Between God.* London: SCM, 2004.

Thielicke, H. *The Evangelical Faith.* Grand Rapids: Eerdmans, 1974.

Thielman, F. 'Law.' Pages 529-542 in *Dictionary of Paul and His Letters.* Edited by G. F. Hawthorne, Ralph P. Martin, and Daniel G. Reid, eds. Leicester: IVP, 1993.

Thiselton, A. C. *The Two Horizons: New Testament Hermeneutics and Philosophical Description with Special Reference to Heidegger, Bultmann, Gadamer, and Wittgenstein.* Carlisle: Paternoster, 1980.

_____ 'Hermeneutics.' Pages 293-297 in *New Dictionary of Theology.* Edited by S. B. Ferguson, D. F. Wright and J. I Packer. Leicester: IVP, 1988.

_____ *New Horizons in Hermeneutics.* London: HarperCollins, 1992.

_____ *The First Epistle to the Corinthians: A Commentary on the Greek Text.* Grand Rapids: Eerdmans; Carlisle: Paternoster, 2000.

_____ *The Holy Spirit: In Biblical Teaching, Through the Centuries, and Today.* London: SPCK, 2013.

Thomas, J. C. 'Women, Pentecostals and the Bible: An Experiment in Pentecostal Hermeneutics.' *Journal of Pentecostal Theology* 5 (1994): 41-56.

Thompson, D., ed. *The Concise Oxford Dictionary.* 9th Edition. Oxford: Clarendon 1995.

Thompson, M. M. *1-3 John.* Leicester: IVP, 1992.

Thomson, J. B. 'Time for Church? Evangelicals, Scripture and Conversational Hermeneutics.' *Anvil* Vol. 21 No. 4 (2004): 245–257.

Thomson, J. *Modern Trinitarian Perspectives.* Oxford: Oxford University Press, 1994.

Thrall, M. E. *The Second Epistle to the Corinthians.* Vol. 1. Edinburgh: T&T Clark, 1994.

Tomlinson, D. 'Issues in Modern Hermeneutics.' *Evangel* (Autumn 1995): 89–95.

Torrance, T. F. *The Christian Doctrine of God, One Being, Three Persons.* Edinburgh: T&T Clark, 1996.

Towner, P. H. *1 Timothy & Titus.* Leicester: IVP, 1994.

_____ 'Pauline Theology or Pauline Tradition in the Pastoral Epistles: The Question of Method.' *Tyndale Bulletin* 46:2 (1995): 287–314.

_____ 'The Pastoral Epistles.' Pages 330–336 in *New Dictionary of Biblical Theology.* Edited by T. Desmond Alexander and B. S. Rosner. Leicester: IVP, 2000.

Trembath, K. R. 'Biblical Inspiration and the Believing Community.' *The Evangelical Quarterly* Vol. LVIII No. 3 (July 1986): 245–256.

Treier, Daniel J. *Introducing Theological Interpretation of Scripture: Recovering a Christian Practice.* Nottingham: Apollos, 2008.

Tuckett, C. 'Paul, Scripture and Ethics: Some Reflections.' *New Testament Studies* Vol. 46 (2000): 403–424.

Turner, M. M. B. 'Holy Spirit.' Pages 341–351 in *Dictionary of Jesus and the Gospels.* Edited by J. B. Green, S. McKnight and I. Howard Marshall. Leicester: IVP, 1992.

Turner, M. M. B *Power from on High: The Spirit in Israel's Restoration and Witness in Luke-Acts.* Sheffield Academic Press, 1996.

_____ *The Holy Spirit and Spiritual Gifts.* Carlisle: Paternoster, 1996.

Van der Horst, P. W. *Hellenism-Judaism-Christianity: Essays on their Interaction.* Leuven: Peeters, 1998.

Van Engen, J. 'Tradition.' Page 1104 in *Evangelical Dictionary of Theology.* Edited by. W. A. Elwell. Grand Rapids: Baker, 1984.

Vandervelde, G. '"Church, Evangelization, and the Bonds of *Koinonia*." A Report of the International Consultation between the Catholic Church and the World Evangelical Alliance (1993–2002).' *Evangelical Review of Theology* Vol. 29 No. 2 (April 2005): 100–130.

Vanhoozer, K. J. 'The Spirit of Understanding: Special Revelation and General Hermeneutics.' Pages 131–172 in *Disciplining Hermeneutics: Interpretation in Christian Perspective*. Edited by Roger Lundin. Leicester: Apollos/IVP 1997.

_____ *Is There a Meaning in this Text? The Bible, the Reader and the Morality of Literary Knowledge*. Leicester: Apollos/IVP, 1998.

_____ 'Exegesis and Hermeneutics.' Pages 52–64 in *New Dictionary of Biblical Theology*. Edited by T. D. Alexander and B. Rosner. Leicester: IVP, 2000.

_____ 'The Promise of Consensus: Towards a Communicative Hermeneutic.' *The Bible in TransMission* (Spring 2001): 6–7.

_____ *First Theology: God Scripture and Hermeneutics*. Leicester: Apollos/IVP, 2002.

Vanhoozer, K. J., Craig G. Bartholomew, Daniel J. Treier and N. T. Wright. *Dictionary for Theological Interpretation of the Bible*. Grand Rapids: Baker, 2005.

Veenhof, J. 'The Holy Spirit and Hermeneutics.' *Scottish Bulletin of Evangelical Theology* Vol. 5 No. 1 (Spring 1987): 105–122.

Vermes, G. *An Introduction to the Complete Dead Sea Scrolls*. Minneapolis: Fortress, 1999.

Vondey, W. 'The Holy Spirit and Time in Contemporary Catholic and Protestant Theology.' *Scottish Journal of Theology* Vol. 58 No. 4 (2005): 393–409.

Ward, T. *Word and Supplement: Speech Acts, Biblical Texts, and the Sufficiency of Scripture*. Oxford: Oxford University Press, 2002.

Ware, T. Letter to *The Times* dated 3rd May 2003.

Warfield, B. B. *The Inspiration and Authority of the Bible*. Philadelphia, PA: Presbyterian and Reformed Publishing Company, 1948.

Warwick, Montgomery J., ed. *God's Inerrant Word: An International Symposium on the Trustworthiness of Scripture*. Minneapolis: Bethany House, 1974.

Watson, F. *Text, Church and World: Biblical Interpretation in Theological Perspective*. Edinburgh: T&T Clark, 1994.

Welker, M. *God the Spirit*. Minneapolis: Fortress, 1994.

Wells, D. *No Place for Truth: Or Whatever happened to Evangelical Theology?* Leicester: IVP, 1992.

Wells, P. R. *James Barr and the Bible: Critique of a New Liberalism*. Phillipsburg, NJ: Presbyterian and Reformed Publishing Company, 1980.

Wenham, D. *Paul: Follower of Jesus or Founder of Christianity?* Grand Rapids: Eerdmans, 1995.

Wenham, D. Review of *Jesus Remembered: Christianity in the Making,* Vol. 1 by J. D. G. Dunn in *Evangelical Quarterly* 77.2 (2005): 171–174.

Wenk, M. *Community-Forming Power: The Socio-Ethical Role of the Spirit in Luke-Acts.* Sheffield: Sheffield Academic Press, 2000.

_____ 'The Fullness of the Spirit: Pentecostalism and the Spirit.' *Evangel* 21:2 (Summer 2003): 40–44.

Westcott, B. F. *The Gospel According to St. John.* London: John Murray, 1903.

Westerholm, S. *Israel's Law and the Church's Faith: Paul and his Recent Interpreters.* Grand Rapids: Eerdmans, 1988.

Whiteley, D. E. H. *The Theology of St. Paul.* Oxford: Blackwell, 1974.

Wiarda, T. 'The Jerusalem Council and the Theological Task.' *Journal of the Evangelical Theological Society* Vol. 46, No. 2 (June 2003): 233–248.

Williams, D. 'Music and the Spirit.' *Evangel* 23:1 (Spring 2005): 10–16.

Wilson, W. T. 'Hellenistic Judaism.' Page 477 in *Dictionary of New Testament Background.* Edited by C. A. Evans and S. E. Porter. Leicester: IVP, 2000.

Wimberly, E. P. *African American Pastoral Care.* Nashville: Abingdon, 1991.

Winter, S. 'More Light & Truth? Biblical Interpretation in Covenantal Perspective.' *Whitley Lecture 2007.* Oxford: Whitely, 2007.

Witherington, B. *Conflict and Community in Corinth: A Socio-Rhetorical Commentary on 1 and 2 Corinthians.* Grand Rapids: Eerdmans; Carlisle: Paternoster, 1995.

_____ *John's Wisdom - A Commentary on the Fourth Gospel.* Cambridge: Lutterworth, 1995.

_____ *Acts of the Apostles: A Socio-Rhetorical Commentary.* Carlisle: Paternoster, 1998.

Work, T. *Living and Active Scripture in the Economy of Salvation.* Grand Rapids: Eerdmans, 2002.

Wright, N. G. *God on the Inside: The Holy Spirit in Holy Scripture.* Oxford: Bible Reading Fellowship, 2006.

Wright, N. T. *The Climax of the Covenant: Christ & The Law in Pauline Theology.* London: T&T Clark, 1991.

_____ *The New Testament and The People of God.* London: SPCK, 1992.

_____ *Jesus and the Victory of God.* London: SPCK, 1996.

_____ *Scripture and the Authority of God.* London: SPCK, 2005.

Yoder, J. H. 'The Hermeneutics of Anabaptists.' Pages 291–307 in *Essays on Biblical Interpretation: Anabaptist-Mennonite Perspectives.* Edited by Willard M. Swartley. Elkhart, IN: Institute of Mennonite Studies, 1984.

_____ *Body Politics: Five Practices of the Christian Community Before the Watching World.* Scottdale, PA: Herald, 1992; reprint 2001.

Yong, A. *Spirit-Word-Community: Theological Hermeneutics in Trinitarian Perspective.* Aldershot: Ashgate, 2002.

_____ *Beyond the Impasse: Toward a Pneumatological Theology of Religions.* Carlisle: Paternoster, 2003.

_____ 'As the Spirit Gives Utterance: Pentecost, Intra-Christian Ecumenism and the Wider Oikoumene.' *International Review of Mission* Vol. xcii No. 366 (July 2003): 299–305.

Young, F. *The Making of the Creeds.* London: SCM, 1991.

Ziesler, J. *Pauline Christianity.* Revised Edition. Oxford: Oxford University Press, 1990.

Zizioulas, J. D. *Being As Communion: Studies in Personhood and the Church.* Crestwood, NY: St Vladimir's Seminary Press; London: Darton Longman and Todd, 1985.

www.ingramcontent.com/pod-product-compliance
Lightning Source LLC
Chambersburg PA
CBHW070015010526
44117CB00011B/1582